THE
Gabbitas
GUIDE TO
Independent
Schools

Publisher's note
The information supplied in this Guide has been published in good faith on
the basis of information submitted by the schools listed. Neither Kogan Page
nor Gabbitas Educational Consultants can guarantee the accuracy of the
information in this guide and accept no responsibility for any error or
misrepresentation. All liability for loss, disappointment, negligence or other
damage caused by the reliance on the information contained in this Guide, or
in the event of bankruptcy or liquidation or cessation of trade of any
company, individual or firm mentioned, is hereby excluded.

Photographs on front cover supplied with kind permission of (top to bottom)
Box Hill School, Surrey; The Leys School, Cambridge; Tonbridge School, Kent.

First published in 1995
This edition published in 1996

Kogan Page Ltd
120 Pentonville Road
London N1 9JN

© Kogan Page 1996

British Library Cataloguing in Publication Data
A CIP record for this book is available from the British Library
ISBN 0 7494 1797 8

Typeset by Barrall Word and Data Processing, Studley, Warwickshire
Printed and bound by Biddles Ltd, Guildford and Kings Lynn

THE
Gabbitas
GUIDE TO
Independent
Schools

The definitive guide
to independent education
in the UK

SECOND EDITION

GABBITAS
EDUCATIONAL CONSULTANTS

Contents

Introduction

Independent Schools – Full Steam Ahead

Robin Peverett

Independent schools have often had to look behind them to forestall possible attacks from the rear, and so their speed of progress has been cautious and slow. But I believe that in the coming years they will keep their gaze on the future and go full steam ahead. This is not just because political realities have changed, but rather more because the schools are offering education of a higher quality than ever before. Quality is what pupils need, it is what parents want, and it is what both obtain from the independent sector. There are real concerns about league tables, but they do demonstrate the extraordinary academic achievements of our schools. It is unfortunate that the silly squabble about the relative standards of girls in single sex and co-educational schools has at times blurred the vital message about overall standards. Heads need knocking together and certain associations should sign a peace treaty ending internecine strife.

There is another message that is in danger of being obscured, and that is the triumph of those schools that are not selective, but help the average, the below average and the educationally needy. Their results are often breathtakingly good, but they are dimmed by the trumpeting about A grades and the top ten schools. We must continue to clarify and broaden the message, but the essential core is always there for all to see – independent schools deliver the academic goods.

They deliver so much else as well. Care is a broad term, but there is no doubt that the schools care about their pupils, and care for them. That rightly produces a responsive chord in the hearts of parents. It is ironic that the philosophical and economic shift away from boarding has greatly improved boarding provision. Slimmer and fitter, boarding has re-considered its aims and its ideals, and it is now a very attractive option. It will never suit every pupil, but the challenge of greater self-sufficiency should be on offer to all. It is my belief that the term 'boarding' is now outdated and should be discarded, for it no longer reflects the variety and value of what is on offer. 'Adventure Residence' has a better ring, a real life specialism offered by the most experienced, best-provided and totally dedicated schools.

Resident or non-resident, the range of provision in independent schools remains unchallenged. Sport is still a pearl without price and frequently beyond the tightened purse strings of other schools. Activities from music and art to community involvement and information technology ensure that in a changing and less secure employment market minds and bodies can still be stretched in bad times as well as good. Equally important are the known boundaries of behaviour that lead to self-discipline. All in all it is a formidable menu that requires the right staff to guide, the right Heads to lead and the right Governors to oversee.

But something more is needed, and that is quality control. It can only come from inspection, and all independent schools within the Independent Schools Joint Council (ISJC) *are* inspected. HMI/Ofsted can only inspect occasionally, but the essential regular inspection is provided by the Accreditation Review and Consultancy Service (ARCS). Close collaboration with Ofsted ensures that the inspections are stringent and the inspectors properly trained. It is a safeguard that gives parents confidence and defeats complacency in schools.

An area that is often overlooked is the increasingly important part that independent schools play in the national educational debate and in academic innovation. The old image of an isolated group hacking its way through its own educational jungle has been replaced by the understanding that we are a group of professionals with close links with government and national educational bodies. Being independent our schools can speak freely and, where necessary, forcefully. Successful battles have been fought about the early idiocies of the National Curriculum and the flaws in the national tests, and cool wisdom has been injected into the A level debate, developments at GCSE and vouchers for the under fives. The fact that advice is sought as well as given is evidence that a proper balance has been achieved between independence and isolation.

Arrogance might once have been the besetting sin of the independent schools, but now the difficulties they have had to overcome in recent years have replaced it with a more realistic modesty. There has been no immunity from the economic problems that have been nationwide, and no magic formula against the changes in social and business attitudes. Parents have become more demanding, slower to decide whether and where to spend their money, quicker to complain or withdraw. New style Governors have flexed their muscles and Heads have rolled. It has been a harder time for schools, a salutary reminder that paying parents and selected pupils are not a protection against the realities of life. Some schools have closed, some have merged, some have saved themselves by rapid change. It has left the independent sector tougher and more flexible.

It has driven home another lesson, too. Parents may choose an independent school because they want their children to have high standards, inspirational teaching, a wide range of experiences, challenging companionship, support and control and the best chance in the future. But they have to be certain they can pay the fees, for many years, at a time when job security is increasingly uncertain. Through facing difficulties themselves, independent schools have gained a greater understanding of the economic problems potential and existing parents may face, and a greater determination to help. Many schools have raised money for the specific purpose of helping parents who fall on hard times, who become redundant or whose children clearly need the education the parental income cannot cover. It is typical of this spirit that last year, a hard year, more money was spent in this way than ever before, helping 18.2 per cent of the pupils. It is all part of that higher than ever quality that signals full steam ahead for the independent schools.

Robin Peverett
Headmaster, Dulwich College Preparatory School, Cranbrook
1970–1990
Director of Education IAPS 1990–1995
IAPS Counsellor 1995–

How To Use The Guide

This Guide has been designed to provide you with a range of starting points, depending on the factors most important in your search. The editorial section which follows and the reference section at the back will also give you valuable information about the independent sector as a whole, on examinations, fee-planning, scholarships and bursaries as well as guidance on choosing a school. The main index at the back contains details of all page references for each individual school.

Selecting a school in a particular location

If you are looking for a school in a specific area, turn to the directory section (Part Two), which is arranged geographically by postal town and county. The exceptions are London, for which schools are listed under their postal areas, and Scotland, where schools are listed by regions rather than counties. Each entry gives the name, address and telephone number of the school, together with the name of the Head, details of the type and age range of pupils accepted, the number of pupils, number of boarders (where applicable) and the annual fees.

Schools which have an asterisk also appear in the advertisement section, where more detailed information will be provided, and have a map reference to show the school's exact location.

To locate any other references to the school, for example to find out whether it offers scholarships or accepts pupils on the Assisted Places Scheme, turn to the main index at the back.

Scholarships, Bursaries and Reserved Entrance Awards

Many schools offer scholarships for children with a particular talent; bursaries where there is financial hardship or reserved entrance awards for children with a parent in a specific profession such as the Clergy or HM Forces. The reference section at the back contains a complete list of schools, by county, which offer such awards.

Once you have selected a few schools for further investigation, turn to the main index to find the school's other listings.

This section is necessarily only a brief guide to awards available. Some schools have given more detailed information about scholarship and similar awards in the special section which begins on p xxx. More specific information can be obtained from individual schools.

The Assisted Places Scheme

The Assisted Places Scheme is a government-funded scheme which exists to provide additional financial help to those pupils who demonstrate particular academic ability but whose parents may have difficulty in meeting independent school fees.

If you are interested in applying for an Assisted Place, the reference section at the back contains a summary of the scheme and eligibility for applications together with a full list of participating schools and the type of pupils accepted.

Religious affilation

If schools with a particular religious affiliation are to form the basis of your selection, the index under this heading in Part Four will provide a full list of schools under appropriate headings. The main index will tell you where to find further information about individual schools.

Single-sex schools

Single-sex education forms a significant part of the independent sector. If this is an important factor in your choice, you may find it helpful to refer firstly to the full index of single-sex schools, both boys' and girls', which appears in the final section (Part Four) of the book. Page references may be found in the main index.

For general guidance on any aspect of independent education and choosing a school, consult the articles at the front of the book. A full list of these is given in the Contents.

Acknowledgements

Gabbitas would like to express their thanks to all those who have helped in the preparation of this Guide, in particular to Dr John Cook, formerly Headmaster, Epsom College; Mrs Anne Feek, Managing Director, School Fees Insurance Agency Ltd; Robin Peverett, IAPS Counsellor, Director of Education IAPS 1990 – 1995 and former Headmaster, Dulwich College Preparatory School, Cranbrook; and to the Heads and schools who have provided so much of the information required for publication.

Gabbitas Educational Consultants Ltd
1995

PART ONE: THE INDEPENDENT SECTOR

1.1
What is an Independent School?

Independent schools educate some 7.5 per cent of the school population. While subject to certain regulations set centrally by the Department for Education and Employment (DFEE), they are largely self-governing. They are distinct from state schools in various aspects of funding, organisation, management and regulation. The key features are set out below.

In recent years the government has frequently stated its commitment to increased choice for parents and has taken steps to develop greater independence for state schools. The introduction of Local Management of Schools has given state schools greater control over the allocation of available resources. Grant-maintained schools, which receive funding directly from central government, have complete control over their budgets. However, these schools are still subject to regulations governing the provision of state education and in most cases must comply with new legislation or government initiatives on such matters as the curriculum, testing and assessment of pupils and teachers' salaries and conditions of employment.

Status and funding

Independent schools are usually funded by the fees charged to parents, although some also have generous endowments which allow them to keep fees at a lower level. Most are run as charitable trusts under a Board of Governors, which constitutes the policy-making body for the school. Schools with charitable status are effectively non-profit-making concerns; any surplus funds are allocated at the discretion of the Governors. Frequently they may go towards investment in new facilities or in scholarships and bursaries for new or existing pupils. A few schools are still privately-owned but these are in the minority.

The appointment of staff, financial management, administration, curriculum, admission of pupils and most other aspects of school life are controlled entirely by the individual school.

There is sometimes confusion over the terms used to describe independent schools. 'Public schools', as it refers to the independent sector, is a term generally applied to the old-established schools in membership of the Headmasters' Conference (HMC). Many of these date back to the days when education was a luxury, received chiefly through private tutors. A public school was therefore simply a school to which the public could be admitted. Most schools now prefer to be described as 'independent'. A private school simply means any school at which fees are paid.

Organisation, management and staff

The Board of Governors is responsible for appointment of the Head, allocation of finances and for other major decisions affecting the school. In the rare event of a dispute between a parent and the school, for example over a pupil's breach of school rules and any disciplinary action taken as a result, the Governors are the final arbiters. Once the child is formally registered as a pupil at the school, there is in effect a formal contract between the parents and the school, the terms of which must be heeded by both parties. Should parents wish to take further action after a Governors' decision which they dispute, the only option is to take out private legal proceedings. In practice however, issues of concern are normally resolved without recourse to such extreme measures.

Day-to-day responsibility for the running of the school is delegated to the Head, who is accountable to the Board of Governors. Other key figures in senior management include the Bursar, who has significant influence over the allocation of financial resources, and the Director of Studies, frequently appointed to manage academic life on a daily basis as Heads are compelled to pay greater attention to management and marketing.

Academic staff in independent schools are not legally required to hold teaching qualifications, but schools almost always insist on a first degree in a subject which normally forms a part of the secondary school curriculum and a PGCE (Postgraduate Certificate in Education). All schools look for enthusiastic and committed staff with flair and ability. Independent schools generally offer higher salaries than state schools, which enables them to attract high-calibre teachers.

Curriculum, testing and assessment

Independent schools are not bound to follow the National Curriculum, although most have chosen to do so. Almost all are preparing pupils for the public examinations at GCSE and A/AS level, or in Scotland, for Standard and Higher Grade examinations.

Assessment and monitoring of pupils' progress is a matter for individual schools to decide. There is no compulsion for pupils to sit the SATs (Standard Assessment Tests) introduced by the government within state schools. In practice most schools have regular assessments throughout the term and set formal, internal examinations two or three times a year, the results of which are included in the end of term report.

Registration and inspection of independent schools

All independent schools, like their counterparts in the maintained sector, are subject to inspection by Her Majesty's Inspectors (HMI), who provide the professional arm of OFSTED (the Office for Standards in Education).

OFSTED is the chief body and 'watchdog' responsible for monitoring the performance of schools in England. It is a non-ministerial government department and is separate from the Department for Education and Employment (DFEE). It has been set up to monitor a national service on a disinterested basis and is entirely independent in its work.

School inspections in the maintained sector are carried out on a four-year cycle by independent teams of inspectors. Each team is led by a Registered Inspector (RI) trained by OFSTED. Other members of the scheme must also have completed the OFSTED training scheme and may be drawn from a wide variety of career backgrounds. Inspection teams are invited by OFSTED to tender for individual school inspections. OFSTED is responsible for the awarding of contracts. Inspections are carried out according to specific formal procedures. Once the final report is published, copies are publicly available free of charge.

All independent schools are required to register with the DFEE or the Scottish Education Department if they have five or more pupils between the ages of five and sixteen. Before registration can be finalised the DFEE asks HMI to visit the school, which must satisfy set standards for premises, accommodation, staffing, curriculum and teaching, management and welfare of pupils.

Registered schools are visited on a regular basis by HMI to ensure that they still meet the standards required for registration. It is anticipated that independent schools will be visited every five years. The DFEE may also request a visit to any school which it feels to be deficient in specific aspects of provision.

The Children Act 1989 also requires independent schools to ensure and promote the welfare of boarding pupils. Independent boarding schools are therefore also subject to inspection by the Local Authority Social Services Department.

In addition to the inspection visits connected with registration, HMI undertakes about thirty full inspections by an HMI team every year. The purpose of all HMI inspection activity is to inform Her Majesty's Chief Inspector (HMCI) and the Secretary of State about standards in independent schools. Reports on full inspections are published and are available to parents of the school concerned free of charge.

Self-regulation within the independent sector

For many years, independent schools have maintained their own self-regulating systems. Most schools are members of one of the main associations, which form the constituent bodies of the Independent Schools Joint Council (ISJC). The associations are strict in setting rigorous standards to which members must conform. They include the Headmasters' Conference (HMC), the Girls' School Association (GSA) (including the Girls' Public Day School Trust GPDST), the Society of Headmasters and Headmistresses of Independent Schools (SHMIS), the Incorporated Association of Preparatory Schools (IAPS), the Independent Schools Association Incorporated (ISAI), the Governing Bodies Association (GBA), the Governing Bodies of Girls' Schools Association (GBGSA) and the Independent Schools Bursars' Association (ISBA). In some cases it is the Head not the school who is in membership, which is granted by election. The total comprised membership of ISJC is about 1400 schools. The equivalent body in Scotland is the Scottish Council of Independent Schools (SCIS) which represents most of the independent school sector in Scotland.

Until 1978, the DFEE (then the Department of Education and Science) operated an inspection scheme for independent schools in England and Wales, which, upon a satisfactory report from Her Majesty's Inspectorate of Schools, could be granted the status 'recognised as efficient'.

Following the withdrawal of this scheme in 1978, independent schools and their associations sought to replace it with another means of monitoring and maintaining educational standards. In 1980 a new Accreditation scheme was established under the auspices of the ISJC. This is now administered by the ISJC Accreditation, Review and Consultancy Service. Accreditation is not a legal requirement, but all schools seeking membership of one of the ISJC constituent associations must be accredited. Those schools already in membership and previously designated 'recognised as efficient' have not been required to seek accreditation.

Accreditation involves a visit to the school, lasting two to three days, by a team of inspectors led by a former HMI Inspector and including serving Heads of the association of which the school is a member. Inspection covers all aspects of the school – premises, facilities, staffing and management, financial management, administration, teaching standards, accommodation, boarding facilities, pastoral care and so on.

The phrase 'Accredited by ISJC' means that the school concerned has had such a visit or that there is an arrangement for one to take place, in accordance with the policy of the association of which it is a member. Accreditation is given only when the required standards have been met.

HMC has recently developed its own inspection system. A team of experienced lead inspectors was selected from recently retired HMC Headmasters, HMI and current HMC Heads. All have been fully trained, as have the subject inspectors, with the arrangements requiring everyone to be assessed before they can begin an inspection, and then to have their performance appraised during an actual inspection. In this way, HMC ensures that high and consistent standards are maintained in its inspections. The subject inspectors are mainly drawn from those currently teaching in HMC schools. Although this arrangement is different from that used by OFSTED, it is seen by HMC as a real strength because the inspectors should then be fully sensitive to the prevailing situation in a school.

The inspections cover all aspects of life in a school. As with OFSTED inspections, a full report is produced for the Governors and Head of the school. However, only a summary of the report has to be published, although many schools have chosen to make the full report available to parents and others who are interested. The recommendations of each report are followed up by HMC to ensure that the schools have benefited from the work of the inspectors.

1.2
The Independent Sector

There are over 2,200 independent schools in Britain. Schools cover all age ranges; some offer education from nursery level through to 18, others are junior or senior only. Many are day schools but a large number offer boarding or weekly boarding facilities. There is a variety of co-educational and single-sex schools; many of the latter, particularly boys' schools, offer co-education at sixth-form level.

The following is a summary of entry requirements, curriculum, examinations and assessment and other aspects of school life at the various stages of independent schooling. This is offered as a general picture; individual schools may vary considerably and parents should check specific details with those schools in which they are interested.

Entry requirements

Nursery and pre-preparatory schools

Pupils under the age of five are rarely required to meet more than the very basic practical requirements, although the Head will wish to meet the child in advance. Most schools offer entry at the beginning of each term. Pre-preparatory generally refers to the period of schooling between ages five and seven although many preparatory schools now have their own pre-preparatory and nursery departments.

Preparatory schools

Preparatory schools generally take children from age 5 or 7 to 13 and normally accept entry at any age in between. Entry is usually dependent upon an interview with the Head and a satisfactory report from the previous school. Some schools also set verbal or written entrance tests in English and Mathematics, although pupils entering the preparatory department of a pre-preparatory school which they already attend may be exempted from such tests.

Entry is normally in September, but is possible at other times depending on circumstances. Schools which prepare children primarily for the Common Entrance examination may test older entrants more rigorously to ensure that they have the capacity to pass at 11 or 13. Places are offered at the discretion of the Head, whose decision is final.

Senior schools

Senior schools generally admit pupils from 11 – 18, although some boys' schools still maintain the traditional age of entry at 13. Entry at sixth-form level is also a popular option.

Not all independent schools educate highly academic children, but there is always some form of selection. While some schools will only accept pupils able to keep pace with a fast moving curriculum, there are many others which cater for children of more average ability and some which specialise in helping those in need of more individual attention in a less academic environment.

Schools with their own preparatory department may offer a straightforward transfer into the senior school but most demand successful completion of entrance tests. Some schools, particularly day schools, set their own entrance tests in English, mathematics and a general paper. Many use the Common Entrance examination, which pupils may take at 11+, 12+ or 13+.

Many senior schools also offer a range of scholarships for pupils demonstrating exceptional talent and potential in such areas as academic study, music and art. Examinations are normally held in February and March for entry in September.

Entry to the sixth form of most schools is dependent upon interview, together with specified results at GCSE, which will vary from one school to another. Some schools also offer scholarships at this level.

Curriculum and teaching

Independent schools are not required to follow the National Curriculum but most have chosen to do so, while at the same time supplementing it with additional options or areas of study as desired. In Scotland new curriculum guidelines for state schools are currently under debate. Although Scottish independent schools are free to form their own curriculum policy – like their English counterparts – it is likely that they will have regard for any new developments once these are finally implemented. The following is a guide to studies and activities at each level.

Nursery and pre-preparatory schools

Very young children usually begin nursery school by attending mornings or afternoons only, progressing gradually to a full day at school. The emphasis is on the development of academic, social, language and aesthetic skills through play, music, art, drama and handicrafts. Children cover basic letter and number work, handwriting and spelling which will equip them for school life. Exploration of mathematical concepts, for example, is encouraged through the use of simple apparatus such as puzzles, sand and clay. Language skills are developed with rhymes, stories and singing, physical development through music and movement and games. The development of general knowledge and enjoyment of learning is encouraged through topics and project work, cooking, nature work and outings.

Classes are usually between 10 and 15 in number, usually with three members of staff on hand, normally a teacher plus ancillary staff or trained nursery nurses to supervise groups of about five pupils.

Approaches vary, from traditional teaching styles to more modern 'child-centred' teaching, which encourages children to learn by discovery, working at their own pace under supervision. Classes may often be divided into smaller sub-groups which work at different activities on a rotating basis. One group, for example, might be absorbed in a maths-based activity while another concentrates on English or art. Montessori schools teach according to the principles developed by Maria Montessori earlier this century.

Preparatory schools

Most preparatory schools are preparing pupils for Common Entrance in anticipation of entry to senior boarding or day schools. Some parts of the country retain the old examinations for entry to local grammar schools, which require no formal preparation. The destination of school leavers and the main academic thrust of the school may well be influenced by available provision at senior level.

Pupils are normally taught by class teachers until the age of about eight. After this they may be grouped according to ability and are more likely to have some subjects taught by subject specialists. At the age of nine or ten, there is increasing emphasis on individual subject teaching and close attention to the requirements of GCSE and the National Curriculum. Within the upper age range pupils are often based as a form with a form teacher but move to their various groups for all subject teaching. Class sizes may be anything from 12 to 20 but normally average between 15 and 18.

The normal curriculum might include English, mathematics, art, computing, arts and crafts, drama, French, German, music, scripture, sciences, history, geography and Latin. Many schools also offer CDT (Craft, Design and Technology), which encourages the development of artistic, design and construction skills. Some schools also offer Greek. Other elements of the curriculum might include current affairs and topical studies, group activities and projects as well as field trips and expeditions to supplement studies in all subjects. Computers are now an integral part of the curriculum and many schools have facilities which are used across the whole subject spectrum.

Most pupils are set homework, 10–15 minutes for very young pupils, increasing gradually to about an hour or more for older pupils and those preparing for Common Entrance.

Many schools also offer excellent library facilities, which pupils are encouraged to use both for reference purposes and to instil an enjoyment of reading and a spirit of enquiry. Reading is encouraged both for studies and for leisure, during the school holidays as well as in term time.

The Arts are considered an important part of the curriculum. Many pupils take individual music lessons in addition to class music studies and most schools have a variety of orchestral, choral and drama groups to give performances during Chapel, at school concerts and often at festivals and concerts outside school. Most schools also organise visits to concerts, opera and ballet.

Games and PE are also an important element. All schools offer a range of team games as part of the timetabled curriculum, together with other sporting and activity options to allow for all interests and abilities. Inter-school matches are a regular part of school-life and training is often given to a very high standard.

Senior schools

All schools are preparing pupils for GCSE and A levels. Some also offer a more limited range of AS levels. GCSEs are taken at the age of 16 after a two-year course. A levels normally involve a further two years' study after GCSE. In Scotland most schools prepare pupils for the Scottish Certificate of Education Standard Grade examinations (broadly equivalent to GCSEs in England), taken at 16+, Higher Grade examinations taken at 17+ or 18+ and the Certificate of Sixth Year Studies taken at 18+. Boarding schools in Scotland usually follow the English examination system although many also offer Highers as an option. Further information about these examinations is given in the Reference Section which begins on page 492.

The curriculum for new entrants will vary according to the school's age of entry, normally 11 or 13. However, as a general rule, pupils study a curriculum of English, mathematics, physics, chemistry and biology (although some schools combine the Sciences as Integrated Sciences), French, history, geography, religious education, information technology, physical education, art, drama, music and technology or CDT. Many schools also offer German or Spanish, Latin, Classical studies and home economics.

Class size at the lower end of the age range normally averages 15 to 20, GCSE groups about 12 to 18. Most schools teach pupils in sets or streams according to ability. Setting is based on a pupil's ability in individual subjects; therefore a pupil good at French would be placed in a set with other pupils of equal ability in the subject, but might be placed in a lower set for weaker subjects. Streaming groups children by ability on a cross-curricular basis.

At 14 pupils begin the two-year GCSE course. Most pupils take eight or nine subjects, although very able students may take 10 or 11. In some cases the brightest pupils may take some GCSE subjects after one year rather than two. The GCSE course normally combines a balance of academic subjects, including English, mathematics and the Sciences, modern languages, geography, history, Classics, Greek, Latin and religious education, with studies in art and design, music, CDT, drama, physical education and home economics. Some schools offer GCSEs which combine the Sciences. Teaching and careers staff discuss GCSE options with pupils before a final choice is made, to take into account interests and aptitudes and future plans. Schools try to be as flexible as possible within timetabling constraints, to allow pupils to take their preferred combination of subjects. In Scotland pupils generally take seven to eight Standard Grade subjects.

Music, art and drama are key aspects of the curriculum at all levels. A large of number of pupils receive individual music tuition in a wide variety of instruments and most schools have a full programme of vocal and instrumental concerts, plays and musicals performed in school, within the local community and further afield at festivals and in school competitions. Most schools prepare pupils for examinations set by the Associated Board of the Royal Schools of Music, the London Academy of Music and Dramatic Art (LAMDA) and similiar bodies.

Competitive team sports are timetabled as a regular part of the curriculum. The main games include football, cricket, rugby and tennis for boys and netball, tennis, rounders, gymnastics, hockey and lacrosse for girls. Other sports might include athletics, cross-country running, basketball, volleyball and swimming.

Many schools recognise, however, that not all pupils enjoy team games and in recent years there has been an increase in the number of alternative options offered in the form of more individual and non-competitive sports and activities such as squash, trampolining, horse-riding, archery, badminton, sailing and golf, to cater for all interests and abilities.

Teaching in all subjects often incorporates a range of activities outside school, on field study trips for geography, the Sciences and Classics, visits to galleries, concerts, the theatre and so on.

Sixth form

Pupils at sixth-form level are encouraged to develop a more independent approach to their studies and responsibilities, to learn how to determine priorities and manage their time wisely. As well as timetabled lessons, they will normally have periods set aside for individual study.

Most pupils take three A level subjects. Very able pupils may take four. Some schools also offer AS levels, which are as demanding in academic terms as an A level, but are lesser in terms of volume and so designed to take up only half the time required for an A level. Two AS levels may therefore be taken in place of one A level, which allows pupils to broaden the range of their sixth form studies or take a complementary subject. Teaching groups at this level may contain anything from 4 to 12 pupils, sometimes more.

A level subjects available will usually be the same as those offered at GCSE, but often with additional options. Some A level options may be started from scratch as an accelerated course which leads to A level within the two years. Business studies, law and modern languages such as Russian or Japanese are examples. The range of A levels available is very wide indeed. More recent subjects introduced include history of art, theatre studies and media studies. Pupils are encouraged to seek the guidance of staff and to consider their plans after A levels before making a final choice.

A few schools offer the International Baccalaureate, a demanding two-year course taken in place of A levels. The IB is broader in scope than A levels, including six subject groups which together make up a balanced curriculum of arts and sciences. The IB is accepted as an alternative to A levels by all British universities.

Some schools also run one-year courses for students who do not wish to take a full sixth-form examination course but may wish to take a general course which includes the opportunity to take additional GCSEs, supplemented by options such as business studies, secretarial studies or vocational studies.

Full-time vocational studies such as BTEC or RSA programmes leading to GNVQ and NVQ qualifications are offered in a few schools. These cover a range of vocational areas such as such as computing, business and finance, secretarial work and information technology.

In Scotland, the Higher Grade examinations taken at 17+ form the basis for entry to Higher Education. The Higher Grade is offered in a wide range of subjects. Most pupils stay on after the first round of Higher Grade examinations to study for the Certificate of Sixth Year Studies (CSYS). Most students take two or three CSYS subjects and may also take additional Highers at the same time.

Some schools also offer vocational programmes leading to SCOTVEC (Scottish Vocational Education Council) qualifications, which cover a range of areas similar to those offered by BTEC and RSA programmes mentioned above.

Exams, testing and assessment

Independent schools use their own methods of assessment to monitor a pupil's progress. The Government has introduced assessment tests for pupils in state schools in England to monitor progress through the Key Stages of the National Curriculum, but independent schools are not obliged to use them.

Preparatory schools

Teachers keep a constant eye on the progress of their pupils. On a more formal basis pupils may be tested or assessed on a regular basis during the term to monitor levels of achievement and efforts made. Some schools operate a points system, with marks for good work contributed to a pupil's record, which will include assessments of behaviour and efforts made in sports and other activities as well as academic performance. Formal exams are normally set twice a year or at the end of each term. Grades and position in the class are entered in the termly report for parents.

Senior schools

Pupils are graded for achievement in every subject throughout the term and regular assessments made. More formal examinations are normally taken two or three times a year. In addition, many schools have a tutorial system with a House tutor assigned to each pupil to monitor educational, social and personal development. The pupil and tutor meet regularly to discuss progress and reports from teachers and to identify any areas where help is required, particularly important at sixth-form level. Full subject reports are written at the end of each term and sent to parents.

Mock examinations may be taken by GCSE and A level candidates in the spring preceding the real examinations. These are marked internally by the school and give an indication of likely performance in the summer, together with areas in need of further revision.

Extra-curricular activities

Independent schools at all levels take care to encourage pupils to develop their interests outside the classroom as well as their academic ability. The range of options is now very wide indeed, offering pupils everything from art appreciation to abseiling, from fencing to fishing, often at very high standards. Most schools have a range of musical activities – orchestras, choir, madrigal groups, wind ensembles, to name but a few; and there are usually ample opportunities for individual music tuition. Most sports form part of extra-curricular activities as well as timetabled lessons. Other alternatives might include chess, badminton, canoeing, Duke of Edinburgh Award, horse-riding, Brownies and Scout groups, ballet, cookery, gardening, trampolining, rowing, golf, billiards, ball games, furniture restoration, stamps, sailing, carpentry, model-making, CDT, pottery, drama, French clubs, community service and outward bound activities. Individual schools will be happy to supply parents with a list of their activities. Some list over 50!

Boarding

Boarding still forms a major part of the independent sector, although boarding numbers overall have declined over the years. Children whose parents live overseas, whether British or foreign nationals, clearly have a need for boarding provision, but many parents based in Britain simply choose it in preference to a day school because of the benefits it offers their children. Boarding does not suit all children, but for those who feel happy as boarders it encourages independence and self-reliance and fosters long-lasting friendships. Staff are always on hand to help with academic work, and pupils generally have immediate access to a range of activities on-site which could not possibly be provided at home.

There are some 700 independent schools offering boarding places, including a good mix of single-sex and co-educational options, although most now take day pupils as well. The proportion of boarding pupils within the school varies enormously; a school of 300 pupils may have as many as 200 boarders or as few as 50. Such variations clearly have a bearing on the ethos and character of a school, so it is wise to check the proportions with schools, whether your interest is in a boarding or a day place.

Boarders may start from the age of eight, although a few schools will accept them at seven. Pupils are often accommodated in separate Houses with a homely, comfortable atmosphere and facilities which are second to none. The traditional-style dormitories have been replaced with cheerful, carpeted and well-heated bedrooms which house small groups of children, perhaps seven to eight in the lower age range, normally reducing in size as children get older. Fifth- and sixth-form pupils often have shared- or single-study bedrooms. There are normally recreation and common rooms for games, films or general relaxation as well as study areas. Meals may be taken in-House or in a central dining hall. Older pupils may also have the use of kitchen facilities to allow them greater flexibility.

The Housemaster or Housemistress is normally assisted by a qualified Matron and one or two assistants, depending on the number of children in the House. Older pupils are encouraged to take care of younger ones and may have in-House duties to assist in running the House.

From 9.00 am to 4.30 pm the school day for both boarders and day pupils will be the same. The boarding routine before and after lessons varies from one school to another, but typically might run as given in the example of a school day later in this section.

Weekends are normally a very active time in boarding schools, with a multitude of options laid on. Some schools still have Saturday morning school, which day pupils must also attend, but this is declining. On Saturday afternoons there may be sports matches, rambles, outings or opportunities to pursue a favourite hobby as well as free time for pupils to relax. After tea there may be a film, concert or school entertainment, or in summer a walk. On Sundays pupils attend Chapel and have time for letter-writing and their own activities. Day pupils are often invited to take part in weekend activities although this is not normally compulsory unless they are required for school matches or concerts etc.

Weekends out, commonly known as 'exeats', vary in frequency. Some schools may allow one per term, others allow children to go home almost weekly, although any weekend commitments in school must come first.

Weekly boarding on a regular basis is increasingly popular among parents and is now offered by many boarding schools. It offers pupils all the advantages of a boarding education during the working week whilst allowing weekends to be spent at home with parents. The length of the 'weekend' will vary according to individual schools. Some may allow pupils to leave on Friday evening and return on Sunday evening. Others may require pupils to stay at school on Saturday morning for lessons or other activities. The fees charged for weekly boarding are generally the same or a little less than the full boarding fees.

Structure of the school day

Nursery schools

Young children normally begin on a half-day basis, attending mornings or afternoons only. A morning session might run from 9.00 – 11.45 am, afternoons 12.45 – 3.45 pm. By the age of four most children will be attending school all day.

Preparatory and senior schools

A typical day will vary from one school to another, but the following offers an illustration one might expect in a boarding and day school:

General	
7.00 am	Boarders rise
7.15 – 7.45 am	Breakfast
7.45 – 8.15 am	Bedmaking, tidying up, teeth brushing, music practice or time to finish work or read
8.30 am	Chapel or Assembly
Prep schools	
9.00 – 10.45 am	Lessons

10.45 – 11.15 am	Break
11.15 am – 12.30 pm	Lessons
12.30 – 1.30 pm	Lunch, followed by various activities: choir practice, clubs or time to see staff
1.30 – 2.45 pm	Afternoon school
3.00 – 4.15 pm	Games or further lessons
4.15 pm	Day pupils leave. Some may stay at school for activities/prep and tea
4.30 – 5.30 pm	Supervised prep
5.30 pm	Tea
6.15 – 6.45 pm	Further prep for older pupils
6.45 –	Clubs, societies and activities
7.30 pm	Younger pupils to bath and bed
8.30 pm	Older pupils to bath and bed

Senior schools

9.00 – 10.45 am	Lessons
10.45 – 11.15 am	Break
11.15 am – 1.00 pm	Lessons
1.15 – 2.15 pm	Lunch
2.15 – 5.30 pm	Games and/or further lessons or activities
5.30 pm	Day pupils leave. Some may stay at school for prep and supper
6.00 – 6.45 pm	Supper
6.45 – 9.00 pm	Prep and other activities
9.30 – 10.30 pm	Lights out

At weekends, boarding schools offer a range of activities and allow free time for pupils to relax or go home. Some may allow senior pupils to go out of school into the nearby village or town, but only with specific permission and under strictly-observed conditions and time limits.

Discipline

Most schools keep rules simple, encouraging self-discipline and common sense in their pupils and giving praise for good behaviour. Corporal punishment is rare. A pupil who has produced good work or shown particular merit in some aspect of school life may be rewarded with extra points or certain privileges. This might mean being made a prefect or being allowed to bring a radio to school. Points might be deducted for silliness or bad behaviour. Other sanctions imposed might include limitations on leaving school premises or detention.

A breach of school rules with regard to smoking or alcohol may mean suspension. Breaches involving illegal drugs always mean immediate expulsion.

Schools should make parents aware of their disciplinary code from the outset and keep them informed about any breach of school rules by their child and any sanctions imposed as a result.

The House system

Most independent schools, whether boarding or day, operate a House system, which divides pupils into a smaller community groups for the purposes of inter-school competitions in such areas as sports, music and drama and, in boarding schools, for pastoral care, with pupils accommodated in smaller groups in their own 'House'. The Housemaster or Housemistress is in charge of pastoral care and will also go through the school report with each child at the end of term. House staff monitor overall progress, keep the Head informed about each child and, in boarding schools, may be the first point of contact for parents. The system provides a more homely, family-like boarding environment for pupils and also encourages a spirit of competition.

Religion

Spiritual growth is an important aspect of life in most independent schools, whatever their affiliation. The range includes Church of England, Roman Catholic, Quaker, Methodist, Jewish and others. Most adopt an inter-denominational approach and are happy to accept children of other faiths, but parents should check with individual schools the extent to which their child, if of a faith other than the majority of pupils, will be expected to participate in school worship. Children in a minority group can sometimes feel a little isolated in such situations. An index of schools by religious affiliation starts on page 541.

Contact with parents

Every child receives a termly report which is sent home to parents. Schools also hold parents' evenings at regular intervals to allow parents to discuss with teaching and pastoral staff any issues of concern and to be fully briefed on their child's progress. The school report will also contain results of any internal exams held during the term.

Parents are often invited to attend school sporting, musical or theatrical events, whether or not their child is taking part, and sometimes to help with school projects such as trips out of school or fundraising activities.

School staff – who's who?

Governors

The planning and policy-making body which controls the administration and finance of the school. Some may also be parents of children at the school. They are responsible for the appointment of the Head and for all major decisions affecting the school. Governors give their time voluntarily. Many are individuals with expertise in their professional lives, for example in law or accountancy, who can contribute their knowledge for the benefit of the school.

Head

Accountable to the Governors for the safety and welfare of pupils and the competence of staff, the Head is responsible for all aspects of the day-to-day management of the school, including appointment of staff, pupil recruitment and selection, staffing and administrative structure, curriculum content and management. As figureheads for their schools, many Heads also regard the marketing of their school as a key part of their rôle, although some schools now recruit staff specifically for the purpose. Most Heads also include several hours' teaching in the week, which helps them to keep in touch and get to know pupils individually.

Bursar

The Bursar, in conjunction with the Governors, is responsible for financial matters within the school and is an important part of the management team. The Bursar also takes charge of maintenance of the grounds, premises, buildings, catering and so on.

Director of Studies

Management of the curriculum is becoming an increasingly complex issue. Yet the demands on the Head, continually called upon to attract pupils to the school in a competitive market place, mean that some of the more traditional aspects of the rôle are being delegated. Many schools now have a Director of Studies who is responsible for day-to-day curriculum matters and timetabling and ensuring that staff are kept informed of new developments.

Registrar

The Registrar is responsible for the admission of pupils, making arrangements for parents to visit the school and meet the Head. The Registrar also takes care of the practical aspects of registration and joining.

Housemaster/Housemistress

The Housemaster or Housemistress takes care of the welfare and overall progress of children in the House and is normally the first point of contact for parents. They keep the Head informed of each child's progress and may often be the first to hear of any problems. Serious issues are always referred to the Head.

Subject teachers

Subject teachers are responsible for the academic progress of pupils and will produce a termly report for those taking their subject. Open evenings offer parents the opportunity to discuss any matters of concern with subject teachers.

Chaplain

The Chaplain has a special rôle within school. Independent of academic or disciplinary considerations, he is responsible for the spiritual development of pupils and can often provide a sympathetic ear to children who seek guidance on issues of concern.

Matron

The Matron looks after the practical aspects of boarding life, supervising and arranging laundry. Separate Houses normally have their own Matron. She often knows children well individually and can provide sympathetic and homely support for those, particularly young children, who are homesick or temporarily unhappy.

Sister

The Sister is a qualified nurse responsible for medical arrangements. She looks after pupils who may be admitted into the sanatorium with minor ailments and may require a few days in bed. Within a boarding school, serious medical matters are always referred to the school doctor and where necessary children will be taken to hospital.

Student positions

Independent schools encourage their pupils to take on positions of responsibility as part of school life. Senior pupils who show good sense and have contributed to the school by their achievements in academic work, musical or sporting activities for example, may be granted suitable senior positions in recognition of their efforts. Hence an excellent sportsman may be made Games Captain or an outstanding chorister Head of Choir. Pupils with an excellent academic record or who deserve merit for other contributions may be given the posts of Head Boy or Girl. Prefects have responsibility for some of the daily routines in school and are encouraged to set a good example to younger pupils.

1.3
Choosing Your School

'Which is the best school?'

The most commonly asked question, but impossible to answer! There is no one 'best school' able to provide the best possible education for every child. The independent sector offers enormous variety; some schools cater for exceptionally able children, others cater for those of more average ability, some offer a dynamic, fast-moving and competitive environment in which able, ambitious and gregarious children will thrive, others specialise in ensuring a more homely, less demanding atmosphere. You will undoubtedy hear differing views about individual schools, but do remember that you are the best judge of your own child's needs; the question to ask is 'which one will suit my child best?'

When to start

Requests for recommendations before birth are not uncommon! However, while places at the large city day schools may be in demand, in reality there is no need to panic at such an early stage. Waiting lists tend to disappear as September approaches and places are taken up. For entry to preparatory school at seven or eight, you should be thinking about your choice once your child reaches the age of about four. This allows you to be clearer about his or her academic potential while allowing plenty of time for your research. For entry to senior schools, most parents start to look at the options two to three years ahead. Clearly the earlier you start, the more time you will have to make an informed decision, but remember that much can change in a school in five years.

Establishing your criteria

Where do we start? With the multitude of information sources now available and the variety of options, parents may find the initial task of compiling a list of 'possibles' rather daunting. It may help if you can set some basic ground rules first.

Would you prefer single-sex or co-education? Some argue that single-sex education, particularly for girls, enables pupils to achieve at a higher level without the distraction of the opposite sex. Others believe that co-education offers a more natural environment. There are protagonists on both sides, but try not to be browbeaten by either camp. Consider it as just one of the factors in your decision.

Are you looking for day or boarding? For some parents there may be no option. Those based overseas or required to move regularly often appreciate the continuity and stability which boarding offers their child. For foreign pupils the need is obvious. The traditional attractions however, continue to draw British-based parents as well. Boarding encourages a sense of independence and self-confidence at an early age and helps to foster tolerance and consideration for others in pupils living as part of a large community. Many boarding schools also offer a range of opportunities and activities which parents at home could not possibly provide. That said, boarding does not suit all children. How would your child respond?

Weekly boarding has become increasingly popular. Working parents who may have little time from Monday to Friday can devote the week to professional commitments, allowing time to spend with the family at the weekend. City-based parents are often attracted by the benefits of a quieter, cleaner, more rural environment where the distractions of city life and travel problems are eliminated. Some children like the arrangement; others may find the constant change of environment unsettling.

Location may not seem immediately important for those looking for a boarding school, but in practice most parents these days choose schools within about two hours' drive. If you have children at more than one school, remember that the round trip for collection and delivery at the beginning and end of the holidays can turn into a marathon if the schools are very distant.

The religious affiliation of the school may be a further important factor. Will you only consider those of your own denomination or are you willing to include others in your choice? If you are not keen on too great an emphasis on religious aspects, a school which openly promotes a strong Christian tradition may seem a little overwhelming. If your child is of a faith other than that of the majority of pupils, will he or she be expected to participate in the school's usual worship? What allowances will be made for the observance of his or her own religion and principles? Ask the Head about the school's approach. Most schools will be happy to accept pupils of other faiths, but if the religious aspect of the school is very strong, a pupil of another faith is likely to be in a minority and may feel a little left out or 'different'.

Your child's needs

Once the basics have been worked out, go on to consider your child's needs. Academic considerations are always top priority. You may have a very able child, but most children are of more average ability. Be realistic about his or her potential. Trying to gain a place at a very academic school when your child is not really up to it generally does more harm than good. Failing the entrance test can knock a child's confidence, particularly if you show disappointment. Even if a place is offered, the entrance exam is only the first of many hurdles. If the pace of the school is too fast, your child will continue to struggle, and nothing will be more demoralising than constantly coming bottom!

Academic matters aside, your child probably has other interests which he or she wishes to pursue. If there is a particular talent in music or a passionate interest in the outdoors, this should form part of your selection criteria.

The atmosphere and ethos is different in every school. Consider your child's overall personality. Is there a need for a highly active environment offering a multitude of stimuli and the company of other lively and confident youngsters? Or is he or she in need of a gentler approach and a smaller, more family-oriented school?

Finding out

You should not find it difficult to obtain information. The Head of your child's present school will probably be able to recommend suitable choices. Friends and parents of children at schools you are considering may also be able to help. There are also published guides available such as this one which offer an overview of overall options. You may also find the objective opinion of an educational consultant helpful. Ask those schools which interest you to send you a prospectus. This will tell you something about the main thrust of the school, the curriculum and other areas of activity in which the school has a particular interest.

Coming from overseas

If you live overseas, the best advice is to plan early. If your child is to board, the location of the school may be determined in part by the proximity of friends or relatives living in Britain, but try not to restrict your selection too narrowly. There are excellent boarding schools throughout Britain, which is well served with rail, road and air links to the major cities and airports.

Parents can ask schools direct for a prospectus or alternatively may wish to seek guidance from an educational consultant at home or in Britain, who can provide an overview and give guidance on the suitability of options available.

It will be helpful if you can plan your visit to Britain well in advance, so that you can arrange to see the schools which interest you and give yourself time to make an informed decision. If possible, visit schools during term-time, normally early September to mid-December, early January to late March and mid-April to early July.

If your child has been educated abroad, find out what levels of achievement the school will seek from your child in overall academic terms. If your child's first language is not English, how willing is the school to provide additional language support? Is this done by a qualified teacher? How many hours a week? Does this involve absence from certain lessons or does it take place outside normal lessons? Some schools encourage children with little English to be involved first with those lessons not requiring a good grasp of it, for example sport or art, the remainder of the time occupied with English language teaching. Children are gradually introduced those subjects which they will be studying at their senior school. Parents should be able to obtain guidance on English language support from the schools in which they are interested or from an educational consultant.

For some pupils the best option may be an international school. These specialise in education for children whose stay in Britain may be limited, for example where foreign staff are posted to Britain for fixed term contracts of one or two years. The student body normally comprises a strong mix of nationalities and the curriculum is sufficiently flexible to allow a smooth transition both into the school and afterwards into a British, American or international school elsewhere. Some schools follow an American curriculum, others prepare pupils for the International Baccalaureate, an academically demanding alternative to A levels which offers a broader programme of study and which is recognised for admission purposes by universities throughout Britain, Europe and other parts of the world. Non-native English speakers are given particular support, but teaching may be offered in a range of languages.

Visiting schools

Whatever the prospectus, your friends and your instincts tell you, the only way to find out whether or not you like a school is to see it for yourself. Do take your child with you if at all possible. Your visit will enable you to meet the staff who will be responsible for your child and the pupils who will be his or her schoolmates and to get a 'feel' for the school. You, and your child, must be positive that this is a school where he or she will feel happy.

Try to visit more than one school, so that you have a means of comparison. Most parents visit at least two, some three or four. You may be invited to an Open Day, but the best time to visit is on a normal day during term time. Then you can see the day to day routine in place and the children at their usual activities.

In most cases the Head will meet parents and interview the child. Afterwards you will probably be given a tour of the school, by the Head, another member of staff or sometimes by a pupil. The latter can be a useful and honest source of opinion on such matters as extra-curricular activities, boarding life and the food! After your visit it is wise to make a few notes; if you visit more than one school it is surprisingly easy to confuse your impressions and information.

Your interview with the Head

Don't be frightened to ask questions, however trivial you may think they sound. Heads are used to answering all sorts of questions and should be happy to spend time with you clearing up any worries or discussing matters of particular concern. If not, you should ask yourself whether this is really the school for you. You are about to make a heavy investment in financial terms, quite apart from the issue of maximising your child's one and only opportunity of education. You may even wish to ask the Head about the financial stability of the school, although clearly this is a sensitive area. Checklists of questions may be self-defeating; going armed with a standard list for all schools is by nature not very helpful. The prospectus will answer some of your queries in each case, so do read it first. Then think about the aspects of the individual school which have not been covered; gear your questions to those elements which are most important to you personally.

There are certain fundamental areas however, in which you will wish to be fully briefed, either by asking the Head or by using your eyes as you go round the school:

Academic thrust

Let us assume for a moment that your aim is to give your child a sound preparatory school education and then enter him or her into one of the excellent local maintained grammar schools in your area. If the Head tells you that all pupils are being prepared for Common Entrance and that 95 per cent go on to major boarding schools, is this really what you want? What are the usual leavers' destinations? Similarly, a senior school with a high university entry rate in academic subjects may not be the best option for a pupil with ambitions in more practical spheres. Try to get a picture of the range and nature of ability for which the school provides. How many subjects do pupils take at GCSE and A/AS level? Are there any areas of the curriculum in which the school really excels? If your child has strengths in specific areas or subjects, how are these taught? Are they offered at GCSE and A/AS level?

If possible it is better to avoid changing schools while children are in the middle of GCSE or A/AS level courses to avoid disruption but in some cases it may be unavoidable. If so, find out which syllabuses the school uses for your child's subjects. If they are not the same as those he or she is following, can the school offer any additional help to ensure that all the necessary ground is covered? How willing is the school to help with the transition? At secondary level the sixth form is an important measure of the school's performance. How many pupils stay on after GCSE? If a significant number leaves, what is the reason for this?

Teaching staff and methods

Are all the staff suitably qualified? How much experience do they have? Are they specialists in the subjects they teach or do they cover a range of subjects other than their own? Is there a high staff turnover? If so, why? Is there a reasonably broad age range among staff? Older staff may have more knowledge and experience, younger ones perhaps a fresh approach and a good rapport with pupils who find them closer to their own age.

How is teaching organised? Are children streamed or setted according to ability? If it is a prep school you may wish to find out at what age pupils begin individual subject studies.

Class size

As a very rough guide, schools may have classes of between 14 and 23. Classes for GCSE and sixth-form studies are generally smaller. At A level, numbers may be anything from two or three for more unusual subjects to 10 or 12 for more popular options. Look at the class sizes as you go round the school.

Exam results

Interesting, but not the only factor. Schools should be happy to let you see past GCSE and A level exam results. Be careful how you interpret them. A 100 per cent pass rate in an A level subject may look impressive, but how many pupils are included? Three or 33? Were all those who studied the subject actually entered for the exam? Some schools pre-select candidates, which inevitably improves the pass rate statistics. League tables have been much debated. Although interesting, they should be treated with some caution, largely because of the important information which they omit. A school with a highly selective academic intake and consequently a very able set of sixth-form pupils will inevitably score well. It might be argued that a less selective school with equally good results has put in greater effort and achieved far more with more average pupils. A school specialising in less able pupils may have achieved a miracle if one of their pupils achieves a grade D at A level, but the school may be a long way down the table.

Testing and assessment

How often are formal assessments made? Are parents informed of the results? What other systems are in place to monitor a pupil's progress? If there is a particular problem, are all staff made aware? How much communication is there between teaching and pastoral staff on general progress?

Extra-curricular activities

Does the school have any special strengths? If your child is talented in music, for example, how seriously is this taken by the school? Is there an orchestra, choir, wind ensemble? Do pupils give performances for fellow pupils and at events outside school? Are they encouraged to enter competitions for performing, singing or composing? The same principles apply whether your child is an artist or an ornithologist. What encouragement will he or she receive and what activities and facilities are available?

Special needs

Many children require additional help at some time in their school career to cope with learning difficulties or dyslexia. If you have selected the school as an option with this in mind, exactly what provision is made? Some schools bring in a visiting teacher once a week; others may have a complete unit in which children are taught on an extraction basis, taken out of certain lessons for additional individual tuition to help them cope with all their studies. How much help does your child need and how does the Head respond?

 If your child is dyslexic, you can obtain further information about suitable provision from organisations such as the Dyslexia Institute, the British Dyslexia Association and CReSTeD. See the 'Useful addresses' section for details.

Gifted children also often need special help and attention. If your child displays particular ability well above that of other children of the same age, how would the school make provision for this?

Day pupils

If your child is to be one of a minority of day pupils in what is chiefly a boarding school, will he or she be classed as a second-class citizen? Are the activities offered to boarders in the evenings and at weekends also open to or even compulsory for day pupils? How many in practice actually take part in optional activities? Do boarders and day pupils mix well socially during the school day or do they tend to keep apart? Does the House system mix boarders and day pupils or keep them separate?

Working parents might wish to find out whether the school is able to accept day pupils early in the morning and provide for them after school, with tea and activities until parents can collect. Some city day schools are well-practised in this.

Scholarships and bursaries

If your child is exceptionally talented in a specific area, there may well be scholarship opportunities which may reduce the fees by as much as 50 per cent or possibly more. If financial hardship is an issue, bursaries may be available to help top up the shortfall. The decision to grant a bursary will be taken according to individual circumstances. Academically able pupils may also qualify for financial help under the Assisted Places Scheme. Details of the Scheme and other forms of financial assistance are given on page 35. A list of schools participating in the Assisted Places Scheme starts on page 523.

Educational guidance

What guidance is given to pupils as they choose their GCSE and A/AS level subjects? How much information and advice is available on higher education and careers? Is there a careers library and what does it contain? A few dusty box files or a comprehensive, up–to–date, well-organised and maintained library of information on the wide range of options available? Is there a dedicated team of experienced and qualified careers staff or is this a part-time role given on a rotating basis to whichever member of staff draws the short straw?

Are there timetabled careers guidance sessions, visiting speakers, work experience opportunities, visits to companies or industrial centres? Does every pupil receive a formal careers assessment, interview practice and individual guidance?

Fees

What does the basic fee cover? What is not included? How much are parents normally asked to pay during the term for additional expenses such as school lunches, school trips, sports kit, music lessons and so on?

Boarding

What is the boarding routine? What happens in the evenings and at weekends? How much free time is available? How much supervision is there? Who takes care of pastoral matters? Ask to meet the House staff who will be taking care of your child. You must have complete confidence in them. Make sure you see the boarding accommodation. Most schools offer very comfortable accommodation these days and you can expect high standards. Are the bedrooms, bathrooms and common rooms clean, warm and welcoming? Are there spacious lockers and areas available for clothes and personal effects? What are pupils permitted to bring to school? What is forbidden? Radios, pets, pocket money and clothes may all be at issue here.

Are pupils allowed out of school? At what age? Are they supervised? What restrictions are there? How many exeats are there each term? May pupils telephone home at any time?

Medical matters are a further issue. Do boarders receive regular medical and dental checks? Is there always a doctor available? Make sure you are shown the sanatorium and meet the Sister in charge. Would you be happy to entrust these people with your sick child? In the unlikely event of serious accident or illness, what is the procedure? Suppose parents cannot be contacted in an emergency? What is the school's responsibility?

Seeing the school

Your first impressions may be surprisingly accurate. How easy was it to find the school/Headmaster's office? Was it signposted? Were you welcomed by a member of staff clearly expecting you or greeted as an unwelcome disruption by someone who wasn't? Is there a sense of organisation and purpose? If you passed any pupils did they offer to show you the way? Were they neat and tidy?

How do the pupils behave towards staff and visitors? Do they stand up in class, stand aside to let you pass or ignore you? Do they talk easily and sensibly to adults? How do they respond to teachers in class? Are they interested and enthusiastic? Is their work well displayed on the walls? Is there a sense of variety in the work displayed and teaching styles used or does the classroom seem 'tired'? The Head is a crucial figure. Is there a good rapport with staff and pupils or is he or she a distant figure?

How full and up to date are the notice boards? These will give you a good idea of what is going on, how often and how much interest is generated.

Are the buildings and grounds well kept and decorated? Some schools occupy very elaborate buildings, but others take equal pride in more ordinary premises. In many schools the standards of design and architecture in new buildings are outstanding.

Registration

Registering with a school commits neither you nor the school. The length of waiting lists at some schools may be more mythical than actual but schools are understandably reluctant to dispel such perceptions. That said, the longer you delay registering your child, the more likely it is that places may no longer be available by the time you apply.

Schools normally charge a non-refundable registration fee to discourage parents who are not genuinely interested. This may be anything up to £75 for a senior school, less for younger pupils. Always have a 'fall-back' registration in case no place is offered or available at your first choice. As the proposed entry date approaches, normally about a year in advance, you will need to make up your mind. Once you have formally accepted a place there is a contract between you and the school and your deposit, should you change your mind, may or may not be refundable depending on the terms set by the school.

Making your mind up

After your visits, go back to your original criteria. How far do the schools conform? Which aspects take priority? Take notice of your child's responses too. Ten-year-olds have different criteria. They may have fears about individual schools which can easily be allayed or they may have noticed other factors which could prove a real problem. If your child really dislikes the feel of the school as a whole, don't ignore the signals, but don't let your child make the final decision. It must clearly be your choice. If your child agrees, so much the better. If you allow your child to choose, there is a danger later on of guilt and recriminations should things go wrong. The responsibility must be yours. If ultimately you have difficulty deciding on a final choice, the answer is to trust your instincts. The right school is the one which will allow your child to develop to his or her full potential in the company of liked and trusted staff and pupils in an environment where he or she feels happy and at home.

1.4
How do Parents Pay for School Fees?

Anne Feek, Managing Director, School Fees Insurance Agency Limited

The majority of parents still continue to pay fees as they arise from taxed income. However, there are far better ways of managing such a major financial commitment.

Currently starting at around £1,500 for a day pupil at preparatory level, termly fees can rise to more than £4,000 for senior boarding. After that, because maintenance grants are means tested and those with higher incomes are unlikely to qualify for support, the costs of university or further specialist training can prove equally expensive.

But, having taken the decision to pursue an education in the independent sector for their children, the question for most parents is not whether they can afford it, but how.

There are basically three methods of planning for school fees:

- capital investment;
- regular savings;
- borrowing on a secured or unsecured basis.

If parents (or grandparents) have capital available or are able to save on a regular basis, the same basic principles apply. Any plan or plans should take into consideration the individual's personal financial circumstances eg the level of fees and when they will be required, whether there is any existing provision in place and the current and potential rate of income tax. Attitude to risk is also an important factor. But for school fees planning the safe and secure route, especially for fees required in the shorter term, is advisable. It should also be a major consideration to mitigate any tax liability.

Parents considering capital investment should look for an arrangement where the capital is protected. Bank and building society deposit accounts obviously come to mind as do national savings, provided the timescales fit. In addition, parents who are totally committed to independent education should definitely consider educational trusts. These are specifically designed to meet termly fees and provide advantageous tax benefits when the proceeds are to be used for education. If the child is due to start school in less than a year it may also be worth enquiring whether or not the school will offer a discount if fees are paid by lump sum in advance. However, it is still important to check how this money is secured.

Some parents may like to consider the more traditional insurance products such as bonds, particularly with-profit bonds. For investors who are a little more adventurous, the tax efficiency of Personal Equity Plans is hard to beat and with Corporate Bond PEPs there is the option to invest with a more conservative approach.

For a regular savings plan to provide effectively a fund on which to draw fees, it must run for a minimum of five years and preferably longer. Again, PEPs should be considered because of their tax efficiency and, in addition, protection to ensure continuance of the payments in the event of death, critical illness or if a parent is unable to work.

National savings and TESSAs are an option for the very cautious, as are traditional life insurance products which incorporate life cover, such as maximum investment plans and endowments.

Some parents will fund fees from a combination of capital investment and regular savings. However, flexibility is the key word because circumstances may change and the money may be required earlier or later than originally anticipated or perhaps will be not used for fees at all.

The third category of plans is for those who require immediate help with school fees. In these circumstances, one of the most common ways of raising money is to arrange for an equity within the parents' house to be released on a termly drawdown basis thereby allowing the family to borrow the money at very competitive rates and only pay interest on the amounts actually drawn down. A number of banks and building societies now offer this facility as a means of keeping the initial cost substantially lower than the fees that are currently being funded. The loan is then repaid across a longer period.

Alternatively, for parents who may not wish to draw upon the equity of their property or would prefer to repay a loan over a shorter period of time, unsecured lending facilities specifically for the purpose of funding education are available. Again, monies are drawn down termly to keep interest payments at a minimum. Repayment is over a 10 to 15 year period with extremely competitive interest rates, but earlier repayment is without penalty. Typically the limit for this type of lending is £20,000, but sometimes it may be higher.

In conclusion, the earlier parents start planning, the better, but for those who are late planners, there are still ways of making costs more manageable.

1.5
Scholarships, Bursaries, Assisted Places and Other Awards

In addition to the many financial planning schemes available, assistance with the payment of fees may be obtainable from a variety of other sources.

Scholarships

Many senior schools offer scholarship opportunities. These are awarded, at the discretion of the school, to pupils displaying particular ability or promise, either in academic subjects, as an all-rounder or in specific areas such as music or art. Candidates are normally assessed on the basis of their performance in an examination or audition. Scholarship examinations are normally held in the February or March preceding September entry. Pupils awarded scholarships in for example, music or art, may be required to sit the Common Entrance examination to ensure that they meet the normal academic requirements of the awarding school.

Scholarships are normally offered upon the normal age of entry to the school. Some schools also offer awards for sixth-form entry, for example for students who have performed particularly well in the GCSE examinations. These awards may be restricted to pupils already attending the school or may also be open to prospective entrants coming from other schools.

Scholarships vary in value, although full-fee scholarships are now less frequently available. Scholarships are awarded as a percentage of the full tuition fee to allow for inflation.

Fewer scholarships are available at preparatory school level. Choristers, however, are a special category. Choir schools generally offer much reduced fees for choristers, well below the normal day fee. Help may also be available at senior schools, although in practice it is common for choristers to gain music scholarships at their senior schools.

For a general guide to scholarships offered by individual schools, turn to the scholarships index in the reference section (Part Four). More detailed information about individual school awards may be found in the advertisement section entitled Scholarship Profiles.

Bursaries

Bursaries are intended primarily to ensure that children obtain provision suited to their needs and ability in cases where parents cannot afford the normal fees. They are awarded on the basis of financial hardship, rather than particular ability. All pupils applying for a bursary, however, will be required to show, normally by passing Common Entrance or the school's own entry tests, that they meet academic requirements. The size of the award is entirely at the discretion of the school.

A list of schools able to offer bursaries is given in the reference section.

For further information about bursaries contact the Educational Grants Advisory Service, administered by Mrs Judith Crawford, 62 Park Lane, Norwich, Norfolk NR2 3EF.

Reserved Entrance Awards

Some schools reserve awards for children with parents in a specific profession, for example in HM Forces, the clergy or in teaching. These are similar to bursaries in that the child must meet the normal entry requirements of the school, but eligibility for the award will be dependent upon fulfilment of one of the criteria stated above. Normally schools will reserve only a few places on this basis. Once a place for a specific award has been filled, it will not become available again until the pupil currently in receipt leaves the school. Hence the award may be available only once every five years or so.

A list of schools and brief summary of the reserved entrance awards offered by each is given in the reference section. The awards covered include those offered to children with one or both parents working in any of HM Forces, the Foreign Office, the medical profession, teaching, the clergy or as Christian missionaries.

Other Awards

Schools may also offer concessions for brothers and sisters or for the children of former pupils.

Assisted Places Scheme

The Government Assisted Places Scheme is for academically able boys and girls whose parents cannot afford the full tuition fees at an independent school. Pupils may be given an Assisted Place regardless of the type of school attended previously, but in practice most schools have to offer Assisted Places to pupils from state schools. There are about 5,700 Assisted Places each year at participating schools in England and Wales. There is also an Assisted Places Scheme in Scotland but with certain significant differences.

The normal age of entry is 11 or 13, but this varies from one school to another. Places may also be available at sixth-form level. Pupils may also be able to get Assisted Places at other ages but only if they are entering a class with other pupils with Assisted Places who entered in a previous year. To be eligible a pupil must have been resident in the UK, Channel Islands or the Isle of Man for two years before taking up the place, but some children who have been resident abroad may also be eligible. There are special rules for the children of workers from the UK and other European Economic Area (EEA) countries moving within the EEA, and for refugees.

The amount of help given with payment of tuition fees depends on family income. In some instances families may be eligible for help with other expenses such as school meals. No assistance is available with boarding fees but if parents wish their child to board, some schools offer bursaries to children with Assisted Places to help with payment of boarding fees.

The contribution due from parents towards payment of tuition fees is based upon 'relevant income', normally the total income (before tax) of both parents from all sources and any unearned income of all dependent children. An allowance of £1,165 (in 1995–96) is taken off this total for each dependent child (other than the Assisted Place holder) and also for each dependent relative of parents. Relevant income is normally assessed for the tax year before the school year in question. Special rules apply for divorced or separated parents and parents receiving disability benefits.

For the school year 1995–96 parents do not have to pay anything towards tuition fees if the relevant income for the tax year 1994–95 is £9,572 or less. The table overleaf is a guide to parental contributions for the year 1995–96. Note that the table can be extended beyond the £29,000 shown but you will not in any case have to pay more than the amount of the fees. Different rules apply if there are three or more Assisted Place holders in the family. The schools in the Scheme have complete scales of contributions and will work out the amount you have to pay. You will normally be asked to pay your share of the fees in three equal instalments, one at the start of each term. The assistance given is reviewed each year.

Your contribution to fees 1995 – 1996 school year

Relevant income (1994–95) (after allowances for dependents)	One Assisted Place holder	For each of two Assisted Place holders
£	£	£
9,573	15	9
10,000	51	39
11,000	165	123
12,000	312	234
13,000	480	360
14,000	690	516
15,000	900	675
17,000	1,371	1,029
19,000	1,887	1,416
21,000	2,547	1,911
23,000	3,207	2,406
25,000	3,867	2,901
27,000	4,527	3,396
29,000	5,187	3,891

A full list of schools in England, Wales and Scotland offering Assisted Places is given in the reference section at the back. Further information about the scheme may be obtained from the following addresses: **Department for Education and Employment**, Assisted Places Team, Mowden Hall, Darlington, Co Durham DL3 9BG *Tel*: 01325 392163 (for schools in England); **Welsh Office Education Department**, Cathays Park, Cardiff CF1 3NQ *Tel*: 01222 825111 (for schools in Wales); **Scottish Office Education Department**, Room 4/08, New St Andrew's House, St James Centre, Edinburgh EH1 3TG *Tel*: 0131 244 5521 (for schools in Scotland).

Other government grants

Assistance with the payment of fees is also offered to personnel employed by the Foreign and Commonwealth Office and by the Ministry of Defence, where a boarding education may be the only feasible option for parents whose professional lives demand frequent moves or postings overseas.

The FCO termly boarding allowance from September 1995 is £3,693 for senior pupils and £3,218 for junior pupils. Parents in need of further information should contact the FCO Personnel Services Department on 0171 210 8159.

Services personnel may seek guidance from the Service Children's Education Authority (SCEA) who can advise on schools and on the boarding allowance made. In 1995–96 the boarding allowance is £1,883 per term for junior pupils, £2,248 per term for senior pupils and £2,998 per term for children with special needs. Further information may be obtained from SCEA, HQ DGAGC, Worthy Down, Winchester, Hampshire SO21 2RG Tel: 01962 887934.

Parents may also find it helpful to consult the list of schools offering reserved entrance awards. Some schools may be able to supplement allowances offered by employers through a reserved entrance award offered to pupils who meet the relevant criteria, eg with a parent in HM Forces.

Grant-giving Trusts

There are various educational and charitable Trusts which exist to provide financial help for parents unable to meet the cost of independent school fees. Usually the criteria restrict eligibility to particular groups, for example orphans, children with parents in the teaching profession or in cases of sudden and unforeseen financial hardship. Applications are normally considered on an individual basis by an appointed committee. The criteria for eligibility and for the award of a grant will vary according to individual policy. In some cases several Trusts may each contribute an agreed sum towards one individual case in order to make up the fees required. It should be noted that such Trusts receive many more applications for grants than can possibly be issued and competition is fierce. Parents may find it helpful to consult the Educational Grants Directory, published by the Directory of Social Change.

Local Authority grants

Grants from local authorities are sometimes available where a need for a child to board can be demonstrated, for example where the child has special educational needs which cannot be met in a day school environment or where travel on a daily basis is not feasible. Such grants are few in number. Awards for boarding fees at an independent school may not be granted unless it can be shown that there is no boarding place available at one of the state boarding schools, of which there are about 40 nationwide.

Awards from Local Authorities are a complex issue. Parents wishing to find out more should contact the Director of Education for the Authority in which they live.

Note on information given in the directory section

Type of school

The directory comprises schools listed within the Department for Education and Employment Register of Independent Schools. State schools, grant-maintained schools, special schools, independent colleges and overseas schools are not included.

Each school is given a brief description, which explains whether the school is single-sex or co-educational. In some cases schools take small numbers of the opposite sex within a specified age range. These are indicated where appropriate, eg:

Boys boarding and day 3-18 (Day girls 16-18)

Schools are described as 'boarding' (which indicates boarding pupils only), 'boarding and day', 'day and boarding' (indicating a predominance of day pupils) or 'day' only.

Number of boarders

Where necessary these are divided into full boarders (F) and weekly boarders (W). Weekly boarding arrangements vary according to individual school policy.

Fees

All fees are given annually from September 1995 unless otherwise stated. It should be remembered, however, that some schools increase fees during the year and the figures shown may therefore be subject to change after September 1995. Where the date given is other than September 1995, the information provided is the latest available from the school. Figures are shown for full boarding (FB), weekly boarding (WB) and day fees. In some instances the fees for full and weekly boarding are the same (F/WB). A minimum and a maximum fee are given for each range. These figures are intended as a guide only. For more precise information schools should be contacted direct.

School profiles

*denotes that the school has a profile in Part Three.

PART TWO: FULL GEOGRAPHICAL DIRECTORY

2.1
ENGLAND

(* denotes school has a profile in Part Three)

AVON

BATH

BATH HIGH SCHOOL GPDST
Hope House, Lansdown, Bath, Avon
BA1 5ES
Tel: (01225) 422931
Head: Miss M A Winfield
Type: Girls Day 4-18
No of Pupils: 620
Fees: (September 95) £2928 - £3984

DOWNSIDE SCHOOL
Stratton-on-the-Fosse, Bath, Avon
BA3 4RJ
Tel: (01761) 232206
Head: Dom Antony Sutch
Type: Boys Boarding 10-18
No of Pupils: 300 No of Boarders
F300
Fees: (September 95) FB £8929 -
£11130 DAY £6324 - £7134

KING EDWARD'S JUNIOR SCHOOL
North Road, Bath, Avon BA2 6JA
Tel: (01225) 463218
Head: P M Garner
Type: Boys Day 7-11
No of Pupils: 183
Fees: (September 95) £3155

KING EDWARD'S SCHOOL, BATH
North Road, Bath, Avon BA2 6HU
Tel: (01225) 464313
Head: P J Winter
Type: Boys Day 7-18 (Co-ed VIth
form)
No of Pupils: B817 G48
Fees: (September 95) £3135 - £4293

KINGSWOOD DAY PREPARATORY SCHOOL
College Road, Bath, Avon BA1 5SD
Tel: (01225) 310468
Head: Mrs M H Newbery
Type: Co-educational Day 3-11
No of Pupils: B50 G47
Fees: (September 95) £2685 - £3285

KINGSWOOD SCHOOL*
Lansdown, Bath, Avon BA1 5RG
Tel: (01225) 734300
Head: G M Best
Type: Co-educational Boarding &
Day 11-18
No of Pupils: B254 G184 No of
Boarders F249
Fees: (September 95) F/WB £8793 -
£11160 DAY £5484 - £6999

MONKTON COMBE JUNIOR SCHOOL
Combe Down, Bath, Avon BA2 7ET
Tel: (01225) 837912
Head: E J D Clarke
Type: Co-educational Day &
Boarding 3-13
No of Pupils: B147 G50 No of
Boarders F52
Fees: (September 95) FB £8685 DAY
£1860 - £6120

MONKTON COMBE SCHOOL*
Bath, Avon BA2 7HG
Tel: (01225) 721102
Head: M J Cuthbertson
Type: Co-educational Boarding &
Day 11-18
No of Pupils: B218 G105 No of
Boarders F275
Fees: (September 95) FB £9645 -
£11685 DAY £6585 - £8085

PARAGON SCHOOL
Lyncombe House, Lyncombe Vale,
Bath, Avon BA2 4LT
Tel: (01225) 310837
Head: D J Martin
Type: Co-educational Day 3-11
No of Pupils: B135 G133
Fees: (September 95) £2535 - £2826

THE PARK SCHOOL
Weston Lane, Bath, Avon BA1 4AQ
Tel: (01225) 421681
Head: Revd R M Clarke
Type: Boys Day 3-11 (Girls nursery
only)
No of Pupils: 140
Fees: (September 95) £2595 - £3885

PRIOR PARK COLLEGE*
Bath, Avon BA2 5AH
Tel: (01225) 835353
Head: J W Goulding
Type: Co-educational Boarding &
Day 11-18
No of Pupils: B267 G189 No of
Boarders F140 W18
Fees: (September 95) F/WB £10074
DAY £5334 - £5571

THE ROYAL SCHOOL*
Lansdown, Bath, Avon BA1 5SZ
Tel: (01225) 313877
Head: Mrs E McKendrick
Type: Girls Boarding & Day 3-18
(Boys 3-7)
No of Pupils: B17 G345 No of
Boarders F225
Fees: (September 95) FB £9258 -
£11001 DAY £2781 - £5886

BRISTOL

AMBERLEY HOUSE SCHOOL
42 Apsley Road, Clifton, Bristol,
Avon BS8 2SU
Tel: (0117) 973 5515
Head: Mrs H Tallis
Type: Co-educational Day 2-11
No of Pupils: B100 G70
Fees: (September 94) £710 - £2130

BADMINTON SCHOOL*
Westbury-on-Trym, Bristol, Avon
BS9 3BA
Tel: (0117) 962 3141
Head: C J Gould
Type: Girls Boarding & Day 5-18
No of Pupils: 360 No of Boarders
F230
Fees: (September 95) FB £8250 -
£11250 DAY £2985 - £6225

BRISTOL CATHEDRAL SCHOOL
College Square, Bristol, Avon
BS1 5TS
Tel: (0117) 929 1872
Head: K J Riley
Type: Boys Day 10-18 (Co-ed VIth form)
No of Pupils: B435 G25
Fees: (September 95) £4041

BRISTOL GRAMMAR SCHOOL
University Road, Bristol, Avon
BS8 1SR
Tel: (0117) 973 6006
Head: C Martin
Type: Co-educational Day 7-18
No of Pupils: B871 G332
Fees: (September 95) £2340 - £3888

BRISTOL WALDORF SCHOOL
Park Place, Clifton, Bristol, Avon
BS8 1JR
Tel: (0117) 926 0440
Type: Co-educational Day 3-14
No of Pupils: 263
Fees: On application

CLEVE HOUSE SCHOOL
254 Wells Road, Bristol, Avon
BS4 2PN
Tel: (0117) 977 7218
Head: D Lawson and Mrs E Lawson
Type: Co-educational Day 2-11
No of Pupils: B115 G95
Fees: (September 95) £2025 - £2160

CLIFTON COLLEGE*
32 College Road, Bristol, Avon
BS8 3JH
Tel: (0117) 973 9187
Head: A H Monro
Type: Co-educational Boarding & Day 13-18
No of Pupils: B450 G250 No of Boarders F390
Fees: (September 95) FB £12150 DAY £8430

CLIFTON COLLEGE PREPARATORY SCHOOL
The Avenue, Clifton, Bristol, Avon
BS8 3HE
Tel: (0117) 973 7264
Head: Dr R J Acheson
Type: Co-educational Boarding & Day 3-13
No of Pupils: B370 G100 No of Boarders F90 W20
Fees: (September 94) FB £8487 WB £8178 DAY £1230 - £6135

CLIFTON HIGH SCHOOL
College Road, Clifton, Bristol, Avon
BS8 3JD
Tel: (0117) 973 0201
Head: Mrs J D Walters
Type: Girls Day 3-18 (Boarders 16-18, day boys 3-11)
No of Pupils: B73 G677 No of Boarders F25 W5
Fees: (September 95) FB £8160 WB £7755 DAY £810 - £4275

COLSTON'S COLLEGIATE SCHOOL
Stapleton, Bristol, Avon BS16 1BJ
Tel: (0117) 965 5207
Head: D G Crawford
Type: Co-educational Boarding & Day 3-18
No of Pupils: B453 G99 No of Boarders F72
Fees: (September 95) FB £8400 - £10080 WB £8100 - £9630 DAY £3810 - £5475

COLSTON'S GIRLS' SCHOOL
Cheltenham Road, Bristol, Avon
BS6 5RD
Tel: (0117) 942 4328
Head: Mrs J P Franklin
Type: Girls Day 10-18
No of Pupils: 500
Fees: (September 95) £3585

THE DOWNS SCHOOL*
Wraxall, Bristol, Avon BS19 1PF
Tel: (01275) 852008
Head: J K Macpherson
Type: Co-educational Boarding & Day 3-13
No of Pupils: B250 G50 No of Boarders F60
Fees: (September 95) F/WB £7080 DAY £2205 - £5100

FAIRFIELD PNEU SCHOOL
Fairfield Way, Farleigh Road, Backwell, Bristol, Avon BS19 3PD
Tel: (01275) 462743
Head: Mrs A Nosowska
Type: Co-educational Day 3-11
No of Pupils: B53 G63
Fees: (September 95) £975 - £3120

GRACEFIELD PREPARATORY SCHOOL
266 Overndale Road, Fishponds, Bristol, Avon BS16 2RG
Tel: (0117) 956 7977
Head: Mrs M Garman
Type: Co-educational Day 4-11
No of Pupils: B45 G45
Fees: (September 95) £1662 - £1839

MANDER PORTMAN WOODWARD
10 Elmdale Road, Clifton, Bristol, Avon BS8 1SL
Tel: (0117) 925 5688
Head: Ms F A Eldridge
Type: Co-educational Day & Residential 14-20
No of Pupils: B50 G30
Fees: (September 95) DAY £1785 - £8970

OAK HILL SCHOOL
Okebourne Road, Brentry, Bristol, Avon BS10 6QY
Tel: (0117) 959 1083
Head: Mrs H Jelfs
Type: Co-educational Day 4-11
No of Pupils: 90
Fees: On application

OVERNDALE SCHOOL
Chapel Lane, Old Sodbury, Bristol, Avon BS17 6NQ
Tel: (01454) 310332
Head: M R Wallis-Eade
Type: Co-educational Day 3-11
No of Pupils: B55 G45
Fees: (September 95) £2040

QUEEN ELIZABETH'S HOSPITAL
Berkeley Place, Clifton, Bristol, Avon BS8 1JX
Tel: (0117) 929 1856
Head: Dr R Gliddon
Type: Boys Day & Boarding 11-18
No of Pupils: 500 No of Boarders F90
Fees: (September 95) FB £6957 DAY £3915

THE RED MAIDS' SCHOOL
Westbury-on-Trym, Bristol, Avon BS9 3AW
Tel: (0117) 962 2641
Head: Miss S Hampton
Type: Girls Boarding & Day 11-18
No of Pupils: 500 No of Boarders F100
Fees: (September 95) FB £7440 DAY £3720

REDLAND HIGH SCHOOL
Redland Court, Redland, Bristol, Avon BS6 7EF
Tel: (0117) 924 5796
Head: Mrs C Lear
Type: Girls Day 4-18
No of Pupils: 655
Fees: (September 95) £1950 - £3966

SACRED HEART PREPARATORY SCHOOL
Chew Magna, Bristol, Avon
BS18 8PT
Tel: (0117) 933 2470
Head: Sr V Kavanagh
Type: Co-educational Day 3-11
No of Pupils: 140
Fees: (September 95) £2190 - £2490

ST URSULA'S HIGH SCHOOL*
Brecon Road, Westbury-on-Trym,
Bristol, Avon BS9 4DT
Tel: (0117) 962 2616
Head: Mrs M A Macnaughton
Type: Girls Day 3-18 (Boys 3-11)
No of Pupils: B80 G300
Fees: (September 95) £1125 - £3450

SILVERHILL SCHOOL
Swan Lane, Winterbourne, Bristol,
Avon BS17 1RL
Tel: (01454) 772156
Head: Mrs G J Clewer
Type: Co-educational Day 2-13
No of Pupils: B164 G142
Fees: (September 95) £2085 - £3630

TOCKINGTON MANOR
Tockington, Bristol, Avon BS12 4NY
Tel: (01454) 613229
Head: R G Tovey
Type: Co-educational Day &
Boarding 3-14
No of Pupils: B100 G60 No of
Boarders F50
Fees: (September 95) FB £8640 DAY
£3420 - £5970

TORWOOD HOUSE SCHOOL
29 Durdham Park, Redland, Bristol,
Avon BS6 6XE
Tel: (0117) 973 5620
Head: Mrs S Sheppard
Type: Co-educational Day 2-11
No of Pupils: 190
Fees: (September 94) £560 - £2100

WESTWING SCHOOL
Kyneton House, Thornbury, Bristol,
Avon BS12 2JZ
Tel: (01454) 412311
Head: Mrs A Rispin
Type: Girls Boarding & Day 4-18
No of Pupils: 110 No of Boarders F60
W10
Fees: (September 95) FB £7773 -
£8223 WB £7530 - £7998 DAY
£2871 - £4059

CLEVEDON

RYDAL PRE-PREPARATORY SCHOOL
11 Albert Road, Clevedon, Avon
BS21 7RP
Tel: (01275) 874127
Head: Mrs E A Humby
Type: Co-educational Day 4-11
No of Pupils: B15 G15
Fees: (September 94) £2100

ST BRANDON'S SCHOOL
Elton Road, Clevedon, Avon BS21
7SD
Tel: (01275) 875092
Head: Mrs S Vesey
Type: Co-educational Day 3-11
No of Pupils: 160
Fees: (September 95) £450 - £2805

WESTON-SUPER-MARE

ASHBROOKE HOUSE
9 Ellenborough Park North,
Weston-Super-Mare, Avon BS23
1XH
Tel: (01934) 629515
Head: J C Teasdale
Type: Co-educational Day 3-11
No of Pupils: B65 G20
Fees: (September 95) £885 - £1863

LANCASTER HOUSE SCHOOL
38 Hill Road, Weston-Super-Mare,
Avon BS23 2RY
Tel: (01934) 624116
Head: Mrs S Lewis
Type: Co-educational Day 4-11
No of Pupils: B30 G40
Fees: (September 95) £1020 - £1080

WYNCROFT
5 Charlton Road,
Weston-Super-Mare, Avon
Tel: (01934) 626556
Head: Mrs E M Thorn
Type: Co-educational Day 4-11
No of Pupils: 100
Fees: On application

WINSCOMBE

THE HALL SCHOOL SIDCOT
Pre-Preparatory School for Sidcot,
Winscombe, Avon BS25 1PD
Tel: (01934) 844118
Head: Mrs W Wardman
Type: Co-educational Day 3-9
No of Pupils: 60
Fees: (September 94) £1425 - £2790

SIDCOT SCHOOL*
Winscombe, Avon BS25 1PD
Tel: (01934) 843102
Head: C Greenfield
Type: Co-educational Boarding &
Day 9-18
No of Pupils: B224 G185 No of
Boarders F180
Fees: (September 95) F/WB £9561
DAY £4230 - £5718

BEDFORDSHIRE

BEDFORD

ACORN SCHOOL
15 St Andrews Road, Bedford
MK40 2LL
Tel: (01234) 343449
Head: Mrs M Mason
Type: Co-educational Day 2-9
No of Pupils: 100
Fees: (September 95) £780 - £2208

BEDFORD HIGH SCHOOL*
Bromham Road, Bedford MK40 2BS
Tel: (01234) 360221
Head: Mrs B Stanley
Type: Girls Day & Boarding 7-18
No of Pupils: 960 No of Boarders F69
Fees: (September 95) FB £8589 WB
£8490 DAY £3474 - £4749

BEDFORD MODERN SCHOOL*
Manton Lane, Bedford MK41 7NT
Tel: (01234) 364331
Head: P J Squire
Type: Boys Day & Boarding 7-18
No of Pupils: 1170 No of Boarders
F50 W5
Fees: (September 95) FB £7590 -
£8640 WB £6339 - £7731 DAY
£3099 - £4491

BEDFORD SCHOOL*
Burnaby Road, Bedford MK40 2TU
Tel: (01234) 340444
Head: Dr I P Evans
Type: Boys Day & Boarding 13-18
No of Pupils: 713 No of Boarders
F217
Fees: (September 95) FB £11145 DAY
£7005

BEDFORD PREPARATORY
SCHOOL
Burnaby Road, Bedford MK20 2TU
Tel: (01234) 352007
Head: Rev Dr B A Rees
Type: Boys Boarding & Day 7-12
No of Pupils: 407 No of Boarders F27
Fees: (September 95) FB £7875 -
£9195 WB £7485 - £8805 DAY
£4785 - £6105

DAME ALICE HARPUR
SCHOOL
Cardington Road, Bedford MK42 0BX
Tel: (01234) 340871
Head: Mrs R Randle
Type: Girls Day 7-18
No of Pupils: 951
Fees: (September 95) £3144 - £4338

GEORGINA PERKINS
Young Life Centre, 163 Tavistock
Street, Bedford MK40 2SD
Tel: (01234) 219734
Head: Mrs B A Hartley
Type: Co-educational Day
No of Pupils: B15 G15
Fees: (September 95) £864 - £954

POLAM SCHOOL
45 Lansdowne Road, Bedford
MK40 2BY
Tel: (01234) 261864
Head: A R Brown
Type: Co-educational Day 3-9
No of Pupils: B128 G128
Fees: (September 95) £1392 - £2427

RUSHMOOR SCHOOL
58-60 Shakespeare Road, Bedford
MK40 2DL
Tel: (01234) 352031
Head: P J Owen
Type: Boys Day 4-16
No of Pupils: 245
Fees: (September 95) £2115 - £4110

ST ANDREW'S SCHOOL
78 Kimbolton Road, Bedford
MK40 2PA
Tel: (01234) 267272
Head: Mrs J M Mark
Type: Girls Day 5-16
No of Pupils: 320
Fees: (September 95) £2145 - £3555

WALMSLEY HOUSE SCHOOL
23 Kimbolton Road, Bedford
MK40 2NY
Tel: (01234) 359686
Head: W Anderson
Type: Co-educational Day 3-11
No of Pupils: B130 G130
Fees: (September 95) £1185 - £2286

DUNSTABLE

ST GEORGE'S
28 Priory Road, Dunstable,
Bedfordshire
Tel: (01582) 661471
Head: Mrs Plater
Type: Co-educational Day 3-9
No of Pupils: B35 G35
Fees: (September 95) £2295

LEIGHTON BUZZARD

PARKSIDE KINDERGARTEN
AND PREPARATORY SCHOOL
41-43 Grove Road, Leighton
Buzzard, Bedfordshire LU7 8SF
Tel: (01525) 379293
Head: Mrs M S Fuller
Type: Co-educational Day 0-7
No of Pupils: B7 G8
Fees: On application

SUTHERLANDS SCHOOL
Stoke Road, Linslade, Leighton
Buzzard, Bedfordshire LU7 7SR
Tel: (01525) 373360
Head: Mrs A Goulding
Type: Co-educational Day 3-10
No of Pupils: B25 G25
Fees: (September 94) £2100

LUTON

BROADMEAD SCHOOL
117 Tennyson Road, Luton,
Bedfordshire LU1 3RR
Tel: (01582) 22570
Head: A F Compton
Type: Co-educational Day 2-11
No of Pupils: B65 G65
Fees: (September 95) £2352

MOORLANDS SCHOOL
Leagrave Hall, Luton, Bedfordshire
LU4 9LE
Tel: (01582) 573376
Head: A Cook
Type: Co-educational Day 2-11
No of Pupils: 180
Fees: (September 95) £1464 - £2925

BERKSHIRE

ASCOT

HEATHFIELD SCHOOL
London Road, Ascot, Berkshire SL5
8BQ
Tel: (01344) 882955
Head: Mrs J Benammar
Type: Girls Boarding 11-18
No of Pupils: 210 No of Boarders
F210
Fees: (September 95) FB £12525

LICENSED VICTUALLERS'
SCHOOL*
London Road, Ascot, Berkshire
SL5 8DR
Tel: (01344) 882770
Head: Mrs P Cowley
Type: Co-educational Boarding &
Day 5-18
No of Pupils: B423 G244 No of
Boarders F100 W110
Fees: (September 95) FB £8139 -
£9570 WB £3537 - £9510 DAY
£2916 - £5370

MARIST CONVENT SENIOR
SCHOOL*
The Rosary, Sunninghill, Ascot,
Berkshire SL5 7PS
Tel: (01344) 24291
Head: Sister M Gaffney
Type: Girls Day 11-18
No of Pupils: 382
Fees: (September 95) £3900

PAPPLEWICK*
Ascot, Berkshire SL5 7LH
Tel: (01344) 21488
Head: D R Llewellyn
Type: Boys Boarding & Day 7-13
No of Pupils: 185 No of Boarders
F115
Fees: (September 95) FB £9345 DAY
£7176

ST GEORGE'S SCHOOL*
Ascot, Berkshire SL5 7DZ
Tel: (01344) 20273
Head: Mrs A M Griggs
Type: Girls Boarding & Day 11-18
No of Pupils: 295 No of Boarders
F180
Fees: (September 95) FB £11625 DAY
£6825

ST MARY'S SCHOOL*
Ascot, Berkshire SL5 9JF
Tel: (01344) 23721
Head: Sister Frances Orchard
Type: Girls Boarding & Day 11-18
No of Pupils: 330 No of Boarders
F320
Fees: (September 95) FB £11833 DAY
£7101

STUBBINGTON HOUSE
Earlywood, Ascot, Berkshire SL5 9JU
Tel: (01344) 20257
Head: Mrs P E Godwin
Type: Co-educational Boarding &
Day 3-13
No of Pupils: 100 No of Boarders F10
Fees: (September 95) FB £9000 WB
£8100 DAY £1650 - £5310

BRACKNELL

BRACKNELL MONTESSORI
SCHOOL
Windlesham Centre, Priestwood,
Bracknell, Berkshire RG12 1UD
Tel: (01344) 50922
Head: Mrs E Ashcroft
Type: Co-educational Day 2-6
No of Pupils: B30 G30
Fees: (September 95) £1098 - £2598

LAMBROOK*
Winkfield Row, Bracknell, Berkshire
RG42 6LU
Tel: (01344) 882717
Head: R Badham-Thornhill
Type: Boys Boarding & Day 4-13
No of Pupils: 120 No of Boarders F55
Fees: (September 95) FB £6090 -
£8550 DAY £3165 - £6090

NEWBOLD SCHOOL
Popeswood Road, Binfield, Bracknell,
Berkshire RG12 5AH
Tel: (01344) 421088
Head: M Brooks
Type: Co-educational Day 3-11
No of Pupils: 80
Fees: (September 95) £1410 - £1770

CROWTHORNE

OUR LADY'S PREPARATORY
SCHOOL
The Avenue, Crowthorne, Berkshire
Tel: (01344) 773394
Head: Mrs S T Hayden
Type: Co-educational Day 3-11
No of Pupils: B75 G75
Fees: (September 95) £272 - £743

WAVERLEY SCHOOL
Ravenswood Avenue, Crowthorne,
Berkshire RG11 6AY
Tel: (01344) 772379
Head: S G Melton
Type: Co-educational Day 3-11
No of Pupils: B87 G75
Fees: (September 95) £1536 - £3249

WELLINGTON COLLEGE
Crowthorne, Berkshire RG11 7PU
Tel: (01344) 772261
Head: C J Driver
Type: Boys Boarding & Day 13-18
(Co-ed VIth form)
No of Pupils: B762 G54 No of
Boarders F662
Fees: (September 95) FB £12270 -
£12555 DAY £8955

MAIDENHEAD

CLAIRES COURT SCHOOL
Ray Mill Road East, Maidenhead,
Berkshire SL6 8TE
Tel: (01628) 411470
Head: J T Wilding
Type: Boys Day 10-17
No of Pupils: 270
Fees: (September 95) £4425 - £5280

HERRIES SCHOOL
Dean Lane, Cookham Dean,
Maidenhead, Berkshire SL6 9BD
Tel: (01628) 483350
Head: D G Hare
Type: Co-educational Day 2-13
No of Pupils: B31 G80
Fees: (September 95) £480 - £1165

HIGHFIELD SCHOOL
2 West Road, Maidenhead, Berkshire
SL6 1PD
Tel: (01628) 24918
Head: Mrs C M A Lane
Type: Co-educational Day B3-7
G3-11
No of Pupils: B47 G207
Fees: (September 95) £1725 - £4035

MAIDENHEAD COLLEGE
CLAIRES COURT GIRLS
1 College Avenue, Maidenhead,
Berkshire SL6 6AW
Tel: (01628) 411480
Head: Dr M Marwick
Type: Girls Day 3-18 (Boys 3-7)
No of Pupils: B35 G200
Fees: (September 95) £3165 - £5280

RIDGEWAY SCHOOL
(CLAIRES COURT JUNIOR)
Maidenhead Thicket, Maidenhead,
Berkshire SL6 3QE
Tel: (01628) 822609
Head: Miss K M Boyd
Type: Boys Day 4-11
No of Pupils: 222
Fees: (September 95) £1160 - £1475

ST PIRAN'S PREPARATORY
SCHOOL
Gringer Hill, Maidenhead, Berkshire
SL6 7LZ
Tel: (01628) 27316
Head: A P Blumer
Type: Co-educational Day 3-13
No of Pupils: 210
Fees: (September 95) £2550 - £5400

SILCHESTER HOUSE SCHOOL
Silchester House, Bath Road,
Taplow, Maidenhead, Berkshire
SL6 0AP
Tel: (01628) 20549
Head: Mrs D J Austen
Type: Co-educational Day 2-12
No of Pupils: B81 G65
Fees: (September 95) £1725 - £3655

WINBURY SCHOOL
Hibbert Road, Bray, Maidenhead,
Berkshire SL6 1UU
Tel: (01628) 27412
Head: Mrs P L Prewett
Type: Co-educational Day 2-8
No of Pupils: B60 G40
Fees: (September 94) £1230 - £2470

NEWBURY

BROCKHURST & MARLSTON
HOUSE PRE-PREPARATORY
SCHOOL
Ridge House, Cold Ash, Newbury,
Berkshire RG18 9HX
Tel: (01635) 863259
Head: Mrs R A Fleming
Type: Co-educational Day 2-7
No of Pupils: 42
Fees: (September 95) £512 - £1024

BROCKHURST SCHOOL
Hermitage, Newbury, Berkshire
RG18 9UL
Tel: (01635) 200293
Head: A J Pudden
Type: Boys Boarding & Day 6-13
No of Pupils: 112 No of Boarders F33
Fees: (September 94) F/WB £8565
DAY £3990 - £6615

CHEAM HAWTREYS*
Headley, Newbury, Berkshire
RG19 8LD
Tel: (01635) 268242
Head: C C Evers
Type: Boys Boarding & Day 7-13
No of Pupils: 155 No of Boarders
F114
Fees: (September 95) FB £9045 DAY
£6390

DOWNE HOUSE SCHOOL*
Cold Ash, Newbury, Berkshire
RG16 9JJ
Tel: (01635) 200286
Head: Miss S Cameron
Type: Girls Boarding & Day 11-18
No of Pupils: 550 No of Boarders
F517
Fees: (September 95) FB £12420 DAY
£9000

HORRIS HILL
Newtown, Newbury, Berkshire
RG20 9DJ
Tel: (01635) 40594
Head: M J Innes
Type: Boys Boarding 8-13
No of Pupils: 150 No of Boarders
F130
Fees: (September 95) FB £9300
DAY £6600

MARLSTON HOUSE SCHOOL
Hermitage, Newbury, Berkshire
RG18 9UL
Tel: (01635) 200293
Head: A J Pudden
Type: Girls Boarding & Day 6-13
Fees: (September 95) F/WB £8565
DAY £3990 - £6615

NEWBURY PREPARATORY
SCHOOL
84 Enborne Road, Newbury,
Berkshire RG14 6AN
Tel: (01635) 41638
Head: B A Freer
Type: Co-educational Day 2-11
No of Pupils: B60 G60
Fees: (September 95) £2541 - £3267

PRIORS COURT
PREPARATORY SCHOOL
Chieveley, Newbury, Berkshire
RG16 8XW
Tel: (01635) 248209
Head: Paul High
Type: Co-educational Boarding &
Day 3-13
No of Pupils: B112 G50 No of
Boarders F80
Fees: (September 95) FB £8400
DAY £3000 - £5700

ST GABRIEL'S SCHOOL
Sandleford Priory, Newbury,
Berkshire RG15 9BB
Tel: (01635) 40663
Head: D Cobb
Type: Girls Day 3-16 (Boys 3-8)
No of Pupils: B10 G356
Fees: (September 95) £1776 - £4980

THORNGROVE SCHOOL
The Mount, Highclere, Newbury,
Berkshire RG15 9PS
Tel: (01635) 253172
Head: N J Broughton
Type: Co-educational Day 4-13
No of Pupils: 120
Fees: (September 94) £3375 - £4377

READING

THE ABBEY SCHOOL*
17 Kendrick Road, Reading,
Berkshire RG1 5DZ
Tel: (01734) 872256
Head: Miss B C Sheldon
Type: Girls Day 4-18 (Boys 4-7)
No of Pupils: B1 G1010
Fees: (September 95) £3300 - £4140

ALDER BRIDGE SCHOOL
Mill Lane, Padworth, Reading,
Berkshire RG7 4JU
Tel: (01734) 714471
Type: Co-educational Day 3-9
No of Pupils: B21 G23
Fees: (September 95) £1920 - £2226

THE ARK SCHOOL
School Road, Padworth, Reading,
Berkshire RG7 4JA
Tel: (01734) 834802
Head: John S Hartley
Type: Co-educational Day 2-8
No of Pupils: B35 G29
Fees: (September 95) £1980 - £8100

BRADFIELD COLLEGE
Bradfield, Reading, Berkshire
RG7 6AR
Tel: (01734) 744203
Head: P B Smith
Type: Boys Boarding & Day 13-18
(Co-ed VIth form)
No of Pupils: B510 G88 No of
Boarders F560
Fees: (September 95) FB £12225
DAY £9156

CHILTERN COLLEGE SCHOOL
16 Peppard Road, Caversham,
Reading, Berkshire RG4 8JZ
Tel: (01734) 471847
Head: Mrs P Ardrey
Type: Co-educational Day 4-8
No of Pupils: 45
Fees: (September 95) £880

CROSFIELDS SCHOOL
Shinfield, Reading, Berkshire
RG2 9BL
Tel: (01734) 871810
Head: F G Skipwith
Type: Boys Day 4-13
No of Pupils: 320
Fees: (September 94) £2700 - £4995

DOLPHIN SCHOOL
Hurst, Twyford, Reading, Berkshire
RG10 0BP
Tel: (01734) 341277
Head: Dr N E Follett
Type: Co-educational Day 3-13
No of Pupils: B122 G119
Fees: (September 93) £2355 - £3900

DOUAI SCHOOL*
Upper Woolhampton, Reading,
Berkshire RG7 5TH
Tel: (01734) 715200
Head: Dom E Power
Type: Co-educational Boarding &
Day 10-18
No of Pupils: 220 No of Boarders
F100 W36
Fees: (September 95) FB £8445 -
£10545 WB £8145 - £10245
DAY £5535 - £6780

ELSTREE SCHOOL
Woolhampton, Reading, Berkshire
RG7 5TD
Tel: (01734) 713302
Head: S M Hill
Type: Boys Boarding & Day 3-13
No of Pupils: 175 No of Boarders F90
Fees: (September 95) FB £9210
DAY £3900 - £6540

FOXLEY PNEU SCHOOL
Manor Drive, Shurlock Row,
Reading, Berkshire RG10 0PX
Tel: (01734) 343578
Head: Miss M J Fallon
Type: Co-educational Day 4-7
No of Pupils: B18 G17
Fees: (September 95) £1122 - £2046

HEMDEAN HOUSE SCHOOL
Hemdean Road, Caversham,
Reading, Berkshire RG4 7SD
Tel: (01734) 472590
Head: Mrs P L Pethybridge
Type: Co-educational Day B3-11
G3-16
No of Pupils: B50 G120
Fees: (September 95) £2250 - £3225

LEIGHTON PARK SCHOOL
Shinfield Road, Reading, Berkshire
RG2 7DH
Tel: (01734) 872065
Head: J A Chapman
Type: Co-educational Boarding &
Day 11-18
No of Pupils: B300 G75 No of
Boarders F215
Fees: (September 95) FB £9522 -
£11196 DAY £7065 - £8397

THE ORATORY
PREPARATORY SCHOOL
Goring Heath, Reading, Berkshire
RG8 7SF
Tel: (01734) 844511
Head: D L Sexon
Type: Co-educational Day &
Boarding 4-13
No of Pupils: B230 G64 No of
Boarders F51
Fees: (September 95) FB £8283
DAY £1599 - £5815

THE ORATORY SCHOOL
Woodcote, Reading, Berkshire
RG8 0PJ
Tel: (01491) 680207
Head: S W Barrow
Type: Boys Boarding & Day 11-18
No of Pupils: 395 No of Boarders
F270
Fees: (September 95) FB £9255 -
£11760 DAY £6675 - £8220

PADWORTH COLLEGE
Padworth, Reading, Berkshire
RG7 4NR
Tel: (01734) 832644
Head: Dr Sheila Villazon
Type: Girls Residential & Day 14-20
No of Pupils: 140
Fees: (September 95) FB £10935

PANGBOURNE COLLEGE*
Pangbourne, Reading, Berkshire
RG8 8LA
Tel: (01734) 842101
Head: A B Hudson
Type: Co-educational Boarding &
Day 11-18
No of Pupils: 390 No of Boarders 305
Fees: (September 95) FB £11310
DAY £7920

PRESENTATION COLLEGE
63 Bath Road, Reading, Berkshire
RG30 2BB
Tel: (01734) 572861
Head: Rev Brother S Sullivan
Type: Boys Day 5-18 (Co-ed VIth
Form)
No of Pupils: 405
Fees: (September 95) £2550 - £3330

QUEEN ANNE'S SCHOOL*
6 Henley Road, Caversham, Reading,
Berkshire RG4 0DX
Tel: (01734) 471582
Head: Mrs D Forbes
Type: Girls Boarding & Day 11-18
No of Pupils: 350 No of Boarders
F207 W39
Fees: (September 95) F/WB £11250
DAY £7380

READING BLUE COAT
SCHOOL*
Holme Park, Sonning, Reading,
Berkshire RG4 0SU
Tel: (01734) 441005
Head: Rev A C Sanders
Type: Boys Day & Boarding 11-18
(Co-ed VIth form)
No of Pupils: B530 G30 No of
Boarders F25 W40
Fees: (September 95) FB £9570 WB
£9270 DAY £5250

ST ANDREW'S SCHOOL
Buckhold, Pangbourne, Reading,
Berkshire RG8 8QA
Tel: (01734) 744276
Head: J M Snow
Type: Co-educational Day &
Boarding 4-13
No of Pupils: B174 G83 No of
Boarders F44
Fees: (September 95) FB £8100 -
£8250 DAY £3300 - £5940

ST EDWARDS SCHOOL
64 Tilehurst Road, Reading,
Berkshire RG3 2JH
Tel: (01734) 574345
Head: A McComas
Type: Boys Day 7-14
No of Pupils: 117
Fees: (September 95) £2985 - £3090

ST JOSEPH'S CONVENT
SCHOOL*
64 Upper Redlands Road, Reading,
Berkshire RG1 5JT
Tel: (01734) 661000
Head: Mrs V Brookes
Type: Girls Day 11-18
No of Pupils: 400
Fees: (September 95) £3675 - £3795

ST JOSEPH'S PREPARATORY SCHOOL

66 Upper Redlands Road, Reading, Berkshire RG1 5JT
Tel: (01734) 351717
Head: Sister Helen-Marie
Type: Girls Day 3-11 (Boys 3-7)
No of Pupils: B20 G160
Fees: (September 95) £2160

SLOUGH

ETON END PNEU

35 Eton Road, Datchet, Slough, Berkshire SL3 9AX
Tel: (01753) 541075
Head: Mrs B E Ottley
Type: Girls Day 3-12 (Boys 3-7)
No of Pupils: B85 G140
Fees: (September 95) £2052 - £3591

LANGLEY MANOR SCHOOL

St Marys Road, Langley, Slough, Berkshire SL3 6BZ
Tel: (01753) 825368
Head: Mrs S Eaton
Type: Co-educational Day 3-12
No of Pupils: B138 G121
Fees: (September 95) £3042 - £3168

LONG CLOSE SCHOOL

Upton Court Road, Slough, Berkshire SL3 7LU
Tel: (01753) 520095
Head: M H Kneath
Type: Co-educational Day 3-13
No of Pupils: B149 G25
Fees: (September 95) £1881 - £5400

ST BERNARD'S PREPARATORY SCHOOL

Hawtrey Close, Slough, Berkshire SL1 1TB
Tel: (01753) 21821
Head: Sister Francis Mary
Type: Co-educational Day 3-12
No of Pupils: B40 G220
Fees: (September 95) £3120 - £3310

SUNNINGDALE

HURST LODGE*

Charters Road, Sunningdale, Berkshire SL5 9QG
Tel: (01344) 22154
Head: Mrs A M Smit
Type: Girls Day & Boarding 3-18 (Boys 3-7)
No of Pupils: B20 G170 No of Boarders 40
Fees: (September 95) FB £9900 DAY £1800 - £5850

SUNNINGDALE SCHOOL

Sunningdale, Berkshire SL5 9PY
Tel: (01344) 20159
Head: A J N Dawson & T M E Dawson
Type: Boys Boarding 8-13
No of Pupils: 120 No of Boarders F120
Fees: (September 95) FB £6885

TILEHURST

THE HIGHLANDS SCHOOL

Wardle Avenue, Tilehurst, Berkshire RG3 6JR
Tel: (01734) 427186
Head: Miss E D Lind-Smith
Type: Co-educational Day B3-8 G3-11
No of Pupils: B53 G117
Fees: (September 95) £1998 - £3168

TWYFORD

CEDAR PARK SCHOOL

Bridge Farm Road, Twyford, Berkshire RG10 9PP
Tel: (01734) 340118
Head: Mrs Bradley & Mrs Christie
Type: Co-educational Day 2-7
No of Pupils: B38 G38
Fees: (September 95) £660 - £4560

WINDSOR

THE BRIGIDINE SCHOOL

King's Road, Windsor, Berkshire SL4 2AX
Tel: (01753) 863779
Head: Mrs M B Cairns
Type: Girls Day 3-18 (Boys 3-7)
No of Pupils: B8 G355
Fees: (September 95) £3033 - £4425

ETON COLLEGE

Windsor, Berkshire SL4 6DW
Tel: (01753) 671000
Head: J E Lewis
Type: Boys Boarding 13-18
No of Pupils: 1262
Fees: (September 95) FB £12888

HAILEYBURY JUNIOR SCHOOL*

Clewer Manor, Imperial Road, Windsor, Berkshire SL4 3RS
Tel: (01753) 866330
Head: B J Hare
Type: Boys Boarding & Day 7-14
No of Pupils: 164 No of Boarders F35 W11
Fees: (September 95) FB £7875 DAY £6075

ST GEORGE'S SCHOOL

Windsor Castle, Windsor, Berkshire SL4 1QF
Tel: (01753) 865553
Head: Rev R Marsh
Type: Boys Boarding & Day 7-13
No of Pupils: 82 No of Boarders F37 W8
Fees: (September 95) FB £8580 WB £8430 DAY £5790 - £6390

ST JOHN'S BEAUMONT

Windsor, Berkshire SL4 2JN
Tel: (01784) 432428
Head: D St Gogarty
Type: Boys Boarding & Day 4-13
No of Pupils: 186 No of Boarders F24 W20
Fees: (September 95) FB £9954 WB £8331 DAY £3429 - £6027

UPTON HOUSE SCHOOL

115 St Leonard's Road, Windsor, Berkshire SL4 3DF
Tel: (01753) 862610
Head: Mrs J G Woodley
Type: Girls Day 3-11 (Boys 3-7)
No of Pupils: B65 G148
Fees: (September 95) £1644 - £3753

WOKINGHAM

BEARWOOD COLLEGE*

Bearwood, Wokingham, Berkshire RG41 5BG
Tel: (01734) 786915
Head: Dr R J Belcher
Type: Co-educational Boarding & Day 11-18
No of Pupils: 204 No of Boarders F80 W25
Fees: (September 95) F/WB £9045 - £10050 DAY £4995 - £5550

HOLME GRANGE SCHOOL

Heathlands Road, Wokingham, Berkshire RG40 3AL
Tel: (01734) 781566
Head: N J Brodrick
Type: Co-educational Day 4-13
No of Pupils: B154 G105
Fees: (September 95) £3588 - £4608

LUCKLEY- OAKFIELD SCHOOL*

Luckley Road, Wokingham, Berkshire RG41 3EU
Tel: (01734) 784175
Head: R C Blake
Type: Girls Day & Boarding 11-18
No of Pupils: 274 No of Boarders F150
Fees: (September 95) FB £7950 WB £7794 DAY £4929

LUDGROVE
Wokingham, Berkshire RG11 3AB
Tel: (01734) 789881
Head: G W P Barber & C N J Marston
Type: Boys Boarding 8-13
No of Pupils: 180 No of Boarders
F180
Fees: (September 95) FB £8700

**WHITE HOUSE
PREPARATORY SCHOOL**
Finchampstead Road, Wokingham,
Berkshire RG11 3HD
Tel: (01734) 785151
Head: Mrs M L Blake
Type: Co-educational Day B3-7
G3-11
No of Pupils: B20 G92
Fees: (September 95) £2835 - £3240

BUCKINGHAMSHIRE

AMERSHAM

THE BEACON SCHOOL
Chesham Bois, Amersham,
Buckinghamshire HP6 5PF
Tel: (01494) 433654
Head: J V Cross
Type: Boys Day 3-13
No of Pupils: 300
Fees: (September 95) £1710 - £5478

HEATHERTON HOUSE
SCHOOL
Copperkins Lane, Chesham Bois,
Amersham, Buckinghamshire HP6
5QB
Tel: (01494) 726433
Head: Mrs P K Thomson
Type: Girls Day 3-13 (Boys 3-5)
No of Pupils: B17 G135
Fees: (September 95) £1440 - £3975

AYLESBURY

ASHFOLD SCHOOL*
Dorton, Aylesbury,
Buckinghamshire HP18 9NG
Tel: (01844) 238237
Head: D H Dalrymple
Type: Co-educational Boarding &
Day 3-14
No of Pupils: B120 G54 No of
Boarders F8 W22
Fees: (September 95) F/WB £8175
DAY £1995 - £6225

LADYMEDE
Little Kimble, Aylesbury,
Buckinghamshire HP17 0XP
Tel: (01844) 346154
Head: Mrs V Cloutt
Type: Co-educational 3-12
No of Pupils: B18 G91 No of
Boarders F8
Fees: (September 95) DAY £1650 -
£4440

BEACONSFIELD

DAVENIES*
Station Road, Beaconsfield,
Buckinghamshire
HP9 1AA
Tel: (01494) 674169
Head: J R Jones
Type: Boys Day 4-13
No of Pupils: 240
Fees: (September 95) £3885 - £4275

HIGH MARCH SCHOOL
23 Ledborough Lane, Beaconsfield,
Buckinghamshire HP9 2PZ
Tel: (01494) 675186
Head: Mrs P A Forsyth
Type: Girls Day 3-13 (Boys 3-7)
No of Pupils: B12 G292
Fees: (September 95) £1350 - £4170

BUCKINGHAM

AKELEY WOOD SCHOOL
Buckingham, MK18 5AE
Tel: (01280) 814110
Head: J C Lovelock
Type: Co-educational Day 10-18
No of Pupils: B225 G135
Fees: (September 95) £3930 - £4605

STOWE SCHOOL*
Buckingham, MK18 5EH
Tel: (01280) 813164
Head: J G Nichols
Type: Boys Boarding & Day 13-18
(Co-ed VIth form)
No of Pupils: B459 G86
Fees: (September 95) FB £12789
DAY £8955

CHESHAM

CHESHAM PREPARATORY
SCHOOL
Orchard Leigh, Chesham,
Buckinghamshire HP5 3QF
Tel: (01494) 782619
Head: R J Ford
Type: Co-educational Day 5-13
No of Pupils: B158 G137
Fees: (September 95) £2985 - £3795

FARNHAM ROYAL

CALDICOTT*
Crown Lane, Farnham Royal,
Buckinghamshire SL2 3SL
Tel: (01753) 646214
Head: M C Spens
Type: Boys Boarding & Day 7-13
No of Pupils: 250 No of Boarders
F130
Fees: (September 95) FB £8910
DAY £6600

DAIR HOUSE SCHOOL TRUST
LTD
Bishops Blake, Beaconsfield Road,
Farnham Royal, Buckinghamshire
SL2 3BY
Tel: (01753) 643964
Head: Mrs T A Devonside
Type: Co-educational Day 3-8
No of Pupils: B94 G36
Fees: (September 95) £3072 - £3192

GERRARDS CROSS

GAYHURST SCHOOL
Bull Lane, Gerrards Cross,
Buckinghamshire SL9 8RJ
Tel: (01753) 882690
Head: A J Sims
Type: Boys Day 4-13
No of Pupils: 230
Fees: (September 94) £3255 - £4185

HOLY CROSS CONVENT
The Grange, Chalfont St Peter,
Gerrards Cross, Buckinghamshire
SL9 9DW
Tel: (01753) 882583
Head: Sister K Russell
Type: Girls Day & Boarding 5-18
No of Pupils: 400 No of Boarders F60
W10
Fees: (September 95) FB £9000
DAY £2850 - £3000

KINGSCOTE SCHOOL
Oval Way, Gerrards Cross,
Buckinghamshire SL9 8PZ
Tel: (01753) 885535
Head: Mrs S A Tunstall
Type: Boys Day 4-7
No of Pupils: 108
Fees: (September 95) £3450

MALTMANS GREEN SCHOOL
Maltman's Lane, Gerrards Cross,
Buckinghamshire SL9 8RR
Tel: (01753) 883022
Head: Mrs M Evans
Type: Girls Day 3-13
No of Pupils: 330
Fees: (September 95) £1480 - £4800

ST MARY'S SCHOOL
Packhorse Road, Gerrards Cross,
Buckinghamshire SL9 8JQ
Tel: (01753) 883370
Head: Mrs F Balcombe
Type: Girls Day 3-18
No of Pupils: 290
Fees: (September 95) £2655 - £5085

THORPE HOUSE SCHOOL
Oval Way, Gerrards Cross,
Buckinghamshire SL9 8PZ
Tel: (01753) 882474
Head: J Scaife
Type: Boys Day 4-13
No of Pupils: 301
Fees: (September 95) £3350 - £4750

GREAT MISSENDEN

GATEWAY SCHOOL
1 High Street, Great Missenden,
Buckinghamshire HP16 9AA
Tel: (01494) 862407
Head: J H Wade and J L Wade
Type: Co-educational Day 2-13
No of Pupils: B190 G155
Fees: (September 95) £1140 - £8825

HAMPDEN MANOR SCHOOL
Little Hampden, Great Missenden,
Buckinghamshire HP16 9PS
Tel: (01296) 622101
Head: N Lloyd-Webb
Type: Boys Boarding & Day 4-13
(Girls 4-7)
No of Pupils: B90 G5 No of Boarders
W20
Fees: (September 93) WB £5850
DAY £3060 - £4290

HIGH WYCOMBE

CROWN HOUSE SCHOOL
19 London Road, High Wycombe,
Buckinghamshire HP11 1BJ
Tel: (01494) 529927
Head: L Clark
Type: Co-educational Day 4-12
No of Pupils: B81 G67
Fees: (September 95) £3030

GODSTOWE PREPARATORY SCHOOL*
Shrubbery Road, High Wycombe,
Buckinghamshire HP13 6PR
Tel: (01494) 529273
Head: Mrs F I Henson
Type: Girls Day & Boarding 4-13
(Boys 4-8)
No of Pupils: B30 G340 No of
Boarders F127
Fees: (September 95) FB £8730
DAY £2745 - £4845

PIPERS CORNER SCHOOL*
Great Kingshill, High Wycombe,
Buckinghamshire HP15 6LP
Tel: (01494) 718255
Head: Dr M M Wilson
Type: Girls Boarding & Day 4-18
No of Pupils: 350 No of Boarders F39
W41
Fees: (September 95) FB £7635 -
£9330 WB £7266 - £8757
DAY £2700 - £5580

WYCOMBE ABBEY SCHOOL
High Wycombe, Buckinghamshire
HP11 1PE
Tel: (01494) 520381
Head: Mrs J M Goodland
Type: Girls Boarding 11-18 (A few
day places)
No of Pupils: 490 No of Boarders
F480
Fees: (September 95) FB £12240
DAY £9180

MILTON KEYNES

BURY LAWN SCHOOL
Soskin Drive, Stantonbury Fields,
Milton Keynes, Buckinghamshire
MK14 6DP
Tel: (01908) 220345
Head: Mrs H Kiff
Type: Co-educational Day 2-18
No of Pupils: B220 G200
Fees: (September 94) £3165 - £4470

GYOSEI INTERNATIONAL SCHOOL UK
Japonica Lane, Willen Park, Milton
Keynes, Buckinghamshire MK15 9JX
Tel: (01908) 690100
Head: T Sakai
Type: Co-educational Boarding &
Day 11-18
No of Pupils: B187 G107 No of
Boarders F283
Fees: (September 95) FB £12240 -
£12350 DAY £7490 - £7600

MILTON KEYNES PREPARATORY SCHOOL
Tattenhoe Lane, Milton Keynes,
Buckinghamshire MK3 7EG
Tel: (01908) 642111
Head: Mrs H A Pauley
Type: Co-educational Day 1-13
No of Pupils: 420
Fees: (September 94) £3960 - £4530

SWANBOURNE HOUSE SCHOOL
Swanbourne, Milton Keynes,
Buckinghamshire MK17 0HZ
Tel: (01296) 720264
Head: T V More
Type: Co-educational Boarding &
Day 3-13
No of Pupils: B170 G110 No of
Boarders F14 W31
Fees: (September 95) F/WB £8235
DAY £3660 - £6330

THORNTON COLLEGE CONVENT OF JESUS AND MARY
Thornton, Milton Keynes,
Buckinghamshire MK17 0HJ
Tel: (01280) 812610
Head: Mrs E E Speddy
Type: Girls Day & Boarding 3-16
(Boys 3-7)
No of Pupils: 268 No of Boarders F53
W16
Fees: (September 95) FB £6760 -
£7760 WB £6430 - £7400 DAY
£3800 - £4780

NEWPORT PAGNELL

FILGRAVE SCHOOL
Filgrave, Newport Pagnell,
Buckinghamshire MK16 9ET
Tel: (01234) 711534
Head: Mrs S Marriott
Type: Co-educational Day
No of Pupils: B27 G30
Fees: (September 95) £2670

PRINCES RISBOROUGH

ST TERESA'S SCHOOL*
Aylesbury Road, Princes Risborough,
Buckinghamshire HP27 0JW
Tel: (01844) 345005
Head: Mrs C M Sparkes & Mrs A M
Broom Smith
Type: Co-educational Day 3-12
No of Pupils: B77 G97
Fees: (September 95) £852 - £2501

CAMBRIDGESHIRE

CAMBRIDGE

CAMBRIDGE ARTS & SCIENCES (CATS)*
13/14 Round Church Street,
Cambridge CB5 8AD
Tel: (01223) 314431
Head: Miss E R Armstrong
Type: Co-educational Day &
Residential 15-19
No of Pupils: B72 G88
Fees: (September 95) FB £10800 -
£12300 DAY £7500 - £9000

CAMBRIDGE CENTRE FOR VITH FORM STUDIES*
1 Salisbury Villas, Station Road,
Cambridge CB1 2JF
Tel: (01223) 316890
Head: Dr A M Dawson & P C Redhead
Type: Co-educational Residential &
Day 14+
No of Pupils: B96 G122
Fees: (September 95) FB £11355 -
£12915 DAY £8295 - £8670

HORLERS PRE-PREPARATORY SCHOOL
20 Green End, Comberton,
Cambridge CB3 7DY
Tel: (01223) 263189
Head: Mrs A Horler
Type: Co-educational Day 4-8
No of Pupils: B15 G15
Fees: (September 95) £1190

KING'S COLLEGE SCHOOL*
West Road, Cambridge CB3 9DN
Tel: (01223) 365814
Head: A S Corbett
Type: Co-educational Day &
Boarding 4-13 (Day girls only)
No of Pupils: B187 G88 No of
Boarders F23 W30
Fees: (September 95) WB £8412
DAY £4092 - £5430

THE LEYS SCHOOL*
Cambridge CBA 2AD
Tel: (01223) 355327
Head: Rev Dr J C A Barrett
Type: Co-educational Boarding &
Day 13-18
No of Pupils: B300 G120 No of
Boarders F267
Fees: (September 95) FB £11940
DAY £8700

MADINGLEY SCHOOL
Cambridge Road, Madingley,
Cambridge CB3 8AH
Tel: (01954) 210309
Head: Mrs J West
Type: Co-educational Day 3-11
No of Pupils: 55
Fees: (September 95) £1740 - £2475

MANDER PORTMAN WOODWARD
3/4 Brookside, Cambridge CB2 1JE
Tel: (01223) 350158
Head: Mrs Daphne Bigmore
Type: Co-educational Day 13-21
No of Pupils: 180
Fees: (September 95) 3 A Levels
£7620 5 GCSEs £8331

THE MONTESSORI SCHOOL, CAMBRIDGE
St Andrews Hall, Chapel Street,
Chesterton, Cambridge CB4 1DY
Tel: (01223) 350743
Head: Ms Julie Carroll-Watts
Type: Co-educational Day 2-7
No of Pupils: 30
Fees: (September 95) £1785 - £2355

THE PERSE SCHOOL
Hills Road, Cambridge CB2 2QF
Tel: (01223) 568300
Head: N P V Richardson
Type: Boys Day 7-18 (Co-ed VIth
form)
No of Pupils: 670
Fees: (September 95) £4524

THE PERSE SCHOOL FOR GIRLS
Union Road, Cambridge CB2 1HF
Tel: (01223) 568300
Head: Miss H S Smith
Type: Girls Day 7-18
No of Pupils: 710
Fees: (September 95) £4005 - £4656

ST ANDREW'S
2A Free School Lane, Cambridge
CB2 3QA
Tel: (01223) 60040
Head: Mervyn Martin
& K C Easterbrook
Type: Co-educational Day 14+
No of Pupils: B72 G32
Fees: (September 95) 3 A Levels
£7650- £8055
5 GCSEs £6750

ST COLETTE'S SCHOOL*
Tenison Road, Cambridge CB1 2DP
Tel: (01223) 353696
Head: Mrs B Boyton
Type: Co-educational Day 2-7
No of Pupils: B41 G115
Fees: (September 95) £1350 - £2955

ST FAITHS SCHOOL*
Trumpington Road, Cambridge
CB2 2AG
Tel: (01223) 352073
Head: R A Dyson
Type: Co-educational Day 4-13
No of Pupils: 420
Fees: (September 95) £3870 - £4920

ST JOHN'S COLLEGE SCHOOL
73 Grange Road, Cambridge CB3 9AB
Tel: (01223) 353532
Head: K L Jones
Type: Co-educational Day &
Boarding 4-13
No of Pupils: 440 No of Boarders F50
Fees: (September 95) F/WB £8058
DAY £3765 - £5100

ST MARY'S SCHOOL
Bateman Street, Cambridge CB2 1LY
Tel: (01223) 353253
Head: Miss M Conway
Type: Girls Day & Boarding 11-18
No of Pupils: 600 No of Boarders
W80
Fees: (September 95) WB £6930
DAY £3870

SANCTON WOOD SCHOOL
2 St Paul's Road, Cambridge CB1 2EZ
Tel: (01223) 359488
Head: Mrs J Sturdy
Type: Co-educational Day 3-16
No of Pupils: B100 G100
Fees: (September 95) £1512 - £3546

ELY

THE KING'S SCHOOL
Ely, Cambridgeshire CB7 4DB
Tel: (01353) 662824
Head: R H Youdale
Type: Co-educational Boarding &
Day 4-18
No of Pupils: B463 G325 No of
Boarders F118 W99
Fees: (September 95) FB £6900 -
£11487 WB £6660 - £11187
DAY £1860 - £7326

HUNTINGDON

DEAN GRANGE PREPARATORY SCHOOL*
Upper Dean, Huntingdon,
Cambridgeshire PE18 0LT
Tel: (01234) 708243
Head: David Roach
Type: Co-educational Day &
Boarding 4-13 (Nursery 2-4)
No of Pupils: B45 G48 No of Boarders
F16
Fees: (September 95) FB £5520 -
£6285 WB £5160 - £5925 DAY
£2220 - £2985

KIMBOLTON SCHOOL*
Kimbolton, Huntingdon,
Cambridgeshire PE18 0EA
Tel: (01480) 860505
Head: R V Peel
Type: Co-educational Boarding &
Day 7-18 (Boarders from 11)
No of Pupils: B383 G343 No of
Boarders F62
Fees: (September 95) FB £8985 DAY
£4350 - £5235

PETERBOROUGH

LAXTON JUNIOR SCHOOL
North Street, Oundle, Peterborough,
Cambridgeshire PE8 4AL
Tel: (01832) 273673
Head: Miss S C Thomas
Type: Co-educational Day 4-11
No of Pupils: B79 G60
Fees: (September 94) £2814

LAXTON SCHOOL*
Oundle, Peterborough,
Cambridgeshire PE8 4AR
Tel: (01832) 273569
Head: R I Briggs
Type: Co-educational Day 11-18
No of Pupils: B123 G78
Fees: (September 95) £5004

OUNDLE SCHOOL
Peterborough, Cambridgeshire
PE8 4EN
Tel: (01832) 273536
Head: D B McMurray
Type: Co-educational Boarding 11-19
No of Pupils: 830 No of Boarders
F830
Fees: (September 95) FB £9795 -
£12825

PETERBOROUGH HIGH SCHOOL
Westwood House, Thorpe Road,
Peterborough, Cambridgeshire
PE3 6JF
Tel: (01733) 343357
Head: Mrs A J V Storey
Type: Girls Day & Boarding 4-18
(Boys 4-8)
No of Pupils: B10 G300 No of
Boarders F80
Fees: (September 94) F/WB £7380 -
£7863 DAY £1935 - £3915

WISBECH

ST AUDREY'S CONVENT SCHOOL
Alexandra Road, Wisbech,
Cambridgeshire PE13 1HW
Tel: (01945) 583465
Head: Sister Anna Patricia Pereira
Type: Co-educational Day 3-11
No of Pupils: B77 G56
Fees: (September 95) £1020 - £2382

ST PAULS SCHOOL
Gote Lane, Gorefield, Wisbech,
Cambridgeshire PE13
Tel: (01945) 870444
Head: J Jennings
Type: Co-educational Day 4-18
No of Pupils: B30 G25
Fees: (September 95) £795 - £995

WISBECH GRAMMAR SCHOOL
North Brink, Wisbech,
Cambridgeshire PE13 1JX
Tel: (01945) 583631
Head: Mr R S Repper
Type: Co-educational Day 11-18
No of Pupils: B333 G305
Fees: (September 95) £4650

CHANNEL ISLANDS

ALDERNEY

ORMER HOUSE PREPARATORY SCHOOL
La Vallee, Alderney, Channel Islands
Tel: (01481) 823287
Head: A J Roberts
Type: Co-educational Day & Boarding 3-13
No of Pupils: B26 G15 No of Boarders W3
Fees: (September 95) WB £4620 DAY £1935 - £2850

GUERNSEY

CONVENT OF MERCY
Cordier Hill, St Peter Port, Guernsey, Channel Islands
Tel: (01481) 720729
Head: Sister Carmel
Type: Co-educational Day 3-7
No of Pupils: 115
Fees: (September 95) £1200

ELIZABETH COLLEGE
Guernsey, Channel Islands GY1 2PY
Tel: (01481) 726544
Head: J H F Doulton
Type: Boys Day & Boarding 7-18 (Girls 16-18)
No of Pupils: B700 G14 No of Boarders F40
Fees: (September 95) FB £6135 DAY £2460

THE LADIES' COLLEGE
Les Graves, St Peter Port, Guernsey, Channel Islands GY1 1RW
Tel: (01481) 721602
Head: Miss M E Macdonald
Type: Girls Day 3-18 (Boys 3-7)
No of Pupils: B30 G511
Fees: (September 95) £2055 - £2190

JERSEY

ASHDOWN SCHOOL AND NURSERY
47 St Mark's Road, Saint Helier, Jersey, Channel Islands JE2 4LD
Tel: (01534) 34229
Head: Mrs S Wilton
Type: Co-educational Day 3-5
No of Pupils: 110
Fees: On application

BEAULIEU CONVENT SCHOOL
Wellington Road, Saint Helier, Jersey, Channel Islands JE2 4RJ
Tel: (01534) 31280
Head: Mrs R A Hill
Type: Girls Day 4-18
No of Pupils: 600
Fees: (September 95) £1800

DE LA SALLE COLLEGE
The Beeches, Wellington Road, Saint Helier, Jersey, Channel Islands JE2 7TH
Tel: (01534) 26548
Head: Brother L Hughes
Type: Boys Day 4-18
No of Pupils: 700
Fees: (September 95) £1725

FCJ PRIMARY SCHOOL
Deloraine Road, St Saviour, Jersey, Channel Islands JE2 4LB
Tel: (01534) 23063
Head: Sister Cecilia Connolly
Type: Co-educational Day 4-11
No of Pupils: 290
Fees: (September 95) £1290

HELVETIA HOUSE SCHOOL
14 Elizabeth Place, St Helier, Jersey, Channel Islands JE2 3PN
Tel: (01534) 24928
Head: Mrs A E Atkinson
Type: Girls Day 4-11
No of Pupils: 100
Fees: (September 95) £1395

ST GEORGE'S PREPARATORY SCHOOL
La Hague Manor, Rue de la Hague, St Peter, Jersey, Channel Islands JE3 7DB
Tel: (01534) 481593
Head: T Clare
Type: Co-educational Day 3-11
No of Pupils: B62 G65
Fees: (September 95) £1875 - £4500

ST MICHAEL'S PREPARATORY SCHOOL
Five Oaks, St Saviour, Jersey, Channel Islands JE2 7UG
Tel: (01534) 856904
Head: R De Figueiredo
Type: Co-educational Day 3-13
No of Pupils: B142 G127
Fees: (September 95) £4974 - £6396

VICTORIA COLLEGE
St Helier, Jersey, Channel Islands JE2 4RA
Tel: (01534) 37591
Head: J Hydes
Type: Boys Day 11-19 (VIth with Jersey girls college)
No of Pupils: 605
Fees: (September 95) £5175

VICTORIA COLLEGE PREPARATORY SCHOOL
Pleasant Street, St Helier, Jersey, Channel Islands
Tel: (01534) 23465
Head: J H Hibbs
Type: Boys Day 7-11
No of Pupils: 298
Fees: (September 95) £1875

CHESHIRE

ALDERLEY EDGE

MOUNT CARMEL SCHOOL
Wilmslow Road, Alderley Edge,
Cheshire SK9 7QB
Tel: (01625) 583028
Head: Mrs K Mills
Type: Girls Day 4-18
No of Pupils: 602
Fees: (September 95) £2340 - £3588

THE RYLEYS
Ryleys Lane, Alderley Edge, Cheshire
SK9 7UY
Tel: (01625) 583241
Head: J R Bridgeland
Type: Boys Day & Boarding 3-13
(Weekly boarding only)
No of Pupils: 272 No of Boarders
W14
Fees: (September 95) DAY £1320 -
£4050

ST HILARY'S SCHOOL
Alderley Edge, Cheshire SK9 7AG
Tel: (01625) 583532
Head: Mrs G M Case
Type: Girls Day 3-18
No of Pupils: 272
Fees: (September 95) £2175 - £4041

ALTRINCHAM

ALTRINCHAM PREPARATORY
SCHOOL
'Highbury', 6 West Road, Bowdon,
Altrincham, Cheshire WA14 2LE
Tel: (0161) 928 3366
Head: R J McCay
Type: Boys Day 4-12
No of Pupils: 325
Fees: (September 95) £2440 - £3025

BOWDON PREPARATORY
SCHOOL FOR GIRLS
48 Stamford Road, Bowdon,
Altrincham, Cheshire WA14 2JP
Tel: (0161) 928 0678
Head: Mrs J H Tan
Type: Girls Day 2-12
Fees: (September 94) £2340

CULCHETH HALL
Ashley Road, Altrincham, Cheshire
WA14 2LT
Tel: (0161) 928 1862
Head: C D Taylor
Type: Girls Day 3-18
No of Pupils: 250
Fees: (September 95) £1860 - £3690

FOREST SCHOOL
Moss Lane, Timperley, Altrincham,
Cheshire WA15 6LJ
Tel: (0161) 980 4075
Head: Mrs J Quest
Type: Co-educational Day 3-11
No of Pupils: B95 G72
Fees: (September 95) £2355 - £2670

HALE PREPARATORY SCHOOL
Broomfield Lane, Hale, Altrincham,
Cheshire WA15 9AS
Tel: (0161) 928 2386
Head: J Connor
Type: Co-educational Day 4-12
No of Pupils: B110 G69
Fees: (September 95) £2295

LORETO CONVENT
GRAMMAR SCHOOL
Dunham Road, Altrincham, Cheshire
WA14 4AH
Tel: (0161) 928 3703
Head: Sister Aileen McEvoy
Type: Girls Day 11-18
No of Pupils: 800
Fees: (September 95) £2892

LORETO CONVENT
PREPARATORY SCHOOL
Dunham Road, Altrincham, Cheshire
WA14 4AH
Tel: (0161) 928 8310
Head: Sister C A Fay
Type: Girls Day 4-11 (Boys 4-7)
No of Pupils: 198
Fees: (September 95) £1830

NORTH CESTRIAN GRAMMAR
SCHOOL
Dunham Road, Altrincham, Cheshire
WA14 4AJ
Tel: (0161) 928 1856
Head: P F Morton
Type: Boys Day 11-18
No of Pupils: 370
Fees: (September 95) £3450

ST AMBROSE COLLEGE
Hale Barns, Altrincham, Cheshire
WA15 0HF
Tel: (0161) 980 2711
Head: G E Hester
Type: Boys Day 11-18
No of Pupils: 720
Fees: (September 95) £3450

ST AMBROSE PREPARATORY
SCHOOL
Hale Barns, Altrincham, Cheshire
WA15 0HF
Tel: (0161) 903 9193
Head: M J Lochery
Type: Boys Day 4-11
No of Pupils: 195
Fees: (September 95) £2460

CHEADLE

CHEADLE HULME SCHOOL
Claremont Road, Cheadle Hulme,
Cheadle, Cheshire SK8 6EF
Tel: (0161) 485 4142
Head: D J Wilkinson
Type: Co-educational Day 7-18
No of Pupils: B558 G571
Fees: (September 95) £3273 - £4086

GREENBANK
Heathbank Road, Cheadle Hulme,
Cheadle, Cheshire SK8 6HU
Tel: (0161) 485 3724
Head: N Brown
Type: Co-educational Day 3-11
(Nursery 2-4)
No of Pupils: B102 G71
Fees: (September 95) £1671 - £2886

HULME HALL SCHOOLS
75 Hulme Hall Road, Cheadle
Hulme, Cheadle, Cheshire SK8 6LA
Tel: (0161) 485 4638
Head: G Kellock
Type: Co-educational Day 11-16
No of Pupils: 325
Fees: (September 95) £1890 - £3570

HULME HALL SCHOOLS
(JUNIOR SECTION)
70 Swann Lane, Cheadle Hulme,
Cheadle, Cheshire SK8 7HU
Tel: (0161) 486 9970
Head: Mrs J Carr
Type: Co-educational Day 3-11
No of Pupils: 200
Fees: (September 95) £1785 - £2550

LADY BARN HOUSE SCHOOL
Langlands, Schools Hill, Cheadle
Hulme, Cheadle, Cheshire SK8 1JE
Tel: (0161) 428 2912
Head: E J Bonner
Type: Co-educational Day 3-11
No of Pupils: B260 G157
Fees: (September 94) £2310 - £2625

RAMILLIES HALL SCHOOL
Cheadle Hulme, Cheadle, Cheshire
SK8 7AJ
Tel: (0161) 485 3804
Head: M F Brown & Mrs A L Poole
Type: Co-educational Boarding &
Day 2-13
No of Pupils: B75 G49 No of
Boarders F16 W5
Fees: (September 95) FB £6600 -
£7500 WB £6150 - £6900 DAY
£2955 - £3855

CHESTER

ABBEY GATE COLLEGE
Saighton Grange, Saighton, Chester,
Cheshire CH3 6EG
Tel: (01244) 332077
Head: E W Mitchell
Type: Co-educational Day 8-18
No of Pupils: B165 G131
Fees: (September 95) £4020

ABBEY GATE SCHOOL
Victoria Road, Chester, Cheshire CH2
2AY
Tel: (01244) 380552
Head: Mrs S T Gill
Type: Co-educational Day 3-11
No of Pupils: 160
Fees: (September 95) £1725 - £1815

THE FIRS SCHOOL
45 Newton Lane, Upton, Chester,
Cheshire CH2 1HB
Tel: (01244) 322443
Head: M Ellis
Type: Co-educational Day 4-11
No of Pupils: B128 G98
Fees: (September 95) £2121 - £2271

HAMMOND SCHOOL
Hoole Bank House, Mannings Lane,
Chester, Cheshire CH2 2PB
Tel: (01244) 328542
Head: Mrs M P Dangerfield
Type: Girls Day & Boarding 11-16
No of Pupils: B4 G117 No of
Boarders F30
Fees: (September 95) FB £10800 DAY
£3840

THE KING'S SCHOOL
Wrexham Road, Chester, Cheshire
CH4 7QL
Tel: (01244) 680026
Head: A R Wickson
Type: Boys Day 7-18
No of Pupils: 680
Fees: (September 95) £2640 - £4032

MERTON HOUSE
(DOWNSWOOD)
Downswood Drive, West Bank, Off
Abbots Park, Chester, Cheshire CH1
4BD
Tel: (01244) 377165
Head: P J Watts and E Watts
Type: Co-educational Day 4-11
No of Pupils: 130
Fees: (September 94) £2100 - £2400

THE QUEEN'S SCHOOL
City Walls Road, Chester, Cheshire
CH1 2NN
Tel: (01244) 312078
Head: Miss D M Skilbeck
Type: Girls Day 5-18 (Boys 5-8)
No of Pupils: B34 G585
Fees: (September 94) £1980 - £4050

CONGLETON

PREPARATORY SCHOOL
The Daintry Hall, North Rode,
Congleton, Cheshire CW12 2PF
Tel: (01260) 223568
Head: Mrs M Leyland
Type: Co-educational Day 3-11
No of Pupils: B35 G15
Fees: (September 95) £2190 - £2340

ST PETER'S NURSERY
SCHOOL
Chapel Street, Congleton, Cheshire
CW12 4AB
Tel: (01260) 276085
Head: Ms D L Birdsall
Type: Co-educational Day 0-5
No of Pupils: 50
Fees: On application

HOLMES CHAPEL

TERRA NOVA SCHOOL
Jodrell Bank, Holmes Chapel,
Cheshire CW4 8BT
Tel: (01477) 571251
Head: T R Lewis
Type: Co-educational Boarding &
Day 3-13
No of Pupils: B149 G59 No of
Boarders F48 W38
Fees: (September 95) F/WB £7725
DAY £1605 - £6255

KNUTSFORD

YORSTON LODGE SCHOOL
18 St John's Road, Knutsford,
Cheshire WA16 0DP
Tel: (01565) 633177
Head: I N Cumpsty
Type: Co-educational Day 4-11
No of Pupils: B62 G41
Fees: (September 95) £1935

MACCLESFIELD

BEECH HALL SCHOOL
Beech Hall Drive, Tytherington,
Macclesfield, Cheshire SK10 2EG
Tel: (01625) 422192
Head: J S Fitz-Gerald
Type: Co-educational Day 4-13
(Kindergarten 2-5)
No of Pupils: B114 G61
Fees: (September 95) £2940 - £4620

THE KING'S SCHOOL
Macclesfield, Cheshire SK10 1DA
Tel: (01625) 618586
Head: A G Silcock
Type: Co-educational Day 7-18
(Single sex education)
No of Pupils: B980 G310
Fees: (September 95) £3330 - £4245

REGENCY PREPARATORY
SCHOOL
142 Chester Road, Macclesfield,
Cheshire SK11 8PX
Tel: (01625) 422315
Head: O T Allmand-Smith
Type: Co-educational Day 1-8
No of Pupils: 75
Fees: (September 95) £2100

ST BRIDE'S SCHOOL
154 Cumberland Street,
Macclesfield, Cheshire SK10 1BP
Tel: (01625) 423255
Head: Mrs H Clayton
Type: Co-educational Day 3-8
No of Pupils: B53 G9
Fees: (September 95) £2205

NORTHWICH

CRANSLEY SCHOOL
Belmont Hall, Great Budworth,
Northwich, Cheshire CW9 6NQ
Tel: (01606) 891747
Head: M A Eagar
Type: Girls Day 3-16 (Boys 3-11)
No of Pupils: B15 G176
Fees: (September 95) £2310 - £4155

THE GRANGE SCHOOL*
Bradburns Lane, Hartford,
Northwich, Cheshire CW8 1LU
Tel: (01606) 74007
Head: E S Marshall
Type: Co-educational Day 4-18
No of Pupils: B559 G528
Fees: (September 95) £2625 - £3675

SALE

FOREST PARK SCHOOL
Lauriston House, 27 Oakfield, Sale,
Cheshire M33 6NB
Tel: (0161) 973 4835
Head: Mrs R Smart
Type: Co-educational Day 3-11
No of Pupils: B70 G50
Fees: (September 95) £2355 - £2670

SOUTHFIELDS SCHOOL
Raglan Road, Sale, Cheshire M33
4AN
Tel: (0161) 973 7223
Head: Mrs J Fildes
Type: Co-educational Day 3-11
No of Pupils: B50 G50
Fees: (September 95) £2100

SANDBACH

SANDBACH SCHOOL
Crewe Road, Sandbach, Cheshire
CW11 0NT
Tel: (01270) 767321
Head: C R Brown
Type: Boys Day 11-18
No of Pupils: 900
Fees: On application

SOUTH WIRRAL

MOSTYN HOUSE SCHOOL
Parkgate, South Wirral, Cheshire
L64 6SG
Tel: (0151) 336 1010
Head: A D J Grenfell
Type: Co-educational Day 4-18
No of Pupils: B189 G136
Fees: (September 95) £1320 - £4485

STALYBRIDGE

TRINITY SCHOOL
Wirbeck Street, Stalybridge, Cheshire
K15 1SH
Tel: (0161) 303 0674
Head: Mrs S Baker
Type: Co-educational Day 4-16
No of Pupils: B60 G48
Fees: On application

STOCKPORT

BRABYNS SCHOOL
34-36 Arkwright Road, Marple,
Stockport, Cheshire SK6 7DB
Tel: (0161) 427 2395
Head: Mrs A D Briggs
Type: Co-educational Day 2-11
No of Pupils: B91 G93
Fees: (September 95) £1530 - £2346

HILLCREST GRAMMAR SCHOOL
Beech Avenue, Stockport, Cheshire
SK3 8HB
Tel: (0161) 480 0329
Head: D K Blackburn
Type: Co-educational Day 3-16
No of Pupils: B190 G120
Fees: (September 95) £2265 - £3120

ORIEL BANK HIGH SCHOOL
Devonshire Park Road, Davenport,
Stockport, Cheshire SK2 6JP
Tel: (0161) 483 2935
Head: Mrs A P Perrett
Type: Girls Day 3-16
No of Pupils: 200
Fees: (September 95) £1455 - £3540

ST CATHERINE'S PREPARATORY SCHOOL
Hollins Lane, Marple Bridge,
Stockport, Cheshire SK6 5BB
Tel: (0161) 449 8800
Head: Mrs M A Sidwell
Type: Co-educational Day 3-11
No of Pupils: B85 G75
Fees: (September 94) £2055 - £2160

STELLA MARIS JUNIOR SCHOOL
St Johns Road, Heaton, Mersey,
Stockport, Cheshire SK4 3BR
Tel: (0161) 432 0532
Head: Miss I L Gannon
Type: Co-educational Day 4-11
No of Pupils: B56 G43
Fees: (September 95) £1728 - £1920

STOCKPORT GRAMMAR SCHOOL
Buxton Road, Stockport, Cheshire
SK2 7AF
Tel: (0161) 456 9000
Head: D R J Bird
Type: Co-educational Day 4-18
No of Pupils: B510 G495
Fees: (September 95) £2916 - £3897

SYDDAL PARK SCHOOL
33 Syddal Road, Bramhall,
Stockport, Cheshire SK7 1AB
Tel: (0161) 439 1751
Head: Mrs P Hamel
Type: Co-educational Day 3-7
No of Pupils: 85
Fees: (September 95) £1470 - £2370

WOODFORD PREP & NURSERY SCHOOL
Chester Road, Woodford, Stockport,
Cheshire SK7 1PS
Tel: (0161) 439 9302
Head: Mrs V E Blundell
Type: Co-educational 2-11
No of Pupils: B40 G50
Fees: (September 95) DAY £1200 -
£2730

WILMSLOW

POWNALL HALL SCHOOL
Wilmslow, Cheshire SK9 5DW
Tel: (01625) 523141
Head: J J Meadmore
Type: Boys Day 3-13
No of Pupils: 250
Fees: (September 95) £1200 - £4275

WILMSLOW PREPARATORY SCHOOL
Grove Avenue, Wilmslow, Cheshire
SK9 5EG
Tel: (01625) 524246
Head: Miss J Ballance
Type: Girls Day 3-11
No of Pupils: 180
Fees: (September 95) £900 - £3600

CLEVELAND

HARTLEPOOL

SHEILA BRUCE COMMUNITY ARTS EDUCATIONAL ESTABLISHMENT
Wilton Grange, Grange Road, Hartlepool, Cleveland TS26 8LX
Tel: (01429) 264976
Head: Mrs Sheila Bruce
Type: Co-educational Day 2-16
No of Pupils: B17 G23
Fees: (September 95) £1620

MIDDLESBROUGH

MILL HILL SCHOOL
Green Lane, Middlesbrough, Cleveland TS5 7RY
Tel: (01642) 816875
Head: T M Duncanson
Type: Co-educational Day 3-16
No of Pupils: B50 G45
Fees: (September 95) £2010 - £2670

STOCKTON-ON-TEES

RED HOUSE SCHOOL
36 The Green, Norton, Stockton-on-Tees, Cleveland TS20 1DX
Tel: (01642) 553370
Head: M England
Type: Co-educational Day 4-16
No of Pupils: B233 G180
Fees: (September 95) £2625 - £3030

TEESSIDE HIGH SCHOOL
The Avenue, Eaglescliffe, Stockton-on-Tees, Cleveland TS16 9AT
Tel: (01642) 782095
Head: Miss J F Hamilton
Type: Girls Day 3-18
No of Pupils: 570
Fees: (September 95) £2625 - £3705

YARM

YARM SCHOOL
The Friarage, Yarm, Cleveland TS15 9EJ
Tel: (01642) 786023
Head: R Neville Tate
Type: Boys Day 5-18 (Co-ed VIth form)
No of Pupils: B680 G20
Fees: (September 94) £2457 - £4584

CORNWALL

BODMIN

TREMORE CHRISTIAN SCHOOL
Tremore Manor, Lanivet, Bodmin, Cornwall PL30 5JT
Tel: (01208) 831713
Head: Miss A Whitaker
Type: Co-educational Day 3-16
No of Pupils: B12 G11
Fees: (September 95) £540

BUDE

ST PETROC'S SCHOOL
Ocean View Road, Bude, Cornwall EX23 8NJ
Tel: (01288) 352876
Head: M J Glen
Type: Co-educational Boarding & Day 3-13
No of Pupils: B66 G43 No of Boarders F10 W10
Fees: (September 95) FB £6330 WB £5940 DAY £2370 - £3945

LAUNCESTON

ST JOSEPH'S SCHOOL*
15 St Stephen's Hill, Launceston, Cornwall PL15 8HN
Tel: (01566) 772988
Head: P S Larkman
Type: Girls Day & Boarding 3-16 (Boys 3-11)
No of Pupils: B39 G161 No of Boarders F1 W23
Fees: (September 95) FB £6960 - £7770 WB £5760 - £6570 DAY £2506 - £3594

PAR

ROSELYON SCHOOL
St Blazey Road, Par, Cornwall PL24 2HZ
Tel: (01726) 812110
Head: Mrs J M Argent
Type: Co-educational Day 3-11
No of Pupils: B40 G40
Fees: (September 95) £855 - £2670

PENRYN

TREMOUGH CONVENT SCHOOL
Penryn, Cornwall TR10 9EZ
Tel: (01326) 372226
Head: Mrs M Biscoe
Type: Girls Boarding & Day 3-18 (Boys 3-11)
No of Pupils: B20 G240 No of Boarders W56
Fees: (September 95) WB £4440 - £4590 DAY £2790 - £2940

TRURO

THE DUCHY GRAMMAR SCHOOL
Tregye, Carnon Downs, Truro, Cornwall TR3 6JH
Tel: (01872) 862289
Head: M L Fuller
Type: Co-educational Day & Boarding 3-18
No of Pupils: B72 G37 No of Boarders F13 W16
Fees: (September 95) FB £7494 - £8364 WB £7212 - £8082 DAY £2130 - £4845

POLWHELE HOUSE SCHOOL
Newquay Road, Truro, Cornwall
TR4 9AE
Tel: (01872) 73011
Head: Mr and Mrs R I White
Type: Co-educational Day &
Boarding 3-13
No of Pupils: B127 G93 No of
Boarders W18
Fees: (September 94) WB £7425 -
£7665 DAY £480 - £4320

TRURO

ST PIRAN'S SCHOOL
Trelissick Road, Hayle, Cornwall
TR27 4HY
Tel: (01736) 752612
Head: D G Jones
Type: Co-educational Day 3-12
No of Pupils: B25 G25
Fees: (September 95) £280 - £610

TRELISKE SCHOOL
Truro, Cornwall TR1 3QN
Tel: (01872) 72616
Head: R L Hollins
Type: Co-educational Day &
Boarding 3-11
No of Pupils: B148 G54 No of
Boarders F19
Fees: (September 95) FB £7479 DAY
£552 - £4194

TRESCOL VEAN SCHOOL
Baldhu, Truro, Cornwall TR3 6EG
Tel: (01872) 560788
Head: Mrs S M Baron
Type: Co-educational Day 3-7
No of Pupils: B36 G36
Fees: (September 95) £756 - £2520

TRURO HIGH SCHOOL
Falmouth Road, Truro, Cornwall
TR1 2HU
Tel: (01872) 72830
Head: J Graham Brown
Type: Girls Boarding & Day 3-18
(Boys 3-5)
No of Pupils: 400 No of Boarders F46
W42
Fees: (September 95) FB £7683 -
£7995 WB £7578 - £7890 DAY
£4068 - £4380

TRURO SCHOOL
Trennick Lane, Truro, Cornwall TR1
1TH
Tel: (01872) 72763
Head: G A Dodd
Type: Co-educational Day &
Boarding 11-18
No of Pupils: B548 G252 No of
Boarders F142
Fees: (September 95) F/WB £8580
DAY £4608

CUMBRIA

BARROW-IN-FURNESS

OUR LADY'S, CHETWYNDE
Croslands, Rating Lane,
Barrow-in-Furness, Cumbria LA13
0NY
Tel: (01229) 824210
Head: Mrs M M Stones
Type: Co-educational Day 3-18
No of Pupils: B252 G254
Fees: (September 95) £2182

CARLISLE

AUSTIN FRIARS SCHOOL*
St Ann's Hill, Carlisle, Cumbria CA3
9PB
Tel: (01228) 28042
Head: M G Taylor
Type: Co-educational Boarding &
Day 11-18 (Day girls)
No of Pupils: B143 G113 No of
Boarders F34
Fees: (September 95) FB £7578 WB
£7371 DAY £4518

LIME HOUSE SCHOOL
Holm Hill, Dalston, Carlisle,
Cumbria CA5 7BX
Tel: (01228) 710225
Head: N A Rice
Type: Co-educational Boarding &
Day 4-18
No of Pupils: B190 G110 No of
Boarders F200 W20
Fees: (September 95) FB £5000 -
£8100 WB £4000 - £6750 DAY
£1650 - £3450

ST MONICA'S SCHOOL
Saint Ann's Hill, Carlisle, Cumbria
CA3 9PL
Tel: (01228) 37458
Head: Mrs F M Willacy
Type: Co-educational Day 4-11
No of Pupils: 120
Fees: (September 94) £2091

EGREMONT

ST BEES SCHOOL*
Egremont, Cumbria CA27 0DS
Tel: (01946) 822263
Head: P A Chamberlain
Type: Co-educational Boarding &
Day 11-18
No of Pupils: B145 G143 No of
Boarders F90 W35
Fees: (September 95) FB £7675 -
£10492 WB £7070 - £9991 DAY
£5853 - £7220

KENDAL

**HOLME PARK PREPARATORY
SCHOOL**
Hill Top, New Hutton, Kendal,
Cumbria LA8 0AH
Tel: (01539) 721245
Head: N J Curry
Type: Co-educational Boarding &
Day 4-13 (Nursery 3-4)
No of Pupils: B63 G17 No of Boarders
W28
Fees: (September 94) WB £5418 DAY
£3218 - £4266

PENRITH

HUNTER HALL SCHOOL
Frenchfield, Penrith, Cumbria CA11
8UA
Tel: (01768) 891291
Head: Mrs L Dexter
Type: Co-educational Day 4-11
No of Pupils: B45 G50
Fees: (September 95) £2640

SEASCALE

HARECROFT HALL SCHOOL
Gosforth, Seascale, Cumbria CA20 1HS
Tel: (01946) 725220
Head: D G Hoddy
Type: Co-educational Boarding & Day 2-16
No of Pupils: B47 G39 No of Boarders F7 W5
Fees: (September 95) FB £6840 WB £6525 DAY £3402 - £4755

SEDBERGH

SEDBERGH SCHOOL
Sedbergh, Cumbria LA10 5HG
Tel: (01539) 620535
Head: C H Hirst
Type: Boys Boarding 11-18
No of Pupils: 400 No of Boarders F390
Fees: (September 95) FB £8280 - £11640 DAY £5790 - £8145

WIGTON

ST URSULAS CONVENT SCHOOL
Burnfoot, Wigton, Cumbria CA7 9HL
Tel: (01697) 344359
Head: Ms M A Horrocks
Type: Co-educational Day 2-11
No of Pupils: B59 G32
Fees: (September 95) £1980

WINDERMERE

ST ANNE'S*
Browhead, Windermere, Cumbria LA23 1NW
Tel: (01539) 446164
Head: C M G R Jenkins
Type: Girls Boarding & Day 3-18 (Boys 3-11)
No of Pupils: B17 G336 No of Boarders F209
Fees: (September 95) FB £7350 - £9126 WB £6420 DAY £1200 - £6051

DERBYSHIRE

ASHBOURNE

ASHBOURNE PNEU SCHOOL
St Monica's House, Windmill Lane, Ashbourne, Derbyshire DE6 1EY
Tel: (01335) 343294
Head: M A Broadbent
Type: Co-educational Day 3-13
No of Pupils: B52 G66
Fees: (September 94) £540 - £2985

BAKEWELL

ST ANSELM'S
Bakewell, Derbyshire DE45 1DP
Tel: (01699) 812734
Head: R J Foster
Type: Co-educational Boarding & Day 3-13
No of Pupils: B120 G50 No of Boarders F90
Fees: (September 95) FB £8750 DAY £608 - £6650

BUXTON

NORMANTON SCHOOL
St John's Road, Buxton, Derbyshire SK17 6SJ
Tel: (01298) 22745/77111
Head: D M Sanderson
Type: Co-educational Boarding & Day 3-18
No of Pupils: B60 G60 No of Boarders F60 W3
Fees: (September 95) FB £8250 WB £7500 DAY £1800 - £2400

CHESTERFIELD

BARLBOROUGH HALL SCHOOL*
Barlborough, Chesterfield, Derbyshire S43 4TJ
Tel: (01246) 810511
Head: A J Taylor
Type: Co-educational Day & Boarding 3-13
No of Pupils: B88 G61 No of Boarders F32
Fees: (September 95) FB £6771 DAY £2651 - £4818

ST JOSEPH'S CONVENT
42 New Bold Road, Chesterfield, Derbyshire S41 7PL
Tel: (01246) 232392
Head: Sister M Carolan
Type: Co-educational Day 3-11
No of Pupils: B96 G84
Fees: (September 95) £1914 - £2295

ST PETER & ST PAUL SCHOOL
Penmore House Precinct, Hasland Road, Chesterfield, Derbyshire S41 0SJ
Tel: (01246) 278522
Head: Mrs B Beet
Type: Co-educational Day 3-11
No of Pupils: B85 G80
Fees: (September 95) £1785 - £1875

DERBY

DERBY HIGH SCHOOL
Hillsway, Littleover, Derby DE3 7DT
Tel: (01332) 514267
Head: Dr G H Goddard
Type: Girls Day 3-18 (Boys 3-11)
No of Pupils: B78 G480
Fees: (September 95) £3210 - £4350

EMMANUEL SCHOOL
Juniper Lodge, 43 Kedleston Road, Derby DE22 1FP
Tel: (01332) 340505
Head: Mrs G Hart
Type: Co-educational Day 4-11
No of Pupils: B40 G35
Fees: (September 95) £300 - £1560

OCKBROOK SCHOOL
The Settlement, Ockbrook, Derby DE7 3RJ
Tel: (01332) 673532
Head: Miss D P Bolland
Type: Girls Day & Boarding 3-18 (Boys 3-11)
No of Pupils: B49 G328 No of Boarders F14 W5
Fees: (September 95) F/WB £5703 - £6906 DAY £2520 - £3723

THE OLD VICARAGE SCHOOL
Church Lane, Darley Abbey, Derby
DE22 1EW
Tel: (01332) 557130
Head: G C Holbrow & Mrs M
Holbrow
Type: Co-educational Day 3-11
Fees: (September 95) £2835 - £3045

REPTON PREPARATORY
SCHOOL
Foremarke Hall, Milton, Derby
DE65 6EJ
Tel: (01283) 703269
Head: R C Theobald
Type: Co-educational Boarding &
Day 7-13
No of Pupils: B253 G106 No of
Boarders F42 W66
Fees: (September 95) F/WB £7689
DAY £5787

HEANOR

MICHAEL HOUSE SCHOOL
The Field, Shipley, Heanor,
Derbyshire DE75 7JH
Tel: (01773) 718050
Head: A Peacock
Type: Co-educational Day 4-16
No of Pupils: B85 G75
Fees: (September 95) £900 - £3000

ILKESTON

GATEWAY CHRISTIAN
SCHOOL
Moor Lane, Dale Abbey, Ilkeston,
Derbyshire DE7 4PP
Tel: (0115) 944 0609
Head: Ms S E Down
Type: Co-educational Day 3-11
No of Pupils: B28 G17
Fees: On application.

MATLOCK

ST ELPHIN'S SCHOOL
Darley Dale, Matlock, Derbyshire
DE4 2HA
Tel: (01629) 732687
Head: Mrs V Fisher
Type: Girls Boarding & Day 3-18
(Co-ed junior school)
No of Pupils: B4 G226 No of Boarders
F49 W21
Fees: (September 95) FB £8760 -
£9711 WB £8322 - £9226 DAY
£2259 - £5658

STANCLIFFE HALL
Darley Dale, Matlock, Derbyshire
DE4 2HJ
Tel: (01629) 732310
Head: A R R Wareham
Type: Co-educational Boarding &
Day 3-14
No of Pupils: B130 G51 No of
Boarders F31 W35
Fees: (September 95) F/WB £7560
DAY £2730 - £6090

REPTON

REPTON SCHOOL
The Hall, Repton, Derbyshire
DE65 6FH
Tel: (01283) 702375
Head: G E Jones
Type: Co-educational Boarding &
Day 13-18
No of Pupils: B440 G132 No of
Boarders F403
Fees: (September 95) FB £11604 DAY
£8730

ST WYSTAN'S SCHOOL
11A High Street, Repton, Derbyshire
DE6 6GE
Tel: (01283) 703258
Head: Mrs J E Roberts
Type: Co-educational Day 2-11
No of Pupils: B74 G70
Fees: (September 95) £1320 - £3000

DEVON

ASHBURTON

SANDS SCHOOL
Greylands, 48 East Street,
Ashburton, Devon TQ13 7AX
Tel: (01364) 53666
Head: S Bellamy
Type: Co-educational Day 11-18
No of Pupils: B24 G19
Fees: (September 95) £3375

BARNSTAPLE

ST MICHAEL'S
Tawstock Court, Barnstaple, Devon
EX31 3HY
Tel: (01271) 43242
Head: R K Yetzes
Type: Co-educational Boarding &
Day 3-13
No of Pupils: B125 G80 No of
Boarders F30
Fees: (September 95) F/WB £5850 -
£7920 DAY £2430 - £4875

WEST BUCKLAND
PREPARATORY SCHOOL
Langholme, West Buckland,
Barnstaple, Devon EX32 0SX
Tel: (01598) 760545
Head: G D Benfield
Type: Co-educational Day &
Boarding 5-11
No of Pupils: B63 G31 No of Boarders
F17
Fees: (September 95) FB £5460 -
£7275 DAY £2460 - £4275

WEST BUCKLAND SCHOOL
Barnstaple, Devon EX32 0SX
Tel: (01598) 760281
Head: M Downward
Type: Co-educational Boarding &
Day 11-18
No of Pupils: B280 G173 No of
Boarders F145
Fees: (September 95) FB £8970 DAY
£4866

BEAWORTHY

SHEBBEAR COLLEGE
Shebbear, Beaworthy, Devon
EX21 5HJ
Tel: (01409) 281228
Head: R J Buley
Type: Co-educational Boarding &
Day 3-18
No of Pupils: 290
Fees: (September 95) FB £5775 -
£9330 DAY £2040 - £5010

BIDEFORD

EDGEHILL COLLEGE*
Northdown Road, Bideford, Devon
EX39 3LY
Tel: (01237) 471701
Head: Mrs E M Burton
Type: Co-educational Boarding &
Day 3-19
No of Pupils: B98 G408 No of
Boarders F107 W25
Fees: (September 95) FB £6870 -
£9570 WB £6210 - £8655 DAY
£2535 - £5265

GRENVILLE COLLEGE
Bideford, Devon EX39 3JR
Tel: (01237) 472212
Head: Dr M C Cane
Type: Co-educational Boarding &
Day 2-18 (Boarders from 9)
No of Pupils: B275 G270 No of
Boarders F175
Fees: (September 95) FB £7725 -
£9816 DAY £1875 - £4881

SMALL SCHOOL
Fore Street, Hartland, Bideford,
Devon EX39 6AB
Tel: (01237) 441672
Head: R Secombe
Type: Co-educational Day 11-16
No of Pupils: 40
Fees: On application

BRIXHAM

GRAMERCY HALL SCHOOL
Churston Ferrers, Brixham, Devon
TQ5 0HR
Tel: (01803) 844338
Head: G L Nickerson
Type: Co-educational Day 3-16
No of Pupils: B75 G35
Fees: (September 95) £1200 - £3885

CHULMLEIGH

OSHO KO HSUAN SCHOOL
Chawleigh, Chulmleigh, Devon
EX18 7EX
Tel: (01769) 580896
Head: R A Jones
Type: Co-educational Boarding 9-16
No of Pupils: B30 G30 No of
Boarders F60
Fees: (September 95) FB £5175

CREDITON

SHOBROOKE HOUSE SCHOOL
Shobrooke, Crediton, Devon EX17
1AP
Tel: (01363) 22715
Head: P G Spencer
Type: Co-educational Day 3-11
No of Pupils: B32 G28
Fees: (September 95) £660 - £1950

DAWLISH

LANHERNE SCHOOL
18 Longlands, Dawlish, Devon EX7
9NG
Tel: (01626) 863091
Head: R Hazeldene
Type: Co-educational Day 1-11
No of Pupils: 60
Fees: (September 94) £1050 - £1500

EXETER

BENDARROCH SCHOOL
Aylesbeare, Exeter, Devon EX5 2BY
Tel: (01395) 233553
Head: N R Home
Type: Co-educational Day 5-13
No of Pupils: B20 G20
Fees: (September 94) £2175 - £2565

BRAMDEAN GRAMMAR
SCHOOL
Richmond Lodge, Homefield Road,
Heavitree, Exeter, Devon EX1 2QR
Tel: (01392) 73387
Head: D A Connett
Type: Boys Boarding & Day 11-17
(Co-ed VIth form)
No of Pupils: 180 No of Boarders
W25
Fees: (September 94) WB £1990 -
£5478 DAY £1264 - £3480

BRAMDEAN PREPARATORY &
GRAMMAR SCHOOL
Richmond Lodge, Homefield Road,
Heavitree, Exeter, Devon EX1 2QR
Tel: (01392) 73387
Head: D Stoneman
Type: Boys Boarding & Day 7-11
No of Pupils: B140 G6 No of
Boarders W20
Fees: (September 94) WB £5970 DAY
£3792

ELM GROVE SCHOOL
Elm Grove Road, Topsham, Exeter,
Devon EX3 0EQ
Tel: (01392) 873031
Head: B E Parsons & Mrs K M
Parsons
Type: Co-educational Day 3-7
No of Pupils: B30 G30
Fees: (September 95) £1800

EMMANUEL SCHOOL
36-38 Blackboy Road, Exeter, Devon
EX4 6SZ
Tel: (01392) 58150
Head: P Gedye
Type: Co-educational Day 4-16
No of Pupils: B25 G21
Fees: (September 95) £1100

EXETER CATHEDRAL SCHOOL
The Chantry, Palace Gate, Exeter,
Devon EX1 1HX
Tel: (01392) 55298
Type: Co-educational Day &
Boarding 4-13
No of Pupils: 149 No of Boarders F25
W15
Fees: (September 95) FB £6750 -
£6900 WB £6540 - £6690 DAY
£2325 - £4230

EXETER PREPARATORY
SCHOOL
Victoria Park Road, Exeter, Devon
EX2 4NS
Tel: (01392) 58712
Head: J B Lawford
Type: Boys Day 7-11
No of Pupils: 100
Fees: (September 95) £3615 - £3912

EXETER SCHOOL
Exeter, Devon EX2 4NS
Tel: (01392) 73679
Head: N W Gamble
Type: Boys Boarding & Day 11-18
(Co-ed VIth form)
No of Pupils: B657 G48 No of
Boarders F60
Fees: (September 95) F/WB £7950
DAY £3615 - £4200

HYLTON KINDERGARTEN &
PRE-PREPARATORY SCHOOL
13A Lyndhurst Road, Exeter, Devon
EX2 4PA
Tel: (01392) 54755
Head: Mrs B J Glass
Type: Co-educational Day 4-8
No of Pupils: 48
Fees: (September 95) £1575 - £2250

MAGDALEN COURT SCHOOL
Uplands, 81 Heavitree Road, Exeter,
Devon EX1 2LX
Tel: (01392) 494919
Head: Mrs J J Jenner
Type: Co-educational Day 2-18
No of Pupils: B40 G60
Fees: (September 95) £1800 - £2850

THE MAYNARD SCHOOL
Denmark Road, Exeter, Devon EX1
1SJ
Tel: (01392) 73417
Head: Miss F Murdin
Type: Girls Day 7-18
No of Pupils: 560
Fees: (September 95) £3354 - £4173

MOUNT ST MARY'S
CONVENT SCHOOL
Wonford Road, Exeter, Devon EX2
4PF
Tel: (01392) 436770
Head: Sister Eileen Delaney
Type: Girls Day 3-18 (Boys 3-7)
No of Pupils: B25 G405
Fees: (September 95) £595 - £1150

NEW SCHOOL
Exe Vale, Exminster, Exeter, Devon
EX6 8AT
Tel: (01392) 496122
Head: Mrs G Redman
Type: Co-educational Day 4-8
No of Pupils: B19 G24
Fees: (September 95) £1485 - £2085

ST MARGARET'S EXETER
Magdalen Road, Exeter, Devon EX2
4TS
Tel: (01392) 73197
Head: Mrs M D'Albertanson
Type: Girls Day 5-18
No of Pupils: 440
Fees: (September 95) £2625 - £4083

ST WILFRID'S SCHOOL
25 St David's Hill, Exeter, Devon
EX4 4DA
Tel: (01392) 76171
Head: J G Bushrod
Type: Co-educational Day 3-16
Fees: (September 94) £1770 - £2835

EXMOUTH

CASTLE DOWN SCHOOL
Littleham Road, Exmouth, Devon
EX8 2RD
Tel: (01395) 269998
Head: Miss H Lee
Type: Co-educational Day 3-7
No of Pupils: B16 G24
Fees: (September 95) £690 - £1350

THE DOLPHIN SCHOOL
Raddenstile Lane, Exmouth, Devon
EX8 2JH
Tel: (01395) 272418
Head: Mrs J Bishop
Type: Co-educational Day 3-13
No of Pupils: 60
Fees: (September 94) £1920

ST PETER'S SCHOOL
Harefield, Lympstone, Exmouth,
Devon EX8 5AU
Tel: (01395) 272148
Head: C N Abram
Type: Co-educational Day &
Boarding 5-13
No of Pupils: B147 G67 No of
Boarders W42
Fees: (September 95) WB £6285 DAY
£3075 - £4380

HONITON

MANOR HOUSE SCHOOL
Springfield House, Honiton, Devon
EX14 8TL
Tel: (01404) 42026
Head: P A Eyles
Type: Co-educational Boarding &
Day 3-13
No of Pupils: B100 G80 No of
Boarders W10
Fees: (September 95) WB £4850 DAY
£2200 - £2800

KINGSBRIDGE

KINGSBRIDGE PREPARATORY
SCHOOL
The Gatehouse, Embankment Road,
Kingsbridge, Devon TQ7 1JN
Tel: (01548) 852703
Head: Mrs A S Johnson
Type: Co-educational Day 2-11
No of Pupils: 75
Fees: (September 95) £2895 - £3090

LUSTLEIGH

LUSTLEIGH SCHOOL
Church House, Lustleigh, Newton
Abbot, Devon
TQ1 9TJ
Tel: (01647) 277399
Head: Mrs Jane Dennis
Type: Co-educational Day 3-7
No of Pupils: B8 G10
Fees: (September 95) £885 - £1785

NEWTON ABBOT

ABBOTSBURY SCHOOL
90 Torquay Road, Newton Abbot,
Devon TQ12 2JD
Tel: (01626) 52164
Head: Mrs S M Manley
Type: Co-educational Day 2-7
No of Pupils: B50 G50
Fees: (September 95) £390 - £1380

ST BERNARD'S
PREPARATORY SCHOOL
9 Courtenay Road, Newton Abbot,
Devon TQ12 1HP
Tel: (01626) 65424
Head: R Dudley-Cooke
Type: Co-educational Day 2-11
No of Pupils: 100
Fees: (September 95) £765 - £2730

STOVER SCHOOL
Newton Abbot, Devon TQ12 6QG
Tel: (01626) 54505
Head: P E Bujak
Type: Girls Boarding & Day 10-18
No of Pupils: 160 No of Boarders F56
W22
Fees: (September 95) FB £8475 WB
£8250 DAY £4425

WOLBOROUGH HILL SCHOOL
South Road, Newton Abbot, Devon
TQ12 1HH
Tel: (01626) 54078
Head: S J Day
Type: Co-educational Day &
Boarding 4-13
No of Pupils: B202 G32 No of
Boarders W29
Fees: (September 95) WB £6600 DAY
£990 - £1500

PAIGNTON

GREYLANDS SCHOOL
9 Belle Vue Road, Paignton, Devon
TQ4 6ES
Tel: (01803) 557298
Head: Mrs P M Adams
Type: Co-educational Day 3-11
No of Pupils: 100
Fees: (September 95) £1785 - £2085

TOWER HOUSE SCHOOL
Fisher Street, Paignton, Devon
TQ4 5EW
Tel: (01803) 557077
Head: M Robinson
Type: Co-educational Day 2-16
No of Pupils: B95 G95
Fees: (September 95) £2505 - £3795

PLYMOUTH

FLETEWOOD SCHOOL
88 North Road East, Plymouth,
Devon PL4 6AN
Tel: (01752) 663782
Head: J Martin
Type: Co-educational Day 3-11
No of Pupils: B35 G35
Fees: (September 95) £1590

KING'S SCHOOL
Hartley Road, Mannamead,
Plymouth, Devon PL3 5LW
Tel: (01752) 771789
Head: Mrs J Lee
Type: Co-educational Day 3-11
No of Pupils: B71 G75
Fees: (September 95) £1830 - £2175

PLYMOUTH COLLEGE
Ford Park, Plymouth, Devon
PL4 6RN
Tel: (01752) 228596
Head: A J Morsley
Type: Co-educational Day &
Boarding 11-18
No of Pupils: B580 G40 No of
Boarders F40 W49
Fees: (September 95) FB £8910 WB
£8850 DAY £4650

PLYMOUTH COLLEGE
PREPARATORY SCHOOL
Hartley Road, Plymouth, Devon
PL3 5LW
Tel: (01752) 772283
Head: G Pessell
Type: Co-educational Day 4-11
No of Pupils: B230 G120
Fees: (September 95) £2250 - £3180

ST DUNSTAN'S ABBEY
SCHOOL
Plymouth, Devon PL1 5DH
Tel: (01752) 663998
Head: R A Bye
Type: Girls Day & Boarding 4-18
(Boys 4-7)
No of Pupils: 473 No of Boarders F2
W44
Fees: (September 95) FB £6030 -
£8010 WB £5130 - £7110 DAY
£2280 - £4500

SEATON

WHITE HOUSE SCHOOL
Old Beer Road, Seaton, Devon
EX12 2PX
Tel: (01297) 20614
Head: H R Doran
Type: Co-educational Day 4-13
No of Pupils: B50 G44
Fees: (September 95) £1705 - £2115

SIDMOUTH

ST JOHN'S SCHOOL
Broadway, Sidmouth, Devon
EX10 8RG
Tel: (01395) 513984
Head: N R Pockett
Type: Co-educational Day &
Boarding 3-13
No of Pupils: B140 G128 No of
Boarders F70 W35
Fees: (September 95) F/WB £6195
DAY £2190 - £3675

TAVISTOCK

KELLY COLLEGE*
Tavistock, Devon PL19 0HZ
Tel: (01822) 612010
Head: M Turner
Type: Co-educational Boarding &
Day 11-18
No of Pupils: B241 G62 No of
Boarders F122 W46
Fees: (September 95) FB £11385 WB
£10905 DAY £5085 - £7155

KELLY COLLEGE JUNIOR
SCHOOL - ST MICHAEL'S
Hazeldon House, Parkwood Road,
Tavistock, Devon PL19 0JS
Tel: (01822) 612919
Head: M J Nicholls
Type: Co-educational Day 4-11
No of Pupils: B45 G55
Fees: (September 95) £2565 - £3225

MOUNT HOUSE SCHOOL
Tavistock, Devon PL19 9JL
Tel: (01822) 612244
Head: C D Price
Type: Boys Boarding & Day 7-14
No of Pupils: 160 No of Boarders
F130
Fees: (September 95) FB £8169 DAY
£5922

TEIGNMOUTH

TRINITY SCHOOL
Buckeridge Road, Teignmouth,
Devon TQ6 9RA
Tel: (01626) 774138
Head: C J Ashby
Type: Co-educational Day &
Boarding 3-18
No of Pupils: B143 G119 No of
Boarders F77 W6
Fees: (September 95) FB £7500 -
£8340 WB £7290 - £8130 DAY
£2580 - £4110

TIVERTON

BLUNDELL'S SCHOOL*
Tiverton, Devon EX16 4DN
Tel: (01884) 252543
Head: J Leigh
Type: Co-educational Boarding &
Day 13-18
No of Pupils: B375 G48 No of
Boarders F330
Fees: (September 95) FB £11550 DAY
£5640

ST AUBYNS SCHOOL
Howden Court, Tiverton, Devon
EX16 5PB
Tel: (01884) 252393
Head: A C Herniman
Type: Co-educational Day &
Boarding 3-13
No of Pupils: B165 G100 No of
Boarders F20 W15
Fees: (September 95) F/WB £5940 -
£6894 DAY £528 - £4356

TORQUAY

THE ABBEY SCHOOL
Hampton Court, St Marychurch,
Torquay, Devon TQ1 4PR
Tel: (01803) 327868
Head: Mrs S J Greinig
Type: Co-educational Day 2-11
No of Pupils: B235 G225
Fees: (September 94) £300 - £2850

STOODLEY KNOWLE
CONVENT SCHOOL
Ansteys Cove Road, Torquay, Devon
TQ1 2JB
Tel: (01803) 293160
Head: Sister Perpetua
Type: Girls Boarding & Day 4-18
(Weekly boarding only)
No of Pupils: 200 No of Boarders
W65
Fees: (September 95) WB £3933 -
£4443 DAY £2310 - £3003

TOTNES

PARK SCHOOL
Park Road, Dartington, Totnes,
Devon TQ9 6EQ
Tel: (01803) 864588
Head: C Nicolls
Type: Co-educational Day 3-11
No of Pupils: B30 G30
Fees: (September 95) £1740 - £2214

RUDOLF STEINER SCHOOL
Hood Manor, Buckfastleigh Road,
Dartington, Totnes, Devon TQ9 6AB
Tel: (01803) 762528
Head: C R Cooper
Type: Co-educational Day 3-16
No of Pupils: B122 G130
Fees: (September 95) £1350 - £2499

ST CHRISTOPHERS SCHOOL
Mount Barton, Staverton, Totnes,
Devon TQ9
Tel: (01803) 762202
Head: Mrs J E Kenyon
Type: Co-educational Day 3-11
No of Pupils: B20 G12
Fees: (September 95) £535 - £855

DORSET

BLANDFORD FORUM

BRYANSTON SCHOOL
Blandford Forum, Dorset DT11 0PX
Tel: (01258) 452411
Head: T D Wheare
Type: Co-educational Boarding &
Day 13-18
No of Pupils: B400 G260
Fees: (September 95) FB £13230 DAY
£8820

**CLAYESMORE PREPARATORY
SCHOOL**
Iwerne Minster, Blandford Forum,
Dorset DT11 8PH
Tel: (01747) 811707
Head: M G Cooke
Type: Co-educational Boarding &
Day 3-13
No of Pupils: B110 G90 No of
Boarders F60 W10
Fees: (September 95) F/WB £8430
DAY £2850 - £6000

CLAYESMORE SCHOOL
Iwerne Minster, Blandford Forum,
Dorset DT11 8LL
Tel: (01747) 812122
Head: D J Beeby
Type: Co-educational Boarding &
Day 13-18
No of Pupils: B184 G102 No of
Boarders F215
Fees: (September 95) FB £11190 DAY
£7830

CROFT HOUSE SCHOOL*
Shillingstone, Blandford Forum,
Dorset DT11 0QS
Tel: (01258) 860295
Head: M Hawkins
Type: Girls Boarding & Day 11-18
No of Pupils: 130 No of Boarders F77
W29
Fees: (September 95) F/WB £9750
DAY £6885

HANFORD SCHOOL
Childe Okeford, Blandford Forum,
Dorset DT11 8HL
Tel: (01258) 860219
Head: Miss S Canning & Mrs R A
McKenzie Johnston
Type: Girls Boarding 7-13
No of Pupils: 140 No of Boarders
F140
Fees: (September 95) FB £8250

KNIGHTON HOUSE
Durweston, Blandford Forum,
Dorset DT11 0PY
Tel: (01258) 452065
Head: R P Weatherly
Type: Co-educational Boarding &
Day B4-7 G4-13
No of Pupils: B20 G160 No of
Boarders F100
Fees: (September 95) FB £8760 DAY
£2385 - £6435

MILTON ABBEY SCHOOL
Blandford Forum, Dorset DT11 0BZ
Tel: (01258) 880484
Head: J Hughes-D'Aeth
Type: Boys Boarding & Day 13-18
No of Pupils: 209 No of Boarders
F200
Fees: (September 95) FB £11604 DAY
£7746

BOURNEMOUTH

**HOMEFIELD SCHOOL
(PREPARATORY)**
Iford Lane, Southbourne,
Bournemouth, Dorset BH6 5NQ
Tel: (01202) 429483
Head: A C Partridge
Type: Co-educational Boarding &
Day 3-12
No of Pupils: B175 G75
Fees: (September 95) FB £9675 DAY
£2580 - £3525

THE PARK SCHOOL
45 Queen's Park, South Drive,
Bournemouth, Dorset BH8 9BJ
Tel: (01202) 396640
Head: M Smyth
Type: Co-educational Day 4-12
No of Pupils: 225
Fees: (September 95) £2115 - £2865

ST MARTIN'S SCHOOL
15 Stokewood Road, Bournemouth,
Dorset BH3 7NA
Tel: (01202) 554483
Head: T Shenton
Type: Co-educational Day 4-12
No of Pupils: B50 G50
Fees: (September 95) £1560 - £2025

**ST THOMAS GARNET'S
SCHOOL**
Parkwood Road, Boscombe,
Bournemouth, Dorset BH5 2DE
Tel: (01202) 420172
Head: P R Gillings
Type: Co-educational Day 2-11
No of Pupils: B80 G70
Fees: (September 95) £2280 - £2610

TALBOT HEATH*
Rothesay Road, Bournemouth,
Dorset BH4 9NJ
Tel: (01202) 761881
Head: Mrs C Dipple
Type: Girls Day & Boarding 3-18
No of Pupils: 548 No of Boarders F25
W4
Fees: (September 95) FB £6930 -
£9150 WB £7170 - £8910 DAY
£1650 - £5250

**TALBOT HOUSE
PREPARATORY SCHOOL**
8 Firs Glen Road, Bournemouth,
Dorset BH9 2LR
Tel: (01202) 510348
Head: Mrs E H Stevenson
Type: Co-educational Day 4-12
No of Pupils: B69 G74
Fees: (September 95) £1719 - £1950

WENTWORTH MILTON MOUNT

College Road, Bournemouth, Dorset BH5 2DY
Tel: (01202) 423266
Head: Miss S Coe
Type: Girls Boarding & Day 11-18
No of Pupils: 265 No of Boarders F70 W30
Fees: (September 95) F/WB £8835 DAY £5541

BRIDPORT

ST RONAN'S

Asker Mead, Bridport, Dorset DT6 4DA
Tel: (01308) 422128
Head: Mrs J A Fairbrother
Type: Co-educational Day 3-19
No of Pupils: 60
Fees: (September 94) £1650

CHRISTCHURCH

HOMEFIELD SCHOOL

Salisbury Road, Winkton, Christchurch, Dorset BH23 7AR
Tel: (01202) 476644
Head: A C Partridge
Type: Co-educational Boarding & Day 11-16
No of Pupils: B250 G100
Fees: (September 95) FB £9675 DAY £3735 - £4020

DORCHESTER

DORCHESTER PREPARATORY SCHOOL

25/26 Icen Way, Dorchester, Dorset DT1 1EP
Tel: (01305) 264925
Head: J Rose
Type: Co-educational Day 3-13
No of Pupils: B120 G80
Fees: (September 95) £1110 - £2820

SUNNINGHILL PREPARATORY SCHOOL

Herringston Road, Dorchester, Dorset DT1 2BS
Tel: (01305) 262306
Head: C Pring
Type: Co-educational Day 3-13
No of Pupils: B72 G97
Fees: (September 95) £1491 - £2805

LYME REGIS

ALLHALLOWS COLLEGE*

Rousdon, Lyme Regis, Dorset DT7 3RA
Tel: (01297) 626100
Head: J E Muller
Type: Co-educational Boarding & Day 11-18
No of Pupils: B159 G81 No of Boarders F180
Fees: (September 95) FB £9600 WB £8250 DAY £3600 - £4800

POOLE

BUCKHOLME TOWERS

18 Commercial Road, Parkstone, Poole, Dorset BH14 0JW
Tel: (01202) 742871
Head: Mrs C B M Westhead
Type: Co-educational Day 3-12
No of Pupils: B79 G79
Fees: (September 95) £975 - £2355

ST JOSEPH'S CONVENT NURSERY SCHOOL

37 Parkstone Road, Poole, Dorset BH15 2NU
Tel: (01202) 674515
Head: Sister Germaine
Type: Co-educational Day 3-5
No of Pupils: 40
Fees: On application

ST MONICA'S SCHOOL

The Yarrells, Upton, Poole, Dorset BH16 5EU
Tel: (01202) 622229
Head: Mrs Covell
Type: Co-educational Day 3-12
No of Pupils: B42 G153
Fees: (September 95) £1355 - £4413

UPLANDS SCHOOL

40 St Osmund's Road, Parkstone, Poole, Dorset BH14 9JY
Tel: (01202) 742626
Head: Mrs L Dummett
Type: Co-educational Day 3-16
No of Pupils: B185 G160
Fees: (September 95) £1515 - £3675

SHAFTESBURY

MOTCOMBE GRANGE SCHOOL

The Street, Motcombe, Shaftesbury, Dorset SP7 9HJ
Tel: (01747) 52426
Head: Mrs M R Williams
Type: Co-educational Day 3-11
No of Pupils: B60 G50
Fees: (January 95) £2385

PORT REGIS

Motcombe Park, Shaftesbury, Dorset SP7 9QA
Tel: (01747) 852566
Head: P A Dix
Type: Co-educational Boarding & Day 4-13
No of Pupils: B200 G116 No of Boarders F204 W30
Fees: (September 94) F/WB £10065 DAY £7350

ST MARY'S SCHOOL*

Shaftesbury, Dorset SP7 9LP
Tel: (01747) 854005
Head: Sister M Campion Livesey
Type: Girls Boarding & Day 9-18
No of Pupils: 300 No of Boarders F200
Fees: (September 95) FB £9150 - £9600 DAY £5850 - £6150

SHERBORNE

NEWELL HOUSE SCHOOL

Cornhill, Sherborne, Dorset DT9 3PL
Tel: (01935) 812584
Head: P J Dale
Type: Co-educational Day 3-12
No of Pupils: B35 G25
Fees: (September 95) £1875 - £2175

ST ANTONY'S-LEWESTON PREPARATORY SCHOOL

Sherborne, Dorset DT9 6EN
Tel: (01963) 210790
Head: Mrs S M Cook
Type: Co-educational Boarding & Day 3-11
No of Pupils: 90
Fees: (September 95) FB £6795 DAY £1290 - £3885

ST ANTONY'S-LEWESTON SCHOOL

Sherborne, Dorset DT9 6EN
Tel: (01963) 210691
Head: Miss C Denley Lloyd
Type: Girls Boarding & Day 11-18
No of Pupils: 285 No of Boarders F160
Fees: (September 95) FB £10515 DAY £6861

SHERBORNE PREPARATORY SCHOOL*
Acreman Street, Sherborne, Dorset
DT9 3NY
Tel: (01935) 812097
Head: R T M Lindsay
Type: Co-educational Day &
Boarding 3-13
No of Pupils: B134 G64 No of
Boarders F34 W14
Fees: (September 95) F/WB £7479
DAY £1215 - £4986

SHERBORNE SCHOOL
Abbey Road, Sherborne, Dorset
DT9 3AP
Tel: (01935) 812249
Head: P H Lapping
Type: Boys Boarding 13-18
No of Pupils: 640 No of Boarders
F615
Fees: (September 95) FB £12555 DAY
£9570

SHERBORNE SCHOOL FOR GIRLS*
Bradford Road, Sherborne, Dorset
DT9 3QN
Tel: (01935) 812245
Head: Miss J M Taylor
Type: Girls Boarding & Day 12-18
No of Pupils: 453 No of Boarders
F442
Fees: (September 95) FB £11550 DAY
£7950

SHERBORNE SCHOOL INTERNATIONAL STUDY CENTRE*
Newell Grange, Sherborne, Dorset
DT9 4EZ
Tel: (01935) 814743
Head: R W Mowat
Type: Boys Boarding 10-16
No of Pupils: 75
Fees: (September 95) FB £15300

SWANAGE

THE OLD MALTHOUSE
Langton Matravers, Swanage,
Dorset BH19 3HB
Tel: (01929) 422302
Head: J H L Phillips
Type: Boys Boarding & Day 4-13
(Girls 4-7)
No of Pupils: B113 G9 No of Boarders
F56 W14
Fees: (September 95) F/WB £8610
DAY £2475 - £6525

WEYMOUTH

THORNLOW JUNIOR SCHOOL
Connaught Road, Weymouth,
Dorset DT4 0SA
Tel: (01305) 785703
Head: Mrs J D Crocker
Type: Co-educational Day &
Boarding 4-11
No of Pupils: B32 G18 No of Boarders
F5 W12
Fees: (September 95) FB £8175 WB
£7860 DAY £2315 - £3660

THORNLOW SENIOR SCHOOL
101 Buxton Road, Weymouth,
Dorset DT4 9PR
Tel: (01305) 782977
Head: D H Crocker
Type: Co-educational Boarding &
Day 11-16
No of Pupils: B93 G37 No of Boarders
F39 W24
Fees: (September 94) FB £7200 WB
£6540 DAY £2970 - £3330

WIMBORNE

CANFORD SCHOOL
Wimborne, Dorset BH21 3AD
Tel: (01202) 841254
Head: J D Lever
Type: Co-educational Boarding &
Day 13-18
No of Pupils: B405 G85 No of
Boarders F345
Fees: (September 95) FB £12380 DAY
£9285

CASTLE COURT PREPARATORY SCHOOL
The Knoll House, Knoll Lane, Corfe
Mullen, Wimborne, Dorset BH21 3RF
Tel: (01202) 694438
Head: R E T Nicholl
Type: Co-educational Day 3-13
No of Pupils: B171 G104
Fees: (September 95) £3375 - £6570

DUMPTON SCHOOL
Deans Grove House, Wimborne,
Dorset BH21 7AF
Tel: (01202) 883818
Head: A G M Watson
Type: Co-educational Day &
Boarding 3-13
No of Pupils: 220 No of Boarders F40
Fees: (September 95) F/WB £7725
DAY £2040 - £5970

COUNTY DURHAM

BARNARD CASTLE

BARNARD CASTLE SCHOOL
Barnard Castle, County Durham
DL12 8UN
Tel: (01833) 690222
Head: F S McNamara
Type: Co-educational Boarding &
Day 7-18
No of Pupils: 610
Fees: (September 95) FB £6405 -
£8358 DAY £3441 - £4947

BISHOP AUCKLAND

ST ANNE'S CONVENT HIGH SCHOOL
Angate Square, Wolsingham, Bishop
Auckland, County Durham
DL13 3AL
Tel: (01388) 527298
Head: Sister M Michael
Type: Girls Day 3-16 (Boys 4-11)
No of Pupils: B22 G190
Fees: (September 95) £2430 - £2610

DARLINGTON

HURWORTH HOUSE SCHOOL
The Green, Hurworth-on-Tees,
Darlington, County Durham
DL2 2AD
Tel: (01325) 720645
Head: Dr M Rymer
Type: Boys Day 4-16
No of Pupils: 180
Fees: (September 95) £2775 - £4567

POLAM HALL
Darlington, County Durham
DL1 5PA
Tel: (01325) 463383
Head: Mrs H C Hamilton
Type: Girls Boarding & Day 4-18
No of Pupils: 420 No of Boarders F45
W10
Fees: (September 95) FB £7050 -
£8724 WB £6975 - £8649
DAY £1968 - £4266

RAVENTHORPE
PREPARATORY SCHOOL
96 Carmel Road, Darlington, County
Durham DL3 8JB
Head: Mrs C Hermione Jacques
Type: Co-educational
No of Pupils: 150
Fees: On application

DURHAM

BOW SCHOOL
South Road, Durham DH1 3LS
Tel: (0191) 384 8233
Head: J P Wansey
Type: Boys Day & Boarding 4-13
No of Pupils: 113 No of Boarders F5
Fees: (September 95) FB £6732 DAY
£3000 - £4788

THE CHORISTER SCHOOL
The College, Durham DH1 3EL
Tel: (0191) 384 2935
Head: C S S Drew
Type: Boys Day & Boarding 4-13
(Day girls)
No of Pupils: 171 No of Boarders F27
W11
Fees: (September 95) F/WB £6207
DAY £2880 - £4140

DURHAM HIGH SCHOOL
Farewell Hall, Durham DH1 3TB
Tel: (0191) 384 3226
Head: Miss M L Walters
Type: Girls Day 4-18 (Boys 4-7)
No of Pupils: 423
Fees: (September 95) £2592 - £4377

DURHAM SCHOOL*
Durham DH1 4SZ
Tel: (0191) 384 7977
Head: M A Lang
Type: Boys Boarding & Day 11-18
(Co-ed VIth form)
No of Pupils: B283 G39 No of
Boarders F141
Fees: (September 95) FB £9693 -
£11406 DAY £5085 - £7419

ESSEX

BILLERICAY

ST JOHN'S SCHOOL
Stock Road, Billericay, Essex
CM12 0AR
Tel: (01277) 623070
Head: Mrs S Hillier & Mrs F Armour
Type: Co-educational Day 3-16
No of Pupils: B180 G150
Fees: (September 95) £1560 - £3894

BRENTWOOD

BELL HOUSE SCHOOL
Brizes Park, Ongar Road, Kelvedon
Hatch, Brentwood, Essex CM15 0DG
Tel: (01277) 373613
Head: Mrs B J Morton
Type: Girls Day 3-16 (Boys 3-7)
No of Pupils: B66 G155
Fees: (September 94) £1830 - £4539

BRENTWOOD SCHOOL*
Ingrave Road, Brentwood, Essex
CM15 8AS
Tel: (01277) 212271
Head: J A B Kelsall
Type: Co-educational Boarding &
Day B7-18 G11-18
No of Pupils: B942 G304 No of
Boarders F60
Fees: (September 95) FB £9615
DAY £4212 - £5496

HERINGTON HOUSE SCHOOL
Mount Avenue, Hutton, Brentwood,
Essex CM13 2NS
Tel: (01277) 211595
Head: R Dudley-Cooke
Type: Co-educational Day 3-11
No of Pupils: B32 G110
Fees: (September 95) £1605 - £3405

BUCKHURST HILL

BRAESIDE SCHOOL FOR GIRLS
130 High Road, Buckhurst Hill,
Essex IG9 5SD
Tel: (0181) 504 1133
Head: Mrs C Naismith
Type: Girls Day 4-16
No of Pupils: 220
Fees: (September 95) £2955 - £3900

DAIGLEN SCHOOL
68 Palmerston Road, Buckhurst Hill,
Essex IG9 5LG
Tel: (0181) 504 7108
Head: D Wood
Type: Boys Day 4-11
No of Pupils: 152
Fees: (September 95) £2505

LOYOLA PREPARATORY
SCHOOL
103 Palmerston Road, Buckhurst
Hill, Essex IG9 5NH
Tel: (0181) 504 7372
Head: P G Nicholson
Type: Boys Day 4-11 (Nursery 3-4)
No of Pupils: 185
Fees: (September 95) £3120

CHELMSFORD

ELM GREEN PREPARATORY
SCHOOL
Parsonage Lane, Little Baddow,
Chelmsford, Essex CM3 4SU
Tel: (01245) 225230
Head: Mrs E L Mimpriss
Type: Co-educational Day 4-11
No of Pupils: B117 G93
Fees: (September 95) £3090

HEATHCOTE SCHOOL
Eves Corner, Danbury, Chelmsford,
Essex CM3 4QB
Tel: (01245) 223131
Head: Mr & Mrs R H Greenland
Type: Co-educational Day 4-11
No of Pupils: B103 G100
Fees: (September 95) £2865

NEW HALL SCHOOL*
Boreham, Chelmsford, Essex
CM3 3HT
Tel: (01245) 467588
Head: Sister Margaret Mary
Type: Girls Boarding & Day 4-18
(Boys day 4-11)
No of Pupils: 427 No of Boarders
F123 W84
Fees: (September 95) FB £7164 -
£10314 WB £7164 - £10110 DAY
£3060 - £6603

ST ANNE'S PREPARATORY
SCHOOL
154 New London Road, Chelmsford,
Essex CM2 0AW
Tel: (01245) 353488
Head: Mrs K Darby
Type: Co-educational Day 3-11
No of Pupils: B58 G82
Fees: (September 95) £2310 - £2715

ST CEDD'S SCHOOL
Maltese Road, Chelmsford, Essex
CM1 2PB
Tel: (01245) 354380
Head: Dr S A Foster
Type: Co-educational Day 4-11
No of Pupils: B172 G161
Fees: (September 95) £2700 - £3099

WIDFORD LODGE
Widford Road, Chelmsford, Essex
CM2 9AN
Tel: (01245) 352581
Head: H C Witham
Type: Boys Day 4-13 (Co-ed 2-4)
No of Pupils: 150
Fees: (September 95) £2610 - £3720

CHIGWELL

CHIGWELL SCHOOL
High Road, Chigwell, Essex IG7 6QF
Tel: (0181) 500 1396
Head: A R Little
Type: Boys Day & Boarding 7-18
(Co-ed VIth form)
No of Pupils: B624 G30 No of
Boarders F28 W42
Fees: (September 95) FB £6360 -
£9471 WB £6012 - £8967 DAY
£4572 - £6750

CLACTON-ON-SEA

ST CLARE'S DAY NURSERY
18 Holland Road, Clacton-On-Sea,
Essex CO15 6EG
Tel: (01255) 425344
Type: Co-educational Day 5-11
Fees: On application

COLCHESTER

COLCHESTER BOYS HIGH
SCHOOL
Wellesley Road, Colchester, Essex
CO3 3HD
Tel: (01206) 573389
Head: A T Moore
Type: Boys Day 3-16 (Girls 4-11)
No of Pupils: B350 G15
Fees: (September 95) £2835 - £3600

HOLMWOOD HOUSE
Chitts Hill, Lexden, Colchester, Essex
CO3 5ST
Tel: (01206) 574305
Head: H S Thackrah
Type: Co-educational Day &
Boarding 4-14
No of Pupils: B223 G107 No of
Boarders F38
Fees: (September 95) FB £7965 -
£8925 DAY £3885 - £6915

LITTLEGARTH SCHOOL
(DEDHAM) LTD
Horkesley Park, Nayland,
Colchester, Essex CO6 4JR
Tel: (01206) 262332
Head: Mrs M L Harvey
Type: Co-educational Day 2-12
No of Pupils: B89 G116
Fees: (September 95) £960 - £2880

OXFORD HOUSE SCHOOL
2 Lexden Road, Colchester, Essex
CO3 3NE
Tel: (01206) 576686
Head: R P Spendlove
Type: Co-educational Day 2-11
No of Pupils: B65 G65
Fees: (September 95) £1545 - £3075

ST MARY'S SCHOOL*
91 Lexden Road, Colchester, Essex
CO3 3RB
Tel: (01206) 572544
Head: Mrs G M Mouser
Type: Girls Day 4-17
No of Pupils: 500
Fees: (September 95) £2640 - £3690

DUNMOW

FELSTED PREPARATORY
SCHOOL
Felsted, Dunmow, Essex CM6 3JL
Tel: (01371) 820252
Head: M P Pomphrey
Type: Co-educational Boarding &
Day 4-13
No of Pupils: 234 No of Boarders F35
Fees: (September 95) FB £9225 DAY
£2760 - £6750

FELSTED SCHOOL
Felsted, Dunmow, Essex CM6 3LL
Tel: (01371) 820258
Head: S C Roberts
Type: Co-educational Boarding &
Day 13-18
No of Pupils: B295 G68 No of
Boarders F303
Fees: (September 94) FB £11880 WB
£9375 DAY £8685

EPPING

COOPERSALE HALL SCHOOL*
Flux's Lane, off Steward's Green
Road, Epping, Essex CM16 7PE
Tel: (01992) 577133
Head: Mrs F Best
Type: Co-educational Day 3-11
No of Pupils: B112 G110
Fees: (September 95) £1987 - £3585

FRINTON-ON-SEA

ST PHILOMENA'S
PREPARATORY SCHOOL
Hadleigh Road, Frinton-on-Sea,
Essex CO13 9HQ
Tel: (01255) 674492
Head: Mrs B Buck
Type: Co-educational Day 3-11
No of Pupils: B50 G51
Fees: (September 95) £1494

HALSTEAD

GOSFIELD SCHOOL
Halstead Road, Gosfield, Halstead,
Essex CO9 1PF
Tel: (01787) 474040
Head: J Shaw
Type: Co-educational Boarding &
Day 4-18
No of Pupils: B109 G24 No of
Boarders F62
Fees: (September 95) FB £6850 -
£9000 DAY £3230 - £5050

ST MARGARET'S SCHOOL
Gosfield Hall Park, Gosfield,
Halstead, Essex CO9 1SE
Tel: (01787) 472134
Head: J Dann
Type: Co-educational Day 4-13
(Nursery 2-4)
No of Pupils: B65 G80
Fees: (September 95) £2650 - £3160

HARLOW

ST NICHOLAS SCHOOL
Hillingdon House, Hobbs Cross
Road, Harlow, Essex CM17 0NJ
Tel: (01279) 429910
Head: G W Brant
Type: Co-educational Day 4-16
No of Pupils: B140 G144
Fees: (September 95) £1995 - £4080

HORNCHURCH

GOODRINGTON SCHOOL
17 Walden Road, Emerson Park,
Hornchurch, Essex RM11 2JT
Tel: (01708) 448349
Head: Mrs J Lauchlan
Type: Co-educational Day 3-11
No of Pupils: 65
Fees: (September 95) £1194 - £1944

ILFORD

BEEHIVE PREPARATORY SCHOOL
233 Beehive Lane, Redbridge, Ilford,
Essex IG4 5ED
Tel: (0181) 550 3224
Head: C J Beasant
Type: Co-educational Day 4-11
No of Pupils: 95
Fees: (September 95) £1615

CLARKS PREPARATORY SCHOOL
81/85 York Road, Ilford, Essex
Tel: (0181) 478 6510
Head: Ms M L Jones
Type: Co-educational Day 1-7
No of Pupils: B34 G37
Fees: (September 95) £2445 - £4680

CRANBROOK COLLEGE*
Mansfield Road, Ilford, Essex
IG1 3BD
Tel: (0181) 554 1757
Head: G T Reading
Type: Boys Day 4-16
No of Pupils: 220
Fees: (September 95) £2850 - £3660

EASTCOURT INDEPENDENT SCHOOL
1 Eastwood Road, Goodmayes,
Ilford, Essex IG3 8UW
Tel: (0181) 590 5472
Head: Mrs C Redgrave
Type: Co-educational Day 4-11
No of Pupils: B141 G174
Fees: (September 95) £2100

GLENARM COLLEGE
20 Coventry Road, Ilford, Essex
IG1 4QR
Tel: (0181) 554 1760
Head: Mrs V Mullooly
Type: Co-educational Day B4-8
G4-11
No of Pupils: B14 G120
Fees: (September 95) £2460

ILFORD PREPARATORY SCHOOL
Carnegie Buildings, 785 High Road,
Ilford, Essex IG3 8RR
Tel: (0181) 599 8822
Head: Mrs B P M Wiggs
Type: Co-educational Day 3-11
No of Pupils: B85 G85
Fees: (September 95) £750 - £900

ILFORD URSULINE HIGH SCHOOL*
Morland Road, Ilford, Essex IGI 4QS
Tel: (0181) 554 1995
Head: Miss J Reddington
Type: Girls Day 11-18
No of Pupils: 369
Fees: (September 95) £4329

MANSFIELD LODGE
29 Mansfield Road, Ilford, Essex
IG1 3BA
Tel: (0181) 553 0212
Head: Ms Anna Meshora
Type: Co-educational 1-7
No of Pupils: B19 G26
Fees: (September 95) DAY £65 - £95

PARK SCHOOL FOR GIRLS
20 Park Avenue, Ilford, Essex
IG1 4RS
Tel: (0181) 554 2466
Head: Mrs N O'Brien
Type: Girls Day 7-18
No of Pupils: 235
Fees: (September 95) £2730 - £3630

INGATESTONE

LANDRY SCHOOL
Whites Hill, Stock, Ingatestone,
Essex CM4 9QD
Tel: (01277) 840338
Head: Miss E Prior
Type: Co-educational Day 4-8
No of Pupils: B7 G8
Fees: (September 95) £1275

LEIGH-ON-SEA

COLLEGE SAINT-PIERRE
16 Leigh Road, Leigh-on-Sea, Essex
SS9 1LE
Tel: (01702) 74164
Head: G Bragard
Type: Co-educational Day 3-11
No of Pupils: B70 G40
Fees: (September 95) £1230 - £2340

ST MICHAEL'S SCHOOL
198 Hadleigh Road, Leigh-on-Sea,
Essex SS9 2LP
Tel: (01702) 78719
Head: Mrs S Stokes
Type: Co-educational Day 3-11
No of Pupils: B141 G151
Fees: (September 95) £2589

LOUGHTON

OAKLANDS SCHOOL*
8 Albion Hill, Loughton, Essex
IG10 4RA
Tel: (0181) 508 3517
Head: Mrs A Hagger
Type: Co-educational Day B3-7
G3-11
No of Pupils: B58 G177
Fees: (September 95) £2100 - £3240

MALDON

MALDON COURT PREPARATORY SCHOOL
Silver Street, Maldon, Essex CM9 7QE
Tel: (01621) 853529
Head: A G Sutton
Type: Co-educational Day 4-11
No of Pupils: 125
Fees: (September 95) £2775

ONGAR

SPRINGFIELD PNEU SCHOOL LTD
Stondon Road, Ongar, Essex
CM5 9RG
Tel: (01277) 362945
Head: Mrs S G Jeans-Jakobsson
Type: Co-educational Day 4-13
No of Pupils: B80 G80
Fees: (September 95) £2100 - £4050

ROCHFORD

CROWSTONE PREPARATORY SCHOOL (SUTTON ANNEXE)
Fleethall Lane, Shockland Road,
Rochford, Essex SS4 1LL
Tel: (01702) 540629
Head: J P Thayer
Type: Co-educational Day 3-11
No of Pupils: B75 G75
Fees: (September 93) £2655

ROMFORD

GIDEA PARK COLLEGE
Balgores House, 2 Balgores Lane,
Romford, Essex RM2 5JR
Tel: (01708) 740381
Head: Mrs V S Lee
Type: Co-educational Day 2-11
No of Pupils: B110 G75
Fees: (September 95) £2946

IMMANUEL SCHOOL
Havering Grange Centre, Havering
Road North, Romford, Essex
RM1 4HR
Tel: (01708) 764449
Head: D J Van Rooyen
Type: Co-educational Day 4-16
No of Pupils: 78
Fees: (September 94) £2280

RAPHAEL INDEPENDENT SCHOOL
Park Lane, Romford, Essex
RM11 1XY
Tel: (01708) 744735
Head: N W Malicka
Type: Co-educational Day 4-16
No of Pupils: 140
Fees: (September 95) £2385 - £4095

ST MARY'S HARE PARK SCHOOL
South Drive, Gidea Park, Romford,
Essex
Tel: (01708) 761220
Head: Mrs J C Guilford
Type: Girls Day 3-11 (Boys 3-7)
No of Pupils: 180
Fees: (September 95) £2250

SAFFRON WALDEN

DAME JOHANE BRADBURY'S SCHOOL*
Ashdon Road, Saffron Walden, Essex
CB10 2AL
Tel: (01799) 522348
Head: Mrs R M Rainey
Type: Co-educational Day 4-11
No of Pupils: B108 G160
Fees: (September 95) £2355 - £3120

FRIENDS' SCHOOL
Mount Pleasant Road, Saffron
Walden, Essex CB11 3EB
Tel: (01799) 525351
Head: Miss S H Evans
Type: Co-educational Boarding &
Day 3-18
No of Pupils: B125 G146 No of
Boarders F135
Fees: (September 95) F/WB £7512 -
£10014 DAY £3357 - £6066

SOUTHEND-ON-SEA

ALLEYN COURT AND ETON HOUSE SCHOOL*
Wakering Road, Great Wakering,
Southend-on-Sea, Essex SS3 0PW
Tel: (01702) 582553
Head: S Bishop & P Green
Type: Co-educational Day 2-16
No of Pupils: B301 G49
Fees: (September 95) £1767 - £4560

THORPE HALL SCHOOL
Wakering Road, Southend-on-Sea,
Essex SS1 3RD
Tel: (01702) 582340
Head: T Fawell
Type: Co-educational Day 3-16
No of Pupils: 380
Fees: (September 95) £2340 - £3360

WESTCLIFF-ON-SEA

CROWSTONE PREPARATORY SCHOOL
121-123 Crowstone Road,
Westcliff-on-Sea, Essex SS0 8LH
Tel: (01702) 346758
Head: J P Thayer
Type: Co-educational Day 3-11
No of Pupils: 170
Fees: (September 93) £2655

QUEENSLAND PREPARATORY SCHOOL
100 Crowstone Road,
Westcliff-on-Sea, Essex SS0 8LQ
Tel: (01702) 340664
Head: Miss R G Waltham
Type: Co-educational Day 3-11
No of Pupils: 48
Fees: (September 94) £1500 - £1590

ST HILDA'S SCHOOL
15 Imperial Avenue,
Westcliff-on-Sea, Essex SS0 8NE
Tel: (01702) 344542
Head: Mrs V M Tunnicliffe
Type: Girls Day 3-16 (Boys 3-7)
No of Pupils: 200
Fees: (September 95) £2556 - £3150

WESTMINSTER PREPARATORY SCHOOL
9 Westminster Drive,
Westcliff-on-Sea, Essex SS0 9SJ
Tel: (01702) 74144
Head: Mrs J Perfitt-Harvey
Type: Co-educational Day 4-11
No of Pupils: B19 G16
Fees: (September 95) £1500 - £1800

WOODFORD GREEN

AVON HOUSE
490 High Road, Woodford Green,
Essex IG8 0PN
Tel: (0181) 504 1749
Head: Mrs S Ferrari
Type: Co-educational Day 3-11
No of Pupils: 300
Fees: (September 95) £2760 - £3300

BANCROFTS SCHOOL*
Woodford Green, Essex IG8 0RF
Tel: (0181) 505 4821
Head: Dr P C Southern
Type: Co-educational Day 7-18
No of Pupils: B451 G486
Fees: (September 95) £4308 - £5694

ST AUBYN'S SCHOOL
Bunces Lane, Woodford Green, Essex
IG8 9DU
Tel: (0181) 504 1577
Head: G James
Type: Boys Day 4-13
No of Pupils: 240
Fees: (September 95) £2745 - £4062

WOODFORD GREEN PREPARATORY SCHOOL
Glengall Road, Snakes Lane,
Woodford Green, Essex IG8 0BQ
Tel: (0181) 504 5045
Head: I P Stroud
Type: Co-educational Day 3-11
No of Pupils: B161 G215
Fees: (September 95) £1350 - £2880

GLOUCESTERSHIRE

CHELTENHAM

AIRTHRIE SCHOOL
29 Christ Church Road, Cheltenham,
Gloucestershire GL50 2NY
Tel: (01242) 512837
Head: Mrs A E Sullivan
Type: Co-educational Day 3-11
No of Pupils: B90 G90
Fees: (September 95) £2238 - £2832

BERKHAMPSTEAD SCHOOL
Pittville Circus Road, Cheltenham,
Gloucestershire GL52 2PZ
Tel: (01242) 523263
Head: W R Marsh
Type: Co-educational Day 3-11
No of Pupils: B79 G150
Fees: (September 95) £1125 - £3480

CHELTENHAM COLLEGE
Bath Road, Cheltenham,
Gloucestershire GL53 7LD
Tel: (01242) 513540
Head: P D Wilkes
Type: Boys Boarding & Day 13-18
(Co-ed VIth Form)
No of Pupils: B480 G100 No of
Boarders F370
Fees: (September 95) FB £12210 DAY
£9225

CHELTENHAM COLLEGE
JUNIOR SCHOOL
Thirlestaine Road, Cheltenham,
Gloucestershire GL53 7AB
Tel: (01242) 522697
Head: N I Archdale
Type: Boys Boarding & Day 3-13
(Girls 3-10)
Fees: (September 95) FB £6930 -
£8610 DAY £2115 - £6660

CHELTENHAM LADIES'
COLLEGE*
Bayshill Road, Cheltenham,
Gloucestershire GL50 3EP
Tel: (01242) 520691
Head: Miss E Castle
Type: Girls Boarding & Day 11-18
No of Pupils: 850 No of Boarders
F660
Fees: (September 95) FB £12285
DAY £7800

DEAN CLOSE JUNIOR
SCHOOL*
Lansdown Road, Cheltenham,
Gloucestershire GL51 6QS
Tel: (01242) 512217
Head: I F Ferguson
Type: Co-educational Boarding &
Day 4-13
No of Pupils: B128 G108 No of
Boarders F75
Fees: (September 95) FB £8880 WB
£7500 DAY £6075

DEAN CLOSE SCHOOL*
Cheltenham, Gloucestershire
GL51 6HE
Tel: (01242) 522640
Head: C J Bacon
Type: Co-educational Boarding &
Day 12-18
No of Pupils: B254 G194 No of
Boarders F274
Fees: (September 95) FB £12225 DAY
£8535

THE RICHARD PATE SCHOOL
Southern Road, Cheltenham,
Gloucestershire GL53 9RP
Tel: (01242) 522086
Head: E L Rowland
Type: Co-educational Day 3-11
No of Pupils: B164 G120
Fees: (September 95) £1311 - £3042

ST EDWARD'S SCHOOL
Ashley Road, Charlton Kings,
Cheltenham, Gloucestershire
GL52 6NT
Tel: (01242) 526697
Head: A J Martin
Type: Co-educational Day 2-18
No of Pupils: B348 G349
Fees: (September 95) £2985 - £5385

CINDERFORD

ST ANTHONYS SCHOOL
93 Bellevue Road, Cinderford,
Gloucestershire GL14 2AA
Tel: (01594) 823558
Head: Sister M C McKenna
Type: Co-educational Day 3-11
No of Pupils: B56 G62
Fees: (September 95) £1590 - £2040

CIRENCESTER

HATHEROP CASTLE
PREPARATORY SCHOOL*
Hatherop, Cirencester,
Gloucestershire GL7 3NB
Tel: (01285) 750206
Head: P Easterbrook
Type: Co-educational Boarding &
Day 2-13
No of Pupils: B80 G88 No of
Boarders F10 W15
Fees: (September 95) F/WB £7500
DAY £3000 - £4800

INGLESIDE PNEU SCHOOL
The Beeches, Cirencester,
Gloucestershire GL7 1BN
Tel: (01285) 654046
Head: Mrs P F Cox
Type: Co-educational Day 4-11
No of Pupils: B40 G50
Fees: (September 95) £1800 - £2190

THE QUERNS SCHOOL
Querns Lane, Cirencester,
Gloucestershire GL7 1RL
Tel: (01285) 652953
Head: Mrs M Paine
Type: Co-educational Day 4-11
No of Pupils: B45 G70
Fees: (September 95) £2055 - £2880

RENDCOMB COLLEGE*
Rendcomb, Cirencester,
Gloucestershire GL7 7HA
Tel: (01285) 831213
Head: J N Tolputt
Type: Co-educational Boarding &
Day 11-18
No of Pupils: B182 G58 No of
Boarders F200
Fees: (September 95) FB £8307 -
£10674 DAY £6432 - £8442

GLOUCESTER

GLOUCESTERSHIRE ISLAMIC
SCHOOL
Sinope Street, off Widden Street,
Gloucester
Tel: (01452) 300465
Type: Girls Day 11-16
No of Pupils: 35
Fees: (September 95) £400

THE KING'S SCHOOL*
Pitt Street, Gloucester GL1 2BG
Tel: (01452) 521251
Head: P R Lacey
Type: Co-educational Boarding &
Day 4-19
No of Pupils: B403 G191 No of
Boarders F50 W5
Fees: (September 95) FB £8800 -
£9400 WB £8000 - £9000 DAY
£2040 - £5670

SELWYN SCHOOL
Matson House, Matson Lane,
Gloucester GL4 9DY
Tel: (01452) 305663
Head: Miss L Brown
Type: Girls Day & Boarding 3-18
(Boys 3-11)
No of Pupils: B47 G310 No of
Boarders F46 W12
Fees: (September 95) FB £6540 -
£8430 WB £6060 - £7950 DAY
£2046 - £4800

WYNSTONES SCHOOL
Whaddon Green, Gloucester GL4 0UF
Tel: (01452) 522475
Type: Co-educational Day &
Boarding 3-18
No of Pupils: B133 G144 No of
Boarders F11 W7
Fees: (September 95) FB £6509 -
£6680 DAY £1335 - £3576

LECHLADE

ST CLOTILDE'S SCHOOL
Lechlade Manor, Lechlade,
Gloucestershire GL7 3BB
Tel: (01367) 252259
Head: Miss A Wood
Type: Girls Boarding & Day 3-18
(Boarders from 11, day boys 3-9)
No of Pupils: B21 G140 No of
Boarders W15
Fees: (September 95) WB £8490 DAY
£1380 - £5070

MORETON-IN-MARSH

THE DORMER HOUSE PNEU
SCHOOL
High Street, Moreton-in-Marsh,
Gloucestershire GL56 0AD
Tel: (01608) 650758
Head: Ms D A Trembath
Type: Co-educational Day 3-11
No of Pupils: B48 G46
Fees: (September 95) £1470 - £2460

KITEBROOK HOUSE
Moreton-in-Marsh, Gloucestershire
GL56 0RP
Tel: (01608) 674350
Head: Mrs A McDermott
Type: Girls Boarding & Day 4-13
(Boys 4-8)
No of Pupils: B44 G136
Fees: (September 94) WB £6870 DAY
£1590 - £4470

NAILSWORTH

ACORN SCHOOL
Church Street, Nailsworth,
Gloucestershire GL6 0BP
Tel: (01453) 836508
Head: G E B Whiting
Type: Co-educational Boarding &
Day 3-19
No of Pupils: B19 G30 No of Boarders
F2
Fees: (September 95) FB £1440 -
£2520 DAY £300 - £2775

STONEHOUSE

HOPELANDS SCHOOL
38 Regent Street, Stonehouse,
Gloucestershire GL10 2AD
Tel: (01453) 822164
Head: Mrs B J Janes
Type: Co-educational Day 3-11
No of Pupils: B17 G43
Fees: (September 95) £2250 - £2775

WYCLIFFE COLLEGE*
Stonehouse, Gloucestershire
GL10 2JQ
Tel: (01453) 822432
Head: D C Prichard
Type: Co-educational Boarding &
Day 13-18
No of Pupils: B227 G104 No of
Boarders F193
Fees: (September 95) FB £11610 -
£11985 DAY £8190

WYCLIFFE COLLEGE JUNIOR
SCHOOL
Stonehouse, Gloucestershire
GL10 2LD
Tel: (01453) 823233
Head: R Outwin-Flinders
Type: Co-educational Boarding &
Day 2-13
No of Pupils: B180 G120 No of
Boarders F40 W20
Fees: (September 95) FB £6315 -
£8070 WB £6120 - £7785 DAY
£2430 - £5775

STOW ON THE WOLD

LEVERETS SCHOOL
Maugersbury Manor, Stow on the
Wold, Gloucestershire GL54 1DR
Tel: (01451) 831599
Head: Mrs S Gould
Type: Co-educational Day 3-11
No of Pupils: B26 G19
Fees: (September 95) £837 - £1386

STROUD

BEAUDESERT PARK*
Minchinhampton, Stroud,
Gloucestershire GL6 9AF
Tel: (01453) 832072
Head: J R W Beasley
Type: Co-educational Boarding &
Day 4-13
No of Pupils: B149 G124 No of
Boarders F34 W47
Fees: (September 95) F/WB £8559
DAY £3150 - £6300

UPFIELD PREPARATORY
SCHOOL LTD
Paganhill, Stroud, Gloucestershire
GL5 4AY
Tel: (01453) 764820
Head: P S Harris
Type: Co-educational Day 3-11
No of Pupils: B60 G50
Fees: (September 95) £1300 - £1795

TETBURY

WESTONBIRT SCHOOL*
Tetbury, Gloucestershire GL8 8QG
Tel: (01666) 880333
Head: Mrs G Hylson-Smith
Type: Girls Boarding & Day 11-18
No of Pupils: 242 No of Boarders
F212
Fees: (September 95) FB £10785 DAY
£6936

TEWKESBURY

THE ABBEY SCHOOL
Church Street, Tewkesbury,
Gloucestershire GL20 5PD
Tel: (01684) 294460
Head: J H Milton
Type: Co-educational Day &
Boarding 3-13
No of Pupils: B71 G37 No of Boarders
W8
Fees: (September 95) WB £6420 -
£7365 DAY £990 - £5295

BREDON SCHOOL*
Pull Court, Bushley, Tewkesbury,
Gloucestershire GL20 6AH
Tel: (01684) 293156
Head: C E Wheeler
Type: Co-educational Boarding &
Day 3-18
No of Pupils: B247 G53 No of
Boarders F154 W44
Fees: (September 95) FB £8130 -
£12150 WB £7950 - £11970 DAY
£2400 - £6960

WOTTON-UNDER-EDGE

ROSE HILL SCHOOL
Alderley, Wotton-under-Edge,
Gloucestershire GL12 7QT
Tel: (01453) 843196
Head: R C Lyne-Pirkis
Type: Co-educational Boarding &
Day 3-13
No of Pupils: B89 G66 No of
Boarders F15 W21
Fees: (September 94) F/WB £6120 -
£8100 DAY £2790 - £6120

HAMPSHIRE

ALDERMASTON

CEDARS SCHOOL
Church Road, Aldermaston,
Hampshire RG7 4LR
Tel: (01734) 714251
Head: Mrs A E Ludlow
Type: Co-educational Day 4-11
No of Pupils: B18 G18
Fees: (September 95) £2685

ALDERSHOT

STOCKTON HOUSE SCHOOL
Stockton Avenue, Fleet, Aldershot,
Hampshire GU13 8NF
Tel: (01252) 616323
Head: Mrs C Tweedie-Smith
Type: Co-educational Day 2-8
No of Pupils: 120
Fees: (September 95) £795 - £2205

ALTON

**CONVENT OF OUR LADY OF
PROVIDENCE SCHOOL**
Anstey Lane, Alton, Hampshire
GU34 2NG
Tel: (01420) 82070
Head: F Martin & Sister Madeleine
Type: Girls Day 4-18 (Co-ed junior
school)
No of Pupils: B45 G367
Fees: (September 95) £2850 - £3150

**MAYFIELD PREPARATORY
SCHOOL**
103 Anstey Road, Alton, Hampshire
GU34 2RN
Tel: (01420) 83105
Head: T T Incles & Mrs C E Incles
Type: Co-educational Day 2-11
No of Pupils: B62 G50
Fees: (September 95) £907 - £2757

ANDOVER

FARLEIGH SCHOOL*
Red Rice, Andover, Hampshire
SP11 7PW
Tel: (01264) 710766
Head: Mr J E Murphy
Type: Co-educational Day &
Boarding 3-13
No of Pupils: B240 G92 No of
Boarders F87
Fees: (September 95) F/WB £8367
DAY £1356 - £5940

ROOKWOOD SCHOOL*
Weyhill Road, Andover, Hampshire
SP10 3AL
Tel: (01264) 352855
Head: Mrs S Hindle
Type: Girls Day & Boarding 3-16
(Day boys 3-11)
No of Pupils: B82 G191 No of
Boarders F2 W21
Fees: (September 95) FB £6600 -
£8631 WB £6075 - £8106 DAY
£2595 - £4536

**ST BENEDICT'S CONVENT
SCHOOL**
Penton Lodge, Andover, Hampshire
SP11 0RD
Tel: (01264) 772291
Head: Mrs R M Wheelwright
Type: Girls Boarding & Day 3-16
No of Pupils: 116
Fees: (September 94) FB £5610 -
£6840 DAY £1500 - £2985

BASINGSTOKE

DANESHILL HOUSE
Stratfield Turgis, Basingstoke,
Hampshire RG27 0AR
Tel: (01256) 882707
Head: S V Spencer
Type: Co-educational Day 3-12
No of Pupils: B122 G197
Fees: (September 95) £3090 - £4080

**GREY HOUSE PREPARATORY
SCHOOL**
Mount Pleasant Road, Hartley
Wintney, Basingstoke, Hampshire
RG27 8PW
Tel: (01252) 842353
Head: Mrs E M Purse
Type: Co-educational Day 4-11
No of Pupils: B70 G81
Fees: (September 95) £2925 - £3600

INHURST HOUSE SCHOOL
Baughurst, Basingstoke, Hampshire
RG26 5JJ
Tel: (01734) 813388
Head: Mrs M Smallwood
Type: Co-educational Day B3-8
G3-11
No of Pupils: B31 G89
Fees: (September 95) £3435 - £3750

**LORD WANDSWORTH
COLLEGE***
Long Sutton, Basingstoke,
Hampshire RG25 1TB
Tel: (01256) 862482
Head: G de Waller
Type: Boys Boarding & Day 11-18
(Co-ed VIth form)
No of Pupils: B409 G35 No of
Boarders F67 W258
Fees: (September 95) F/WB £9084 -
£9492 DAY £7092 - £7380

ST NEOT'S SCHOOL

Eversley, Basingstoke, Hampshire
RG27 0PN
Tel: (01734) 732118
Head: R J Thorp
Type: Boys Day & Boarding 3-13
(Day girls 3-13)
No of Pupils: B110 G60 No of
Boarders W16
Fees: (September 95) WB £7710 DAY
£3045 - £5886

CHANDLER'S FORD

PIXIE SCHOOL HAMPSHIRE

120 Kingsway, Chandler's Ford,
Hampshire SO5 1DW
Tel: (01703) 253815
Head: Mrs D M Munro
Type: Co-educational Day 3-8
No of Pupils: 30
Fees: (September 94) £930 - £1380

WOODHILL SCHOOL

61 Brownhill Road, Chandler's Ford,
Hampshire SO53 2EH
Tel: (01703) 268012
Head: Mrs M Dacombe
Type: Co-educational Day 3-11
No of Pupils: B60 G60
Fees: (September 95) £1164 - £2265

EASTLEIGH

SHERBORNE HOUSE SCHOOL

Lakewood Road, Chandler's Ford,
Eastleigh, Hampshire SO53 1EU
Tel: (01703) 252440
Head: Mrs S M Warner
Type: Girls Day 3-11 (Boys 3-8)
No of Pupils: B20 G150
Fees: (September 95) £2550 - £2700

FAREHAM

BOUNDARY OAK SCHOOL

Roche Court, Fareham, Hampshire
PO17 5BL
Tel: (01329) 280955
Head: R B Bliss
Type: Boys Boarding & Day 3-13
(Girls 3-9)
No of Pupils: B210 G15 No of
Boarders F5 W30
Fees: (September 95) F/WB £6015 -
£7740 DAY £1485 - £5175

MEONCROSS SCHOOL

Burnt House Lane, Stubbington,
Fareham, Hampshire PO14 2EF
Tel: (01329) 662182
Head: C Ford
Type: Co-educational Day 4-16
No of Pupils: B184 G219
Fees: (September 95) £2820 - £3876

SEAFIELD SCHOOL

Westlands Grove, Portchester,
Fareham, Hampshire PO16 9AA
Tel: (01705) 377158
Head: Mrs E G Jones
Type: Co-educational Day 3-8
No of Pupils: B40 G25
Fees: (September 95) £1110 - £1440

WEST HILL PARK PREPARATORY SCHOOL

Titchfield, Fareham, Hampshire
PO14 4BS
Tel: (01329) 842356
Head: E P Hudson
Type: Co-educational Boarding &
Day 3-13
No of Pupils: B188 G71 No of
Boarders F70
Fees: (September 95) FB £7860 DAY
£5415 - £5865

WYKEHAM HOUSE SCHOOL*

17 East Street, Fareham, Hampshire
PO16 0BW
Tel: (01329) 280178
Head: Mrs R M Kamaryc
Type: Girls Day 4-16
No of Pupils: 300
Fees: (September 95) £1560 - £3870

FARNBOROUGH

FARNBOROUGH HILL*

Farnborough, Hampshire GU14 8AT
Tel: (01252) 545197
Head: Sr E McCormack
Type: Girls Day 11-18
No of Pupils: 520
Fees: (September 95) £4428

KWABENA MONTESSORI SCHOOL

17 Closeworth Road, Farnborough,
Hampshire GU14 6JH
Tel. (01252) 547607
Head: Mrs A M Phoenix
Type: Co-educational Day 3-7
Fees: (September 95) £1620 – £1758

RUSHMOOR INDEPENDENT SCHOOL

40 Reading Road, Farnborough,
Hampshire GU14 6NB
Tel: (01252) 544738
Head: Mrs A Rendell
Type: Co-educational Day 2-16
No of Pupils: B50 G24
Fees: (September 95) £360 - £2694

SALESIAN COLLEGE

Farnborough, Hampshire GU14 6PA
Tel: (01252) 542919
Head: Rev Br M Delmer
Type: Boys Day 11-18
No of Pupils: 495
Fees: (September 95) £2994

FLEET

ST NICHOLAS SCHOOL

Branksomewood Road, Fleet,
Hampshire GU13 8JT
Tel: (01252) 614864
Head: Mrs L G Smith
Type: Girls Day 4-16 (Boys 4-7)
No of Pupils: B5 G406
Fees: (September 95) £1818 - £3750

FORDINGBRIDGE

FORRES SANDLE MANOR*

Fordingbridge, Hampshire SP6 1NS
Tel: (01425) 653181
Head: R P Moore
Type: Co-educational Boarding &
Day 3-13
No of Pupils: B150 G105 No of
Boarders F52 W30
Fees: (September 95) F/WB £8385
DAY £1788 - £5985

GOSPORT

MARYCOURT SCHOOL

27 Crescent Road, Alverstoke,
Gosport, Hampshire PO12 2DJ
Tel: (01705) 581766
Head: Mrs M Crane
Type: Co-educational Day 3-11
No of Pupils: 120
Fees: (September 95) £1101 - £1977

HAVANT

GLENHURST SCHOOL

Beechworth Road, Havant,
Hampshire PO9 1AX
Tel: (01705) 484054
Head: Mrs E A Newman
Type: Co-educational Day 3-9
No of Pupils: B60 G44
Fees: (September 95) £1195 - £1485

HOOK

NORTH FORELAND LODGE

Reading Road, Sherfield-on-Loddon,
Hook, Hampshire RG27 0HT
Tel: (01256) 882431
Head: Miss D L Matthews
Type: Girls Boarding & Day 11-18
No of Pupils: 170 No of Boarders
F170
Fees: (September 95) FB £10800

LEE-ON-THE-SOLENT

ST ANNE'S SCHOOL
13 Milvil Road, Lee-on-the-Solent,
Hampshire PO13 9LU
Tel: (01705) 550820
Head: Mrs J G Bottomley
Type: Co-educational Day 3-8
No of Pupils: B21 G24
Fees: (September 95) £1440 - £1740

LIPHOOK

BROOKHAM SCHOOL
Highfield Lane, Liphook, Hampshire
GU30 7LQ
Tel: (01428) 722005
Head: Miss G Di Duca
Type: Co-educational Day 3-8
No of Pupils: 78
Fees: (September 95) £1050 - £3900

HIGHFIELD SCHOOL
Liphook, Hampshire GU30 7LQ
Tel: (01428) 722228
Head: N O Ramage
Type: Co-educational Boarding &
Day 7-13
No of Pupils: B110 G65 No of
Boarders F145
Fees: (September 95) FB £7950 -
£8970 DAY £6000 - £6960

LITTLEFIELD SCHOOL
Midhurst Road, Liphook, Hampshire
GU30 7HT
Tel: (01428) 723187
Head: G Milne
Type: Co-educational Day 2-11
No of Pupils: 138
Fees: (September 95) £1005 - £3255

LYMINGTON

HORDLE HOUSE
Milford-on-Sea, Lymington,
Hampshire SO41 0NW
Tel: (01590) 642104
Head: R H C Phillips
Type: Co-educational Boarding &
Day 2-13
No of Pupils: B107 G80 No of
Boarders F52 W12
Fees: (September 95) F/WB £6750 -
£7950 DAY £3150 - £5970

WALHAMPTON SCHOOL
Walhampton, Lymington,
Hampshire SO41 5ZG
Tel: (01590) 672013
Head: A W Robinson
Type: Co-educational Boarding &
Day 4-13
No of Pupils: B135 G89 No of
Boarders F105
Fees: (September 95) FB £9480 DAY
£3300 - £7020

NEW MILTON

BALLARD COLLEGE
New Milton, Hampshire BH25 5JL
Tel: (01425) 611090
Head: Rev A J Folks
Type: Co-educational Boarding &
Day B13-18 G11-18
Fees: (September 95) FB £8385 WB
£7890 DAY £5310

BALLARD LAKE
PREPARATORY SCHOOL
Fernhill Lane, New Milton,
Hampshire BH25 5SU
Tel: (01425) 611153
Head: Miss G R Morris
Type: Co-educational Boarding &
Day 3-13
Fees: (September 95) FB £7845 WB
£7335 DAY £810 - £5310

DURLSTON COURT
Becton Lane, Barton-on-Sea, New
Milton, Hampshire BH25 7AQ
Tel: (01425) 610010
Head: J T Seddon
Type: Co-educational Day &
Boarding 3-14
No of Pupils: B160 G110 No of
Boarders F60
Fees: (September 95) F/WB £7920
DAY £1650 - £5610

PETERSFIELD

BEDALES SCHOOL*
Petersfield, Hampshire GU32 2DG
Tel: (01730) 263286
Head: Mrs Alison Willcocks
Type: Co-educational Boarding &
Day 13-18
No of Pupils: B193 G213 No of
Boarders F346
Fees: (September 95) FB £12996 DAY
£9562

CHURCHERS COLLEGE
Portsmouth Road, Petersfield,
Hampshire GU31 4AS
Tel: (01730) 263033
Head: G W Buttle
Type: Co-educational Day 4-18
No of Pupils: B395 G178
Fees: (September 95) £4995

CHURCHERS COLLEGE
JUNIOR DEPARTMENT
The Spain, Petersfield, Hampshire
GU32 3LA
Tel: (01730) 263724
Head: J D Wallis
Type: Co-educational Day 4-11
No of Pupils: B70 G53
Fees: (September 95) £2610 - £2865

DITCHAM PARK SCHOOL*
Ditcham Park, Petersfield,
Hampshire GU31 5RN
Tel: (01730) 825659
Head: Mrs P M Holmes
Type: Co-educational Day 4-16
No of Pupils: B169 G139
Fees: (September 95) £3288 - £5453

DUNHURST (BEDALES
JUNIOR SCHOOL)*
Alton Road, Steep, Petersfield,
Hampshire GU31 2DP
Tel: (01730) 262984
Head: M Heslop and H Heslop
Type: Co-educational Boarding &
Day 8-13
No of Pupils: B82 G87 No of
Boarders F70
Fees: (September 95) FB £8811 -
£9369 DAY £5943 - £6396

PORTSMOUTH

THE PORTSMOUTH
GRAMMAR SCHOOL
High Street, Portsmouth, Hampshire
PO1 2LN
Tel: (01705) 819125
Head: A C Evans
Type: Co-educational Day 4-18
No of Pupils: 1113
Fees: (September 95) £2874 - £4485

PURBROOK

WOODSIDE HOUSE SCHOOL
Woodside House, Purbrook,
Hampshire PO7 5RT
Tel: (01705) 230024
Head: Mrs M J Vernon-Harcourt
Type: Co-educational Day 3-11
No of Pupils: B37 G28
Fees: (September 95) £1350 - £2250

RINGWOOD

AVONLEA SCHOOL
8 Broadshard Lane, Ringwood,
Hampshire BH24 1RR
Tel: (01425) 473994
Head: Mrs C M Palomo
Type: Co-educational Day 2-11
No of Pupils: B20 G55
Fees: (September 95) £1275 - £1875

MOYLES COURT SCHOOL
Moyles Court, Ringwood,
Hampshire BH24 3NF
Tel: (01425) 472856
Head: R A Dean
Type: Co-educational Day &
Boarding 3-16
No of Pupils: B83 G63 No of Boarders
F61
Fees: (September 95) FB £7080 -
£8040 DAY £2985 - £5085

RINGWOOD WALDORF
SCHOOL
Ashley, Ringwood, Hampshire
BH24 2NN
Tel: (01425) 472664
Type: Co-educational Day 4-14
No of Pupils: B70 G70
Fees: (September 93) £600 - £3900

ROMSEY

EMBLEY PARK*
Romsey, Hampshire SO51 6ZE
Tel: (01794) 512206
Head: D F Chapman
Type: Co-educational Boarding &
Day 3-18 (Boarders from 11)
No of Pupils: B250 G105 No of
Boarders F50 W45
Fees: (September 95) F/WB £4635 -
£9570 DAY £2775 - £5835

LA SAGESSE CONVENT
Abbey House, Romsey, Hampshire
SO51 8EL
Tel: (01794) 522320
Head: Sister Thomas Cox
Type: Girls Day 3-16 (Boys 3-11)
No of Pupils: B30 G180
Fees: (September 95) £1134 - £3024

STANBRIDGE EARLS SCHOOL*
Stanbridge Lane, Romsey,
Hampshire SO51 0ZS
Tel: (01794) 516777
Head: H Moxon
Type: Co-educational Boarding &
Day 11-18
No of Pupils: B142 G41 No of
Boarders F175
Fees: (September 95) FB £10665 -
£11655 DAY £7995 - £8745

THE STROUD SCHOOL
Highwood House, Romsey,
Hampshire SO51 9ZH
Tel: (01794) 513231
Head: A J Dodds
Type: Co-educational Day 3-13
No of Pupils: B185 G65
Fees: (September 95) £1629 - £5778

SOUTHAMPTON

THE ATHERLEY SCHOOL FOR
GIRLS
Hill Lane, Southampton, Hampshire
SO9 1GR
Tel: (01703) 772898
Head: Mrs C Madina
Type: Girls Day 3-18 (Boys 3-11)
No of Pupils: 437
Fees: (September 95) £1416 - £4272

THE GREGG SCHOOL
Townhill Park House, Cutbush Lane,
Southampton, Hampshire SO2 2GF
Tel: (01703) 671676
Head: R D Hart
Type: Co-educational Day 11-16
No of Pupils: B150 G130
Fees: (September 95) £4200

KING EDWARD VI SCHOOL
Kellett Road, Southampton,
Hampshire SO15 7UQ
Tel: (01703) 704561
Head: T R Cookson
Type: Co-educational Day 11-18
No of Pupils: B835 G105
Fees: (September 95) £4710

ST CHRISTOPHER'S SCHOOL
Tamarisk Gardens, Bitterne Park,
Southampton, Hampshire SO18 4RA
Tel: (01703) 672010
Head: Mrs J A Naulin
Type: Co-educational Day 3-8
No of Pupils: B20 G20

ST MARY'S COLLEGE
57 Midanbury Lane, Bitterne Park,
Southampton, Hampshire SO18 4DJ
Tel: (01703) 671267
Head: Rev Bro Peter
Type: Boys Day 3-18
No of Pupils: 450
Fees: (September 94) £1095

ST WINIFRED'S SCHOOL
17-19 Winn Road, Southampton,
Hampshire SO17 IEJ
Tel: (01703) 557352
Head: J Collins
Type: Co-educational Day 3-11
No of Pupils: B75 G54
Fees: (September 95) £1950 - £2835

SOUTHAMPTON SMALL
SCHOOL
2 Brookvale Road, Portswood,
Southampton, Hampshire SO17 1QL
Tel: (01703) 322538
Head: Mrs J R Brennan
Type: Co-educational Day 3-11
Fees: (September 95) £1700 - £2500

VINE SCHOOL
Church Lane, Curdridge,
Southampton, Hampshire SO32 2DR
Tel: (01489) 789123
Head: R W Medway
Type: Co-educational Day
No of Pupils: B30 G30
Fees: (September 95) £700

WOODHILL PREPARATORY
SCHOOL
Brook Lane, Botley, Southampton,
Hampshire SO30 2ER
Tel: (01489) 781112
Head: Mrs M Dacombe
Type: Co-educational Day 3-11
No of Pupils: B70 G70
Fees: (September 95) £1164 - £2265

SOUTHSEA

MAYVILLE HIGH SCHOOL
35 St Simon's Road, Southsea,
Hampshire PO5 2PE
Tel: (01705) 734847
Head: Mrs L Owens
Type: Girls Day 2-16 (Boys 2-8)
No of Pupils: B32 G239
Fees: (September 95) £2400 - £3450

PORTSMOUTH HIGH SCHOOL
GPDST
25 Kent Road, Southsea, Hampshire
PO5 3EQ
Tel: (01705) 826714
Head: Mrs J M Dawtrey
Type: Girls Day 4-18
No of Pupils: 750
Fees: (September 95) £2928 - £3984

ST JOHN'S COLLEGE
Grove Road South, Southsea,
Hampshire PO5 3QW
Tel: (01705) 815118
Head: J R Davies
Type: Boys Boarding & Day 4-18
(Co-ed VIth form)
No of Pupils: B770 G9 No of Boarders
F90
Fees: (September 95) FB £6855 -
£7770 DAY £2700 - £3885

WICKHAM

ROOKESBURY PARK SCHOOL*
Wickham, Hampshire PO17 6HT
Tel: (01329) 833108
Head: Miss L A Appleyard
Type: Girls Boarding & Day 3-13
No of Pupils: 150 No of Boarders F45
Fees: (September 95) FB £6645 -
£7815 DAY £1565 - £5370

WINCHESTER

NETHERCLIFFE SCHOOL
Hatherley Road, Winchester,
Hampshire SO22 6RS
Tel: (01962) 854570
Head: R F Whitfield
Type: Co-educational Day 3-11
No of Pupils: B91 G32
Fees: (September 95) £1557 - £3531

THE PILGRIMS SCHOOL*
The Close, Winchester, Hampshire
SO23 9LT
Tel: (01962) 854189
Head: M E Kefford
Type: Boys Boarding & Day 8-13
No of Pupils: 180 No of Boarders F80
Fees: (September 95) FB £8115 DAY
£5925

PRINCE'S MEAD SCHOOL
43 Edgar Road, Winchester,
Hampshire SO23 9TN
Tel: (01962) 853416
Head: Mrs D Moore
Type: Co-educational Day 3-11
No of Pupils: B115 G147
Fees: (April 95) £1415 - £4245

ST SWITHUN'S SCHOOL
Winchester, Hampshire SO21 1HA
Tel: (01962) 861316
Head: Dr H L Harvey
Type: Girls Boarding & Day 11-18
No of Pupils: 458 No of Boarders F83
W140
Fees: (September 95) F/WB £11130
DAY £6720

TWYFORD SCHOOL
Winchester, Hampshire SO21 1NW
Tel: (01962) 712269
Head: P R D Gould
Type: Co-educational Day &
Boarding 3-13
No of Pupils: B194 G66 No of
Boarders F70
Fees: (September 95) FB £8700 DAY
£1770 - £6360

WINCHESTER COLLEGE
College Street, Winchester,
Hampshire SO23 9NA
Tel: (01962) 854328
Head: J P Sabben-Clare
Type: Boys Boarding & Day 13-18
No of Pupils: 667 No of Boarders
F641
Fees: (September 95) FB £13290 DAY
£9966

HEREFORD & WORCESTER

BEWDLEY

MOFFATS SCHOOL
Kinlet Hall, Bewdley, Hereford &
Worcester DY12 3AY
Tel: (01299) 841230
Head: Mr & Mrs M Daborn
Type: Co-educational Boarding 7-13
No of Pupils: B50 G28 No of
Boarders F75
Fees: (September 95) FB £6225 DAY
£3780

BROMSGROVE

BROMSGROVE LOWER
SCHOOL*
Cobham House, Conway Road,
Bromsgrove, Hereford & Worcester
B60 2AD
Tel: (01527) 579600
Head: E J Ormerod
Type: Co-educational Boarding &
Day 7-13
No of Pupils: B235 G172 No of
Boarders F80
Fees: (September 95) FB £7545 -
£8685 DAY £4290 - £5625

BROMSGROVE
PRE-PREPARATORY SCHOOL*
28-30 College Road, Bromsgrove,
Hereford & Worcester B60 2NF
Tel: (01527) 873007
Head: Mrs S Pickering
Type: Co-educational Day 3-7
No of Pupils: B73 G68
Fees: (September 95) £1317 - £2712

BROMSGROVE SCHOOL*
Bromsgrove, Hereford & Worcester
B61 7DU
Tel: (01527) 579679
Head: T M Taylor
Type: Co-educational Boarding &
Day 13-18
No of Pupils: B392 G251 No of
Boarders F259
Fees: (September 95) FB £9825 DAY
£6150

MOUNT SCHOOL
Birmingham Road, Bromsgrove,
Hereford & Worcester B61 0EP
Tel: (01527) 877772
Head: B J Maybee
Type: Co-educational Day 3-12
No of Pupils: B77 G67
Fees: (September 95) £2397 - £3288

WHITFORD HALL SCHOOL
Bromsgrove, Hereford & Worcester
B61 7LB
Tel: (01527) 31631
Head: Mrs S Brooks
Type: Co-educational Day B3-11
G3-13
No of Pupils: B43 G138
Fees: (September 95) £1440 - £3930

BROMYARD

ST RICHARD'S
Bredenbury Court, Bromyard,
Hereford & Worcester HR7 4TD
Tel: (01885) 482491
Head: R E Coghlan
Type: Co-educational Boarding &
Day 4-13
No of Pupils: B69 G57 No of
Boarders F55 W10
Fees: (September 95) FB £7140 WB
£6675 DAY £4842

DROITWICH

DODDERHILL SCHOOL
Crutch Lane, Droitwich, Hereford &
Worcester WR9 0BE
Tel: (01905) 778290
Head: Mrs M A Maybee
Type: Girls Day 9-16
No of Pupils: 110
Fees: (September 95) £3855 - £4335

EVESHAM

GREEN HILL SCHOOL
Evesham, Hereford & Worcester
WR11 4NG
Tel: (01386) 442364
Head: O Lister
Type: Co-educational Day &
Boarding 3-16
No of Pupils: B55 G45 No of Boarders
F20
Fees: (September 95) FB £6000 -
£7200 WB £6000 DAY £1750 -
£3090

HEREFORD

THE HEREFORD CATHEDRAL
JUNIOR SCHOOL
28 Castle Street, Hereford HR1 2NW
Tel: (01432) 353726
Head: S A Sides
Type: Co-educational Day &
Boarding 3-11
No of Pupils: 246 No of Boarders F16
W2
Fees: (September 95) F/WB £5910 -
£6585 DAY £2475 - £3555

HEREFORD CATHEDRAL
SCHOOL*
Old Deanery, Cathedral Close,
Hereford HR1 2NG
Tel: (01432) 346522
Head: Dr H C Tomlinson
Type: Co-educational Day &
Boarding 11-18
No of Pupils: B325 G305 No of
Boarders F40
Fees: (September 95) FB £7980 DAY
£4530

THE MARGARET ALLEN
SCHOOL
32 Broomy Hill, Hereford HR4 0LH
Tel: (01432) 273594
Head: Lady Mynors
Type: Girls Day 3-11
No of Pupils: 106
Fees: (September 95) £2310 - £3030

KIDDERMINSTER

BOWBROOK SCHOOL
Hartlebury, Kidderminster, Hereford
& Worcester DY11 7TE
Tel: (01299) 250258
Head: D R Bolam
Type: Co-educational Day 3-16
No of Pupils: 140
Fees: (September 93) £885 - £4305

HEATHFIELD SCHOOL
Wolverley, Kidderminster, Hereford
& Worcester DY10 3QE
Tel: (01562) 850204
Head: G L Sinton
Type: Co-educational Day 3-16
No of Pupils: B184 G75
Fees: (September 95) £855 - £4065

HOLY TRINITY SCHOOL
Birmingham Road, Kidderminster,
Hereford & Worcester DY10 2BY
Tel: (01562) 822929
Head: Mrs S M Bell
Type: Girls Day 3-18
No of Pupils: 306
Fees: (September 95) £1875 - £3549

THE KNOLL SCHOOL
33 Manor Avenue, Kidderminster,
Hereford & Worcester DY11 6EA
Tel: (01562) 822622
Head: N J Humphreys
Type: Co-educational Day 3-11
No of Pupils: B78 G55
Fees: (April 95) £630 - £2400

LEA HOUSE SCHOOL
The Lea, Bewdley Hill,
Kidderminster, Hereford &
Worcester DY11 6JR
Tel: (01562) 822376
Head: Mrs F Williams
Type: Co-educational Day 2-11
No of Pupils: B51 G49
Fees: (September 95) £2025 - £2850

WINTERFOLD HOUSE
Chaddesley Corbett, Kidderminster,
Hereford & Worcester DY10 4PL
Tel: (01562) 777234
Head: S D Arbuthnott
Type: Co-educational Boarding &
Day 3-13
No of Pupils: 125 No of Boarders
W30
Fees: (September 94) WB £5670 DAY
£4470

MALVERN

CROFTDOWN
Abbey Road, Malvern, Hereford &
Worcester WR14 3HE
Tel: (01684) 575083
Head: Mrs J Myring
Type: Girls Boarding & Day 3-12
No of Pupils: 64 No of Boarders F19
Fees: (September 95) F/WB £6420
DAY £1470 - £4410

THE DOWNS SCHOOL*
Colwall, Malvern, Hereford &
Worcester WR13 6EY
Tel: (01684) 540277
Head: Mrs J M Griggs
Type: Co-educational Boarding &
Day 3-13
No of Pupils: B108 G80 No of
Boarders F74 W17
Fees: (September 95) F/WB £7935
DAY £1545 - £5832

THE ELMS
Colwall, Malvern, Hereford &
Worcester WR13 6EF
Tel: (01684) 540344
Head: L A Ashby
Type: Co-educational Boarding &
Day 3-13
No of Pupils: B114 G59 No of
Boarders F94
Fees: (September 95) FB £8400 DAY
£2250 - £7200

HILLSIDE SCHOOL
171-179 Worcester Road, Malvern,
Hereford & Worcester WR14 1EX
Tel: (01684) 893345
Head: J A Quibell-Smith
Type: Co-educational Day 3-12
No of Pupils: 200
Fees: (September 94) £950 - £2700

HILLSTONE SCHOOL
(MALVERN COLLEGE JUNIOR
SCHOOL)
Abbey Road, Malvern, Hereford &
Worcester WR14 3HF
Tel: (01684) 573057
Head: R G Gillard
Type: Co-educational Boarding &
Day 3-13
No of Pupils: B108 G52 No of
Boarders F43
Fees: (September 94) F/WB £7500
DAY £1290 - £5670

MALVERN COLLEGE
College Road, Malvern, Hereford & Worcester WR14 3DF
Tel: (01684) 892333
Head: R de C Chapman
Type: Co-educational Boarding & Day 13-18
No of Pupils: 664 No of Boarders F555
Fees: (September 95) FB £12210 DAY £8880

MALVERN GIRLS' COLLEGE*
Avenue Road, Malvern, Hereford & Worcester WR14 3BA
Tel: (01684) 892288
Head: Dr A Lee
Type: Girls Boarding & Day 11-18
No of Pupils: 487 No of Boarders F427
Fees: (September 95) FB £11700 DAY £7800

ST JAMES'S & THE ABBEY*
West Malvern, Malvern, Hereford & Worcester WR14 4DF
Tel: (01684) 560851
Head: Miss E Mullenger
Type: Girls Boarding & Day 11-18
No of Pupils: 200 No of Boarders 148
Fees: (September 95) FB £10962 DAY £7308

MALVERN WELLS

THE ABBEY COLLEGE
253 Wells Road, Malvern Wells, Hereford & Worcester WR14 4JF
Tel: (01684) 892300
Head: L James
Type: Co-educational Boarding 12+
No of Pupils: B70 G50
Fees: (September 95) 3 A levels £4750 5 GCSEs £5000

PERSHORE

BOWBROOK HOUSE SCHOOL
Peopleton, Pershore, Hereford & Worcester WR10 2EE
Tel: (01905) 841242
Head: S W Jackson
Type: Co-educational Day 3-16
No of Pupils: B59 G60
Fees: (September 95) £1530 - £3450

TENBURY WELLS

ST MARY'S PREPARATORY SCHOOL
Rochford, Tenbury Wells, Hereford & Worcester
Tel: (01584) 781233
Head: Mrs L A Bush
Type: Co-educational Day B3-8 G3-11
No of Pupils: B20 G31
Fees: (September 95) £350 - £550

WORCESTER

ABBERLEY HALL
Worcester WR6 6DD
Tel: (01299) 896275
Head: M V D Haggard
Type: Boys Boarding & Day 2-13 (Girls 2-7)
No of Pupils: 225 No of Boarders F130
Fees: (September 94) F/WB £7980 DAY £5985

THE ALICE OTTLEY SCHOOL
Upper Tything, Worcester WR1 1HW
Tel: (01905) 27061
Head: Miss C Sibbit
Type: Girls Day 3-19
No of Pupils: 703
Fees: (September 95) £2226 - £4785

AYMESTREY SCHOOL
Crown East, Worcester WR2 5TR
Tel: (01905) 425619
Head: D H Griffith
Type: Boys Day & Boarding 7-13
No of Pupils: 35 No of Boarders F18
Fees: (September 95) FB £5055 DAY £3750

BARBOURNE PREPARATORY SCHOOL
Cypress House, 47 Waterworks Road, Worcester WR1 3EY
Tel: (01905) 24785
Head: N S Ridley
Type: Co-educational Day 3-11
No of Pupils: 70
Fees: (September 95) £2208 - £2460

HAWFORD LODGE SCHOOL
Hawford Lodge, Worcester WR3 7SE
Tel: (01905) 451292
Head: A Race
Type: Co-educational Day 3-13
No of Pupils: 176
Fees: (September 94) £2640 - £4788

THE KING'S SCHOOL
Worcester WR1 2LH
Tel: (01905) 23016
Head: Dr J M Moore
Type: Co-educational Day & Boarding 7-18
No of Pupils: B660 G264 No of Boarders F67
Fees: (September 95) FB £7002 - £8793 DAY £3300 - £5091

ROYAL GRAMMAR SCHOOL WORCESTER
Upper Tything, Worcester WR1 1HP
Tel: (01905) 613391
Head: W A Jones
Type: Boys Day 7-18
No of Pupils: 923
Fees: (September 95) £3474 - £4338

ST MARY'S CONVENT SCHOOL
Mount Battenhall, Worcester WR5 2HP
Tel: (01905) 357786
Head: Miss G M Morrissey
Type: Girls Day 3-18 (Boys 3-8)
No of Pupils: B18 G400
Fees: (September 95) £2145 - £3600

SUNNYSIDE SCHOOL
Barbourne Terrace, Worcester
Tel: (01905) 23973
Head: Mrs J M Douglas-Pennant
Type: Co-educational Day 3-9
No of Pupils: B100 G50
Fees: (September 95) £1100 - £2900

HERTFORDSHIRE

ALDENHAM

EDGE GROVE SCHOOL
Aldenham, Hertfordshire WD2 8BL
Tel: (01923) 855724
Head: K J Waterfield
Type: Boys Boarding & Day 2-13
(Girls 2-7)
No of Pupils: 140 No of Boarders F80
Fees: (September 95) FB £8175 WB
£7875 DAY £4500 - £5850

ST CHRISTOPHER'S
Edge Grove, High Cross, Aldenham,
Hertfordshire WD2 8BL
Tel: (01923) 855745
Head: Mrs E Cornelissen
Type: Co-educational Day 2-8
No of Pupils: B45 G45
Fees: (September 95) £1725 - £2970

BARNET

FIRST IMPRESSIONS
MONTESSORI SCHOOLS
The Old Bull Arts Centre, Studio 4,
68 High Street, Barnet, Hertfordshire
EN5 5SJ
Tel: (0181) 447 1565
Head: Mrs Vickerman
Type: Co-educational Day 2-5
No of Pupils: 125
Fees: (September 95) £1560

LYONSDOWN SCHOOL TRUST
LTD
3 Richmond Road, New Barnet,
Barnet, Hertfordshire EN5 1SA
Tel: (0181) 449 0225
Head: Mrs R Miller
Type: Co-educational Day B4-7
G4-11
No of Pupils: B40 G140
Fees: (September 95) £2970 - £3285

ST MARTHA'S SENIOR
SCHOOL*
Camlet Way, Hadley, Barnet,
Hertfordshire EN5 5PX
Tel: (0181) 449 6889
Head: Sister M Cecile Archer
Type: Girls Day 11-18
No of Pupils: 311
Fees: (September 95) £3150

BERKHAMSTED

BERKHAMSTED JUNIOR
SCHOOL
Castle Street, Berkhamsted,
Hertfordshire HP4 2BB
Tel: (01442) 863236
Head: E T Sneddon
Type: Boys Day & Boarding 7-13
No of Pupils: 260
Fees: (September 95) F/WB £9231
DAY £4395 - £5691

BERKHAMSTED SCHOOL
Castle Street, Berkhamsted,
Hertfordshire HP4 2BB
Tel: (01442) 863236
Head: Rev K H Wilkinson
Type: Boys Day & Boarding 10-18
(Co-ed VIth form)
No of Pupils: 700 No of Boarders F80
Fees: (September 95) F/WB £9231 -
£11034 DAY £5691 - £6774

BERKHAMSTED SCHOOL FOR
GIRLS
Kings Road, Berkhamsted,
Hertfordshire HP4 3BG
Tel: (01442) 862168
Head: Miss V E Shepherd
Type: Girls Boarding & Day 3-18
No of Pupils: 550 No of Boarders F24
W30
Fees: (September 95) F/WB £9327
DAY £5487

EGERTON-ROTHESAY SCHOOL
Durrants Lane, Berkhamsted,
Hertfordshire HP4 3UJ
Tel: (01442) 865275
Head: J R Adkins
Type: Co-educational Day 2-18
No of Pupils: B281 G229
Fees: (September 95) £525 - £5280

HARESFOOT PREPARATORY
SCHOOL
Chesham Road, Berkhamsted,
Hertfordshire HP4 2SZ
Tel: (01442) 872742
Head: Mrs G R Waterhouse
Type: Co-educational Day 2-12
No of Pupils: B113 G126
Fees: (September 95) £570 - £3420

HARESFOOT SENIOR SCHOOL
Amersfort, The Common,
Berkhamsted, Hertfordshire HP4 2QF
Tel: (01442) 877215
Head: D L Davies
Type: Co-educational Day 11-18
No of Pupils: B40 G18
Fees: (September 95) £4605 - £5595

MARLIN MONTESSORI
SCHOOL
1 Park View Road, Berkhamsted,
Hertfordshire HP4 3EY
Tel: (01442) 866290
Head: Mrs S O'Neill
Type: Co-educational Day 1-6
No of Pupils: 50
Fees: (September 95) £639 - £3000

BISHOP'S STORTFORD

BISHOP'S STORTFORD
COLLEGE*
Maze Green Road, Bishop's
Stortford, Hertfordshire CM23 2QZ
Tel: (01279) 758575
Head: S G Benson
Type: Co-educational Boarding &
Day 13-18
No of Pupils: B290 G40 No of
Boarders F140
Fees: (September 95) FB £10320 DAY
£7440

CHRISTIAN SCHOOL
(TAKELEY)
Dunmow Road, Brewers End,
Takeley, Bishop's Stortford,
Hertfordshire CM22 6QH
Tel: (01279) 871182
Head: M E Humphries
Type: Co-educational Day 5-16
No of Pupils: B19 G15
Fees: On application

HOWE GREEN HOUSE
SCHOOL
Great Hallingbury, Bishop's
Stortford, Hertfordshire CM22 7UF
Tel: (01279) 657706
Head: Mrs N R J Garrod
Type: Co-educational Day 3-11
Fees: (September 95) £2760 - £4455

THE JUNIOR SCHOOL, BISHOP'S STORTFORD COLLEGE

Maze Green Road, Bishop's Stortford, Hertfordshire CM23 2PH
Tel: (01279) 653616
Head: D J Defoe
Type: Co-educational Boarding & Day 4–13
No of Pupils: 250 No of Boarders F45
Fees: (September 95) FB £7200 – £7860 DAY £3600 – £5970

BUSHEY

CKHR IMMANUEL COLLEGE

87/91 Elstree Road, Bushey, Hertfordshire WD2 3RJ
Tel: (0181) 950 0604
Head: Mrs Myrna Jacobs
Type: Co-educational Day 11–18
No of Pupils: B180 G160
Fees: (September 95) £5350

LITTLE ACORNS MONTESSORI SCHOOL

International University Grounds, The Avenue, Bushey, Hertfordshire WD2 2LN
Tel: (01923) 230705
Head: Ms J Nugent & Ms R Lau
Type: Co-educational Day 3–7
No of Pupils: 24
Fees: (September 94) £1830

LONGWOOD SCHOOL

Aldenham Road, Bushey, Hertfordshire WD2 2ER
Tel: (01923) 253715
Head: Mrs Satoula Livesey
Type: Co-educational Day 3–8
No of Pupils: B78 G67
Fees: (September 95) £1755 – £2655

ST ANDREW'S MONTESSORI SCHOOL

Royal Caledonian Schools, Aldenham Road, Bushey, Hertfordshire
Tel: (01923) 212875
Head: Mrs S O'Neill
Type: Co-educational Day 2–12
No of Pupils: 40
Fees: (September 95) £1575 – £4500

ST HILDA'S SCHOOL

High Street, Bushey, Hertfordshire WD2 3DA
Tel: (0181) 950 1751
Head: Mrs L Cavanagh
Type: Girls Day 3–11
No of Pupils: 150
Fees: (September 95) £2685 – £3945

BUSHEY HEATH

WESTWOOD

6 Hartsbourne Road, Bushey Heath, Hertfordshire WD2 1JH
Tel: (0181) 950 1138
Head: Mrs J Hill
Type: Co-educational Day 4–8
No of Pupils: 72
Fees: (September 95) £2955

ELSTREE

ALDENHAM SCHOOL*

Elstree, Hertfordshire WD6 3AJ
Tel: (01923) 858122
Head: S Borthwick
Type: Boys Boarding & Day 11–18 (Co-ed VIth form)
No of Pupils: B360 G15 No of Boarders F110
Fees: (September 95) F/WB £11460 DAY £4995 – £7860

HABERDASHERS' ASKE'S SCHOOL

Butterfly Lane, Elstree, Hertfordshire WD6 3AF
Tel: (0181) 207 4323
Head: K Dawson
Type: Boys Day 7–18
No of Pupils: 1300
Fees: (September 95) £5136 – £5601

HABERDASHERS' ASKE'S SCHOOL FOR GIRLS*

Aldenham Road, Elstree, Hertfordshire WD6 3BT
Tel: (0181) 953 4261
Head: Mrs P A Penney
Type: Girls Day 4–18
No of Pupils: 1140
Fees: (September 95) £3465 – £4140

HARPENDEN

ALDWICKBURY SCHOOL

Wheathampstead Road, Harpenden, Hertfordshire AL5 1AE
Tel: (01582) 713022
Head: P H Jeffery
Type: Boys Day & Boarding 4–13 (Girls 4–7)
No of Pupils: 270 No of Boarders W40
Fees: (September 95) WB £5475 – £6075 DAY £2685 – £4500

HARPENDEN PREPARATORY SCHOOL

53 Luton Road, Harpenden, Hertfordshire AL5 2UE
Tel: (01582) 712361
Head: Mrs J Cross
Type: Co-educational Day 2–11
No of Pupils: 110
Fees: (September 95) £1608 – £3237

KINGS SCHOOL

Elmfield, Ambrose Lane, Harpenden, Hertfordshire AL5
Tel: (01582) 767566
Head: M J Vincent
Type: Co-educational Day 5–16
No of Pupils: B72 G72
Fees: (September 95) £1800

ST HILDA'S SCHOOL

28 Douglas Road, Harpenden, Hertfordshire AL5 2ES
Tel: (01582) 712307
Head: Mrs M Piachaud
Type: Girls Day 2–11
No of Pupils: 168
Fees: (September 95) £1980 – £3135

HATFIELD

QUEENSWOOD*

Shepherds Way, Brookmans Park, Hatfield, Hertfordshire AL9 6NS
Tel: (01707) 652262
Head: Mrs A M Butler
Type: Girls Boarding & Day 11–18
No of Pupils: 395 No of Boarders F335
Fees: (September 95) FB £10974 – £11442 DAY £6768

HEMEL HEMPSTEAD

ABBOT'S HILL*

Bunkers Lane, Hemel Hempstead, Hertfordshire HP3 8RP
Tel: (01442) 240333
Head: Mrs J S Kingsley
Type: Girls Boarding & Day 11–16
No of Pupils: 168 No of Boarders F29 W65
Fees: (September 95) FB £10275 WB £10200 DAY £6060

LOCKERS PARK

Lockers Park Lane, Hemel Hempstead, Hertfordshire HP1 1TL
Tel: (01442) 251712
Head: N J Chapman and C R Stephens
Type: Boys Boarding & Day 7–13
No of Pupils: 105 No of Boarders F79
Fees: (September 95) FB £8235 DAY £5085 – £5985

ST NICHOLAS HOUSE
Bunkers Lane, Hemel Hempstead,
Hertfordshire HP3 8RP
Tel: (01442) 211156
Head: Mrs D A Harrison
Type: Girls Day 3-11 (Boys 3-7)
No of Pupils: B12 G120
Fees: (September 95) £1075 - £1325

WESTBROOK HAY
Bourne End, London Road, Hemel
Hempstead, Hertfordshire HP1 2RF
Tel: (01442) 256143
Acting Heads: J Coates & D Hill
Type: Co-educational Boarding &
Day 2-13
No of Pupils: B138 G47 No of
Boarders F30
Fees: (September 94) FB £7965 DAY
£945 - £5730

HERTFORD

DUNCOMBE SCHOOL
4 Warren Park Road, Bengeo,
Hertford SG14 3JA
Tel: (01992) 582653
Head: Miss R M Martin
Type: Co-educational Day 4-11
No of Pupils: B109 G116
Fees: (September 95) £1458 - £4101

HAILEYBURY COLLEGE*
Haileybury, Hertford SG13 7NU
Tel: (01992) 463353
Head: D J Jewell
Type: Boys Boarding & Day 11-18
(Co-ed VIth form)
No of Pupils: B520 G80 No of
Boarders F420
Fees: (September 95) FB £12720 DAY
£6135 - £9225

HEATH MOUNT SCHOOL*
Woodhall Park, Watton-at-Stone,
Hertford SG14 3NG
Tel: (01920) 830230
Head: Rev H J Matthews
Type: Co-educational Boarding &
Day 3-13
No of Pupils: B219 G120 No of
Boarders W45
Fees: (September 95) WB £6804 -
£7287 DAY £1575 - £5808

ST JOSEPH'S SCHOOL
The Park, Hertingfordbury, Hertford
SG14 2LX
Tel: (01992) 581378
Head: B C Buckley
Type: Co-educational Day 3-11
No of Pupils: B60 G70
Fees: (September 95) £1575 - £3450

HITCHIN

KINGSHOTT
St Ippolyts, Hitchin, Hertfordshire
SG4 7JX
Tel: (01462) 432009
Head: Rev D Highton
Type: Co-educational Day 4-13
No of Pupils: B210 G115
Fees: (September 95) £3015 - £4050

**THE PRINCESS HELENA
COLLEGE***
Preston, Hitchin, Hertfordshire
SG4 7RT
Tel: (01462) 432100
Head: J Jarvis
Type: Girls Boarding & Day 11-18
No of Pupils: 150
Fees: (September 95) F/WB £9990
DAY £6960

KINGS LANGLEY

RUDOLF STEINER SCHOOL
Langley Hill, Kings Langley,
Hertfordshire WD4 9HG
Tel: (01923) 262505
Type: Co-educational Day 3-19
No of Pupils: 420
Fees: (September 95) £2295 - £3705

LEOMINSTER

**LUCTON PIERREPONT
SCHOOL**
Leominster, Hertfordshire HR6 9PN
Tel: (01568) 780686
Head: N P T Staunton
Type: Co-educational Boarding &
Day 3-16
No of Pupils: B52 G38 No of Boarders
F24
Fees: (September 95) FB £5955 -
£6810 DAY £2160 - £3696

LETCHWORTH

ST CHRISTOPHER SCHOOL*
Barrington Road, Letchworth,
Hertfordshire SG6 3JZ
Tel: (01462) 679301
Head: Colin Reid
Type: Co-educational Boarding &
Day 2-19
No of Pupils: B290 G184 No of
Boarders F171
Fees: (September 95) FB £8742 -
£10920 DAY £2190 - £6186

ST FRANCIS' COLLEGE*
The Broadway, Letchworth,
Hertfordshire SG6 3PJ
Tel: (01462) 670511
Head: Miss M Hegarty
Type: Girls Boarding & Day 3-19
(Boys 3-7)
No of Pupils: B3 G325 No of Boarders
F36 W15
Fees: (September 95) F/WB £8550 -
£9810 DAY £3120 - £5025

POTTERS BAR

LOCHINVER HOUSE SCHOOL*
Heath Road, Little Heath, Potters
Bar, Hertfordshire EN6 1LW
Tel: (01707) 653064
Head: P C E Atkinson
Type: Boys Day 4-13
No of Pupils: 251
Fees: (September 95) £3780 - £5040

**ST JOHN'S PREPARATORY
SCHOOL**
Brownlowes, The Ridgeway, Potters
Bar, Hertfordshire EN6 5QT
Tel: (01707) 657294
Head: Mrs C Tardios
Type: Co-educational Day 4-11
No of Pupils: B78 G49
Fees: (September 95) £3120

STORMONT
The Causeway, Potters Bar,
Hertfordshire EN6 5HA
Tel: (01707) 654037
Head: Mrs M E Johnston
Type: Girls Day 4-11
No of Pupils: 170
Fees: (September 95) £3360 - £4050

RADLETT

**RADLETT PREPARATORY
SCHOOL**
Kendal Hall, Watling Street, Radlett,
Hertfordshire WD7 7LY
Tel: (01923) 856812
Head: W N Warren
Type: Co-educational Day 4-11
No of Pupils: B220 G180
Fees: (September 95) £3120

RICKMANSWORTH

NORTHWOOD PREPARATORY SCHOOL
Moor Farm, Sandy Lodge Road, Rickmansworth, Hertfordshire WD3 1LW
Tel: (01923) 825648
Head: N D Flynn
Type: Boys Day 4-13
No of Pupils: 250
Fees: (September 95) £3570 - £4350

THE RICKMANSWORTH MASONIC SCHOOL*
Chorleywood Road, Rickmansworth, Hertfordshire WD3 4HF
Tel: (01923) 773168
Head: Mrs I M Andrews
Type: Girls Boarding & Day 4-18
No of Pupils: 700 No of Boarders F189 W106
Fees: (September 95) F/WB £5229 - £8811 DAY £2760 - £5361

RICKMANSWORTH PNEU SCHOOL
88 The Drive, Rickmansworth, Hertfordshire WD3 4DU
Tel: (01923) 772101
Head: Mrs S M Marshall-Taylor
Type: Girls Day 3-11 (Boys 3-7)
No of Pupils: B4 G136
Fees: (September 95) £1068 - £3069

YORK HOUSE SCHOOL
Redheath, Croxley Green, Rickmansworth, Hertfordshire WD3 4LW
Tel: (01923) 772395
Head: P B Moore
Type: Boys Day 4-13
No of Pupils: 220
Fees: (September 95) £2754 - £4344

ST ALBANS

BEECHWOOD PARK
Markyate, St Albans, Hertfordshire AL3 8AW
Tel: (01582) 840333
Head: D S Macpherson
Type: Boys Day & Boarding 4-13 (Girls 4-7)
No of Pupils: B278 G19 No of Boarders F38 W3
Fees: (September 95) FB £7674 WB £7263 DAY £3900 - £5321

HOMEWOOD INDEPENDENT SCHOOL
Hazel Road, Park Street, St Albans, Hertfordshire AL2 2AH
Tel: (01727) 873542
Head: Mrs Carol Erwin
Type: Co-educational Day 3-8
Fees: (September 95) £1740 - £2925

ST ALBANS HIGH SCHOOL*
Townsend Avenue, St Albans, Hertfordshire AL1 3SJ
Tel: (01727) 853800
Head: Mrs C Y Daly
Type: Girls Day 7-18
No of Pupils: 720
Fees: (September 95) £3900 - £4710

ST ALBANS SCHOOL
Abbey Gateway, St Albans, Hertfordshire AL3 4HB
Tel: (01727) 855521
Head: A R Grant
Type: Boys Day 11-18 (Co-ed VIth form)
No of Pupils: B610 G40
Fees: (September 95) £5460

ST COLUMBA'S COLLEGE
King Harry Lane, St Albans, Hertfordshire AL3 4AW
Tel: (01727) 855185
Head: J Stuart
Type: Boys Day 11-18
No of Pupils: 500
Fees: (September 95) £4140

STEVENAGE

THE LITTLE FOLKS LAB
22 North Road, Stevenage, Hertfordshire SG1 4AJ
Tel: (01438) 351220
Head: H V Howe & Mrs J E Howe
Type: Co-educational Day 2-7
No of Pupils: B80 G80
Fees: (September 95) £1800

TRING

THE ARTS EDUCATIONAL SCHOOL*
Tring Park, Tring, Hertfordshire HP23 5LX
Tel: (01442) 824255
Head: Mrs J D Billing
Type: Co-educational Boarding & Day 8-18
No of Pupils: 220 No of Boarders F160
Fees: (September 95) FB £8268 - £10812 DAY £4770 - £6678

CONVENT OF ST FRANCIS DE SALES
Aylesbury Road, Tring, Hertfordshire HP23 4DL
Tel: (01442) 822315
Head: Sister Miriam Elizabeth
Type: Girls Day 2-17 (Boys 2-12)
No of Pupils: B42 G118
Fees: (September 95) £3000 - £3600

WARE

ST EDMUND'S COLLEGE*
Old Hall Green, Ware, Hertfordshire SG11 1DS
Tel: (01920) 821504
Head: D J McEwen
Type: Co-educational Day & Boarding 7-18
No of Pupils: B331 G199 No of Boarders F117 W41
Fees: (September 95) FB £7725 - £9555 WB £7260 - £8865 DAY £5085 - £6120

WATFORD

NORTHFIELD SCHOOL
Church Road, Watford, Hertfordshire WD1 3QB
Tel: (01923) 229758
Head: Mrs P Hargreaves
Type: Girls Day 2-18 (Boys 2-7)
No of Pupils: B20 G165
Fees: (September 95) £3180 - £3906

ST MARGARET'S SCHOOL
Merryhill Road, Bushey, Watford, Hertfordshire WD2 1DT
Tel: (0181) 950 1548
Head: Miss M de Villiers
Type: Girls Boarding & Day 4-18
No of Pupils: 425 No of Boarders F85 W51
Fees: (September 95) F/WB £7590 - £8760 DAY £3075 - £5475

STANBOROUGH SCHOOL*
Stanborough Park, Watford, Hertfordshire WD2 6JT
Tel: (01923) 673268
Head: Dr A Luxton
Type: Co-educational Day & Boarding 3-18
No of Pupils: B116 G95 No of Boarders F30 W23
Fees: (September 95) FB £5970 - £7005 WB £5130 - £6165 DAY £1830 - £2910

WELWYN

SHERRARDSWOOD SCHOOL*
Lockleys, Welwyn, Hertfordshire
AL6 0BJ
Tel: (01707) 322281
Head: M C Lloyd
Type: Co-educational Day &
Boarding 3-18
No of Pupils: B176 G150 No of
Boarders F36
Fees: (September 95) F/WB £6804 -
£8385 DAY £2706 - £4437

NORTH HUMBERSIDE

HESSLE

HESSLE MOUNT SCHOOL
Jenny Brough Lane, Hessle, North
Humberside HU13 0JX
Tel: (01482) 643371
Head: Mrs Cutting
Type: Co-educational Day 4-8
No of Pupils: 160
Fees: (September 95) £1950 - £2310

HULL

FROEBEL HOUSE SCHOOL
5 Marlborough Avenue, Hull, North
Humberside HU5 3JP
Tel: (01482) 342272
Head: Mrs L A Roberts
Type: Co-educational Day 4-11
No of Pupils: 120
Fees: (September 95) £1800

HULL HIGH SCHOOL
Tranby Croft, Anlaby, Hull, North
Humberside HU10 7EH
Tel: (01482) 657016
Head: Mrs M A Benson
Type: Girls Day 3-18 (Boys 4-11)
No of Pupils: B56 G320
Fees: (September 95) £2526 - £3957

HYMERS COLLEGE
Hymers Avenue, Hull, North
Humberside HU3 1LW
Tel: (01482) 343555
Head: J C Morris
Type: Co-educational Day 8-18
No of Pupils: B595 G325
Fees: (September 94) £2925 - £3300

KINGSTON-UPON-HULL

HULL GRAMMAR SCHOOL*
Cottingham Road,
Kingston-Upon-Hull, North
Humberside HU5 2DL
Tel: (01482) 440144
Head: R Haworth
Type: Co-educational Day 3-18
No of Pupils: 370
Fees: (September 95) £2250 - £3825

SOUTH HUMBERSIDE

BRIGG

**BRIGG PREPARATORY
SCHOOL**
Bigby Street, Brigg, South
Humberside DN20 8EF
Tel: (01652) 653237
Head: T Green
Type: Co-educational Day 4-11
No of Pupils: B87 G85

Fees: (September 95) £2175 - £2310

GRIMSBY

ST JAMES' SCHOOL*
22 Bargate, Grimsby, South
Humberside DN34 4SY
Tel: (01472) 362093
Head: D J Berisford
Type: Co-educational Day &
Boarding 4-18
No of Pupils: B155 G95 No of
Boarders F46 W19
Fees: (September 95) FB £6168 -
£7983 WB £5772 - £7584 DAY
£2235 - £5710

**ST MARTIN'S PREPARATORY
SCHOOL**
63 Bargate, Grimsby, South
Humberside DN34 5AA
Tel: (01472) 878907
Head: Mrs M Preston
Type: Co-educational Day 3-11
No of Pupils: B109 G130
Fees: (September 95) £1215 - £2325

SCUNTHORPE

LYNTON PREPARATORY SCHOOL
250 Frodingham Road, Scunthorpe,
South Humberside DN15 7NW
Tel: (01724) 850 881
Head: Mrs E J Broadbent
Type: Co-educational Day 3-11
No of Pupils: B45 G55
Fees: (September 94) £1320 - £1380

ISLE OF MAN

CASTLETOWN

THE BUCHAN SCHOOL
West Hill, Castletown, Isle of Man
Tel: (01624) 822526
Head: P Moody
Type: Co-educational Day &
Boarding 4-11
No of Pupils: B88 G81 No of
Boarders F9
Fees: (September 95) F/WB £6615 -
£8490 DAY £3405 - £5280

KING WILLIAM'S COLLEGE
Castletown, Isle of Man IM9 1TP
Tel: (01624) 822551
Head: S A Westley
Type: Co-educational Boarding &
Day 11-18
No of Pupils: B195 G145 No of
Boarders F104
Fees: (September 95) FB £8955 -
£11160 DAY £5745 - £7950

ISLE OF WIGHT

BEMBRIDGE

BEMBRIDGE SCHOOL*
Bembridge, Isle of Wight PO35 5PH
Tel: (01983) 872101
Head: J High
Type: Co-educational Boarding &
Day 7-18
No of Pupils: B170 G73 No of
Boarders F185 W15
Fees: (September 95) FB/WB £7680 -
£9270 DAY £4470 - £4620

NEWPORT

WESTMONT SCHOOL
Carisbrooke Road, Newport, Isle of
Wight PO30 1BY
Tel: (01983) 523051
Head: Mrs J S Maclean
Type: Co-educational Day 3-13
No of Pupils: B56 G41
Fees: (September 95) £1755 - £2148

RYDE

RYDE SCHOOL WITH UPPER CHINE
Queen's Road, Ryde, Isle of Wight
PO33 3BE
Tel: (01983) 562229
Head: M D Featherstone
Type: Co-educational Day &
Boarding 3-18
No of Pupils: 690
Fees: (September 95) FB £8535 WB
£8019 DAY £1725 - £4182

SANDOWN

PRIORY SCHOOL
The Broadway, Sandown, Isle of
Wight PO36 9BY
Tel: (01983) 406866
Head: Mrs E J Goldthorpe
Type: Co-educational Day 3-16
No of Pupils: B27 G36
Fees: (September 95) £1170 - £2370

KENT

ASHFORD

ASHFORD SCHOOL*
East Hill, Ashford, Kent TN24 8PB
Tel: (01233) 625171
Head: Mrs P Metham
Type: Girls Day & Boarding 3-18
No of Pupils: 558 No of Boarders F70
W19
Fees: (September 95) FB £9021 -
£10479 WB £8886 - £10344 DAY
£954 - £5850

FRIARS SCHOOL*
Great Chart, Ashford, Kent TN23 3DJ
Tel: (01233) 620493
Head: P M Ashley
Type: Co-educational Boarding &
Day 2-13
No of Pupils: B95 G50 No of Boarders
W10
Fees: (September 95) WB £7425 DAY
£1200 - £5325

HOLLINGTON SCHOOL
Hollington Place, Ashford, Kent
TN24 8UN
Tel: (01233) 621000
Head: Mrs M J Cox
Type: Co-educational Day 2-11
No of Pupils: B53 G42
Fees: (September 95) £585 - £3015

SPRING GROVE SCHOOL
Harville Road, Wye, Ashford, Kent
TN25 5EX
Tel: (01233) 812337
Head: N Washington-Jones
Type: Co-educational Day 2-11
No of Pupils: B80 G80
Fees: (September 95) £1350 - £3900

BECKENHAM

EDEN PARK SCHOOL
204 Upper Elmers End Road,
Beckenham, Kent BR3 3HE
Tel: (0181) 650 0365
Head: Mrs B Hunter
Type: Co-educational Day 3-11
No of Pupils: B94 G92
Fees: (September 95) £1680 - £2295

ST CHRISTOPHER'S SCHOOL
49 Bromley Road, Beckenham, Kent
BR3 2PA
Tel: (0181) 650 2200
Head: Mrs G M Scales
Type: Co-educational Day 3-11
No of Pupils: B110 G105
Fees: (September 95) £1185 - £2991

BROADSTAIRS

HADDON DENE SCHOOL
57 Gladstone Road, Broadstairs, Kent
CT10 2HY
Tel: (01843) 861176
Head: Dr P J Smith
Type: Co-educational Day 3-11
No of Pupils: 200
Fees: (September 95) £1980 - £2340

ST JOSEPH'S CONVENT
SCHOOL
53 St Peter's Park Road, Broadstairs,
Kent CT10 2BA
Tel: (01843) 861738
Head: Mrs S Coppins
Type: Co-educational Day 3-11
No of Pupils: 110
Fees: (September 94) £1950 - £2085

WELLESLEY HOUSE SCHOOL
Broadstairs, Kent CT10 2DG
Tel: (01843) 862991
Head: R R Steel
Type: Co-educational Boarding &
Day 8-13
No of Pupils: B111 G52 No of
Boarders F132 W20
Fees: (September 95) FB £8850 WB
£8550 DAY £6450

BROMLEY

ASHGROVE SCHOOL
116 Widmore Road, Bromley, Kent
BR1 3BE
Tel: (0181) 460 4143
Head: Dr P Ash
Type: Co-educational Day 4-11
No of Pupils: B50 G50
Fees: (September 95) £3315

BASTON SCHOOL
Baston Road, Hayes, Bromley, Kent
BR2 7AB
Tel: (0181) 462 1010
Head: C R C Wimble
Type: Girls Day & Boarding 3-18
No of Pupils: 237 No of Boarders F25
W3
Fees: (September 95) FB £8700 WB
£8550 DAY £990 - £4455

BICKLEY PARK SCHOOL*
2 Southborough Road, Bickley,
Bromley, Kent BR1 2DY
Tel: (0181) 467 2195
Head: D J A Cassell
Type: Boys Day 8-13
No of Pupils: 380
Fees: (September 95) £5010 - £5490

BICKLEY PARVA SCHOOL
14 Page Heath Lane, Bickley,
Bromley, Kent BR1 2DS
Tel: (0181) 460 9800
Head: Mrs M P Dorning
Type: Co-educational Day B2-8 G2-5
No of Pupils: 238
Fees: (September 95) £1095 - £2985

BISHOP CHALLONER SCHOOL
Bromley Road, Shortlands, Bromley,
Kent BR2 0BS
Tel: (0181) 460 3546
Head: T Robinson
Type: Co-educational Day 3-18
No of Pupils: 350
Fees: (September 95) £2355 - £3720

BREASIDE PREPARATORY
SCHOOL*
41-43 Orchard Road, Bromley,
Kent BR1 2PR
Tel: (0181) 460 0916
Head: N Murray
Type: Co-educational Day 3-11
No of Pupils: B168 G41
Fees: (September 95) £1800 - £3360

BROMLEY HIGH SCHOOL
GPDST
Blackbrook Lane, Bickley, Bromley,
Kent BR1 2TW
Tel: (0181) 468 7981
Head: Mrs E J Hancock
Type: Girls Day 4-18
No of Pupils: 791
Fees: (September 95) £3576 - £4644

HOLY TRINITY COLLEGE
81 Plaistow Lane, Bromley, Kent
BR1 3LL
Tel: (0181) 313 0399
Head: Mrs D Bradshaw
Type: Girls Day 3-18 (Boys 3-5)
No of Pupils: 600
Fees: (September 95) £3030 - £4140

CANTERBURY

THE FAMILY SCHOOL
5-6 The Borough, Canterbury, Kent
CT1 2DR
Tel: (01227) 764 197
Head: A B Andreae
Type: Co-educational Day 4-16
No of Pupils: B13 G13
Fees: (September 95) £312 - £936

JUNIOR KING'S SCHOOL
Milner Court, Sturry, Canterbury,
Kent CT2 0AY
Tel: (01227) 710245
Head: R G Barton
Type: Co-educational Day &
Boarding 4-13
No of Pupils: B172 G92 No of
Boarders F64
Fees: (September 95) F/WB £8460
DAY £3300 - £5910

KENT COLLEGE*
Canterbury, Kent CT2 9DT
Tel: (01227) 763231
Head: E B Halse
Type: Co-educational Boarding &
Day 11-18
No of Pupils: 520 No of Boarders
F210
Fees: (September 95) FB £10098 DAY
£5664

**VERNON HOLME (KENT
COLLEGE INFANT & JUNIOR
SCHOOL)**
Harbledown, Canterbury, Kent
CT2 9AQ
Tel: (01227) 762436
Head: T J Smith
Type: Co-educational Day &
Boarding 3-11
No of Pupils: B83 G79 No of
Boarders F10 W2
Fees: (September 94) F/WB £6945
DAY £850 - £5145

THE KING'S SCHOOL*
Canterbury, Kent CT1 2ES
Tel: (01227) 595501
Head: Rev Canon A C Phillips
Type: Co-educational Boarding &
Day 13-18
No of Pupils: B444 G290 No of
Boarders F605
Fees: (September 95) FB £12795 DAY
£8835

**PERRY COURT RUDOLF
STEINER SCHOOL**
Garlinge Green, Chartham,
Canterbury, Kent CT4 5RU
Tel: (01227) 738285
Type: Co-educational Day 4-17
No of Pupils: B110 G90
Fees: (September 95) £2505 - £3510

ST CHRISTOPHER'S SCHOOL
48 New Dover Road, Canterbury,
Kent CT1 3DT
Tel: (01227) 462960
Head: J D Archer
Type: Co-educational Day 3-11
No of Pupils: 150
Fees: (September 95) £2160

**ST EDMUND'S JUNIOR
SCHOOL**
Canterbury, Kent CT2 8HU
Tel: (01227) 454575
Head: D C Gahan
Type: Co-educational Day &
Boarding 4-13
No of Pupils: B150 G70 No of
Boarders F62
Fees: (September 95) FB £8310 -
£8415 DAY £3090 - £5880

ST EDMUND'S SCHOOL*
Canterbury, Kent CT2 8HU
Tel: (01227) 454575
Head: A N Ridley
Type: Co-educational Day &
Boarding 3-18
No of Pupils: B341 G155 No of
Boarders F170
Fees: (September 95) FB £12030 -
£12360 DAY £7860

ST FAITH'S AT ASH SCHOOL
5 The Street, Ash, Canterbury, Kent
CT3 2HH
Tel: (01304) 813409
Head: Mrs J A Dredge
Type: Co-educational Day 3-11
No of Pupils: B90 G90
Fees: (September 95) £365 - £910

CHISLEHURST

BABINGTON HOUSE SCHOOL*
Grange Drive, Chislehurst, Kent
BR7 5ES
Tel: (0181) 467 5537
Head: Mrs E V Walter
Type: Girls Day 3-16 (Boys 3-7)
No of Pupils: B59 G189
Fees: (September 95) £3405 - £4350

**FARRINGTONS & STRATFORD
HOUSE***
Perry Street, Chislehurst, Kent
BR7 6LR
Tel: (0181) 467 0256
Head: Mrs B J Stock
Type: Girls Boarding & Day 3-18
No of Pupils: 600 No of Boarders
F187 W35
Fees: (September 95) FB £8295 -
£9561 DAY £3447 - £4962

CRANBROOK

BEDGEBURY SCHOOL
Bedgebury Park, Goudhurst,
Cranbrook, Kent TN17 2SH
Tel: (01580) 211954
Head: Mrs L J Griffin
Type: Girls Boarding & Day 3-18
(Boys Day 3-7)
No of Pupils: 370 No of Boarders
F104 W103
Fees: (September 95) F/WB £7089 -
£10788 DAY £1566 - £6678

BENENDEN SCHOOL
Cranbrook, Kent TN17 4AA
Tel: (01580) 240592
Head: Mrs G duCharme
Type: Girls Boarding 11-18
No of Pupils: 440 No of Boarders
F440
Fees: (September 95) FB £12630

BETHANY SCHOOL
Goudhurst, Cranbrook, Kent TN17
1LB
Tel: (01580) 211273
Head: W M Harvey
Type: Co-educational Boarding &
Day 11-18
No of Pupils: 265 No of Boarders
F142
Fees: (September 95) F/WB £9441 -
£9954 DAY £6039 - £6552

**DULWICH COLLEGE
PREPARATORY SCHOOL***
Coursehorn, Cranbrook, Kent TN17
3NP
Tel: (01580) 712179
Head: M C Wagstaffe
Type: Co-educational Day &
Boarding 3-13
No of Pupils: B272 G262 No of
Boarders F26 W46
Fees: (September 95) FB £8595 WB
£8355 DAY £1935 - £5595

DEAL

**NORTHBOURNE PARK
SCHOOL***
Betteshanger, Deal, Kent CT14 0NW
Tel: (01304) 611215
Head: F W Roche
Type: Co-educational Day &
Boarding 3-13
No of Pupils: B124 G88 No of
Boarders F45
Fees: (September 95) FB £8040 DAY
£3210 - £5745

DOVER

DOVER COLLEGE*
Effingham Crescent, Dover, Kent
CT17 9RH
Tel: (01304) 205969
Head: M P Wright
Type: Co-educational Boarding &
Day 11-18
No of Pupils: B163 G87 No of
Boarders F150
Fees: (September 95) FB £11175 WB
£10560 DAY £3600 - £5970

DUKE OF YORK'S ROYAL
MILITARY SCHOOL*
Dover, Kent CT15 5EQ
Tel: (01304) 245029
Head: Col G H Wilson
Type: Co-educational Boarding 11-18
No of Pupils: B388 G102 No of
Boarders F490
Fees: (September 95) FB £750

EDENBRIDGE

ST ANDREW'S PREPARATORY
SCHOOL
Eden Hall, Edenbridge, Kent
TN8 5NN
Tel: (01342) 850388
Head: Mrs S Brown
Type: Co-educational Day 3-11
No of Pupils: 120
Fees: (September 95) £1400 - £2600

FAVERSHAM

LORENDEN PREPARATORY
SCHOOL
Painter's Forstal, Faversham, Kent
ME13 0EN
Tel: (01795) 590030
Head: Mrs A Hannaford
Type: Co-educational Day 3-11
No of Pupils: B54 G66
Fees: (September 95) £870 - £1170

FOLKESTONE

ST MARY'S COLLEGE
Ravenlea Road, Folkestone, Kent
CT20 2JU
Tel: (01303) 851363
Head: Sister B Milligan
Type: Co-educational Day 4-16
No of Pupils: B75 G165
Fees: (September 95) £2977 - £5324

ST NICHOLAS NURSERY
SCHOOL
18 Wiltie Gardens, Folkestone, Kent
CT19 5AX
Tel: (01303) 254578
Head: Mrs C F Carlile
Type: Co-educational Day 2-7
No of Pupils: B11 G11
Fees: On application

SIBTON PARK*
Lyminge, Folkestone, Kent CT18 8HB
Tel: (01303) 862284
Head: Mrs P F Blackwell & C E R
Blackwell
Type: Girls Boarding & Day 2-13
(Boys 2-8)
No of Pupils: B20 G100 No of
Boarders F50
Fees: (September 95) F/WB £6864 -
£8985 DAY £1935 - £5871

WESTBROOK HOUSE SCHOOL
Westbrook House, Shorncliffe Road,
Folkestone, Kent CT20 2NQ
Tel: (01303) 851222
Head: R Lewis
Type: Co-educational Boarding &
Day 3-13
No of Pupils: B111 G74 No of
Boarders F44 W2
Fees: (September 95) FB £7725 WB
£6810 DAY £1350 - £5100

GILLINGHAM

BRYONY SCHOOL
Marshall Road, Rainham,
Gillingham, Kent ME8 0AJ
Tel: (01634) 231511
Head: D E Edmunds & Mrs M P Edmunds
Type: Co-educational Day 2-11
No of Pupils: B120 G122
Fees: (September 95) £2047 - £2388

GRAVESEND

BRONTE SCHOOL
5-7 Parrock Road, Gravesend, Kent
DA12 1PY
Tel: (01474) 533805
Head: Mrs R M Roberts
Type: Co-educational Day 3-11
No of Pupils: B48 G47
Fees: (September 95) £2750

COBHAM HALL*
Cobham, Gravesend, Kent DA12 3BL
Tel: (01474) 824319
Head: Mrs R McCarthy
Type: Girls Boarding & Day 11-18
No of Pupils: 200 No of Boarders
F180
Fees: (September 95) F/WB £12855
DAY £6600 - £8250

CONVENT PREPARATORY
SCHOOL
46 Old Road East, Gravesend, Kent
DA12 1NR
Tel: (01474) 533012
Head: Sr Anne
Type: Co-educational Day 3-11
No of Pupils: B126 G129
Fees: (September 95) £2025

HAWKHURST

MARLBOROUGH HOUSE
SCHOOL
High Street, Hawkhurst, Kent TN18
4PY
Tel: (01580) 753555
Head: D N Hopkins
Type: Co-educational Boarding &
Day 3-13
No of Pupils: B118 G75 No of
Boarders F35
Fees: (September 94) FB £8385 WB
£8325 DAY £1680 - £6390

ST RONAN'S
Hawkhurst, Kent TN18 5DJ
Tel: (01580) 752271
Head: J R Vassar-Smith
Type: Boys Boarding & Day 3-13
(Girls 3-8)
No of Pupils: 90 No of Boarders F16
W25
Fees: (September 95) F/WB £7680
DAY £1665 - £5955

MAIDSTONE

EYLESDEN COURT
PREPARATORY SCHOOL
Bearsted House, Bearsted,
Maidstone, Kent ME14 4EB
Tel: (01622) 737845
Head: R G Dean Hughes
Type: Co-educational Day 3-13
No of Pupils: 160
Fees: (September 95) £2520 - £3885

SHERNOLD SCHOOL
Hill Place, Queens Avenue,
Maidstone, Kent ME16 0ER
Tel: (01622) 752868
Head: Mrs C Birtwell
Type: Girls Day 3-13
No of Pupils: 144
Fees: (September 94) £2025 - £2880

SUTTON VALENCE JUNIOR
SCHOOL
Chart Sutton, Maidstone, Kent
ME17 3RF
Tel: (01622) 842117
Type: Co-educational Day 3-11
Fees: (September 95) FB £8700
£4035 - £5550

SUTTON VALENCE SCHOOL*
Sutton Valence, Maidstone, Kent
ME17 3HL
Tel: (01622) 842281
Head: N A Sampson
Type: Co-educational Boarding &
Day 11-18
No of Pupils: B225 G125 No of
Boarders F140
Fees: (September 95) FB £11250 WB
£10875 DAY £3705 - £6150

PEMBURY

KENT COLLEGE
Pembury, Kent TN2 4AX
Tel: (01892) 822006
Head: Miss B J Crompton
Type: Girls Boarding & Day 3-18
No of Pupils: 380 No of Boarders F77
W33
Fees: (September 95) FB £8268 -
£10584 WB £7275 - £9828 DAY
£2835 - £6330

RAMSGATE

**THE JUNIOR SCHOOL,
ST LAWRENCE COLLEGE**
Ramsgate, Kent CT11 7AF
Tel: (01843) 591788
Head: Rev D D R Blackwell
Type: Co-educational Boarding &
Day 4-13
No of Pupils: B91 G55 No of
Boarders F69 W2
Fees: (September 95) F/WB £8370
DAY £2400 - £5490

**ST LAWRENCE COLLEGE IN
THANET***
Ramsgate, Kent CT11 7AE
Tel: (01843) 592680
Head: J H Binfield
Type: Co-educational Boarding &
Day 11-18
No of Pupils: B220 G150 No of
Boarders F200
Fees: (September 95) FB £8370 -
£11160 DAY £5490 - £7455

ROCHESTER

GAD'S HILL SCHOOL
Higham, Rochester, Kent ME3 7AA
Tel: (01474) 822366
Head: Mrs A Everitt
Type: Girls Day 3-18 (Boys 3-11)
No of Pupils: 150
Fees: (September 95) £1269 - £2772

**KING'S PREPARATORY
SCHOOL, ROCHESTER**
King Edward Road, Rochester, Kent
ME1 1UB
Tel: (01634) 843657
Head: C J Nickless
Type: Co-educational Day &
Boarding 8-13
No of Pupils: B187 G23 No of
Boarders F10 W7
Fees: (September 95) F/WB £9546 -
£10122 DAY £5451 - £6027

KING'S SCHOOL
Satis House, Boley Hill, Rochester,
Kent ME1 1TE
Tel: (01634) 843913
Head: Dr I R Walker
Type: Co-educational Day &
Boarding 13-18
No of Pupils: B340 G40 No of
Boarders F60
Fees: (September 95) F/WB £9546 -
£11682 DAY £3363 - £6702

**ROCHESTER TUTORS
INDEPENDENT COLLEGE**
New Road House, 3 New Road,
Rochester, Kent ME1 1BD
Tel: (01634) 828115
Head: S de Belder & B Pain
Type: Co-educational Day &
Residential 14+
No of Pupils: B62 G62
Fees: (September 95) 3 A Levels/5
GCSEs £6350

ST ANDREW'S SCHOOL
24-28 Watts Avenue, Rochester,
Kent ME1 1SA
Tel: (01634) 843479
Head: D M McKenna
Type: Co-educational Day 4-11
No of Pupils: B150 G150
Fees: (September 95) £2070 - £2205

SEVENOAKS

COMBE BANK SCHOOL*
Sundridge, Sevenoaks, Kent TN14
6AE
Tel: (01959) 563720
Head: Miss N Spurr
Type: Girls Day 3-18
No of Pupils: 415
Fees: (September 95) £1785 - £5460

THE GRANVILLE SCHOOL
Sevenoaks, Kent TN13 3LJ
Tel: (01732) 453039
Head: Mrs J D Evans
Type: Girls Day 3-11
No of Pupils: 200
Fees: (September 95) £1575 - £3960

**MARGARET MAY SCHOOLS
LTD**
Apple Tree Cottage School, Seal
Chart, Sevenoaks, Kent TN15 0ES
Tel: (01732) 761097
Head: Mrs M May
Type: Co-educational Day 3-8
No of Pupils: B17 G18
Fees: (September 95) £1050

THE NEW BEACON SCHOOL
Brittains Lane, Sevenoaks, Kent
TN13 2PB
Tel: (01732) 452131
Head: R Constantine
Type: Boys Day & Boarding 5-13
No of Pupils: 358 No of Boarders
W35
Fees: (September 95) WB £7080 DAY
£2535 - £4470

RUSSELL HOUSE SCHOOL
Station Road, Otford, Sevenoaks,
Kent TN14 5QU
Tel: (01959) 522352
Head: A Duffy & Mrs E Lindsay
Type: Co-educational Day 3-11
No of Pupils: B99 G100
Fees: (September 95) £2100 - £4500

ST MICHAEL'S SCHOOL
Otford Court, Otford, Sevenoaks,
Kent TN14 5SA
Tel: (01959) 522137
Head: Simon Cummins
Type: Co-educational Day 2-13
No of Pupils: B226 G124
Fees: (September 95) £3000 - £4500

**SEVENOAKS PREPARATORY
SCHOOL**
Fawke Cottage, Godden Green,
Sevenoaks, Kent TN15 0JU
Tel: (01732) 762336
Head: E H Oatley
Type: Co-educational Day 3-13
No of Pupils: B220 G36
Fees: (September 95) £2760 - £4200

SEVENOAKS SCHOOL*
Sevenoaks, Kent TN13 1HU
Tel: (01732) 455133
Head: R P Barker
Type: Co-educational Day &
Boarding 11-18
No of Pupils: B517 G428 No of
Boarders F323
Fees: (September 95) FB £11619 DAY
£7074

SOLEFIELD SCHOOL
Solefields Road, Sevenoaks, Kent
TN13 1PH
Tel: (01732) 452142
Head: J R Baugh
Type: Boys Day 4-13
No of Pupils: 200
Fees: (September 95) £820 - £1395

WALTHAMSTOW HALL
Hollybush Lane, Sevenoaks, Kent
TN13 3UL
Tel: (01732) 451334
Head: Mrs J S Lang
Type: Girls Day & Boarding 3-18
No of Pupils: 540 No of Boarders F40
W12
Fees: (September 95) F/WB £9555 -
£11775 DAY £270 - £6345

WEST HEATH SCHOOL
Sevenoaks, Kent TN13 1SR
Tel: (01732) 452541
Head: Mrs A Williamson
Type: Girls Boarding & Day 11-18
No of Pupils: 102 No of Boarders F83
Fees: (September 95) FB £11040 DAY
£7755

SHEERNESS

ELLIOTT PARK SCHOOL
Marina Drive, Minster, Isle of
Sheppey, Sheerness, Kent ME12 2DP
Tel: (01795) 873372
Head: C G Hudson
Type: Co-educational Day 4-11
No of Pupils: B45 G40
Fees: (September 94) £1980 - £2100

SIDCUP

HARENC SCHOOL TRUST
167 Rectory Lane, Footscray, Sidcup,
Kent DA14 5BU
Tel: (0181) 309 0619
Head: S H Cassidy
Type: Boys Day 3-11
No of Pupils: 160
Fees: (September 95) £2595 - £3135

MERTON COURT
PREPARATORY SCHOOL
38 Knoll Road, Sidcup, Kent DA14
4QU
Tel: (0181) 300 2112
Head: Mrs E Price
Type: Co-educational Day 2-11
No of Pupils: B140 G110
Fees: (September 95) £2805 - £3105

WEST LODGE PREPARATORY
SCHOOL
36 Station Road, Sidcup, Kent DA15
7DU
Tel: (0181) 300 2489
Head: Mrs J V Barrett
Type: Girls Day 3-11 (Boys 3-7)
No of Pupils: B32 G114
Fees: (September 95) £1500 - £2730

TONBRIDGE

BICKIES
Somerhill, Tonbridge, Kent TN11 0NJ
Tel: (01732) 352124
Head: C F Woodmansee
Type: Co-educational Day 3-7
No of Pupils: 146
Fees: (September 95) £1485 - £3885

DERWENT LODGE SCHOOL
FOR GIRLS
Somerhill, Tonbridge, Kent TN11 0NJ
Tel: (01732) 352124
Head: Mrs C M York
Type: Girls Day 7-11
No of Pupils: 76
Fees: (September 95) £4425

HILDEN GRANGE SCHOOL
62 Dry Hill Park Road, Tonbridge,
Kent TN10 3BX
Tel: (01732) 352706
Head: J A Stewart & J Withers
Type: Co-educational Day 3-13
No of Pupils: B210 G78
Fees: (September 95) £1125 - £4800

HILDEN OAKS SCHOOL
38 Dry Hill Park Road, Tonbridge,
Kent TN10 3BU
Tel: (01732) 353941
Head: Mrs H J Bacon
Type: Co-educational Day B3-7
G3-11
No of Pupils: B30 G151
Fees: (September 95) £1485 - £3225

SACKVILLE SCHOOL
Tonbridge Road, Hildenborough,
Tonbridge, Kent TN11 9HN
Tel: (01732) 838888
Head: J Langdale
Type: Co-educational Day 11-16
No of Pupils: 127
Fees: (September 95) £1540 - £1931

TONBRIDGE SCHOOL
Tonbridge, Kent TN9 1JP
Tel: (01732) 365555
Head: J M Hammond
Type: Boys Boarding & Day 13-18
No of Pupils: 660 No of Boarders
F430
Fees: (September 95) FB £12969 DAY
£9153

YARDLEY COURT
Somerhill, Tonbridge, Kent TN11 0NJ
Tel: (01732) 352124
Head: A M Brooke
Type: Boys Day 7-13
No of Pupils: 137
Fees: (September 95) £5085 - £5805

TUNBRIDGE WELLS

BEECHWOOD SCHOOL,
SACRED HEART*
Pembury Road, Tunbridge Wells,
Kent TN2 3QD
Tel: (01892) 532747
Head: T Hodkinson
Type: Girls Boarding & Day 3-18
(Boys 3-7)
No of Pupils: 219 No of Boarders F83
Fees: (September 95) FB £8160 -
£10605 WB £5985 - £8430 DAY
£2550 - £6330

HOLMEWOOD HOUSE*
Langton Green, Tunbridge Wells,
Kent TN3 0EB
Tel: (01892) 862088
Head: D G Ives
Type: Co-educational Boarding &
Day 3-13
No of Pupils: B312 G144 No of
Boarders F62
Fees: (September 95) F/WB £10455
DAY £1905 - £7020

THE MEAD SCHOOL
16 Frant Road, Tunbridge Wells,
Kent TN2 5SN
Tel: (01892) 525837
Head: Mrs A Culley
Type: Co-educational Day 3-11
No of Pupils: B70 G70
Fees: (September 95) £1440 - £3480

ROSE HILL SCHOOL*
Culverden Down, Tunbridge Wells,
Kent TN4 9SY
Tel: (01892) 525591
Head: J G Parker
Type: Co-educational Day 3-13
No of Pupils: B136 G60
Fees: (September 95) £1770 - £5430

WEST WICKHAM

GREENHAYES SCHOOL FOR BOYS*
83 Corkscrew Hill, West Wickham, Kent BR4 9BA
Tel: (0181) 777 2093
Head: D J Cozens
Type: Boys Day 4-11 (Girls 3-5)
No of Pupils: 104
Fees: (September 95) £2250 - £2490

ST DAVID'S COLLEGE
Justin Hall, Beckenham Road, West Wickham, Kent BR4 0QS
Tel: (0181) 777 5852
Head: Mrs P A Johnson
Type: Co-educational Day 4-11
No of Pupils: B105 G94
Fees: (September 95) £2250 - £2400

WESTERHAM

CROFT HALL (HILL SCHOOL JUNIOR DEPARTMENT)
London Road, Westerham, Kent
Tel: (01959) 563381
Head: Miss P Wilkinson
Type: Co-educational Day 3-7
No of Pupils: B25 G20
Fees: (September 94) £1485 - £2190

THE HILL PREPARATORY SCHOOL
Pilgrims' Way, Westerham, Kent TN16 2DU
Tel: (01959) 563381
Head: N J Sanceau
Type: Co-educational Day 3-13
No of Pupils: B73 G25
Fees: (September 95) £1575 - £4080

WESTGATE-ON-SEA

CHARTFIELD SCHOOL
45 Minster Road, Westgate-on-Sea, Kent CT8 8DA
Tel: (01843) 831716
Head: Mrs J L Prebble
Type: Co-educational Day 4-11
No of Pupils: B35 G34
Fees: (September 95) £1455 - £1590

URSULINE COLLEGE*
225 Canterbury Road, Westgate-on-Sea, Kent CT8 8LN
Tel: (01843) 834431
Head: Sister Alice Montgomery
Type: Girls Boarding & Day 10-18
No of Pupils: 250 No of Boarders F125
Fees: (September 95) FB £9180 - £10563 DAY £5355

LANCASHIRE

BLACKBURN

OAKHILL COLLEGE
Wiswell Lane, Whalley, Blackburn, Lancashire BB7 9AF
Tel: (01254) 823546
Head: Mrs Finley
Type: Co-educational Day 3-16
No of Pupils: 204
Fees: (September 94) £2358 - £3807

QUEEN ELIZABETH'S GRAMMAR SCHOOL
Blackburn, Lancashire BB2 6DF
Tel: (01254) 59911
Head: Dr D S Hempsall
Type: Boys Day 7-18 (Co-ed VIth form)
No of Pupils: B1100 G70
Fees: (September 95) £3120 - £3942

WESTHOLME SCHOOL
Wilmar Lodge, Meins Road, Blackburn, Lancashire BB2 6QU
Tel: (01254) 53447
Head: Mrs L Croston
Type: Girls Day 4-18 (Boys 4-8)
No of Pupils: B74 G925
Fees: (September 95) £2505 - £3525

BLACKPOOL

ARNOLD SCHOOL
Lytham Road, Blackpool, Lancashire FY4 1JG
Tel: (01253) 346391
Head: W T Gillen
Type: Co-educational Day & Boarding 11-18
No of Pupils: B453 G366 No of Boarders F57 W6
Fees: (September 95) FB £3795 WB £2709 DAY £2883 - £3735

ELMSLIE GIRLS' SCHOOL
194 Whitegate Drive, Blackpool, Lancashire FY3 9HL
Tel: (01253) 763775
Head: Miss E M Smithies
Type: Girls Day 3-18
No of Pupils: 300
Fees: (September 95) £2895 - £3885

BOLTON

BOLTON MUSLIM GIRLS SCHOOL
High Street, Bolton, Lancashire BL3 6TA
Tel: (01204) 361103
Head: A Ghodiwala
Type: Girls Day
No of Pupils: 250
Fees: (September 95) On application.

BOLTON SCHOOL (BOYS' DIVISION)
Chorley New Road, Bolton, Lancashire BL1 4PA
Tel: (01204) 840201
Head: A W Wright
Type: Boys Day 8-18
No of Pupils: 1000
Fees: (September 95) £3225 - £4476

BOLTON SCHOOL (GIRLS' DIVISION)
Chorley New Road, Bolton, Lancashire BL1 4PB
Tel: (01204) 840201
Head: Miss E J Panton
Type: Girls Day 4-18
No of Pupils: 1137
Fees: (September 95) £3225 - £4476

CLEVELANDS PREPARATORY SCHOOL
Chorley New Road, Bolton, Lancashire BL1 5DA
Tel: (01204) 843898
Head: Mrs E M Davies
Type: Co-educational Day 4-11
No of Pupils: B90 G92
Fees: (September 95) £2505

LORD'S COLLEGE
53 Manchester Road, Bolton, Lancashire BL2 1ES
Tel: (01204) 523731
Head: Mrs D Wittle
Type: Co-educational Day 10-17
No of Pupils: 100
Fees: (September 94) £1350

BURNLEY

ST JOSEPH'S CONVENT SCHOOL
Park Hill, Padiham Road, Burnley, Lancashire BB12 6TG
Tel: (01282) 455622
Head: Sister Mary Clement
Type: Co-educational Day 4-11
No of Pupils: B101 G103
Fees: (September 95) £1200

SUNNY BANK PREPARATORY SCHOOL
171-173 Manchester Road, Burnley, Lancashire BB11 4HR
Tel: (01282) 421336
Head: Mrs J M Taylor
Type: Co-educational Day 3-11
No of Pupils: B35 G30
Fees: (September 94) £1620 - £1740

BURY

BURY CATHOLIC PREPARATORY SCHOOL
Arden House, 172 Manchester Road, Bury, Lancashire BL9 9BH
Tel: (0161) 764 2346
Head: Mrs S F Entwistle
Type: Co-educational Day 3-11
No of Pupils: B75 G75
Fees: (September 95) £2190

BURY GRAMMAR SCHOOL
Tenterden Street, Bury, Lancashire BL9 0HN
Tel: (0161) 797 2700
Head: K Richards
Type: Boys Day 7-18
No of Pupils: 825
Fees: (September 95) £2637 - £3702

BURY GRAMMAR SCHOOL (GIRLS')
Bridge Road, Bury, Lancashire BL9 0HH
Tel: (0161) 797 2808
Head: Miss J M Lawley
Type: Girls Day 4-18 (Boys 4-7)
No of Pupils: B72 G1048
Fees: (September 95) £2520 - £3702

CARNFORTH

CASTERTON SCHOOL*
Kirkby Lonsdale, Carnforth, Lancashire LA6 2SG
Tel: (01524) 271202
Head: A F Thomas
Type: Girls Boarding & Day 4-18 (Boys 4-7)
No of Pupils: 345 No of Boarders F270 W3
Fees: (September 95) FB £7230 - £9030 WB £7050 - £7554 DAY £4920 - £5664

CHORLEY

CHORCLIFFE PREPARATORY SCHOOL
The Old Manse, Park Street, Chorley, Lancashire PR7 1ER
Tel: (01257) 268807
Head: Ms H Mayer
Type: Co-educational Day 8-13
No of Pupils: B11 G6
Fees: (September 95) £3753 - £4170

CLITHEROE

MOORLAND SCHOOL
Ribblesdale Avenue, Clitheroe, Lancashire BB7 2JA
Tel: (01200) 23833
Head: J Harrison
Type: Co-educational Boarding & Day 2-16
No of Pupils: B81 G89 No of Boarders F40 W13
Fees: (September 95) FB £7059 - £7413 WB £6969 - £7323 DAY £1980 - £3348

STONYHURST COLLEGE
Stonyhurst, Clitheroe, Lancashire BB7 9PZ
Tel: (01254) 826345
Head: Dr R G G Mercer
Type: Boys Boarding & Day 13-18 (Girls 16-18)
No of Pupils: B392 G5 No of Boarders F350
Fees: (September 95) FB £11472 DAY £7125

FLEETWOOD

EMMANUEL CHRISTIAN SCHOOL
Elm Street, Fleetwood, Lancashire
Tel: (01253) 770646
Head: M Brunton Smith
Type: Co-educational Day 3-16
No of Pupils: B39 G41
Fees: (September 95) £1200 - £1608

ROSSALL PREPARATORY SCHOOL
Fleetwood, Lancashire FY7 8JW
Tel: (01253) 774222
Head: A N Rostron
Type: Co-educational Day & Boarding 2-11
No of Pupils: B143 G114 No of Boarders F60
Fees: (September 95) FB £7710 DAY £1950 - £2700

ROSSALL SCHOOL
Fleetwood, Lancashire FY7 8JW
Tel: (01253) 774247
Head: R D Rhodes
Type: Co-educational Boarding & Day 11-18
No of Pupils: B288 G143 No of Boarders F431
Fees: (September 95) FB £7710 - £11400 DAY £4200

LANCASTER

BENTHAM SCHOOL
Bentham, Lancaster, Lancashire LA2 7DB
Tel: (01524) 261275
Head: T K Halliwell
Type: Co-educational Boarding & Day 3-18
No of Pupils: B158 G125 No of Boarders F140
Fees: (September 94) F/WB £6897 - £8394 DAY £2175 - £4194

LYTHAM ST ANNES

KING EDWARD VII SCHOOL
Clifton Drive, Lytham St Annes, Lancashire FY8 1DT
Tel: (01253) 736459
Head: P J Wilde
Type: Boys Day 3-18
No of Pupils: 557
Fees: (September 95) £2460 - £3690

QUEEN MARY SCHOOL
Lytham St Annes, Lancashire FY8 1DS
Tel: (01253) 723246
Head: Miss M C Ritchie
Type: Girls Day 7-18
No of Pupils: 600
Fees: (September 95) £2460 - £3690

ST ANNE'S COLLEGE GRAMMAR SCHOOL
293 Clifton Drive South, St
Annes-on-Sea, Lytham St Annes,
Lancashire FY8 1HN
Tel: (01253) 725815
Head: Mr & Mrs S R Welsby
Type: Co-educational Day 2-18
No of Pupils: B106 G106
Fees: (September 94) £1950 - £2475

OLDHAM

FARROWDALE HOUSE PREPARATORY SCHOOL
Farrow Street, Shaw, Oldham,
Lancashire OL2 7AD
Tel: (01706) 844533
Head: Mrs A Graydon
Type: Co-educational Day 4-11
No of Pupils: B70 G70
Fees: (September 95) £1935 - £2010

GRASSCROFT INDEPENDENT SCHOOL
Lydgate Parish Hall, Stockport Road,
Lydgate, Oldham, Lancashire
OL4 4JJ
Tel: (01457) 820485
Head: Mrs B Donough
Type: Co-educational Day 3-7
No of Pupils: B36 G46
Fees: (September 95) £741 - £1833

THE HULME GRAMMAR SCHOOL
Chamber Road, Oldham, Lancashire
OL8 4BX
Tel: (0161) 624 4497
Head: G F Dunkin
Type: Boys Day 7-18
No of Pupils: 860
Fees: (September 95) £2502 - £3510

THE HULME GRAMMAR SCHOOL FOR GIRLS
Chamber Road, Oldham, Lancashire
OL8 4BX
Tel: (0161) 624 2523
Head: Miss M S Smolenski
Type: Girls Day 7-18
No of Pupils: 620
Fees: (September 94) £2445 - £3426

WERNETH PRIVATE PREPARATORY SCHOOL
Plum Street, Oldham, Lancashire
OL8 1TJ
Tel: (0161) 624 2947
Head: Mrs M J Press
Type: Co-educational Day 3-11
No of Pupils: B90 G60
Fees: (September 95) £1950 - £2451

ORMSKIRK

SCARISBRICK HALL SCHOOL
Ormskirk, Lancashire L40 9RQ
Tel: (01704) 880200
Head: D M Raynor
Type: Co-educational Day 3-18
No of Pupils: B260 G265
Fees: (September 95) £1779 - £2682

PRESTON

HIGHFIELD PRIORY SCHOOL
Fulwood Row, Fulwood, Preston,
Lancashire PR2 6SL
Tel: (01772) 709624
Head: B C Duckett
Type: Co-educational Day 2-11
No of Pupils: B180 G150
Fees: (September 95) £2445

KINGSFOLD CHRISTIAN SCHOOL
Moss Lane, Hesketh Bank, Preston,
Lancashire PR4 6AA
Tel: (01772) 813824
Head: S D Lamin
Type: Co-educational Day
No of Pupils: B26 G22
Fees: (September 95) £936 - £1020

KIRKHAM GRAMMAR SCHOOL
Ribby Road, Kirkham, Preston,
Lancashire PR4 2BH
Tel: (01772) 671079
Head: B Stacey
Type: Co-educational Boarding &
Day 4-18
No of Pupils: B277 G243 No of
Boarders F52 W16
Fees: (September 95) FB £6975 WB
£6810 DAY £2775 - £3675

ST PIUS X PREPARATORY SCHOOL
200 Garstang Road, Fulwood,
Preston, Lancashire PR2 8RD
Tel: (01772) 719937
Head: Miss B Banks
Type: Co-educational Day 3-11
No of Pupils: B160 G168
Fees: (September 95) £2220 - £2475

WOODLANDS SCHOOL
162 Ribbleton Ave, Preston,
Lancashire PR2 6DB
Tel: (01772) 792484
Head: Mrs J G Hirst
Type: Co-educational Day 2-11
No of Pupils: B50 G50
Fees: (September 95) £2205 - £2643

ROCHDALE

BEECH HOUSE SCHOOL
184 Manchester Road, Rochdale,
Lancashire OL11 4JQ
Tel: (01706) 46309
Head: I R Barber
Type: Co-educational Day 3-17
No of Pupils: B95 G99
Fees: (September 95) £1740 - £2340

CONVENT PRIMARY SCHOOL
Beechwood, Manchester Road,
Rochdale, Lancashire OL11 4LU
Tel: (01706) 46627
Head: Sister R Steinbach
Type: Co-educational Day 3-11
No of Pupils: B109 G99
Fees: (September 95) £1650 - £1920

GLEBE HOUSE SCHOOL
Broadfield Stile, Rochdale, Lancashire
OL16 1UT
Tel: (01706) 45985
Head: K Bayliss
Type: Co-educational Day 3-7
No of Pupils: B42 G49
Fees: (September 95) £1530 - £2040

STONYHURST

ST MARY'S HALL
Stonyhurst, Lancashire BB7 9PU
Tel: (01254) 826242
Head: R F O'Brien
Type: Boys Boarding & Day 7-13
No of Pupils: 175 No of Boarders F75
Fees: (September 95) FB £7625 DAY
£3772 - £5438

LEICESTERSHIRE

ASHBY-DE-LA-ZOUCH

MANOR HOUSE SCHOOL
South Street, Ashby-de-la-Zouch,
Leicestershire LE65 1BR
Tel: (01530) 412932
Head: R J Sill
Type: Co-educational Day 3-14
No of Pupils: 230
Fees: (September 95) £2544 - £4020

LEICESTER

ALL SAINTS SCHOOL
2 St Pauls Road, Leicester LE3 9DE
Tel: (0116) 253 6409
Head: Rev Anthony Ballard
Type: Co-educational Day
No of Pupils: B17 G7
Fees: (September 95) £3300

BROOKE HOUSE COLLEGE
Brooke House, Market Harborough,
Leicester LE16 7AU
Tel: (01858) 462452
Head: Mrs F Colyer
Type: Co-educational Residential
14-18
No of Pupils: B55 G45
Fees: FB £11355 DAY £6570

FOSSE WAY SCHOOL
72 Fosse Road South, Leicester LE3
0QD
Tel: (0116) 254 1115
Head: Mrs S J Cooper
Type: Co-educational Day 3-11
No of Pupils: B30 G31
Fees: (September 95) £1524 - £2178

GRACE DIEU MANOR SCHOOL
Grace Dieu, Thringstone, Leicester
LE67 5UG
Tel: (01530) 222276
Head: Rev Fr G J Duffy
Type: Co-educational Boarding &
Day 3-13
No of Pupils: B257 G93 No of
Boarders F30 W15
Fees: (September 95) FB £6624 WB
£6543 DAY £2550 - £4416

IRWIN COLLEGE*
164 London Road, Leicester LE2 1ND
Tel: (0116) 255 2648
Head: A J Elliott
Type: Co-educational Residential &
Day 13-23
No of Pupils: B43 G21
Fees: (September 95) FB £8910
DAY £5040

LEICESTER GRAMMAR
JUNIOR SCHOOL
Evington Hall, Spencefield Lane,
Leicester LE5 6HN
Tel: (0116) 241 2000
Head: J Greathead
Type: Co-educational Day 3-11
No of Pupils: B143 G105
Fees: (September 95) £2880 - £2985

LEICESTER GRAMMAR
SCHOOL*
8 Peacock Lane, Leicester LE1 5PX
Tel: (0116) 262 1221
Head: J B Sugden
Type: Co-educational Day 10-18
No of Pupils: B285 G300
Fees: (September 95) £4080

LEICESTER HIGH SCHOOL
FOR GIRLS
454 London Road, Leicester LE2 2PP
Tel: (0116) 270 5338
Head: Mrs P A Watson
Type: Girls Day 3-18
No of Pupils: 406
Fees: (September 95) £2685 - £4275

RATCLIFFE COLLEGE*
Fosse Way, Ratcliffe on the Wreake,
Leicester LE7 4SG
Tel: (01509) 817000
Head: Rev K A Tomlinson
Type: Co-educational Boarding &
Day 10-18
No of Pupils: B318 G140 No of
Boarders F151 W29
Fees: (September 95) FB £9096 WB
£7233 - £9096 DAY £4824 - £6066

ST CRISPIN'S SCHOOL
St Mary's Road, Leicester LE2 1XA
Tel: (0116) 270 7648
Head: B Harrild
Type: Co-educational Day 2-13
No of Pupils: 200
Fees: (September 94) £1140 - £3255

STONEYGATE SCHOOL
254 London Road, Leicester LE2 1RP
Tel: (0116) 270 7536
Head: J B Josephs
Type: Co-educational Day 3-13
No of Pupils: 385
Fees: (September 95) £2640 - £4125

LOUGHBOROUGH

FAIRFIELD SCHOOL
Leicester Road, Loughborough,
Leicestershire LE11 2AE
Tel: (01509) 215172
Head: T A Eadon
Type: Co-educational Day 4-11
No of Pupils: B262 G208
Fees: (September 95) £3096

LOUGHBOROUGH GRAMMAR
SCHOOL
Burton Walks, Loughborough,
Leicestershire LE11 2DU
Tel: (01509) 233233
Head: D N Ireland
Type: Boys Day & Boarding 10-18
No of Pupils: 940 No of Boarders F70
Fees: (September 95) FB £8208 WB
£7218 DAY £4428

LOUGHBOROUGH HIGH
SCHOOL
Burton Walks, Loughborough,
Leicestershire LE11 2DU
Tel: (01509) 212348
Head: Miss J E Harvatt
Type: Girls Day 11-18
No of Pupils: 540
Fees: (September 95) £3969

OUR LADY'S CONVENT
SCHOOL
Burton Street, Loughborough,
Leicestershire LE11 2DT
Tel: (01509) 263901
Head: Sister Mary Mark Fynn
Type: Girls Day 3-18 (Boys 3-5)
No of Pupils: B11 G547
Fees: (September 95) £2040 - £3450

PNEU SCHOOL
8 Station Road, East Leake,
Loughborough, Leicestershire
LE12 6LQ
Tel: (01509) 852229
Head: Mrs B G Warder
Type: Co-educational Day 3-11
No of Pupils: B46 G40
Fees: (September 95) £2880 - £3005

MARKET BOSWORTH

THE DIXIE GRAMMAR
SCHOOL
Market Bosworth, Leicestershire
CV13 0LE
Tel: (01455) 292244
Head: R S Willmott
Type: Co-educational Day 10-18
Fees: (September 95) £3450

**THE WOLSTAN
PREPARATORY SCHOOL**
Market Bosworth, Leicestershire
CV13 0LE
Tel: (01445) 292244
Head: R S Wilmott
Type: Co-educational Day 4-9
Fees: (September 95) £2580 - £2940

MARKET HARBOROUGH

NEVILL HOLT SCHOOL
Market Harborough, Leicestershire
LE16 8EG
Tel: (01858) 565234
Head: I D Mackenzie
Type: Co-educational Boarding &
Day 4-13
No of Pupils: B80 G48 No of
Boarders F12 W18
Fees: (September 95) FB £7755 WB
£7440 DAY £2580 - £5610

OAKHAM

BROOKE PRIORY SCHOOL
Brooke, Oakham, Leicestershire LE15
8DG
Tel: (01572) 724778
Head: Mrs S Allen
Type: Co-educational Day 4-11
No of Pupils: B66 G54
Fees: (September 95) £2391 - £2760

OAKHAM SCHOOL
Chapel Close, Oakham, Leicestershire
LE15 6DT
Tel: (01572) 758500
Head: G Smallbone
Type: Co-educational Boarding &
Day 10-18
No of Pupils: B498 G490 No of
Boarders F571
Fees: (September 95) FB £11670 DAY
£6450

UPPINGHAM SCHOOL*
Oakham, Leicestershire LE15 9QE
Tel: (01572) 822216
Head: Dr S C Winkley
Type: Boys Boarding & Day 13-18
(Co-ed VIth form)
No of Pupils: B500 G110 No of
Boarders F600
Fees: (September 95) FB £12750 DAY
£7650

UPPINGHAM

WINDMILL HOUSE SCHOOL
22 Stockerston Road, Uppingham,
Leicestershire LE15 9UD
Tel: (01572) 823593
Head: Mrs J Taylor
Type: Co-educational Day 4-11
No of Pupils: B51 G37
Fees: (September 94) £1770 - £2655

LINCOLNSHIRE

BOSTON

**CONWAY PREPARATORY
SCHOOL**
Tunnard Street, Boston, Lincolnshire
PE21 6PL
Tel: (01205) 363150
Head: Mrs J Nyman
Type: Co-educational Day 3-11
No of Pupils: B90 G90
Fees: (September 94) £1440

BOURNE

WITHAM HALL
Witham-on-the-Hill, Bourne,
Lincolnshire PE10 0JJ
Tel: (01778) 590222
Head: D H Burston
Type: Co-educational Boarding &
Day 4-13
No of Pupils: B102 G54 No of
Boarders F60
Fees: (September 95) F/WB £7350
DAY £2970 - £5490

GAINSBOROUGH

**HANDEL HOUSE
PREPARATORY SCHOOL**
Northolme Road, Gainsborough,
Lincolnshire DN21 2JB
Tel: (01427) 612426
Head: Mrs M Hornsey
Type: Co-educational Day 3-12
No of Pupils: B34 G30
Fees: (September 95) £1200 - £2000

GRANTHAM

DUDLEY HOUSE SCHOOL
1 Dudley Road, Grantham,
Lincolnshire NG31 9AA
Tel: (01476) 61173
Head: E J Winch
Type: Co-educational Day 3-11
No of Pupils: B40 G29
Fees: (September 95) £675

**HEATHLANDS PREPARATORY
SCHOOL**
Gorse Lane, Grantham, Lincolnshire
NG31 7UF
Tel: (01476) 593293
Head: Mrs P A Anderson
Type: Co-educational Day 3-11
No of Pupils: B57 G66
Fees: (September 94) £2565

HORNCASTLE

MAYPOLE HOUSE
Horncastle, Lincolnshire LN9 5AE
Tel: (01507) 462764
Head: Mr and Mrs M White
Type: Co-educational Day 3-16
No of Pupils: B70 G50
Fees: (September 95) £1800 - £2200

LINCOLN

THE CATHEDRAL SCHOOL
Eastgate, Lincoln LN2 1QE
Tel: (01522) 523769
Head: Rev Canon R G Western
Type: Co-educational Day &
Boarding 2-13
No of Pupils: B69 G11 No of
Boarders F15 W3
Fees: (September 94) F/WB £6600
DAY £1170 - £3555

ST JOSEPH'S SCHOOL
Upper Lindum Street, Lincoln
LN2 5RW
Tel: (01522) 543764
Head: Mrs M Bradley
Type: Girls Day & Boarding 4-18
(Boys 4-11)
No of Pupils: 225 No of Boarders F17
W17
Fees: (September 95) FB £8000 -
£9000 WB £5000 - £6000 DAY
£4000 - £4500

ST MARY'S SCHOOL
5 Pottergate, Lincoln LN2 1PH
Tel: (01522) 524622
Head: P H Brewster
Type: Co-educational Day 2-11
No of Pupils: B92 G81
Fees: (September 95) £3300 - £3450

STONEFIELD HOUSE
Church Lane, Lincoln LN2 1QR
Tel: (01552) 541741
Head: J P S Child
Type: Co-educational Day 3-16
No of Pupils: B84 G52
Fees: (September 95) £2700 - £4530

SLEAFORD

THE FEN PREPARATORY SCHOOL
Side Bar Lane, Heckington Fen,
Sleaford, Lincolnshire NG34 9LY
Tel: (01529) 460966
Head: Mrs J M Dunkley
Type: Co-educational Day 2-16
No of Pupils: B19 G11
Fees: (September 94) £1764 - £4095

SPALDING

AYSCOUGHFEE HALL SCHOOL
Welland Hall, London Road,
Spalding, Lincolnshire PE11 2TE
Tel: (01775) 724733
Head: B Chittick
Type: Co-educational Day 3-11
No of Pupils: B78 G77
Fees: (September 95) £1815 - £2175

STAMFORD

COPTHILL SCHOOL
Barnack Road, Uffington, Stamford,
Lincolnshire PE6 4TD
Tel: (01780) 57506
Head: Mrs A M Teesdale
Type: Co-educational Day 2-11
No of Pupils: B96 G109
Fees: (September 95) £525 - £2997

STAMFORD HIGH SCHOOL
St Martin's, Stamford, Lincolnshire
PE9 2LJ
Tel: (01780) 62330
Head: Miss G K Bland
Type: Girls Day & Boarding 4-18
(Boys 4-8)
No of Pupils: B63 G925 No of
Boarders F97 W21
Fees: (September 95) FB £7362 -
£8178 WB £7284 - £8100 DAY
£3273 - £4089

STAMFORD SCHOOL
St Paul's Street, Stamford,
Lincolnshire PE9 2BS
Tel: (01780) 62171
Head: G J Timm
Type: Boys Day & Boarding 8-18
(Co-ed 4-8)
No of Pupils: 920 No of Boarders
F220
Fees: (September 95) FB £7323 -
£8130 DAY £3258 - £4065

WHITE HOUSE SCHOOL
Stamford Road, Easton-on-the-Hill,
Stamford, Lincolnshire PE9 3NU
Tel: (01780) 53405
Head: Mrs C M Coleman
Type: Co-educational Day 2-9
No of Pupils: B30 G28
Fees: (September 94) £936 - £3120

WOODHALL SPA

ST HUGH'S SCHOOL
Cromwell Avenue, Woodhall Spa,
Lincolnshire LN10 6TQ
Tel: (01526) 352169
Head: P M Wells
Type: Co-educational Boarding &
Day 4-13
No of Pupils: B92 G50 No of Boarders
F90
Fees: (September 95) F/WB £7275 -
£7446 DAY £2976 - £5508

LONDON

E1

ISLAMIC COLLEGE LONDON
16 Settles Street, London, E1 1JP
Tel: (0171) 377 1595
Head: A Sayeed
Type: Boys Day 11-16
No of Pupils: 50
Fees: (September 94) £1000 - £1500

MADNI GIRLS SCHOOL
15-17 Rampart Street, London,
E1 2LA
Tel: (0171) 791 3531
Head: Mrs F R Liyawdeen
Type: Girls Day 12-18
No of Pupils: 65
Fees: On application

E2

GATEHOUSE SCHOOL
Sewardstone Road, Victoria Park,
London, E2 9JG
Tel: (0181) 980 2978
Head: Miss A Eversole
Type: Co-educational Day 2-11
No of Pupils: 126
Fees: (September 95) £3070

E4

NORMANHURST SCHOOL
68/74 Station Road, Chingford,
London, E4 7BA
Tel: (0181) 529 4307
Head: J Leyland
Type: Co-educational Day 4-16
No of Pupils: B100 G80
Fees: (September 95) £3810 - £4725

E7

CEDAR SCHOOL
5-7 Stafford Road, Forest Gate,
London, E7 8NL
Tel: (0181) 472 5723
Head: S J Sherwood
Type: Co-educational Day 4-11
No of Pupils: B17 G10
Fees: (September 95) £2385

GRANGEWOOD INDEPENDENT SCHOOL
Chester Road, Forest Gate, London,
E7 8QT
Tel: (0181) 472 3552
Head: B Davies
Type: Co-educational Day 4-11
No of Pupils: 120
Fees: (September 94) £2580

E11

ST JOSEPH'S CONVENT SCHOOL
59 Cambridge Park, London, E11 2PR
Tel: (0181) 989 4700
Head: Mrs C Youle
Type: Girls Day 4-11
No of Pupils: 195
Fees: (September 95) £1905

E17

FOREST GIRLS' SCHOOL
Snaresbrook, London, E17 3PY
Tel: (0181) 521 7477
Head: Mrs R Martin
Type: Girls Day 11-18
No of Pupils: 360
Fees: (September 95) £5484

FOREST JUNIOR SCHOOL
Snaresbrook, London, E17 3PY
Tel: (0181) 520 1744
Head: R T Cryer
Type: Boys Day & Boarding 7-13
(Day girls 7-11)
No of Pupils: B333 G64 No of
Boarders F2
Fees: (September 95) FB £8610 WB
£5736 DAY £3753 - £5484

FOREST SCHOOL
College Place, Snaresbrook, London,
E17 3PY
Tel: (0181) 520 1744
Head: A Boggis
Type: Boys Day & Boarding 13-18
No of Pupils: 474 No of Boarders F31
Fees: (September 95) FB £6033 -
£8610 WB £5736 DAY £3753 -
£5484

HYLAND HOUSE
896 Forest Road, Walthamstow,
London, E17 4AE
Tel: (0181) 520 4186
Head: Mrs T Thorpe
Type: Co-educational Day 3-11
No of Pupils: 100
Fees: (September 95) £1500 - £1800

E18

SNARESBROOK COLLEGE
75 Woodford Road, South
Woodford, London, E18 2EA
Tel: (0181) 989 2394
Head: Mrs L J Chiverrell
Type: Co-educational Day 3-11
No of Pupils: B74 G87
Fees: (September 95) £2832 - £3765

EC1

THE CHARTERHOUSE SQUARE SCHOOL
40 Charterhouse Square, London,
EC1M 6EA
Tel: (0171) 600 3805
Head: Mrs J Malden
Type: Co-educational Day 4-11
No of Pupils: B60 G70
Fees: (September 95) £4500

DALLINGTON SCHOOL
8 Dallington Street, London,
EC1V 0BQ
Tel: (0171) 251 2284
Head: Mrs M C Hercules
Type: Co-educational Day 3-11
No of Pupils: B75 G102
Fees: (September 95) £2871 - £3918

ITALIA CONTI ACADEMY OF THEATRE ARTS
23 Goswell Road, London, EC1M 7BB
Tel: (0171) 608 0047
Head: C Vote
Type: Co-educational Day 9-21
No of Pupils: B45 G200
Fees: (September 94) £4200 - £6300

EC2

CITY OF LONDON SCHOOL FOR GIRLS
Barbican, London, EC2Y 8BB
Tel: (0171) 628 0841
Head: Dr Y Burne
Type: Girls Day 7-18
No of Pupils: 640
Fees: (September 95) £5094

EC4

CITY OF LONDON SCHOOL
Queen Victoria Street, London,
EC4V 3AL
Tel: (0171) 489 0291
Head: R Dancey
Type: Boys Day 10-18
No of Pupils: 870
Fees: (September 95) £5832

ST PAUL'S CATHEDRAL CHOIR SCHOOL*
2 New Change, London, EC4M 9AD
Tel: (0171) 248 5156
Head: S A Sides
Type: Boys Boarding & Day 7-13
No of Pupils: 100 No of Boarders F40
Fees: (September 95) FB £2970 DAY
£4950

N1

WOODLEE ACADEMY THEATRE SCHOOL
Trinity Centre, Bletchley Street,
Islington, London, N1 7QG
Tel: (0171) 251 2879
Head: B Benson
Type: Co-educational Day
No of Pupils: B9 G32
Fees: (September 95) £2850 - £3750

N2

ANNEMOUNT SCHOOL
18 Holne Chase, London, N2 0QN
Tel: (0181) 455 2132
Head: Mrs G Tausig
Type: Co-educational Day 3-7
No of Pupils: B30 G20
Fees: (September 95) £1950 - £3300

KEREM HOUSE
18 Kingsley Way, London, N2 0ER
Tel: (0181) 455 7524
Head: Mrs A Kennard
Type: Co-educational Day 3-5
Fees: On application

THE KEREM SCHOOL
Norrice Lea, London, N2 0RE
Tel: (0181) 455 0909
Head: Mrs R Goulden
Type: Co-educational Day 4-11
No of Pupils: B79 G81
Fees: (September 95) £3609

N3

AKIVA SCHOOL
The Manor House, 80 East End
Road, London, N3 2SY
Tel: (0181) 349 4980
Head: Mrs J Roback
Type: Co-educational 4-11
No of Pupils: B82 G56
Fees: (September 95) DAY £3645

PARDES GRAMMAR BOYS' SCHOOL
Hendon Lane, London, N3 1SA
Tel: (0181) 343 3568
Head: Rabbi D Dunner
Type: Boys Day 5-17
No of Pupils: 460
Fees: On application

N4

HOLLY PARK MONTESSORI
The Holly Park Methodist Church,
Crouch Hill, London, N4 4BY
Tel: (0171) 263 6563
Head: Mrs A Lake
Type: Co-educational Day 2-9
No of Pupils: B33 G32
Fees: (September 95) £650 - £1020

N6

CHANNING JUNIOR SCHOOL
Fairseat, 1 Highgate High Street,
London, N6 5JR
Tel: (0181) 342 9862
Head: Miss E Krispinussen
Type: Girls Day 5-11
No of Pupils: 146
Fees: (September 95) £4860 - £5250

CHANNING SCHOOL
Highgate, London, N6 5HF
Tel: (0181) 340 2328
Head: Mrs I R Raphael
Type: Girls Day 11-18
No of Pupils: 334
Fees: (September 95) £5700

HIGHFIELD SCHOOL
1 Bloomfield Road, Highgate,
London, N6 4ET
Tel: (0181) 340 5981
Head: Mrs L Hayes
Type: Co-educational Day B3-7
G3-11
No of Pupils: B87 G75
Fees: (September 95) £1845 - £3690

HIGHGATE JUNIOR SCHOOL
Cholmeley House, 3 Bishopswood
Road, Highgate, London, N6 4PL
Tel: (0181) 340 9193
Head: H S Evers
Type: Boys Day 7-13
No of Pupils: 360
Fees: (September 95) £6375

HIGHGATE
PRE-PREPARATORY SCHOOL
7 Bishopswood Road, Highgate,
London, N6
Tel: (0181) 340 9196
Head: Mrs B Rock
Type: Co-educational Day 3-7
No of Pupils: 128
Fees: (September 95) £2745 - £5640

HIGHGATE SCHOOL
North Road, London, N6 4AY
Tel: (0181) 340 1524
Head: R P Kennedy
Type: Boys Day 13-18
No of Pupils: 625
Fees: (September 95) £7125

RAINBOW MONTESSORI
SCHOOL
Highgate URC, Pond Square,
London, N6 6BA
Tel: (0171) 328 8986
Head: Mrs Linda Madden
Type: Co-educational Day 2-5
No of Pupils: 50
Fees: (September 94) £1650 - £2550

N10

THE MONTESSORI HOUSE
SCHOOL
5 Princes Avenue, Muswell Hill,
London, N10 3LS
Tel: (0181) 444 4399
Head: Mrs N Forsyth
Type: Co-educational Day 2-5
No of Pupils: 60
Fees: (September 95) £1545 - £3615

NORFOLK HOUSE SCHOOL
10 Muswell Avenue, London,
N10 2EG
Tel: (0181) 883 4584
Head: R Howat
Type: Co-educational Day 4-11
No of Pupils: B50 G50
Fees: (September 95) £2985

PRINCES AVENUE SCHOOL
5 Princes Avenue, Muswell Hill,
London, N10 3LS
Tel: (0181) 444 4399
Head: Mrs N Forsyth
Type: Co-educational Day 5-7
No of Pupils: 24
Fees: (September 95) £4695

N11

FRIERN BARNET GRAMMAR
SCHOOL
Friern Barnet Road, London,
N11 3DR
Tel: (0181) 368 3777
Head: John Pearman
Type: Boys Day 10-16
No of Pupils: 150
Fees: (September 94) £4260

N12

WOODSIDE PARK SCHOOL
Woodside Lane, London, N12 8SY
Tel: (0181) 445 2333
Head: R F Metters
Type: Co-educational Day B2-13
G2-11
No of Pupils: B275 G75
Fees: (September 95) £2025 - £4800

N14

SALCOMBE SCHOOL
224-226 Chase Side, Southgate,
London, N14 4PL
Tel: (0181) 441 5282
Head: A J Blackhurst
Type: Co-educational Day 2-11
No of Pupils: B210 G125
Fees: (September 95) £3285

VITA ET PAX SCHOOL
Priory Close, Green Road, Southgate,
London, N14 4AT
Tel: (0181) 449 8336
Head: Miss P M Condon
Type: Co-educational Day 4-11
No of Pupils: B90 G90
Fees: (September 95) £2550

N16

LUBAVITCH HOUSE SENIOR
SCHOOL FOR BOYS
107-115 Stamford Hill, Hackney,
London, N16 5RP
Tel: (0181) 800 0022
Type: Boys Day 11-18
No of Pupils: 120
Fees: (September 95) £5000

MECHINAH LIYESHIVAH
ZICHRON MOSHE
86 Amhurst Park, London, N16 5AR
Tel: (0181) 800 5892
Head: Rabbi M Halpern
Type: Boys Day 11-16
No of Pupils: 60
Fees: (September 95) £4000

TALMUD TORAH JEWISH
SCHOOL
112-114 Bethune Road, London, N16
Tel: (0181) 802 2512
Head: S Harris
Type: Boys Day 3-11
No of Pupils: 60
Fees: On application

YESODEY HATORAH JEWISH
SCHOOL
2-4 Amhurst Park, London, N16 5AE
Tel: (0181) 800 8612
Head: Rabbi Abraham Pinter
Type: Co-educational Day 3-16
(Single-sex education)
No of Pupils: B250 G710
Fees: On application

YETEV LEV DAY SCHOOL FOR BOYS
111-115 Cazenove Road, London, N16 6AX
Tel: (0181) 806 3834
Head: I Greenbaum
Type: Boys Day 3-13
No of Pupils: 240
Fees: On application

N17

THE JOHN LOUGHBOROUGH SCHOOL
Holcombe Road, Tottenham, London, N17 9AD
Tel: (0181) 808 7837
Head: Dr C Valley
Type: Co-educational Day 9-16
No of Pupils: 200
Fees: (September 95) £1425 - £2100

N21

GRANGE PARK PREPARATORY SCHOOL
13 The Chine, Grange Park, Winchmore Hill, London, N21 2EA
Tel: (0181) 360 1469
Head: Mrs R J Jeans
Type: Girls Day 3-11
No of Pupils: 105
Fees: (September 95) £1320 - £2340

KEBLE PREPARATORY SCHOOL
Wades Hill, Winchmore Hill, London, N21 1BG
Tel: (0181) 360 3359
Head: G C Waite
Type: Boys Day 4-13
No of Pupils: 200
Fees: (September 95) £2070 - £4770

PALMERS GREEN HIGH SCHOOL
Hoppers Road, Winchmore Hill, London, N21 3LJ
Tel: (0181) 886 1135
Head: Mrs Sian Grant
Type: Girls Day 3-16
No of Pupils: 320
Fees: (September 95) £1536 - £4020

NW1

THE CAVENDISH SCHOOL*
179 Arlington Road, London, NW1 7EY
Tel: (0171) 485 1958
Head: Mrs L J Harris
Type: Co-educational Day B3-7 G3-11
No of Pupils: B7 G143
Fees: (September 95) £3675 - £3936

FRANCIS HOLLAND SCHOOL
Clarence Gate, Ivor Place, London, NW1 6XR
Tel: (0171) 723 0176
Head: Mrs P H Parsonson
Type: Girls Day 11-18
No of Pupils: 370
Fees: (September 95) £5205

INTERNATIONAL COMMUNITY SCHOOL
4 York Terrace East, Regent's Park, London, NW1 4PT
Tel: (0171) 935 1206
Head: P Hurd & Ms B Townley
Type: Co-educational Day 3-18
No of Pupils: 215
Fees: (September 95) £5393 - £6493

NORTH BRIDGE HOUSE LOWER SCHOOL*
1 Gloucester Avenue, London, NW1 7AB
Tel: (0171) 485 0661
Head: Miss E J Battye
Type: Co-educational Day 7-10
No of Pupils: B115 G145
Fees: (September 95) £5250

NORTH BRIDGE HOUSE UPPER SCHOOL*
1 Gloucester Avenue, London, NW1 7AB
Tel: (0171) 267 6266
Head: R L Shaw & J C Lovelock
Type: Co-educational Day 10-16
No of Pupils: B165 G54
Fees: (September 95) £5250

SYLVIA YOUNG THEATRE SCHOOL
Rossmore Road, Marylebone, London, NW1 6NJ
Tel: (0171) 402 0673
Head: Miss M T Melville
Type: Co-educational Day 7-16
No of Pupils: 132
Fees: (September 95) £2970 - £3840

NW2

THE MULBERRY HOUSE SCHOOL
7 Minster Road, West Hampstead, London, NW2 3SD
Tel: (0181) 452 7340
Head: Ms J Pedder & Mrs B Lewis-Powell
Type: Co-educational Day 2-8
No of Pupils: 140
Fees: On application

WELSH SCHOOL OF LONDON
265 Willesden Lane, London, NW2 5JG
Tel: (0181) 459 2690
Head: Miss S Edwards
Type: Co-educational Day 4-11
No of Pupils: 28
Fees: (September 94) £1350

NW3

CHALCOT MONTESSORI SCHOOL AMI
9 Chalcot Gardens, London, NW3 4YB
Tel: (0171) 722 1386
Head: Ms Joanna Morfey
Type: Co-educational Day 2-6
No of Pupils: 24
Fees: (September 95) £2160

DEVONSHIRE HOUSE PREPARATORY SCHOOL*
2 Arkwright Road, Hampstead, London, NW3 6AD
Tel: (0171) 435 1916
Head: Mrs S P Donovan
Type: Co-educational Day 2-12
No of Pupils: 300
Fees: (September 95) £3765 - £4980

FINE ARTS COLLEGE
85 & 81b Belsize Park Gardens, Hampstead, London, NW3 4NJ
Tel: (0171) 586 0312
Head: Ms Candida Cochrane Cave
Type: Co-educational Day 15+
No of Pupils: B30 G50
Fees: (September 95) 3 A Levels/5 GCSEs £8985

THE HALL SCHOOL
23 Crossfield Road, Hampstead, London, NW3 4NU
Tel: (0171) 722 1700
Head: P F Ramage
Type: Boys Day 5-13
No of Pupils: 364
Fees: (September 95) £5520 - £5670

HAMPSTEAD HILL PRE-PREPARATORY & NURSERY SCHOOL*
St Stephen's Hall, Pond Street, Hampstead, London, NW3 2PP
Tel: (0171) 435 6262
Head: Mrs Andrea Taylor
Type: Co-educational Day 2-9
No of Pupils: B140 G80
Fees: (September 95) £3500 - £5200

HEATHSIDE PREPARATORY SCHOOL*
16 New End, Hampstead, London, NW3 1JA
Tel: (0171) 794 5857
Head: Ms M Remus & Mrs J White
Type: Co-educational Day 2-13
No of Pupils: 85
Fees: (September 95) £3960

HEREWARD HOUSE SCHOOL
14 Strathray Gardens, Hampstead, London, NW3 4NY
Tel: (0171) 794 4820
Head: Mrs L Sampson
Type: Boys Day 4-13
No of Pupils: 170
Fees: (September 95) £4785 - £5325

THE HILLTOP NURSERY SCHOOL
Christchurch, Hampstead Square, London, NW3 1AB
Tel: (0171) 435 7010
Head: Mrs G Tausig
Type: Co-educational Day 2-5
No of Pupils: 24
Fees: (September 95) £1950 - £3300

LYNDHURST HOUSE PREPARATORY SCHOOL
24 Lyndhurst Gardens, Hampstead, London, NW3 5NW
Tel: (0171) 435 4936
Head: M O Spilberg
Type: Boys Day 7-13
No of Pupils: 140
Fees: (September 95) £5430

MARIA MONTESSORI CHILDREN'S HOUSE
26 Lyndhurst Gardens, Hampstead, London, NW3 5NW
Tel: (0171) 435 3646
Head: Mrs L Lawrence
Type: Co-educational Day 2-6
No of Pupils: 30
Fees: (September 95) £1275 - £3060

NORTH BRIDGE HOUSE JUNIOR SCHOOL
8 Netherhall Gardens, London, NW3 5RR
Tel: (0171) 435 2884
Head: Miss J Raines
Type: Co-educational Day 5-7
No of Pupils: B110 G110
Fees: (September 95) £5250

NORTH BRIDGE HOUSE SCHOOL
33 Fitzjohn's Avenue, London, NW3 5JY
Tel: (0171) 435 9641
Head: Mrs R Allsopp
Type: Co-educational Day 2-5
No of Pupils: 210
Fees: (September 95) £5250

THE PHOENIX SCHOOL
36 College Crescent, London, NW3 5LF
Tel: (0171) 711 4433
Head: J Clegg
Type: Co-educational Day 3-7
No of Pupils: B48 G20
Fees: (September 95) £800 - £1650

THE ROYAL SCHOOL, HAMPSTEAD*
Vane House, 65 Rosslyn Hill, Hampstead, London, NW3 5UD
Tel: (0171) 794 7708
Head: Mrs C Sibson
Type: Girls Boarding & Day 4-18
No of Pupils: 188 No of Boarders F51
Fees: (September 95) FB £7050 - £8670 WB £6450 - £8070 DAY £3150 - £3690

SOUTHBANK INTERNATIONAL SCHOOL, HAMPSTEAD*
16 Netherhall Gardens, Hampstead, London, NW3
Tel: (0171) 229 8230
Head: Milton Toubkin & Mrs Jane Treftz
Type: Co-educational Day 3-13
Fees: (September 95) £3600 - £8340

ST ANTHONY'S PREPARATORY SCHOOL
90 Fitzjohns Avenue, Hampstead, London, NW3 6NP
Tel: (0171) 435 3597
Head: N Pitel
Type: Boys Day 6-13
No of Pupils: 260
Fees: (September 95) £5025 - £5160

ST CHRISTOPHER'S SCHOOL
32 Belsize Lane, London, NW3 5AE
Tel: (0171) 435 1521
Head: Mrs F Cook
Type: Girls Day 4-11
No of Pupils: 230
Fees: (September 95) £4560 - £4830

ST MARGARET'S SCHOOL*
18 Kidderpore Gardens, London, NW3 7SR
Tel: (0171) 435 2439
Head: Mrs S Meaden
Type: Girls Day 5-16
No of Pupils: 140
Fees: (September 95) £3510 - £4155

ST MARY'S HAMPSTEAD
47 Fitzjohn's Avenue, London, NW3 6PG
Tel: (0171) 435 1868
Head: Mrs W Nash
Type: Girls Day 3-11 (Boys 3-7)
No of Pupils: B45 G155
Fees: (September 95) £4125

SARUM HALL
15 Eton Avenue, London, NW3 3EL
Tel: (0171) 794 2261
Head: Lady Smith-Gordon
Type: Girls Day 3-11 (Boys 3-5)
No of Pupils: 170
Fees: (September 95) £4875

SOUTH HAMPSTEAD HIGH SCHOOL
3 Maresfield Gardens, Camden, London, NW3 5SS
Tel: (0171) 435 2899
Head: Mrs J G Scott
Type: Girls Day 4-18
No of Pupils: 890
Fees: (September 95) £3744 - £4644

TREVOR ROBERTS'
57 Eton Avenue, London, NW3 3ET
Tel: (0171) 586 1444
Head: C Trevor-Roberts
Type: Co-educational Day 5-14
No of Pupils: 109
Fees: (September 95) £7050

UNIVERSITY COLLEGE SCHOOL
Frognal, Hampstead, London, NW3 6XH
Tel: (0171) 435 2215
Head: G D Slaughter
Type: Boys Day 11-18
No of Pupils: 700
Fees: (September 95) £6825

UNIVERSITY COLLEGE SCHOOL, JUNIOR BRANCH
11 Holly Hill, London, NW3 6QN
Tel: (0171) 435 3068
Head: J F Hubbard
Type: Boys Day 7-12
No of Pupils: 250
Fees: (September 95) £6390

THE VILLAGE SCHOOL
2 Parkhill Road, Belsize Park, London, NW3 2YN
Tel: (0171) 485 4673
Head: Mrs F M Prior
Type: Girls Day 4-11
No of Pupils: 140
Fees: (September 94) £3600 - £4470

WILLOUGHBY HALL SCHOOL
1 Willoughby Road, Hampstead, London, NW3 1RP
Tel: (0171) 794 3538
Head: Mrs Gillian McAndrew
Type: Co-educational Day B3-8 G3-11
No of Pupils: 140
Fees: (September 95) £3600 - £4800

NW4

THE ALBANY COLLEGE
23/24 Queen's Road, Hendon, London, NW4 2TL
Tel: (0181) 202 9748
Head: R J Arthy
Type: Co-educational Day 14-19
No of Pupils: B110 G80
Fees: (September 95) 3 A Levels £7200 5 GCSEs £6500

HENDON PREPARATORY SCHOOL
20 Tenterden Grove, Hendon, London, NW4 1TD
Tel: (0181) 203 7727
Head: T Lee
Type: Co-educational Day B3-13 G3-11
No of Pupils: B167 G91
Fees: (September 94) £5088

NW5

L'ILE AUX ENFANTS
22 Vicar's Road, London, NW5 4NL
Tel: (0171) 267 7119
Head: Miss C Chagny
Type: Co-educational Day 2-11
No of Pupils: 150
Fees: (September 95) £2355

NW6

BROADHURST SCHOOL
19 Greencroft Gardens, London, NW6 3LP
Tel: (0171) 328 4280
Head: Miss D Berkery
Type: Co-educational Day 2-5
No of Pupils: B68 G92
Fees: (September 95) £2775 - £465

JEWISH PREPARATORY SCHOOL
21 Andover Place, London, NW6 5ED
Tel: (0171) 328 2802
Head: Mrs K Peters
Type: Co-educational Day 3-11
No of Pupils: B70 G51
Fees: (September 95) £3300 - £4050

RAINBOW MONTESSORI SCHOOL
13 Woodchurch Road, Hampstead, London, NW6 3PL
Tel: (0171) 328 8986
Head: Mrs Linda Madden
Type: Co-educational Day 2-11
No of Pupils: 70
Fees: (January 94) £1650 - £3600

RAINBOW MONTESSORI SCHOOL
St James's Hall, Sherriff Road, West Hampstead, London, NW6 2AP
Tel: (0171) 328 8986
Head: Mrs Linda Madden
Type: Co-educational Day 2-5
No of Pupils: 24
Fees: (September 94) £1500 - £2160

NW7

BELMONT (MILL HILL JUNIOR SCHOOL)
Mill Hill, London, NW7 4ED
Tel: (0181) 959 1431
Head: J R Hawkins
Type: Boys Day 7-13
No of Pupils: 310
Fees: (September 95) £5835

GOODWYN SCHOOL
Hammers Lane, Mill Hill, London, NW7 4DB
Tel: (0181) 959 3756
Head: S W Robertson
Type: Co-educational Day 3-7
No of Pupils: B100 G100
Fees: (September 94) £1854 - £3708

MATHILDA MARKS-KENNEDY SCHOOL
68 Hale Lane, Mill Hill, London, NW7 3RT
Tel: (0181) 959 6089
Head: Mrs J Shindler
Type: Co-educational Day 2-11
No of Pupils: 180
Fees: (September 95) £2985

MILL HILL SCHOOL*
Mill Hill Village, London, NW7 1QS
Tel: (0181) 959 1176
Head: E A MacAlpine
Type: Boys Boarding & Day 13-18 (Co-ed VIth form)
No of Pupils: B490 G30 No of Boarders F190
Fees: (September 95) FB £11640 DAY £7530

THE MOUNT SCHOOL*
Milespit Hill, Mill Hill, London, NW7 2RX
Tel: (0181) 959 3403
Head: Mrs M Pond
Type: Girls Day 5-18
No of Pupils: 400
Fees: (September 95) £3180 - £3555

ST MARTIN'S
22 Goodwyn Avenue, Mill Hill, London, NW7 3RG
Tel: (0181) 959 1965
Head: Mrs S Braud
Type: Co-educational Day B4-7 G4-11
No of Pupils: B30 G85
Fees: (September 95) £1700 - £2000

NW8

ABERCORN PLACE SCHOOL*
28 Abercorn Place, London, NW8 9XP
Tel: (0171) 286 4785
Head: Mrs A S Greystoke
Type: Co-educational Day 2-13
No of Pupils: B100 G95
Fees: (September 95) £3105 - £5685

THE AMERICAN SCHOOL IN LONDON*
2-8 Loudoun Road, London, NW8 0NP
Tel: (0171) 722 0101
Head: Dr J R Glickman
Type: Co-educational Day 4-18
No of Pupils: B653 G591
Fees: (September 95) £8275 - £9750

ARNOLD HOUSE SCHOOL
1-3 Loudoun Road, St John's Wood,
London, NW8 0LH
Tel: (0171) 286 1100
Head: N M Allen
Type: Boys Day 5-13
No of Pupils: 230
Fees: (September 95) £5505

MCCAFFREYS SCHOOL
2 Langford Place, London,
NW8
Tel: (0171) 624 2325
Head: Ms M Deniya
Type: Co-educational Day 3-7
No of Pupils: 70
Fees: (September 95) £2535 - £4485

ST CHRISTINA'S RC PREPARATORY SCHOOL
25 St Edmunds Terrace, Regents
Park, London, NW8 7PY
Tel: (0171) 722 8784
Head: Sister Mary Corr
Type: Girls Day 3-11 (Boys 3-7)
No of Pupils: B40 G180
Fees: (September 95) £3300

NW9

GOWER HOUSE SCHOOL
Blackbird Hill, London, NW9 8RR
Tel: (0181) 205 2509
Head: M Keane
Type: Co-educational Day 2-11
No of Pupils: 200
Fees: (September 95) £2130 - £3105

ST NICHOLAS SCHOOL
22 Salmon Street, London,
NW9
Tel: (0181) 205 7153
Head: Mrs Y Fisher
Type: Co-educational Day 5-11
No of Pupils: 70
Fees: (September 95) £2340

NW11

GOLDERS HILL SCHOOL
666 Finchley Road, London,
NW11 7NT
Tel: (0181) 455 2589
Head: Mrs A Eglash
Type: Co-educational Day 2-7
No of Pupils: B80 G60
Fees: (September 95) £2100 - £4000

THE KING ALFRED SCHOOL*
North End Road, London, NW11 7HY
Tel: (0181) 457 5200
Head: F P Moran
Type: Co-educational Day 4-18
No of Pupils: B232 G224
Fees: (September 95) £3780 - £6450

LES POUSSINS
5 Brunner Close, London, NW11 6NP
Tel: (0181) 882 6980
Type: Co-educational Day 5-11
Fees: On application

MENORAH GRAMMAR SCHOOL
Beverley Gardens, Golders Green,
London, NW11 9DG
Tel: (0181) 458 8354
Head: Rabbi A M Goldblatt
Type: Boys Day 11-18
No of Pupils: 135
Fees: On application

POMME D'API
86 Wildwood Road, Hampstead
Garden Suburb, London, NW11 6UJ
Tel: (0181) 455 1417
Head: Mrs R Gill
Type: Co-educational Day 1-5
No of Pupils: 20
Fees: (September 95) £1200 - £1500

THE TUITION CENTRE
8 Accommodation Road, Golders
Green, London, NW11 8ED
Tel: (0181) 201 8020
Head: B Canetti
Type: Co-educational Day 15+
No of Pupils: B25 G20
Fees: (September 95) 3 A Levels
£6800   5 GCSEs £6100

SE1

HIGHWAY CHRISTIAN SCHOOL
Union Chapel, 255 Tooley Street,
Bermondsey, London, SE1 2LA
Tel: (0171) 403 6192
Head: K R Dilliway
Type: Co-educational Day 5-11
No of Pupils: B38 G32
Fees: (September 95) £1956

SE3

BLACKHEATH HIGH SCHOOL GPDST
Vanbrugh Park, Blackheath,
London, SE3 7AG
Tel: (0181) 853 2929
Head: Miss R K Musgrave
Type: Girls Day 4-18
No of Pupils: 596
Fees: (September 95) £3576 - £4644

CHRISTS COLLEGE*
4 St Germans Place, Blackheath,
London, SE3 0NJ
Tel: (0181) 858 0692
Head: R Bellerby
Type: Co-educational Boarding &
Day 4-19
No of Pupils: 200 No of Boarders F80
Fees: (September 95) FB £8200 -
£9900 WB £7000 - £9200 DAY
£2900 - £4600

HEATH HOUSE PREPARATORY SCHOOL
37 Wemyss Road, Blackheath,
London, SE3 0TG
Tel: (0181) 297 1900
Head: I Laslett
Type: Co-educational Day
No of Pupils: B12 G12
Fees: (September 95) £1150 - £1316

THE POINTER SCHOOL
19 Stratheden Road, Blackheath,
London, SE3 7TH
Tel: (0181) 293 1331
Head: R J S Higgins
Type: Co-educational Day 3-11
No of Pupils: B45 G45
Fees: (September 95) £1785 - £3450

SE4

SHEPHERDS COMMUNITY SCHOOL
71 Tressillian Road, Brockley,
London, SE4
Tel: (0181) 692 5015
Head: D Potts
Type: Co-educational Day 3-8
Fees: (September 95) £680

SE6

PRIORY HOUSE SCHOOL
61 Bromley Road, London,
SE6
Tel: (0181) 697 4518
Head: Mrs H Thomas
Type: Co-educational Day 3-11
No of Pupils: 100
Fees: (September 94) £1980 - £2040

ST DUNSTAN'S COLLEGE*
Stanstead Road, Catford, London,
SE6 4TY
Tel: (0181) 690 1274
Head: J D Moore
Type: Co-educational Day 4-18
No of Pupils: 800
Fees: (September 95) £3465 - £5370

SE9

ELTHAM COLLEGE
Grove Park Road, Mottingham,
London, SE9 4QF
Tel: (0181) 857 1455
Head: D M Green
Type: Boys Day & Boarding 7-18
(Co-ed VIth form)
No of Pupils: B730 G50 No of
Boarders F15
Fees: (September 95) FB £11505 DAY
£4200 - £5451

ST OLAVES PREPARATORY
SCHOOL
106-110 Southwood Road, New
Eltham, London, SE9 3QS
Tel: (0181) 850 9175
Head: P D Stradling
Type: Co-educational Day 3-11
No of Pupils: B110 G90
Fees: (September 95) £1608 - £3672

SE11

TOAD HALL MONTESSORI
NURSERY SCHOOL
37 St Mary's Gardens, Kennington,
London, SE11 4UF
Tel: (0171) 735 5087
Head: Mrs V K Rees
Type: Co-educational Day 2-5
No of Pupils: 40
Fees: (September 95) £1845

SE12

COLFE'S SCHOOL
Horn Park Lane, London, SE12 8AW
Tel: (0181) 852 2283
Head: Dr D Richardson
Type: Boys Day 7-18 (Co-ed 3-6 and
16-18)
No of Pupils: B920 G51
Fees: (September 95) £3225 - £5025

RIVERSTON SCHOOL
63-69 Eltham Road, London,
SE12 8UF
Tel: (0181) 318 4327
Head: D M Lewis
Type: Co-educational Day 2-16
No of Pupils: B410 G180
Fees: (September 95) £2811 - £3729

SE19

VIRGO FIDELIS CONVENT
Central Hill, Upper Norwood,
London, SE19 1RS
Tel: (0181) 670 6917
Head: Sister Madeleine & Sister
Renata
Type: Girls Day 3-18 (Boys 3-8, with
option to stay until 11)
No of Pupils: 370
Fees: (September 95) £1100 - £4275

SE21

DULWICH COLLEGE*
Dulwich, London, SE21 7LD
Tel: (0181) 693 3601
Type: Boys Day & Boarding 7-18
No of Pupils: 1400 No of Boarders
F50 W50
Fees: (September 95) FB £12270 WB
£11775 DAY £5811 - £6135

DULWICH COLLEGE
PREPARATORY SCHOOL
42 Alleyn Park, Dulwich, London,
SE21 7AA
Tel: (0181) 670 3217
Head: G Marsh
Type: Boys Boarding & Day 3-13
(Girls 3-5)
No of Pupils: B723 G12 No of
Boarders W22
Fees: (September 95) WB £8145 -
£8790 DAY £3600 - £5880

DULWICH MONTESSORI
NURSERY SCHOOL
All Saints Church, Rosendale Road,
London, SE21 8LN
Tel: (0181) 761 9560
Head: Mrs E Irwin
Type: Co-educational Day 2-6
No of Pupils: 40
Fees: (September 95) £1545

JAMES ALLEN'S
PREPARATORY SCHOOL
East Dulwich Grove, London,
SE22 8TE
Tel: (0181) 693 0374
Head: P Heyworth
Type: Co-educational Day 4-11
No of Pupils: 295
Fees: (September 95) £4335 - £4515

OAKFIELD PREPARATORY
SCHOOL
Thurlow Park Road, Dulwich,
London, SE21 8HP
Tel: (0181) 670 4206
Head: Mrs A Tompkins
Type: Co-educational Day 2-11
No of Pupils: B285 G232
Fees: (September 95) £3600

ROSEMEAD PREPARATORY
SCHOOL*
70 Thurlow Park Road, London,
SE21 8HZ
Tel: (0181) 670 5865
Head: Mrs R Lait
Type: Co-educational Day 3-11
No of Pupils: B130 G130
Fees: (September 95) £3000 - £3570

SE22

ALLEYN'S SCHOOL
Townley Road, Dulwich, London,
SE22 8SU
Tel: (0181) 693 3422
Head: Dr C H Niven
Type: Co-educational Day 5-18
No of Pupils: B458 G456
Fees: (September 95) £5640

JAMES ALLEN'S GIRLS'
SCHOOL
East Dulwich Grove, London,
SE22 8TE
Tel: (0181) 693 1181
Head: Mrs M Gibbs
Type: Girls Day 11-18
No of Pupils: 740
Fees: (September 95) £5505 - £5700

SE26

SYDENHAM HIGH SCHOOL
19 Westwood Hill, London, SE26 6BL
Tel: (0181) 778 8737
Head: Mrs G Baker
Type: Girls Day 4-18
No of Pupils: 700
Fees: (September 95) £3576 - £4644

SW1

EATON HOUSE SCHOOL
3 and 5 Eaton Gate, Eaton Square,
London, SW1
Tel: (0171) 730 9343
Head: Mrs J Aviss
Type: Boys Day 4-9
No of Pupils: 250
Fees: (September 95) £4560

EATON SQUARE SCHOOL
79 Eccleston Square, London,
SW1V 1PP
Tel: (0171) 931 9469
Head: Miss Y Cuthbert
Type: Co-educational Day 2-11
No of Pupils: B115 G115
Fees: (September 95) £2175 - £5895

FRANCIS HOLLAND SCHOOL
39 Graham Terrace, London,
SW1W 8JF
Tel: (0171) 730 2971
Head: Mrs J A Anderson
Type: Girls Day 4-18
No of Pupils: 350
Fees: (September 95) £5040 - £5940

GARDEN HOUSE SCHOOL*
53 Sloane Gardens, London,
SW1W 8ED
Tel: (0171) 730 1652
Head: Mrs R Whaley
Type: Girls Day 3-11 (Boys 3-8)
No of Pupils: B75 G255
Fees: (September 95) £2700 - £6150

HELLENIC COLLEGE OF LONDON
67 Pont Street, London, SW1X 0BD
Tel: (0171) 581 5044
Head: J Wardrobe
Type: Co-educational Day 2-18
No of Pupils: B100 G110
Fees: (September 95) £3675 - £4785

HILL HOUSE SCHOOL*
17 Hans Place, London, SW1X 0EP
Tel: (0171) 584 1331
Head: Lt Col H S Townend
Type: Co-educational Day 3-13
No of Pupils: 1050
Fees: (September 95) £3800 - £4900

MISS MORLEYS NURSERY SCHOOL
Fountain Court Club Room, Ebury
Square, London, SW1
Tel: (0171) 730 5797
Head: Mrs C Spence
Type: Co-educational Day 2-5
No of Pupils: 25
Fees: (September 95) £1725 - £1950

MORE HOUSE
22-24 Pont Street, Chelsea, London,
SW1X 0AA
Tel: (0171) 235 2855
Head: Miss M Connell
Type: Girls Day 11-18
No of Pupils: 230
Fees: (September 95) £5460

ST JAMES INDEPENDENT SCHOOL FOR BOYS
61 Eccleston Square, London,
SW1V 1PH
Tel: (0171) 834 0471
Head: N Debenham
Type: Boys Day 10-19
No of Pupils: 180
Fees: (September 95) £4620 - £4755

SUSSEX HOUSE SCHOOL
68 Cadogan Square, Knightsbridge,
London, SW1X 0EA
Tel: (0171) 584 1741
Head: N P Kaye
Type: Boys Day 8-13
No of Pupils: 172
Fees: (September 95) £5745

THOMAS'S KINDERGARTEN
14 Ranelagh Grove, London,
SW1W 8PD
Tel: (0171) 730 3596
Head: Miss A Everett-Heath
Type: Co-educational Day 2-5
No of Pupils: B30 G30
Fees: (September 95) £1365 - £2100

WESTMINSTER ABBEY CHOIR SCHOOL
London, SW1P 3NY
Tel: (0171) 222 6151
Head: G Roland-Adams
Type: Boys Boarding 7-13
No of Pupils: 38 No of Boarders F38
Fees: (September 95) FB £2619

WESTMINSTER CATHEDRAL CHOIR SCHOOL
Ambrosden Avenue, London,
SW1P 1QH
Tel: (0171) 798 9081
Head: C Foulds
Type: Boys Boarding & Day 8-13
No of Pupils: 90 No of Boarders F30
Fees: (September 95) FB £2910 -
£3240 DAY £5880

WESTMINSTER SCHOOL
Little Dean's Yard, Westminster,
London, SW1P 3PF
Tel: (0171) 963 1003
Head: D M Summerscale
Type: Boys Boarding & Day 13-18
(Co-ed VIth form)
No of Pupils: B580 G80 No of
Boarders W220
Fees: (September 95) FB £12900 DAY
£8850 - £9675

WESTMINSTER UNDER SCHOOL
Adrian House, 27 Vincent Square,
London, SW1P 2NN
Tel: (0171) 821 5788
Head: G Ashton
Type: Boys Day 8-13
No of Pupils: 260
Fees: (September 95) £6165

YOUNG ENGLAND KINDERGARTEN
St Saviour's Hall, St George's
Square, London, SW1V 2HP
Tel: (0171) 834 3171
Head: Mrs K King
Type: Co-educational Day 2-5
No of Pupils: 75
Fees: (September 95) £1410 - £2175

SW2

SOMERVILLE SCHOOL
12 Wavertree Road, London,
SW2 3SJ
Tel: (0181) 674 5495
Head: Mrs E A Tye
Type: Co-educational Day 3-7
No of Pupils: B40 G30
Fees: (September 95) £2100

SW3

CAMERON HOUSE
4 The Vale, Chelsea, London,
SW3 4AH
Tel: (0171) 352 4040
Head: Mrs F M Stack
Type: Co-educational Day 4-11
No of Pupils: 100
Fees: (September 95) £5760

JAMAHIRIYA SCHOOL
Glebe Place, London, SW3 5JP
Tel: (0171) 352 6642
Head: M Shelli
Type: Co-educational Day 5-15
No of Pupils: B50 G60
Fees: On application

THE KNIGHTSBRIDGE KINDERGARTENS
St Saviours Church, Walton Street,
London, SW3 1RJ
Tel: (0171) 351 0368
Head: Mrs J Ewing-Hoy
Type: Co-educational Day 2-5
No of Pupils: B20 G20
Fees: (September 95) £2250

SW4

EATON HOUSE THE MANOR
58 Clapham Common Northside,
London, SW4 9RU
Tel: (0171) 924 6000
Head: S Hepher & Miss P de Giles
Type: Boys Day 2-13 (Girls 2-4)
No of Pupils: 360
Fees: (September 95) £900 - £5250

PARKGATE MONTESSORI
Parkgate House, 80 Clapham
Common North Side, London,
SW4 9SD
Tel: (0171) 350 2452
Head: Miss C Shanley
Type: Co-educational Day 2-7
No of Pupils: B60 G60
Fees: (September 95) £1785 - £4485

SW5

COLLINGHAM
23 Collingham Gardens, London,
SW5 0HL
Tel: (0171) 244 7414
Head: G Hattee
Type: Co-educational Day 14-19
No of Pupils: B140 G120
Fees: (September 95) £7800

SW6

AL-MUNTADA ISLAMIC SCHOOL
7 Bridges Place, Parsons Green,
London, SW6 4HW
Tel: (0171) 371 7308
Head: Z Chemimi
Type: Co-educational Day 4-11
No of Pupils: B68 G55
Fees: (September 95) £1225

BLOOMSBURY COLLEGE
52a Walham Grove, London,
SW6 1QR
Tel: (0171) 381 0213
Head: S Howse
Type: Co-educational Day 15-22
No of Pupils: B40 G20
Fees: (September 95) 3 A Levels/5
GCSEs £4950

L'ECOLE DES PETITS
2 Hazelbury Road, London, SW6 2NB
Tel: (0171) 371 8350
Type: Co-educational Day 2-6
(Bilingual)
No of Pupils: 120
Fees: (September 95) £2100 - £3060

LE HERISSON
St Peter's Church Hall, St Peter's
Terrace, London, SW6
Tel: (0171) 381 6758
Head: B Rios
Type: Co-educational Day 2-6
No of Pupils: 36
Fees: (September 94) £1740 - £2535

RISING STAR MONTESSORI SCHOOL
St Clement Church Hall, 286 Fulham
Palace Road, London, SW6 6HP
Tel: (0171) 381 3511
Head: Mrs H Casson
Type: Co-educational Day 2-5
No of Pupils: 24
Fees: (September 95) £1560

SINCLAIR HOUSE SCHOOL
159 Munster Road, Fulham, London,
SW6 6AD
Tel: (0171) 736 9182
Head: Mrs E A Sinclair-House
Type: Co-educational Day 2-8
No of Pupils: 55
Fees: (September 95) £1950 - £3750

TWICE TIMES MONTESSORI SCHOOL
The Cricket Pavilion, South Park,
London, SW6 3AF
Tel: (0171) 731 4929
Head: Mrs S Henderson
Type: Co-educational Day 2-5
No of Pupils: B25 G25
Fees: (September 95) £1785

SW7

DUFF MILLER COLLEGE
59 Queen's Gate, London, SW7 5JP
Tel: (0171) 225 0577
Head: Clive Denning and G Dalle
Type: Co-educational Day 13-18
No of Pupils: B73 G77
Fees: (September 95) 3 A Levels
£7050-£7800
5 GCSEs £5985

FALKNER HOUSE*
19 Brechin Place, London, SW7 4QB
Tel: (0171) 373 4501
Head: Mrs J Bird
Type: Girls Day 4-11
No of Pupils: 140
Fees: (September 95) £5250

GLENDOWER PREPARATORY SCHOOL*
87 Queen's Gate, South Kensington,
London, SW7 5JX
Tel: (0171) 370 1927
Head: Mrs B Humber
Type: Girls Day 4-12
No of Pupils: 178
Fees: (September 95) £4800

THE HAMPSHIRE SCHOOL (KNIGHTSBRIDGE UNDER SCHOOL)
5 Wetherby Place, London, SW7 4NX
Tel: (0171) 584 3297
Head: A G Bray
Type: Co-educational Day 3-6
No of Pupils: B45 G45
Fees: (September 95) £2100 - £4428

THE HAMPSHIRE SCHOOL (KNIGHTSBRIDGE UPPER SCHOOL)
63 Ennismore Gardens, London,
SW7 1NH
Tel: (0171) 584 3297
Head: A G Bray
Type: Co-educational Day B6-8
G6-11
No of Pupils: B32 G80
Fees: (September 95) £4740 - £6624

LYCEE FRANCAIS CHARLES DE GAULLE
35 Cromwell Road, London,
SW7 2DG
Tel: (0171) 584 6322
Head: Dr H L Brusa
Type: Co-educational Day 4-19
No of Pupils: B1204 G1336
Fees: (September 95) £1779 - £2916

MANDER PORTMAN WOODWARD*
24 Elvaston Place, London, SW7 5NL
Tel: (0171) 584 8555
Head: Dr N Stout
Type: Co-educational Day 14-19
No of Pupils: 400
Fees: (September 95) 7 GCSEs £9723
3 A Levels £9171

MONTESSORI - ST NICHOLAS SCHOOL
23-24 Prince's Gate, London,
SW7 1PT
Tel: (0171) 589 3095
Head: Mrs R E Hinde
Type: Co-educational Day 3-8
No of Pupils: 85
Fees: (September 95) £1950 - £3000

QUEEN'S GATE SCHOOL*
131-133 Queen's Gate, Kensington,
London, SW7 5LE
Tel: (0171) 589 3587
Head: Mrs A M Holyoak
Type: Girls Day 4-18
No of Pupils: 350
Fees: (September 95) £3480 - £5400

ST JAMES INDEPENDENT SCHOOL FOR BOYS*

91 Queen's Gate, London, SW7 5AB
Tel: (0171) 373 5638
Head: P Moss
Type: Boys Day 4-10
No of Pupils: 147
Fees: (September 95) £3300 - £3750

ST JAMES INDEPENDENT SCHOOL FOR GIRLS*

91 Queen's Gate, London, SW7 5AB
Tel: (0171) 373 5638
Head: P Moss
Type: Girls Day 4-10
No of Pupils: 123
Fees: (September 95) £3300 - £3750

ST PHILIP'S SCHOOL*

6 Wetherby Place, London, SW7 4NE
Tel: (0171) 373 3944
Head: H Biggs-Davison
Type: Boys Day 7-13
No of Pupils: 100
Fees: (September 95) £4305

THE VALE SCHOOL

2 Elvaston Place, London, SW7 5QH
Tel: (0171) 730 9343
Head: Miss S Calder
Type: Co-educational Day B4-9 G4-11
No of Pupils: B40 G60
Fees: (September 95) £4560

SW8

NEWTON PREPARATORY SCHOOL*

149 Battersea Park Road, London, SW8 4BH
Tel: (0171) 720 4091
Head: R Dell
Type: Co-educational Day 3-13
No of Pupils: B150 G100
Fees: (September 95) £4725 - £5415

THE WILLOW SCHOOL

c/o Clapham Baptist Church,
823-825 Wandsworth Road,
London, SW8
Tel: (0171) 498 0319
Head: Mrs C Kane
Type: Co-educational Day 2-5
No of Pupils: 38
Fees: (September 95) £1575 - £1725

SW10

THE BOLTONS NURSERY SCHOOL

262 Fulham Road, London, SW10
Tel: (0171) 351 6993
Head: Miss V Harting
Type: Co-educational Day 2-5
No of Pupils: 60
Fees: (September 95) £1710 - £2190

THE CHELSEA NURSERY SCHOOL

Worlds End Place, Kings Road,
Chelsea, London, SW10 0DR
Tel: (0171) 351 0993
Head: Mrs O Lovelace
Type: Co-educational Day 2-5
No of Pupils: 30
Fees: (September 94) £600 - £1050

KNIGHTSBRIDGE KINDERGARTEN TWO

St Andrews Church, Park Walk,
Chelsea, London, SW10 0AU
Tel: (0171) 351 0368
Head: Miss S Corlett
Type: Co-educational Day 2-5
No of Pupils: B20 G20
Fees: (September 94) £2025

THE OCTAGON SCHOOL

459A Fulham Road, London,
SW10 9UZ
Tel: (0171) 351 4142
Head: E J Cussell
Type: Co-educational Day 3-13
Fees: (September 95) £2490 - £5625

PAINT POTS MONTESSORI SCHOOL CHELSEA

Chelsea Christian Centre, Edith
Grove, London, SW10 0LB
Tel: (0171) 792 0433
Head: Georgina Hood
Type: Co-educational Day 2-5
No of Pupils: 35
Fees: (September 95) £1167 - £3618

REDCLIFFE SCHOOL*

47 Redcliffe Gardens, London,
SW10 9JH
Tel: (0171) 352 9247
Head: Miss R E Cunnah
Type: Co-educational Day B4-8 G4-11
No of Pupils: B37 G60
Fees: (September 95) £4620

SW11

BRIDGE LANE MONTESSORI SCHOOL

23 Bridge Lane, London, SW11 3AD
Tel: (0171) 228 9403
Head: Mrs J Brittain
Type: Co-educational Day 2-6
No of Pupils: 40
Fees: (September 95) £1800 - £2550

CALDER HOUSE SCHOOL

142 Battersea Park Road, London,
SW11 4NB
Tel: (0171) 720 8783
Head: Mrs L Robertson
Type: Co-educational Day 6-13
No of Pupils: 32
Fees: (September 95) £9300

EMANUEL SCHOOL

Battersea Rise, London, SW11 1HS
Tel: (0181) 870 4171
Head: T Jones-Parry
Type: Boys Day 10-19 (Co-ed VIth
form. Girls accepted at 10+, 11+
from September 1996)
No of Pupils: 720
Fees: (September 95) £4287 - £4587

HORNSBY HOUSE SCHOOL

Hearnville Road, London, SW12 8RS
Tel: (0181) 675 1255
Head: Mrs E Nightingale
Type: Co-educational Day 3-11
No of Pupils: B80 G80
Fees: (September 95) £495 - £1515

NORTHCOTE LODGE

26 Bolingbroke Grove, London,
SW11 6EL
Tel: (0171) 924 7170
Head: D Bain
Type: Boys Day 7-13
No of Pupils: 70
Fees: (September 95) £5985

THE PARK NURSERY SCHOOL

St Saviours' Church, 351 Battersea
Park Road, London, SW11 4LH
Tel: (0171) 627 5125
Head: Mrs Alison Dady
Type: Co-educational Day 2-5
No of Pupils: 30
Fees: (September 95) £1560 - £1950

THOMAS'S KINDERGARTEN, BATTERSEA

The Crypt, Saint Mary's Church,
Battersea Church Road, London,
SW11 3NA
Tel: (0171) 738 0400
Head: Miss S Wakefield
Type: Co-educational Day 2-5
No of Pupils: B25 G25
Fees: (September 95) £1365 - £2100

THOMAS'S PREPARATORY SCHOOL

28-40 Battersea High Street, London, SW11 3JB
Tel: (0171) 978 4224
Head: Miss J Kelham
Type: Co-educational Day 4-13
No of Pupils: B228 G225
Fees: (September 95) £5265 - £6150

THOMAS'S PREPARATORY SCHOOL CLAPHAM

Broomwood Road, London, SW11 6JZ
Tel: (0171) 924 5006
Head: Mrs P Evelegh
Type: Co-educational Day 4-13
No of Pupils: 265
Fees: (September 95) £5250 - £6150

SW12

BALHAM PREPARATORY SCHOOL

47a Balham High Road, London, SW12
Tel: (0181) 675 7747
Head: M I Abrahams
Type: Co-educational Day 3-11
No of Pupils: B33 G35
Fees: (September 95) £320 - £400

BROOMWOOD HALL SCHOOL

74 Nightingale Lane, London, SW12 8NR
Tel: (0181) 673 1616
Head: Mrs K A Colquhoun
Type: Co-educational Day B4-8 G4-12
No of Pupils: B110 G170
Fees: (September 95) £4500 - £5280

WALDORF SCHOOL OF SOUTH WEST LONDON

12 Balham Park Road, London, SW12 8DR
Tel: (0181) 769 6587
Type: Co-educational Day 4-11
No of Pupils: B50 G30
Fees: (September 93) £1350 - £1800

WOODENTOPS PRE-PREPARATORY SCHOOL & KINDERGARTEN

72 Thornton Road, Clapham Park, London, SW12 0LF
Tel: (0181) 674 9514
Head: Mrs M E McCahery
Type: Co-educational Day 2-8
No of Pupils: B30 G30
Fees: (September 95) £1635 - £2850

SW13

THE HARRODIAN SCHOOL

Lonsdale Road, London, SW13 9QN
Tel: (0181) 748 6117
Head: Lady Houstoun-Boswall
Type: Co-educational Day 7-13
No of Pupils: 130
Fees: (September 95) £5700

ST PAUL'S PREPARATORY SCHOOL

Colet Court, Lonsdale Road, London, SW13 9JT
Tel: (0181) 748 3461
Head: G J Thompson
Type: Boys Day & Boarding 7-13
No of Pupils: 440 No of Boarders F15
Fees: (September 95) F/WB £9543 DAY £6198

ST PAUL'S SCHOOL

Lonsdale Road, Barnes, London, SW13 9JT
Tel: (0181) 748 9162
Head: R S Baldock
Type: Boys Day & Boarding 13-18
No of Pupils: 777 No of Boarders W80
Fees: (September 95) F/WB £12357 DAY £8082

SW14

TOWER HOUSE SCHOOL

188 Sheen Lane, London, SW14 8LF
Tel: (0181) 876 3323
Head: J D T Wall
Type: Boys Day 5-13
No of Pupils: 170
Fees: (September 95) £4785

SW15

THE HALL SCHOOL WIMBLEDON

Beavers Holt, Stroud Crescent, Putney Vale, London, SW15 3EQ
Tel: (0181) 788 2370
Head: T J Hobbs
Type: Co-educational Day 3-13
No of Pupils: 250
Fees: (September 95) £1500 - £5056

HURLINGHAM PRIVATE SCHOOL

95 & 97 Deodar Road, Putney, London, SW15 2NU
Tel: (0181) 874 1673
Head: Miss R Whitehead
Type: Co-educational Day B4-8 G4-11
No of Pupils: B34 G63
Fees: (September 95) £2550 - £3450

IBSTOCK PLACE, THE FROEBEL SCHOOL*

Clarence Lane, Roehampton, London, SW15 5PY
Tel: (0181) 876 9991
Head: Mrs F Bayliss
Type: Co-educational Day 3-16
No of Pupils: 450
Fees: (September 95) £1650 - £5250

LION HOUSE SCHOOL

The Old Methodist Hall, Gwendolen Avenue, London, SW15 6EH
Tel: (0181) 780 9446
Head: Miss H J Luard
Type: Co-educational Day 3-8
No of Pupils: B44 G41
Fees: (September 95) £300 - £1225

THE MERLIN SCHOOL

4 Carlton Drive, Putney Hill, London, SW15 2BZ
Tel: (0181) 788 2769
Head: Mrs J Addis
Type: Co-educational Day 4-8
No of Pupils: 170
Fees: On application

PROSPECT HOUSE SCHOOL

75 Putney Hill, London, SW15 3NT
Tel: (0181) 780 0456
Head: Mrs Eley
Type: Co-educational Day 3-11
No of Pupils: B90 G100
Fees: (September 95) £720 - £1588

PUTNEY HIGH SCHOOL

35 Putney Hill, London, SW15 6BH
Tel: (0181) 788 4886
Head: Mrs E Merchant
Type: Girls Day 4-18
No of Pupils: 847
Fees: (September 95) £3576 - £4644

PUTNEY PARK SCHOOL

Woodborough Road, London, SW15 6PY
Tel: (0181) 788 8316
Head: Miss J Tweedie-Smith
Type: Girls Day 4-16 (Boys 4-8)
No of Pupils: B93 G233
Fees: (September 95) £3810 - £4380

SW16

STREATHAM HILL AND CLAPHAM HIGH SCHOOL

Abbotswood Road, London, SW16 1AW
Tel: (0181) 677 8400
Head: Miss G M Ellis
Type: Girls Day 4-18
No of Pupils: 610
Fees: (September 95) £3576 - £4644

STREATHAM MODERN SCHOOL
508 Streatham High Road, London, SW16 3QB
Tel: (0181) 764 7232
Head: B Russell-Owen
Type: Boys Day 3-12
No of Pupils: 110
Fees: (September 95) £2250

SW17

THE CHILDREN'S HOUSE MONTESSORI NURSERY SCHOOL
London, SW17 0UQ
Tel: (0181) 947 7359
Head: Mrs C Narain
Type: Co-educational Day 2-5
No of Pupils: 32
Fees: (September 95) £1440

EVELINE DAY SCHOOL
14 Trinity Crescent, Upper Tooting, London, SW17
Tel: (0181) 672 4673
Head: Ms E Drut
Type: Co-educational Day 2-11
No of Pupils: B34 G41
Fees: On application

FINTON HOUSE SCHOOL
171 Trinity Road, London, SW17 7HL
Tel: (0181) 682 0921
Head: Miss T O'Neill
Type: Co-educational Day 4-11
No of Pupils: B90 G100
Fees: (September 95) £4650 - £5250

RED BALLOON NURSERY
St Mary Magdalene Church Hall, Trinity Road, London, SW17 7SD
Tel: (0181) 672 4711
Head: Miss T Millington-Drake
Type: Co-educational Day 2-5
No of Pupils: 70
Fees: (September 95) £1800 - £1860

UPPER TOOTING INDEPENDENT HIGH SCHOOL
169 Trinity Road, Tooting, London, SW17 7HL
Tel: (0181) 672 5676
Head: Mrs A Abbott
Type: Co-educational Day 4-16
No of Pupils: B70 G40
Fees: (September 95) £2085 - £2811

SW18

HIGHFIELD SCHOOL
256 Trinity Road, Wandsworth Common, London, SW18 3RQ
Tel: (0181) 874 2778
Head: Mrs V J Lowe
Type: Co-educational Day 2-11
No of Pupils: B85 G45
Fees: (September 95) £1530 - £3660

THE ROCHE SCHOOL
11 Frogmore, Wandsworth, London, SW18 1HW
Tel: (0181) 877 0823
Head: Mrs C Roche
Type: Co-educational Day 2-11
No of Pupils: B75 G75
Fees: (September 95) £4050 - £4545

SW19

KING'S COLLEGE JUNIOR SCHOOL
Southside, Wimbledon Common, London, SW19 4TT
Tel: (0181) 946 2503
Head: C Holloway
Type: Boys Day 7-13
No of Pupils: 460
Fees: (September 95) £5790 - £6120

KING'S COLLEGE SCHOOL
Wimbledon Common, London, SW19 4TT
Tel: (0181) 255 5300
Head: R M Reeve
Type: Boys Day 13-18
No of Pupils: 720
Fees: (September 95) £5760

MONTESSORI 3-5 NURSERY
58 Queens Road, Wimbledon, London, SW19 8LR
Tel: (0181) 946 8139
Head: Mrs I Hodgson
Type: Co-educational Day 2-6
No of Pupils: B50 G50
Fees: (September 95) £1572 - £2991

THE STUDY PREPARATORY SCHOOL
Camp Road, Wimbledon Common, London, SW19 4UN
Tel: (0181) 947 6969
Head: Mrs L Bond
Type: Girls Day 4-11
No of Pupils: 308
Fees: (September 95) £3960 - £4500

WILLINGTON SCHOOL
Worcester Road, Wimbledon, London, SW19 7QQ
Tel: (0181) 944 7020
Head: J A Hey
Type: Boys Day 4-13
No of Pupils: 200
Fees: (September 95) £3750 - £4485

WIMBLEDON COLLEGE PREP SCHOOL
Donhead Lodge, 33 Edge Hill, Wimbledon, London, SW19 4NP
Tel: (0181) 946 7000
Head: D J O'Leary
Type: Boys Day 7-13
No of Pupils: 300
Fees: (September 95) £3075

WIMBLEDON HIGH SCHOOL
Mansel Road, London, SW19 4AB
Tel: (0181) 946 1756
Head: Dr J Clough
Type: Girls Day 5-18
No of Pupils: 810
Fees: (September 95) £3576 - £4644

SW20

HAZELHURST SCHOOL FOR GIRLS
17 The Downs, Wimbledon, London, SW20 8HF
Tel: (0181) 946 1704
Head: Mrs C W Milner-Williams
Type: Girls Day 4-16 (Co-ed 4-7)
No of Pupils: B10 G145
Fees: (September 95) £3090 - £4620

THE NORWEGIAN SCHOOL
28 Arterberry Road, Wimbledon, London, SW20 8AH
Tel: (0181) 947 6617
Head: Mrs V Ligard
Type: Co-educational Day 3-16
No of Pupils: B52 G52
Fees: On application

THE ROWANS SCHOOL
19 Drax Avenue, Wimbledon, London, SW20 0EG
Tel: (0181) 946 8220
Head: Mrs J Anderson
Type: Co-educational Day 3-8
No of Pupils: 120
Fees: (September 95) £1605 - £3045

URSULINE CONVENT PREPARATORY SCHOOL
18 The Downs, London, SW20 8HR
Tel: (0181) 947 0859
Head: Sister B Perrott
Type: Girls Day 4-13 (Boys 4-7)
No of Pupils: B20 G215
Fees: (September 95) £2385

W1

GREAT BEGINNINGS MONTESSORI SCHOOL
82a Chiltern Street, London, W1M 1PS
Tel: (0171) 486 2276
Head: Mrs W Innes
Type: Co-educational Day 2-6
No of Pupils: B25 G25
Fees: (September 95) £2385 - £3450

LONDON MONTESSORI CENTRE LTD
18 Balderton Street, London, W1Y 1TG
Tel: (0171) 493 0165
Head: Mrs J L Britton
Type: Co-educational Day 2-5
No of Pupils: 30
Fees: (September 95) £3600

QUEEN'S COLLEGE*
43-49 Harley Street, London, W1N 2BT
Tel: (0171) 580 1533
Head: The Hon Lady Goodhart
Type: Girls Day 11-18
No of Pupils: 370
Fees: (September 95) £5820

W2

CONNAUGHT HOUSE
47 Connaught Square, London, W2 2HL
Tel: (0171) 262 8830
Head: F Hampton & Mrs J A Hampton
Type: Co-educational Day 4-11
No of Pupils: B41 G41
Fees: (September 95) £3900 - £5250

DAVIES, LAING AND DICK INDEPENDENT VI FORM COLLEGE*
10 Pembridge Square, London, W2 4ED
Tel: (0171) 727 2797
Head: P W Boorman & E Rickards
Type: Co-educational Day 16-20
No of Pupils: B130 G120
Fees: (September 95) £1539 - £7800

DR ROLFE'S MONTESSORI SCHOOL
10 Pembridge Square, London, W2 4ED
Tel: (0171) 727 8300
Head: Miss A Arnold
Type: Co-educational Day 2-5
No of Pupils: 50
Fees: (September 95) £2085 - £4170

THE HAMPSHIRE SCHOOL (KENSINGTON GARDENS)
9 Queensborough Terrace, London, W2 3TB
Tel: (0171) 229 7065
Head: A G Bray
Type: Co-educational Day 3-13
No of Pupils: B80 G80
Fees: (September 95) £2100 - £6402

KENSINGTON PARK SCHOOL
10 Pembridge Square, London, W2 4ED
Tel: (0171) 221 5748
Head: R Walker
Type: Co-educational Day 11-18
No of Pupils: B50 G40
Fees: (September 95) £5490 - £6000

PAINT POTS MONTESSORI SCHOOL
Bayswater United Reform Church, Newton Road, London, W2 5LS
Tel: (0171) 792 0433
Head: Miss G Hood
Type: Co-educational Day 2-5
No of Pupils: B12 G12
Fees: (September 95) £1167 - £3618

PEMBRIDGE HALL
18 Pembridge Square, London, W2 4EH
Tel: (0171) 229 0121
Head: Mrs L Marani
Type: Girls Day 4-11
No of Pupils: 250
Fees: (September 95) £4695

RAVENSTONE HOUSE PRE-PREPARATORY AND NURSERY
The Long Garden, Albion Street, Marble Arch, London, W2
Tel: (0171) 262 1190
Head: Mrs A Saunders
Type: Co-educational Day 1-7
No of Pupils: 100
Fees: (September 95) £1950 - £4350

WETHERBY SCHOOL
11 Pembridge Square, London, W2 4ED
Tel: (0171) 727 9581
Head: Miss F Blair Turner
Type: Boys Day 4-8
No of Pupils: 150
Fees: (September 95) £5070

W3

BARBARA SPEAKE STAGE SCHOOL
East Acton Lane, London, W3 7EG
Tel: (0181) 743 1306
Head: David R Speake
Type: Co-educational Day 4-16
No of Pupils: B50 G80
Fees: (September 95) £1650 - £1845

EALING MONTESSORI SCHOOL
St Martins Church Hall, Hale Gardens, London, W3
Tel: (0181) 992 4513
Head: Mrs P Jaffer
Type: Co-educational Day 2-6
Fees: (September 95) £1800 - £2775

INTERNATIONAL SCHOOL OF LONDON*
139 Gunnersbury Avenue, London, W3 8LG
Tel: (0181) 992 5823
Head: R Hermon
Type: Co-educational Day 4-19
No of Pupils: B110 G90
Fees: (September 95) £5190 - £8340

THE JAPANESE SCHOOL
87 Creffield Road, Acton, London, W3 9PU
Tel: (0181) 993 7145
Head: S Saito
Type: Co-educational Day 6-15
No of Pupils: B550 G350
Fees: (September 95) £1170

KING FAHAD ACADEMY
Bromyard Avenue, Acton, London, W3 7HD
Tel: (0181) 743 0131
Head: Dr I All-Bassam
Type: Co-educational Day 5-18
No of Pupils: 1050
Fees: (September 94) £1672 - £2272

THE PEGASUS PREP
The Pavilion, Queens Drive Playing Fields, Queens Drive, London, W3
Tel: (0181) 998 2723
Head: Ms T Farrar
Type: Co-educational Day 4-8
Fees: (September 94) £3300

W4

THE ARTS EDUCATIONAL SCHOOLS*
Cone Ripman House, 14 Bath Road, Chiswick, London, W4 1LY
Tel: (0181) 994 9366
Head: P A Fowler
Type: Co-educational Day 8-18
No of Pupils: 340
Fees: (September 95) £3750 - £5850

CATERPILLAR MONTESSORI NURSERY SCHOOL
The Green Hall & The New Hall, St Albans Church, South Parade, Chiswick, London, W4
Tel: (0181) 747 8531
Head: Miss M Ward-Niblett
Type: Co-educational Day 2-5
No of Pupils: B24 G24
Fees: (September 95) £1560 - £1830

CHISWICK AND BEDFORD PARK PREPARATORY SCHOOL
Priory House, Priory Avenue, Bedford Park, London, W4 1TX
Tel: (0181) 994 1804
Head: Mrs M B Morrow
Type: Co-educational Day 4-11
No of Pupils: 195
Fees: (September 95) £2985 - £3825

ELMWOOD MONTESSORI SCHOOL
St Michaels Church Hall, Elmwood Road, London, W4 3DY
Tel: (0181) 994 8177
Head: Mrs S Herbert
Type: Co-educational Day 3-5
No of Pupils: B20 G20
Fees: (September 95) £1920

THE FALCONS PRE-PREPARATORY SCHOOL
2 Burnaby Gardens, Chiswick, London, W4
Tel: (0181) 747 8393
Head: Miss L Wall
Type: Boys Day 3-8
No of Pupils: 154
Fees: (September 95) £1515 - £4545

ORCHARD HOUSE SCHOOL
16 Newton Grove, Bedford Park, London, W4 1LB
Tel: (0181) 742 8544
Head: Mrs S A Hobbs
Type: Co-educational Day 3-7
No of Pupils: 95
Fees: (September 95) £4380

W5

BEACON HOUSE SCHOOL*
15 Gunnersbury Avenue, Ealing, London, W5 3XD
Tel: (0181) 992 5189
Head: Mrs M Milner
Type: Co-educational Day 3-11
No of Pupils: B30 G120
Fees: (September 95) £1362 - £3030

CLIFTON LODGE*
8 Mattock Lane, Ealing, London, W5 5BG
Tel: (0181) 579 3662
Head: D A Blumlein
Type: Boys Day 4-13
No of Pupils: 160
Fees: (September 95) £4200 - £4450

CORFTON HILL EDUCATIONAL ESTABLISHMENT
Corfton Hill, 35 Corfton Road, Ealing, London, W5 2HP
Tel: (0181) 248 9050
Head: Mrs G Levitt
Type: Co-educational Day 6-11
No of Pupils: 12
Fees: (September 95) £2235 - £2820

DURSTON HOUSE
12-14-26 Castlebar Road, Ealing, London, W5 2DR
Tel: (0181) 810 6845
Head: P D Craze
Type: Boys Day 4-13
No of Pupils: 365
Fees: (September 95) £4440 - £5340

HARVINGTON SCHOOL
20 Castlebar Road, Ealing, London, W5 2DS
Tel: (0181) 997 1583
Head: Mrs A Fookes
Type: Girls Day 3-16
No of Pupils: 190
Fees: (September 95) £3150 - £3885

ST ANGELO PREPARATORY SCHOOL
10 Montpelier Road, London, W5 2QP
Tel: (0181) 997 3209
Head: D G Cattini
Type: Boys Day 4-13
No of Pupils: 90
Fees: (September 95) £3255 - £3600

ST AUGUSTINE'S PRIORY
Hillcrest Road, Ealing, London, W5 2JL
Tel: (0181) 997 2022
Head: Mrs F Gumley-Mason
Type: Girls Day 4-18
No of Pupils: 425
Fees: (September 95) £2205 - £3510

ST BENEDICT'S JUNIOR SCHOOL
5 Montpelier Avenue, Ealing, London, W5 2XP
Tel: (0181) 997 9800
Head: Rev M Shipperlee
Type: Boys Day 4-11
No of Pupils: 251
Fees: (September 95) £3390 - £3720

ST BENEDICT'S SCHOOL
54 Eaton Rise, Ealing, London, W5 2ES
Tel: (0181) 997 9828
Head: Dr A J Dachs
Type: Boys Day 11-18 (Co-ed VIth form)
No of Pupils: B555 G40
Fees: (September 95) £4860

W6

BUTE HOUSE PREPARATORY SCHOOL FOR GIRLS
Bute House, Luxemburg Gardens, London, W6 7EA
Tel: (0171) 603 7381
Head: Mrs S Salvidant
Type: Girls Day 4-11
No of Pupils: 270
Fees: (September 95) £4050

ECOLE FRANCAISE JACQUES PREVERT
59 Brook Green, London, W6 7BE
Tel: (0171) 602 6871
Head: M Grolleau
Type: Co-educational Day 4-10
No of Pupils: 260
Fees: (September 95) £1779

THE GODOLPHIN AND LATYMER SCHOOL
Iffley Road, Hammersmith, London, W6 0PG
Tel: (0181) 741 1936
Head: Miss M Rudland
Type: Girls Day 11-18
No of Pupils: 700
Fees: (September 94) £5385

THE JORDANS NURSERY SCHOOL

Kelmscott Gardens Community Centre, Kelmscott Gardens, Askew Road, London, W12
Tel: (0181) 746 3144
Head: Mrs S Jordan
Type: Co-educational Day 2-5
No of Pupils: B40 G38
Fees: (September 95) £1272 - £1854

LATYMER UPPER SCHOOL*

King Street, Hammersmith, London, W6 9LR
Tel: (0181) 741 1851
Head: C Diggory
Type: Boys Day 7-18
No of Pupils: 1061
Fees: (September 95) £5085 - £5802

RAVENSCOURT PARK PREPARATORY SCHOOL

16 Ravenscourt Avenue, London, W6 0SL
Tel: (0181) 846 9153
Head: Mrs M Gardener
Type: Co-educational Day 4-11
No of Pupils: 178
Fees: (September 95) £4542

RAVENSCOURT THEATRE SCHOOL

Tandy House, 30-40 Dalling Road, London, W6 0JB
Tel: (0181) 741 0707
Head: Rev R Blakeley
Type: Co-educational Day 5-16
No of Pupils: B43 G41
Fees: (September 95) £3150

THE ROSE MONTESSORI NURSERY SCHOOL

St Alban's Church Hall, Margravine Road, London, W6
Tel: (0171) 381 6002
Head: Miss K Gould
Type: Co-educational Day 3-5
No of Pupils: B12 G12
Fees: (September 95) £1600

ST PAUL'S GIRLS' SCHOOL

Brook Green, London, W6 7BS
Tel: (0171) 603 2288
Head: Miss J Gough
Type: Girls Day 11-18
No of Pupils: 612
Fees: (September 95) £6282

W7

MANOR HOUSE SCHOOL

16 Golden Manor, Hanwell, London, W7 3EG
Tel: (0181) 567 4101
Head: J Carpenter
Type: Co-educational Day 2-13
No of Pupils: B95 G45
Fees: (September 95) £2310 - £2965

W8

ALLENDALE PREPARATORY SCHOOL

Allen Street, Kensington, London, W8 6BL
Tel: (0171) 937 7576
Head: Mrs M Peake
Type: Co-educational Day B4-9 G4-11
No of Pupils: B25 G50
Fees: (September 95) £2850 - £3000

ASHBOURNE INDEPENDENT SIXTH FORM COLLEGE*

17 Old Court Place, London, W8 4PL
Tel: (0171) 937 3858
Head: M J Hatchard-Kirby
Type: Co-educational Day 16-19
No of Pupils: B97 G49
Fees: (September 95) £8025 - £9750

ASHBOURNE MIDDLE SCHOOL*

17 Old Court Place, London, W8 4PL
Tel: (0171) 937 3858
Head: J Hingley
Type: Co-educational Day 11-15
No of Pupils: 50
Fees: (September 95) £7875

KENSINGTON PREP SCHOOL FOR GIRLS

17 Upper Phillimore Gardens, London, W8 7HF
Tel: (0171) 937 0108
Head: Mrs G M Lumsdon
Type: Girls Day 4-11
No of Pupils: 200
Fees: (September 95) £4704

LADY EDEN'S SCHOOL

39-41 Victoria Road, Kensington, London, W8 5RJ
Tel: (0171) 937 0583
Head: Mrs G A Wayne
Type: Girls Day 3-11
No of Pupils: 160
Fees: (September 95) £2475 - £5685

LANSDOWNE SIXTH FORM COLLEGE

7-9 Palace Gate, London, W8 5LS
Tel: (0171) 581 3307
Head: P J Murphy
Type: Co-educational Day 15+
No of Pupils: B150 G150
Fees: (September 95) 3 A Levels/5 GCSEs £5925

THOMAS'S PREPARATORY SCHOOL

17-19 Cottesmore Gardens, London, W8 5PR
Tel: (0171) 938 1931
Head: Miss K Stayt
Type: Co-educational Day 4-11
No of Pupils: B105 G105
Fees: (September 95) £5265 - £6150

W10

BALES COLLEGE

2(J) Kilburn Lane, London, W10 4AA
Tel: (0181) 960 5899
Head: W B Moore
Type: Co-educational Day 15+
No of Pupils: B50 G50
Fees: (September 95) 3 A Levels £4350

BASSETT HOUSE SCHOOL

60 Bassett Road, London, W10 6JP
Tel: (0181) 969 0313
Head: Mrs A Landen
Type: Co-educational Day 3-8
No of Pupils: B70 G50
Fees: (September 95) £2190 - £4380

PETITE ECOLE FRANCAISE

90 Oxford Gardens, London, W10 5UW
Tel: (0181) 960 1278
Head: Ms A Stones
Type: Co-educational Day 2-5
No of Pupils: 60
Fees: (September 95) £2925

W11

DAVID GAME TUTORIAL
COLLEGE*
69 Notting Hill Gate, London,
W11 3JS
Tel: (0171) 584 9097
Head: D T Game
Type: Co-educational Day &
Residential 14-21
No of Pupils: B120 G90
Fees: (September 95) 3 A Levels
£4150-£5890
5 GCSEs £3250

KENLEY MONTESSORI
SCHOOL
Kenley Walk, Notting Hill, London,
W11 4BA
Tel: (0181) 876 5021
Head: Mrs I Aljovin
Type: Co-educational Day 2-5
No of Pupils: B10 G10
Fees: (September 95) £1485 - £1845

LADBROKE SQUARE
MONTESSORI SCHOOL
43 Ladbroke Square, London,
W11 3ND
Tel: (0171) 229 0125
Head: Mrs S Russell-Cobb
Type: Co-educational Day 2-5
No of Pupils: B50 G50
Fees: (September 95) £615 - £1125

NORLAND PLACE SCHOOL
162-166 Holland Park Avenue,
London, W11 4UH
Tel: (0171) 603 9103
Head: Mrs S J Garnsey
Type: Co-educational Day B4-8
G4-11
No of Pupils: B88 G154
Fees: (September 95) £3510 - £5580

ST JAMES INDEPENDENT
SCHOOL FOR GIRLS
19 Pembridge Villas, London,
W11 3EP
Tel: (0171) 229 2253
Head: Mrs L A Hyde
Type: Girls Day 10-18
No of Pupils: 150
Fees: (September 95) £4620 - £4755

SOUTHBANK
INTERNATIONAL SCHOOL
36-38 Kensington Park Road,
London, W11 3BU
Tel: (0171) 229 8230
Head: Milton Toubkin
Type: Co-educational Day 3-18
No of Pupils: 250
Fees: (September 95) £3600 - £9480

TODDLERS INN MONTESSORI
The Rugby Club, 223 Walmer Road,
London, W11 4EY
Tel: (0171) 727 6309
Head: Mrs M Molavi
Type: Co-educational Day 2-5
No of Pupils: B11 G11
Fees: (September 95) £1695

W12

SHEPHERD'S BUSH DAY
NURSERY
101 Frithville Gardens, London,
W12 7JQ
Tel: (0181) 749 1255
Head: Ms Lisa Rowland
Type: Co-educational Day 1-5
No of Pupils: B17 G17
Fees: (September 95) £7670

W13

AVENUE HOUSE SCHOOL*
70 The Avenue, Ealing, London,
W13 8LS
Tel: 0181 998 9981
Head: Miss C M Barber
Type: Co-educational Day 2-11
Fees: (September 95) £3600

EALING COLLEGE UPPER
SCHOOL
83 The Avenue, Ealing, London,
W13 8JS
Tel: (0181) 997 4346
Head: B Webb
Type: Boys Day 11-18 (Co-ed VIth
form)
No of Pupils: B135 G5
Fees: (September 95) £3900

NOTTING HILL AND EALING
HIGH SCHOOL GPDST
2 Cleveland Road, Ealing, London,
W13 8AX
Tel: (0181) 997 5744
Head: Mrs S Whitfield
Type: Girls Day 5-18
No of Pupils: 830
Fees: (September 95) £3576 - £4644

W14

LITTLE FOLK MONTESSORI &
MUSIC KINDERGARTEN
The Bhavan Centre, 4A Castletown
Road, London, W14
Tel: (0171) 381 8335
Head: Ms M Squires
Type: Co-educational Day 2-5
No of Pupils: 24
Fees: (September 93) £1740

ROYAL BALLET SCHOOL
155 Talgarth Road, Barons Court,
London, W14 9DE
Tel: (0181) 748 6335
Head: J G Mitchell
Type: Co-educational Boarding &
Day 11-18
No of Pupils: B76 G162 No of
Boarders F130
Fees: (September 95) FB £15771 DAY
£11676

WC1

DAVIES'S COLLEGE*
25 Old Gloucester Street, Queen
Square, London, WC1N 3AF
Tel: (0171) 430 1622
Head: A T Williams
Type: Co-educational Day 15+
No of Pupils: B75 G65
Fees: 3 A Levels £9103 5 GCSEs
£6490

WC2

THE URDANG ACADEMY OF
BALLET
20-22 Shelton Street, London,
WC2H 9JJ
Tel: (0171) 836 5709
Head: Miss L Urdang
Type: Co-educational Day 10-16
Fees: (September 94) £6600 - £7200

ECCLES

CLARENDON COTTAGE SCHOOL
Ivy Bank House, Half Edge Lane, Eccles, Greater Manchester M30 9BJ
Tel: (0161) 787 7865
Head: Miss K S Farley & Mrs E A Bagnall
Type: Co-educational Day 1-11
No of Pupils: B30 G30
Fees: On application

MONTON PREPARATORY SCHOOL
Francis Street, Monton, Greater Manchester M30 9PR
Tel: (0161) 789 0472
Head: Miss D S Bradburn
Type: Co-educational Day 2-13
No of Pupils: B100 G100
Fees: On application

MANCHESTER

AMBERLEIGH*
398 Wilbraham Road, Chorlton-cum-Hardy, Manchester M21 1UH
Tel: (0161) 881 1593
Head: P F Hayden
Type: Co-educational Day 4-11
No of Pupils: B76 G40
Fees: (September 95) £1704 - £2528

ASH LEA GRAMMAR SCHOOL
1 Half Edge Lane, Eccles, Manchester M30 9GJ
Tel: (0161) 789 3892
Head: J Swift
Type: Co-educational Day 2-16
No of Pupils: 150
Fees: (September 94) £1485 - £2550

BRANWOOD PREPARATORY SCHOOL
Stafford Road, Monton, Eccles, Manchester M30 9HN
Tel: (0161) 789 1054
Head: W M Howard
Type: Co-educational Day 4-11
No of Pupils: B90 G90
Fees: (September 95) £1227 - £2040

BRIDGEWATER SCHOOL*
Drywood Hall, Worsley Road, Worsley, Manchester M28 2WQ
Tel: (0161) 794 1463
Head: Dr B J Blundell
Type: Co-educational Day 3-18
No of Pupils: 435
Fees: (September 95) £2535 - £3995

CAIUS HOUSE SCHOOL
99 Church Road, Urmston, Manchester M41 9FJ
Tel: (0161) 748 3261
Head: N A Ricketts
Type: Co-educational Day 3-11
No of Pupils: B65 G53
Fees: (September 95) £1500 - £2040

CHETHAM'S SCHOOL OF MUSIC
Long Millgate, Manchester M3 1SB
Tel: (0161) 834 9644
Head: Rev P F Hullah
Type: Co-educational Boarding 8-18
No of Pupils: B120 G166
Fees: (September 95) FB £15600 DAY £12075

KING OF KINGS SCHOOL
142 Dantzic Street, Manchester M4 4DN
Tel: (0161) 834 4214
Head: Mrs B Lewis
Type: Co-educational Day 2-18
No of Pupils: B13 G8
Fees: (September 95) £1170 - £1320

THE MANCHESTER GRAMMAR SCHOOL
Old Hall Lane, Manchester M13 0XT
Tel: (0161) 224 7201
Head: Dr G M Stephen
Type: Boys Day 11-18
No of Pupils: 1415
Fees: (September 95) £4140

MANCHESTER HIGH SCHOOL FOR GIRLS
Grangethorpe Road, Manchester M14 6HS
Tel: (0161) 224 0447
Head: Ms E M Diggory
Type: Girls Day 4-18
No of Pupils: 930
Fees: (September 94) £2475 - £3735

MANCHESTER JEWISH GRAMMAR SCHOOL
Charlton Avenue, Prestwich, Manchester M25 8PH
Tel: (0161) 773 1789
Head: P Pink
Type: Boys Day 11-18
No of Pupils: 150
Fees: (September 95) £3900

MOOR ALLERTON SCHOOL
131 Barlow Moor Road, Manchester M20 2PW
Tel: (0161) 445 4521
Head: M J Clarke
Type: Co-educational Day 3-11
No of Pupils: B98 G52
Fees: (September 95) £1500 - £3150

NORMAN HOUSE SCHOOL
349 Hollinwood Avenue, New Moston, Manchester M40 0JX
Tel: (0161) 681 3097
Head: S Jobling
Type: Co-educational Day 3-11
No of Pupils: B85 G75
Fees: (September 95) £2115 - £2190

ROSECROFT SCHOOL DIDSBURY
826 Wilmslow Road, Didsbury, Manchester M20 0UZ
Tel: (0161) 434 2616
Head: Miss M L Mullins
Type: Girls Day 3-16 (Boys 3-7)
No of Pupils: B20 G110
Fees: (September 95) £2400 - £3450

ST BEDE'S COLLEGE
Alexandra Park, Manchester M16 8HX
Tel: (0161) 226 3323
Head: J Byrne
Type: Co-educational Day 11-19
No of Pupils: B530 G441
Fees: (September 95) £3870

WHITEFIELD PREPARATORY SCHOOL
Holly Bank, Church Lane, Whitefield, Manchester M45 7NF
Tel: (0161) 766 2744
Head: J G Roscoe
Type: Co-educational Day 3-11
No of Pupils: B37 G27
Fees: (September 94) £1680

WILLIAM HULME'S GRAMMAR SCHOOL
Spring Bridge Road, Manchester M16 8PR
Tel: (0161) 226 2054
Head: P D Briggs
Type: Co-educational Day 11-18
No of Pupils: B533 G260
Fees: (September 95) £4071

WITHINGTON GIRLS' SCHOOL
Wellington Road, Fallowfield,
Manchester M14 6BL
Tel: (0161) 224 1077
Head: Mrs M Kenyon
Type: Girls Day 7-18
No of Pupils: 590
Fees: (September 95) £2595 - £3750

PRESTWICH

PRESTWICH PREPARATORY SCHOOL
400 Bury Old Road, Prestwich,
Greater Manchester M25 5PZ
Tel: (0161) 773 1223
Head: D R Sheldon
Type: Co-educational Day 2-11
No of Pupils: B60 G60
Fees: (September 95) £1968

SALFORD

JEWISH HIGH SCHOOL FOR GIRLS
10 Radford Street, Salford, Greater
Manchester M7 0NT
Tel: (0161) 792 2118
Head: Rabbi M I Young
Type: Girls Day 11-18
No of Pupils: 160
Fees: (September 94) £3300

TASHBAR SCHOOL
33 Broom Lane, Salford, Greater
Manchester M7 4EQ
Tel: (0161) 792 8732
Head: Rabbi E Pruim
Type: Boys Day 5-11
No of Pupils: 76
Fees: (September 95) £1500

MERSEYSIDE

BIRKENHEAD

BIRKENHEAD HIGH SCHOOL GPDST
86 Devonshire Place, Birkenhead,
Merseyside L43 1TY
Tel: (0151) 652 5777
Head: Mrs K R Irving
Type: Girls Day 4-18
No of Pupils: 970

Fees: (September 95) £2928 - £3984

BIRKENHEAD SCHOOL
58 Beresford Road, Oxton,
Birkenhead, Merseyside
Tel: (0151) 652 4014
Head: S J Haggett
Type: Boys Day 3-18
No of Pupils: 1093
Fees: (September 95) £2748 - £3663

HIGHFIELD SCHOOL
96 Bidston Road, Oxton, Birkenhead,
Merseyside L43 6TW
Tel: (0151) 652 3708
Head: Mrs S Morris
Type: Co-educational Day B2-11
G2-16
No of Pupils: 150
Fees: (September 95) £2250 - £2700

LIVERPOOL

ATHERTON HOUSE
Alexandra Road, Crosby, Liverpool,
Merseyside L23 7TF
Tel: (0151) 924 5578
Head: Mrs J Warren
Type: Co-educational Day 2-11
No of Pupils: 85
Fees: (September 95) £1130 - £2030

BEECHENHURST PREPARATORY SCHOOL
145 Menlove Avenue, Liverpool,
Merseyside L18 3EE
Tel: (0151) 722 3279
Head: Mrs E M Turner
Type: Co-educational Day 3-11
No of Pupils: B60 G60
Fees: (September 95) £1740 - £1920

THE BELVEDERE SCHOOL GPDST
17 Belvidere Road, Princes Park,
Liverpool, Merseyside L8 3TF
Tel: (0151) 727 1284
Head: Mrs C Evans
Type: Girls Day 3-18
No of Pupils: 641
Fees: (September 95) £2550 - £3984

CARLETON HOUSE PREPARATORY SCHOOL
Lyndhurst Road, Mossley Hill,
Liverpool, Merseyside L18 8AQ
Tel: (0151) 724 4880
Head: Mrs C Line
Type: Co-educational Day 4-11
No of Pupils: 143
Fees: (September 95) £2340

ELLIOTT-CLARKE SCHOOL
63 Rodney Street, Liverpool,
Merseyside L1 9ER
Tel: (0151) 709 3323
Head: Miss A I Thomson
Type: Co-educational Day 7-16
No of Pupils: B8 G41
Fees: (September 95) £2040

LIVERPOOL COLLEGE
Liverpool, Merseyside L18 8BG
Tel: (0151) 724 4000
Head: B R Martin
Type: Co-educational Day 3-18
No of Pupils: B700 G300
Fees: (September 94) £2225 - £3918

MCKEE SCHOOL OF EDUCATION, DANCE & DRAMA
2 Carnforth Road, Liverpool,
Merseyside L18 6JS
Tel: (0151) 724 1316
Head: Mrs K M McKee
Type: Co-educational Day 3-11
No of Pupils: B26 G38
Fees: (September 95) £1275 - £1425

MERCHANT TAYLORS' SCHOOL
Crosby, Liverpool, Merseyside
L23 0QP
Tel: (0151) 928 3308
Head: S J Dawkins
Type: Boys Day 7-18
No of Pupils: 848
Fees: (September 95) £3486 - £3744

MERCHANT TAYLORS' SCHOOL FOR GIRLS
Crosby, Liverpool, Merseyside
L23 5SP
Tel: (0151) 924 3140
Head: Mrs J I Mills
Type: Girls Day 4-18
No of Pupils: 900
Fees: (September 95) £2421 - £3744

NEWBOROUGH SCHOOL
Quarry Street, Woolton, Liverpool,
Merseyside L25 6HD
Tel: (0151) 428 1838
Head: Miss D Prior
Type: Co-educational Day B3-11
G3-16
No of Pupils: B51 G80
Fees: (September 95) £1125 - £1500

ST EDWARD'S COLLEGE
North Drive, Sandfield Park,
Liverpool, Merseyside L12 1LF
Tel: (0151) 228 3376
Head: J E Waszek
Type: Co-educational Day 3-18
No of Pupils: B700 G350
Fees: (September 95) £2400 - £3498

ST MARY'S COLLEGE
Crosby, Liverpool, Merseyside
L23 3AB
Tel: (0151) 924 3926
Head: W Hammond
Type: Co-educational Day 3-18
No of Pupils: B521 G358
Fees: (September 95) £2022 - £3744

STREATHAM HOUSE SCHOOL*
Victoria Road, Crosby, Liverpool,
Merseyside L23 8UQ
Tel: (0151) 924 1514
Head: Mrs C Baxter
Type: Girls Day 2-16 (Boys 2-11)
No of Pupils: B30 G187
Fees: (September 95) £1620 - £2985

NEWTON-LE-WILLOWS

NEWTON BANK SCHOOL
34A High Street,
Newton-Le-Willows, Merseyside
WA12 9SN
Tel: (01925) 225979
Head: Mrs J Butler
Type: Co-educational Day 3-12
No of Pupils: 100
Fees: (September 95) £1480

PRESCOT

TOWER COLLEGE
Mill Lane, Rainhill, Prescot,
Merseyside L35 6NE
Tel: (0151) 426 4333
Head: Miss R J Oxley
Type: Co-educational Day 4-16
No of Pupils: B230 G203
Fees: (September 95) £1743 - £2109

SOUTH WIRRAL

BENTY HEATH SCHOOL AND KINDERGARTEN
Benty Heath Lane, South Wirral,
Merseyside L64 1SB
Tel: (0151) 327 4594
Head: Mrs J E Tedstone
Type: Co-educational Day 3-7
No of Pupils: B20 G22
Fees: (September 95) £220 - £580

SOUTHPORT

KINGSWOOD SCHOOL
26 Westcliffe Road, Birkdale,
Southport, Merseyside PR8 2BU
Tel: (01704) 563211
Head: E J Borowski
Type: Co-educational Day 2-18
No of Pupils: B210 G210
Fees: (September 95) £1380 - £3030

SUNNYMEDE SCHOOL
4 Westcliffe Road, Birkdale,
Southport, Merseyside PR8 2BN
Tel: (01704) 568593
Head: S J Pattinson
Type: Co-educational Day 3-13
No of Pupils: B120 G55
Fees: (September 95) £1965 - £3825

TOWER DENE PREPARATORY SCHOOL
59-76 Cambridge Road, Southport,
Merseyside PR9 9RH
Tel: (01704) 28556
Head: Mrs A Lewin
Type: Co-educational Day 3-11
No of Pupils: B70 G60
Fees: (September 95) £1650 - £2250

WALLASEY

MARYMOUNT CONVENT SCHOOL
Love Lane, Wallasey, Merseyside
L44 5SB
Tel: (0151) 638 8467
Head: Sister C O'Reilly
Type: Girls Day 3-11
No of Pupils: 200
Fees: (September 95) £1500

WESTBOURNE PREPARATORY SCHOOL
45 Penkett Road, Wallasey,
Merseyside
Tel: (0151) 639 2722
Head: T N Cottam
Type: Co-educational Day 4-11
No of Pupils: 110
Fees: (September 95) £1170 - £1245

WIRRAL

AVALON PREPARATORY SCHOOL
Avalon School Ltd, Caldy Road, West
Kirby, Wirral, Merseyside L48 2HE
Tel: (0151) 625 6993
Head: Dr B Scott
Type: Co-educational Day 3-11
No of Pupils: B50 G100
Fees: (September 95) £660 - £2625

HESWALL PREPARATORY SCHOOL
Carberry, Quarry Road East,
Heswall, Wirral, Merseyside L60 6RB
Tel: (0151) 342 7851
Head: Mrs M Hannaford
Type: Co-educational Day 3-11
No of Pupils: B25 G25
Fees: (September 95) £1050 - £2100

KINGSLEY NURSERY SCHOOL
46 Ford Road, Upton, Wirral,
Merseyside L49 0TF
Tel: (0151) 677 5716
Head: E Newbury
Type: Co-educational Day 3-5
No of Pupils: B14 G16
Fees: (September 94) £2086

KINGSMEAD SCHOOL
Bertram Drive, Hoylake, Wirral,
Merseyside L47 0LL
Tel: (0151) 632 3156
Head: E H Bradby
Type: Co-educational Boarding &
Day 3-13
No of Pupils: B118 G67 No of
Boarders F15 W6
Fees: (September 95) FB £6555 -
£7185 WB £6255 - £6885 DAY
£1650 - £4935

PERSHORE HOUSE SCHOOL
Prenton Lane, Birkenhead, Wirral,
Merseyside L42 8LA
Tel: (0151) 608 1170
Head: D B Winterford
Type: Co-educational Day 2-11
No of Pupils: B40 G53
Fees: (September 95) £2070 - £2370

MIDDLESEX

ASHFORD

ST DAVID'S SCHOOL
Church Road, Ashford, Middlesex
TW15 3DZ
Tel: (01784) 252494
Head: Mrs J G Osborne
Type: Girls Day & Boarding 3-18
No of Pupils: 450 No of Boarders F25
W20
Fees: (September 95) FB £8985 WB
£8460 DAY £1470 - £5175

BRENTFORD

PARK SCHOOL
Syon Park, Brentford, Middlesex
TW8 8JF
Tel: (0181) 568 4355
Head: Mrs C Whitehouse
Type: Co-educational Day 4-7
Fees: (September 95) £2550

EDGWARE

HOLLAND HOUSE
1 Broadhurst Avenue, Edgware,
Middlesex HA8 8TP
Tel: (0181) 958 6979
Head: Mrs I Tyk
Type: Co-educational Day 4-11
No of Pupils: B70 G70
Fees: (September 94) £3180

**NORTH LONDON
COLLEGIATE SCHOOL**
Canons Drive, Edgware, Middlesex
HA8 7RJ
Tel: (0181) 952 0912
Head: Mrs J L Clanchy
Type: Girls Day 4-18
No of Pupils: 970
Fees: (September 95) £3912 - £4848

ENFIELD

ST JOHN'S SENIOR SCHOOL
North Lodge, The Ridgeway, Enfield,
Middlesex EN2 8BE
Tel: (0181) 363 4439
Head: A Tardios
Type: Co-educational Day 11-18
No of Pupils: 110
Fees: (September 95) £3600

FELTHAM

HOUNSLOW COLLEGE
The Old Rectory, Park Road,
Hanworth, Feltham, Middlesex
TW13 6PN
Tel: (0181) 751 1710
Head: W R Hamblin
Type: Boys Day 10-19
No of Pupils: 80
Fees: (September 95) £2475

HAMPTON

ATHELSTAN HOUSE SCHOOL
36 Percy Road, Hampton, Middlesex
TW12 2LA
Tel: (0181) 979 1045
Head: Ms E M Woolf
Type: Co-educational Day 3-7
No of Pupils: B28 G55
Fees: (September 95) £1725 - £3060

DENMEAD SCHOOL
41-43 Wensleydale Road, Hampton,
Middlesex TW12 2LP
Tel: (0181) 979 1844
Head: R Jeynes
Type: Boys Day 3-13
No of Pupils: 200
Fees: (September 95) £1650 - £3945

**GRASSROOTS NURSERY
SCHOOL**
The Studio, 24 Ashley Road,
Hampton, Middlesex TW12 2JA
Tel: (0181) 783 1190
Head: Mrs Walters
Type: Co-educational Day 2-5
No of Pupils: 30
Fees: (September 95) £2160

HAMPTON SCHOOL
Hanworth Road, Hampton,
Middlesex TW12 3HD
Tel: (0181) 979 5526
Head: G G Able
Type: Boys Day 11-18
No of Pupils: 940
Fees: (September 95) £4920

JACK AND JILL SCHOOL
30 Nightingale Road, Hampton,
Middlesex TW12 3HX
Tel: (0181) 979 3195
Head: Miss K S Papirnik
Type: Girls Day 3-7 (Boys 3-5)
No of Pupils: B20 G100
Fees: (September 95) £1710 - £3135

**THE LADY ELEANOR HOLLES
SCHOOL**
102 Hanworth Road, Hampton,
Middlesex TW12 3HF
Tel: (0181) 979 1601
Head: Miss E M Candy
Type: Girls Day 7-18
No of Pupils: 867
Fees: (September 95) £4350 - £5040

**TWICKENHAM
PREPARATORY SCHOOL**
Beveree, 43 High Street, Hampton,
Middlesex TW12 2SA
Tel: (0181) 979 6216
Head: G D Malcolm
Type: Co-educational Day B4-13
G4-11
No of Pupils: B59 G76
Fees: (September 95) £2535 - £4050

HARROW

ALPHA PREPARATORY SCHOOL
21 Hindes Road, Harrow, Middlesex HA1 1SH
Tel: (0181) 427 1471
Head: P J Wylie
Type: Boys Day 4-13 (Girls 4-11)
No of Pupils: 170
Fees: (September 95) £3000 - £4050

BUCKINGHAM COLLEGE SENIOR SCHOOL
15 Hindes Road, Harrow, Middlesex HA1 1SH
Tel: (0181) 427 1220
Head: D F Bell
Type: Boys Day 11-18 (Co-ed VIth form)
No of Pupils: B201 G2
Fees: (September 94) £3705 - £4341

THE JOHN LYON SCHOOL
Middle Road, Harrow, Middlesex HA2 0HN
Tel: (0181) 422 2046
Head: Rev T J Wright
Type: Boys Day 11-18
No of Pupils: 505
Fees: (September 95) £5355

ORLEY FARM SCHOOL
South Hill Avenue, Harrow, Middlesex HA1 3NU
Tel: (0181) 422 1525
Head: I S Elliott
Type: Boys Day 4-13 (Girls 4-6)
No of Pupils: 450
Fees: (September 95) £3477 - £4944

THE PURCELL SCHOOL
Oakhurst, Mount Park Road, Harrow, Middlesex HA1 3JS
Tel: (0181) 422 1284
Head: J Bain
Type: Co-educational Day & Boarding 8-18
No of Pupils: B66 G97 No of Boarders F81
Fees: (September 95) FB £12699 - £14400 DAY £6969 - £8514

QUAINTON HALL SCHOOL
91 Hindes Road, Harrow, Middlesex HA1 1RX
Tel: (0181) 427 1304
Head: P J Milner
Type: Boys Day 4-13
No of Pupils: 220
Fees: (September 95) £3240 - £4320

ROXETH MEAD SCHOOL
25 Middle Road, Harrow, Middlesex HA2 0HW
Tel: (0181) 422 2092
Head: Mrs A Collins
Type: Co-educational Day 3-7
No of Pupils: B20 G25
Fees: (September 95) £2850

ST ANDREW'S SENIOR GIRLS' SCHOOL
39, 42-44 Gloucester Road, Harrow, Middlesex HA1 4PW
Tel: (0181) 427 0692
Head: Mrs M Hudson
Type: Girls Day 8-16 (Boys 8-10)
No of Pupils: 100
Fees: (September 95) £2580 - £2970

HARROW ON THE HILL

HARROW SCHOOL
Harrow on the Hill, Middlesex HA1 3HW
Tel: (0181) 869 1200
Head: N R Bomford
Type: Boys Boarding 13-18
No of Pupils: 785 No of Boarders F785
Fees: (September 95) FB £13425

ISLEWORTH

ASHTON HOUSE SCHOOL
50/52 Eversley Crescent, Isleworth, Middlesex TW7 4LW
Tel: (0181) 560 3902
Head: Miss M Regan
Type: Co-educational Day 3-11
No of Pupils: B70 G80
Fees: (September 95) £3450 - £3669

KENTON

BUCKINGHAM COLLEGE LOWER SCHOOL
The Ridgeway, Kenton, Middlesex HA3 0LJ
Tel: (0181) 907 1522
Head: N Wilkins
Type: Boys Day 4-11
No of Pupils: 125
Fees: (September 95) £2970 - £3825

NORTHWOOD

MERCHANT TAYLORS' SCHOOL
Sandy Lodge, Northwood, Middlesex HA6 2HT
Tel: (01923) 820644
Head: J R Gabitass
Type: Boys Day & Boarding 11-18
No of Pupils: 750 No of Boarders F60
Fees: (September 95) FB £11000 DAY £6600

NORTHWOOD COLLEGE
Maxwell Road, Northwood, Middlesex HA6 2YE
Tel: (01923) 825446
Head: Mrs A Mayou
Type: Girls Day 4-18
No of Pupils: 589
Fees: (September 95) £3297 - £4836

ST HELEN'S SCHOOL FOR GIRLS*
Northwood, Middlesex HA6 3AS
Tel: (01923) 828511
Head: Mrs D M Jefkins
Type: Girls Day & Boarding 4-18
No of Pupils: 939 No of Boarders F62
Fees: (September 95) FB £7932 - £8994 WB £7611 - £8673 DAY £3036 - £4773

ST JOHN'S NORTHWOOD
Potter Street Hill, Northwood, Middlesex HA6 3QY
Tel: (0181) 866 0067
Head: C R Kelly
Type: Boys Day 4-13
No of Pupils: 320
Fees: (September 95) £3600 - £4440

ST MARTIN'S SCHOOL*
40 Moor Park Road, Northwood, Middlesex HA6 2DJ
Tel: (01923) 825740
Head: M J Hodgson
Type: Boys Day 3-13
No of Pupils: 360
Fees: (September 95) £1425 - £4770

PINNER

HEATHFIELD SCHOOL
Beaulieu Drive, Pinner, Middlesex HA5 1NB
Tel: (0181) 868 2346
Head: Mrs J Merritt
Type: Girls Day 3-18
No of Pupils: 475
Fees: (September 95) £3576 - £4644

INNELLAN HOUSE, ST ANDREWS SCHOOL GROUP
44 Love Lane, Pinner, Middlesex HA5 3EX
Tel: (0181) 866 1855
Head: Mrs R Edwards
Type: Co-educational Day 3-8
No of Pupils: 105
Fees: (September 95) £2295 - £2490

REDDIFORD
36-38 Cecil Park, Pinner, Middlesex HA5 5HH
Tel: (0181) 866 0660
Head: B Hembry
Type: Co-educational Day 3-11
No of Pupils: B73 G71
Fees: (September 95) £2400 - £3300

SHEPPERTON

HALLIFORD SCHOOL
Russell Road, Shepperton, Middlesex TW17 9HX
Tel: (01932) 223593
Head: J R Crook
Type: Boys Day 11-19 (VIth with local girls' school)
No of Pupils: 275
Fees: (September 95) £4440

STAINES

STAINES PREPARATORY SCHOOL TRUST
3 Gresham Road, Staines, Middlesex TW18 2BT
Tel: (01784) 452916
Head: P A Monger
Type: Co-educational Day 3-11
No of Pupils: B250 G150
Fees: (September 95) £2310 - £2895

STANMORE

PETERBOROUGH & ST MARGARET'S HIGH SCHOOL
Tanglewood Common Road, Stanmore, Middlesex HA7 3JB
Tel: (0181) 950 3600
Head: Mrs D M Tomlinson
Type: Girls Day 4-16
No of Pupils: 211
Fees: (September 95) £2880 - £4260

TWICKENHAM

THE MALL SCHOOL
185 Hampton Road, Twickenham, Middlesex TW2 5NQ
Tel: (0181) 977 2523
Head: T P MacDonogh
Type: Boys Day 4-13
No of Pupils: 285
Fees: (September 95) £3750 - £4350

NEWLAND HOUSE SCHOOL
Waldegrave Park, Twickenham, Middlesex TW1 4TQ
Tel: (0181) 892 7479
Head: D J Ott
Type: Co-educational Day 4-13
No of Pupils: B269 G165
Fees: (September 95) £3620 - £4440

ST CATHERINE'S SCHOOL
Cross Deep, Twickenham, Middlesex TW1 4QJ
Tel: (0181) 891 2898
Head: Miss D Wynter
Type: Girls Day 3-16
No of Pupils: 310
Fees: (September 95) £2790 - £3855

SUNFLOWER MONTESSORI SCHOOL
8 Victoria Road, Twickenham, Middlesex TW1 3HW
Tel: (0181) 891 2675
Head: Ms Joy Colbert
Type: Co-educational Day 2-12
Fees: (September 95) £1605 - £3015

UXBRIDGE

THE AMERICAN COMMUNITY SCHOOLS*
Hillingdon Court, 108 Vine Lane, Uxbridge, Middlesex UB10 0BE
Tel: (01895) 259771
Head: B Duncan
Type: Co-educational Day 4-18
No of Pupils: B299 G271
Fees: (September 95) £3500 - £8740

ST HELEN'S COLLEGE
Parkway, Hillingdon, Uxbridge, Middlesex UB10 9JX
Tel: (01895) 234371
Head: D A Crehan
Type: Co-educational Day 3-11
No of Pupils: B120 G130
Fees: (September 95) £2160 - £2400

WEMBLEY

BUXLOW PREPARATORY SCHOOL
5/6 Castleton Gardens, Wembley, Middlesex HA9 7QJ
Tel: (0181) 904 3615
Head: Mrs B L Lancaster
Type: Co-educational Day 4-11
No of Pupils: B64 G59
Fees: (September 95) £2940

ST CHRISTOPHER'S SCHOOL
71 Wembley Park Drive, Wembley, Middlesex HA9 8HE
Tel: (0181) 902 5069
Head: Mrs S M Morley
Type: Co-educational Day 4-11
No of Pupils: B53 G54
Fees: (September 95) £2640 - £2994

NORFOLK

CROMER

BEESTON HALL SCHOOL
West Runton, Cromer, Norfolk
NR27 9NQ
Tel: (01263) 837324
Head: J M Elder
Type: Co-educational Boarding &
Day 6-13
No of Pupils: B98 G70 No of
Boarders F105
Fees: (September 95) FB £8100 DAY
£6084

DISS

RIDDLESWORTH HALL
Diss, Norfolk IP22 2TA
Tel: (01953) 81246
Head: Miss S A Smith
Type: Girls Boarding & Day 2-13
(Boys 2-8)
No of Pupils: B10 G130 No of
Boarders F70 W30
Fees: (September 95) FB £8820 WB
£8670 DAY £2700 - £5580

HOLT

GRESHAM'S PREPARATORY
SCHOOL
Cromer Road, Holt, Norfolk
NR25 6EY
Tel: (01263) 712227
Head: A H Cuff
Type: Co-educational Day &
Boarding 4-13
No of Pupils: B132 G85 No of
Boarders F52 W17
Fees: (September 95) FB £8205 WB
£7590 DAY £2730 - £5730

GRESHAM'S SCHOOL
Holt, Norfolk NR25 6EA
Tel: (01263) 713271
Head: J H Arkell
Type: Co-educational Boarding &
Day 13-18
No of Pupils: B308 G177 No of
Boarders F314
Fees: (September 94) FB £11220 DAY
£7860

HUNSTANTON

GLEBE HOUSE SCHOOL
2 Cromer Road, Hunstanton,
Norfolk PE36 6HW
Tel: (01485) 532809
Head: M W Spinney
Type: Co-educational Boarding &
Day 2-13
No of Pupils: B53 G35 No of
Boarders W5
Fees: (September 95) WB £6735 -
£6945 DAY £3000 - £5685

KING'S LYNN

SILFIELD SCHOOL
85 Gayton Road, Gaywood, King's
Lynn, Norfolk PE30 4EH
Tel: (01553) 774642
Head: C E K Phillips & Mrs E M
Phillips
Type: Co-educational Day 3-11
No of Pupils: B35 G30
Fees: (September 95) £1095 - £2020

NORTH WALSHAM

ST NICHOLAS
KINDERGARTEN &
PREPARATORY SCHOOL
Yarmouth Road, North Walsham,
Norfolk NR28 9AT
Tel: (01692) 403143
Head: Mrs M Webster
Type: Co-educational Day 3-11
No of Pupils: B72 G70
Fees: (September 95) £1250 - £1545

NORWICH

BUSHEY PLACE SCHOOL
35 Cromer Road, Aylsham, Norwich,
Norfolk NR11
Tel: (01263) 734108
Head: R G Horne
Type: Co-educational Boarding &
Day 7-16
No of Pupils: B37 G10 No of
Boarders F17
Fees: (September 95) FB £6300 -
£15000 DAY £2500 - £5750

CAWSTON COLLEGE
Cawston, Norwich, Norfolk
NR10 4JD
Tel: (01603) 871204
Head: Mrs B Harrison
Type: Co-educational Boarding &
Day 5-18
No of Pupils: B120 G40 No of
Boarders F90 W20
Fees: (September 95) FB £6534 -
£8205 WB £6381 - £8049 DAY
£2226 - £4497

ECCLES HALL SCHOOL
Quidenham, Norwich, Norfolk
NR16 2NZ
Tel: (01953) 887217
Head: S A Simington
Type: Co-educational Boarding &
Day 5-16
No of Pupils: 150 No of Boarders
F135
Fees: (September 95) FB £8985 DAY
£4725

HETHERSETT OLD HALL
SCHOOL
Hethersett, Norwich, Norfolk
NR9 3DW
Tel: (01603) 810390
Head: Mrs V M Redington
Type: Girls Boarding & Day 7-18
No of Pupils: 232 No of Boarders F66
Fees: (September 95) FB £6855 -
£8550 DAY £3330 - £4350

LANGLEY PREPARATORY
SCHOOL & NURSERY*
Beech Hill, 11 Yarmouth Road,
Thorpe St Andrew, Norwich,
Norfolk NR7 0EA
Tel: (01603) 433861
Head: P J Weeks
Type: Co-educational Day 2-12
No of Pupils: 125
Fees: (September 95) £2010 - £3945

LANGLEY SCHOOL*
Langley Park, Nr Loddon, Norwich,
Norfolk NR14 6BJ
Tel: (01508) 520210
Head: S J McArthur
Type: Co-educational Boarding &
Day 10-18
No of Pupils: B211 G56 No of
Boarders F39 W38
Fees: (September 95) FB £8655 -
£10500 WB £7410 - £8520 DAY
£4455 - £5460

THE NEW BUCKENHAM SCHOOL
The Market Place, New Buckenham, Norwich, Norfolk NR16 2AN
Tel: (01953) 860858
Head: Mrs J M T Simington
Type: Co-educational Day 2-12
Fees: On application

THE NORWICH HIGH SCHOOL FOR GIRLS GPDST
95 Newmarket Road, Norwich, Norfolk NR2 2HU
Tel: (01603) 53265
Head: Mrs V C Bidwell
Type: Girls Day 4-18
No of Pupils: 900
Fees: (September 95) £2928 - £3804

NORWICH SCHOOL
School House, 70 The Close, Norwich, Norfolk NR1 4DQ
Tel: (01603) 623194
Head: C D Brown
Type: Boys Day 8-18 (Co-ed VIth form)
No of Pupils: 750
Fees: (September 95) £4353 - £4530

NOTRE DAME PREPARATORY SCHOOL
147 Dereham Road, Norwich, Norfolk NR2 3TA
Tel: (01603) 625593
Head: Mrs A E Mancini
Type: Girls Day 3-12 (Boys 3-8)
No of Pupils: B25 G167
Fees: (September 95) £780 - £1875

ST CHRISTOPHER'S SCHOOL
George Hill, Old Catton, Norwich, Norfolk NR7 6DE
Tel: (01603) 425179
Head: Mrs D Arthur & Mrs C Cunningham
Type: Co-educational Day 2-12
No of Pupils: B77 G57
Fees: (September 95) £399 - £2469

STRETTON SCHOOL
1 Albermarle Road, Norwich, Norfolk NR2 2DF
Tel: (01603) 451285
Head: Mrs Y D Barnett
Type: Co-educational Day 2-9
No of Pupils: 110
Fees: (September 93) £915 - £1470

TAVERHAM HALL
Taverham, Norwich, Norfolk NR8 6HU
Tel: (01603) 868206
Head: W D Lawton
Type: Co-educational Boarding & Day 4-13
No of Pupils: B133 G54 No of Boarders F17 W18
Fees: (September 95) FB £8100 DAY £2805 - £6210

THORPE HOUSE SCHOOL
7 Yarmouth Road, Norwich, Norfolk NR7 0EA
Tel: (01603) 33055
Head: Mrs F M Hunt
Type: Girls Day 3-16
No of Pupils: 324
Fees: (September 95) £1590 - £2475

TOWN CLOSE HOUSE PREPARATORY SCHOOL
14 Ipswich Road, Norwich, Norfolk NR2 2LR
Tel: (01603) 620180
Head: S Higginson
Type: Boys Day & Boarding 3-13 (Girls 3-8)
No of Pupils: B289 G46 No of Boarders W20
Fees: (September 95) WB £6384 DAY £1050 - £4395

WOOD DENE SCHOOL
Aylmerton Hall, Aylmerton, Norwich, Norfolk NR11 8QA
Tel: (01263) 837224
Head: Mrs D M Taylor
Type: Girls Day 2-16 (Boys 2-11)
No of Pupils: B20 G100
Fees: (September 94) £1560 - £2835

SWAFFHAM

CONVENT OF THE SACRED HEART
17 Mangate Street, Swaffham, Norfolk PE37 7QW
Tel: (01760) 721330
Head: Sister Francis Ridler
Type: Co-educational Day & Boarding B3-11 G3-16
No of Pupils: B39 G234 No of Boarders W25
Fees: (September 95) WB £5100 DAY £2340 - £3300

THETFORD

THETFORD GRAMMAR SCHOOL
Bridge Street, Thetford, Norfolk IP24 3AF
Tel: (01842) 752840
Head: J R Weeks
Type: Co-educational Day 7-18
No of Pupils: B148 G122
Fees: (September 95) £3831 - £4161

NORTHAMPTONSHIRE

BLACKTHORN

ST PETER'S INDEPENDENT SCHOOL
Lingswood Park, Blackthorn,
Northamptonshire NN3 4TA
Tel: (01604) 411745
Head: G J Smith
Type: Co-educational Day 4-18
No of Pupils: 185
Fees: (September 93) £1590

BRACKLEY

BEACHBOROUGH SCHOOL
Westbury, Brackley,
Northamptonshire NN13 5LB
Tel: (01280) 700071
Head: A J Boardman
Type: Co-educational Day &
Boarding 2-13
No of Pupils: B118 G62 No of
Boarders F29
Fees: (September 95) WB £7980 DAY
£3480 - £6150

WINCHESTER HOUSE SCHOOL*
Brackley, Northamptonshire
NN13 5AZ
Tel: (01280) 702483
Head: D R Speight
Type: Co-educational Boarding &
Day 8-14
No of Pupils: B130 G60 No of
Boarders F117
Fees: (September 95) FB £8730 DAY
£2760 - £6600

KETTERING

OUR LADY'S CONVENT PREPARATORY SCHOOL
Hall Lane, Kettering,
Northamptonshire NN15 7LJ
Tel: (01536) 513882
Head: Mrs L Burgess
Type: Co-educational Day 2-11
No of Pupils: B68 G89
Fees: (September 95) £2280

ST PETER'S SCHOOL
52 Headlands, Kettering,
Northamptonshire NN15 6DJ
Tel: (01536) 512066
Head: Mrs B Blakeley
Type: Girls Day 3-16 (Co-ed 3-11)
No of Pupils: B53 G117
Fees: (September 95) £2220 - £3675

NORTHAMPTON

BOSWORTH TUTORIAL COLLEGE*
9-12 St George's Avenue,
Northampton NN2 6JA
Tel: (01604) 719988
Head: Mark Broadway
Type: Co-educational Residential &
Day 14-19
No of Pupils: B53 G31
Fees: (September 95) FB £9825 DAY
£5560

GREAT HOUGHTON PREPARATORY SCHOOL
Great Houghton Hall, Northampton
NN4 7AG
Tel: (01604) 761907
Head: M T E Street
Type: Co-educational Day 4-13
No of Pupils: B214 G58
Fees: (September 95) £2325 - £4875

MAIDWELL HALL
Maidwell, Northampton NN6 9JG
Tel: (01604) 686234
Head: P Whitton
Type: Boys Boarding & Day 3-13
(Girls 3-8)
No of Pupils: 83 No of Boarders F81
Fees: (September 95) FB £9300 DAY
£1875 - £5550

NORTHAMPTON HIGH SCHOOL
Newport Pagnell Road,
Hardingstone, Northampton
NN4 0UU
Tel: (01604) 765765
Head: Mrs L A Mayne
Type: Girls Day 3-18
No of Pupils: 797
Fees: (September 95) £2850 - £4110

OVERSTONE PARK SCHOOL
Overstone Park, Overstone,
Northampton NN6 0AD
Tel: (01604) 643787
Head: Mrs M F Brown
Type: Co-educational Day 2-16
No of Pupils: 160
Fees: (September 94) £2016 - £3024

QUINTON HOUSE
The Hall, Upton, Northampton
NN5 6UX
Tel: (01604) 752050
Head: G H Griffiths
Type: Co-educational Day 3-18
No of Pupils: B160 G160 No of
Boarders W12
Fees: (September 95) £2172 - £3693

SPRATTON HALL
Spratton, Northampton NN6 8HP
Tel: (01604) 847292
Head: A P Bickley
Type: Co-educational Day 4-13
No of Pupils: B199 G115
Fees: (September 95) £1200 - £4485

WESTON FAVELL PREPARATORY SCHOOL
473 Wellingborough Road,
Northampton NN3 3HN
Tel: (01604) 712098
Head: Mrs Claire Stanford-Jones
Type: Co-educational Day 4-9
(Montessori pre-school 2-4)
No of Pupils: B40 G40
Fees: (September 95) £2220 - £2295

PITSFORD

NORTHAMPTONSHIRE GRAMMAR SCHOOL*
Pitsford Hall, Pitsford,
Northamptonshire NN6 9AX
Tel: (01604) 880306
Head: P D Hanson
Type: Boys Day 7-18
No of Pupils: 200
Fees: (September 95) £4530 - £4830

TOWCESTER

FALCON MANOR
Greens Norton, Towcester,
Northamptonshire NN12 8BN
Tel: (01327) 50544
Head: G D Priest
Type: Co-educational Boarding &
Day 8-18
No of Pupils: B90 G40 No of
Boarders W120
Fees: (September 95) FB £6953 -
£7725 WB £6210 - £6900 DAY
£3000 - £4650

WELLINGBOROUGH

WELLINGBOROUGH SCHOOL*
Wellingborough, Northamptonshire
NN8 2BX
Tel: (01933) 222427
Head: F R Ullmann
Type: Co-educational Day &
Boarding 4-18 (Boarding 13-18 only)
No of Pupils: B502 G309 No of
Boarders F56
Fees: (September 95) FB £9100 –
£12600 WB £8370 DAY £2480 –
£5175

NORTHUMBERLAND

ALNWICK

ST OSWALD'S SCHOOL
Spring Gardens, South Road,
Alnwick, Northumberland
NE66 2NU
Tel: (01665) 602739
Head: Dr A J Robb
Type: Co-educational Day 3-18
No of Pupils: B36 G76
Fees: (September 95) £1800 – £2970

BERWICK-UPON-TWEED

LONGRIDGE TOWERS SCHOOL
Berwick-upon-Tweed,
Northumberland TD15 2XH
Tel: (01289) 307584
Head: Dr M J Barron
Type: Co-educational Day &
Boarding 4-18
No of Pupils: B140 G152 No of
Boarders F72 W8
Fees: (September 95) FB £7485 –
£8100 WB £7035 – £7650 DAY
£2400 – £4050

HEXHAM

CROFT HOUSE SCHOOL
Leazes Lane, Hexham,
Northumberland NE46 3BB
Tel: (01434) 602082
Head: Mrs J M Peers
Type: Co-educational Day 3-11
No of Pupils: B31 G52
Fees: (September 95) £3240 – £3675

STOCKSFIELD

MOWDEN HALL SCHOOL
Newton, Stocksfield,
Northumberland NE43 7TD
Tel: (01661) 842147
Head: A Lewis
Type: Co-educational Boarding &
Day 4-13
No of Pupils: B110 G40 No of
Boarders F103 W10
Fees: (September 95) F/WB £7980
DAY £3450 – £5955

NOTTINGHAMSHIRE

MANSFIELD

SAVILLE HOUSE SCHOOL
11 Church Street, Mansfield
Woodhouse, Mansfield,
Nottinghamshire NG19 8AH
Tel: (01623) 25068
Type: Co-educational Day 3-11
No of Pupils: B74 G70
Fees: (September 95) £1200 – £1230

NEWARK

EDGEHILL SCHOOL
Main Street, Edingley, Newark,
Nottinghamshire NG22 8BE
Tel: (01623) 882936
Head: Mrs A Burton
Type: Co-educational Day 2-11
No of Pupils: B40 G30
Fees: (September 95) £2420

HIGHFIELDS SCHOOL
London Road, Newark,
Nottinghamshire NG24 3AL
Tel: (01636) 704103
Head: P F Smith
Type: Co-educational Day 2-11
No of Pupils: B122 G93
Fees: (September 95) £2460

RODNEY SCHOOL
Kirklington, Newark,
Nottinghamshire NG22 8NB
Tel: (01636) 813281
Head: Dr C Reynolds
Type: Co-educational Boarding &
Day 8-18
No of Pupils: B59 G47 No of
Boarders F59
Fees: (September 95) F/WB £5550 -
£5775 DAY £3150 - £3375

WELLOW HOUSE SCHOOL
Wellow, Newark, Nottinghamshire
NG22 0EA
Tel: (01623) 861054
Head: Dr M D W Tozer
Type: Co-educational Day &
Boarding 2-13
No of Pupils: B50 G40 No of
Boarders W10
Fees: (September 95) WB £6750 DAY
£2400 - £5025

NOTTINGHAM

**ATTENBOROUGH
PREPARATORY SCHOOL**
The Strand, Attenborough, Beeston,
Nottingham NG9 6AU
Tel: (0115) 943 6725
Head: Mrs M Cahill
Type: Co-educational Day 4-11
No of Pupils: 90
Fees: (September 95) £1095 - £1650

BROADGATE SCHOOL
1 Western Terrace, The Park,
Nottingham NG7 1AF
Tel: (0115) 947 4275
Head: T Osgerby
Type: Co-educational Day 4-16
No of Pupils: B50 G35
Fees: (September 95) £2100 - £3500

COTESWOOD HOUSE SCHOOL
19 Thackeray's Lane, Woodthorpe,
Nottingham NG5 4HT
Tel: (0115) 967 6551
Head: Miss E Gamble
Type: Co-educational Day 3-11
No of Pupils: 44
Fees: (September 95) £1260

DAGFA HOUSE SCHOOL
Broadgate, Beeston, Nottingham
NG9 2FU
Tel: (0115) 925 4100
Head: A Oatway
Type: Co-educational Day 2-16
No of Pupils: B115 G100
Fees: (September 95) £927 - £3345

GREENHOLME SCHOOL
392 Derby Road, Lenton,
Nottingham NG7 2DX
Tel: (0115) 978 7329
Head: Miss P M Breen
Type: Co-educational Day 3-11
No of Pupils: B149 G79
Fees: (September 95) £1980 - £3285

GROSVENOR SCHOOL
Edwalton, Nottingham NG12 4BS
Tel: (0115) 923 1184
Head: C G J Oldershaw
Type: Co-educational Day 4-13
No of Pupils: B127 G50
Fees: (September 95) £2634 - £2904

HOLLYGIRT SCHOOL
Elm Avenue, Nottingham NG3 4GF
Tel: (0115) 958 0596
Head: Mrs M R Banks
Type: Girls Day 4-16
No of Pupils: 320
Fees: (September 95) £2745 - £3636

THE KING'S SCHOOL
Collygate Road, The Meadows,
Nottingham
Tel: (0115) 9539194
Head: R Southey
Type: Co-educational Day 5-16
No of Pupils: B80 G82
Fees: On application

**THE MOUNT PREPARATORY
SCHOOL**
Cranmer Mount, St Ann's Hill,
Woodborough Road, Nottingham
NG3 4LA
Tel: (0115) 960 7439
Head: Mrs J Chadwick-Dobson
Type: Co-educational Day 4-9
No of Pupils: 60
Fees: (September 95) £3101

MOUNTFORD HOUSE SCHOOL
373 Mansfield Road, Nottingham
NG5 2DA
Tel: (0115) 960 5676
Head: Mrs D Williams
Type: Co-educational Day 3-11
No of Pupils: B108 G30
Fees: (September 95) £1287 - £2766

**NOTTINGHAM HIGH SCHOOL
PREPARATORY SCHOOL**
Waverley Mount, Nottingham
NG7 4ED
Tel: (0115) 978 9411
Head: P M Pallant
Type: Boys Day 7-11
No of Pupils: 190
Fees: (September 95) £3699

NOTTINGHAM HIGH SCHOOL
Waverley Mount, Nottingham
NG7 4ED
Tel: (0115) 978 6056
Head: C S Parker
Type: Boys Day 11-18
No of Pupils: 838
Fees: (September 95) £4644

**NOTTINGHAM HIGH SCHOOL
FOR GIRLS**
9 Arboretum Street, Nottingham
NG1 4JB
Tel: (0115) 941 7663
Head: Mrs C Bowering
Type: Girls Day 4-18
No of Pupils: 1090
Fees: (September 95) £2928 - £3984

PLUMTREE SCHOOL
Church Hill, Plumtree, Nottingham
NG12 5ND
Tel: (0115) 937 5859
Head: N White
Type: Co-educational Day 3-11
No of Pupils: B61 G52
Fees: (September 95) £2340 - £2370

PNEU SCHOOL
13 Waverley Street, Nottingham
NG7 4DX
Tel: (0115) 978 3230
Head: T J Collins
Type: Co-educational Day B3-8
G3-11
No of Pupils: B48 G82
Fees: (September 95) £2940 - £3105

**ST JOSEPH'S PREPARATORY
SCHOOL**
33 Derby Road, Nottingham
NG1 5AW
Tel: (0115) 941 8356
Head: Miss M McNamara
Type: Co-educational Day 1-11
No of Pupils: B122 G89
Fees: (September 95) £2640

SALTERFORD HOUSE SCHOOL
Salterford Lane, Calverton,
Nottingham NG14 6NZ
Tel: (0115) 965 2127
Head: Mrs M Venables
Type: Co-educational Day 2-11
No of Pupils: B100 G98
Fees: (September 95) £2325 - £2385

TRENT COLLEGE
Long Eaton, Nottingham NG10 4AD
Tel: (0115) 973 2737
Head: J S Lee
Type: Co-educational Boarding &
Day 11-18
No of Pupils: B567 G90 No of
Boarders F280
Fees: (September 95) FB £8946 -
£10425 DAY £5919 - £6375

TRENT FIELDS PREPARATORY
19/21 Trent Boulevard, West
Bridgford, Nottingham NG2 5BB
Tel: (0115) 982 1685
Head: Mrs G A Robinson
Type: Co-educational Day 4-7
No of Pupils: 16
Fees: (September 95) £3950

**WEST BRIDGFORD HIGH
SCHOOL**
61-63 Musters Road, West
Bridgford, Nottingham NG2 7PY
Tel: (0115) 981 2967
Head: C W Redwood
Type: Boys Day 5-18 (Co-ed VIth
form)
No of Pupils: 100
Fees: (September 95) £2685 - £3525

RETFORD

**AL KARAM SECONDARY
SCHOOL**
Eaton Hall, Retford, Nottinghamshire
Tel: (01777) 706441
Head: I H Pirzada
Type: Boys Boarding 11-18
No of Pupils: 170
Fees: (September 95) FB £1500

BRAMCOTE SCHOOL
Gamston, Retford, Nottinghamshire
DN22 0QQ
Tel: (01777) 838636
Head: D H Fuller
Type: Co-educational Boarding &
Day 2-13
No of Pupils: B120 G50 No of
Boarders F50 W15
Fees: (September 95) F/WB £7050
DAY £2250 - £5400

LORNE HOUSE
London Road, Retford,
Nottinghamshire DN22 7EB
Tel: (01777) 703434
Head: A N Brownridge
Type: Co-educational Day 3-13
No of Pupils: B68 G72
Fees: (September 94) £2025 - £3165

ORCHARD SCHOOL
South Leverton, Retford,
Nottinghamshire DN22 0DJ
Tel: (01427) 880395
Head: Mrs S Fox
Type: Co-educational Day 2-16
No of Pupils: B70 G60
Fees: (September 93) £1500 - £2700

RANBY HOUSE
Retford, Nottinghamshire DN22 8HX
Tel: (01777) 703138
Head: D C Wansey
Type: Co-educational Boarding &
Day 3-13
No of Pupils: B185 G120 No of
Boarders F58
Fees: (September 95) F/WB £7065
DAY £2850 - £5355

SUTTON IN ASHFIELD

LAMMAS SCHOOL
Lammas Road, Sutton In Ashfield,
Nottinghamshire NG17 2AD
Tel: (01623) 516879
Head: C M Peck
Type: Co-educational Day 4-16
No of Pupils: 130
Fees: (September 95) £2100 - £2400

WEST BRIDGFORD

**LOCKSLEY PREPARATORY
SCHOOL**
1 Selby Road, West Bridgford,
Nottinghamshire NG2 7BP
Tel: (0115) 981 2980
Head: A G Todhunter
Type: Co-educational Day 3-11
No of Pupils: 30
Fees: (September 95) £1690

WORKSOP

WORKSOP COLLEGE
Worksop, Nottinghamshire S80 3AP
Tel: (01909) 472391
Head: R A Collard
Type: Co-educational Boarding &
Day 13-18
No of Pupils: B250 G100 No of
Boarders F130 W60
Fees: (September 95) F/WB £10785
DAY £7440

OXFORDSHIRE

ABINGDON

ABINGDON SCHOOL*
Park Road, Abingdon, Oxfordshire
OX14 IDE
Tel: (01235) 521563
Head: M St John Parker
Type: Boys Boarding & Day 11-18
No of Pupils: 765 No of Boarders F50
W75
Fees: (September 95) F/WB £9849
DAY £5262

**COTHILL HOUSE
PREPARATORY SCHOOL**
Frilford Heath, Abingdon,
Oxfordshire OX13 6JL
Tel: (01865) 390800
Head: A D Richardson
Type: Boys Boarding & Day 8-13
No of Pupils: 260 No of Boarders
F253
Fees: (September 95) FB £9600 DAY
£6420

**JOSCA'S PREPARATORY
SCHOOL**
Frilford, Abingdon, Oxfordshire
OX13 5NX
Tel: (01865) 391570
Head: A Savin
Type: Boys Day 4-13 (Girls 4-7)
No of Pupils: B163 G2
Fees: (September 95) £3285 - £4650

MANOR PREPARATORY SCHOOL
Faringdon Road, Abingdon,
Oxfordshire OX13 6LN
Tel: (01235) 523789
Head: Mrs J H Hearnden
Type: Co-educational Day B3-7
G3-11
No of Pupils: B58 G301
Fees: (September 95) £1785 - £3915

MILLBROOK HOUSE*
Milton, Abingdon, Oxfordshire
OX14 4EL
Tel: (01235) 831237
Head: S R Glazebrook
Type: Co-educational Day &
Boarding 7-14
No of Pupils: 50
Fees: (September 95) FB £9900 DAY
£6900

OUR LADY'S CONVENT JUNIOR SCHOOL
St John's Road, Abingdon,
Oxfordshire OX14 2EB
Tel: (01235) 523147
Head: Sister Jean Frances
Type: Co-educational Day 4-11
No of Pupils: B75 G75
Fees: (September 95) £2655 - £2745

OUR LADY'S CONVENT SENIOR SCHOOL
Radley Road, Abingdon, Oxfordshire
OX14 3PS
Tel: (01235) 524658
Head: Sister Deidre Byrne
Type: Girls Day 11-18
No of Pupils: 350
Fees: (September 95) £3975

RADLEY COLLEGE
Abingdon, Oxfordshire OX14 2HR
Tel: (01235) 520294
Head: R M Morgan
Type: Boys Boarding 13-18
No of Pupils: 600 No of Boarders
F600
Fees: (September 95) FB £12300

SCHOOL OF S HELEN & S KATHARINE
Faringdon Road, Abingdon,
Oxfordshire OX14 1BE
Tel: (01235) 520173
Head: Mrs C Hall
Type: Girls Day 9-18 (VIth form
boarders only)
No of Pupils: 528 No of Boarders
W28
Fees: (September 95) WB £8250 DAY
£4500

BANBURY

BLOXHAM SCHOOL*
Bloxham, Banbury, Oxfordshire
OX15 4PE
Tel: (01295) 720206
Head: Mr D K Exham
Type: Boys Boarding & Day 13-18
(Day boys 11-13, co-ed VIth form)
No of Pupils: B300 G60 No of
Boarders F290 W70
Fees: (April 95) FB £11580 DAY
£5985 - £8985

THE CARRDUS SCHOOL
Overthorpe Hall, Banbury,
Oxfordshire OX17 2BS
Tel: (01295) 263733
Head: Miss S Carrdus
Type: Co-educational Day 3-11 (Boys 3-8)
No of Pupils: B18 G111
Fees: (September 95) £1260 - £3930

ST JOHN'S PRIORY SCHOOL
St John's Road, Banbury,
Oxfordshire OX16 8HX
Tel: (01295) 259607
Head: Mrs J M Walker
Type: Co-educational Day 3-11
No of Pupils: 95
Fees: (September 95) £2250 - £2400

SIBFORD SCHOOL
Sibford Ferris, Banbury, Oxfordshire
OX15 5QL
Tel: (01295) 780441
Head: J Dunston
Type: Co-educational Boarding &
Day 6-18
No of Pupils: B207 G113 No of
Boarders F117 W61
Fees: (September 95) F/WB £6885 -
£9600 DAY £3075 - £5085

TUDOR HALL SCHOOL
Banbury, Oxfordshire OX16 9UR
Tel: (01295) 263434
Head: Miss N Godfrey
Type: Girls Boarding 11-18
No of Pupils: 260 No of Boarders
F240
Fees: (September 95) FB £10140 DAY
£6318

FARINGDON

FERNDALE SCHOOL
Faringdon, Oxfordshire SN7 7JF
Tel: (01367) 240618
Head: J R Hunt
Type: Co-educational Day 3-11
No of Pupils: B65 G65
Fees: (September 95) £2685 - £3240

ST HUGH'S SCHOOL
Carswell Manor, Faringdon,
Oxfordshire SN7 8PT
Tel: (01367) 87223
Head: D Cannon
Type: Co-educational Boarding &
Day 4-13
No of Pupils: B158 G72 No of
Boarders F33 W32
Fees: (September 95) F/WB £7950
DAY £2850 - £6150

ST MARY'S PRIORY NURSERY SCHOOL
St Mary's Priory, Fernham,
Faringdon, Oxfordshire SN7 7PP
Tel: (01367) 240133
Head: Sister Mary Stephen
Type: Co-educational Day 3-5
No of Pupils: 25
Fees: On application

HENLEY-ON-THAMES

RUPERT HOUSE
90 Bell Street, Henley-on-Thames,
Oxfordshire RG9 2BN
Tel: (01491) 574263
Head: Mrs S B Dixon
Type: Co-educational Day B4-8
G4-12
No of Pupils: B75 G149
Fees: (September 95) £1785 - £4380

ST MARY'S PREPARATORY SCHOOL
13 St Andrew's Road,
Henley-on-Thames, Oxfordshire
RG9 1HS
Tel: (01491) 573118
Head: Mrs S Bradley
Type: Co-educational Day 2-12
No of Pupils: B33 G64
Fees: (September 95) £975 - £4635

SHIPLAKE COLLEGE
Henley-on-Thames, Oxfordshire
RG9 4BW
Tel: (01734) 402455
Head: N V Bevan
Type: Boys Day & Boarding 13-18
No of Pupils: 310 No of Boarders
F245
Fees: (September 95) FB £11175 DAY
£7530

OXFORD

ABACUS COLLEGE*
Threeways House, George Street,
Oxford OX1 2BJ
Tel: (01865) 240111
Head: Mrs L Brown
Type: Co-educational Day and
Residential
No of Pupils: B75 G45
Fees: (September 95) FB £4635 -
£12625 DAY £1830 - £9150

BRUERN ABBEY SCHOOL
Bruern, Oxford OX7 6PZ
Tel: (01993) 831831
Head: R Woods
Type: Boys Boarding & Day 8-13
No of Pupils: 45
Fees: (September 93) F/WB £7323
DAY £5265

CHRIST CHURCH
CATHEDRAL SCHOOL
3 Brewer Street, Oxford OX1 1QW
Tel: (01865) 242561
Head: A Mottram
Type: Boys Day & Boarding 4-13
No of Pupils: 130 No of Boarders F25
Fees: (September 95) FB £3426 -
£7596 DAY £2961 - £4977

COLLINGHAM BROWN &
BROWN TUTORIAL COLLEGE
31 St Giles, Oxford OX1 3LF
Tel: (01865) 728280
Head: Andrew Shepherd
Type: Co-educational Day 12+
No of Pupils: B24 G29
Fees: 3 A Levels £7800 5 GCSEs
£6750

D'OVERBROECK'S*
1 Park Town, Oxford OX2 6SN
Tel: (01865) 310000
Head: J D Noel
Type: Co-educational Day &
Residential 16-19
No of Pupils: B120 G100
Fees: (September 95) FB £12765
DAY £9165

DRAGON SCHOOL
Bardwell Road, Oxford OX2 6SS
Tel: (01865) 315400
Head: R S Trafford
Type: Co-educational Boarding &
Day 3-13
No of Pupils: B625 G140 No of
Boarders F230
Fees: (September 95) FB £9327 DAY
£3300 - £6111

EDWARD GREENE'S
TUTORIAL ESTABLISHMENT
45 Pembroke Street, Oxford OX1 1BP
Tel: (01865) 248308
Head: E P Greene MA
Type: Co-educational Day
No of Pupils: B31 G24
Fees: (September 95) 3 A Levels
£9360 5 GCSEs £10400

EMMANUAL CHRISTIAN
SCHOOL
359 Woodstock Road, Oxford
OX2 8AA
Tel: (01865) 311828
Head: S McTegart
Type: Co-educational 4-16
No of Pupils: B30 G15
Fees: (September 95) DAY £1200 -
£1890

GREYCOTES SCHOOL
1 Bardwell Road, Oxford OX2 6SU
Tel: (01865) 515647
Head: Mrs S R Hayward
Type: Co-educational Day B3-7
G3-11
No of Pupils: B75 G168
Fees: (September 95) £1890 - £4095

HEADINGTON SCHOOL*
Oxford OX3 7TD
Tel: (01865) 62711
Head: Miss E M Tucker
Type: Girls Day & Boarding 4-18
(Co-ed 4-7)
No of Pupils: B15 G713 No of
Boarders F124 W84
Fees: (September 95) FB £9030 WB
£8940 DAY £4524

KINGHAM HILL SCHOOL*
Kingham, Chipping Norton, Oxford
OX7 6TH
Tel: (01608) 658999
Head: M H Payne
Type: Co-educational Boarding &
Day 11-18
No of Pupils: B164 G46 No of
Boarders F190
Fees: (September 95) FB £9204 -
£9477 DAY £5520 - £5685

MAGDALEN COLLEGE SCHOOL
Cowley Place, Oxford OX4 1DZ
Tel: (01865) 242191
Head: P M Tinniswood
Type: Boys Day & Boarding 9-18
(Boarding for Choristers only)
No of Pupils: 510 No of Boarders F15
Fees: (September 95) FB £9126 DAY
£4809

NEW COLLEGE SCHOOL
2 Savile Road, Oxford OX1 3UA
Tel: (01865) 243657
Head: J Edmunds
Type: Boys Day 7-13
No of Pupils: 132
Fees: (September 95) £4080 - £4470

OXFORD HIGH SCHOOL
GPDST
Belbroughton Road, Oxford OX2 6XA
Tel: (01865) 59888
Head: Mrs J Townsend
Type: Girls Day 9-18
No of Pupils: 650
Fees: (September 95) £2928 - £3984

OXFORD TUTORIAL COLLEGE
16 Gloucester Street, Oxford
OX1 2BN
Tel: (01865) 793333
Head: Ralph Dennison
Type: Co-educational Day 16+
No of Pupils: B40 G40
Fees: (September 95) 3 A Levels
£8892 5 GCSEs £7500

RYE ST ANTONY SCHOOL*
Pullen's Lane, Headington Hill,
Oxford OX3 0BY
Tel: (01865) 62802
Head: Miss A M Jones
Type: Girls Boarding & Day 8-18
No of Pupils: 380 No of Boarders
F120 W30
Fees: (September 95) F/WB £7350 -
£8550 DAY £2250 - £5250

ST CLARE'S, OXFORD*
139 Banbury Road, Oxford OX2 7AL
Tel: (01865) 52031
Head: Mrs M Skarland
Type: Co-educational Residential
16-20
No of Pupils: B106 G169
Fees: (September 95) FB £12820 -
£13040 DAY £5020

ST EDWARD'S SCHOOL
Woodstock Road, Oxford OX2 7NN
Tel: (01865) 319204
Head: D Christie
Type: Boys Boarding & Day 13-18
(Co-ed VIth form)
No of Pupils: B514 G59 No of
Boarders F447
Fees: (September 95) FB £12270 DAY
£9210

THE SQUIRREL SCHOOL
90 Woodstock Road, Oxford
OX2 7ND
Tel: (01865) 58279
Head: Mrs M Easton
Type: Co-educational Day 3-9
No of Pupils: B65 G85
Fees: (September 95) £1380 - £2670

SUMMER FIELDS
Oxford OX2 7EN
Tel: (01865) 54433
Head: N Talbot Rice
Type: Boys Boarding & Day 8-13
No of Pupils: 255 No of Boarders
F241
Fees: (September 95) FB £9690 DAY
£6300

WINDRUSH VALLEY SCHOOL
The Green, London Lane, Chipping
Norton, Oxford OX7 6AN
Tel: (01993) 831793
Head: Mr & Mrs Kean
Type: Co-educational Day
No of Pupils: B55 G55
Fees: (September 95) £515 - £895

WYCHWOOD SCHOOL
74 Banbury Road, Oxford OX2 6JR
Tel: (01865) 57976
Head: Mrs M L Duffill
Type: Girls Boarding & Day 11-18
No of Pupils: 160 No of Boarders F46
W34
Fees: (September 95) FB £6885 DAY
£4350

THAME

CHILTERN HOUSE SCHOOL
30 Queens Road, Thame,
Oxfordshire OX9 3NQ
Tel: (01844) 212932
Head: Mrs J M Dodds
Type: Co-educational Day 3-8
No of Pupils: 80
Fees: (September 95) £480 - £2070

WALLINGFORD

CARMEL COLLEGE
Mongewell Park, Wallingford,
Oxfordshire OX10 8BT
Tel: (01491) 837505
Head: P D Skelker
Type: Co-educational Boarding &
Day 11-18
No of Pupils: B135 G78 No of
Boarders F200
Fees: (September 95) FB £9000 -
£17640 DAY £7305

CRANFORD HOUSE SCHOOL
Moulsford, Wallingford, Oxfordshire
OX10 9HT
Tel: (01491) 651218
Head: Mrs A B Gray
Type: Girls Day 3-16 (Boys 3-7)
No of Pupils: B36 G202
Fees: (September 95) £1053 - £4920

MOULSFORD PREPARATORY
SCHOOL
Moulsford, Wallingford, Oxfordshire
OX10 9HR
Tel: (01491) 651438
Head: M J Higham
Type: Boys Boarding & Day 7-13
No of Pupils: 175 No of Boarders
W51
Fees: (September 95) WB £7305 DAY
£5775

WANTAGE

ST ANDREW'S
Wallingford Street, Wantage,
Oxfordshire OX12 8AZ
Tel: (01235) 762345
Head: Mrs M A Farley & Mrs M E
Macbeth
Type: Co-educational Day 3-11
No of Pupils: B65 G65
Fees: (September 95) £1194 - £2775

ST MARY'S SCHOOL*
Wantage, Oxfordshire OX12 8BZ
Tel: (01235) 763571
Head: Mrs S Bodinham
Type: Girls Boarding 11-18 (a few
day places)
No of Pupils: 230 No of Boarders
F230
Fees: (September 95) FB £10860 DAY
£7200

WITNEY

COKETHORPE SCHOOL*
Witney, Oxfordshire OX8 7PU
Tel: (01993) 703921
Head: P J S Cantwell
Type: Co-educational Boarding &
Day 9-18 (Day girls only)
No of Pupils: 210 No of Boarders F50
W40
Fees: (September 95) F/WB £9495 -
£11940 DAY £4050 - £7860

THE KING'S SCHOOL
New Yatt Road, Witney, Oxfordshire
OX8 6TA
Tel: (01993) 778463
Head: D W Freeman
Type: Co-educational Day 5-16
No of Pupils: 175
Fees: (September 94) £2250

SHROPSHIRE

BUCKNELL

BEDSTONE COLLEGE*
Bedstone, Bucknell, Shropshire
SY7 0BG
Tel: (01547) 530303
Head: M S Symonds
Type: Co-educational Boarding &
Day 4-19
No of Pupils: B111 G73 No of
Boarders F159
Fees: (September 95) F/WB £9639
DAY £4131 - £6006

ELLESMERE

ELLESMERE COLLEGE
Ellesmere, Shropshire SY12 9AB
Tel: (01691) 622321
Head: D R Du Croz
Type: Boys Day & Boarding 10-18
(Girls 10-13 and 16-18)
No of Pupils: B300 G50 No of
Boarders F221
Fees: (September 95) FB £10500 DAY
£4500 - £6999

LUDLOW

MOOR PARK SCHOOL
Ludlow, Shropshire SY8 4EA
Tel: (01584) 876061
Head: J R Badham
Type: Co-educational Boarding &
Day 3-14
No of Pupils: B135 G92 No of
Boarders F35 W67
Fees: (September 94) F/WB £7485
DAY £600 - £5370

NEWPORT

CASTLE HOUSE SCHOOL
Chetwynd End, Newport, Shropshire
TF10 7JE
Tel: (01952) 811035
Head: Mrs A E Davies
Type: Co-educational Day 3-11
No of Pupils: B65 G65
Fees: (September 95) £1275 - £2565

OSWESTRY

BELLAN HOUSE PREPARATORY SCHOOL
Bellan House, Church Street,
Oswestry, Shropshire SY11 2ST
Tel: (01691) 653453
Head: Mrs S L Durham
Type: Co-educational Day 2-9
No of Pupils: B87 G92
Fees: (September 95) £765 - £3255

MORETON HALL*
Weston Rhyn, Oswestry, Shropshire
SY11 3EW
Tel: (01691) 773671
Head: J Forster
Type: Girls Boarding & Day 11-18
No of Pupils: 280 No of Boarders
F265
Fees: (September 94) FB £10950 DAY
£7590

OSWESTRY JUNIOR SCHOOL
The Quarry, Upper Brook Street,
Oswestry, Shropshire SY11 2TJ
Tel: (01691) 653209
Head: C J Rickart
Type: Co-educational Day &
Boarding 8-13
No of Pupils: B90 G73 No of Boarders
F33
Fees: (September 95) FB £8616 -
£9090 DAY £4875 - £5316

OSWESTRY SCHOOL
Upper Brook Street, Oswestry,
Shropshire SY11 2TL
Tel: (01691) 655711
Head: P K Smith
Type: Co-educational Boarding &
Day 13-18
No of Pupils: B179 G103 No of
Boarders F107
Fees: (September 95) FB £9090 DAY
£5316

QUEEN'S PARK SCHOOL
Queen's Road, Oswestry, Shropshire
SY11 2HZ
Tel: (01691) 652416
Head: Mrs D Baur
Type: Co-educational Boarding &
Day 8-16
No of Pupils: 50
Fees: (September 95) FB £11433 -
£11997 WB £10797 - £11325 DAY
£8385 - £8784

SHREWSBURY

ADCOTE SCHOOL
Little Ness, Shrewsbury, Shropshire
SY4 2JY
Tel: (01939) 260202
Head: Mrs S B Cecchet
Type: Girls Boarding & Day 5-18
No of Pupils: 102 No of Boarders F32
W11
Fees: (September 95) FB £7260 -
£9195 WB £6405 - £8340 DAY
£2850 - £5100

CONCORD COLLEGE*
Acton Burnell Hall, Shrewsbury,
Shropshire SY5 7PF
Tel: (01694) 731631
Head: A L Morris
Type: Co-educational Residential &
Day 12-20
No of Pupils: B140 G110
Fees: (September 95) FB £11850

KINGSLAND GRANGE
Old Roman Road, Shrewsbury,
Shropshire SY3 9AH
Tel: (01743) 232132
Head: M C James
Type: Boys Day & Boarding 4-13
No of Pupils: 165 No of Boarders
W12
Fees: (September 95) WB £5100 DAY
£2280   £1200

PACKWOOD HAUGH*
Ruyton XI Towns, Shrewsbury,
Shropshire SY4 1HX
Tel: (01939) 260217
Head: P J F Jordan
Type: Co-educational Boarding &
Day 4-13
No of Pupils: B130 G90 No of
Boarders F130
Fees: (September 95) FB £8064 DAY
£2724 - £6270

PRESTFELDE PREPARATORY SCHOOL
London Road, Shrewsbury,
Shropshire SY2 6NZ
Tel: (01743) 356500
Head: J R Bridgeland
Type: Boys Day & Boarding 3-13
No of Pupils: 257 No of Boarders F67
Fees: (September 95) FB £6690 DAY
£1470 - £5025

ST WINEFRIDE'S CONVENT SCHOOL
Belmont, Shrewsbury, Shropshire
SY1 1LS
Tel: (01743) 69883
Head: Sister Felicity
Type: Co-educational Day 4-11
No of Pupils: B40 G80
Fees: (September 95) £1425 - £1470

SHREWSBURY HIGH SCHOOL GPDST
32 Town Walls, Shrewsbury,
Shropshire SY1 1TN
Tel: (01743) 362872
Head: Miss S Gardner
Type: Girls Day 4-18
No of Pupils: 581
Fees: (September 95) £2928 - £3984

SHREWSBURY SCHOOL
The Schools, Kingsland, Shrewsbury,
Shropshire SY3 7BA
Tel: (01743) 344537
Head: F E Maidment
Type: Boys Boarding & Day 13-18
No of Pupils: 695 No of Boarders
F550
Fees: (September 95) FB £12375 DAY
£8700

TELFORD

THE OLD HALL SCHOOL
Holyhead Road, Wellington, Telford,
Shropshire TF1 2DN
Tel: (01952) 223117
Head: R J Ward
Type: Co-educational Day &
Boarding 3-13
No of Pupils: B150 G160 No of
Boarders W34
Fees: (September 95) WB £5655 DAY
£2805 - £4410

WREKIN COLLEGE*
Wellington, Telford, Shropshire
TF1 3BH
Tel: (01952) 240131
Head: P M Johnson
Type: Co-educational Boarding &
Day 11-19
No of Pupils: 260 No of Boarders
F182
Fees: (September 95) FB £10890 DAY
£5085 - £5970

WHITCHURCH

WHITE HOUSE SCHOOL
Heath Road, Whitchurch, Shropshire
SY13 2AA
Tel: (01948) 662730
Head: Mrs E Hall
Type: Co-educational Day 4-11
No of Pupils: B80 G80
Fees: (September 95) £1440

SOMERSET

BRIDGWATER

QUANTOCK SCHOOL
Over Stowey, Bridgwater, Somerset
TA5 1HD
Tel: (01278) 732252
Head: D T Peaster
Type: Co-educational Day &
Boarding 8-16
No of Pupils: B120 G60
Fees: (September 94) FB £6000 -
£7800 WB £5700 - £7500 DAY
£2100 - £3600

BRUTON

BRUTON SCHOOL FOR GIRLS*
Sunny Hill, Bruton, Somerset
BA10 0NT
Tel: (01749) 812277
Head: Mrs J M Wade
Type: Girls Day & Boarding 8-18
No of Pupils: 540 No of Boarders
F160 W70
Fees: (September 95) F/WB £6354 -
£6990 DAY £3150 - £3786

KING'S SCHOOL
Bruton, Somerset BA10 0ED
Tel: (01749) 813326
Head: R I Smyth
Type: Boys Boarding & Day 13-18
(Co-ed VIth form)
No of Pupils: B291 G20 No of
Boarders F248
Fees: (September 95) FB £10965 DAY
£7770

BURNHAM-ON-SEA

**SOUTHLEIGH
KINDERGARTEN**
11 Rectory Road, Burnham on Sea,
Somerset
Tel: (01278) 783999
Head: Mrs J Murray
Type: Co-educational Day 2-9
No of Pupils: B31 G20
Fees: (September 95) £1665 - £1860

ST CHRISTOPHER'S
93 Berrow Road, Burnham-on-Sea,
Somerset TA8 2NY
Tel: (01278) 782234
Head: Mrs S P Morrell-Davies
Type: Girls Day & Boarding 3-13
(Boys 3-11)
No of Pupils: 126 No of Boarders F17
Fees: (September 95) F/WB £7350
DAY £2250 - £4410

CHARD

**CHARD INDEPENDENT
SCHOOL**
Fore Street, Chard, Somerset
TA20 1QE
Tel: (01460) 63234
Head: C Organ
Type: Co-educational Day 3-11
No of Pupils: B63 G40
Fees: (September 95) £2000 - £2200

CREWKERNE

PERROTT HILL SCHOOL*
North Perrott, Crewkerne, Somerset
TA18 7SL
Tel: (01460) 72051
Head: J E Barnes
Type: Co-educational Boarding &
Day 3-13
No of Pupils: B109 G37 No of
Boarders F16 W18
Fees: (September 95) F/WB £7539
DAY £1620 - £5424

**ST MARTIN'S INDEPENDENT
SCHOOL**
24 Abbey Street, Crewkerne,
Somerset TA18 7HY
Tel: (01460) 73265
Head: Mrs J A Murrell
Type: Co-educational Day 4-13
No of Pupils: B50 G50
Fees: (September 95) £1200 - £2850

GLASTONBURY

ABBEY SCHOOL
Magdalene Street, Glastonbury,
Somerset BA6 9EJ
Tel: (01458) 832902
Head: Mrs K L Cookson
Type: Co-educational Day 3-8
No of Pupils: B87 G63
Fees: (September 95) £2400 - £2550

EDGARLEY HALL*
Glastonbury, Somerset BA6 8LD
Tel: (01458) 832446
Head: R J Smyth
Type: Co-educational Boarding &
Day 8-13
No of Pupils: B262 G174 No of
Boarders F254
Fees: (September 95) FB £9735 DAY
£6330

HIGHBRIDGE

ROSSHOLME SCHOOL
East Brent, Highbridge, Somerset
TA9 4JA
Tel: (01278) 760219
Head: Mrs S J Webb
Type: Girls Boarding & Day 7-16
(Co-ed 3-7)
No of Pupils: B4 G72 No of Boarders
F14
Fees: (September 95) FB £6495 -
£6990 WB £6375 - £6870 DAY
£1590 - £3570

SHEPTON MALLET

ALL HALLOWS*
Cranmore Hall, East Cranmore,
Shepton Mallet, Somerset BA4 4SF
Tel: (01749) 880227
Head: C J Bird
Type: Co-educational Boarding &
Day 3-14
No of Pupils: B125 G87 No of
Boarders F73 W10
Fees: (September 95) F/WB £8280
DAY £2700 - £5400

STREET

CEDAR SCHOOL
Friends Meeting House, High Street,
Street, Somerset BA16 0EB
Tel: (01458) 442533
Head: Mrs P Thomas
Type: Co-educational Day 3-7
No of Pupils: B19 G14
Fees: (September 95) £354 - £1200

MILLFIELD SCHOOL
Street, Somerset BA16 0YD
Tel: (01458) 442291
Head: C S Martin
Type: Co-educational Boarding &
Day 13-19
No of Pupils: B733 G516 No of
Boarders F953
Fees: (September 95) FB £13320 DAY
£8310

TAUNTON

BEEHIVE SCHOOL
68 Wellington Road, Taunton,
Somerset TA1 5AP
Tel: (01823) 333638
Head: J P Garrett
Type: Co-educational Day 4-11
No of Pupils: B70 G70
Fees: (September 95) £1305 - £1320

KING'S COLLEGE
Taunton, Somerset TA1 3DX
Tel: (01823) 272708
Head: R S Funnell
Type: Co-educational Boarding &
Day 13-18
No of Pupils: B333 G133 No of
Boarders F381
Fees: (September 95) FB £11490 DAY
£7560

KING'S HALL SCHOOL
Pyrland, Kingston Road, Taunton,
Somerset TA2 8AA
Tel: (01823) 272431
Head: Mrs M Willson
Type: Co-educational Boarding &
Day 3-13
No of Pupils: B225 G171 No of
Boarders F40 W26
Fees: (September 95) FB £4800 -
£8040 WB £4530 - £7770 DAY
£1800 - £5700

QUEEN'S COLLEGE
Trull Road, Taunton, Somerset
TA1 4QS
Tel: (01823) 272559
Head: C Bradnock
Type: Co-educational Boarding &
Day 8-18
No of Pupils: B352 G324 No of
Boarders F215
Fees: (September 95) FB £9270 DAY
£6075

QUEEN'S COLLEGE JUNIOR SCHOOL
Trull Road, Taunton, Somerset
TA1 4QR
Tel: (01823) 272990
Head: P N Lee-Smith
Type: Co-educational Day &
Boarding 8-12
No of Pupils: B85 G85 No of Boarders
F50
Fees: (September 95) FB £4320 -
£7830 DAY £2790 - £5175

TAUNTON PREPARATORY SCHOOL
Staplegrove Road, Taunton,
Somerset TA2 6AE
Tel: (01823) 349250
Head: A D Wood
Type: Co-educational Day &
Boarding 3-12
No of Pupils: 410 No of Boarders F45
Fees: (September 95) FB £4290 -
£8310 DAY £1320 - £5490

TAUNTON SCHOOL
Taunton, Somerset TA2 6AD
Tel: (01823) 349200/349223
Head: B B Sutton
Type: Co-educational Boarding &
Day 13-18
No of Pupils: B275 G231 No of
Boarders F221
Fees: (September 95) FB £11355 DAY
£7260

WATCHET

BUCKLAND SCHOOL
7 St Decumans Road, Watchet,
Somerset TA23 0HR
Tel: (01984) 631314
Type: Co-educational Day 2-9
No of Pupils: 40
Fees: (September 94) £1344

WELLINGTON

WELLINGTON SCHOOL
South Street, Wellington, Somerset
TA21 8NT
Tel: (01823) 668800
Head: A J Rogers
Type: Co-educational Boarding &
Day 10-19
No of Pupils: B443 G335 No of
Boarders F170
Fees: (September 95) FB £8040 DAY
£4398

WELLS

WELLS CATHEDRAL JUNIOR SCHOOL
10 New Street, Wells, Somerset
BA5 2LQ
Tel: (01749) 672291
Head: N M Wilson
Type: Co-educational Boarding &
Day 4-11
No of Pupils: B92 G72 No of Boarders
F30
Fees: (September 95) FB £7962 DAY
£2556 - £4911

WELLS CATHEDRAL SCHOOL
Wells, Somerset BA5 2ST
Tel: (01749) 672117
Head: J S Baxter
Type: Co-educational Boarding &
Day 4-18
No of Pupils: B415 G392 No of
Boarders F303
Fees: (September 95) FB £9114 DAY
£5352

YEOVIL

CHILTON CANTELO SCHOOL
Chilton Cantelo, Yeovil, Somerset
BA22 8BG
Tel: (01935) 850555
Head: D S von Zeffman
Type: Co-educational Boarding &
Day 8-18
No of Pupils: B70 G60 No of
Boarders F80
Fees: (September 95) FB £6300 –
£8460 DAY £3180 – £4830

KING'S BRUTON
PRE-PREPARATORY &
JUNIOR SCHOOL
Hazlegrove House, Sparkford,
Yeovil, Somerset BA22 7JA
Tel: (01963) 440314
Head: Rev B Bearcroft
Type: Co-educational Day &
Boarding 3-13
No of Pupils: 230 No of Boarders F86
Fees: (September 95) FB £7650 –
£8730 DAY £5160 – £6240

THE PARK SCHOOL
Yeovil, Somerset BA20 1DH
Tel: (01935) 23514
Head: P W Bate
Type: Co-educational Day &
Boarding 3-16
No of Pupils: B45 G132 No of
Boarders F15 W3
Fees: (September 95) FB £7200 –
£8100 WB £6600 – £7500 DAY
£1680 – £4680

STAFFORDSHIRE

ABBOTS BROMLEY

SCHOOL OF S MARY AND
S ANNE*
Abbots Bromley, Staffordshire
WS15 3BW
Tel: (01283) 840232/840225
Head: A J Grigg
Type: Girls Boarding & Day 5-19
No of Pupils: 290 No of Boarders 170
Fees: (September 95) FB £9015 –
£10665 DAY £2520 – £7110

BURTON-UPON-TRENT

HOWITT HOUSE SCHOOL
New Lodge, Hanbury,
Burton-upon-Trent, Staffordshire
DE13 8TG
Tel: (01283) 820236
Head: M H Davis
Type: Co-educational Day 3-12
No of Pupils: B45 G47
Fees: (September 95) £2580

CANNOCK

LYNCROFT HOUSE SCHOOL
Convent Close, St John's Road,
Cannock, Staffordshire WS11 3UR
Tel: (01543) 502388
Head: M W Mash
Type: Co-educational Day &
Boarding 5-18
No of Pupils: B114 G69 No of
Boarders F15 W20
Fees: (September 95) FB £8010 WB
£5502 DAY £2778 – £4005

LICHFIELD

LICHFIELD CATHEDRAL
SCHOOL (ST CHAD'S)
The Palace, Lichfield, Staffordshire
WS13 7LH
Tel: (01543) 263326
Head: Rev A F Walters
Type: Co-educational Day &
Boarding 4-13
No of Pupils: B133 G57 No of
Boarders F22 W10
Fees: (September 94) FB £6645 –
£6870 WB £6045 – £6270 DAY
£4485 – £4710

ST JOHN'S PREPARATORY
SCHOOL
28 St John Street, Lichfield,
Staffordshire
Tel: (01543) 263345
Head: Ms S P DeGruchy
Type: Co-educational Day 2-11
No of Pupils: 70
Fees: (September 95) £2313 – £2826

NEWCASTLE-UNDER-LYME

EDENHURST SCHOOL
Westlands Avenue,
Newcastle-under-Lyme,
Staffordshire ST5 2PU
Tel: (01782) 619348
Head: N H F Copestick
Type: Co-educational Day 3-14
No of Pupils: B110 G90
Fees: (September 95) £1950 – £3654

NEWCASTLE-UNDER-LYME
SCHOOL
Mount Pleasant,
Newcastle-under-Lyme,
Staffordshire ST5 1DB
Tel: (01782) 633604
Head: Dr R M Reynolds
Type: Co-educational Day 8-18
No of Pupils: B635 G660
Fees: (September 95) £3078 – £3540

WOLSTANTON
PREPARATORY SCHOOL
30 Woodland Avenue, Wolstanton,
Newcastle-under-Lyme,
Staffordshire ST5 8AZ
Tel: (01782) 626675
Head: Mrs E A Cooper
Type: Co-educational Day 3-11
No of Pupils: B25 G21
Fees: (September 95) £2277

STAFFORD

BROOKLANDS SCHOOL
Eccleshall Road, Stafford ST16 1PD
Tel: (01785) 51399
Head: C T O'Donnell
Type: Co-educational Day 3-13
No of Pupils: B64 G64
Fees: (September 95) £1980 – £3486

ST BEDE'S SCHOOL*
Bishton Hall, Wolseley Bridge,
Stafford ST17 0XN
Tel: (01889) 881277
Head: A H Stafford Northcote &
H C Stafford Northcote
Type: Co-educational Boarding &
Day 2-13
No of Pupils: B78 G57 No of
Boarders F47
Fees: (September 95) FB £5940 DAY
£2400 – £4500

ST DOMINIC'S SCHOOL

32 Bargate Street, Brewood, Stafford
ST19 9BA
Tel: (01902) 850248
Head: Mrs K S Butwilowska
Type: Girls Day 2-18 (Co-ed 2-7)
No of Pupils: 450
Fees: (September 95) £2250 - £3825

STAFFORD GRAMMAR
SCHOOL

Burton Manor, Stafford ST18 9AT
Tel: (01785) 49752
Head: M S James
Type: Co-educational Day 11-18
No of Pupils: B153 G130
Fees: (September 95) £3945

YARLET HALL*

Stafford, ST18 9SU
Tel: (01889) 508240
Head: R S Plant
Type: Co-educational Boarding &
Day 3-13
No of Pupils: 111 No of Boarders F52
Fees: (September 95) FB £7170 DAY
£2715 - £5850

STOKE-ON-TRENT

ST DOMINIC'S INDEPENDENT
JUNIOR SCHOOL

Hartshill Road, Stoke-on-Trent,
Staffordshire ST4 7LY
Tel: (01782) 48588
Head: Mrs J A Oliver
Type: Co-educational Day 3-12
No of Pupils: B76 G74
Fees: (September 95) £1680 - £2142

ST JOSEPH'S COLLEGE

Trent Vale, Stoke-on-Trent,
Staffordshire ST4 5NT
Tel: (01782) 48008
Head: J E Stoer
Type: Co-educational Day 4-18
No of Pupils: B336 G133
Fees: (September 95) £2040 - £3294

STONE

ST DOMINIC'S PRIORY
SCHOOL

21 Station Road, Stone, Staffordshire
ST15 8EN
Tel: (01785) 814181
Head: Mrs J Hildreth
Type: Girls Day 3-18 (Boys 3-8)
No of Pupils: B27 G346
Fees: (September 95) £2853 - £3294

UTTOXETER

ABBOTSHOLME SCHOOL

Rocester, Uttoxeter, Staffordshire
ST14 5BS
Tel: (01889) 590217
Head: D J Farrant
Type: Co-educational Boarding &
Day 11-18
No of Pupils: B158 G88 No of
Boarders F169
Fees: (September 95) F/WB £11391
DAY £7614

DENSTONE COLLEGE

Uttoxeter, Staffordshire ST14 5HN
Tel: (01889) 590484
Head: H C K Carson
Type: Co-educational Boarding &
Day 11-18
No of Pupils: B210 G84 No of
Boarders F162
Fees: (September 95) F/WB £10890
DAY £5364 - £7770

DENSTONE COLLEGE
PREPARATORY SCHOOL*

Smallwood Manor, Uttoxeter,
Staffordshire ST14 8NS
Tel: (01889) 562083
Head: A C Ninham
Type: Co-educational Boarding &
Day 3-13
No of Pupils: 187 No of Boarders F39
W5
Fees: (September 95) F/WB £6663 -
£7119 DAY £2418 - £5313

SUFFOLK

BECCLES

THE OLD SCHOOL

Henstead, Beccles, Suffolk NR34 7LG
Tel: (01502) 741150
Head: M J Hewett
Type: Co-educational Day 4-13
Fees: (September 95) £2070 - £2790

BURY ST EDMUNDS

CHERRY TREES SCHOOL

Flempton Road, Risby, Bury St
Edmunds, Suffolk IP28 6QJ
Tel: (01284) 760531
Head: Ms W Compson
Type: Co-educational Boarding &
Day 2-13
No of Pupils: B110 G107
Fees: (September 94) FB £5190 -
£5895 DAY £3105 - £3810

CULFORD SCHOOL

Bury St Edmunds, Suffolk IP28 6TX
Tel: (01284) 728615
Head: John Richardson
Type: Co-educational Boarding &
Day 2-18
No of Pupils: B345 G268 No of
Boarders F206
Fees: (September 95) FB £8211 -
£10401 WB £7311 - £8085 DAY
£5274 - £6771

MORETON HALL

Mount Road, Bury St Edmunds,
Suffolk IP32 7BJ
Tel: (01284) 753532
Head: M E Higgins
Type: Co-educational Boarding &
Day 2-13
No of Pupils: 90 No of Boarders F20
Fees: (September 95) FB £8100 DAY
£3105 - £6075

SHI-TENNOJI SCHOOL IN UK

Herringswell, Bury St Edmunds,
Suffolk IP28 6SW
Tel: (01638) 750234
Head: J Deguchi
Type: Co-educational Boarding 9-17
No of Pupils: B113 G80
Fees: On application

SOUTH LEE PREPARATORY
SCHOOL

Nowton Road, Bury St Edmunds,
Suffolk IP33 2BT
Tel: (01284) 754654
Head: Mrs R Williamson
Type: Co-educational Day 2-13
No of Pupils: B99 G168
Fees: (September 95) £3540 - £4440

HALESWORTH

SOUTHFIELD PNEU SCHOOL & STARTING POINTS PRE SCHOOL

School Lane, Halesworth, Suffolk
IP19 8BW
Tel: (01986) 874569
Head: Mrs J J Jones
Type: Co-educational Day 2-8
No of Pupils: 60
Fees: (September 95) £2500 - £2750

HAVERHILL

BARNARDISTON HALL PREPARATORY SCHOOL

Barnardiston, Haverhill, Suffolk
CB9 7TG
Tel: (01440) 786316
Head: Lt Col K A Boulter
Type: Co-educational Day & Boarding 2-13
No of Pupils: B110 G110
Fees: (September 95) FB £7050 WB £6300 DAY £2080 - £3870

IPSWICH

AMBERFIELD SCHOOL

Nacton, Ipswich, Suffolk IP10 0HL
Tel: (01473) 659265
Head: Mrs L Amphlett Lewis
Type: Girls Day 3-16 (Boys 3-7)
No of Pupils: B15 G280
Fees: (September 95) £2580 - £3710

IPSWICH HIGH SCHOOL GPDST

Woolverstone, Ipswich, Suffolk
IP9 1AZ
Tel: (01473) 780201
Head: Miss V C MacCuish
Type: Girls Day 4-18 (Boys 4-7)
No of Pupils: B25 G650
Fees: (September 94) £2808 - £3804

IPSWICH PREPARATORY SCHOOL

Henley Road, Ipswich, Suffolk
IP1 3SQ
Tel: (01473) 255730
Head: D Williams
Type: Co-educational Day 7-11
No of Pupils: 150
Fees: (September 95) £3270 - £3402

IPSWICH SCHOOL

Henley Road, Ipswich, Suffolk
IP1 3SG
Tel: (01473) 255313
Head: I G Galbraith
Type: Boys Day & Boarding 11-19
(VIth form day girls)
No of Pupils: B563 G39 No of Boarders F25 W10
Fees: (September 95) FB £7665 - £8652 WB £7533 - £8406 DAY £4791 - £5052

OLD BUCKENHAM HALL SCHOOL

Brettenham, Ipswich, Suffolk
IP7 7PH
Tel: (01449) 740252
Head: H D Cocke
Type: Boys Day & Boarding 3-13
No of Pupils: 156
Fees: (September 95) FB £8400 WB £8100 DAY £3075 - £6525

ORWELL PARK

Nacton, Ipswich, Suffolk IP10 0ER
Tel: (01473) 659225
Head: A H Auster
Type: Co-educational Boarding & Day 3-13
No of Pupils: 200 No of Boarders F90 W85
Fees: (September 95) FB £8025 - £8880 DAY £2535 - £6375

ROYAL HOSPITAL SCHOOL

Holbrook, Ipswich, Suffolk IP9 2RX
Tel: (01473) 328342
Head: N K D Ward
Type: Co-educational Boarding 11-18 (VIth form day pupils)
No of Pupils: 600 No of Boarders F600
Fees: (September 95) FB £77 - £7800 DAY £3900

ST JOSEPH'S COLLEGE

Birkfield, Ipswich, Suffolk IP2 9DR
Tel: (01473) 690281
Head: J Regan
Type: Boys Day & Boarding 11-18
(Boarding from 13, co-ed VIth form)
No of Pupils: B520 G16 No of Boarders F95
Fees: (September 95) FB £7566 - £8436 WB £6810 - £7593 DAY £4191 - £4830

ST JOSEPH'S PREPARATORY SCHOOL

Oak Hill Lane, Ipswich, Suffolk
IP2 9AN
Tel: (01473) 601927
Head: D Evans
Type: Co-educational Day 4-11
No of Pupils: B154 G18
Fees: (September 94) £2889 - £3663

SCHOOL OF JESUS AND MARY

Woodbridge Road, Ipswich, Suffolk
IP4 4BB
Tel: (01473) 728112
Head: Mrs E A McKay
Type: Girls Day 3-16 (Boys 3-7)
No of Pupils: B32 G305
Fees: (September 95) £2775 - £4080

LEISTON

SUMMERHILL SCHOOL

Leiston, Suffolk IP16 4HY
Tel: (01728) 830540
Head: Mrs Z S Readhead
Type: Co-educational Boarding & Day 6-16
No of Pupils: B35 G30 No of Boarders F60
Fees: (September 94) FB £4590 - £5670 DAY £1860 - £2805

LOWESTOFT

BRIAR SCHOOL

8 Gunton Cliff, Lowestoft, Suffolk
NR32 4PE
Tel: (01502) 583481
Head: C A Middleditch
Type: Co-educational Day 3-13
No of Pupils: 120
Fees: (September 95) £2460 - £2850

NEWMARKET

FAIRSTEAD HOUSE SCHOOL

Fordham Road, Newmarket, Suffolk
CB8 7AA
Tel: (01638) 662318
Head: D J Wedgwood
Type: Co-educational Day 4-11
No of Pupils: B55 G65
Fees: (September 95) £2310 - £2700

SAXMUNDHAM

FAIRFIELD PREPARATORY SCHOOL

North Lodge, Saxmundham, Suffolk
IP17 1AY
Tel: (01728) 602293
Head: R Neve
Type: Co-educational Day 2-12
No of Pupils: 30
Fees: (September 94) £2770 - £2860

SOUTHWOLD

EVERSLEY SCHOOL
Southwold, Suffolk IP18 6AH
Tel: (01502) 723302
Head: B E Nelson
Type: Co-educational Day &
Boarding 4-13 (Weekly boarding
only)
No of Pupils: B46 G15 No of Boarders
W14
Fees: (September 93) WB £3510 DAY
£1575 - £2812

ST FELIX*
Southwold, Suffolk IP18 6SD
Tel: (01502) 722175
Head: Mrs S Campion
Type: Girls Boarding & Day 11-18
No of Pupils: 229 No of Boarders
F145
Fees: (September 95) F/WB £10350
DAY £6750

ST GEORGE'S SCHOOL
Southwold, Suffolk IP18 6SD
Tel: (01502) 723314
Head: Mrs W H Holland
Type: Girls Day & Boarding 2-11
(Boys day only)
No of Pupils: 106 No of Boarders F5
Fees: (September 95) FB £7200 DAY
£2460 - £4185

STOWMARKET

FINBOROUGH SCHOOL
The Hall, Great Finborough,
Stowmarket, Suffolk IP14 3EF
Tel: (01449) 674479
Head: J Sinclair
Type: Co-educational Boarding &
Day 2-18
No of Pupils: B150 G100 No of
Boarders F200
Fees: (September 95) FB £6390 -
£7980 WB £4320 - £5400 DAY
£1575 - £3630

HILLCROFT PREPARATORY SCHOOL
Walnutree Manor, Haughley Green,
Stowmarket, Suffolk IP14 3RQ
Tel: (01449) 673003
Head: F R G J Rapsey & Mrs G O
Rapsey
Type: Co-educational Day 2-13
No of Pupils: B50 G51
Fees: (September 95) £1050 - £3900

SUDBURY

STOKE COLLEGE
Stoke by Clare, Sudbury, Suffolk
CO10 8JE
Tel: (01787) 278141
Head: D Marshall
Type: Co-educational Day &
Boarding 3-16
No of Pupils: B116 G93 No of
Boarders W30
Fees: (September 95) WB £7335 -
£8118 DAY £3264 - £4863

WOODBRIDGE

THE ABBEY SCHOOL
Woodbridge, Suffolk IP13 9HA
Tel: (01394) 382673
Head: M S Booth
Type: Co-educational Day 4-11
No of Pupils: 242
Fees per term: (September 95) £875 -
£1461

ALEXANDERS INTERNATIONAL SCHOOL*
Bawdsey Manor, Bawdsey,
Woodbridge, Suffolk IP12 3AZ
Tel: (01394) 411633
Head: Niels Toettcher
Type: Co-educational Boarding 10-18
No of Pupils: B60 G40
Fees: (September 95) FB £9000

FRAMLINGHAM COLLEGE*
Framlingham, Woodbridge, Suffolk
IP13 9EY
Tel: (01728) 723789
Head: Mrs G Randall
Type: Co-educational Boarding &
Day 13-18
No of Pupils: B300 G140 No of
Boarders F305
Fees: (September 95) FB £9687 DAY
£6216

FRAMLINGHAM COLLEGE JUNIOR SCHOOL
Brandeston Hall, Woodbridge,
Suffolk IP13 7AQ
Tel: (01728) 685331
Head: N Johnson
Type: Co-educational Boarding &
Day 4-13
No of Pupils: B170 G120 No of
Boarders F35 W25
Fees: (September 95) FB £7638 DAY
£2700 - £4737

MOAT BARN MONTESSORI
Hasketon, Woodbridge, Suffolk
IP13 6JW
Tel: (01473) 738282
Head: Mrs J Millar
Type: Co-educational Day 3-5
No of Pupils: 50
Fees: (September 95) £300 - £1260

WOODBRIDGE SCHOOL*
Woodbridge, Suffolk IP12 4JH
Tel: (01394) 385547
Head: S H Cole
Type: Co-educational Day &
Boarding 11-18
No of Pupils: B242 G253 No of
Boarders F36
Fees: (September 95) F/WB £8796
DAY £5352

SURREY

ASHTEAD

CITY OF LONDON FREEMEN'S SCHOOL
Ashtead, Surrey KT21 1ET
Tel: (01372) 277933
Head: D C Haywood
Type: Co-educational Day &
Boarding 7-18
No of Pupils: B325 G395 No of
Boarders F24 W23
Fees: (September 95) FB £7610 -
£9090 WB £7326 - £8806 DAY
£4338 - £5823

DOWNSEND LODGE
22 Oakfield Road, Ashtead, Surrey
KT21 2RE
Tel: (01372) 273778
Head: Mrs M R New
Type: Co-educational Day 2-7
No of Pupils: B55 G46
Fees: (September 95) £885 - £3285

PARSONS MEAD*
Ottways Lane, Ashtead, Surrey
KT21 2PE
Tel: (01372) 276401
Head: Miss E B Plant
Type: Girls Day & Boarding 3-18
No of Pupils: 370 No of Boarders
W10
Fees: (September 95) WB £8169 -
£8829 DAY £2946 - £5025

BAGSHOT

HALL GROVE SCHOOL
Bagshot, Surrey GU19 5HZ
Tel: (01276) 473059
Head: A R Graham
Type: Boys Day 4-14
No of Pupils: 230
Fees: (September 95) £3615 - £4530

BANSTEAD

GREENACRE SCHOOL FOR GIRLS*
Sutton Lane, Banstead, Surrey
SM7 3RA
Tel: (01737) 352114
Head: Mrs P M Wood
Type: Girls Day 3-18
No of Pupils: 390
Fees: (September 95) £1260 - £4980

OAKLAND NURSERY SCHOOL
Palmersfield Road, Banstead, Surrey
SM7 2LD
Tel: (01737) 351157
Head: Mrs M Dollimore
Type: Co-educational Day 3-5
No of Pupils: B30 G30
Fees: (September 95) £705 - £1170

PRIORY SCHOOL*
Bolters Lane, Banstead, Surrey
SM7 2AJ
Tel: (01737) 354479
Head: I R Chapman
Type: Boys Day 3-13
No of Pupils: 185
Fees: (September 95) £1620 - £4290

CAMBERLEY

CHESWYCKS SCHOOL
Guildford Road, Frimley Green,
Camberley, Surrey GU16 6PB
Tel: (01252) 835669
Head: B Parsons
Type: Co-educational Day 2-11
No of Pupils: B101 G94
Fees: (September 95) £323 - £3235

CLEWBOROUGH HOUSE PREPARATORY SCHOOL
Clewborough Drive, Camberley,
Surrey GU15 1NX
Tel: (01276) 64799
Head: Commander M F Clarke
Type: Co-educational Day 2-13
No of Pupils: B120 G80
Fees: (September 95) £3100 - £4400

EAGLE HOUSE
Sandhurst, Camberley, Surrey
GU17 8PH
Tel: (01344) 772134
Head: S J Carder
Type: Boys Day & Boarding 4-13
(Girls 4-7)
No of Pupils: 190 No of Boarders F26
W30
Fees: (September 95) F/WB £9060
DAY £3705 - £6375

ELMHURST BALLET SCHOOL
Heathcote Road, Camberley, Surrey
GU15 2EV
Tel: (01276) 65301
Head: J McNamara
Type: Co-educational Boarding &
Day 9-19
No of Pupils: B35 G218 No of
Boarders F216
Fees: (September 95) FB £8580 -
£9120 DAY £6015 - £6690

HAWLEY PLACE SCHOOL
Fernhill Road, Blackwater,
Camberley, Surrey GU17 9HU
Tel: (01276) 32028
Head: Mr & Mrs T G Pipe
Type: Girls Day 2-16 (Boys 2-11)
No of Pupils: 166
Fees: (September 95) £2940 - £3750

LYNDHURST SCHOOL
Sumner Lodge, The Avenue,
Camberley, Surrey GU15 3NE
Tel: (01276) 22895
Head: R L Cunliffe
Type: Co-educational Day 3-12
No of Pupils: B106 G90
Fees: (September 95) £1410 - £3600

ST CATHERINE'S SCHOOL
Park Road, Camberley, Surrey
GU15 2LL
Tel: (01276) 23511
Head: R W Burt & Mrs H M Burt
Type: Girls Day 3-12 (Boys 3-5)
No of Pupils: B30 G130
Fees: (September 95) £1500 - £3840

YATELEY MANOR PREPARATORY SCHOOL*
51 Reading Road, Yateley,
Camberley, Surrey GU17 7UQ
Tel: (01252) 873298
Head: F G Howard
Type: Co-educational Day 3-13
No of Pupils: B319 G171
Fees: (September 95) £1407 - £4707

CATERHAM

CATERHAM SCHOOL*
Harestone Valley Road, Caterham, Surrey CR3 6YA
Tel: (01883) 343028
Head: R A E Davey
Type: Co-educational Day & Boarding 11-18
No of Pupils: 750 No of Boarders F140
Fees: (September 95) FB £10596 - £11196 DAY £5796

CATERHAM SCHOOL PREPARATORY
Mottrams, Harestone Valley Road, Caterham, Surrey CR3 6YB
Tel: (01883) 342097
Head: A D Moy
Type: Co-educational Day 3-10
No of Pupils: 250
Fees: (September 95) £2910 - £5520

ESSENDENE LODGE SCHOOL
Essendene Road, Caterham, Surrey CR3 5PB
Tel: (01883) 348349
Head: Mrs S A Haydock
Type: Co-educational Day 2-11
No of Pupils: 200
Fees: (September 95) £750 - £2205

OAKHYRST GRANGE SCHOOL
160 Stanstead Road, Caterham, Surrey CR3 6AF
Tel: (01883) 343344
Head: Mrs D F Cooper
Type: Boys Day 3-11
No of Pupils: 120
Fees: (September 95) £1110 - £2790

WOLDINGHAM SCHOOL*
Marden Park, Woldingham, Caterham, Surrey CR3 7YA
Tel: (01883) 349431
Head: Dr P Dineen
Type: Girls Boarding & Day 11-18
No of Pupils: 495
Fees: (September 95) FB £11436 DAY £6927

CHEAM

AMBLESIDE PNEU SCHOOL
1 West Drive, Cheam, Surrey SM2 7NB
Tel: (0181) 642 2862
Head: Mrs L M Vaughan-Stevens
Type: Co-educational Day 3-7
No of Pupils: 80
Fees: (September 95) £1560 - £3219

GLAISDALE SCHOOL
14 Arundel Road, Cheam, Surrey SM2 7AD
Tel: (0181) 642 4266
Head: Mrs H M Steel
Type: Co-educational Day 3-11
No of Pupils: 152
Fees: (September 95) £900 - £2520

CHERTSEY

SIR WILLIAM PERKINS'S SCHOOL
Guildford Road, Chertsey, Surrey KT16 9BN
Tel: (01932) 562161
Head: Miss Susan Ross
Type: Girls Day 11-18
No of Pupils: 590
Fees: (September 95) £3945

COBHAM

THE AMERICAN COMMUNITY SCHOOLS*
'Heywood', Portsmouth Road, Cobham, Surrey KT11 1BL
Tel: (01932) 867251
Head: T Lehman
Type: Co-educational Boarding & Day 3-18
No of Pupils: 1091
Fees: (September 95) FB £14310 WB £12750 DAY £3500 - £8740

THE COBHAM MONTESSORI NURSERY SCHOOL
23 Spencer Road, Cobham, Surrey KT11 2AF
Tel: (01306) 876465
Head: Mrs S Hall
Type: Co-educational Day 2-5
No of Pupils: 40
Fees: On application

FELTONFLEET SCHOOL
Cobham, Surrey KT11 1DR
Tel: (01932) 862264
Head: D T Cherry
Type: Co-educational Boarding & Day 3-13
No of Pupils: 175 No of Boarders F40
Fees: (September 95) F/WB £7650 DAY £3600 - £5685

NOTRE DAME PREPARATORY SCHOOL
Burwood House, Cobham, Surrey KT11 1HA
Tel: (01932) 862152
Head: Sister J Lanaghan
Type: Girls Day 2-11 (Boys 2-6)
No of Pupils: B38 G281
Fees: (September 95) £1575 - £3600

NOTRE DAME SENIOR SCHOOL
Burwood House, Cobham, Surrey KT11 1HA
Tel: (01932) 863560
Head: Sister Faith Ede
Type: Girls Day 11-18
No of Pupils: 300
Fees: (September 95) £4320 - £4500

PARKSIDE SCHOOL
The Manor, Stoke D'Abernon, Cobham, Surrey KT11 3PX
Tel: (01932) 862749
Head: R L Shipp
Type: Boys Day & Boarding 4-14 (Co-ed 2-5)
No of Pupils: 320 No of Boarders F8 W15
Fees: (September 95) FB £8325 WB £7848 DAY £3480 - £5430

REED'S SCHOOL*
Sandy Lane, Cobham, Surrey KT11 2ES
Tel: (01932) 863076
Head: D E Prince
Type: Boys Boarding & Day 11-18 (Co-ed VIth form)
No of Pupils: B340 G20 No of Boarders F150
Fees: (September 95) FB £8649 - £10239 DAY £6486 - £7740

YEHUDI MENUHIN SCHOOL
Stoke D'Abernon, Cobham, Surrey KT11 3QQ
Tel: (01932) 864739
Head: N Chisholm
Type: Co-educational Boarding 8-18
No of Pupils: B21 G28 No of Boarders F49
Fees: (September 95) FB £19443

CRANLEIGH

CRANLEIGH PREPARATORY SCHOOL*
Cranleigh, Surrey GU6 8QH
Tel: (01483) 274199
Head: M R Keppie
Type: Boys Boarding & Day 7-13
No of Pupils: 180 No of Boarders F89
Fees: (September 95) FB £8310 DAY £6270

CRANLEIGH SCHOOL*
Cranleigh, Surrey GU6 8QQ
Tel: (01483) 273997
Head: T A A Hart
Type: Boys Boarding & Day 13-18
(Co-ed VIth form)
No of Pupils: B435 G76 No of
Boarders F430
Fees: (September 95) FB £12400 DAY
£9330

DUKE OF KENT SCHOOL*
Peaslake Road, Ewhurst, Cranleigh,
Surrey GU6 7NS
Tel: (01483) 277313
Head: R K Wilson
Type: Co-educational Boarding &
Day 4-13
No of Pupils: B100 G55 No of
Boarders F100
Fees: (September 95) FB £7365 -
£8235 DAY £2250 - £5760

CROYDON

NEW LIFE CHRISTIAN
SCHOOL
Cairo New Road, Croydon, Surrey
CR0 1XP
Tel: (0181) 680 7671
Type: Co-educational Day 4-11
No of Pupils: B38 G28
Fees: (September 95) £1824

OLD PALACE SCHOOL OF
JOHN WHITGIFT
Old Palace Road, Croydon, Surrey
CR0 1AX
Tel: (0181) 688 2027
Head: Miss K L Hilton
Type: Girls Day 4-18
No of Pupils: 789
Fees: (September 95) £2925 - £3978

ROYAL RUSSELL SCHOOL*
Coombe Lane, Croydon, Surrey CR9
5BX
Tel: (0181) 657 4433
Head: R D Balaam
Type: Co-educational Boarding &
Day 3-18
No of Pupils: B435 G247 No of
Boarders F95 W45
Fees: (September 95) F/WB £10035
DAY £2745 - £5295

TRINITY SCHOOL*
Shirley Park, Croydon, Surrey CR9
7AT
Tel: (0181) 656 9541
Head: B J Lenon
Type: Boys Day 10-18
No of Pupils: 850
Fees: (September 95) £5304

WARLINGHAM PARK SCHOOL
Chelsham Common, Warlingham,
Croydon, Surrey CR6 4PB
Tel: (01883) 626844
Head: M R Donald
Type: Co-educational Day 2-11
No of Pupils: B57 G47
Fees: (September 95) £1485 - £2790

DORKING

BELMONT SCHOOL*
Feldemore, Holmbury St Mary,
Dorking, Surrey RH5 6LQ
Tel: (01306) 730852
Head: D Gainer
Type: Co-educational Boarding &
Day 4-13
No of Pupils: B190 G60 No of
Boarders W40
Fees: (September 95) WB £7545 DAY
£2670 - £5175

BOX HILL SCHOOL*
Mickleham, Dorking, Surrey
RH5 6EA
Tel: (01372) 373382
Head: Dr Rodney Atwood
Type: Co-educational Boarding &
Day 11-18
No of Pupils: B176 G93 No of
Boarders F112 W51
Fees: (September 95) FB £10200 WB
£9840 DAY £6150

HURTWOOD HOUSE*
Holmbury St Mary, Dorking, Surrey
RH5 6NU
Tel: (01483) 277416
Head: K R Jackson
Type: Co-educational Residential 15+
No of Pupils: B130 G130
Fees: (September 95) FB £13500 -
£16500

NOWER LODGE SCHOOL
Coldharbour Lane, Dorking, Surrey
RH4 3BT
Tel: (01306) 882448
Head: Mrs S Watt
Type: Co-educational Day 3-13
No of Pupils: 120
Fees: (September 95) £2850 - £3975

ST TERESA'S SCHOOL*
Effingham Hill, Dorking, Surrey
RH5 6ST
Tel: (01372) 452037
Head: L Allan
Type: Girls Boarding & Day 3-18
(Boys 3-5)
No of Pupils: 532 No of Boarders
F140
Fees: (September 95) F/WB £10785
DAY £5070

STANWAY SCHOOL
Chichester Road, Dorking, Surrey
RH4 1LR
Tel: (01306) 882151
Head: Mrs C A Belk
Type: Girls Day 3-13 (Boys 3-8)
No of Pupils: B40 G140
Fees: (September 95) £639 - £4050

EFFINGHAM

ST TERESA'S PREPARATORY
SCHOOL
Grove House, Guildford Road,
Effingham, Surrey KT24 5QA
Tel: (01372) 453456
Head: Mrs M Head
Type: Girls Day & Boarding 2-11
No of Pupils: 200 No of Boarders F6
Fees: (September 95) F/WB £9585
DAY £1560 - £4230

EGHAM

THE AMERICAN COMMUNITY
SCHOOL*
'Woodlee', London Road (A30),
Egham, Surrey TW20 0HS
Tel: (01784) 430611
Head: Mrs K Alderdice
Type: Co-educational Day and
Boarding 3-14
Fees: (September 95) FB £12750 -
£14310 DAY £3500 - £8740

SCAITCLIFFE SCHOOL
Englefield Green, Egham, Surrey
TW20 0YJ
Tel: (01784) 432109
Head: W A Constable
Type: Boys Day & Boarding 3-13
(Day Girls 3-7)
No of Pupils: 125 No of Boarders
W30
Fees: (September 95) WB £7839 DAY
£1800 - £5796

TASIS ENGLAND AMERICAN
SCHOOL*
Coldharbour Lane, Thorpe, Egham,
Surrey TW20 8TE
Tel: (01932) 565252
Head: L D Rigg
Type: Co-educational Boarding &
Day 4-18
No of Pupils: 650
Fees: (September 95) FB £13500 DAY
£3575 - £8185

EPSOM

DOWNSEND LODGE (EPSOM)
6 Norman Avenue, Epsom, Surrey
KT17 3AB
Tel: (01372) 721824
Head: Mrs G Brooks
Type: Co-educational Day 2-7
No of Pupils: 110
Fees: (September 95) £885 - £3105

EPSOM COLLEGE
Epsom, Surrey KT17 4JQ
Tel: (01372) 723621
Head: A H Beadles
Type: Boys Boarding & Day 13-18
(Co-ed VIth form. Fully Co-ed from
September 1996)
No of Pupils: B596 G61 No of
Boarders F145 W209
Fees: (September 95) FB £11595 WB
£11436 DAY £8616

EWELL CASTLE SCHOOL*
Church Street, Ewell, Epsom, Surrey
KT17 2AW
Tel: (0181) 393 1413
Head: R A Fewtrell
Type: Boys Day 3-18 (Girls 3-11 and
16-18)
No of Pupils: B430 G20
Fees: (September 95) £2352 - £4425

KINGSWOOD HOUSE SCHOOL
56 West Hill, Epsom, Surrey
KT19 8LF
Tel: (01372) 723590
Head: M Harvey
Type: Boys Day 3-13
No of Pupils: 210
Fees: (September 95) £2940 - £4305

LYNTON PREPARATORY
SCHOOL
Epsom Road, Ewell, Epsom, Surrey
KT17 1LJ
Tel: (0181) 393 4169
Head: Mrs V M Thorns
Type: Co-educational Day 4-12
No of Pupils: B60 G100
Fees: (September 95) £1740 - £1995

ST CHRISTOPHER'S SCHOOL
6 Downs Road, Epsom, Surrey
KT18 5HE
Tel: (01372) 721807
Head: Miss J A Luckman
Type: Co-educational Day 3-7
No of Pupils: B69 G77
Fees: (September 95) £1476 - £2856

ESHER

CLAREMONT FAN COURT
SCHOOL*
Claremont Drive, Esher, Surrey
KT10 9LY
Tel: (01372) 467841
Head: Mrs P B Farrar
Type: Co-educational Day &
Boarding 3-18
No of Pupils: B319 G345 No of
Boarders F20
Fees: (September 95) FB £8640 -
£8985 DAY £1665 - £5685

EMBERHURST
94 Ember Lane, Esher, Surrey
Tel: (0181) 398 2933
Head: Mrs P Chadwick
Type: Co-educational Day 3-8
No of Pupils: 55
Fees: (September 95) £1200 - £1980

GRANTCHESTER HOUSE
5 Hinchley Way, Hinchley Wood,
Esher, Surrey KT10 0BD
Tel: (0181) 398 1157
Head: Mrs A E Fry
Type: Co-educational Day 3-7
No of Pupils: B47 G46
Fees: (September 95) £1818 - £3315

MILBOURNE LODGE SCHOOL
43 Arbrook Lane, Esher, Surrey
KT10 9EG
Tel: (01372) 462737
Head: N R Hale
Type: Boys Day 8-13
No of Pupils: B180 G20
Fees: (September 95) £4350 - £4500

ROWAN PREPARATORY
SCHOOL
6 Fitzalan Road, Claygate, Esher,
Surrey KT10 0LX
Tel: (01372) 462627
Head: Mrs E Brown
Type: Girls Day 3-11
No of Pupils: 300
Fees: (September 95) £1425 - £4535

FARNHAM

BARFIELD SCHOOL
Runfold, Farnham, Surrey GU10 1PB
Tel: (01252) 782271
Head: B Hoar
Type: Co-educational Day 3-13
No of Pupils: B152 G85
Fees: (September 95) £1710 - £5385

EDGEBOROUGH*
Frensham, Farnham, Surrey
GU10 3AH
Tel: (01252) 792495
Head: R A Jackson
Type: Co-educational Boarding &
Day 3-13
No of Pupils: B150 G65 No of
Boarders F45
Fees: (September 95) F/WB £8115 -
£8970 DAY £3705 - £6855

FRENSHAM HEIGHTS
SCHOOL*
Rowledge, Farnham, Surrey
GU10 4EA
Tel: (01252) 792134
Head: P de Voil
Type: Co-educational Boarding &
Day 11-18
No of Pupils: B144 G146 No of
Boarders F116
Fees: (September 95) F/WB £11670
DAY £7470

MORE HOUSE SCHOOL
Moons Hill, Frensham, Farnham,
Surrey GU10 3AW
Tel: (01252) 792303
Head: B G Huggett
Type: Boys Boarding & Day 10-16
No of Pupils: 110 No of Boarders F48
W31
Fees: (September 95) FB £10050 DAY
£6150

ST GEORGE'S FRENSHAM
Armoury Court, Pierrepont,
Frensham, Farnham, Surrey GU10
3DN
Tel: (01252) 792006
Head: A J Melbourne
Type: Co-educational Day 2-11
No of Pupils: B25 G20
Fees: (September 94) £743 - £944

GODALMING

ALDRO SCHOOL
Shackleford, Godalming, Surrey
GU8 6AS
Tel: (01483) 810266
Head: I M Argyle
Type: Boys Boarding & Day 7-13
No of Pupils: 216 No of Boarders F90
Fees: (September 95) FB £8505 DAY
£6570

BARROW HILLS SCHOOL
Roke Lane, Witley, Godalming,
Surrey GU8 5NY
Tel: (01428) 683639
Head: M Connolly
Type: Co-educational Day 4–13
No of Pupils: 150
Fees: (September 95) £3795 – £6345

CHARTERHOUSE
Godalming, Surrey GU7 2DJ
Tel: (01483) 291600
Type: Boys Boarding & Day 13–18
(Co-ed VIth form)
No of Pupils: B620 G80 No of
Boarders F680
Fees: (September 95) FB £12765 DAY
£10548

**KING EDWARD'S SCHOOL
WITLEY***
Petworth Road, Wormley,
Godalming, Surrey GU8 5SG
Tel: (01428) 682572
Head: R J Fox
Type: Co-educational Boarding &
Day 11–18
No of Pupils: B260 G248 No of
Boarders F407
Fees: (September 95) FB £8970 DAY
£6720

PRIOR'S FIELD SCHOOL*
Priorsfield Road, Godalming, Surrey
GU7 2RH
Tel: (01483) 810551
Head: Mrs J McCallum
Type: Girls Boarding & Day 11–18
No of Pupils: 220 No of Boarders F40
W80
Fees: (September 95) F/WB £9810
DAY £6555

ST HILARY'S SCHOOL
Holloway Hill, Godalming, Surrey
GU7 1RZ
Tel: (01483) 416551
Head: Mrs M I Thomas
Type: Co-educational Day B3–8
G3–12
No of Pupils: B75 G260
Fees: (September 95) £3300 – £3750

GUILDFORD

DRAYTON HOUSE SCHOOL
35 Austen Road, Guildford, Surrey
GU13 3NP
Tel: (01483) 504707
Head: Mrs J Tyson-Jones
Type: Co-educational Day 3–8 (Day
Nursery 1–3)
No of Pupils: B51 G43
Fees: (September 95) £1830 – £2595

**GUILDFORD HIGH SCHOOL
(CHURCH SCHOOLS CO LTD)**
London Road, Guildford, Surrey
GU1 1SJ
Tel: (01483) 61440
Head: Mrs S H Singer
Type: Girls Day 4–18
No of Pupils: 725
Fees: (September 95) £3024 – £5100

LANESBOROUGH
Maori Road, Guildford, Surrey
GU1 2EL
Tel: (01483) 502060
Head: S Deller
Type: Boys Day 4–13
No of Pupils: 300
Fees: (September 95) £1755 – £4620

**LONGACRE PREPARATORY
SCHOOL**
Shamley Green, Guildford, Surrey
GU5 0NQ
Tel: (01483) 893225
Head: Mrs L Prince
Type: Co-educational Day 2–11
No of Pupils: B65 G100
Fees: (September 95) £840 – £3900

ROYAL GRAMMAR SCHOOL
High Street, Guildford, Surrey
GU1 3BB
Tel: (01483) 502424
Head: T M Young
Type: Boys Day 11–18
No of Pupils: 830
Fees: (September 95) £5715 – £5985

**RYDE'S HILL PREPARATORY
SCHOOL**
Aldershot Road, Guildford, Surrey
GU2 6BP
Tel: (01483) 63160
Head: Mrs J Lenahan
Type: Girls Day 3–11 (Boys 3–7)
No of Pupils: 170
Fees: (September 95) £1140 – £3540

ST CATHERINE'S SCHOOL*
Bramley, Guildford, Surrey GU5 0DF
Tel: (01483) 893363
Head: Mrs C M Oulton
Type: Girls Day & Boarding 4–18
No of Pupils: 630 No of Boarders F68
W73
Fees: (September 95) F/WB £8355 –
£9255 DAY £2940 – £5655

SURREY COLLEGE
St Michael's House, 53 Woodbridge
Road, Guildford, Surrey GU1 4RF
Tel: (01483) 65887
Head: Dr G P Connolly
Type: Co-educational Day &
Residential 14+
No of Pupils: B160 G120
Fees: (September 95) 3 A Levels
£8395 5 GCSEs £8375

TORMEAD SCHOOL
27 Cranley Road, Guildford, Surrey
GUI 2JD
Tel: (01483) 575101
Head: Mrs H E M Alleyne
Type: Girls Day 4–18
No of Pupils: 610
Fees: (September 95) £2400 – £5100

HASLEMERE

**HASLEMERE PREPARATORY
SCHOOL**
The Heights, Hill Road, Haslemere,
Surrey GU27 2JP
Tel: (01428) 642350
Head: A C Morrison
Type: Boys Day 5–14
No of Pupils: 200
Fees: (September 95) £3840 – £4950

ST IVES
Three Gates Lane, Haslemere, Surrey
GU27 2ES
Tel: (01428) 643734
Head: Mrs M S Greenway
Type: Girls Day 3–11 (Boys 3–5)
No of Pupils: 140
Fees: (September 95) £3540 – £4575

WISPERS SCHOOL
High Lane, Haslemere, Surrey
GU27 1AD
Tel: (01428) 643646
Head: L H Beltran
Type: Girls Boarding & Day 11–18
No of Pupils: 150 No of Boarders F90
Fees: (September 95) F/WB £9135
DAY £5880

HINDHEAD

AMESBURY SCHOOL*
Hazel Grove, Hindhead, Surrey
GU26 6BL
Tel: (01428) 604322
Head: N Taylor
Type: Co-educational Day &
Boarding 3–13
No of Pupils: B120 G50 No of
Boarders W20
Fees: (September 94) F/WB £6465 –
£7305 DAY £2400 – £5925

THE ROYAL SCHOOL*

Hindhead, Surrey GU26 6BW
Tel: (01428) 605407
Head: C Brooks
Type: Girls Day & Boarding 5-18
No of Pupils: 430
Fees: (September 95) FB £8070 -
£9507 DAY £3465 - £6057

ST EDMUND'S SCHOOL*

Portsmouth Road, Hindhead, Surrey
GU26 6BH
Tel: (01428) 604808
Head: A Fowler-Watt
Type: Boys Boarding & Day 7-13
(Co-ed day 2-6)
No of Pupils: 110 No of Boarders F55
Fees: (September 95) FB £8475 DAY
£3675 - £6375

HORLEY

REDEHALL PREPARATORY SCHOOL

Redehall Road, Smallfield, Horley,
Surrey RH6 9QA
Tel: (01342) 842987
Head: Mrs E A Blow
Type: Co-educational Day 4-12
No of Pupils: B45 G45
Fees: (September 95) £1255

KINGSTON-UPON-THAMES

CANBURY SCHOOL*

Kingston Hill,
Kingston-upon-Thames, Surrey
KT2 7LN
Tel: (0181) 549 8622
Head: J G Wyatt
Type: Co-educational Day 10-17
No of Pupils: B42 G11
Fees: (September 95) £4725

HOLY CROSS PREPARATORY SCHOOL

Coombe Ridge House, George Road,
Kingston Hill, Kingston-upon-
Thames, Surrey
KT2 7NU
Tel: (0181) 942 0729
Head: Mrs K Hayes
Type: Co-educational Day B4-7
G4-11
No of Pupils: B15 G226
Fees: (September 95) £3075

KINGSTON GRAMMAR SCHOOL*

70-72 London Road,
Kingston-upon-Thames, Surrey KT2
6PY
Tel: (0181) 546 5875
Head: C D Baxter
Type: Co-educational Day 10-19
No of Pupils: B385 G211
Fees: (September 95) £5130 - £5385

MARYMOUNT INTERNATIONAL SCHOOL*

George Road,
Kingston-upon-Thames, Surrey KT2
7PE
Tel: (0181) 949 0571
Head: Sister R Sheridan
Type: Girls Day & Boarding 11-18
No of Pupils: 200 No of Boarders F96
W6
Fees: (September 95) FB £12550 -
£13350 WB £12350 - £13150 DAY
£6900 - £7700

PARK HILL SCHOOL

8 Queens Road,
Kingston-upon-Thames, Surrey
KT2 7SH
Tel: (0181) 546 5496
Head: Mrs M D Christie
Type: Co-educational Day B3-8
G3-11
No of Pupils: B40 G85
Fees: (September 95) £1755 - £3225

ROKEBY SCHOOL

George Road,
Kingston-upon-Thames, Surrey
KT2 7PB
Tel: (0181) 942 2247
Head: R M Moody
Type: Boys Day 4-13
No of Pupils: 365
Fees: (September 95) £3651 - £5268

SURBITON HIGH SCHOOL*

Surbiton Crescent,
Kingston-upon-Thames, Surrey
KT1 2JT
Tel: (0181) 546 5245
Head: Miss M G Perry
Type: Girls Day 4-18 (Boys 4-11)
No of Pupils: B108 G812
Fees: (September 95) £2916 - £4860

LEATHERHEAD

ACORN MONTESSORI SCHOOL

Methodist Church Hall, 10 Church
Road, Leatherhead, Surrey
Tel: (0181) 876 5021
Head: Mrs I Aljovin
Type: Co-educational Day 2-5
Fees: On application

CRANMORE SCHOOL

West Horsley, Leatherhead, Surrey
KT24 6AT
Tel: (01483) 284137
Head: K A Cheney
Type: Boys Day 3-13
Fees: (September 95) £2400 - £4290

DANES HILL PREPARATORY SCHOOL

Leatherhead Road, Oxshott,
Leatherhead, Surrey KT22 0JG
Tel: (01372) 842509
Head: R Parfitt
Type: Co-educational Day 3-13
No of Pupils: 680
Fees: (September 94) £705 - £4914

DOWNSEND GIRLS' PREPARATORY SCHOOL

1 Leatherhead Road, Leatherhead,
Surrey KT22 8TJ
Tel: (01372) 362668
Head: Mrs D M Harvey
Type: Girls Day 7-11
No of Pupils: 90
Fees: (September 95) £4275

DOWNSEND LODGE (ROWANS)

13 Epsom Road, Leatherhead, Surrey
KT22 8ST
Tel: (01372) 372123
Head: Mrs M Kekwick
Type: Co-educational Day 2-7
No of Pupils: B69 G48
Fees: (September 95) £885 - £3330

DOWNSEND SCHOOL

1 Leatherhead Road, Leatherhead,
Surrey KT22 8TJ
Tel: (01372) 372197
Head: A D White
Type: Boys Day 7-13
No of Pupils: 350
Fees: (September 95) £4275

GLENESK SCHOOL

Ockham Road North, East Horsley,
Leatherhead, Surrey KT24 6NS
Tel: (01483) 282329
Head: Mrs S P Johnson
Type: Co-educational Day 2-8
No of Pupils: B80 G100
Fees: (September 95) £1350 - £4035

MANOR HOUSE SCHOOL

Manor House Lane, Little Bookham,
Leatherhead, Surrey KT23 4EN
Tel: (01372) 458538
Head: Mrs L A Mendes
Type: Girls Boarding & Day 3-16
(Boys 3-8)
No of Pupils: B32 G296 No of
Boarders W14
Fees: (September 94) WB £6240 -
£7569 DAY £1320 - £5184

ST JOHN'S SCHOOL*

Epsom Road, Leatherhead, Surrey
KT22 8SP
Tel: (01372) 372021
Head: C H Tongue
Type: Boys Boarding & Day 13-18
(Co-ed VIth form)
No of Pupils: B350 G50 No of
Boarders F120
Fees: (September 95) F/WB £10500
DAY £7200

LINGFIELD

NOTRE DAME SCHOOL

Lingfield, Surrey RH7 6PH
Tel: (01342) 833176
Head: Mrs N E Shepley
Type: Girls Day 2-18 (Boys 2-11 &
16-18)
No of Pupils: 400
Fees: (September 95) £2010 - £4125

NEW MALDEN

BRETBY HOUSE SCHOOL

39 Woodlands Avenue, New Malden,
Surrey KT3 3UL
Tel: (0181) 942 5779
Head: Mrs S M Mallin
Type: Co-educational Day 3-8
No of Pupils: B61 G60
Fees: (September 95) £3291 - £3750

THE STUDY SCHOOL

57 Thetford Road, New Malden,
Surrey KT3 5DP
Tel: (0181) 942 0754
Head: J H Hudson
Type: Co-educational Day 3-11
No of Pupils: B80 G50
Fees: (September 95) £1545 - £4000

WESTBURY HOUSE

80 Westbury Road, New Malden,
Surrey KT3 5AS
Tel: (0181) 942 5885
Head: Mrs M T Morton
Type: Co-educational Day 3-12
No of Pupils: B105 G80
Fees: (September 94) £450 - £1005

OXTED

HAZELWOOD SCHOOL

Wolf's Hill, Limpsfield, Oxted,
Surrey RH8 0QU
Tel: (01883) 712194
Head: A M Synge
Type: Co-educational Day &
Boarding 3-13
No of Pupils: B232 G65 No of
Boarders W20
Fees: (September 95) WB £7245 DAY
£1545 - £5520

LAVEROCK SCHOOL

19 Bluehouse Lane, Oxted, Surrey
RH8 0AA
Tel: (01883) 714171
Head: Mrs A C Paterson
Type: Girls Day 3-11
No of Pupils: 155
Fees: (September 95) £1485 - £3420

ST MICHAEL'S SCHOOL

Wolf's Row, Limpsfield, Oxted,
Surrey RH8 0QR
Tel: (01883) 712311
Head: Dr M J Hustler
Type: Girls Boarding & Day 3-18
(Boys 3-8)
No of Pupils: B16 G191 No of
Boarders F91 W6
Fees: (September 95) F/WB £7950 -
£10500 DAY £2970 - £5985

PURLEY

COMMONWEAL LODGE
SCHOOL

Woodcote Lane, Purley, Surrey
CR8 3HB
Tel: (0181) 660 3179
Head: Mrs S Law
Type: Girls Day 4-18
No of Pupils: 250
Fees: (September 95) £2025 - £4515

DOWNSIDE PREPARATORY
SCHOOL

1 Woodcote Lane, Woodcote, Purley,
Surrey CR8 3HB
Tel: (0181) 660 0558
Head: T M Andrews
Type: Boys Day 3-14
No of Pupils: 240
Fees: (September 95) £1680 - £4275

ST DAVID'S SCHOOL

23 Woodcote Valley Road, Purley,
Surrey CR8 3AL
Tel: (0181) 660 0723
Head: Mrs L Randall
Type: Co-educational Day 3-11
No of Pupils: B85 G85
Fees: (September 95) £2025 - £2460

SHAFTESBURY
INDEPENDENT SCHOOL

Godstone Road, Purley, Surrey
CR8 2AN
Tel: (0181) 668 8080
Head: P A Gowlland
Type: Co-educational Day 3-18
No of Pupils: B40 G20
Fees: (September 95) £2640 - £4275

WEST DENE SCHOOL

167 Brighton Road, Purley, Surrey
CR8 4HE
Tel: (0181) 660 2404
Head: Mrs G Charkin
Type: Co-educational Day 3-9
No of Pupils: B65 G85
Fees: (September 95) £1560 - £2490

REDHILL

DOODS BROW SCHOOL

54 High Street, Nutfield, Redhill,
Surrey RH1 4HQ
Tel: (01737) 823372
Head: Mrs B D Wadlow
Type: Co-educational Day 2-11
No of Pupils: B52 G57
Fees: (September 94) £495 - £2040

THE HAWTHORNS SCHOOL

Pendell Court, Bletchingley, Redhill,
Surrey RH1 4QJ
Tel: (01883) 743048
Head: T R Johns
Type: Co-educational Day 2-13
No of Pupils: B252 G79
Fees: (September 95) £1035 - £4470

REIGATE

BURYS COURT SCHOOL

Leigh, Reigate, Surrey RH2 8RE
Tel: (01306) 611372
Head: D V White
Type: Co-educational Day 3-13
No of Pupils: B70 G50
Fees: (September 95) £1800 - £1920

CONISTON

22 Alma Road, Reigate, Surrey
RH2 0DH
Tel: (01737) 243370
Head: Mrs M Harvey
Type: Co-educational Day 3-8
No of Pupils: B42 G48
Fees: (September 95) £966 - £2436

DUNOTTAR SCHOOL*

High Trees Road, Reigate, Surrey
RH2 7EL
Tel: (01737) 761945
Head: Miss J Burnell
Type: Girls Day 4-18
No of Pupils: 435
Fees: (September 95) £2760 - £4530

MICKLEFIELD SCHOOL

10/12 Somers Road, Reigate, Surrey
RH2 9DU
Tel: (01737) 242615
Head: Mrs C Belton
Type: Girls Day 2-12 (Boys 2-7)
No of Pupils: B43 G200
Fees: (September 95) £747 - £3756

REIGATE GRAMMAR SCHOOL

Reigate Road, Reigate, Surrey
RH2 0QS
Tel: (01737) 222231
Head: J G Hamlin
Type: Co-educational Day 10-18
No of Pupils: B700 G100
Fees: (September 95) £4872

REIGATE ST MARY'S PREPARATORY AND CHOIR SCHOOL

Chart Lane, Reigate, Surrey RH2 7RN
Tel: (01737) 244880
Head: J A Hart
Type: Boys Day 3-13
No of Pupils: 236
Fees: (September 95) £825 - £4113

RICHMOND

BROOMFIELD HOUSE

10 Broomfield Road, Kew Gardens,
Richmond, Surrey TW9 3HS
Tel: (0181) 940 3884
Head: Mrs I O Harrow
Type: Co-educational Day 3-11
No of Pupils: B70 G80
Fees: (September 95) £1782 - £3564

THE GERMAN SCHOOL

Douglas House, Petersham Road,
Richmond, Surrey TW10 7AH
Tel: (0181) 948 3410
Head: E Backhaus
Type: Co-educational Day 5-19
No of Pupils: B302 G283
Fees: (September 95) £1725 - £2640

KEW COLLEGE

24/26 Cumberland Road, Kew,
Richmond, Surrey
Tel: (0181) 940 2039
Head: Mrs D E Lyness
Type: Co-educational Day 3-11
No of Pupils: 196
Fees: (September 95) £2550

KING'S HOUSE SCHOOL

68 King's Road, Richmond, Surrey
TW10 6ES
Tel: (0181) 940 1878
Head: R Armitage
Type: Boys Day 4-13
No of Pupils: 340
Fees: (September 95) £3360 - £4725

OLD VICARAGE SCHOOL

48 Richmond Hill, Richmond, Surrey
TW10 6QX
Tel: (0181) 940 0922
Head: Miss J C Reynolds
Type: Girls Day 4-11
No of Pupils: 168
Fees: (September 95) £3300 - £4020

UNICORN SCHOOL

238 Kew Road, Richmond, Surrey
TW9 3JX
Tel: (0181) 948 3926
Head: Mrs F Timmis
Type: Co-educational Day 3-11
No of Pupils: B78 G86
Fees: (September 95) £710 - £1320

SOUTH CROYDON

BEECH HOUSE PREPARATORY SCHOOL

15 Church Way, Sanderstead, South
Croydon, Surrey CR2 0JT
Tel: (0181) 660 6919
Head: Mrs M Robinson
Type: Co-educational Day 3-7
No of Pupils: B25 G25
Fees: (September 95) £1320 - £1815

CROHAM HURST SCHOOL*

79 Croham Road, South Croydon,
Surrey CR2 7YN
Tel: (0181) 680 3064
Head: Miss S C Budgen
Type: Girls Day 4-18
No of Pupils: 500
Fees: (September 95) £2220 - £4590

CROYDON HIGH SCHOOL GPDST

Old Farleigh Road, Selsdon, South
Croydon, Surrey CR2 8YB
Tel: (0181) 651 5020
Head: Mrs P E Davies
Type: Girls Day 4-18
No of Pupils: 1050
Fees: (September 95) £1192 - £1548

CUMNOR HOUSE SCHOOL

168 Pampisford Road, South
Croydon, Surrey CR2 6DA
Tel: (0181) 660 3445
Head: A A Jeans
Type: Boys Day 4-13
No of Pupils: 350
Fees: (September 95) £3750 - £4260

ELMHURST SCHOOL

44-48 South Park Hill Road, South
Croydon, Surrey CR2 7DW
Tel: (0181) 688 0661
Head: B K Dighton
Type: Boys Day 4-11
No of Pupils: 240
Fees: (September 95) £3150 - £3750

LALEHAM LEA PREPARATORY SCHOOL

29 Peaks Hill, South Croydon,
Surrey CR8 3JJ
Tel: (0181) 660 3351
Head: A C Baseley
Type: Co-educational Day 4-11
No of Pupils: 120
Fees: (September 95) £2400

SANDERSTEAD JUNIOR SCHOOL

29 Purley Oaks Road, Sanderstead,
South Croydon, Surrey CR2 0NW
Tel: (0181) 660 0801
Head: Mrs A Barns
Type: Co-educational Day 3-12
No of Pupils: 100
Fees: (September 95) £1800 - £3050

WHITGIFT SCHOOL

Haling Park, South Croydon, Surrey
CR2 6YT
Tel: (0181) 688 9222
Head: Dr C A Barnett
Type: Boys Day 10-18
No of Pupils: 1050
Fees: (September 95) £5497

SURBITON

LINLEY HOUSE

6 Berrylands Road, Surbiton, Surrey
KT5 8RA
Tel: (0181) 399 4979
Head: Mrs S Dainty
Type: Co-educational Day 3-7
No of Pupils: 32
Fees: (September 94) £1980

SHREWSBURY HOUSE SCHOOL
107 Ditton Road, Surbiton, Surrey KT6 6RL
Tel: (0181) 399 3066
Head: C M Ross
Type: Boys Day 7-13
No of Pupils: 250
Fees: (September 95) £5136

SURBITON PREPARATORY SCHOOL
3 Avenue Elmers, Surbiton, Surrey KT6 4SP
Tel: (0181) 546 5245
Head: S J Pryce
Type: Boys Day 5-11
No of Pupils: 110
Fees: (September 94) £925 - £1265

SUTTON

HOMEFIELD PREPARATORY SCHOOL
Western Road, Sutton, Surrey SM1 2TE
Tel: (0181) 642 0965
Head: P R Mowbray
Type: Boys Day 5-13
No of Pupils: 270
Fees: (September 93) £2340 - £3690

SEATON HOUSE
67 Banstead Road South, Sutton, Surrey SM2 5LH
Tel: (0181) 642 2332
Head: Mrs J Harrison
Type: Girls Day 3-11 (Boys 3-5)
No of Pupils: B20 G180
Fees: (September 95) £1290 - £2730

STOWFORD
95 Brighton Road, Sutton, Surrey SM2 5SJ
Tel: (0181) 661 9444
Head: A J Hennessy
Type: Co-educational Day 7-17
No of Pupils: B65 G26
Fees: (September 95) £2898 - £4647

SUTTON HIGH SCHOOL (GPDST)
55 Cheam Road, Sutton, Surrey SM1 2AX
Tel: (0181) 642 0594
Head: Mrs A J Coutts
Type: Girls Day 4-18
No of Pupils: 760
Fees: (September 95) £3576 - £4644

TADWORTH

ABERDOUR SCHOOL
Brighton Road, Burgh Heath, Tadworth, Surrey KT20 6AJ
Tel: (01737) 354119
Head: A Barraclough
Type: Co-educational Day 3-13
No of Pupils: 240
Fees: (September 95) £1650 - £4410

BRAMLEY SCHOOL
Chequers Lane, Walton-on-the-Hill, Tadworth, Surrey KT20 7ST
Tel: (01737) 812004
Head: Mrs B Johns
Type: Girls Day 3-12
No of Pupils: 115
Fees: (September 95) £1575 - £3450

CHINTHURST SCHOOL
Tadworth Street, Tadworth, Surrey KT20 5QZ
Tel: (01737) 812011
Head: T J Egan
Type: Boys Day 3-13
No of Pupils: 390
Fees: (September 95) £1260 - £3675

ST JOHN'S NURSERY SCHOOL
59 The Avenue, Tadworth, Surrey KT20 5AB
Tel: (01737) 813032
Head: Mrs Scarll
Type: Co-educational Day 3-5
No of Pupils: B15 G15
Fees: (September 95) £945

THAMES DITTON

WESTON GREEN SCHOOL
Weston Green Road, Thames Ditton, Surrey KT7 0JN
Tel: (0181) 398 2778
Head: Mrs J Winser
Type: Co-educational Day 3-11
No of Pupils: 150
Fees: (September 95) £600 - £1050

VIRGINIA WATER

VIRGINIA WATER PREPARATORY SCHOOL
Gorse Hill Road, Virginia Water, Surrey GU25 4AU
Tel: (01344) 843138
Head: Mrs S M Winson
Type: Co-educational Day B2-8 G2-11
No of Pupils: B43 G72
Fees: (September 95) £3285 - £3585

WALLINGTON

COLLINGWOOD SCHOOL
3 Springfield Road, Wallington, Surrey SM6 0BD
Tel: (0181) 647 4607
Head: D W Sweet
Type: Co-educational Day 3-11
No of Pupils: 135
Fees: (September 95) £900 - £2865

WALTON-ON-THAMES

DANESFIELD PREPARATORY SCHOOL
Rydens Avenue, Walton-on-Thames, Surrey KT12 3JB
Tel: (01932) 220930
Head: Mrs T Yates
Type: Co-educational Day 4-11
No of Pupils: B52 G90
Fees: (September 95) £1830 - £3015

WESTWARD PREPARATORY SCHOOL
47 Hersham Road, Walton-on-Thames, Surrey KT12 1LE
Tel: (01932) 220911
Head: Mrs P Townley
Type: Co-educational Day 3-11
No of Pupils: 140
Fees: (September 95) £1260 - £2685

WEYBRIDGE

ST GEORGE'S COLLEGE
Weybridge Road, Addlestone, Weybridge, Surrey KT15 2QS
Tel: (01932) 854811
Head: J A Peake
Type: Boys Day 11-18 (Co-ed VIth form)
No of Pupils: B460 G80
Fees: (September 95) £5745 - £6495

ST GEORGE'S COLLEGE JUNIOR SCHOOL
Weybridge Road, Addlestone, Weybridge, Surrey KT15 2QS
Tel: (01932) 845784
Head: Rev M D Ashcroft
Type: Boys Day 2-11 (Girls 2-7)
No of Pupils: 200
Fees: (September 95) £540 - £4434

ST MAUR'S CONVENT SCHOOL
Thames Street, Weybridge, Surrey KT13 8NL
Tel: (01932) 851411
Head: Mrs M E Dodds
Type: Girls Day 2-18 (Boys 2-7)
No of Pupils: 700
Fees: (September 95) £2265 - £4725

WALLOP SCHOOL
Hanger Hill, Weybridge, Surrey
KT13 9YD
Tel: (01932) 852885
Head: P D Westcombe
Type: Co-educational Day B3-13
G3-11
No of Pupils: B124 G17
Fees: (September 95) £2796 - £4728

WINDLESHAM

WOODCOTE HOUSE SCHOOL
Snows Ride, Windlesham, Surrey
GU20 6PF
Tel: (01276) 472115
Head: N H Paterson
Type: Boys Boarding & Day 7-14
No of Pupils: 110 No of Boarders
F100
Fees: (September 95) FB £7305 DAY
£5100

WOKING

CABLE HOUSE SCHOOL
Horsell Rise, Woking, Surrey
GU21 4AY
Tel: (01483) 760759
Head: R Elvidge
Type: Co-educational Day 3-11
No of Pupils: B55 G55
Fees: (September 95) £1515 - £3090

COWORTH PARK SCHOOL
Valley End, Chobham, Woking,
Surrey GU24 8TE
Tel: (01276) 855707
Head: Mrs P S Middleton
Type: Co-educational Day B3-7
G3-11
No of Pupils: B35 G115
Fees: (September 95) £1860 - £4095

FLEXLANDS SCHOOL
Station Road, Chobham, Woking,
Surrey GU24 8AG
Tel: (01276) 858841
Head: Mrs S J Shaw
Type: Girls Day 3-11 (Boys 3-4)
No of Pupils: 170
Fees: (September 95) £1614 - £4218

GREENFIELD SCHOOL
Brooklyn Road, Woking, Surrey
GU22 7UU
Tel: (01483) 772525
Head: Mrs J S Becker
Type: Co-educational Day 3-11
No of Pupils: B80 G100
Fees: (September 95) £500 - £850

HALSTEAD PREPARATORY
SCHOOL
Woodham Rise, Woking, Surrey
GU21 4EE
Tel: (01483) 772682
Head: Mrs A Hancock
Type: Girls Day 3-11
No of Pupils: 200
Fees: (September 95) £1845 - £3825

HOE BRIDGE SCHOOL*
Hoe Place, Old Woking, Woking,
Surrey GU22 8JE
Tel: (01483) 760018
Head: R W K Barr & P G Tame
Type: Co-educational Boarding &
Day 7-13
No of Pupils: 195 No of Boarders
W20
Fees: (September 95) WB £7650 -
£8415 DAY £5100 - £5865

OAKFIELD*
Coldharbour Lane, Pyrford, Woking,
Surrey GU22 8SJ
Tel: (01932) 342465
Head: Mrs R C Brothers
Type: Co-educational Day B2-11
G2-16
No of Pupils: B30 G150
Fees: (September 95) £2070 - £5250

RIPLEY COURT SCHOOL*
Rose Lane, Ripley, Woking, Surrey
GU23 6NE
Tel: (01483) 225217
Head: J W Dudgeon
Type: Co-educational Boarding &
Day 4-13
No of Pupils: B248 G15 No of
Boarders F12 W22
Fees: (September 95) F/WB £6639
DAY £2688 - £4323

ST ANDREW'S SCHOOL*
Church Hill House, Horsell, Woking,
Surrey GU21 4QW
Tel: (01483) 760943
Head: A Brownridge
Type: Boys Day 3-13 (Girls 3-4)
No of Pupils: 160
Fees: (September 95) £2235 - £5985

THE TREES
PRE-PREPARATORY SCHOOL
Hoe Place, Woking, Surrey GU22 8JE
Tel: (01483) 772194
Head: Mrs L Renfrew
Type: Co-educational Day 3-7
No of Pupils: 180
Fees: (September 95) £1687 - £3720

EAST SUSSEX

BATTLE

BATTLE ABBEY SCHOOL
Battle, East Sussex TN33 0AD
Tel: (01424) 772385
Head: D J Teall
Type: Co-educational Boarding &
Day 2-18
No of Pupils: B115 G115 No of
Boarders F50 W5
Fees: (September 95) F/WB £7290 -
£9090 DAY £3090 - £5625

WILTON HOUSE SCHOOL
Catsfield Place, Battle, East Sussex
TN33 9BS
Tel: (01424) 830234
Head: Mrs F Auer
Type: Co-educational Boarding &
Day 13-18
No of Pupils: B112 G89 No of
Boarders F105
Fees: (September 95) FB £6825 -
£8580 DAY £3105 - £5010

BEXHILL-ON-SEA

AMBERLEY SCHOOL
9 Buckhurst Road, Bexhill-on-sea,
East Sussex TN40 1QF
Tel: (01424) 212472
Head: Mrs B A Sparks
Type: Co-educational Day 3-7
No of Pupils: 60
Fees: (September 95) £850 - £1150

BRIGHTON

BRIGHTON AND HOVE HIGH SCHOOL GPDST
Montpelier Road, Brighton, East Sussex BN1 3AT
Tel: (01273) 734112
Head: Miss R A Woodbridge
Type: Girls Day 4-18
No of Pupils: 750
Fees: (September 95) £2928 - £3984

BRIGHTON COLLEGE*
Eastern Road, Brighton, East Sussex BN2 2AL
Tel: (01273) 605788
Head: J D Leach
Type: Co-educational Day & Boarding 13-18
No of Pupils: B350 G122 No of Boarders F36 W66
Fees: (September 95) FB £11940 WB £10680 DAY £7854

BRIGHTON COLLEGE JUNIOR SCHOOL
Walpole Lodge, Walpole Road, Brighton, East Sussex BN2 2EU
Tel: (01273) 606845
Head: G H Brown
Type: Co-educational Boarding & Day 8-13 (Weekly boarders only)
No of Pupils: B160 G60
Fees: (September 95) WB £7230 DAY £5916

BRIGHTON COLLEGE JUNIOR SCHOOL (PRE-PREPARATORY)*
Brighton College, Sutherland Road, Brighton, East Sussex BN2 2EQ
Tel: (01273) 603495
Head: G H Brown
Type: Co-educational Day 3-8
No of Pupils: 140
Fees: (September 95) £1320 - £3015

DHARMA SCHOOL
White House, Ladies Mile Road, Patcham, Brighton, East Sussex BN1 8TB
Tel: (01273) 502055
Head: Ms L M Medhina
Type: Co-educational Day 4-11
No of Pupils: B4 G7
Fees: (September 95) £2000

ROEDEAN SCHOOL
Brighton, East Sussex BN2 5RQ
Tel: (01273) 603181
Head: Mrs A Longley
Type: Girls Boarding & Day 11-18
No of Pupils: 430 No of Boarders F430
Fees: (September 95) FB £12975 DAY £7365

ST AUBYN'S
High Street, Rottingdean, Brighton, East Sussex BNZ 7JN
Tel: (01273) 302170
Head: J A James
Type: Boys Boarding & Day 7-14
No of Pupils: 115 No of Boarders F85
Fees: (September 95) FB £8805 DAY £6525

ST MARY'S HALL*
Eastern Road, Brighton, East Sussex BN2 5JF
Tel: (01273) 606061
Head: Mrs P J James
Type: Girls Day & Boarding 3-18 (Boys 3-8)
No of Pupils: B7 G424 No of Boarders F97
Fees: (September 95) FB £7317 - £8955 WB £6975 - £8555 DAY £1170 - £5940

EASTBOURNE

EASTBOURNE COLLEGE
Old Wish Road, Eastbourne, East Sussex BN21 4JX
Tel: (01323) 737655
Head: C M Bush
Type: Co-educational Boarding & Day 13-18
No of Pupils: B408 G69 No of Boarders F296
Fees: (September 95) FB £11619 DAY £8592

MOIRA HOUSE JUNIOR SCHOOL*
Upper Carlisle Road, Eastbourne, East Sussex BN20 7TE
Tel: (01323) 644144
Head: Mrs A Harris
Type: Girls Day & Boarding 2-11
No of Pupils: 95 No of Boarders F6
Fees: (September 95) FB £10260 DAY £3210 - £5370

MOIRA HOUSE SENIOR SCHOOL*
Upper Carlisle Road, Eastbourne, East Sussex BN20 7TE
Tel: (01323) 644144
Head: A R Underwood
Type: Girls Boarding & Day 11-18
No of Pupils: 380 No of Boarders F130
Fees: (September 95) FB £10260 - £10710 DAY £5850 - £6900

ST ANDREW'S SCHOOL*
Meads, Eastbourne, East Sussex BN20 7RP
Tel: (01323) 33203
Head: H Davies Jones
Type: Co-educational Boarding & Day 3-13
No of Pupils: B254 G147 No of Boarders F100
Fees: (September 95) F/WB £7725 DAY £3000 - £5340

ST BEDE'S*
Duke's Drive, Eastbourne, East Sussex BN20 7XL
Tel: (01323) 734222
Head: P Pyemont
Type: Co-educational Boarding & Day 2-13
No of Pupils: B280 G150 No of Boarders F80
Fees: (September 95) F/WB £8970 DAY £1680 - £5670

FOREST ROW

ASHDOWN HOUSE SCHOOL
Forest Row, East Sussex RH18 5JY
Tel: (01342) 822574
Head: M V Williams
Type: Co-educational Boarding & Day 8-13
No of Pupils: B145 G54 No of Boarders F185
Fees: (September 95) FB £9330 DAY £7500

GREENFIELDS SCHOOL
Priory Road, Forest Row, East Sussex RH18 5JD
Tel: (01342) 822845
Head: A M McQuade
Type: Co-educational Day & Boarding 3-18
No of Pupils: B86 G74
Fees: (September 94) FB £7395 - £8910 WB £6495 - £8010 DAY £1779 - £4860

MICHAEL HALL*
Kidbrooke Park, Forest Row, East Sussex RH18 5JB
Tel: (01342) 822275
Type: Co-educational Day & Boarding 3-18
No of Pupils: B262 G240 No of Boarders F45 W15
Fees: (September 95) FB £6900 - £8025 DAY £1575 - £3675

HAILSHAM*

ST BEDE'S SCHOOL
The Dicker, Hailsham, East Sussex
BN27 3QH
Tel: (01323) 843252
Head: R A Perrin
Type: Co-educational Boarding &
Day 12-19
No of Pupils: B235 G146 No of
Boarders F248 W10
Fees: (September 95) FB £11400 DAY
£7050

HASTINGS

BROOMHAM SCHOOL
Guestling, Hastings, East Sussex
TN35 4LT
Tel: (01424) 814456
Head: J Auer
Type: Co-educational Boarding &
Day 4-13
No of Pupils: 120 No of Boarders F38
Fees: (September 95) FB £6150 DAY
£2229 - £2910

HOVE

BELLERBYS' COLLEGE
Pitblado House, 44 Cromwell Road,
Hove, East Sussex BN3 3ER
Tel: (01273) 723911
Head: L Denholm & P Corcut
Type: Co-educational Residential &
Day 15+
No of Pupils: B200 G160
Fees: (September 95) FB £11500
-£11850

DEEPDENE SCHOOL
195 New Church Road, Hove, East
Sussex BN3 4ED
Tel: (01273) 418984
Head: Mrs B Cameron
Type: Girls Day 2-11 (Boys 2-7)
No of Pupils: B20 G75
Fees: (September 95) £114 - £2700

THE FOLD SCHOOL
201 New Church Road, Hove, East
Sussex BN3 4ED
Tel: (01273) 410901
Head: Mrs B Cameron
Type: Co-educational Day 3-9
No of Pupils: B35 G35
Fees: (September 95) £2040 - £2190

MOWDEN SCHOOL
The Droveway, Hove, East Sussex
BN3 6LU
Tel: (01273) 503452
Head: C E Snell
Type: Boys Day & Boarding 7-13
No of Pupils: 103 No of Boarders
W15
Fees: (September 95) WB £6675 DAY
£5580

ST CHRISTOPHER'S SCHOOL
33 New Church Road, Hove, East
Sussex BN3 4AD
Tel: (01273) 735404
Head: R J Saunders
Type: Boys Day 5-14
No of Pupils: 240
Fees: (September 95) £2760

STONELANDS SCHOOL OF BALLET
3 Hove Business Centre, Fonthill
Road, Hove, East Sussex BN3 6HA
Tel: (01626) 866708
Head: Mrs J E Filipi
Type: Girls Boarding & Day 3-16
(Boys 3-5, boarders from 7)
No of Pupils: 30; No of Boarders F30
Fees: (September 95) FB £1810 -
£2555 DAY £750 - £1495

LEWES

THE OLD GRAMMAR SCHOOL
136 High Street, Lewes, East Sussex
BN7 1XS
Tel: (01273) 472634
Head: Dr A Hodd
Type: Co-educational Day 4-18
No of Pupils: B260 G130
Fees: (September 95) £2334 - £4173

MAYFIELD

HILLHOUSE PREPARATORY SCHOOL
Mayfield College, Little Trodgers
Lane, Mayfield, East Sussex
TN20 6PL
Tel: (01435) 873713
Head: Mrs M Child
Type: Co-educational 3-11
No of Pupils: B52 G43
Fees: (September 95) DAY £2100

MAYFIELD COLLEGE*
Mayfield, East Sussex TN20 6PL
Tel: (01435) 872041
Head: C P Vroege
Type: Boys Boarding & Day 11-18
(Day girls)
No of Pupils: 90 No of Boarders F47
W13
Fees: (September 95) FB £6075 -
£11850 WB £5895 - £9315 DAY
£3000 - £6120

ST LEONARDS-MAYFIELD SCHOOL*
The Old Palace, Mayfield, East
Sussex TN20 6PH
Tel: (01435) 873055
Head: Sister Jean Sinclair
Type: Girls Boarding & Day 11-18
No of Pupils: 525 No of Boarders
F315 W50
Fees: (September 95) F/WB £10350
DAY £6900

SKIPPERS HILL MANOR PREPARATORY SCHOOL
Five Ashes, Mayfield, East Sussex
TN20 6HR
Tel: (01825) 830234
Head: T W Lewis
Type: Co-educational Day 3-13
No of Pupils: B93 G62
Fees: (September 95) £1590 - £4950

ROBERTSBRIDGE

BODIAM MANOR SCHOOL
Bodiam, Robertsbridge, East Sussex
TN32 5UJ
Tel: (01580) 830225
Head: P L and Mrs S J Northen
Type: Co-educational Day 2-13
No of Pupils: B77 G78
Fees: (September 94) £2514 - £4581

VINEHALL SCHOOL
Robertsbridge, East Sussex TN32 5JL
Tel: (01580) 880413
Head: D C Chaplin
Type: Co-educational Boarding &
Day 4-14
No of Pupils: B197 G113 No of
Boarders F82
Fees: (September 95) FB £8250 DAY
£3360 - £6135

SEAFORD

NEWLANDS MANOR SCHOOL*
Sutton Place, Seaford, East Sussex
BN25 3PL
Tel: (01323) 890309
Head: B F Underwood
Type: Co-educational Boarding &
Day 13-19
No of Pupils: B169 G79 No of
Boarders F179 W10
Fees: (September 95) FB £8955 -
£10185 WB £8865 - £10095 DAY
£5670

NEWLANDS PREPARATORY
SCHOOL*
Eastbourne Road, Seaford, East
Sussex BN25 4NP
Tel: (01323) 892334
Head: R Clark
Type: Co-educational Boarding &
Day 7-13
No of Pupils: B149 G82 No of
Boarders F103 W1
Fees: (September 95) FB £8430 -
£8580 WB £8340 DAY £4170 -
£5130

ST LEONARDS-ON-SEA

CLAREMONT SCHOOL
Baldslow, St Leonards-on-Sea, East
Sussex TN37 7PW
Tel: (01424) 751555
Head: J G Hill
Type: Co-educational Day 2-14
No of Pupils: B100 G100
Fees: (September 95) £2080 - £4560

WESTERLEIGH
Hollington Park, St Leonards-on-Sea,
East Sussex TN38 0SE
Tel: (01424) 440760
Head: Mrs P Wheeler
Type: Co-educational Day 2-13
No of Pupils: B100 G60
Fees: (September 95) £540 - £4740

WINTON HOUSE SCHOOL
4 Dane Road, St Leonards-on-Sea,
East Sussex TN38 0QU
Tel: (01424) 421117
Head: Miss J Casey
Type: Co-educational Day 2-11
No of Pupils: B6 G8
Fees: (September 95) £1980

UCKFIELD

BUCKSWOOD GRANGE
Uckfield, East Sussex TN22 3PU
Tel: (01825) 761666
Head: M B Reiser
Type: Co-educational Day &
Boarding 4-16
No of Pupils: B90 G52 No of
Boarders F80 W3
Fees: (September 95) FB £7500 -
£10000 DAY £3000 - £5000

TEMPLE GROVE*
Heron's Ghyll, Uckfield, East Sussex
TN22 4DA
Tel: (01825) 712112
Head: M G Lee
Type: Co-educational Boarding &
Day 3-13
No of Pupils: B118 G93 No of
Boarders 35
Fees: (September 95) FB £6885 -
£8190 DAY £3795 - £6690

WADHURST

BRICKLEHURST MANOR
PREPARATORY
Stonegate, Wadhurst, East Sussex
TN5 7EL
Tel: (01580) 200448
Head: Mrs R A Lewis
Type: Co-educational Day B4-8
G4-11
No of Pupils: B17 G76
Fees: (September 95) £1665 - £3645

MICKLEFIELD WADHURST
INCORPORATING THE LEGAT
SCHOOL OF CLASSICAL
BALLET*
Mayfield Lane, Wadhurst, East
Sussex TN5 6JA
Tel: (01892) 783193
Head: Miss A M Phillips & E Reynolds
Type: Girls Boarding & Day 10-18
(Boys Ballet only 10-18)
No of Pupils: 180 No of Boarders F80
Fees: (September 95) FB £10110 WB
£10020 DAY £6210 - £6420

SACRED HEART RC PRIMARY
SCHOOL
Mayfield Lane, Durgates, Wadhurst,
East Sussex TN5 6DQ
Tel: (01892) 783414
Head: Mrs H Castle
Type: Co-educational Day 3-11
No of Pupils: B50 G50
Fees: (September 95) £900 - £2280

WEST SUSSEX

ARUNDEL

SLINDON COLLEGE*
Slindon House, Slindon, Arundel,
West Sussex BN18 0RH
Tel: (01243) 814320
Head: D Morris
Type: Boys Boarding & Day 11-18
No of Pupils: 100 No of Boarders F40
W40
Fees: (September 95) F/WB £9150
DAY £5985

BURGESS HILL

BURGESS HILL SCHOOL*
Keymer Road, Burgess Hill, West
Sussex RH15 0EG
Tel: (01444) 241050
Head: Mrs R F Lewis
Type: Girls Day & Boarding 3-18
No of Pupils: B22 G600 No of
Boarders F60
Fees: (September 95) FB £8325 -
£9285 DAY £2565 - £5520

ST PETER'S SCHOOL
Upper St John's Road, Burgess Hill,
West Sussex RH15 8HB
Tel: (01444) 235880
Head: Mrs R H Stevens
Type: Co-educational Day 2-8
No of Pupils: B85 G76
Fees: (September 95) £408 - £2727

CHICHESTER

GREAT BALLARD SCHOOL
Eartham, Chichester, West Sussex
PO18 0LR
Tel: (01243) 814236
Head: R E Jennings
Type: Co-educational Boarding &
Day 3-13
No of Pupils: B123 G39 No of
Boarders F17 W32
Fees: (September 95) F/WB £7242
DAY £1623 - £5112

LAVANT HOUSE-ROSEMEAD*
Chichester, West Sussex PO18 9AB
Tel: (01243) 527211
Head: Mrs M Scott
Type: Girls Day & Boarding 3-18
(Boys 3-8)
No of Pupils: 200 No of Boarders F50
Fees: (September 95) F/WB £7875 -
£9990 DAY £3585 - £5985

LITTLEMEAD GRAMMAR
SCHOOL
Woodfield House, Oving, Chichester,
West Sussex PO20 6EU
Tel: (01243) 787551
Head: I F Bowler
Type: Co-educational Day &
Boarding 3-16
No of Pupils: B74 G63 No of Boarders
F15 W10
Fees: (September 95) FB £5829 -
£6951 WB £5349 - £6471 DAY
£1248 - £4251

NORTHGATE HOUSE SCHOOL
38 North Street, Chichester, West
Sussex PO19 1LX
Tel: (01243) 784828
Head: Mrs W E Shoesmith
Type: Co-educational Day 4-8
No of Pupils: B45 G45
Fees: (September 95) £630 - £930

OAKWOOD SCHOOL
Oakwood, Chichester, West Sussex
PO18 9AN
Tel: (01243) 575209
Head: S J Whittle
Type: Co-educational Boarding &
Day 3-11
No of Pupils: B103 G51 No of
Boarders F11 W17
Fees: (September 95) FB £7350 WB
£6798 DAY £1308 - £5124

THE PREBENDAL SCHOOL
53 West Street, Chichester, West
Sussex PO19 1RT
Tel: (01243) 782026
Head: Rev Canon G C Hall
Type: Co-educational Day &
Boarding 7-14
No of Pupils: B108 G88 No of
Boarders F17 W27
Fees: (September 95) FB £6780 WB
£6480 DAY £4980

WESTBOURNE HOUSE
SCHOOL
Shopwyke, Chichester, West Sussex
PO20 6BH
Tel: (01243) 782739
Head: S L Rigby
Type: Co-educational Boarding &
Day 3-13
No of Pupils: B181 G50 No of
Boarders F92
Fees: (September 95) FB £7725 DAY
£3120 - £6240

CRAWLEY

COPTHORNE SCHOOL
Effingham Lane, Crawley, West
Sussex RH10 3HR
Tel: (01342) 712311
Head: D Newton
Type: Co-educational Day &
Boarding 4-14
No of Pupils: B176 G66 No of
Boarders W25
Fees: (September 95) WB £7260 DAY
£3285 - £5970

WORTH SCHOOL
Worth Abbey, Turners Hill,
Crawley, West Sussex RH10 4SD
Tel: (01342) 715911
Head: Fr C Jamison
Type: Boys Boarding 9-18
No of Pupils: 370 No of Boarders F40
Fees: (September 95) FB £8490 -
£11490 DAY £5670 - £7665

EAST GRINSTEAD

BRAMBLETYE SCHOOL
Brambletye, East Grinstead, West
Sussex RH19 3PD
Tel: (01342) 321004
Head: D G Fowler-Watt
Type: Boys Boarding & Day 7-14
No of Pupils: 216 No of Boarders
F185
Fees: (September 95) FB £8775 DAY
£6450

FONTHILL
Coombe Hill Road, East Grinstead,
West Sussex RH9 4LY
Tel: (01342) 321635
Head: Mrs J Griffiths
Type: Co-educational Day B2-8
G2-11
No of Pupils: 151
Fees: (September 95) £1182 - £4497

NEW LIFE CHRISTIAN
SCHOOL
Maypole Road, East Grinstead, West
Sussex RH19
Tel: (01342) 322724
Head: Mrs A Coggins
Type: Co-educational Day 3-18
No of Pupils: B20 G18
Fees: (September 95) £720 - £1236

STOKE BRUNSWICK
Ashurstwood, East Grinstead, West
Sussex RH19 3PF
Tel: (01342) 822233
Head: W M Ellerton
Type: Co-educational Boarding &
Day 3-13
No of Pupils: B100 G55 No of
Boarders F20 W10
Fees: (September 95) FB £8475 DAY
£3075 - £6165

HASSOCKS

HURSTPIERPOINT COLLEGE
Hassocks, West Sussex BN6 9JS
Tel: (01273) 833636
Head: S D M Meek
Type: Co-educational Boarding &
Day 7-18
No of Pupils: 460 No of Boarders
F260
Fees: (September 95) FB £7680 -
£11370 DAY £4800 - £9060

HAYWARDS HEATH

ARDINGLY COLLEGE*
Haywards Heath, West Sussex
RH17 6SQ
Tel: (01444) 892577
Head: J W Flecker
Type: Co-educational Boarding &
Day 13-18
No of Pupils: B266 G204 No of
Boarders F313
Fees: (September 95) FB £11640 DAY
£9195

ARDINGLY COLLEGE JUNIOR SCHOOL*
Haywards Heath, West Sussex
RH17 6SQ
Tel: (01444) 892279
Head: P Thwaites
Type: Co-educational Boarding &
Day 2-13
No of Pupils: B89 G74 No of
Boarders F66
Fees: (September 95) FB £8250
DAY £5625 - £5750

CUMNOR HOUSE SCHOOL
Danehill, Haywards Heath, West
Sussex RH17 7HT
Tel: (01825) 790347
Head: N J Milner-Gulland
Type: Co-educational Boarding &
Day 4-13
No of Pupils: B111 G87 No of
Boarders F76
Fees: (September 95) FB £8160 -
£8580 DAY £2640 - £6585

GREAT WALSTEAD
Lindfield, Haywards Heath,
West Sussex RH16 2QL
Tel: (01444) 483528
Head: H J Lowries
Type: Co-educational Boarding &
Day 3-13
No of Pupils: B178 G104 No of
Boarders F47
Fees: (September 95) FB £6900 DAY
£552 - £5580

HANDCROSS PARK SCHOOL
Handcross, Haywards Heath,
West Sussex RH17 6HF
Tel: (01444) 400526
Head: W J Hilton
Type: Co-educational Boarding &
Day 2-13
No of Pupils: B138 G103 No of
Boarders W15
Fees: (September 95) WB £7380 DAY
£270 - £6105

TAVISTOCK & SUMMERHILL SCHOOL
Summerhill Lane, Haywards Heath,
West Sussex RH16 1RP
Tel: (01444) 450256
Head: M Barber
Type: Co-educational Day 4-13
No of Pupils: B110 G50
Fees: (September 95) £2400 - £4275

HORSHAM

CHRISTS HOSPITAL*
Horsham, West Sussex RH13 7LS
Tel: (01403) 252547
Head: R C Poulton
Type: Co-educational Boarding 11-18
No of Pupils: B481 G328 No of
Boarders F815
Fees: (September 95) FB up to £10688

FARLINGTON SCHOOL*
Strood Park, Horsham, West Sussex
RH12 3PN
Tel: (01403) 254967
Head: Mrs P Mawer
Type: Girls Day & Boarding 4-18
No of Pupils: 311 No of Boarders F9
W31
Fees: (September 95) FB £8280 -
£9360 WB £8160 - £9240 DAY
£2520 - £5790

PENNTHORPE SCHOOL
Rudgwick, Horsham, West Sussex
RH12 3HJ
Tel: (01403) 822391
Head: Rev J E Spencer
Type: Co-educational Day 2-14
No of Pupils: B145 G74
Fees: (September 95) £2175 - £5655

LANCING

LANCING COLLEGE
Lancing, West Sussex BN15 0RW
Tel: (01273) 452213
Head: C J Saunders
Type: Boys Boarding & Day 13-18
(Co-ed VIth form)
No of Pupils: B461 G54
Fees: (September 95) FB £12030 DAY
£9045

SOMPTING ABBOTTS*
Lancing, West Sussex BN15 0AZ
Tel: (01903) 235960
Head: N A Sinclair
Type: Boys Day & Boarding 3-13
No of Pupils: 175 No of Boarders
W15
Fees: (September 95) WB £5685 DAY
£2025 - £3885

LITTLEHAMPTON

NEW WEST PRESTON MANOR NURSERY SCHOOL
39 Park Drive, Rustington,
Littlehampton, West Sussex
BN16 3DY
Tel: (01903) 774649
Head: Mrs J M Drury
Type: Co-educational Day 2-5
No of Pupils: 38
Fees: On application

MIDHURST

CONIFERS SCHOOL
Egmont Road, Midhurst,
West Sussex GU29 9BG
Tel: (01730) 813243
Head: Mrs J Peel
Type: Co-educational Day 3-11
No of Pupils: B50 G100
Fees: (September 95) £970 - £2910

ST MARGARET'S JUNIOR SCHOOL CONVENT OF MERCY
Petersfield Road, Midhurst,
West Sussex GU29 9JN
Tel: (01730) 813956
Head: Sister M Joan
Type: Co-educational Day 3-11
No of Pupils: B120 G270
Fees: (September 95) £1080 - £1875

ST MARGARET'S SENIOR SCHOOL CONVENT OF MERCY
Petersfield Road, Midhurst,
West Sussex GU29 9JN
Tel: (01730) 813899
Head: Sister Aquinus
Type: Girls Day 11-16
No of Pupils: 300
Fees: (September 95) £2475

PEASE POTTAGE

COTTESMORE SCHOOL*
Buchan Hill, Pease Pottage,
West Sussex RH11 9AU
Tel: (01293) 520648
Head: M A Rogerson
Type: Co-educational Boarding 7-13
No of Pupils: B110 G40 No of
Boarders F145
Fees: (September 95) FB £8730

PETWORTH

SEAFORD COLLEGE*
Lavington Park, Petworth,
West Sussex GU28 0NB
Tel: (01798) 867392
Head: R C Hannaford
Type: Boys Boarding 11-18 (Day
boys 11-13, co-ed VIth form)
No of Pupils: 340 No of Boarders
F280
Fees: (September 95) F/WB £8250 -
£9630 DAY £5265 - £5925

PULBOROUGH

ARUNDALE PREPARATORY SCHOOL
Lower Street, Pulborough,
West Sussex RH20 2BX
Tel: (01798) 872520
Head: Miss K Lovejoy
Type: Co-educational Day B3-8
G3-12
No of Pupils: B24 G84
Fees: (September 95) £1260 - £4705

DORSET HOUSE SCHOOL*
The Manor, Bury, Pulborough,
West Sussex RH20 1PB
Tel: (01798) 831456
Head: A L James
Type: Boys Boarding & Day 4-13
No of Pupils: 119 No of Boarders
F3 W40
Fees: (September 95) F/WB £8040
DAY £3330 - £6705

ST JOSEPH'S DOMINICAN CONVENT
The Abbey, Greyfriars Lane,
Storrington, Pulborough, West
Sussex RH20 4HE
Tel: (01903) 743279
Head: Sister Loretta
Type: Co-educational Day 4-11
No of Pupils: B40 G80
Fees: (September 95) £2400

WINDLESHAM HOUSE*
Washington, Pulborough,
West Sussex RH20 4AY
Tel: (01903) 873207
Acting Heads: Mr & Mrs S Goodhart
Type: Co-educational Boarding 7-13
No of Pupils: 300
Fees: (September 95) FB £8925

SHOREHAM-BY-SEA

SHOREHAM COLLEGE
St Julian's Lane, Shoreham-by-Sea,
West Sussex BN43 6YW
Tel: (01273) 592681
Head: D R Jarman
Type: Co-educational Day 3-16
No of Pupils: B123 G37
Fees: (September 95) £2520 - £5505

STEYNING

SOUTHDOWN PRE-PREPARATORY SCHOOL AND NURSERY
Gervays Hall, Jarvis Lane, Steyning,
West Sussex BN44 3GL
Tel: (01903) 814581
Head: Mrs R A Hoare
Type: Co-educational Day 4-8
(Nursery 3-5)
No of Pupils: B26 G24
Fees: (September 95) £390 - £1470

THE TOWERS CONVENT SCHOOL
Upper Beeding, Steyning,
West Sussex BN44 3TF
Tel: (01903) 812185
Head: Sister M Andrew
Type: Girls Day & Boarding 3-16
No of Pupils: 210 No of Boarders F68
Fees: (September 95) FB £5430 -
£5730 WB £5130 - £5400 DAY
£2895 - £3195

WEST GRINSTEAD

YAGO SCHOOL
Steyning Road, West Grinstead,
West Sussex RH13 8LS
Tel: (01403) 710538
Head: Ramon Resa
Type: Co-educational Boarding &
Day 7-18
No of Pupils: B75 G75 No of Boarders
F50
Fees: On application.

WORTHING

BROADWATER MANOR SCHOOL
Broadwater Road, Worthing,
West Sussex BN14 8HU
Tel: (01903) 236687
Head: D Telfer
Type: Co-educational Day 2-13
No of Pupils: B258 G172
Fees: (September 95) £300 - £3465

OUR LADY OF SION SCHOOL
Gratwicke Road, Worthing,
West Sussex BN11 4BL
Tel: (01903) 204063
Head: B Sexton
Type: Co-educational Day 2-18
No of Pupils: B198 G247
Fees: (September 95) £2985 - £4455

SANDHURST SCHOOL
101 Brighton Road, Worthing,
West Sussex BN11 2EL
Tel: (01903) 201933
Head: Mrs C Skomski
Type: Co-educational Day 3-13
No of Pupils: B82 G105
Fees: (September 95) £1410 - £1725

TYNE AND WEAR

GATESHEAD

GATESHEAD JEWISH PRIMARY SCHOOL
18-20 Gladstone Terrace, Gateshead,
Tyne and Wear NE8 4EA
Head: Rabbi S Wagschal
Fees: On application

NEWCASTLE UPON TYNE

AKHURST PREPARATORY SCHOOL
The Grove, Jesmond, Newcastle
upon Tyne, Tyne and Wear NE2 2PN
Tel: (0191) 281 2116
Head: Mr & Mrs R J Derham
Type: Co-educational Day 2-12
No of Pupils: B155 G60
Fees: (September 94) £1470 - £2940

ASCHAM HOUSE SCHOOL
30 West Avenue, Gosforth,
Newcastle upon Tyne, Tyne and
Wear NE3 4ES
Tel: (0191) 285 1619
Head: S H Reid
Type: Boys Day 4-13
No of Pupils: 270
Fees: (September 95) £3225

CENTRAL NEWCASTLE HIGH SCHOOL GPDST

Eskdale Terrace, Newcastle upon Tyne, Tyne and Wear NE2 4DS
Tel: (0191) 281 1768
Head: Mrs A M Chapman
Type: Girls Day 4–18
No of Pupils: 885
Fees: (September 95) £2928 – £3984

DAME ALLAN'S BOYS SCHOOL

Fowberry Crescent, Fenham, Newcastle upon Tyne, Tyne and Wear NE4 9YJ
Tel: (0191) 275 0608
Head: T A Willcocks
Type: Boys Day 8–18 (Co-ed VIth form)
No of Pupils: 470
Fees: (September 94) £2679 – £3432

DAME ALLAN'S GIRLS SCHOOL

Fowberry Crescent, Fenham, Newcastle upon Tyne, Tyne and Wear NE4 9YJ
Tel: (0191) 275 0708
Head: T A Willcocks
Type: Girls Day 8–18 (Co-ed VIth form)
No of Pupils: 460
Fees: (September 94) £2679 – £3432

EASTCLIFFE GRAMMAR SCHOOL*

The Grove, Gosforth, Newcastle upon Tyne, Tyne and Wear NE3 1NE
Tel: (0191) 285 4873
Head: G D Pearson
Type: Co-educational Day 3–18
No of Pupils: B170 G60
Fees: (September 95) £2400 – £4080

GRAINGER GRAMMAR SCHOOL

35 Grainger Park Road, Newcastle upon Tyne, Tyne and Wear NE4 8SA
Tel: (0191) 273 3426
Head: Mrs J Smith
Type: Co-educational Day 7–16
No of Pupils: B45 G14
Fees: (September 95) £2322 – £3312

LA SAGESSE CONVENT HIGH SCHOOL

North Jesmond, Newcastle upon Tyne, Tyne and Wear NE2 3RJ
Tel: (0191) 281 3474
Head: Miss L Clark
Type: Girls Day 3–18
No of Pupils: 500
Fees: (September 94) £1680 – £3540

LINDEN SCHOOL

72 Station Road, Forest Hall, Newcastle upon Tyne, Tyne and Wear NE12 9BQ
Tel: (0191) 266 2943
Head: Colonel A K Johnson
Type: Co-educational Day 3–11
No of Pupils: B75 G70
Fees: (September 95) £2040

NEWCASTLE PREPARATORY SCHOOL

6 Eslington Road, Jesmond, Newcastle upon Tyne, Tyne and Wear NE2 4RH
Tel: (0191) 281 1769
Head: G Clayton
Type: Co-educational Day 2–13
No of Pupils: 230
Fees: (September 95) £2925 – £3375

NEWCASTLE UPON TYNE CHURCH HIGH SCHOOL

Tankerville Terrace, Jesmond, Newcastle upon Tyne, Tyne and Wear NE2 3BA
Tel: (0191) 281 4306
Head: Miss P E Davies
Type: Girls Day 3–18
No of Pupils: 665
Fees: (September 95) £2625 – £3735

NEWLANDS SCHOOL

34 The Grove, Gosforth, Newcastle upon Tyne, Tyne and Wear NE3 1NH
Tel: (0191) 285 2208
Head: N R Barton
Type: Boys Day 4–14
No of Pupils: 230
Fees: (September 95) £2595 – £3405

ROYAL GRAMMAR SCHOOL

Eskdale Terrace, Newcastle upon Tyne, Tyne and Wear NE2 4DX
Tel: (0191) 281 5711
Head: J F X Miller
Type: Boys Day 8–18
No of Pupils: 1130
Fees: (September 95) £2970 – £3609

WESTFIELD SCHOOL

Oakfield House, Oakfield Road, Gosforth, Newcastle upon Tyne, Tyne and Wear NE3 4HS
Tel: (0191) 285 1948
Head: Mrs M Farndale
Type: Girls Day 3–18
No of Pupils: 360
Fees: (September 95) £1398 – £4140

NORTH SHIELDS

THE KING'S SCHOOL

Huntington Place, Tynemouth, North Shields, Tyne and Wear NE30 4RF
Tel: (0191) 258 5995
Head: Dr D Younger
Type: Co-educational Day 4–18
No of Pupils: 900
Fees: (September 95) £2580 – £3720

SOUTH SHIELDS

ST ANNE'S MIXED HIGH SCHOOL

52 Sunderland Road, South Shields, Tyne and Wear NE34 0SW
Tel: (0191) 455 2310
Head: Mrs A B Smith
Type: Co-educational Day 3–16
No of Pupils: B20 G50
Fees: (September 94) £930 – £2685

SUNDERLAND

ARGYLE HOUSE SCHOOL

19/20 Thornhill Park, Sunderland, Tyne and Wear SR2 7LA
Tel: (0191) 510 0726
Head: J N Johnson
Type: Boys Day 3–16
No of Pupils: 230
Fees: (September 95) £1860 – £3030

CRAIGIEVAR SCHOOL*

37 Roker Park Road, Sunderland, Tyne and Wear SR6 9PL
Tel: (0191) 548 5468
Head: Mrs M Chadwick
Type: Girls Day 2–18 (Boys 4–7)
No of Pupils: B8 G50
Fees: (September 95) £1500 – £2400

FULWELL GRANGE CHRISTIAN SCHOOL

2 Viewforth Terrace, Fulwell Mill, Sunderland, Tyne and Wear SR5 1PZ
Tel: (0191) 548 6531
Head: Mrs E Gray
Type: Co-educational Day 4–16
No of Pupils: B42 G67
Fees: (September 95) £1710 – £2305

ST ANTHONY'S MONTESSORI SCHOOL

Tunstall Road, Sunderland, Tyne and Wear SR2 7JR
Tel: (0191) 567 7893
Head: J Ward
Type: Co-educational Day 3–11
No of Pupils: B84 G132
Fees: (September 95) £1950 – £2340

SUNDERLAND HIGH SCHOOL
Mowbray Road, Sunderland, Tyne
and Wear SR2 8HY
Tel: (0191) 567 4984
Head: Ms C M Rendle-Short
Type: Co-educational Day 3-18
No of Pupils: B220 G295
Fees: (September 95) £2355 - £3915

WHICKHAM

CHASE SCHOOL
Rectory Lane, Whickham, Tyne and
Wear NE6 4PD
Tel: (0191) 4960016
Head: Mrs A Nelson
Type: Co-educational Day
No of Pupils: B21 G10
Fees: (September 95) £2460 - £2520

WARWICKSHIRE

ATHERSTONE

TWYCROSS HOUSE SCHOOL
Twycross, Atherstone, Warwickshire
CV9 3PL
Tel: (01827) 880651
Head: R V Kirkpatrick
Type: Co-educational Day 8-19
No of Pupils: B140 G140
Fees: (September 95) £3060 - £4050

KENILWORTH

ABBOTSFORD SCHOOL
Bridge Street, Kenilworth,
Warwickshire CV8 1BP
Tel: (01926) 52826
Head: Mrs B Chitty
Type: Co-educational Day 3-11
No of Pupils: B87 G41
Fees: (September 95) £2448 - £2706

ST JOSEPH'S SCHOOL
Kenilworth, Warwickshire CV8 2FT
Tel: (01926) 55348
Head: Mrs F Rimmer
Type: Girls Day 4-18 (Boys 4-11)
No of Pupils: B7 G349
Fees: (September 95) £2430 - £3450

LEAMINGTON SPA

ARNOLD LODGE SCHOOL
Kenilworth Road, Leamington Spa,
Warwickshire CV32 5TW
Tel: (01926) 424737
Head: G Hill
Type: Co-educational Day &
Boarding 3-13
No of Pupils: B250 G100 No of
Boarders W40
Fees: (September 94) WB £6045 DAY
£1245 - £4080

THE KINGSLEY SCHOOL*
Beauchamp Avenue, Leamington
Spa, Warwickshire CV32 5RD
Tel: (01926) 425127
Head: Mrs M A Webster
Type: Girls Day 2-18 (Boys 2-7)
No of Pupils: B6 G579
Fees: (September 95) £4245

NEW COLLEGE
61 Kenilworth Road, Leamington
Spa, Warwickshire CV32 6JU
Tel: (01926) 424058
Head: P S Fulcher
Type: Co-educational Day 2-18
No of Pupils: 60
Fees: (September 95) £1200 - £2100

RUGBY

BILTON GRANGE*
Dunchurch, Rugby, Warwickshire
CV22 6QU
Tel: (01788) 810217
Head: Q G Edwards
Type: Co-educational Boarding &
Day 4-13
No of Pupils: 275 No of Boarders F70
W20
Fees: (September 95) F/WB £8595
DAY £2361 - £6876

THE CRESCENT SCHOOL
Bawnmore Road, Bilton, Rugby,
Warwickshire CV22 7QH
Tel: (01788) 521595
Head: I J Wren
Type: Co-educational Day 2-12
No of Pupils: B87 G98
Fees: (September 95) £1020 - £2865

PRINCETHORPE COLLEGE
Leamington Road, Princethorpe,
Rugby, Warwickshire CV23 9PX
Tel: (01926) 632147
Head: Rev A R Whelan
Type: Co-educational Day &
Boarding B11-18 G16-18 (Girls day
only, 11-16)
No of Pupils: 474 No of Boarders F35
W19
Fees: (September 95) FB £8097 WB
£7287 DAY £3765

RUGBY SCHOOL
Rugby, Warwickshire CV22 5EH
Tel: (01788) 543465
Head: M B Mavor
Type: Co-educational Boarding &
Day 12-18
No of Pupils: B501 G169 No of
Boarders F532
Fees: (September 95) FB £12270 DAY
£7545

STRATFORD-UPON-AVON

THE CROFT SCHOOL
Alveston Hill, Loxley Road, Stratford
upon Avon, Warwickshire CV37 7RL
Tel: (01789) 293795
Head: Mrs L Wolfe
Type: Co-educational Day 2-11
No of Pupils: B177 G146
Fees: (September 95) £110 - £1320

**STRATFORD PREPARATORY
SCHOOL**
Church House, Old Town,
Stratford-upon-Avon, Warwickshire
CV37 6BG
Tel: (01789) 297993
Head: Mrs C Quinn
Type: Co-educational Day 2-11
Fees: (September 95) £355 - £1025

WARWICK

EMSCOTE LAWN SCHOOL
Emscote Road, Warwick CV34 5QD
Tel: (01926) 491961
Head: J H Riley and C D Riley
Type: Co-educational Day &
Boarding 3-13
No of Pupils: B301 G143 No of
Boarders W42
Fees: (September 95) WB £6324 DAY
£2823 - £4287

THE KING'S HIGH SCHOOL
FOR GIRLS
Smith Street, Warwick CV34 4HJ
Tel: (01926) 494485
Head: Mrs J M Anderson
Type: Girls Day 10-18
No of Pupils: 550
Fees: (September 95) £4095

WARWICK PREPARATORY
SCHOOL
Bridge Field, Banbury Road,
Warwick CV34 6PL
Tel: (01926) 491545
Head: Mrs C E Prichard
Type: Co-educational Day B3-6
G3-10
No of Pupils: B108 G315
Fees: (September 95) £2940 - £4050

WARWICK SCHOOL
Myton Road, Warwick CV34 6PP
Tel: (01926) 492484
Head: Dr P J Cheshire
Type: Boys Day & Boarding 7-18
No of Pupils: 995 No of Boarders F26
W24
Fees: (September 95) FB £9300 -
£9840 WB £8640 - £9180 DAY
£4050 - £4590

WROXALL ABBEY SCHOOL
Warwick CV35 7NB
Tel: (01926) 484220
Head: Mrs J Gowen
Type: Girls Boarding & Day 2-18
(Boys day 2-7)
No of Pupils: B2 G100 No of
Boarders F25 W15
Fees: (September 95) WB £8079 -
£9660 DAY £2838 - £4935

WEST MIDLANDS

BIRMINGHAM

ABBEY TUTORIAL COLLEGE
53-55 Cornwall Street, Birmingham,
West Midlands B3 2DH
Tel: (0121) 236 7474
Head: K Byrne
Type: Co-educational Day 14+
No of Pupils: B60 G60
Fees: (September 95) 3 A Levels
£6900-£8400
5 GCSEs £3024

AL HIJRAH SCHOOL
Midland House, 71 Hob Moor Road,
Smallheath, Birmingham, West
Midlands B10 9AZ
Tel: (0121) 7665454
Head: M A K Saqib
Type: Co-educational Day 7-16
(Single-sex education)
No of Pupils: B55 G80
Fees: (September 95) £1050 - £1200

ASTWELL PREPARATORY
SCHOOL
144/146 Hampstead Road,
Hansworth, Birmingham, West
Midlands B20 2QR
Tel: (0121) 554 5791
Head: Miss M Kavanagh
Type: Co-educational Day 3-11
No of Pupils: B75 G65
Fees: (September 95) £1680 - £2541

THE BLUE COAT SCHOOL*
Somerset Road, Edgbaston,
Birmingham, West Midlands
B17 0HR
Tel: (0121) 454 1425
Head: B P Bissell
Type: Co-educational Boarding &
Day 3-13
No of Pupils: B226 G176 No of
Boarders F41 W35
Fees: (September 95) F/WB £6690
DAY £1980 - £4380

DARUL ULOOM ISLAMIC
HIGH SCHOOL & COLLEGE
521-527 Coventry Road,
Smallheath, Birmingham, West
Midlands B10 0LL
Tel: (0102) 772 6408
Head: Dr A A Rahim
Type: Co-educational Boarding &
Day (Single-sex education)
No of Pupils: B101 G7 No of
Boarders F16
Fees: (September 95) FB £800 -
£2000 DAY £300 - £500

EASTBOURNE HOUSE
SCHOOL
111 Yardley Road, Acocks Green,
Birmingham, West Midlands B27 6LL
Tel: (0121) 706 2013
Head: P J Moynihan
Type: Co-educational Day 3-11
No of Pupils: B60 G65
Fees: (September 95) £2040 - £2310

ECCLESTON SCHOOL
22 St Peter's Road, Harborne,
Birmingham, West Midlands
B17 0AX
Tel: (0121) 427 2329
Head: Miss G Thompson
Type: Co-educational Day 5-11
No of Pupils: B53 G49
Fees: (September 95)
£1575

EDGBASTON CHURCH OF
ENGLAND COLLEGE
31 Calthorpe Road, Birmingham,
West Midlands B15 1RX
Tel: (0121) 454 1392
Head: Mrs A P Varley-Tipton
Type: Girls Day 3-18
No of Pupils: 379
Fees: (September 94) £2580 - £4185

EDGBASTON COLLEGE
249 Bristol Road, Birmingham, West
Midlands B5 7UH
Tel: (0121) 472 1034
Head: Father A W Ledwich
Type: Co-educational Day 2-18
No of Pupils: B157 G60
Fees: (September 95) £2475 - £4590

EDGBASTON HIGH SCHOOL FOR GIRLS
Westbourne Road, Edgbaston, Birmingham, West Midlands B15 3TS
Tel: (0121) 454 5831
Head: Mrs S J Horsman
Type: Girls Day 2-18
No of Pupils: 931
Fees: (September 95) £1680 - £4215

HALLFIELD SCHOOL
48 Church Road, Edgbaston, Birmingham, West Midlands B15 3SJ
Tel: (0121) 454 1496
Head: J G Cringle
Type: Co-educational Day 2-13
No of Pupils: 390
Fees: (September 95) £2790 - £4020

HIGHCLARE SCHOOL
10 Sutton Road, Erdington, Birmingham, West Midlands B23 6QL
Tel: (0121) 373 7400
Head: Mrs C A Hanson
Type: Girls Day 3-18 (Boys 3-7 and 16-18)
No of Pupils: B20 G346
Fees: (September 95) £2145 - £4155

HOLY CHILD SCHOOL
39 Sir Harry's Road, Edgbaston, Birmingham, West Midlands B15 2UR
Tel: (0121) 440 4103
Head: Mrs J Hill
Type: Girls Day 3-18 (Boys 3-11)
No of Pupils: B22 G290
Fees: (September 95) £2385 - £4500

HONEYBOURNE SCHOOL
621 Fox Hollies Road, Hall Green, Birmingham, West Midlands B28 9DW
Tel: (0121) 777 3778
Head: Mrs J A Hillstead
Type: Co-educational Day 2-7
No of Pupils: 65
Fees: (September 94) £1455

KING EDWARD VI HIGH SCHOOL FOR GIRLS
Edgbaston Park Road, Birmingham, West Midlands B15 2UB
Tel: (0121) 472 1834
Head: Miss E W Evans
Type: Girls Day 11-18
No of Pupils: 545
Fees: (September 95) £4230

KING EDWARD'S SCHOOL
Edgbaston Park Road, Birmingham, West Midlands B15 2UA
Tel: (0121) 472 1672
Head: H R Wright
Type: Boys Day 11-18
No of Pupils: 870
Fees: (September 95) £4440

NORFOLK HOUSE SCHOOL
4 Norfolk Road, Edgbaston, Birmingham, West Midlands B15 3PS
Tel: (0121) 454 7021
Head: Mrs A Harding
Type: Co-educational Day 3-11
No of Pupils: B72 G75
Fees: (September 95) £1650 - £2394

RATHVILLY SCHOOL
119 Bunbury Road, Birmingham, West Midlands B31 2NB
Tel: (0121) 475 1509
Head: D Jones
Type: Co-educational Day 2-11
No of Pupils: B50 G50
Fees: (September 95) £1770 - £2565

ROSSLYN SCHOOL
1597 Stratford Road, Hall Green, Birmingham, West Midlands BS8
Tel: (0121) 744 2743
Head: Mrs J Taylor
Type: Co-educational Day 3-11
No of Pupils: 140
Fees: (September 95) £1200 - £1800

WEST HOUSE SCHOOL
24 St James's Road, Edgbaston, Birmingham, West Midlands B15 2NX
Tel: (0121) 440 4097
Head: G K Duce
Type: Boys Day 3-13
No of Pupils: 203
Fees: (September 95) £1485 - £4275

COVENTRY

BABLAKE SCHOOL
Coundon Road, Coventry, West Midlands CV1 4AU
Tel: (01203) 228388
Head: Dr S Nuttall
Type: Co-educational Day 7-19
No of Pupils: B475 G450
Fees: (September 95) £2775 - £3750

CHESHUNT PRE-PREPARATORY SCHOOL
8 Park Road, Coventry, West Midlands CV1 2LH
Tel: (01203) 221677
Head: Mrs F Ward
Type: Co-educational Day 3-8
No of Pupils: B66 G59
Fees: (September 95) £2070 - £2220

COVENTRY MUSLIM SCHOOL
283-287 Stoney Stanton Road, Coventry, West Midlands CV1 4FR
Tel: (01203) 257524
Head: Mrs F Farook
Type: Co-educational Day
No of Pupils: B4 G60
Fees: (September 95) £250 - £300

COVENTRY PREPARATORY SCHOOL
Kenilworth Road, Coventry, West Midlands CV3 6PT
Tel: (01203) 675289
Head: D Clark
Type: Co-educational Day 3-13
No of Pupils: B116 G37
Fees: (September 95) £2295 - £4125

DAVENPORT LODGE SCHOOL
21 Davenport Road, Earlsdon, Coventry, West Midlands CV5 6QA
Tel: (01203) 675051
Head: Mrs M D Martin
Type: Co-educational Day 2-8
No of Pupils: B79 G89
Fees: (September 95) £2070 - £2145

KING HENRY VIII SCHOOL
Warwick Road, Coventry, West Midlands CV3 6AQ
Tel: (01203) 673442
Head: T J Vardon
Type: Co-educational Day 7-18
No of Pupils: B561 G484
Fees: (September 95) £2275   £3750

PATTISON'S COLLEGE*
90 Binley Road, Coventry, West Midlands CV3 1FQ
Tel: (01203) 455031
Head: Miss B Pattison
Type: Co-educational Day & Boarding 3-16
No of Pupils: 150 No of Boarders F20 W6
Fees: (September 95) FB £4965 - £5610 WB £4845 - £5490 DAY £1650 - £2985

SOLIHULL

ARDENHURST SCHOOL
Henley-in-Arden, Solihull, West
Midlands B95 6AB
Tel: (01564) 792308
Head: J H Riley
Type: Co-educational Day 3-11
Fees: (September 94) £1076 - £1433

EVERSFIELD PREPARATORY SCHOOL
Warwick Road, Solihull, West
Midlands B91 1AT
Tel: (0121) 705 0354
Head: K U Madden
Type: Boys Day 3-13
No of Pupils: B185 G2
Fees: (January 95) £4271 - £4890

KINGSLEY PREPARATORY SCHOOL
53 Hanbury Road, Dorridge,
Solihull, West Midlands B93 8DW
Tel: (01564) 774144
Head: Mrs J A Scott
Type: Co-educational Day 3-11
No of Pupils: B20 G20
Fees: (September 95) £1800 - £2700

KINGSWOOD SCHOOL
St James Place, Shirley, Solihull,
West Midlands B90 2BA
Tel: (0121) 744 7883
Head: P Callaghan
Type: Co-educational Day 3-11
No of Pupils: 100
Fees: (September 94) £1104 - £2865

RUCKLEIGH SCHOOL
17 Lode Lane, Solihull, West
Midlands B91 2AB
Tel: (0121) 705 2773
Head: D N Carr-Smith
Type: Co-educational Day 3-11
No of Pupils: B163 G101
Fees: (September 95) £3528 - £3558

ST MARTIN'S SCHOOL
Malvern Hall, Brueton Avenue,
Solihull, West Midlands B91 3EN
Tel: (0121) 705 1265
Head: Mrs S J Williams
Type: Girls Day 3-18
No of Pupils: 460
Fees: (September 95) £1440 - £4419

SOLIHULL SCHOOL
Warwick Road, Solihull, West
Midlands B91 3DJ
Tel: (0121) 705 4273
Head: A Lee
Type: Boys Day 7-18 (Co-ed VIth
form)
No of Pupils: B935 G60
Fees: (September 95) £2976 - £4284

STOURBRIDGE

ELMFIELD RUDOLF STEINER SCHOOL
14 Love Lane, Stourbridge, West
Midlands DY8 2EA
Tel: (01384) 394633
Type: Co-educational Day &
Boarding 3-17
No of Pupils: B138 G130 No of
Boarders F13
Fees: (September 95) FB £5295 -
£5640 WB £4665 - £5010 DAY
£1590 - £3330

SUTTON COLDFIELD

CHETWYND HOUSE SCHOOL
6 Streetly Lane, Sutton Coldfield,
West Midlands B74 4TT
Tel: (0121) 308 0332
Head: W P Coldrick
Type: Boys Day 4-12
No of Pupils: 100
Fees: (September 95) £2400

ST PAUL'S CONVENT
88 Lichfield Road, Sutton Coldfield,
West Midlands B74 2SY
Tel: (0121) 355 8205
Head: Sister Maureen Marston
Type: Co-educational Day 3-11
No of Pupils: 170
Fees: (September 95) £1740 - £2175

THE SHRUBBERY SCHOOL
Walmley Ash Road, Walmley,
Sutton Coldfield, West Midlands
B76 1HY
Tel: (0121) 351 1582
Head: Miss J M Rankin
Type: Co-educational Day 3-11
No of Pupils: B152 G118
Fees: (September 95) £1872 - £2709

WYLDE GREEN COLLEGE
245 Birmingham Road, Sutton
Coldfield, West Midlands B72 1EA
Tel: (0121) 354 1505
Head: P J Burd
Type: Co-educational Day 2-11
No of Pupils: 160
Fees: (September 95) £2310 - £3180

WALSALL

HYDESVILLE TOWER SCHOOL
25 Broadway North, Walsall, West
Midlands WS1 2QG
Tel: (01922) 24374
Head: T D Farrell
Type: Co-educational Day 3-16
No of Pupils: B208 G136
Fees: (September 94) £1710 - £4065

MAYFIELD PREPARATORY SCHOOL
Sutton Road, Walsall, West
Midlands WS1 2PD
Tel: (01922) 24107
Head: Mrs C M Jones
Type: Co-educational Day 3-11
No of Pupils: B121 G94
Fees: (September 95) £2250 - £2775

WARLEY

HADEN HILL SCHOOL
High Harcourt House, 154 Barrs
Road, Cradley Heath, Warley, West
Midlands B64 7EX
Tel: (01384) 569318
Head: Mrs B M Simons
Type: Co-educational Day 3-11
No of Pupils: B115 G83
Fees: (September 93) £1830 - £2970

WOLVERHAMPTON

BIRCHFIELD SCHOOL
Albrighton, Wolverhampton, West
Midlands WV7 3AF
Tel: (01902) 372534
Head: J F N Benwell
Type: Boys Boarding & Day 4-13
No of Pupils: 195 No of Boarders F18
Fees: (September 95) WB £5655 DAY
£2985 - £4725

THE DRIVE SCHOOL
Wrottesley Road, Tettenhall,
Wolverhampton, West Midlands
WV6 8SE
Tel: (01902) 751125
Head: Mrs P M Yates
Type: Co-educational Day 3-7
No of Pupils: B39 G13
Fees: (January 95) £1770 - £2601

NEWBRIDGE PREPARATORY SCHOOL
51 Newbridge Crescent, Tettenhall,
Wolverhampton, West Midlands
WV6 0LH
Tel: (01902) 751088
Head: Miss M J Coulter
Type: Girls Day 3-11 (Boys 3-4)
No of Pupils: B6 G140
Fees: (September 95) £2175 - £3315

THE ROYAL WOLVERHAMPTON JUNIOR SCHOOL

Penn Road, Wolverhampton, West Midlands WV3 0EF
Tel: (01902) 341230
Head: Mrs M Saunders
Type: Co-educational Day & Boarding 2-11
No of Pupils: B135 G95 No of Boarders F8 W7
Fees: (September 95) F/WB £7110 DAY £2490 - £3840

THE ROYAL WOLVERHAMPTON SCHOOL*

Penn Road, Wolverhampton, West Midlands WV3 0EG
Tel: (01902) 341230
Head: Mrs Evans
Type: Co-educational Boarding & Day 11-18
No of Pupils: B172 G125 No of Boarders F108 W41
Fees: (September 95) FB £9045 WB £8700 DAY £5175

ST JOSEPH'S PREPARATORY SCHOOL

24 Sandy Lane, Tettenhall, Wolverhampton, West Midlands WV6 9EB
Tel: (01902) 753371
Head: Mrs H Burdon
Type: Co-educational Day 3-11
No of Pupils: 120
Fees: (September 94) £750 - £1500

TETTENHALL COLLEGE

College Road, Wolverhampton, West Midlands WV6 8QX
Tel: (01902) 751119
Head: P C Bodkin
Type: Co-educational Boarding & Day 7-18
No of Pupils: B240 G139 No of Boarders F79
Fees: (September 95) FB £7509 - £9147 WB £6000 - £7500 DAY £4517 - £5640

WOLVERHAMPTON GRAMMAR SCHOOL

Compton Road, Wolverhampton, West Midlands WV3 9RB
Tel: (01902) 21326
Head: B St J Trafford
Type: Co-educational Day 11-18
No of Pupils: B575 G150
Fees: (September 95) £4800

WILTSHIRE

CALNE

ST MARY'S SCHOOL

Calne, Wiltshire SN11 0DF
Tel: (01249) 815899
Head: Miss D H Burns
Type: Girls Boarding & Day 11-18
No of Pupils: 318 No of Boarders F285
Fees: (September 95) FB £11550 DAY £6825

CHIPPENHAM

GRITTLETON HOUSE SCHOOL

Grittleton, Chippenham, Wiltshire SN14 6AP
Tel: (01249) 782434
Head: P Moore
Type: Co-educational Day 3-16
No of Pupils: B125 G70
Fees: (September 95) £1755 - £3375

THE INTERNATIONAL SCHOOL OF CHOUEIFAT*

Ashwicke Hall, Marshfield, Chippenham, Wiltshire SN14 8AG
Tel: (01225) 891841
Acting Head: S Ayche
Type: Co-educational Boarding 8-18
No of Pupils: B100 G17 No of Boarders F117
Fees: (September 95) FB £8700 - £9500

CORSHAM

HEYWOOD PREPARATORY SCHOOL

The Priory, Priory Street, Corsham, Wiltshire SN13 0AP
Tel: (01249) 713379
Head: M Hall & P Hall
Type: Co-educational Day 3-11
No of Pupils: B109 G93
Fees: (September 95) £2145 - £2535

DEVIZES

DAUNTSEY'S SCHOOL*

West Lavington, Devizes, Wiltshire SN10 4HE
Tel: (01380) 812446
Head: C R Evans
Type: Co-educational Boarding & Day 11-18
No of Pupils: B356 G282 No of Boarders F292
Fees: (September 95) FB £10542 DAY £6492

THE MILL SCHOOL

Potterne, Devizes, Wiltshire SN10 5TE
Tel: (01380) 723011
Head: J M Eman
Type: Co-educational Day 3-11
No of Pupils: B39 G28
Fees: (September 95) £1485 - £3270

MARLBOROUGH

KINGSBURY HILL HOUSE*

34 Kingsbury Street, Marlborough, Wiltshire SN8 1JA
Tel: (01672) 512680
Head: M Innes Williams
Type: Co-educational Day 3-13
No of Pupils: 120
Fees: (September 95) £1080 - £4635

MARLBOROUGH COLLEGE

Marlborough, Wiltshire SN8 1PA
Tel: (01672) 892300
Head: E J H Gould
Type: Co-educational Boarding 13-18
No of Pupils: B550 G250 No of Boarders F770
Fees: (September 95) FB £12750 DAY £8985

ST ANDREW SCHOOL

Ogbourne St Andrew, Marlborough, Wiltshire
Tel: (01672) 841291
Head: Miss S Platt
Type: Co-educational Day 3-11
No of Pupils: B18 G23
Fees: (September 95) £1920 - £3135

MELKSHAM

STONAR SCHOOL*
Melksham, Wiltshire SN12 8NT
Tel: (01225) 702309
Head: Mrs S Hopkinson
Type: Girls Boarding & Day 4-18
No of Pupils: 480 No of Boarders 255
Fees: (September 95) F/WB £8742 -
£9546 DAY £2340 - £5289

PEWSEY

ST FRANCIS SCHOOL
Marlborough Road, Pewsey,
Wiltshire SN9 5NT
Tel: (01672) 563228
Head: P W Blundell
Type: Co-educational Day 3-11
No of Pupils: B87 G89
Fees: (September 95) £1425 - £4050

SALISBURY

CHAFYN GROVE SCHOOL
Bourne Avenue, Salisbury, Wiltshire
SP1 1LR
Tel: (01722) 333423
Head: D P Duff-Mitchell
Type: Co-educational Boarding &
Day 4-13
No of Pupils: B154 G89 No of
Boarders F42 W31
Fees: (September 95) F/WB £7542
DAY £2640 - £5634

FLAMBEAUX MONTESSORI
SCHOOL/DAY NURSERY
18 Burford Road, Salisbury,
Wiltshire SP2 8AN
Tel: (01722) 322179
Head: Mrs N M Brinn
Type: Co-educational Day 1-7
No of Pupils: 100
Fees: (September 95) £162 - £960

THE GODOLPHIN SCHOOL*
Milford Hill, Salisbury, Wiltshire
SP1 2RA
Tel: (01722) 333059
Head: Mrs H A Fender
Type: Girls Boarding & Day 7-18
(Boarding from 11)
No of Pupils: 435 No of Boarders
F210
Fees: (September 95) F/WB £10779
DAY £5199 - £6456

LA RETRAITE LEEHURST
SCHOOL
Campbell Road, Salisbury, Wiltshire
SP1 3BQ
Tel: (01722) 333094
Head: Mrs R Simmons
Type: Girls Day 2-18 (Boys 2-7)
No of Pupils: B10 G180
Fees: (September 95) £2520 - £4575

LEADEN HALL*
70 The Close, Salisbury, Wiltshire
SP1 2EP
Tel: (01722) 334700
Head: Mrs D Watkins
Type: Girls Day & Boarding 3-12
No of Pupils: 200 No of Boarders F30
Fees: (September 95) FB £6240 WB
£5310 DAY £2895 - £3480

NORMAN COURT*
West Tytherley, Salisbury, Wiltshire
SP5 1NH
Tel: (01980) 862345
Head: K N Foyle
Type: Co-educational Boarding &
Day 3-13
No of Pupils: B97 G57 No of
Boarders F41 W34
Fees: (September 95) F/WB £7830
DAY £2760 - £5820

SALISBURY CATHEDRAL
SCHOOL
1 The Close, Salisbury, Wiltshire
SP1 2EQ
Tel: (01722) 322652
Head: C J Helyer
Type: Co-educational Day &
Boarding 3-13
No of Pupils: 311 No of Boarders F82
Fees: (September 95) FB £7875 DAY
£1275 - £5925

SANDROYD
Tollard Royal, Salisbury, Wiltshire
SP5 5QD
Tel: (01725) 516264
Head: M J Hatch
Type: Boys Boarding 8-13 (a few day
places)
No of Pupils: 130 No of Boarders
F125
Fees: (September 95) FB £8850 DAY
£7500

SWAN SCHOOL FOR BOYS
26 Elm Grove Road, Salisbury,
Wiltshire
Tel: (01722) 334522
Head: Mrs B L Healy
Type: Boys Day 3-11
No of Pupils: 130
Fees: (September 95) £2250

SWINDON

PINEWOOD SCHOOL*
Bourton, Swindon, Wiltshire
SN6 8HZ
Tel: (01793) 782205
Head: H G Boddington
Type: Co-educational Boarding &
Day 4-13
No of Pupils: B124 G72 No of
Boarders F34
Fees: (September 95) FB £7950 DAY
£2850 - £6075

PRIOR PARK PREPARATORY
SCHOOL
Cricklade, Swindon, Wiltshire
SN6 6BB
Tel: (01793) 750275
Head: G B Hobern
Type: Co-educational Boarding &
Day 7-13 (Pre-prep 2-6)
No of Pupils: B120 G74 No of
Boarders F117
Fees: (September 95) F/WB £6678 -
£6700 DAY £4665 - £4695

TROWBRIDGE

ROUNDSTONE
PREPARATORY SCHOOL
Courtfield House, Polebarn Road,
Trowbridge, Wiltshire BA14 7EG
Tel: (01225) 752847
Head: Mrs M E Pearce
Type: Co-educational Day 4-11
No of Pupils: B72 G75
Fees: (September 95) £1800 - £1950

WARMINSTER

STOURBRIDGE HOUSE
SCHOOL
Castle Street, Mere, Warminster,
Wiltshire BA12 6JQ
Tel: (01747) 860165
Head: Mrs E Coward
Type: Co-educational Day 3-8
No of Pupils: B30 G30
Fees: (September 95) £2280 - £2400

WARMINSTER SCHOOL
Church Street, Warminster,
Wiltshire BA12 8PJ
Tel: (01985) 213038
Head: T D Holgate
Type: Co-educational Boarding &
Day 4-18
No of Pupils: B265 G220 No of
Boarders F300
Fees: (September 95) FB £8460 -
£9270 DAY £1650 - £5370

NORTH YORKSHIRE

BEDALE

AYSGARTH PREPARATORY SCHOOL*
Bedale, North Yorkshire DL8 1TF
Tel: (01677) 450240
Head: J C Hodgkinson
Type: Boys Boarding 8-13 (Coed Day 3-8)
No of Pupils: B111 G7 No of Boarders F87
Fees: (September 95) F/WB £8226 DAY £2400 - £5760

GREAT AYTON

AYTON SCHOOL*
High Green, Great Ayton, North Yorkshire TS9 6BN
Tel: (01642) 722141
Head: Alice Meager
Type: Co-educational Day & Boarding 4-18
No of Pupils: 240 No of Boarders F25
Fees: (September 95) FB £9495 WB £8355 DAY £3000 - £4425

HARROGATE

ASHVILLE COLLEGE*
Harrogate, North Yorkshire HG2 9JR
Tel: (01423) 566358
Head: M H Crosby
Type: Co-educational Day & Boarding 4-18
No of Pupils: B410 G290 No of Boarders F120 W30
Fees: (September 95) FB £7944 - £8754 WB £7974 - £8754 DAY £2400 - £4680

BELMONT-BIRKLANDS SCHOOL
68 Kent Road, Harrogate, North Yorkshire HG1 2NH
Tel: (01423) 502465
Head: Miss V Arthur
Type: Girls Day 2-11 (Boys 2-4)
No of Pupils: B27 G123
Fees: (September 95) £483 - £2727

BRACKENFIELD SCHOOL
128 Duchy Road, Harrogate, North Yorkshire HG1 2HE
Tel: (01423) 508558
Head: Mrs M Sutcliffe
Type: Co-educational Day 3-11
No of Pupils: B80 G98
Fees: (September 95) £2376 - £2784

GROSVENOR HOUSE SCHOOL
Swarcliffe Hall, Birstwith, Harrogate, North Yorkshire HG3 2JG
Tel: (01423) 771029
Head: G J Raspin
Type: Boys Day & Boarding 3-14 (Sisters by arrangement)
No of Pupils: B187 G10 No of Boarders F6 W5
Fees: (September 94) F/WB £5772 - £6300 DAY £1350 - £3900

HARROGATE LADIES' COLLEGE*
Clarence Drive, Harrogate, North Yorkshire HG1 2QG
Tel: (01423) 504543
Acting Head: G F Hazell
Type: Girls Boarding & Day 10-18
No of Pupils: 370 No of Boarders F200
Fees: (September 95) FB £8985 WB £8760 DAY £5985

HARROGATE TUTORIAL COLLEGE
2 The Oval, Harrogate, North Yorkshire HG2 9BA
Tel: (01423) 501041
Head: K W Pollard
Type: Co-educational Day 15-20
No of Pupils: B50 G50
Fees: (September 95) 3 A Levels/5 GCSEs £6600

WEST END SCHOOL
4 The Oval, Harrogate, North Yorkshire HG2 9BA
Tel: (01423) 503444
Head: Mrs A M B Wayman
Type: Co-educational Day 2-11
Fees: (September 95) £455 - £730

MALTON

ST ANDREWS PREPARATORY SCHOOL
West Royd, Castle Howard Road, Malton, North Yorkshire YO17 0AY
Tel: (01653) 695232
Type: Co-educational Day 4-11
No of Pupils: B24 G32
Fees: (September 95) £1470 - £2178

WOODLEIGH SCHOOL
Langton, Malton, North Yorkshire YO17 9QN
Tel: (01653) 658215
Head: D M England
Type: Co-educational Boarding & Day 3-13
No of Pupils: B39 G14 No of Boarders F17 W9
Fees: (September 95) F/WB £6330 DAY £1500 - £3900

RIPON

RIPON CATHEDRAL CHOIR SCHOOL*
Whitcliffe Lane, Ripon, North Yorkshire HG4 2LA
Tel: (01765) 602134
Head: R H Moore
Type: Co-educational Boarding & Day 4-13
No of Pupils: B55 G47 No of Boarders 20
Fees: (September 95) FB £6615 WB £6135 DAY £3330 - £4845

SCARBOROUGH

BAIRNSWOOD PREPARATORY SCHOOL
Lady Edith's Park, Scarborough, North Yorkshire YO12 5PB
Tel: (01723) 363100
Head: Mrs A Johnstone
Type: Co-educational Day 3-6
No of Pupils: B25 G25
Fees: (September 94) £575 - £1197

BRAMCOTE SCHOOL
Filey Road, Scarborough, North Yorkshire YO11 2TT
Tel: (01723) 373086
Head: J G Walker
Type: Co-educational Boarding 8-13
No of Pupils: 104
Fees: (September 95) FB £7950 DAY £5520

SCARBOROUGH COLLEGE*
Filey Road, Scarborough, North Yorkshire YO11 3BA
Tel: (01723) 360620
Head: T Kirkup
Type: Co-educational Boarding & Day 11-18
No of Pupils: B235 G178 No of Boarders F53
Fees: (September 95) FB £9420 DAY £5106

SCARBOROUGH COLLEGE JUNIOR SCHOOL

Lisvane, Sandybed Lane,
Scarborough, North Yorkshire
YO12 5LJ
Tel: (01723) 361595
Head: R N Baird
Type: Co-educational Boarding &
Day 3-11
No of Pupils: B81 G81 No of
Boarders F4
Fees: (September 95) FB £6900 DAY
£2547 - £3642

SELBY

READ SCHOOL*

Drax, Selby, North Yorkshire
YO8 8NL
Tel: (01757) 618248
Head: A J Saddler
Type: Co-educational Boarding &
Day 5-18
No of Pupils: 255 No of Boarders F80
W10
Fees: (September 95) FB £6780 -
£7455 WB £6345 - £6975 DAY
£2595 - £3615

SETTLE

CATTERAL HALL

Giggleswick, Settle, North Yorkshire
BD24 0DG
Tel: (01729) 822527
Head: M J Morris
Type: Co-educational Boarding &
Day 8-13
No of Pupils: B80 G57 No of
Boarders F95
Fees: (September 95) FB £8787 -
£9432 DAY £5868 - £6312

GIGGLESWICK SCHOOL*

Giggleswick, Settle, North Yorkshire
BD24 0DE
Tel: (01729) 823545
Head: A P Millard
Type: Co-educational Boarding &
Day 13-18
No of Pupils: B197 G102 No of
Boarders F254
Fees: (September 94) FB £11100 DAY
£7362

SKIPTON

MALSIS SCHOOL

Cross Hills, Skipton, North
Yorkshire BD20 8DT
Tel: (01535) 633027
Head: J D Clark
Type: Boys Boarding 7-14
No of Pupils: 175 No of Boarders
F175
Fees: (September 95) FB £7950

THIRSK

QUEEN MARY'S SCHOOL*

Baldersby Park, Topcliffe, Thirsk,
North Yorkshire YO7 3BZ
Tel: (01845) 577425
Head: Mr and Mrs P Belward
Type: Girls Boarding & Day 3-16
No of Pupils: 250 No of Boarders 130
Fees: (September 95) FB £7680 -
£8595 WB £7530 - £7965 DAY
£1935 - £5355

WHITBY

FYLING HALL SCHOOL

Robin Hood's Bay, Whitby, North
Yorkshire YO22 4QD
Tel: (01947) 880261
Acting Head: Alex Gregg
Type: Co-educational Boarding &
Day 5-18
No of Pupils: B99 G109 No of
Boarders F162
Fees: (September 95) FB £5520 -
£6060 DAY £2385 - £2775

ST HILDA'S SCHOOL*

Sneaton Castle, Whitby, North
Yorkshire YO21 3QN
Tel: (01947) 600051
Head: Mrs M E Blain
Type: Co-educational Boarding &
Day 2-18
No of Pupils: B93 G148 No of
Boarders F83 W3
Fees: (September 95) FB £7080 -
£8475 WB £6930 - £8310
DAY £2775 - £4575

YORK

AMPLEFORTH COLLEGE

York, North Yorkshire YO6 4ER
Tel: (01439) 788224
Head: Rev G F L Chamberlain
Type: Boys Boarding 13-18
No of Pupils: 552 No of Boarders
F552
Fees: (September 95) F/WB £12015
DAY £6195 - £9735

AMPLEFORTH COLLEGE JUNIOR SCHOOL*

The Castle, Gilling East, York, North
Yorkshire YO6 4HP
Tel: (01439) 788238
Head: Rev J A Sierla & G J Sasse
Type: Boys Boarding & Day 8-13
No of Pupils: 106 No of Boarders
F110
Fees: (September 95) F/WB £8415
DAY £5175 - £6540

BOOTHAM SCHOOL

Bootham, York, North Yorkshire
YO3 7BU
Tel: (01904) 623636
Head: I M Small
Type: Co-educational Boarding &
Day 11-18
No of Pupils: B220 G110 No of
Boarders F92
Fees: (September 95) F/WB £9924
DAY £6441

CLIFTON PREPARATORY SCHOOL

13 The Avenue, Clifton, York, North
Yorkshire YO3 6AS
Tel: (01904) 623716
Head: Mrs J Greenwood
Type: Co-educational Day 3-11
No of Pupils: B60 G70
Fees: (September 95) £1470 - £2700

CUNDALL MANOR SCHOOL

Helperby, York, North Yorkshire
YO6 2RW
Tel: (01423) 360200
Head: J F Napier
Type: Co-educational Boarding &
Day B4-13 G4-14
No of Pupils: B154 G54 No of
Boarders F60
Fees: (September 95) FB £5600 -
£6800 WB £5400 - £6450 DAY
£3000 - £4900

EBOR PREPARATORY SCHOOL

116 Clifton, York, North Yorkshire
YO3 6BA
Tel: (01904) 655021
Head: Ms V Tildesley
Type: Co-educational Day 3-11
No of Pupils: B70 G50
Fees: (September 95) £1020 - £1800

HOWSHAM HALL

York, North Yorkshire YO6 7PJ
Tel: (01653) 618374
Head: S J Knock
Type: Boys Boarding 5-14
No of Pupils: 75 No of Boarders F75
Fees: (September 95) FB £5100 -
£5700 DAY £1920 - £3450

THE MINSTER SCHOOL
Deangate, York, North Yorkshire
YO1 2JA
Tel: (01904) 625217
Head: R J Shephard
Type: Co-educational Day 4-13
No of Pupils: B100 G50
Fees: (September 95) £1380 - £3825

THE MOUNT SCHOOL*
Dalton Terrace, York, North
Yorkshire YO2 4DD
Tel: (01904) 654823
Head: Miss B J Windle
Type: Girls Boarding & Day 11-18
(Day boys)
No of Pupils: 299 No of Boarders
F192
Fees: (September 95) F/WB £9690
DAY £5955

THE MOUNT SCHOOL
JUNIOR DEPARTMENT
Dalton Terrace, York, North
Yorkshire YO2 4DD
Tel: (01904) 622275
Head: Mrs L Atkinson
Type: Co-educational Day 3-11
No of Pupils: 80
Fees: (September 95) £2370 - £3675

MRS RADCLIFFE'S
MONTESSORI SCHOOL
40 The Horseshoe, York, North
Yorkshire YO2 2LX
Tel: (01904) 705041
Head: Mrs N Radcliffe
Type: Co-educational Day 2-6
No of Pupils: 16
Fees: (September 95) £1575

POCKLINGTON SCHOOL*
West Green, Pocklington, York,
North Yorkshire YO4 2NJ
Tel: (01759) 303125
Head: J N Gray
Type: Co-educational Boarding &
Day 7-18
No of Pupils: 753 No of Boarders
F143
Fees: (September 95) FB £7197 -
£8688 DAY £2868 - £4842

QUEEN ETHELBURGA'S
COLLEGE*
Thorpe Underwood Hall, Ouseburn,
York, North Yorkshire YO5 9SZ
Tel: (01423) 331480
Head: Mrs G L Richardson
Type: Girls Boarding & Day 2-18
(Day boys 2-11)
No of Pupils: 300 No of Boarders
F160
Fees: (September 95) F/WB £7077 -
£10497 DAY £1497 - £6777

QUEEN MARGARET'S
SCHOOL*
Escrick Park, York, North Yorkshire
YO4 6EU
Tel: (01904) 728261
Head: G A Chapman
Type: Girls Boarding & Day 11-18
No of Pupils: 350 No of Boarders
F325
Fees: (September 95) F/WB £10218
DAY £6474

RED HOUSE SCHOOL
Moor Monkton, York, North
Yorkshire YO5 8JQ
Tel: (01904) 738256
Head: Major A V Gordon
Type: Co-educational Boarding &
Day 3-13
No of Pupils: B30 G20 No of Boarders
F20
Fees: (September 95) FB £6860 DAY
£2660 - £4630

ST MARTIN'S SCHOOL
Kirkdale Manor, Nawton, York,
North Yorkshire YO6 5UA
Tel: (01439) 71215
Head: S M Mullen
Type: Co-educational Boarding &
Day 3-14
No of Pupils: B63 G42 No of Boarders
F30 W20
Fees: (September 95) F/WB £6411 -
£6573 DAY £2064 - £4329

ST OLAVE'S SCHOOL (JUNIOR
OF ST PETER'S)
Clifton, York, North Yorkshire
YO3 6AB
Tel: (01904) 623269
Head: T Mulryne
Type: Co-educational Day &
Boarding 8-13
No of Pupils: B180 G100 No of
Boarders F60
Fees: (September 95) FB £7638 -
£8715 DAY £3825 - £4962

ST PETER'S SCHOOL
Clifton, York, North Yorkshire
YO3 6AB
Tel: (01904) 623213
Head: A F Trotman
Type: Co-educational Boarding &
Day 13-18
No of Pupils: 480 No of Boarders
F180
Fees: (September 95) FB £10116 -
£10386 DAY £5889 - £6183

TERRINGTON HALL
Terrington, York, North Yorkshire
YO6 4PR
Tel: (01653) 648227
Head: J D Gray
Type: Co-educational Boarding &
Day 3-13
No of Pupils: B72 G41 No of Boarders
F62 W8
Fees: (September 95) F/WB £6960
DAY £2100 - £4740

YORK COLLEGE FOR GIRLS
62 Petergate, York, North Yorkshire
YO1 2HZ
Tel: (01904) 646421
Head: Mrs E Taylor
Type: Girls Day 3-18 (Boys 3-8)
No of Pupils: B21 G214
Fees: (September 95) £1290 - £5250

SOUTH YORKSHIRE

BARNSLEY

BARNSLEY CHRISTIAN SCHOOL
Fellowship House, Blucher Street, Barnsley, South Yorkshire S70 1AP
Tel: (01226) 200262
Type: Co-educational Day 5-16
No of Pupils: B39 G22
Fees: (September 95) £1200 - £1284

DONCASTER

HILL HOUSE PREPARATORY SCHOOL
Rutland Street, Doncaster, South Yorkshire DN1 2JD
Tel: (01302) 323563
Head: A Cruickshank
Type: Co-educational Day 3-13
No of Pupils: B175 G112
Fees: (September 95) £2769 - £4167

ST MARY'S SCHOOL
65 Bawtry Road, Doncaster, South Yorkshire DM4 7AD
Tel: (01302) 535926
Head: Mrs A Donald
Type: Co-educational Day 3-16
No of Pupils: B37 G143
Fees: (September 95) £2865 - £4440

SYCAMORE HALL PREPARATORY SCHOOL
1 Hall Flat Lane, Balby, Doncaster, South Yorkshire DN4 8PT
Tel: (01302) 856800
Head: Miss J Spencer
Type: Co-educational Day 4-12
No of Pupils: B28 G28
Fees: (September 95) £1935

ROTHERHAM

RUDSTON PREPARATORY SCHOOL
59-63 Broom Road, Rotherham, South Yorkshire S60 2SW
Tel: (01709) 364291
Head: A W Cartner
Type: Co-educational Day 4-11
No of Pupils: B89 G81
Fees: (September 94) £2100

SHEFFIELD

ASHDELL PREPARATORY SCHOOL
266 Fulwood Road, Sheffield, South Yorkshire S10 3BL
Tel: (0114) 266 3835
Head: Mrs J Upton
Type: Girls Day 4-11
No of Pupils: 140
Fees: (September 95) £3660 - £4020

BIRKDALE SCHOOL
Oakholme Road, Sheffield, South Yorkshire S10 3DH
Tel: (0114) 266 8408
Head: Revd M D Hepworth
Type: Boys Day 4-18 (Co-ed VIth form)
No of Pupils: 770
Fees: (September 95) £3120 - £4425

BRANTWOOD INDEPENDENT SCHOOL FOR GIRLS*
1 Kenwood Bank, Sheffield, South Yorkshire S7 1NU
Tel: (0114) 258 1747
Head: Mrs E M Swynnerton
Type: Girls Day 4-17
No of Pupils: 190
Fees: (September 95) £2730 - £3375

MOUNT ST MARY'S COLLEGE
Spinkhill, Sheffield, South Yorkshire S31 9YL
Tel: (01246) 433388
Head: P B Fisher
Type: Co-educational Boarding & Day 13-18
No of Pupils: B198 G92 No of Boarders F154 W40
Fees: (September 95) FB £8970 WB £8301 DAY £6063

MYLNHURST CONVENT SCHOOL
Button Hill, Sheffield, South Yorkshire S11 9HJ
Tel: (0114) 236 1411
Head: Mrs P Fuller
Type: Co-educational Day 3-11
No of Pupils: B65 G60
Fees: (September 95) £1902 - £2580

SHEFFIELD HIGH SCHOOL GPDST
10 Rutland Park, Sheffield, South Yorkshire S10 2PE
Tel: (0114) 266 0324
Head: Mrs M Houston
Type: Girls Day 4-18
No of Pupils: 781
Fees: (September 95) £2928 - £3984

WESTBOURNE PREPARATORY SCHOOL
50-54 Westbourne Road, Sheffield, South Yorkshire S10 2QQ
Tel: (0114) 266 0374
Head: C R Wilmshurst
Type: Boys Day 4-13
No of Pupils: 180
Fees: (September 95) £2985 - £4215

WEST YORKSHIRE

APPERLEY BRIDGE

ASHDOWN LODGE
Apperley Bridge, West Yorkshire
BD10 0PQ
Tel: (0113) 250 0938
Head: Mrs C Robinson
Type: Co-educational Day 3-7
No of Pupils: 78
Fees: (September 95) £2985

WOODHOUSE GROVE
SCHOOL
Apperley Bridge, West Yorkshire
BD10 0NR
Tel: (0113) 250 2477
Head: D W Welsh
Type: Co-educational Boarding &
Day 11-18
No of Pupils: B400 G200 No of
Boarders F160
Fees: (September 95) FB £8940 DAY
£5265

BATLEY

BATLEY GRAMMAR SCHOOL
Carlinghow Hill, Batley, West
Yorkshire WF17 0AD
Tel: (01924) 474980
Head: W M Duggan
Type: Boys Day 11-18 (Co-ed VIth
form)
No of Pupils: B560 G20
Fees: (September 95) £3627

BINGLEY

LADY LANE PARK SCHOOL
Lady Lane, Bingley, West Yorkshire
BD16 4AP
Tel: (01274) 551168
Head: Mrs K L Thornton
Type: Co-educational Day 2-11
Fees: On application

BRADFORD

BRADFORD GIRLS'
GRAMMAR SCHOOL
Squire Lane, Bradford, West
Yorkshire BD9 6RB
Tel: (01274) 545395
Head: Mrs L J Warrington
Type: Girls Day 3-18
No of Pupils: 880
Fees: (September 95) £2400 - £3996

BRADFORD GRAMMAR
SCHOOL
Keighley Road, Bradford, West
Yorkshire BD9 4JP
Tel: (01274) 542492
Head: D A G Smith
Type: Boys Day 8-18 (Co-ed VIth
form)
No of Pupils: B1078 G28
Fees: (September 95) £3234 - £4101

BRONTE HOUSE SCHOOL
Apperley Bridge, Bradford, West
Yorkshire BD10 0PQ
Tel: (0113) 250 2811
Head: F F Watson
Type: Co-educational Boarding &
Day 3-11 (Boarding 7-11)
No of Pupils: B155 G75 No of
Boarders F25 W10
Fees: (September 95) F/WB £7650
DAY £2985 - £4500

FOX'S SCHOOL OF
COMMERCE
23 Claremont, Morley Street,
Bradford, West Yorkshire BD7 1BG
Tel: (01274) 725468
Head: Mrs D Whiteley
Type: Co-educational Day 13-19
No of Pupils: B10 G60
Fees: (September 95) £1800 - £1905

NETHERLEIGH SCHOOL
Lynton Drive, Heaton, Bradford,
West Yorkshire BD9 5JH
Tel: (01274) 543162
Head: P Nelson
Type: Co-educational Day 3-8
No of Pupils: B40 G40
Fees: (September 95) £1113 - £1920

ROSSEFIELD SCHOOL
Parsons Road, Heaton, Bradford,
West Yorkshire BD9 4AY
Tel: (01274) 543549
Head: P Nelson
Type: Co-educational Day 4-11
No of Pupils: B98 G118
Fees: (September 95) £1173 - £2100

SHAW HOUSE SCHOOL
150-152 Wilmer Road, Heaton,
Bradford, West Yorkshire BD9 4AH
Tel: (01274) 496299
Head: Mrs J B Eccles
Type: Co-educational Day 9-16
No of Pupils: 100
Fees: (September 95) £2535 - £2850

HALIFAX

THE GLEDDINGS SCHOOL
Birdcage Lane, Halifax, West
Yorkshire HX3 0JB
Tel: (01422) 354605
Head: Mrs D Brearley
Type: Co-educational Day 3-11
No of Pupils: B70 G70
Fees: (September 95) £1550 - £2600

HIPPERHOLME GRAMMAR
SCHOOL
Bramley Lane, Hipperholme,
Halifax, West Yorkshire HX3 8JE
Tel: (01422) 201660
Head: C C Robinson
Type: Co-educational Day 11-18
No of Pupils: B180 G170
Fees: (September 95) £3450 - £3616

LIGHTCLIFFE PREPARATORY
Wakefield Road, Wakefield, Halifax,
West Yorkshire HX3 8AQ
Tel: (01422) 201330
Head: Mrs J A Pickersgill
Type: Co-educational Day 3-11
No of Pupils: 160
Fees: (September 94) £2610

HUDDERSFIELD

KAYES' COLLEGE
New North Road, Huddersfield, West
Yorkshire HD1 5NE
Tel: (01484) 531835
Head: Mrs E J Jackson
Type: Co-educational Day 9-16
No of Pupils: B46 G63
Fees: (September 94) £2295 - £2925

MOUNT SCHOOL
3 Binham Road, Edgerton,
Huddersfield, West Yorkshire
HD2 2AJ
Tel: (01484) 426432
Head: Nigel M Smith
Type: Co-educational Day 3-11
No of Pupils: B79 G85
Fees: (September 95) £550 - £850

MOUNTJOY HOUSE SCHOOL
63 New North Road, Huddersfield,
West Yorkshire HD1 5ND
Tel: (01484) 429967
Head: Mrs D Lemm
Type: Co-educational Day 3-11
Fees: (September 95) £1185 - £2250

ROSEMEADE SCHOOL

12 Bank End Lane, Almondbury,
Huddersfield, West Yorkshire
HD5 8ES
Tel: (01484) 421076
Head: Mrs H M Hebblethwaite
Type: Co-educational Day 3-11
No of Pupils: B40 G55
Fees: (September 95) £2040 - £2100

ST DAVID'S SCHOOL

Royds Mount, Luck Lane, Marsh,
Huddersfield, West Yorkshire
HD1 4QX
Tel: (01484) 424549
Head: Mrs R A Knighton
Type: Co-educational Day 3-16
No of Pupils: B209 G145
Fees: (September 95) £2868 - £3543

ILKLEY

CLEVEDON HOUSE

Ben Rhydding, Ilkley, West
Yorkshire LS29 8BJ
Tel: (01943) 608515
Head: I A Mullins
Type: Co-educational Day &
Boarding 3-16
No of Pupils: B131 G72 No of
Boarders F54
Fees: (September 95) F/WB £6024 -
£7920 DAY £2610 - £4380

GHYLL ROYD SCHOOL

71 Grove Road, Ilkley, West
Yorkshire LS29 9QE
Tel: (01943) 607657
Head: Mrs E Shepherd
Type: Boys Day 3-11
No of Pupils: 120
Fees: (September 95) £1095 - £3105

MOORFIELD SCHOOL

Wharfedale Lodge, Ben Rhydding
Road, Ilkley, West Yorkshire
LS29 8RL
Tel: (01943) 607285
Head: Mrs P Brown
Type: Girls Day 2-11
No of Pupils: 160
Fees: (September 95) £1305 - £2850

WESTVILLE HOUSE
PREPARATORY SCHOOL

Carters Lane, Middleton, Ilkley, West
Yorkshire LS29 0DQ
Tel: (01943) 608053
Head: Dr M B Tait
Type: Co-educational Day 3-13
No of Pupils: B65 G55
Fees: (September 95) £1620 - £3255

KEIGHLEY

KEIGHLEY PREPARATORY
SCHOOL

West Cliffe, Skipton Road, Keighley,
West Yorkshire BD21 2TA
Tel: (01535) 602773
Head: A M Russell
Type: Co-educational Day 4-11
No of Pupils: B40 G40
Fees: (September 93) £2295 - £2385

LEEDS

THE FROEBELIAN SCHOOL

Clarence Road, Horsforth, Leeds,
West Yorkshire LS18 4LB
Tel: (0113) 258 3047
Head: J Tranmer
Type: Co-educational Day 3-11
No of Pupils: B94 G98
Fees: (September 95) £1545 - £2355

GATEWAYS SCHOOL

Harewood, Leeds, West Yorkshire
LS17 9LE
Tel: (0113) 288 6345
Head: Mrs J E Stephen
Type: Girls Day 3-18
No of Pupils: 300
Fees: (September 95) £2280 - £3540

LEEDS CHRISTIAN SCHOOL

48 Call Lane, Leeds, West Yorkshire
LS1 6DT
Tel: (0113) 245 3906
Head: Ms D C Dacre
Type: Co-educational Day 3-18
No of Pupils: B12 G17
Fees: (September 95) £522 - £828

LEEDS GIRLS' HIGH SCHOOL

Headingley Lane, Leeds, West
Yorkshire LS6 1BN
Tel: (0113) 274 4000
Head: Miss P A Randall
Type: Girls Day 3-19 (Boys 3-8)
No of Pupils: B20 G950
Fees: (September 95) £2169 - £4236

LEEDS GRAMMAR SCHOOL

Moorland Road, Leeds, West
Yorkshire LS6 1AN
Tel: (0113) 243 3417
Head: B W Collins
Type: Boys Day 7-18
No of Pupils: 1184
Fees: (September 95) £3618 - £4395

MOORLANDS SCHOOL

Foxhill, Weetwood Lane, Leeds, West
Yorkshire LS16 5PF
Tel: (0113) 278 5286
Head: N Woolnough
Type: Co-educational Day 3-13
No of Pupils: 180
Fees: (September 95) £1620 - £3630

NORTH LEEDS & ST
EDMUND'S HALL
PREPARATORY SCHOOL

North Park House, North Park
Avenue, Leeds, West Yorkshire
LS8 1HS
Tel: (0113) 268 1830
Head: Mrs M K Lynch
Type: Co-educational Day 0-11
No of Pupils: B99 G78
Fees: (September 95) £2640 - £2895

RICHMOND HOUSE SCHOOL

170 Otley Road, Leeds, West
Yorkshire LS16 5LG
Tel: (0113) 275 2670
Head: J F Kellett
Type: Co-educational Day 3-11
No of Pupils: B167 G133
Fees: (September 95) £2090 - £3456

ST AGNES PNEU SCHOOL

25 Burton Crescent, Leeds, West
Yorkshire LS6 4DN
Tel: (0113) 278 6722
Head: Mrs C Burrows
Type: Co-educational Day 2-8
No of Pupils: B35 G10
Fees: (September 95) £2085 - £3060

WAKEFIELD TUTORIAL
PREPARATORY SCHOOL

Commercial Street, Morley, Leeds,
West Yorkshire LS27 8HY
Tel: (0113) 253 4033
Head: R Favell
Type: Co-educational Day 4-11
No of Pupils: B50 G50
Fees: (September 95) £1500 - £1590

PONTEFRACT

ACKWORTH SCHOOL*

Barnsley Road, Ackworth,
Pontefract, West Yorkshire WF7 7LT
Tel: (01977) 611401
Head: M Dickinson
Type: Co-educational Boarding &
Day 7-18
No of Pupils: B182 G253 No of
Boarders F140
Fees: (September 95) F/WB £9333
DAY £5316

INGLEBROOK SCHOOL
Northgate Close, Pontefract, West
Yorkshire WF8 1HT
Tel: (01977) 700120
Head: Mrs J Bellamy
Type: Co-educational Day 2-11
No of Pupils: 230
Fees: (September 95) £1716 - £1860

PUDSEY

FULNECK SCHOOL
Fulneck, Pudsey, West Yorkshire
LS28 8DS
Tel: (0113) 257 0235
Head: Mrs B A Heppell
Type: Co-educational Day &
Boarding 3-18
No of Pupils: B289 G281 No of
Boarders F54
Fees: (September 95) FB £7320 -
£8655 WB £6810 - £7710 DAY
£1740 - £4620

RISHWORTH

RISHWORTH SCHOOL*
Rishworth, West Yorkshire HX6 4QA
Tel: (01422) 822217
Head: M J Elford
Type: Co-educational Day &
Boarding 4-18
No of Pupils: B363 G274
Fees: (September 95) F/WB £8556 -
£9288 DAY £2394 - £4800

SHIPLEY

VICTORIA PARK
PREPARATORY SCHOOL
7 Victoria Park, Shipley, West
Yorkshire BD18 4RL
Tel: (01274) 581680
Head: Ms Phyllis Sanderson
Type: Co-educational Day 4-9
No of Pupils: B40 G30
Fees: (September 95) £2073 - £2085

WAKEFIELD

CLIFF SCHOOL
St John's Lodge, 2 Leeds Road,
Wakefield, West Yorkshire WF1 3JT
Tel: (01924) 373597
Head: E J C Wallace
Type: Co-educational Day B3-9
G3-11
No of Pupils: B54 G121
Fees: (September 95) £2520

QUEEN ELIZABETH
GRAMMAR SCHOOL
154 Northgate, Wakefield, West
Yorkshire WF1 3QX
Tel: (01924) 373943
Head: R P Mardling
Type: Boys Day 7-18
No of Pupils: 975
Fees: (September 95) £2982 - £4122

ST HILDA'S SCHOOL
Dovecote Lane, Horbury, Wakefield,
West Yorkshire WF4 6BB
Tel: (01924) 260706
Head: Mrs A R Mackenzie
Type: Co-educational Day B3-7
G3-11
No of Pupils: B82 G48
Fees: (September 95) £2580 - £2625

SILCOATES SCHOOL
Wrenthorpe, Wakefield, West
Yorkshire WF2 0PD
Tel: (01924) 291614
Head: A P Spillane
Type: Co-educational Day 7-18
No of Pupils: B438 G150
Fees: (September 95) £3126 - £5244

SUNNY HILL HOUSE SCHOOL
Wrenthorpe Lane, Wrenthorpe,
Wakefield, West Yorkshire WF2 0QB
Tel: (01924) 291717
Head: Mrs C Byrne
Type: Co-educational Day 3-7
No of Pupils: B66 G22
Fees: (September 95) £2580

WAKEFIELD GIRLS' HIGH
SCHOOL
Wentworth Street, Wakefield, West
Yorkshire WF1 2QS
Tel: (01924) 372490
Head: Mrs P A Langham
Type: Girls Day 4-18
No of Pupils: 1060
Fees: (September 95) £2910 - £4122

WETHERBY

HIGH TREES SCHOOL
Cinder Lane, Clifford, Wetherby,
West Yorkshire LS23 6HH
Tel: (01937) 541020
Head: Mrs H J Shaw
Type: Co-educational Day 2-8
No of Pupils: 30
Fees: (September 95) £600

2.2
NORTHERN IRELAND

COUNTY ANTRIM

BELFAST

BELFAST ROYAL ACADEMY
7 Cliftonville Road, Belfast, County
Antrim BT14 6JL
Tel: (01232) 740423
Head: W M Sillery
Type: Co-educational Day 4–19
No of Pupils: B813 G862
Fees: On application

CABIN HILL SCHOOL
562-594 Upper Newtownards Road,
Knock, Belfast, County Antrim
BT4 3HJ
Tel: (01232) 653368
Head: C A I Dyer
Type: Boys Day & Boarding 4–13
No of Pupils: 394 No of Boarders F11
W26
Fees: (September 95) FB £4610 –
£6230 WB £4510 – £6130 DAY
£860 – £2830

CAMPBELL COLLEGE
Belfast, County Antrim BT4 2ND
Tel: (01232) 763076
Head: Dr R J I Pollock
Type: Boys Boarding & Day 11–18
No of Pupils: 680 No of Boarders F20
W40
Fees: (September 95) F/WB £4610 –
£5290 DAY £860 – £993

HUNTERHOUSE COLLEGE
Finaghy, Belfast, County Antrim
BT10 0LE
Tel: (01232) 612293
Head: Miss D E M Hunter
Type: Girls Day & Boarding 5–19
No of Pupils: 800 No of Boarders F90
Fees: (September 95) F/WB £2895 –
£5394 DAY £65

METHODIST COLLEGE
1 Malone Road, Belfast, County
Antrim BT9 6BY
Tel: (01232) 669558
Head: T W Mulryne
Type: Co-educational Day &
Boarding 4–19
No of Pupils: B1309 G1121 No of
Boarders F177
Fees: (September 95) FB £4185 –
£5465 DAY £1215 – £2495

**ROYAL BELFAST
ACADEMICAL INSTITUTION**
College Square East, Belfast, County
Antrim BT1 6DL
Tel: (01232) 240461
Head: R M Ridley
Type: Boys Day 11–18
No of Pupils: 1020
Fees: (September 95) £390

VICTORIA COLLEGE BELFAST
Cranmore Park, Belfast, County
Antrim BT9 6JA
Tel: (01232) 661506
Head: Mrs M Andrews
Type: Girls Day & Boarding 4–18
No of Pupils: 976 No of Boarders F47
Fees: (September 95) F/WB £3435 –
£6135 DAY £195

LISBURN

FRIENDS' SCHOOL
Magheralave Road, Lisburn, County
Antrim BT28 3BH
Tel: (01846) 662156
Head: J T Green
Type: Co-educational Day &
Boarding 4–19
No of Pupils: B546 G592 No of
Boarders F15 W30
Fees: (September 95) FB £3200 WB
£3075 DAY £850 – £2510

COUNTY ARMAGH

ARMAGH

THE ROYAL SCHOOL
College Hill, Armagh, County
Armagh BT61 9DH
Tel: (01861) 522807
Head: T Duncan
Type: Co-educational Boarding &
Day 4–19
No of Pupils: B288 G259
Fees: On application

COUNTY DOWN

BANGOR

BANGOR GRAMMAR SCHOOL
13 College Avenue, Bangor, County
Down BT20 5HJ
Tel: (01247) 473734
Head: T W Patton
Type: Boys Day 11-18
No of Pupils: 920
Fees: (September 95) £182

HOLYWOOD

THE HOLYWOOD RUDOLF STEINER SCHOOL
The Highlands, 34 Croft Road,
Holywood, County Down BT18 0PR
Tel: (01232) 428029
Head: Ms C Haupt
Type: Co-educational Day 4-17
No of Pupils: 210
Fees: On application

ROCKPORT PREPARATORY SCHOOL
Craigavad, Holywood, County
Down BT18 0DD
Tel: (01232) 428372
Head: Mrs H G Pentland
Type: Co-educational Boarding &
Day 3-13
No of Pupils: B125 G75 No of
Boarders W47
Fees: (September 93) WB £5475 DAY
£1725 - £4425

COUNTY LONDONDERRY

COLERAINE

COLERAINE ACADEMICAL INSTITUTION
Castlerock Road, Coleraine, County
Londonderry BT51 3LA
Tel: (01265) 44331
Head: R S Forsythe
Type: Boys Day & Boarding 11-19
No of Pupils: 850 No of Boarders F50
W50
Fees: (September 95) FB £5970 DAY
£2730

COUNTY TYRONE

DUNGANNON

ROYAL SCHOOL DUNGANNON
Northland Row, Dungannon,
County Tyrone BT71 6AP
Tel: (01868) 722710
Head: P D Hewitt
Type: Co-educational Day &
Boarding 4-19
No of Pupils: B310 G320 No of
Boarders F12 W8
Fees: (September 95) F/WB £4700 -
£6090 DAY £1089 - £2789

2.3
SCOTLAND

BORDERS

MELROSE

ST MARY'S PREPARATORY SCHOOL
Abbey Park, Melrose, Borders TD6 9LN
Tel: (01896) 822517
Head: R M Common
Type: Co-educational Boarding & Day 4-13
No of Pupils: B47 G45 No of Boarders F13 W12
Fees: (September 95) FB £8220 WB £8055 DAY £4830

CENTRAL

DOLLAR

DOLLAR ACADEMY
Dollar, Central FK14 7DU
Tel: (01259) 742511
Head: J S Robertson
Type: Co-educational Day & Boarding 5-18
No of Pupils: B566 G455 No of Boarders F220
Fees: (September 95) FB £8181 - £9195 WB £7701 - £8715 DAY £3135 - £4149

DUNBLANE

QUEEN VICTORIA SCHOOL
Dunblane, Central FK15 0JY
Tel: (01786) 822288
Head: B Raine
Type: Boys Boarding 10-18
No of Pupils: 270 No of Boarders F270
Fees: On application

STIRLING

BEACONHURST GRANGE
52 Kenilworth Road, Bridge of Allan, Stirling FK9 4RR
Tel: (01786) 832146
Head: D R Clegg
Type: Co-educational Day 3-18
No of Pupils: 245
Fees: (August 95) £1047 - £4239

DUMFRIES & GALLOWAY

CASTLE DOUGLAS

KILQUHANITY HOUSE SCHOOL
Castle Douglas, Dumfries & Galloway DG7 3DB
Tel: (01556) 650242
Head: R Jones
Type: Co-educational Day 5-14
No of Pupils: 50
Fees: (September 93) £1000 - £2100

THORNHILL

CADEMUIR INTERNATIONAL SCHOOL
Moniaive, Thornhill, Dumfries & Galloway DG3 4HG
Tel: (01848) 200212
Head: R Mulvey
Type: Co-educational Boarding & Day 3-18+
No of Pupils: 86
Fees: (September 95) FB £10500 WB £9450 DAY £1800 - £5700

FIFE

DUNFERMLINE

INCHKEITH PRIVATE SCHOOL
Balgownie, Culross, Dunfermline,
Fife KY12 8JJ
Tel: (01383) 880330
Head: Mrs J M Poustie
Type: Co-educational Day 3-11
No of Pupils: 60
Fees: (September 95) £1086 - £1800

KIRKCALDY

SEA VIEW PRIVATE SCHOOL
102 Loughborough Road, Kirkcaldy,
Fife KY1 3DD
Tel: (01592) 652244
Head: Mrs E A Mason
Type: Co-educational Day 3-12
No of Pupils: B32 G33
Fees: (September 95) £1200 - £2400

ST ANDREWS

NEW PARK SCHOOL
98 Hepburn Gardens, St Andrews,
Fife KY16 9LN
Tel: (01334) 472017
Head: A Donald
Type: Co-educational Day &
Boarding 3-13
No of Pupils: B89 G40 No of Boarders
F9 W2
Fees: (September 95) FB £8100 WB
£7050 DAY £825 - £4425

ST KATHARINES GIRLS PREPARATORY SCHOOL*
The Pends, St Andrews, Fife
KY16 9RB
Tel: (01334) 472446
Head: T C R Bayley & G J
Robson-Bayley
Type: Girls Boarding & Day 7-12
No of Pupils: 54 No of Boarders F37
Fees: (September 95) FB £8922 WB
£8622 DAY £3300 - £4800

ST LEONARDS SCHOOL*
St Andrews, Fife KY16 9QU
Tel: (01334) 472126
Head: Mrs Mary James
Type: Girls Boarding & Day 12-18
No of Pupils: 280 No of Boarders
F230
Fees: (September 95) FB £11775 DAY
£6225

GRAMPIAN

ABERDEEN

ABERDEEN WALDORF SCHOOL
111 Gallowgate, Aberdeen AB1 1BU
Tel: (01224) 646111
Type: Co-educational Day 4-16
No of Pupils: B75 G79
Fees: (September 95) £720 - £3516

ALBYN SCHOOL FOR GIRLS*
17-23 Queens Road, Aberdeen
AB9 2PA
Tel: (01224) 322408
Head: Miss N H Smith
Type: Girls Day 3-18 (Boys 3-5)
No of Pupils: B12 G420
Fees: (September 95) £1210 - £3925

AMERICAN SCHOOL IN ABERDEEN
Craigton Road, Cults, Aberdeen
AB1 9QD
Tel: (01224) 868927
Type: Co-educational Day 4-18
No of Pupils: 263
Fees: (September 95) £8400 - £9000

ROBERT GORDONS COLLEGE
Schoolhill, Aberdeen AB9 1FE
Tel: (01224) 646346
Head: G A Allan
Type: Co-educational Day 5-18
No of Pupils: B923 G427
Fees: (September 95) £2535 - £3900

ST MARGARET'S SCHOOL FOR GIRLS*
17 Albyn Place, Aberdeen AB9 1RH
Tel: (01224) 584466
Head: Miss L M Ogilvie
Type: Girls Day 3-18 (Boys 3-5)
No of Pupils: B4 G412
Fees: (September 95) £666 - £3702

TOTAL OIL MARINE FRENCH SCHOOL
Whitehall Place, Aberdeen AB1 2QR
Tel: (01224) 645545
Head: M Le Bresne
Type: Co-educational Day 5-18
No of Pupils: 160
Fees: (September 94) £6000

ABERLOUR

ABERLOUR HOUSE
Aberlour, Grampian AB38 9LJ
Tel: (01340) 871267
Head: J W Caithness
Type: Co-educational Boarding &
Day 8-13
No of Pupils: B66 G45 No of Boarders
F111
Fees: (September 95) FB £8235 DAY
£5640

ELGIN

GORDONSTOUN SCHOOL*
Elgin, Grampian IV30 2RF
Tel: (01343) 830445
Head: M C Pyper
Type: Co-educational Boarding &
Day 13-18
No of Pupils: B250 G215 No of
Boarders F435
Fees: (September 95) FB £12105 DAY
£7809

ROSEBRAE SCHOOL
Spynie, Elgin, Grampian IV30 3XT
Tel: (01343) 544841
Head: Mrs Bell
Type: Co-educational Day 3-10
No of Pupils: B30 G30
Fees: (September 95) £1155 - £2475

LOTHIAN

DUNBAR

BELHAVEN HILL
Dunbar, Lothian EH42 1NN
Tel: (01368) 862785
Head: I M Osborne
Type: Boys Boarding & Day 7-13
No of Pupils: 75 No of Boarders F62 W9
Fees: (September 95) FB £8385 WB £8310 DAY £5850

EDINBURGH

CARGILFIELD
Barnton Avenue West, Edinburgh, Lothian EH4 6HU
Tel: (0131) 336 2207
Head: A J S Bateman
Type: Co-educational Boarding & Day 3-13
No of Pupils: B127 G68 No of Boarders F47 W33
Fees: (September 94) F/WB £8310 DAY £1350 - £5925

DUNEDIN SCHOOL
Millar Hill, 5 Gilmerton Road, Edinburgh, Lothian EH16 5TY
Tel: (0131) 664 1328
Type: Co-educational Day 5-18
No of Pupils: 11
Fees: On application

THE EDINBURGH ACADEMY
42 Henderson Row, Edinburgh, Lothian EH3 5BL
Tel: (0131) 556 4603
Head: J V Light
Type: Boys Day & Boarding 11-18 (Co-ed VIth form)
No of Pupils: B498 G39 No of Boarders F55
Fees: (September 95) FB £10842 DAY £5085

EDINBURGH ACADEMY PREPARATORY SCHOOL
10 Arboretum Road, Edinburgh, Lothian EH3 5PL
Tel: (0131) 552 3690
Head: C R F Paterson
Type: Boys Day & Boarding 3-11 (Girls 3-5)
No of Pupils: B371 G16
Fees: (September 95) FB £9123 - £9324 DAY £2478 - £3567

EDINBURGH TUTORIAL COLLEGE AND AMERICAN SCHOOL
29 Chester Street, Edinburgh, Lothian EH3 7EN
Tel: (0131) 225 9888
Head: A W Morris
Type: Co-educational Day & Boarding 15-18
No of Pupils: 40
Fees: (September 95) FB £7990 DAY £4995

FETTES COLLEGE*
Carrington Road, Edinburgh, Lothian EH4 1QX
Tel: (0131) 332 2281
Head: M T Thyne
Type: Co-educational Boarding & Day 10-18
No of Pupils: B257 G221 No of Boarders F371
Fees: (September 95) FB £8355 - £12255 DAY £5235 - £8235

GEORGE HERIOT'S SCHOOL
Lauriston Place, Edinburgh, Lothian EH3 9EQ
Tel: (0131) 229 7263
Head: K P Pearson
Type: Co-educational Day 4-18
No of Pupils: B846 G631
Fees: (September 95) £2145 - £3750

GEORGE WATSON'S COLLEGE
Colinton Road, Edinburgh, Lothian EH10 5EG
Tel: (0131) 447 7931
Head: F E Gerstenberg
Type: Co-educational Day & Boarding 3-18
No of Pupils: B1194 G950 No of Boarders F62
Fees: (September 95) FB £8280 DAY £1392 - £4140

THE MARY ERSKINE SCHOOL
Ravelston, Edinburgh, Lothian EH4 3NT
Tel: (0131) 337 2391
Head: P F Tobin
Type: Girls Day & Boarding 11-18
No of Pupils: 625 No of Boarders F32
Fees: (September 95) FB £7290 - £8280 DAY £1740 - £4140

MERCHISTON CASTLE SCHOOL*
Colinton, Edinburgh, Lothian EH13 0PU
Tel: (0131) 441 1722
Head: D M Spawforth
Type: Boys Boarding & Day 10-18
No of Pupils: 406 No of Boarders F284
Fees: (September 95) FB £8310 - £11505 DAY £5310 - £7440

THE RUDOLF STEINER SCHOOL
60 Spylaw Road, Edinburgh, Lothian EH10 5BR
Tel: (0131) 337 3410
Type: Co-educational Day 3-18
No of Pupils: 350
Fees: (September 95) £1290 - £3702

ST DENIS AND CRANLEY SCHOOL*
Ettrick Road, Edinburgh, Lothian EH10 5BJ
Tel: (0131) 229 1500
Head: Mrs J M Munro
Type: Girls Boarding & Day 5-18
No of Pupils: 180 No of Boarders 50
Fees: (September 95) F/WB £7140 - £9150 DAY £2175 - £4485

ST GEORGE'S SCHOOL FOR GIRLS
Garscube Terrace, Edinburgh, Lothian EH12 6BG
Tel: (0131) 332 4575
Head: Dr J McClure
Type: Girls Boarding 3-18 (Boys 3-5)
No of Pupils: 880 No of Boarders F87
Fees: (September 95) FB £7395 - £8655 DAY £2415 - £4485

ST MARGARET'S
East Suffolk Road, Edinburgh, Lothian EH16 5PJ
Tel: (0131) 668 1986
Head: Miss A Mitchell
Type: Girls Day & Boarding 3-18 (Boys day 3-8)
No of Pupils: B15 G660 No of Boarders F45 W10
Fees: (September 95) FB £7397 - £8324 WB £6500 - £8324 DAY £2324 - £4120

ST SERF'S SCHOOL
5 Wester Coates Gardens,
Edinburgh, Lothian EH12 5LT
Tel: (0131) 337 1015
Head: Mrs K D Hume
Type: Co-educational Day 5-18
No of Pupils: B128 G132
Fees: (September 95) £1500 - £1960

STEWART'S MELVILLE COLLEGE
Queensferry Road, Edinburgh,
Lothian EH4 3EZ
Tel: (0131) 332 7925
Head: P F Tobin
Type: Boys Day & Boarding 11-18
No of Pupils: 754 No of Boarders F34
Fees: (September 95) FB £8280 DAY
£4140

HADDINGTON

THE COMPASS SCHOOL
West Road, Haddington, Lothian
EH41 3RD
Tel: (01620) 822642
Head: Miss C R Budge
Type: Co-educational Day 4-11
No of Pupils: B44 G57
Fees: (September 95) £1680 - £3360

MUSSELBURGH

LORETTO JUNIOR SCHOOL
North Esk Lodge, Musselburgh,
Central EH21 6JA
Tel: (0131) 665 2628
Head: D P Clark
Type: Co-educational Boarding &
Day 8-13
No of Pupils: 76 No of Boarders F55
Fees: (September 95) FB £8700 DAY
£5838

LORETTO SCHOOL*
Musselburgh, Lothian EH21 7RE
Tel: (0131) 665 2567
Head: K J Budge
Type: Co-educational Boarding 13-18
No of Pupils: B270 G60 No of
Boarders F330
Fees: (September 95) FB £11610 DAY
£7740

NEWBRIDGE

CLIFTON HALL
Newbridge, Lothian EH28 8LQ
Tel: (0131) 333 1359
Head: M Adams
Type: Co-educational Boarding &
Day 3-13 (Weekly boarding only)
No of Pupils: B86 G50 No of Boarders
W8
Fees: (September 95) DAY £1350 -
£5400

STRATHCLYDE

AYR

DRUMLEY HOUSE SCHOOL
Mossblown, Ayr KA6 5AT
Tel: (01292) 520340
Head: C F Robinson
Type: Co-educational Day 3-13
No of Pupils: B100 G20
Fees: (September 95) £1230 - £4545

WELLINGTON SCHOOL
Carleton Turrets, Ayr KA7 2XH
Tel: (01292) 269321
Head: Mrs D A Gardner
Type: Co-educational Day 3-18
No of Pupils: 400
Fees: (September 94) £1320 - £4470

DUMBARTON

KEIL SCHOOL
Helenslee Road, Dumbarton,
Strathclyde G82 4AL
Tel: (01389) 763855
Head: J A Cummings
Type: Co-educational Boarding &
Day 10-18
No of Pupils: B150 G70 No of
Boarders F125
Fees: (September 95) F/WB £9195 -
£9357 DAY £4494 - £5241

GLASGOW

BELMONT HOUSE
Sandringham Avenue, Newton
Mearns, Glasgow, Strathclyde
G77 5DU
Tel: (0141) 639 2922
Head: J Mercer
Type: Boys Day 3-18
No of Pupils: 390
Fees: (September 94) £765 - £3594

CRAIGHOLME SCHOOL
72 St Andrews Drive, Glasgow,
Strathclyde G41 4HS
Tel: (0141) 427 0375
Head: Mrs G Burt
Type: Girls Day 3-18 (Boys 3-8)
No of Pupils: 500
Fees: (September 95) £1200 - £3795

DAIRSIE HOUSE SCHOOL
54 Newlands Road, Glasgow,
Strathclyde G43 2JG
Tel: (0141) 632 0736
Head: Mrs J W Penman
Type: Co-educational Day 3-9
No of Pupils: B54 G58
Fees: (September 94) £1509 - £2580

FERNHILL SCHOOL
Fernbrae Avenue, Rutherglen,
Glasgow, Strathclyde G73 4SG
Tel: (0141) 634 2674
Head: Mrs L M McLay
Type: Girls Day 4-18 (Junior boys
only)
No of Pupils: B50 G260
Fees: (September 95) £2760 - £2955

GASK HOUSE SCHOOL
28 Colston Drive, Bishopbriggs,
Glasgow, Strathclyde G64 2AZ
Tel: (0141) 772 4708
Head: Miss V P Henderson
Type: Co-educational Day 2-9
No of Pupils: 120
Fees: (September 95) £900 - £2490

GLASGOW ACADEMY
Colebrooke Street, Kelvinbridge,
Glasgow, Strathclyde G12 8HE
Tel: (0141) 334 8558
Head: D Comins
Type: Co-educational Day 4-18
No of Pupils: 1050
Fees: (September 95) £2745 - £4290

THE HIGH SCHOOL OF GLASGOW
637 Crow Road, Glasgow,
Strathclyde G13 1PL
Tel: (0141) 954 9628
Head: R G Easton
Type: Co-educational Day 3-18
No of Pupils: B496 G493
Fees: (September 95) £1494 - £4266

HUTCHESONS' GRAMMAR SCHOOL
21 Beaton Road, Glasgow,
Strathclyde G41 4NW
Tel: (0141) 423 2933
Head: D R Ward
Type: Co-educational Day 5-18
No of Pupils: B951 G862
Fees: (September 95) £3114 - £3834

THE KELVINSIDE ACADEMY
33 Kirklee Road, Glasgow,
Strathclyde G12 0SW
Tel: (0141) 357 3376
Head: J H Duff
Type: Boys Day 4-18
No of Pupils: 560
Fees: (September 95) £2385 - £4425

LAUREL BANK SCHOOL
4 Lilybank Terrace, Glasgow,
Strathclyde G12 8RX
Tel: (0141) 339 9127
Head: Mrs E Surber
Type: Girls Day 3-18 (Boys 3-4)
No of Pupils: B15 G373
Fees: (September 95) £2583 - £4266

THE PARK SCHOOL
25 Lynedoch Street, Glasgow,
Strathclyde G3 6EX
Tel: (0141) 332 0426
Head: Mrs M E Myatt
Type: Girls Day 3-18
No of Pupils: 400
Fees: (September 95) £1314 - £3969

ST ALOYSIUS' COLLEGE
45 Hill Street, Glasgow, Strathclyde
G3 6RJ
Tel: (0141) 332 3190
Head: Rev Adrian Porter
Type: Co-educational Day 8-18
No of Pupils: B635 G444
Fees: (September 95) £2850 - £3160

ST FRANCIS PRIMARY - MERRYLEE
Broom Road, Newlands, Glasgow,
Strathclyde G43 2TP
Tel: (0141) 637 0740
Head: Mrs J A McGreal
Type: Co-educational Day 3-11
No of Pupils: B68 G60
Fees: (September 94) £2634

SPRINGBANK SCHOOL
8 Albany Drive, Rutherglen,
Glasgow, Strathclyde G73 3QW
Tel: (0141) 647 6647
Head: Mrs M Russell
Type: Co-educational Day 3-9
No of Pupils: B30 G28
Fees: (September 94) £750 - £1500

HAMILTON

HAMILTON COLLEGE
Bothwell Road, Hamilton,
Strathclyde ML3 6AA
Tel: (01698) 282700
Head: S J Mitchell
Type: Co-educational Day 4-18
Fees: (September 95) £2100 - £2850

HELENSBURGH

LOMOND SCHOOL
10 Stafford Street, Helensburgh,
Strathclyde G84 9JX
Tel: (01436) 672476
Head: A D Macdonald
Type: Co-educational Day & Boarding 3-19
No of Pupils: B256 G258 No of Boarders F68
Fees: (September 95) FB £9930 WB £9615 DAY £1290 - £4545

PARK LODGE SCHOOL
17 Charlotte Street, Helensburgh,
Strathclyde G84 7EY
Tel: (01436) 673008
Head: Mrs E S Durward
Type: Co-educational Day 2-12
Fees: (September 95) £588 - £2829

KILMACOLM

ST COLUMBA'S SCHOOL
Duchal Road, Kilmacolm,
Strathclyde PA13 4AU
Tel: (01505) 872238
Head: A Livingstone
Type: Co-educational Day 3-18
No of Pupils: B227 G343
Fees: (September 95) £1125 - £3789

TAYSIDE

BLAIRGOWRIE

BUTTERSTONE SCHOOL
Meigle, Blairgowrie, Tayside PH12
8QY
Tel: (01828) 4528
Head: C G Syers-Gibson
Type: Girls Boarding & Day 2-13
No of Pupils: 52 No of Boarders F30
Fees: (September 95) FB £8964 DAY £2949 - £5565

CRIEFF

ARDVRECK SCHOOL
Gwydyr Road, Crieff, Tayside
PH7 4EX
Tel: (01764) 653112
Head: N Gardner
Type: Co-educational Boarding & Day 4-14
No of Pupils: B85 G40 No of Boarders F90
Fees: (September 95) FB £7950 - £8325 DAY £4875 - £5085

MORRISON'S ACADEMY*
Crieff, Tayside PH7 3AN
Tel: (01764) 653885
Head: H A Ashmall
Type: Co-educational Day & Boarding 5-18
No of Pupils: B286 G219 No of Boarders F79
Fees: (September 95) FB £9519 - £10590 DAY £2250 - £3645

DUNDEE

THE HIGH SCHOOL OF DUNDEE

P O Box 16, Euclid Crescent, Dundee, Tayside DD1 9BP
Tel: (01382) 202921
Head: R Nimmo
Type: Co-educational Day 5-18
No of Pupils: B575 G575
Fees: (September 95) £2745 - £3909

MONTROSE

LATHALLAN SCHOOL*

Montrose, Tayside DD10 0HN
Tel: (01561) 362220
Head: P F Fawkes
Type: Co-educational Boarding & Day 5-13
No of Pupils: B85 G55 No of Boarders F40 W10
Fees: (September 95) FB £8436 WB £8247 DAY £3717 - £5334

PERTH

CRAIGCLOWAN PREPARATORY SCHOOL

Edinburgh Road, Perth, Tayside PH2 8PS
Tel: (01738) 626310
Head: M E Beale
Type: Co-educational Day 4-13
No of Pupils: B110 G110
Fees: (September 95) £4035

GLENALMOND COLLEGE*

Perth, Tayside PH1 3RY
Tel: (01738) 880442
Head: I G Templeton
Type: Co-educational Boarding 12-18
No of Pupils: B236 G53 No of Boarders F260
Fees: (September 95) FB £8985 - £11970 DAY £5985 - £7980

KILGRASTON SCHOOL

(A Sacred Heart School), Bridge of Earn, Perth, Tayside PH2 9BQ
Tel: (01738) 812257
Head: Mrs J L Austin
Type: Girls Boarding & Day 5-18
No of Pupils: 280 No of Boarders F112 W57
Fees: (September 94) F/WB £8310 - £9180 DAY £3330 - £5100

STRATHALLAN SCHOOL

Forgandenny, Perth, Tayside PH2 9EG
Tel: (01738) 812546
Head: A W McPhail
Type: Co-educational Boarding 10-18
No of Pupils: B340 G160 No of Boarders F500
Fees: (September 95) FB £8700 - £11055 DAY £6345 - £7710

PITLOCHRY

CROFTINLOAN SCHOOL

Pitlochry, Tayside PH16 5JR
Tel: (01796) 472057
Head: N J Heuvel
Type: Co-educational Boarding & Day 5-14
No of Pupils: B53 G35 No of Boarders F77
Fees: (September 95) FB £8370 DAY £5898

RANNOCH SCHOOL*

Rannoch, Pitlochry, Tayside PH17 2QQ
Tel: (01882) 632332
Head: M Barratt
Type: Co-educational Boarding & Day 10-18
No of Pupils: B195 G70 No of Boarders F255
Fees: (September 95) FB £8700 - £10350 DAY £5490

2.4
WALES

CLWYD

COLWYN BAY

LYNDON SCHOOL
Grosvenor Road, Colwyn Bay,
Clwyd LL29 7YF
Tel: (01492) 532347
Head: Mrs A Ashworth
Type: Co-educational Day 3-11
No of Pupils: B60 G42
Fees: (September 95) £2025 - £2730

RYDAL PENRHOS PREPARATORY SCHOOL*
Pwllycrochan, Colwyn Bay, Clwyd
LL29 7BP
Tel: (01492) 530381
Head: M J F Andrews
Type: Co-educational Boarding &
Day 2-13
No of Pupils: B162 G55 No of
Boarders F66
Fees: (September 95) F/WB £4209 -
£8400 DAY £1764 - £6114

RYDAL PENRHOS SENIOR SCHOOL (CO-EDUCATIONAL DIVISION)*
Pwllycrochan Avenue, Colwyn Bay,
Clwyd LL29 7BT
Tel: (01492) 530155
Head: N W Thorne
Type: Co-educational Boarding &
Day 13-18
No of Pupils: B207 G103 No of
Boarders F165
Fees: (September 95) FB £9849 DAY
£7104

RYDAL PENRHOS SENIOR SCHOOL (GIRLS' DIVISION)*
Llannerch Road East, Colwyn Bay,
Clwyd LL28 4DA
Tel: (01492) 530333
Head: C M J Allen
Type: Girls Boarding & Day 11-18
No of Pupils: 225 No of Boarders
F111 W10
Fees: (September 95) F/WB £8265 -
£9345 DAY £5985 - £6405

DENBIGH

HOWELL'S SCHOOL
Denbigh, Clwyd LL16 3EN
Tel: (01745) 813631
Head: Mrs Mary Steel
Type: Girls Boarding & Day 3-18
No of Pupils: 304 No of Boarders
F114
Fees: (September 95) FB £5385 -
£9846 WB £5385 - £5823 DAY
£2490 - £6435

RHYL

NORTHGATE PREPARATORY
57 Russell Road, Rhyl, Clwyd
LL18 3DD
Tel: (01745) 342510
Head: P G Orton
Type: Co-educational Day 4-11
No of Pupils: B23 G23
Fees: (September 95) £1765 - £1915

RUTHIN

RUTHIN SCHOOL
Ruthin, Clwyd LL15 1EE
Tel: (01824) 702543
Head: J S Rowlands
Type: Co-educational Boarding &
Day 3-18
No of Pupils: 250 No of Boarders F58
W31
Fees: (September 95) FB £6675 -
£9885 WB £6675 - £8145 DAY
£1950 - £6225

ST ASAPH

FAIRHOLME PREPARATORY SCHOOL
Mount Road, St Asaph, Clwyd
LL17 0DH
Tel: (01745) 583505
Head: Mrs M Cashman
Type: Co-educational Day 3-11
No of Pupils: B71 G60
Fees: (September 95) £1500 - £2100

DYFED

HAVERFORDWEST

**HAYLETT GRANGE PNEU
SCHOOL**
Merlin's Bridge, Haverfordwest,
Dyfed SA62 4LA
Tel: (01437) 762472
Head: Mrs J M Sharpe
Type: Co-educational Day 2-11
No of Pupils: B54 G76
Fees: (September 95) £1000 - £1800

LLANDOVERY

LLANDOVERY COLLEGE*
Llandovery, Dyfed SA20 0EE
Tel: (01550) 720315
Head: Dr C E Evans
Type: Co-educational Boarding &
Day 11-18
No of Pupils: B168 G73 No of
Boarders F168
Fees: (September 95) F/WB £8058 -
£9510 DAY £5520 - £6204

LLANELLI

ST MICHAEL'S SCHOOL
Bryn, Llanelli, Dyfed SA14 9TU
Tel: (01554) 820325
Head: D T Sheehan
Type: Co-educational Day 5-18
No of Pupils: B187 G130
Fees: (September 95) £1950 - £3255

SAUNDERSFOOT

NETHERWOOD SCHOOL
Saundersfoot, Dyfed SA69 9BE
Tel: (01834) 813360
Head: R H Cope
Type: Co-educational Day &
Boarding 3-16
No of Pupils: B90 G90 No of Boarders
F21 W30
Fees: (September 94) FB £5400 -
£6000 WB £4500 - £5250 DAY
£1650 - £2950

MID GLAMORGAN

PORTHCAWL

ST CLARE'S CONVENT
Newton, Porthcawl, Mid Glamorgan
CF36 5NR
Tel: (01656) 782509
Head: Miss A Jarrett
Type: Co-educational Day 3-18
No of Pupils: B147 G369
Fees: (September 95) £1785 - £3600

ST JOHN'S SCHOOL
Newton, Porthcawl, Mid Glamorgan
CF36 5NP
Tel: (01656) 783404
Head: A J Hughes
Type: Co-educational Day &
Boarding 3-16
No of Pupils: B142 G77 No of
Boarders F13 W34
Fees: (September 95) FB £6405 -
£7350 WB £5775 - £6705 DAY
£2730 - £4680

SOUTH GLAMORGAN

CARDIFF

THE CATHEDRAL SCHOOL
Llandaff, Cardiff, South Glamorgan
CF5 2YH
Tel: (01222) 563179
Head: P L Gray
Type: Co-educational Day &
Boarding 4–13
No of Pupils: B233 G60 No of
Boarders F18 W3
Fees: (September 94) FB £6750 WB
£6600 DAY £2895 – £4350

ELM TREE HOUSE SCHOOL
27 Palace Road, Llandaff, Cardiff,
South Glamorgan CF5 2AG
Tel: (01222) 563386
Head: Mrs C M Thomas
Type: Girls Day 3–11 (Boys 3–7)
No of Pupils: 130
Fees: (September 95) £2625 – £3057

HOWELL'S SCHOOL
LLANDAFF*
Cardiff Road, Llandaff, Cardiff,
South Glamorgan CF5 2YD
Tel: (01222) 562019
Head: Mrs C J Fitz
Type: Girls Day 4–18
No of Pupils: 689
Fees: (September 95) £2928 – £3984

KINGS MONKTON SCHOOL
(PRIMARY)
Clive Hall, Clive Road, Llandaff,
Cardiff, South Glamorgan CF5 1GN
Tel: (01222) 388445
Head: R N Griffin
Type: Co-educational Day 2–11
No of Pupils: B120 G80
Fees: (September 95) £2385 – £2862

KINGS MONKTON SCHOOL
(PRIMARY)
Wordsworth Avenue, Roath, Cardiff,
South Glamorgan CF2 1AR
Tel: (01222) 482854
Head: R N Griffin
Type: Co-educational Day 3–18
No of Pupils: B240 G160
Fees: (September 95) £2385 – £2862

KINGS MONKTON SCHOOL
AND COLLEGE
The Parade, Cardiff, South
Glamorgan CF2 3UA
Tel: (01222) 483130
Head: R N Griffin
Type: Co-educational Day 11–18
No of Pupils: B150 G40
Fees: (September 95) £3465 – £4134

NEW COLLEGE AND SCHOOL
Bute Terrace, Cardiff, South
Glamorgan CF1 2TE
Tel: (01222) 463355
Head: W Hoole
Type: Co-educational Day 3–18
No of Pupils: 352
Fees: (September 95) £2565 – £9750

OUR LADY'S CONVENT
SCHOOL
29 The Walk, Roath, Cardiff, South
Glamorgan CF2 3AG
Tel: (01222) 490907
Head: Sister M Imelda
Type: Girls Day 3–16
No of Pupils: 250
Fees: (September 95) £2100 – £2850

ST JOHN'S COLLEGE
Greenway Road, Cardiff, South
Glamorgan CF3 8QR
Tel: (01222) 778936
Head: Dr D Neville
Type: Co-educational Day 3–16
(Choir School)
No of Pupils: B240 G200
Fees: (September 95) £2100 – £3450

WESTBOURNE SCHOOLS
4 Hickman Road, Penarth, Cardiff,
South Glamorgan CF64 2AJ
Tel: (01222) 707861
Head: A J Bentley-Taylor & R H
Haines
Type: Co-educational Day 3–16
No of Pupils: B136 G51
Fees: (September 95) £2160 – £4380

WEST GLAMORGAN

SWANSEA

CRAIG-Y-NOS SCHOOL
Clyne Common, Bishopston,
Swansea, West Glamorgan SA3 3JB
Tel: (01792) 234288
Head: G W Fursland
Type: Co-educational Day 2–11
No of Pupils: B85 G55
Fees: (September 95) £1905 – £2550

FFYNONE HOUSE SCHOOL
36 St James' Crescent, Swansea,
West Glamorgan SA1 6DR
Tel: (01792) 464967
Head: J R Thomas
Type: Co-educational Day B8–18
G11–18
No of Pupils: 170
Fees: (September 94) £2685 – £3885

OAKLEIGH HOUSE
38 Penlan Crescent, Uplands,
Swansea, West Glamorgan SA2 0RL
Tel: (01792) 298537
Head: Mrs M Evans
Type: Co-educational Day B3–8
G3–11
No of Pupils: B55 G146
Fees: (September 94) £2115 – £2325

GWENT

CHEPSTOW

ST JOHN'S-ON-THE-HILL
Tutshill, Chepstow, Gwent NP6 7LE
Tel: (01291) 622045
Head: I K Etchells
Type: Co-educational Boarding & Day 2-13
No of Pupils: B133 G92 No of Boarders F8 W19
Fees: (September 95) F/WB £6960 DAY £933 - £5154

MONMOUTH

HABERDASHERS' MONMOUTH SCHOOL FOR GIRLS*
Hereford Road, Monmouth, Gwent NP5 3XT
Tel: (01600) 714214
Head: Mrs D L Newman
Type: Girls Day & Boarding 7-18
No of Pupils: 648 No of Boarders F57 W71
Fees: (September 95) F/WB £7272 - £8346 DAY £3501 - £4575

MONMOUTH SCHOOL*
Monmouth, Gwent NP5 3XP
Tel: (01600) 713143
Head: T H P Haynes
Type: Boys Day & Boarding 11-18
No of Pupils: 561 No of Boarders F187
Fees: (September 95) F/WB £8175 DAY £4908

NEWPORT

ROUGEMONT SCHOOL
Llantarnam Hall, Malpas Road, Newport, Gwent NP9 6QB
Tel: (01633) 855560
Head: G R Sims
Type: Co-educational Day 3-18
No of Pupils: 485
Fees: (September 95) £2550 - £4391

GWYNEDD

BANGOR

HILLGROVE SCHOOL
Ffriddoedd Road, Bangor, Gwynedd LL57 2TW
Tel: (01248) 353568
Head: J G Porter
Type: Co-educational Day 3-16
No of Pupils: B100 G66
Fees: (September 95) £1650 - £2640

ST GERARD'S SCHOOL
Ffriddoedd Road, Bangor, Gwynedd LL57 2EL
Tel: (01248) 351656
Head: Miss A Parkinson
Type: Co-educational Day 3-18
No of Pupils: 340
Fees: (September 95) £1755 - £2670

BARMOUTH

TOWER HOUSE
Barmouth, Gwynedd LL42 1RF
Tel: (01341) 280127
Head: Mrs J Pugh
Type: Co-educational Day 4-17
No of Pupils: B83 G64
Fees: (September 95) £2244 - £3150

LLANDUDNO

ST DAVID'S COLLEGE*
Gloddaeth Hall, Llandudno, Gwynedd LL30 1RD
Tel: (01492) 875974
Head: W Seymour
Type: Boys Boarding & Day 11-18
No of Pupils: 220 No of Boarders F170
Fees: (September 95) F/WB £9978 DAY £6489

POWYS

BRECON

CHRIST COLLEGE BRECON*
Brecon, Powys LD3 8AG
Tel: (01874) 623359
Head: S W Hockey
Type: Co-educational Boarding &
Day 11-18
No of Pupils: B291 G55 No of
Boarders F265
Fees: (September 95) FB £9405 DAY
£7290

ST DAVID'S SCHOOL
Glamorgan Street, Brecon, Powys
LD3 7DN
Tel: (01874) 622806
Head: F W Edwards
Type: Co-educational Day 1-16 (Girls
boarding)
No of Pupils: B30 G75 No of
Boarders F5 W10
Fees: (September 95) FB £6915 -
£7995 WB £5115 - £6015 DAY
£1170 - £3675

WELSHPOOL

BROOKLAND HALL SCHOOL & GOLF ACADEMY
Welshpool, Powys SY21 9BU
Tel: (01938) 552326
Head: M J Hutchinson
Type: Boys Boarding 11-16
No of Pupils:: F70
Fees: (September 95) FB £9500 WB
£8500

PART THREE: SCHOOL PROFILES

COUNTIES OF ENGLAND, SCOTLAND AND WALES

NORTHERN ENGLAND

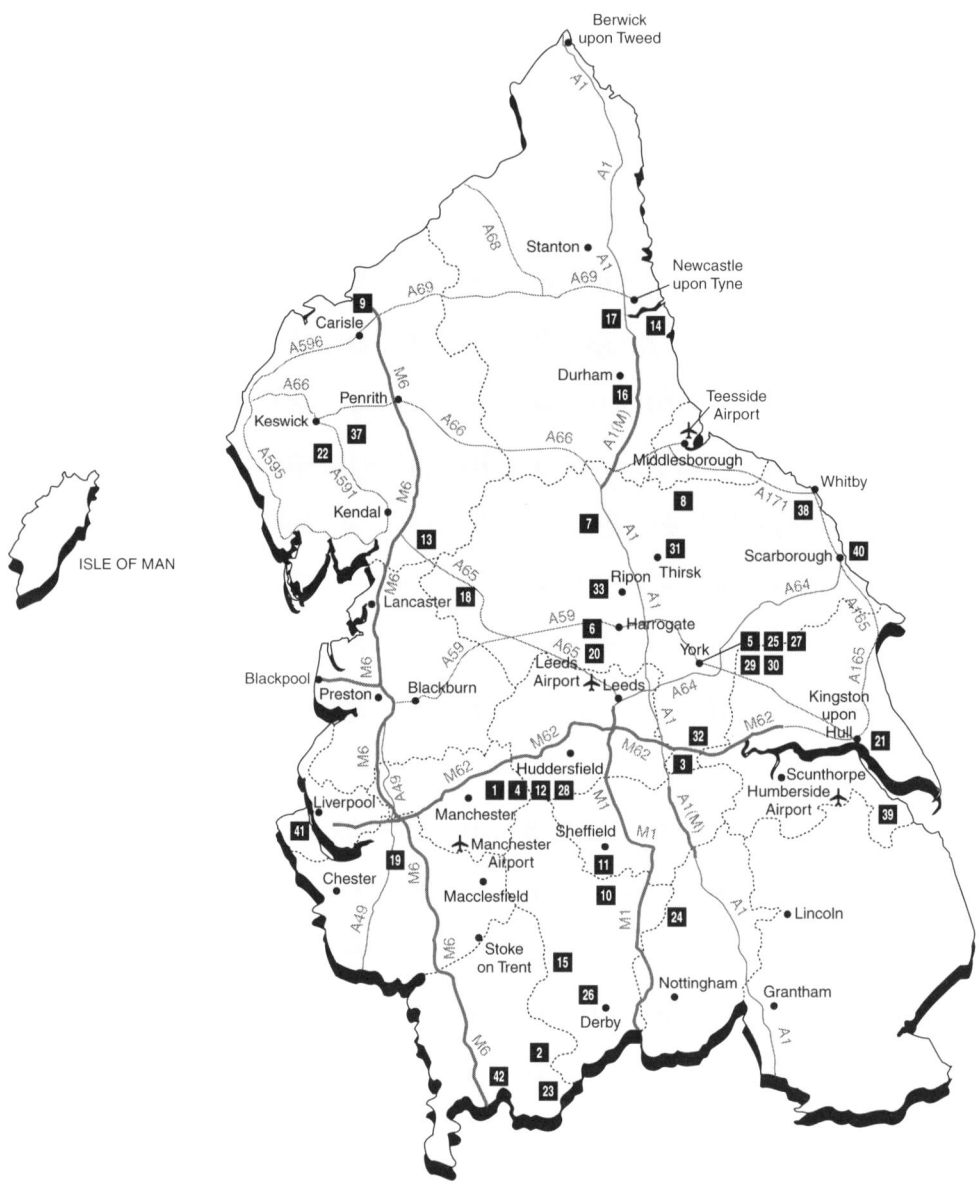

NORTHERN ENGLAND

(Incorporating counties of Cheshire, Cumbria, Derbyshire, Durham, Humberside, Lancashire,
Greater Manchster, Merseyside, Northumberland, Nottinghamshire, Staffordshire, Tyne & Wear, Yorkshire)

MAP OF SOUTH WEST ENGLAND

SOUTH WEST ENGLAND

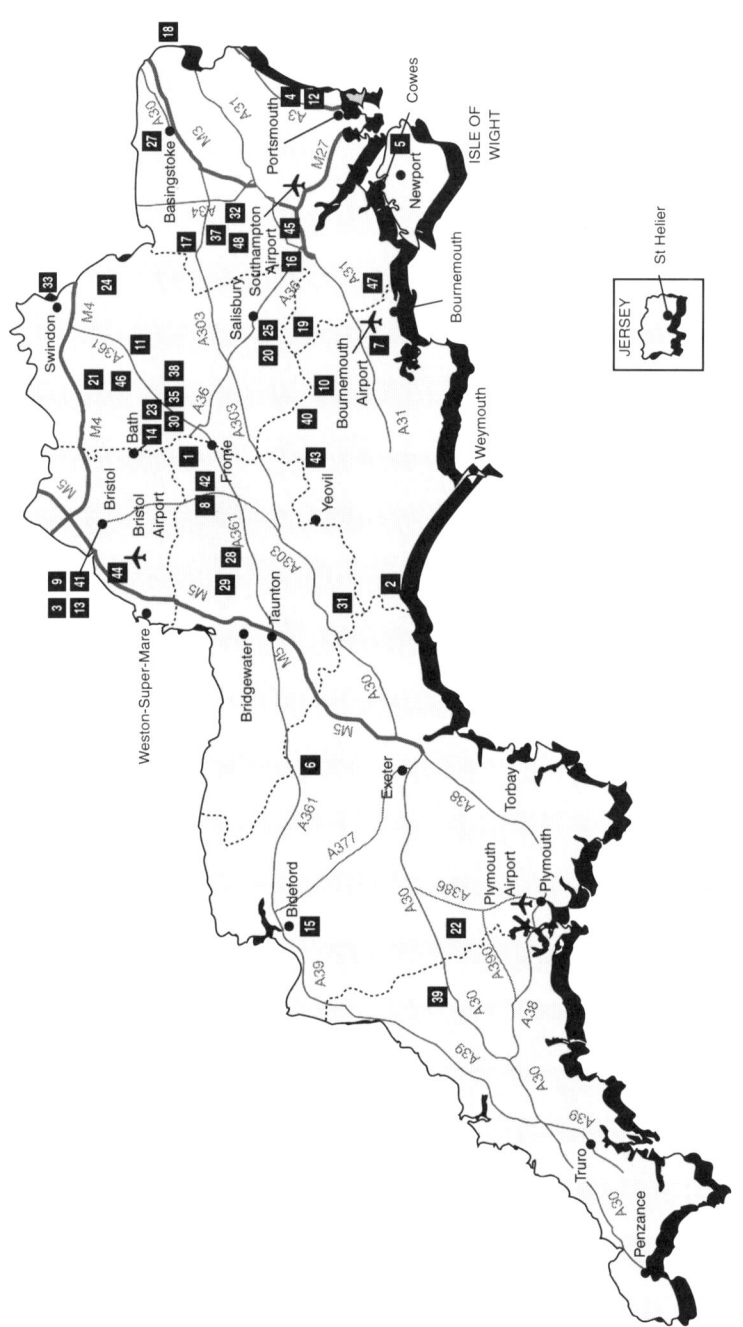

SOUTH WEST ENGLAND

(incorporating the counties of Avon, Cornwall, Devon, Dorset, Hampshire, Isle of Wight, Somerset, Wiltshire)

CENTRAL AND EASTERN ENGLAND

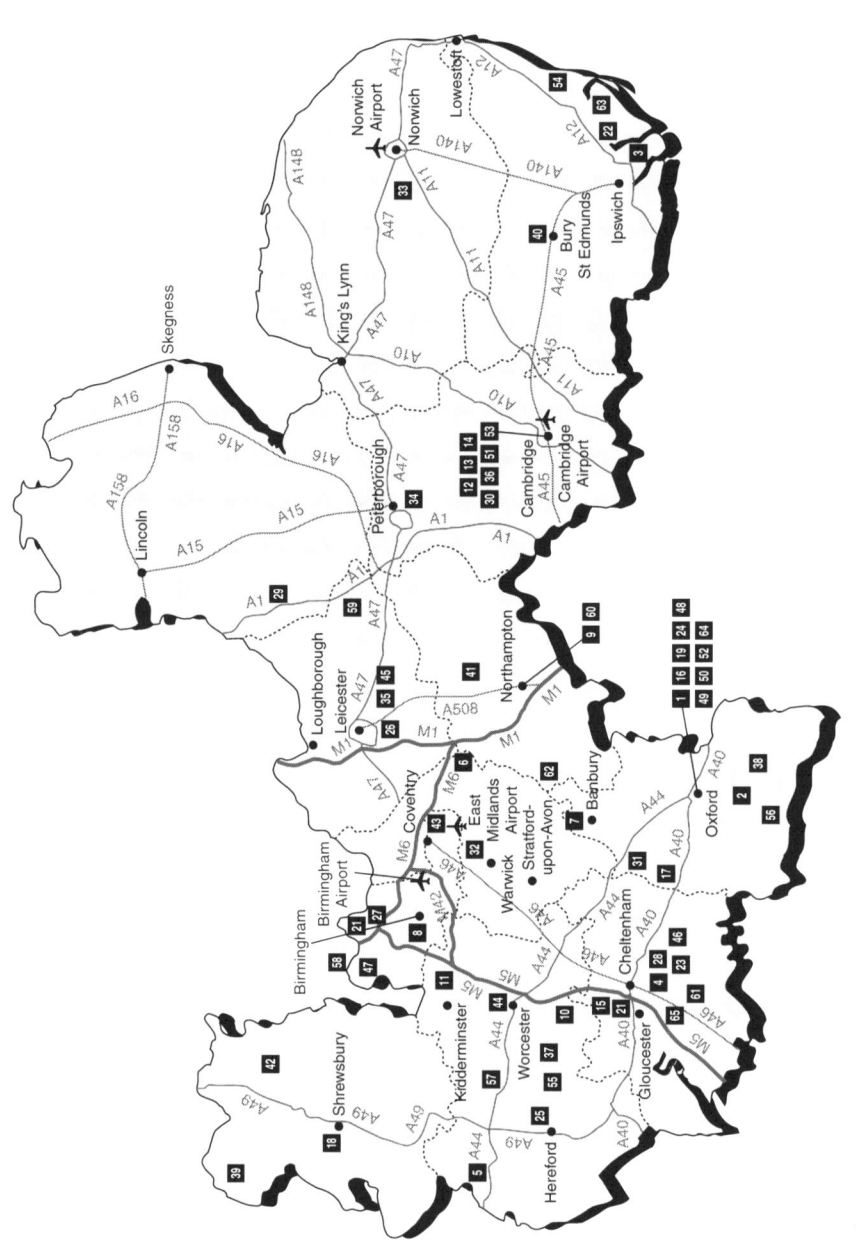

CENTRAL AND EASTERN ENGLAND

(incorporating the counties of Cambridgeshire, Gloucestershire, Hereford & Worcester, Leicestershire, Lincolnshire, West Midlands, Norfolk, Northamptonshire, Oxfordshire, Shropshire, Suffolk, Warwickshire)

HOME COUNTIES

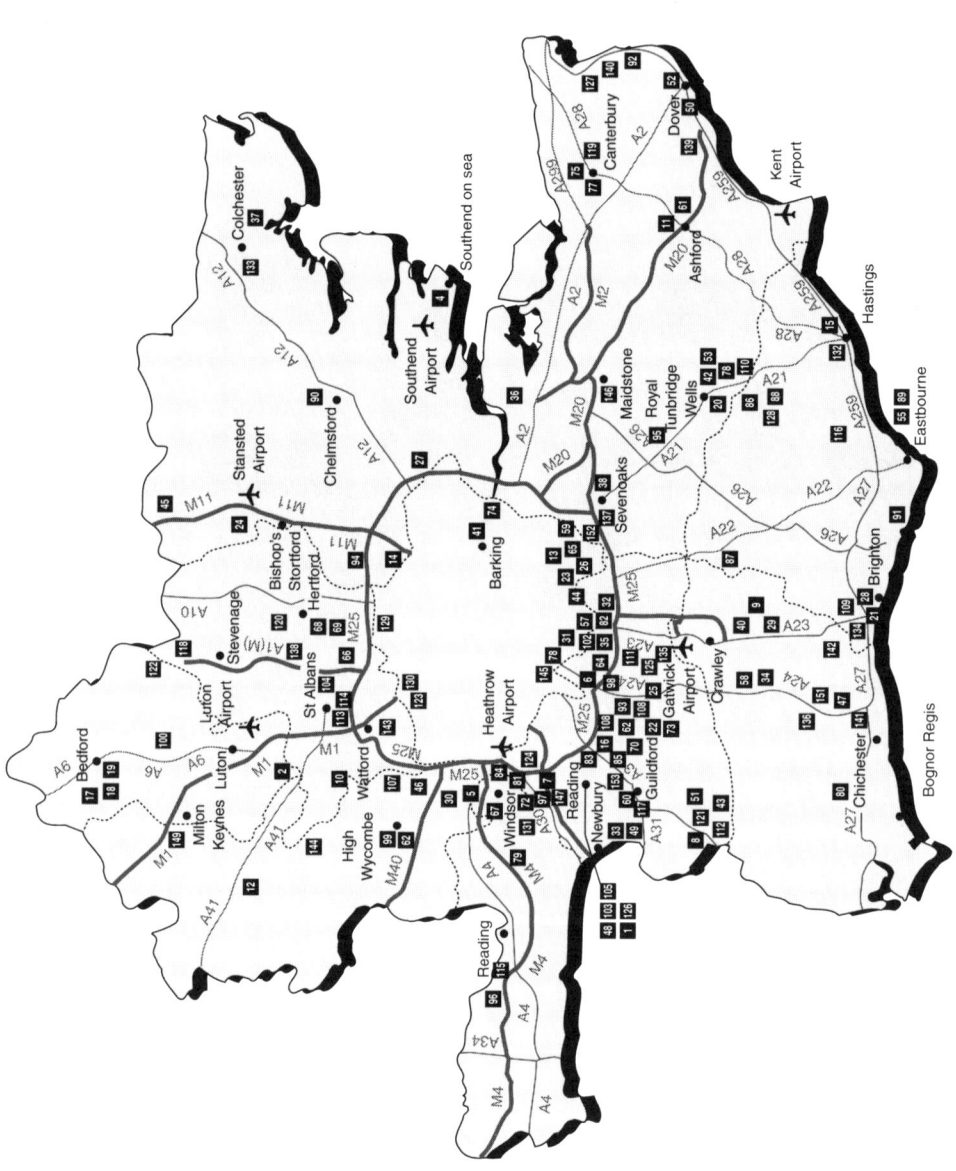

HOME COUNTIES

(incorporating the counties of Bedfordshire, Berkshire, Buckinghamshire, Essex, Hertfordshire, Kent, Middlesex, Surrey, Sussex)

LONDON

30

27 • Barnet

Finchley •

Tottenham •

• Harrow

38 48
Hampstead • 13 19 20 • Islington
33 • St Pancras St.
12 *Euston St*
7 34 City 42
44 11 • Airport Liverpool ✈ • Bow
26 *Paddington St.* Street St. River
5 9 Kensington Thames
Ealing • 2 4 Westminster 16 18 29 31
24 15 25 10 12 23 17 35 40 43 45
3 28 36 Chelsea 21 • Greenwich
Richmond • *Victoria St.* 8
6
32
River Brixton
Thames • Southwark
22 14 37
39
Wimbledon

LONDON

SCOTLAND

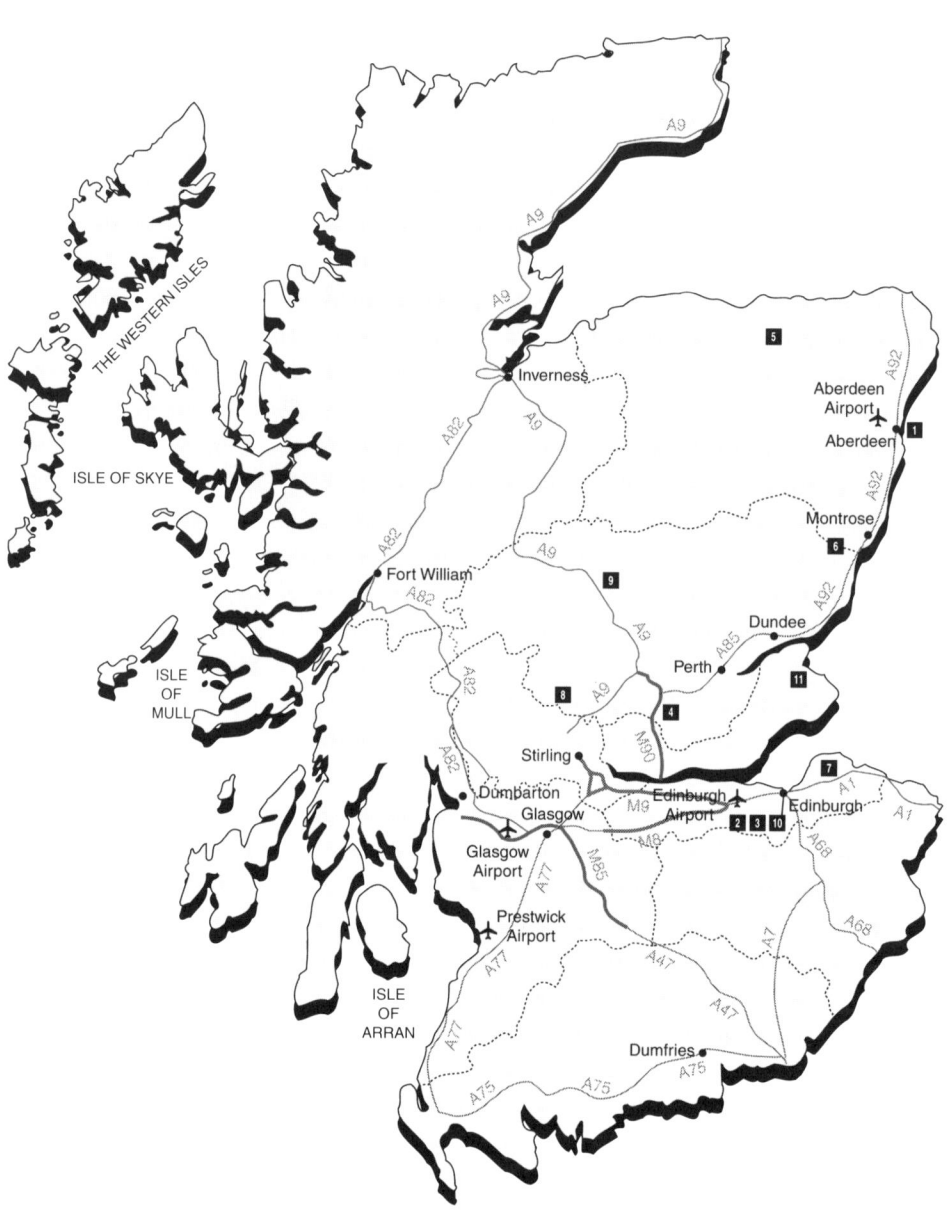

SCOTLAND

WALES

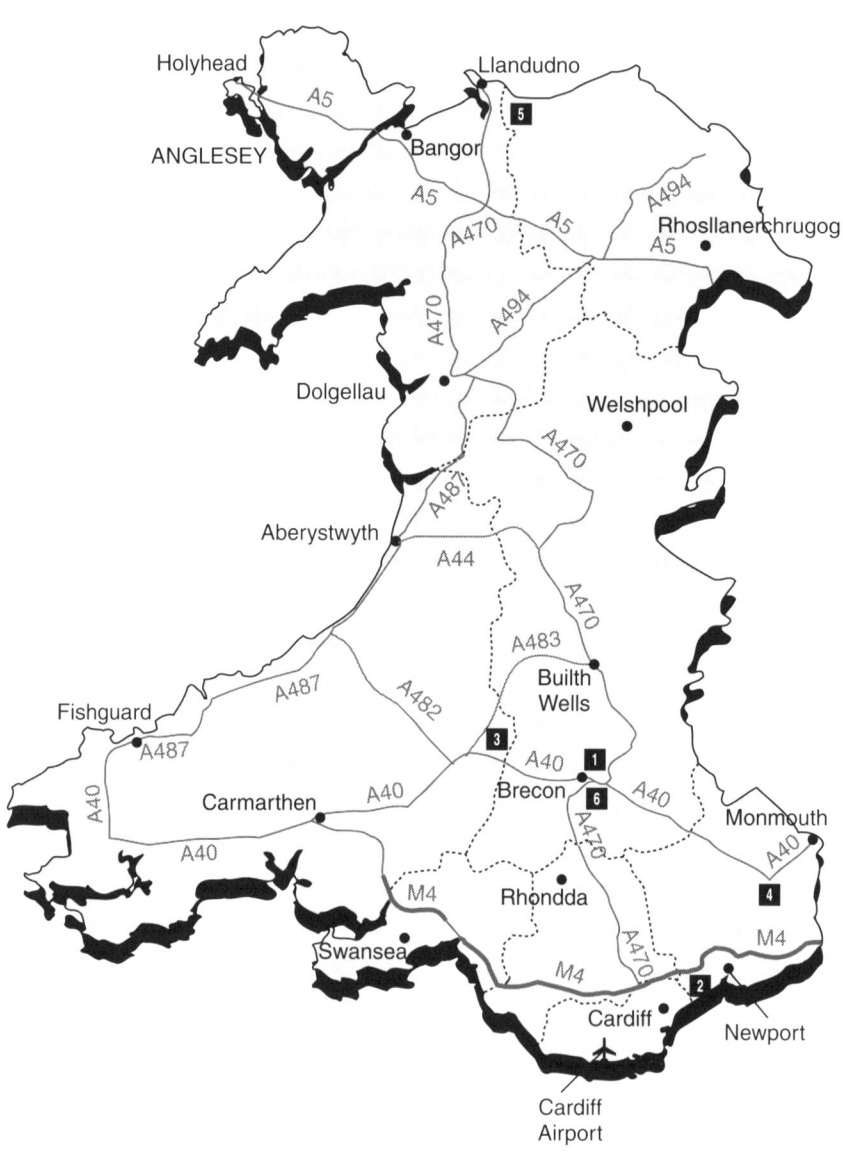

WALES

Map
no

Page
no

Badminton Junior School

Westbury-on-Trym, Bristol, Avon BS9 3BA
Tel: 0117 962 4733

Head Mrs A Lloyd CertEd (Oxon), LGSM
Founded 1858
Type Girls' independent
Religious denomination Church of England
Members of GSA and IAPS
Age range 4 – 11
Girls 75
Fees per term (day) £995 – £1,375; *(boarding)* £2,750

Average size of class: 12–18
Teacher/pupil ratio: 1:8
Curriculum: emphasis on English, maths, technology, spoken French, music, creative arts, games and activities. A balanced day enables a busy and happy atmosphere.

Entry requirements: girls spend a day in the school while we assess their all-round ability and potential. Since entry to the senior school at 11 is automatic, intellectual competence is required. Scholarships for academic, musical or artistic talents.

Badminton Junior School is separate from the senior school but uses its facilities. It has a friendly, welcoming approach with a combination of discipline and warmth which aims to develop self-confidence.

Badminton School

Westbury-on-Trym, Bristol, BS9 3BA
Tel: 0117 962 3141

Head Mr C J T Gould MA
Founded 1858
Type Girls' independent
Religious denomination Inter-denominational
Members of GSA
Age range 4 – 18
No of pupils (day, boarding, weekly boarding) 365
Junior 75 *Senior* 200 *Sixth form* 90
Fees per term (day) £995 (pre-preparatory); £1,150 – £1,375 (junior); £2,075 (senior) *(boarding)* £2,750 (junior); £3,750 (senior)

Curriculum: 18 subjects at GCSE and A level (100 per cent pass rate). A wide range of creative, musical, dramatic and sporting activities. 92 per cent go on to degree courses.

Entry requirements and procedures: entrance exam in English and maths or Common Entrance at 11, 12 and 13. Emphasis on individual potential and all-round education. Numerous scholarships at 11, 12, 13 and 16.

Outskirts of university city with excellent facilities. Emphasis on developing all-round ability, discipline and warmth, hard work and self-confidence. Mature and friendly atmosphere.

Badminton School is a registered charitable trust providing education for children.

Clifton College

32 College Road, Clifton, Bristol, Avon BS8 3JH
Tel: 0117 973 9187 Fax: 0117 946 6826

Head Mr Hugh Monro MA
Founded 1862
Type Co-educational, boarding and day
Religious denomination Church of England and Jewish House
Members of HMC
Age range 13–18 *Boarders from* 7 (in preparatory school)
No of pupils (day) 260; *(boarding)* 390
Girls 200; *Boys* 450
Sixth form 260
Fees per term (day) £2,810; *(boarding)* £4,050
Fees per annum (day) £8,430; *(boarding)* £12,150

Clifton offers a broad and flexible curriculum with an unusually large number of subjects on offer. Entry at 13+ is by Common Entrance or ability tests. Scholarships are available at 11,13 and 16 for academic, art, music and all-round abilities. The school, and the adjoining preparatory school (3 – 13), occupy a superb site in what has been described as 'the handsomest suburb in Europe'. Academic excellence, magnificent buildings, superb sporting and cultural facilities, a pioneering spirit and a high level of pastoral care in a humane and friendly atmosphere characterise the Clifton of the 1990s.

The Downs School

Wraxall, Bristol, Avon BS19 1PF
Tel: 01275 852008 Fax: 01275 855840

Head Mr J K Macpherson
Founded 1894
Type Co-educational
Religious denomination Inter-denominational
Members of IAPS
Age range 3 – 13+ *Boarders from* 8
No of pupils (day) 240 *(boarding)* 60
Girls 50 *Boys* 250
Junior all
Fees per term (day) £735 – £1,700; *(boarding)* £2,360
Fees per annum (day) £2,205 – £5,100; *(boarding)* £7,080

Curriculum: Boys and girls are prepared for scholarships and Common Entrance to many different senior schools, both day and boarding. A significant number take the 13+ entrance examination to the Bristol ex-direct grant schools. The Downs has an enviable academic record with over 100 awards to senior schools in the last 12 years. There is an emphasis on sport, music and a wide range of out-of-class activities. Pupils benefit from the beautiful country location while Bristol, with all the opportunities of a large city, is only 15 minutes away.

Entry requirements: individual assessment in English and maths and informal interview.

The Downs School is a charitable trust which exists to provide education for boys and girls of preparatory school age.

Downside School

Stratton on the Fosse, Bath, Avon BA3 4RJ
Tel: 01761 232206 Fax: 01761 233575

Head Dom Antony Sutch MA
Founded 1607
Type Roman Catholic Boys
Religious denomination Catholic
Members of HMC
Age range 10 – 18 *Boarders from* 10+
No of pupils (day) 10; *(boarding)* 320
Boys 330
Junior 29; *Senior* 150; *Sixth form* 151
Fees per term (day) £1,780 – £1,980; *(boarding)*
£2,976 – £3,710;
Fees per annum (day) £5,340 – £5,940 *(boarding)*
£8,428 – £11,130

Curriculum: complete range of GCSEs and A levels offered. Most pupils take three A levels. Additional subjects: economics and business studies, philosophy and ethics. AS levels. EFL to university standard.
Entry requirements and procedures: entry at 11 based on interview and school reports. At 13, Common Entrance, but special arrangements for those not prepared. Sixth form, entry dependent on GCSE results.
Academic and leisure facilities: IT centre, language laboratories, design, art and ceramics centre. Theatre, music school, sports hall, extensive games fields and all-weather pitches.
Scholarships: academic and music scholarships offered at 11, 13 and for sixth-form entry. Bursaries available.
Boarding facilities: small dormitories. Fifth and sixth individual study bedrooms.

Kingswood School

Lansdown, Bath, Avon BA1 5RG
Tel: 01225 734200 Fax: 01225 734205

Head Gary M Best MA
Founded 1748
Type Boarding and day
Religious denomination Methodist
Members of HMC, SHA, GBA
Age range 11 – 18 *Boarders from* 11
No of pupils (day) 202; *(boarding)* 247
Girls 185; *Boys* 264
Junior 138; *Senior* 164; *Sixth form* 147
Fees per term (day) £1,828 – £2,333; *(boarding)*
£2,931 – £3,720
Fees per annum (day) £5,454 – £6,999;
(boarding) £8,793 – £11,160

Curriculum: from 11 – 13, pupils follow a broad and balanced curriculum. At 14, pupils choose at least eight and up to 12 GCSE subjects. Sixth formers specialise in at least three subjects.
Academic, sports and leisure facilities: Kingswood has excellent facilities set in a superb 218-acre estate overlooking Bath. Recent developments include a theatre and an astro turf. There is on going development in academic and boarding areas.
Boarding facilities: the boarding houses are run by resident housestaff. Two junior houses cater for boys and girls under 14 and there are six senior houses (three girls', three boys'). All day pupils are attached to one of the boarding houses. Each pupil has a personal tutor to monitor progress and welfare.
Entry requirements: Kingswood entrance examination or Common Entrance, school reference. Sixth-form entry: six or more GCSEs at grade C or above.
Scholarships and bursaries: scholarships of up to 50 per cent are offered at 11, 13 and 16. APS places and bursaries available. Remissions for HM Forces, ministers' children.

Monkton Combe School

Bath, Avon BA2 7HG
Tel: 01225 721102 Fax: 01225 721181

Head M J Cuthbertson MA
Founded 1868
Type Independent boarding and day
Religious denomination Church of England
Members of HMC, GBA, SHA
Age range 11 – 18 *Boarders from* 11
No of pupils (day) 48; *(boarding)* 267
Girls 99; *Boys* 221
Sixth form 133
Fees per term (day) £2,195 – £2,695; *(boarding)*
£3,215 – £3,895

Curriculum: a broad range of subjects is offered to the end of the third form. The two years to GCSE are made up of a core of subjects with options to allow pupils to specialise where appropriate. Nineteen subjects are offered at A level and six at AS.

Entry requirements: candidates at age 11 by one-hour tests in English and mathematics, a reasoning test, a school reference and a brief informal interview; candidates at age 13 from preparatory schools by Common Entrance exam; those entering the sixth form require five GCSEs at grade C or above. Scholarships, bursaries and Government Assisted Places are available at all levels.

Facilities: the school is in an incomparable setting, overlooking the Midford and Avon valleys. Recent developments have included two new houses for girls, a chaplaincy centre, the refurbishment of the boys' houses and an astro-turf. Further developments are planned.

Boarding: there are five boys' houses, each under the personal care of a housemaster, and two girls' houses and a junior house for 11 and 12 year olds with married couples as houseparents.

Prior Park College

Bath, Avon BA2 5AH
Tel: 01225 835353 Fax: 01225 835753

Head Mr J W R Goulding MA
Founded 1830
Type Independent
Religious denomination Roman Catholic
Age range 11 – 18 *Boarders from* 13
No of pupils (day) 346; *(boarding)* 155
Girls 209; *Boys* 293
Junior 95; *Senior* 361; *Sixth form* 140
Fees per term (day) £1,778 – £1,857; *(boarding)*
£3,358
Fees per annum (day) £5,334 – £5,571;
(boarding) £10,074

Set in magnificent buildings in the 18th-century estate of Ralph Allen, builder of Georgian Bath, Prior Park offers a wonderful educational opportunity for 450 boarding and day boys and girls aged 11 – 18. Wide-ranging GCSE and A level programmes include all mainstream subjects, and many more; and academic pursuits are enhanced by a richly conceived wider curriculum. The performing and expressive arts are especially strong. Recent buildings include a new music school and recording studio; theatre and sixth-form centre; a design and information technology centre; a library and resources centre; an astro-turf hockey surface and the provision of additional sporting facilities. House-based pastoral care is a central feature of Prior Park: all students are personally supported by a tutor, and the ethos of the school is significantly informed by its Catholic inheritance and its clear yet sensitive emphasis on Christian expectations.

The Royal School, Bath

Lansdown Road, Bath, Avon BA1 5SZ
Tel: 01225 313877 Fax: 01225 420338

Head Mrs Emma McKendrick BA
Founded 1864
Type Girls' independent boarding and day
Religious denomination Church of England
Members of GSA, GBGSA
Age range 2½ – 18 *Boarders from* 7
No of pupils (day) 120; *(boarding)* 225
Girls 345
Junior 70; *Senior* 200; *Sixth form* 80
Fees per term (day) £927 – £1,962; *(boarding)* £3,086 – £3,667
Fees per annum (day) £2,781 – £5,886; *(boarding)* £9,258 – £11,001

Curriculum: full commitment to the National Curriculum with emphasis on the acquisition of the basic skills from the earliest stage. Fully developed programme of modern languages and technology from the age of seven. Academic curiosity and high standards valued. A full range of activities at weekends and after school.

Entry requirements: scholarship examinations, Common Entrance, own assessment and interview days.
Examinations offered: National Curriculum tests, GCSE, A and AS levels, GNVQ Business, LAMDA (drama), Associated Board of Music.
Academic and leisure facilities: modern, light and airy classrooms in a traditional setting on the outskirts of Bath. Refurbished technology area. New careers centre, swimming pool, gymnasium, large playing fields, music centre, chapel. Scholarships awarded at 11+, 13+, 16+. Scholarships awarded for academic potential, ability in sport, gym, dance, music, drama. Boarding facilities have been recently upgraded. Students share smaller bedrooms. There is a separate junior house and sixth-form centre which has individual and shared study bedrooms (two people).

St Ursula's High School

Brecon Road, Westbury-on-Trym, Bristol, Avon BS9 4DT
Tel: 0117 962 2616

Head Mrs M A Macnaughton
Founded 1896
Type Lay Catholic day school
Religious denomination Roman Catholic, open to all
Age range 3 – 16
No of pupils (day) 380
Girls 300; *Boys* 80
Junior 155; *Senior* 190; *Sixth form* 35
Fees per annum (day) £1125 – £3,450

In partnership with parents, we offer a sound academic education, in a happy atmosphere based upon the Christian values of care and respect for the individual pupil.

We hope to educate our pupils with an understanding that it is their contribution to society which will make them happy and fulfilled individuals.

St Ursula's High School has adopted the National Curriculum.

In addition there is a wide variety of extra-curricular activities and particularly flourishing music and drama departments. The house system ensures that all pupils have the opportunity to participate in all school activities and helps the older pupils to develop leadership and motivation skills. Most go on to further education, the majority to university. Careers guidance and advice are given from Year 9 upwards. Boys will enter the school from September 1996.

Although St Ursula's High School is an independent lay Catholic day school the majority of our pupils are not Catholic and we welcome people from all faiths.

Sidcot School

Winscombe, Avon BS25 1PD
Tel: 01934 843102 Fax: 01934 844181

Head Christopher Greenfield MA, MEd
Founded 1699
Type Co-educational day and boarding
Religious denomination Quaker (Society of Friends)
Members of SHMIS, SHA
Age range 9 – 18 *Boarders from* 9
No of pupils (day) 208; *(boarding)* 198
Girls 185; *Boys* 224
Junior 57; *Senior* 233; *Sixth form* 116
Fees per term (day) £1,410 – £1,906; *(boarding)* £3,187
Fees per annum (day) £4,230 – £5,718; *(boarding)* £9,561

Sidcot offers a liberal education, which embraces the National Curriculum and much more. Sidcot looks for average and above in ability. Common Entrance or school's own test.

Sidcot offers music and drama exams, GCSE in usual subjects, GNVQ (Intermediate and Advanced), and A and AS levels in 20 subjects.

Sidcot is now one of the best-equipped schools in the country. New library, sports centre (including swimming pool), horse riding area and science block built in the last three years. New refectory just completed.

Scholarships of up to 50 per cent are offered at 13 and 16.

Between 25 and 50 boarders in each of five houses, each with two to five residential staff.

Bedford High School

Bromham Road, Bedford, Bedfordshire MK40 2BS
Tel: 01234 360221 Fax: 01234 353552

Head Mrs B E Stanley BA
Founded 1882
Type Girls' independent
Religious denomination Non-denominational
Members of GSA
Age range 7 – 18 *Boarders from* 8 – 18
No of pupils (day) 891; *(boarding)* 69
Junior 182; *Senior* 583; *Sixth form* 196
Fees per term (day) £1,158 – £1,583; *(boarding)* £2,863
Fees per annum (day) £3,474 – £4,749; *(boarding)* £8,589

Bedford High School combines excellent academic standards with courses reflecting the latest educational developments. The school is centrally sited in Bedford, convenient for all London airports. Weekly and full boarding are offered in two attractive houses which have recently been refurbished and extended.

The junior school provides an ideal foundation for life at the high school, offering a wide range of subjects beyond the requirements of the National Curriculum. We offer 23 subjects at GCSE, 26 at A level, some AS levels, over 20 sports options and tuition in most musical instruments.

Entrance at all ages is by own examination or GCSE results, report and interview.

Careers guidance begins at 13 and girls receive counselling throughout all major decision-making stages. In the sixth form great care is taken in the preparation of each student's study programme and 90 per cent of students go to university or college, with a number of Oxbridge entrants each year.

Bedford Modern School

Manton Lane, Bedford, Bedfordshire MK41 7NT
Tel: 01234 364331 Fax: 01234 270951

Head Mr P J Squire MA
Type Independent
Religious denomination Non-denominational
Members of HMC, IAPS (Junior)
Age range 7 – 18 *Boarders from* 7
No of pupils (day) 1,085; *(boarding)* 44
Boys 1085
Junior 196; *Senior* 688; *Sixth form* 250
Fees per term (day) £1,033 – £1,497; *(boarding)* £2,416 – £2,880
Fees per annum (day) £3,099 – £4,491; *(boarding)* £7,248 – £8,640

Bedford Modern School is an independent HMC school founded in 1764 and providing continuous education for boys aged 7 - 18+. Boarding or day, the school has first class up-to-date facilities and achieves excellent academic standards. It offers a wide range of GCSE and A level opportunities and the majority of students proceed to higher education. Music, art and drama are strong, some 500 boys learning an instrument. A large extension to the music school was opened in September 1994, and work will be completed on a new sixth-form centre and extra classrooms in September 1996.

All students take part in numerous extra-curricular activities (both sporting and recreational), and apart from the usual inter-school fixtures, many compete at local and national levels.

A great deal of time is spent on pastoral care and our aim is to offer all students the opportunity to fully develop their talents, interests and potential.

We are always delighted to show families around the school.

Bedford School

Burnaby Road, Bedford, Bedfordshire MK40 2TU
Tel: 01234 340444 Fax: 01234 340050

Head Dr I P Evans
Founded 1552
Type Boys' independent boarding and day
Religious denomination Church of England
Members of HMC, IAPS
Age range 7 – 18 *Boarders from* 7 – 18
No of pupils (day) 853; *(boarding)* 247
Boys 1,100
Junior 392; *Senior* 708; *Sixth form*
286
Fees per term (day) £2,335; *(boarding)* £3,715
Fees per annum (day) £7,005; *(boarding)*
£11,145

Situated in a busy market town between the A1
and M1 and near three international airports,
the school's unique mixture means day boys
and boarders are integrated into a well-knit
community.

The curriculum discourages premature
specialisation, placing a strong emphasis on
science and languages and offering a broad
range of options at all levels. Almost all pupils
go on to university.

Pastoral supervision, organised in small tutor
groups, promotes the development of personal
responsibility and responsiveness to others.
Liaison with parents is a priority.

Facilities include first-class science
laboratories and IT, technology and language
suites, a theatre, heated swimming pool,
astro-turf and field study centre. Proud of their
all-round sporting excellence, pupils regularly
win regional and national titles. Music and
drama are notably strong.

Newly modernised senior and junior boarding
accommodation ensures that privacy is
progressively enhanced as pupils mature.

Entry is by Common Entrance or examination
and interview at various ages. General financial
assistance is available in the form of
scholarships, bursaries and GAPs.

Dean Grange Preparatory School

Upper Dean, Huntingdon, Cambridgeshire PE18 0LT (Located on
Northamptonshire/Bedfordshire/Cambridgeshire border)
Tel and fax: 01234 708243

Head David Roach BSc, DipEd
Founded 1947
Type Co-educational preparatory day and
boarding
Religious denomination Inter-denominational
Age range 4 – 11 (Nursery from 2½ – 4)
Girls 46; *Boys* 44
Fees per annum (day) £2,220 – £2,880;
(boarding) £5,520 – £6,180

Curriculum: English, maths, science, French,
history, geography, computer studies, art and
craft, technology, drama, music, games and
scripture. Pupils are prepared for entrance
examinations from 7+ to 11+ years. The usual
range of seasonal sports is played, and there is
a comprehensive inter-school fixture list. The
special needs unit caters for specific learning
difficulties, and also provides remedial
assistance. Extra-curricular activities include
horse-riding, ballet, Cubs, Brownies, Crusaders,
swimming and individual tuition in a variety
of musical instruments.

Entry requirements: interview, and the child will
be informally assessed while spending a day in
the school with his prospective class.

The Abbey School

17 Kendrick Road, Reading, Berkshire RG1 5DZ
Tel: 01734 872256

Head Miss B C L Sheldon BA, Cert Ed, ACE
Founded 1887
Type Girls' independent day
Religious denomination Church of England
Members of GSA, GBGSA
Age range 4 – 18
No of pupils (day) 1,010
Girls 1,009; *Boys* 1
Junior 300; *Senior* 525; *Sixth form* 185
Fees per term (day) £1,100 – £1,380
Fees per annum (day) £3,300 – £4,140

The Abbey School, founded in 1887, provides a broad curriculum for academically able girls. The course includes the three separate sciences, computer studies, Latin and Greek, three modern languages and the humanities. The preparatory department takes pupils from four years. The senior school includes a large sixth-form. All sixth formers (who have their own sixth form centre with tutorial rooms, common rooms and separate dining facilities) study for Advanced level. Almost all proceed to university, many to Oxford or Cambridge, or to art or music colleges. Sixth form applicants are welcome.

The school combines traditional academic standards with modern facilities. There are ten science laboratories, fine libraries, seven computer rooms, a drama studio, specialist music block, and a heated indoor swimming pool. Sport, music and drama flourish.

Pupils travel from throughout Berkshire and from Oxfordshire and Hampshire. Entrance scholarships and Assisted Places may be offered after examination and interview.

Bearwood College

Wokingham, Berkshire RG41 5BG
Tel: 01734 786915 Fax: 01734 773186

Head R J Belcher BSc, PhD, CBiol, MBiol
Founded 1827
Type Independent co-educational day and boarding
Religious denomination Church of England
Members of GBA, SHMIS, ISIS
Age range 11 – 18 *Boarders from* 11
No of pupils (day) 102; *(boarding)* 116
Total 218
Fees per term (day) £1,665 – £1,850; *(boarding)* £3,015 – £3,350
Fees per annum (day) £4,995 – £5,550; *(boarding)* £9,045 – £10,050

Set in magnificent country estate. Good communications network. Local transport support provided. Extensive range of GCSE and A level subjects. CReSTeD accredited Special Learning Support Unit. Enviable sporting and extra-curricular facilities include golf, canoeing, riding, swimming and sailing. Bearwood Outdoor Activities Club and Combined Cadet Force provide additional excitement and challenge. Proven excellence in creative and performing arts. State-of-the-art Bearwood theatre and music school. Separate junior boys' house has full use of all main school facilities. Automatic entry from junior house to senior house at 13. Strong social, pastoral and tutorial welfare support team. Relatively small fully integrated school with generous staff/pupil ratio ensures real focus on structured individual development in a caring family environment, which enables a boy or girl to reach his or her full potential. Wide range of open/closed scholarships and discretionary bursaries available. Full details from the headmaster.

Cheam Hawtreys

Cheam School, Headley, Newbury, Berkshire RG19 8LD
Tel: 01635 268242 Fax: 01635 269345

Head C C Evers
Founded 1645
Type Preparatory
Religious denomination Anglican
Age range 7 – 13 *Boarders from* 8
No of pupils (day) 41; *(boarding)* 114
Boys 155
Fees per term (day) £2,130; *(boarding)* £3,015
Fees per annum (day) £6,390; *(boarding)* £9,045

In September 1994 Cheam joined forces with Hawtreys to create a school with a strong emphasis on boarding. Boys move on to the major public schools: Eton, Harrow and Radley in particular.

Young boarders begin their time in a separate junior house run on family lines.

Recently a major refurbishment of the boarding facilities has taken place. Social Services inspectors said that systems and methods represented 'the best of modern boarding practice'.

Classes never exceed 16 and a three-tier streaming system enables boys to be taught to their individual abilities.

Out-of-school activities abound and team games include rugby, football, cricket and hockey.

There is a sophisticated IT department, a design centre, and a sports hall.

Future plans include the building of a new science block.

Easy access to M3 and M4 and one hour from Heathrow.

Douai School

Upper Woolhampton, Reading, Berkshire RG7 5TH
Tel: 01734 715200 Fax: 01734 715241

Head Dom Edmund Power OSB, BA, BD, PhD
Founded 1615
Type Co-educational senior school
Religious denomination Catholic and Christians of other denominations
Members of HMC
Age range 10 – 18 *Boarders from* 10
No of pupils (day) 88; *(boarding)* 120
Girls 28 *Boys* 190
Junior 41; *Senior* 107; *Sixth form* 60
Fees per term (day) £1,845 – £2,260; *(boarding)* full £2,815 – £3,515; weekly £2,715 – £3,415
Fees per annum (day) £5,535 – £6,780; *(boarding)* full £8,445 – £10,545; weekly £8,145 – £10,245

Founded in Paris in 1615 by English Benedictine monks, the school is set in 150 acres of glorious Berkshire countryside, yet within minutes of the M4 and the towns of Reading, Newbury and Basingstoke. Central London and Gatwick are one hour away and Heathrow 45 minutes. The school is Roman Catholic in foundation, but ecumenical in spirit. Similarly, most pupils currently board, but we have a growing number of day pupils. The school became co-educational in 1993.

The school is small enough to have a family atmosphere and it maintains a tradition of good order and sound discipline. In partnership with parents the expressed aims of Douai are: to develop the academic potential of each pupil successfully and enjoyably; to foster mature, caring behaviour and high standards; to develop talents and skills whether physical, artistic, technical or social; to nurture in each young person the growth of religious faith and spiritual understanding.

Downe House

Cold Ash, Thatcham, Berkshire RG18 9JJ
Tel: 01635 200286 Fax: 01635 202026

Head Miss S R Cameron BA
Founded 1907
Type Girls' independent boarding and day
Religious denomination Church of England
Members of GSA, BSA, ISIS, ISJC, ISBA
Age range 11 – 18 *Boarders from* 11
No of pupils (day) 30; *(boarding)* 584
Girls 618
Junior 69; *Senior* 375; *Sixth form* 170
Fees per term (day) £3,000; *(boarding)* £4,140
Fees per annum (day) £9,000 *(boarding)* £12,420

Curriculum: a wide selection of subjects is available at both GCSE and A level. Girls are also prepared for university entrance.
Entry requirements and procedures: by Common Entrance and assessment. Five passes at grade C or above for an A level course. Scholarships at 11+, 12+, 13+ and sixth form.

The school is situated only five miles from Newbury with easy access to the motorway network, London and Heathrow Airport. The school has an excellent academic record with nearly all pupils going on to university.
Academic and leisure facilities: new sixth form complex with study bedrooms, science block and computer centre. Indoor swimming pool. One term spent in France.

Haileybury Junior School

Imperial Road, Windsor, Berkshire SL4 3RS
Tel: 01753 866330 Fax: 01753 832819

Head B J Hare
Founded 1922
Type Boys' preparatory
Religious denomination Church of England
Members of IAPS
Age range 7 – 13 *Boarders from* 7 – 13
No of pupils (day) 125 *(boarding)* 46
Boys 164
Fees per term (day) £2,050; *(boarding)* £2,625[*]
([*]September 1995)

Boys are prepared through the normal curriculum for scholarship and Common Entrance examinations to Haileybury and other senior independent schools. The curriculum is designed to encourage breadth of thinking as well as depth of study and ample opportunity exists for practical work in sciences and the arts.

Since September 1991, the school has had a special learning unit where boys experiencing problems associated with dyslexia have lessons for two hours per day, in addition to the benefits of other school curriculum and leisure activities.
Entry requirements: entry is by a small test, an interview at the school together with reports from previous schools or other relevant sources.

Hurst Lodge School

Charters Road, Sunningdale, Berkshire SL5 9QG
Tel: 01344 22154 Fax: 01344 22154

Head Mrs Anthea M Smit
Founded 1941
Type Independent
Religious denomination Non-denominational
Members of ISAI, CReSTeD
Age range 2½ – 18 *Boarders from* 6
No of pupils (day) 150; *(boarding)* 40
Girls 170; *Boys* 20
Junior 78; *Senior* 90; *Sixth form* 22
Fees per term (day) £600 – £1,550 (junior); £1,950 (senior); *(boarding)* £3,300
Fees per annum (day) £1,800 – £4,650 (junior); £5,850 (senior); *(boarding)* £9,900

Hurst Lodge is a small friendly school situated in Sunningdale, 50 minutes from central London, half an hour from Heathrow and a few minutes from Sunningdale mainline station. There is a weekly bus service to and from London.

We take day, weekly and full boarders. All students are taught in small classes by enthusiastic staff. GCSE and A level subjects are taught on a tutorial basis with between three and eight students per class. The boarding house with its 40 residents is run like an extended family.

Students receive a broad general education. In addition to all the academic subjects the school has special facilities for studying dance, drama, music, art and media studies. Netball, tennis, swimming and riding are available.

Entry is usually by examination and interview. In some cases a letter of recommendation from the present school is sufficient.

There are academic, art, dance, music and drama scholarships on offer.

The school has an excellent dyslexia department.

Lambrook

Winkfield Row, Bracknell, Berkshire RG42 6LU
Tel: 01344 882717 Fax: 01344 891114

Head Mr R F Badham-Thornhill
Founded 1860
Type Boys' preparatory boarding and day school and pre-preparatory school for boys and girls
Religious denomination Church of England
Members of IAPS
Age range 4 – 13 *Boarders from* 7
No of pupils (day) 63; *(boarding)* 55
Girls 6; *Boys* 112
Fees per term (day) Preparatory £1,495 – £2,030; pre-preparatory £1,055 – £1,260; *(boarding)* Preparatory £2,030 – £2,850
Fees per annum (day) Preparatory £4,485 – £6,090; pre-preparatory £3,165 – £3,780; *(boarding)* Preparatory £6,090 – £8,550

The school is situated in 70 acres of magnificent grounds and is very accessible from the M3, M4, M40 and Heathrow. A wide-ranging curriculum embraces the requirements of

Common Entrance and scholarship exams to major public schools.

Lambrook has a fine record of sporting achievement, and offers a great variety of extra-curricular activities from golf to a thriving magic circle.

The facilities of the school are excellent, the most recent being the sports hall, completed in November 1992. The children are educated in the widest sense. Scholarships and bursaries are available.

Licensed Victuallers' School

London Road, Ascot, Berkshire SL5 8DR
Tel: 01344 882770 Fax: 01344 890648

Head Mrs P M Cowley BA (Hons)
Founded 1803
Type Co-educational day and boarding
Religious denomination Christian
Members of ISAI, ISIS, BSA
Age range 4+ – 18 *Boarders from* Year 3 onwards
No of pupils (day) 456; *(boarding)* 217
Girls 256; *Boys* 417
Junior 186; *Senior* 487; *Sixth form* 70
Fees per term (day) £972 – £1,790; *(boarding)* £2,718 – £3,190
Fees per annum (day) £2,916 – £5,370; *(boarding)* £8,154 – £9,570

Curriculum: courses meeting National Curriculum requirements are taught from 5 to 16, with a wide range of GCSE and A level options, with GNVQs introduced for sixth form. All courses from age 11 are setted by ability.

The curriculum is supported by excellent facilities opened in 1989 when the school relocated to Ascot. These include theatre/drama/music centre, sports complex, art and technology centre, science laboratories, and classrooms supported by a large number of computers.

The school is set in 26 acres of landscaped grounds and offers day boarding and weekly boarding to assist busy families.

Entry requirements: school reports and interviews.

Five open scholarships and one for Society members available for entry at Year 7. There are sixth form scholarships available.

The Society of Licensed Victuallers, which is a registered charity, has always provided education for both boys and girls.

Luckley-Oakfield School

Luckley Road, Wokingham, Berkshire RG11 3EU
Tel: 01734 784175 Fax: 01734 770305

Head Richard C Blake MA (Oxon), MPhil (Soton)
Founded 1918
Type Girls' independent day/boarding
Religious denomination Church of England
Members of GSA, GBGSA, BSA
Age range 11 – 18 *Boarders from* 11
No of pupils (day) 176; *(boarding)* 74
Girls 250
Sixth form 54
Fees per term (day) £1,643; *(boarding)* £2,650
Fees per annum (day) £4,929; *(boarding)* £7,950

Curriculum and examinations: National Curriculum is followed to GCSE with Double Award Modular Science, French and German (Spanish available). Eighteen A levels plus AS, RSA and GNVQ Advanced, ESL.
Entry: by school's own examination and interview mainly at 11, 12 or 13.
Academic and leisure facilities: sixth-form residential block, modern science labs, new IT room, resource centre, studio, music centre,

technology room. Covered swimming pool, sports hall, tennis courts and games field. Extended day option to 5.30pm.
Scholarships: academic awards at 11 and 16. Music scholarship offered.
Boarding facilities: junior and senior boarding houses in main building in addition to separate sixth-form accommodation. High standard of pastoral care. Pleasant setting on edge of town. Easy links to M3, M4 and Heathrow.

Marist Convent Senior School

Sunninghill, Ascot, Berkshire SL5 7PS
Tel: 01344 24291 Fax: 01344 874963

Head Sister M Gaffney
Founded 1870
Type Girls' Roman Catholic day
Religious denomination Roman Catholic
Age range 11 – 18
No of pupils (day) 375
Girls 375
Senior 375; *Sixth form* 70
Fees per term (day) £1,300
Fees per annum (day) £3,900

The school was founded in 1870 and is under the care of the Marist Sisters.
Curriculum: all National Curriculum subjects are offered to GCSE with separate science, Latin, German and Spanish. Twenty-two subjects are offered to A and AS level. There is a wide range of extra-curricular activities.
Entry: at 11+ entry is by written examination or by reports and interview at other levels.
Examinations: school examinations are held once a year. Pupils are also prepared for Key Stage 3, GCSE, RSA, A and AS levels, as well as music and speech examinations.
Facilities: the school stands in its own parkland with hockey pitches and athletics tracks, floodlit all-weather tennis and netball courts and heated indoor swimming pool. There is a separate music block and a well-equipped information technology centre. A new science block opened in 1992 and a suite of sixth-form common rooms opened in 1994.

Pangbourne College

Pangbourne, Berkshire RG8 8LA
Tel: 01734 842101 Fax: 01734 845443

Head A B E Hudson MA, DipEd
Founded 1917
Type Independent
Religious denomination Church of England
Members of HMC, SHMIS, GBSA
Age range 11 – 18 *Boarders from* 11
No of pupils (day) 95; *(boarding)* 305
Junior 45; *Senior* (Middle school) 235; *Sixth form* 120
Fees per term (day) £2,640; *(boarding)* £3,770
Fees per annum (day) £7,920; *(boarding)* £11,310

Curriculum: core and options from 17 subjects to GCSE, 20 A level choices and a strong special needs department. Eighty-five per cent of sixth formers go on to degree courses.

Entry: at 11+ by own examination and interview; at 13+ by Common Entrance; to sixth form by report, interview and GCSE results. There are generous academic scholarships and also music, art, technology and all-round awards.

The beautiful 230-acre rural estate contains six boarding houses, separate junior school and 'Cottage' accommodation for girls. Facilities include the new purpose-built library, language, geography and design technology departments and a sixth form centre. The college is renowned for its lively music and drama and happy atmosphere.
Among the many sports in an unusually strong fixture list, it is especially successful in rugby, hockey, rowing, sailing and judo. It has a strong Combined Cadet Force. The college is easily accessible by road (M4), rail and air (Heathrow).

Papplewick

Windsor Road, Ascot, Berkshire SL5 7LH
Tel: 01344 21488 Fax: 01344 874639

Head Mr Llewellyn
Founded 1947
Type Boys' preparatory
Religious denomination Christian
Members of IAPS
Age range 7 – 13 *Boarders from* 7
No of pupils (day) 70; *(boarding)* 115
Boys 185
Fees per term (day) £2,392; *(boarding)* £3,115

Average size of class: 12
Teacher/pupil ratio: 1:8
Curriculum: all main subjects are studied. Computing is taught throughout the school as are art, design and technology. Steady work towards scholarships and Common Entrance passes is balanced with music, PE and a wide range of competitive sports and games.

Entry requirements and procedures: parental choice and interview followed by placing test. It is essential to register boys well in advance of their sixth birthday.

Papplewick enjoys a spacious rural location on the edge of Windsor Great Park. Convenient links with M4, M3, M25, Heathrow and Gatwick. The quality of care and the dedication of staff are outstanding and remain Papplewick's special hallmark.

Queen Anne's School

6 Henley Road, Caversham, Reading, Berkshire RG4 0DX
Tel: 01734 471582 Fax: 01734 461498

Head Mrs D A Forbes MA
Founded 1894
Type Girls' independent
Religious denomination Church of England
Members of GSA, GBGSA
Age range 11 – 18 *Boarders from* 11
No of pupils (day) 150 *(boarding)* 200
Girls 350
Senior 260; *Sixth form* 90
Fees per term (day) £2,460; *(boarding)* £3,750
Fees per annum (day) £7,380; *(boarding)* £11,250

The school is geographically well placed within a few minutes' journey of Reading from where there is a frequent and fast train service to London and links with Heathrow and Gatwick Airports. Girls enter the school by means of the 11+, 12+ or 13+ Common Entrance examinations or the school's own foundation scholarship examination which offers scholarships of up to full tuition fees.

There is a large sixth form operating on a tutorial system with 90 per cent of girls gaining university entrance. The school buildings include modern science laboratories, a new library, modern languages building and performing arts centre.

Music is a very important part of school life and there is a music scholarship offered each year equivalent to half the fees. There are junior and senior orchestras and choirs. The sports facilities include 24 tennis courts, nine lacrosse pitches, three squash courts, a gymnasium and an indoor heated swimming pool.

Open days are held in the autumn and spring.

Reading Blue Coat School

Holme Park, Sonning-on-Thames, Reading, Berkshire RG4 6SU
Tel: 01734 441005 Fax: 01734 442690

Head Rev A C E Sanders MA (Oxon), MEd
Founded 1646
Type Independent HMC, co-educational sixth form
Religious denomination Church of England
Age range 11 – 18 *Boarders from* 11
No of pupils (day) 500; *(boarding)* 50
Sixth form 170
Fees per term (day) £1,750; *(boarding)* full £3,190; weekly £3,090
Fees per annum (day) £5,250; *(boarding)* full £9,570; weekly £9,270

Curriculum: broad foundation in first and second years including music, art, technology and computer science. GCSE courses in fourth and fifth years. Wide range of A levels leading to university entrance.
Entry requirements and procedures: examinations and interviews for 11+ and 13+.

Entry by grades and interviews for girls and boys wishing to join sixth form. Contact the school for further details and to arrange a visit.
Examinations offered: GCSE and A level.
Academic facilities: full science laboratories, computer and information technology centres, design and technology workshops, music school, art studies, new library.
Leisure facilities: riverside grounds with excellent sports facilities. Extensive activities programme including Combined Cadet Force, adventure training, drama, music.
Scholarships: scholarships and bursaries are provided on merit and need.
Boarding facilities: the boarding house offers full and weekly boarding and boarders still wear the traditional Blue Coats on special occasions.

In 1996 the school celebrates the 350th year of its foundation.

St George's School, Ascot

Ascot, Berkshire SL5 7DZ
Tel: 01344 20273 Fax: 01344 874213

Head Mrs A M Griggs
Founded 1877
Type Girls' independent
Religious denomination Church of England
Age range 11 – 18 *Boarders from* 11
No of pupils (day) 115; *(boarding)* 180
Girls 295
Senior 215; *Sixth form* 80
Fees per term (day) £2,275; *(boarding)* £3,875
Fees per annum (day) £6,825; *(boarding)* £11,625

St George's School, Ascot, is a renowned independent school tucked away in the greenery of Ascot; a winner for young ladies aged 11 – 18.

It lies in the 'golden triangle' formed by the motorways M3, M4 and M25, with easy access to Heathrow and Gatwick.

Entry is at 11, 12 or 13 and, while broadstream, the academic results are outstanding.

Boarders and day girls benefit from the very caring and personal attention of a dedicated teaching and pastoral staff. The main faith is Church of England. Extra-curricular activities are many; particularly strong are music and debating. Sport is excellent and includes lacrosse, tennis, swimming, gymnastics, squash and fitness exercising.

Above all, this is a happy and socially committed school.

St Joseph's Convent School

64 Upper Redlands Road, Reading, Berkshire RG1 5JT
Tel: 01734 661000 Fax: 01734 269932

Head Mrs V M Brookes
Type Girls' Independent school
Religious denomination Roman Catholic
Age range 11 – 18
No of pupils (day) 400
Girls 400
Senior 320; *Sixth form* 80
Fees per term (day) £1,265
Fees per annum (day) £3,795

St Joseph's Convent School was founded by the Sisters of St Marie Madeleine Postel whose aim was to provide a good education in a warm and loving atmosphere. This basic aim is as appropriate today as it was when St Joseph's was founded in 1910.

St Joseph's School combines the best in traditional educational values with a sharp awareness of what is appropriate for girls who need to be prepared for the 21st century. Girls are encouraged to be confident, questioning, independent learners, while at the same time developing a moral and spiritual sense of purpose in their lives and in their studies.

There is a greater emphasis than ever before on scientific and technological education for girls, on practical experience of work and industry and on European understanding through a diversified languages programme.

Examination results at both A and GCSE levels are always well above the national level. Last year 90 per cent of the girls gained five or more grades A–C at GCSE level while over 65 per cent gained grade A–C in eight or more subjects.

St Joseph's Convent School Reading Trust is a charity existing to advance education.

St Mary's School

Ascot, Berkshire SL5 9JF
Tel: 01344 23721 Fax: 01344 873281

Head Sister Frances Orchard IBVM
Founded 1885
Type Independent Roman Catholic boarding
Religious denomination Roman Catholic
Age range 11 – 18 *Boarders from* 11 – 18
No of pupils (day) 10 *(boarding)* 320
Girls 330
Senior 240 *Sixth form* 90

Broad and balanced curriculum to GCSE level including RE, Latin, Spanish and German. Twenty A level subjects.

Entry by school's own assessment and interview at 11+, 13+ and 16+. Applications to the admissions secretary.

Music scholarships at 11+. Science scholarship at 16+. Bursaries.

Strong boarding. Catholic ethos. Academic excellence.

Ashfold School

Dorton House, Dorton, Aylesbury, Buckinghamshire HP18 9NG
Tel: 01844 238237 Fax: 01844 238505

Head D H M Dalrymple MA (Oxon)
Founded 1927
Type Preparatory
Religious denomination Church of England
Members of IAPS
Age range 3 – 13+ *Boarders from* 7
No of pupils (day) 145; *(boarding)* 18
Girls 58; *Boys* 105
Fees per term (day) £665 – £2,075; *(boarding)* £2,725
Fees per annum (day) £1,995 – £6,225; *(boarding)* £8,175

Ashfold lies between the M40 and the A41, 6 miles from Thame, 10 from Bicester, 12 from Aylesbury, 15 from Oxford, within one hour of Heathrow and Luton airports. It is set within 45 acres of playing fields and parkland, with a Jacobean mansion of distinction at its heart.

Entry: by interview and/or written test.
Bursaries: to entrants of exceptional academic, musical, artistic or sporting potential. Discounts for third child and children of service personnel.
Curriculum: English, maths, science, history, geography, RK, art, CDT, IT, music and PE are taught from 7 to 13+. French from eight, Latin from nine.
Facilities: art and CDT centre; music school; science laboratory; sports hall; swimming pool; hard tennis courts; chapel.
Examinations: 13+ Common Entrance or independent senior school scholarships; the Buckinghamshire 12+ or 13+ grammar school entry exams.
Boarding: there are full and weekly boarders, housed in the wings of the main building with matrons on each wing.

Caldicott

Farnham Royal, Buckinghamshire SL2 3SL
Tel: 01753 646214 Fax: 01753 647336

Head M C B Spens Esq MA
Founded 1904
Type IAPS
Religious denomination Church of England
Members of IAPS, BSA
Age range 7 – 13 *Boarders from* 7
No of pupils (day) 120; *(boarding)* 130
Boys 250
Fees per term (day) £2,200; *(boarding)* £2,970
Fees per annum (day) £6,600; *(boarding)* £8,910

Caldicott – a leading IAPS preparatory school for boys with 250 pupils, situated in 20 acres, adjacent to Burnham Beeches, yet only 20 minutes from Heathrow. All boys board during their last two years. Boarding facilities are comfortable and homely. Boys, who are prepared for Common Entrance/scholarship examinations to public schools, achieve a high rate of success. Caldicott boasts well-equipped academic facilities, extensive sports hall, excellent design workshops, computer department, and a purpose-built music school. There are facilities for most games as well as shooting, music, art and drama. Entry via interview and assessment. Prospectus/video available from Headmaster, Caldicott, Farnham Royal, Bucks SL2 3SL.

Davenies

Station Road, Beaconsfield, Buckinghamshire HP9 1AA
Tel: 01494 674169 Fax: 01494 681170

Head J R Jones BEd (Oxon)
Founded 1940
Type Boys' preparatory
Religious denomination None
Members of IAPS
Age range 4 – 13
No of pupils (day) 250
Boys 250
Fees per term (day) £1,295 – £1,425
Fees per annum (day) £3,885 – £4,275

Curriculum: boys largely follow the National Curriculum, and are prepared for scholarship and Common Entrance at 13+, or for entry to Buckinghamshire grammar schools at 12+. French is introduced at seven.

Entry requirements and procedures: between four and seven entry is by interview with parents and child. Over the age of seven, a combination of interview and assessment is followed before places are offered.

Examinations offered: 12+ selection procedure to Buckinghamshire grammar schools, Common Entrance and Public School Scholarship.

Academic and leisure facilities: modern, purpose-built classroom blocks, science laboratory, computer room and specialist facilities for art and design technology.

Sports hall, astro-turf, swimming pool and extensive on-site playing fields.

Godstowe Preparatory School

Shrubbery Road, High Wycombe, Buckinghamshire HP13 6PR
Tel: 01494 529273 Fax: 01494 429001

Head Mrs F J Henson BA
Founded 1900
Type Girls' preparatory and co-educational pre-preparatory
Religious denomination Church of England
Members of IAPS
Age range Preparatory 8 – 13, Pre-preparatory 4 – 7 Boarders from 8 – 13
No of pupils (day) 140 Pre-preparatory 118 *(boarding)* 120
Fees per term (day) £915 – £1,615 *(boarding)* £2,910
Fees per annum (day) £2,745 – £4,845 *(boarding)* £8,370

Godstowe is situated in ten acres of grounds near the centre of High Wycombe and less than an hour from Heathrow. It is within easy reach of London, Oxford, Reading and Windsor.

The school was founded in 1900 as the first preparatory boarding school for girls and it now has 378 pupils, including 100 in the pre-preparatory department for boys and girls. *Curriculum*: the curriculum is broadly based, achieving a balance between pupils' academic, physical, technical and creative abilities. Girls are prepared for Common Entrance and scholarship examinations for senior independent schools at 12+ and 13+, with 100 per cent of girls achieving their first choice school at 13+ Common Entrance in 1995, underlying the school's well-proven record of academic achievement.

Facilities: the school buildings, which were enlarged in 1972 and 1980, include two libraries, science laboratories, design technology workshop, information technology centre, music school, art and textiles room, hall/gymnasium with a well-equipped stage and an indoor swimming pool. Extensive playing fields and tennis courts are on site. Constantly striving to improve facilities, a major new music school and boarding house have recently been completed.

Activities: residential courses and excursions are organised regularly in science, geography, history, environmental studies and languages, and the annual ski trip is a popular excursion.

There are three choirs, an orchestra and regular stage productions, as well as drama workshops and theatre visits.

Clubs and activities include badminton, Brownies, environmental science, gardening, golf, gymnastics, horse riding, information technology, technology and textiles.

Boarding facilities: boarders live in four houses under the care of resident staff. Some 80 per cent of our girls are full boarders and the remainder are weekly. Each boarding house is paired with a day house to ensure integration and to reinforce a sense of community. The school strives for a caring family atmosphere, and arranges regular activities and outings for boarders.

Entry requirements: entry is at four and eight, by chronological order of registration. Prospectus and further details are available on application to the school secretary.

Pipers Corner School

Pipers Lane, Great Kingshill, High Wycombe, Buckinghamshire HP15 6LP
Tel: 01494 718255 Fax: 01494 715391

Head Dr Mary Wilson MèsL, DèsL
Founded 1930
Type Independent
Religious denomination Church of England
Members of GSA, GBGSA
Age range 4 – 18
No of pupils (day) 270; *(boarding)* 80
Junior 70; *Senior* 220; *Sixth form* 60
Fees per term (day) £900 – £1,860; *(boarding)* £2,545 – £3,110

Pipers Corner is situated in its own 36 acres of open country and is easily reached from London, Heathrow, Gatwick and Luton. School coaches are available for local girls.

In addition to girls chosen for sound ability, Pipers welcomes those interested in the expressive arts and sport. A broad-based, balanced curriculum is followed and girls are actively encouraged to achieve high standards.

Our thriving sixth form provides a wide range of A levels and a full-time business studies course. Girls are well prepared for university entrance and prosper in higher education.

A new technology and performing arts centre opened in September 1995.

Housemistresses arrange weekend activities and give boarders a warm and secure environment.

A friendly, lively and challenging educational atmosphere prevails. Our girls' success and happiness from the age of four to entering university is top priority.

Entry requirements: preparatory department by interview and report; senior school by entrance examination, interview and report.

Scholarships: academic and service bursaries and sixth-form scholarships are available.

Stowe

Buckingham, Buckinghamshire MK18 5EH
Tel: 01280 813164 Fax: 01280 822769

Head Jeremy Nichols
Founded 1923
Type Boarding and day
Religious denomination Church of England
Members of Allied Schools, HMC, BSA
Age range 13 – 18 (boys) 16 – 18 (girls) *Boarders from* 13 (boys) 16 (girls)
No of pupils (day) 30; *(boarding)* 515
Girls 86 *Boys* 459
Senior 264 *Sixth form* 281
Fees per term (day) £2,985; *(boarding)* £4,263
Fees per annum (day) £8,955; *(boarding)* £12,789

A Stowe Education – the Best by Every Child
The Stowe curriculum is not a strait jacket into which each child either fits or perishes. Instead it is one designed to encourage each to identify and pursue his or her own specific strengths and interests. It aims to teach pupils to think deeply, to think for themselves and to think about others. It aims also to ensure that its young people become as much the leaders and achievers in a modern, international society as their predecessors were leaders in Britain's public service and Empire.

Stowe's core curriculum recognises the importance of traditional subjects in the sciences, humanities and creative arts. It also reflects the growing importance of a European and international community, seeking to ensure a broad competence in communication skills – in the spoken and written word, in foreign languages and in information technology.

In our pastoral provision, Stowe seeks to develop qualities of consideration for others and their points of view, a sense of responsibility and of what is right. Such a value base demands a secure intellectual, emotional and social environment. This is achieved through small family boarding units and a tutorial system built around each of the ten Houses. Each pupil becomes a member of an extended family of home, tutor group, House and school.

Over 90 per cent of our pupils go on to university. They are young people who are confident in their talents and skills and able to turn opportunity into achievement. They also leave with a sense of self within the communal and spiritual life of society.

A Stowe education is one that is relevant and which looks to the new century ahead; it seeks to do 'the best by every child' so that every child can achieve his or her personal best.

Thornton College

Convent of Jesus and Mary, Thornton, Milton Keynes, Buckinghamshire MK17 0HJ
Tel: 01280 812610 Fax: 01280 824042

Head Mrs Elizabeth E Speddy BA, DipEd
Type Girls' boarding and day; junior boys' day
Religious denomination Roman Catholic but all denominations welcome
No of pupils (day) 162; *(boarding)* 63
Fees per annum (day) £3,800 – £4,780; *(boarding)* full £6,760 – £7,760; weekly £6,430 – £7,400

Curriculum: a full range of subjects is offered to GCSE level.
Entry requirements: school's own assessment tests and interview at any age. Some bursaries available for senior school entry.
Examinations offered: GCSE (SEG and MEG); LAMDA. Overseas pupils are offered Cambridge Examinations in English as a Foreign Language.
Academic and leisure activities: modern sports hall with all indoor games facilities. Games pitches and tennis courts in 25 acres of rural parkland. Swimming pool. Strong music (choral and instrumental) and drama traditions. Interesting range of extra-curricular and weekend activities.

Thornton College is a charitable trust which exists to provide a high quality education in a Christian atmosphere.

Kimbolton School

Kimbolton, Huntingdon, Cambridgeshire PE18 0EA
Tel: 01480 860505 Fax: 01480 860386

Head Mr R V Peel BSc
Founded 1600
Type Independent co-educational boarding and day
Religious denomination Non-denominational
Members of HMC, GBA
Age range 7 – 18 *Boarders from* 11 – 18
No of pupils (day) 660 *(boarding)* 66
Girls 343; *Boys* 383
Junior 170; *Senior* 556
Fees per term (day) 7 – 11: £1,450; 11 – 18: £1,745; *(boarding)* £2,995
Fees per annum (day) 7 – 11: £4,350; 11 – 18: £5,235; *(boarding)* £8,985

Curriculum: a full and wide range of subjects taught to GCSE and A level including art, design technology, economics, home economics, public affairs, Spanish and social biology.

Computer studies throughout the school. Full PE programme. Games include soccer, hockey, cricket, netball and tennis. There is a full programme of indoor activities, including squash, in the new sports complex. Wide range of outdoor pursuits. New concert hall and theatre facilities have recently been provided, along with an art centre. ●

Entry requirements: interview and tests 7 to 11; standardised tests in English, maths and verbal reasoning at 11+. Common Entrance at 13+ (internal examinations where appropriate). Sixth-form entry by GCSE results. Assisted Places available at 11 only. Scholarships and bursaries available at 11, 13 and sixth form.

Kimbolton School Charitable Trust exists to provide high-quality education for local boys and girls from the parish of Kimbolton and also for the education of children from other areas.

King's College School

West Road, Cambridge, Cambridgeshire CB3 9DN
Tel: 01223 365814 Fax: 01223 461388

Head A S R Corbett MA, PGCE
Founded 1441
Type Preparatory, pre-preparatory, choir
Religious denomination Christian (other religions welcome)
Members of BSA, IAPS, CSA
Age range 4 – 13 *Boarders from* 7 – 13
No of pupils (day) 279
Girls 96; *Boys* 183
Fees per term (day) £1,810 (choristers £895, pre-preparatory £1,364) *(boarding)* £2,804
Fees per annum (day) £5,229; (choristers £2,685, pre-preparatory £3,939); *(boarding)* £8,097

Curriculum: broadly National Curriculum plus French from four and Latin from ten. All pupils study art, music, information technology and design technology throughout the school. Music is a speciality.

Entry: at 4+ into pre-prep department by waiting list and visit. Priority to siblings. Entry at 7+ by assessment and interview in January. Other places as available.

Examinations: Common Entrance and scholarship entry to independent schools (15 out of 35 in Year 8 gained music, art and academic awards to major schools last year).

Facilities: specialist rooms for all subjects housed in five buildings, an assembly hall, six games pitches, three tennis courts, two squash courts, and an outdoor swimming pool. Matches are played throughout the year.

Scholarships: two-thirds of boarding/tuition fees are awarded to 22 choristers elected to King's College Choir.

Boarding: modern facilities for 33 weekly boarders approved by the Social Services Department.

Laxton School

North Street, Oundle, Peterborough, Cambridgeshire PE8 4AR
Tel: 01832 273569 Fax: 01832 273564

Head Mr R I Briggs MA (Cantab)
Founded 1556
Type Independent co-educational day
Religious denomination Non-denominational
Members of SHA
Age range 11 – 18
No of pupils (day) 201
Girls 78; *Boys* 123
Junior 57; *Senior* 86; *Sixth form* 58
Fees per term (day) £1,668
Fees per annum (day) £5,004

Laxton School forms the day part and Oundle School the boarding part of the Oundle Schools, governed by the Grocers' Company. All facilities, teaching, games and activities are combined.

The curriculum is initially broad-based, but, by a guided selection of options, is designed to lead to GCSEs, A levels and university entrance. By working in close association with Oundle School, Laxton School provides a full range of facilities both inside the classroom and outside, including specialised classroom blocks, a superb library, extensive workshops, two IT centres, and an indoor swimming pool and sports hall. There are excellent opportunities and facilities for music and drama, and a thriving Combined Cadet Force.

Major sports played are rugby, hockey, soccer, cricket and netball, plus a wide range of minor sports.

Entrance and music scholarships are offered at 11+, 13+ and sixth form. The school participates in the Assisted Places System.

The Leys School

Cambridge, Cambridgeshire CB2 2AD
Tel: 01223 355426/355327 Fax: 01223 357053

Head Rev Dr John C A Barrett MA
Founded 1875
Type Independent
Religious denomination Inter-denominational with Methodist foundation
Age range 13 – 18 *Boarders from* 13
No of pupils (day) 159; *(boarding)* 264
Girls 125; *Boys* 298
Senior 423; *Sixth form* 203
Fees per term (day) £2,900; *(boarding)* £3,980
Fees per annum (day) £8,700; *(boarding)* £11,940

The Leys is a full co-educational boarding and day school, on a prominent site on the edge of the ancient university city of Cambridge. It offers a broad-ranging curriculum, small classes, a high staff-pupil ratio, a wide provision of extra-curricular activities and a liberal education based on strong Christian principles. In addition to the usual subjects, economics, business studies, Latin, Greek, German, Spanish and classical studies are available.

The school is housed in a variety of buildings ranging from late Victorian to the 1990s. Recent developments include a technology centre, a sports hall and an all-weather pitch. Pupils are accommodated in five boys' houses and three girls', and there is a heated indoor swimming-pool, a well-equipped library, a theatre and a music school.

Entry is through Common Entrance or the school's own entrance tests. Scholarships are available at 13+ and 16+.

St Colette's School

Tenison Road, Cambridge, Cambridgeshire CB1 2DP
Tel: 01223 353696

Head Mrs B Y Boyton
Type Nursery, pre-preparatory
Religious denomination Church of England
Members of ISAI
Age range 2½ – 7+
No of pupils (day) 160
Fees per annum (day) £1,350 – £2,955

St Colette's was founded in 1920 and is a very successful co-educational pre-preparatory school catering for day pupils aged from 2½ to 7+ years. It is a small school which encourages pupils to work to a high standard achieving excellent results at the 6+ entrance examination level in a happy and stimulating environment. Drama, speech, music and ballet are a great strength and productions form an integral part of the curriculum. The school aims to offer a programme of learning suited to the child's individual needs and special emphasis is placed on pastoral care. The school encourages a Christian way of thinking, encouraging kindness, honesty and courtesy to others within the community. The headmistress is always available to meet prospective parents and to show them round the school.

St Faith's

Trumpington Road, Cambridge, Cambridgeshire CB2 2AG
Tel: 01223 352073 Fax: 01223 314757

Head Mr Richard A Dyson BA, CertEd
Founded 1884
Type Co-educational preparatory
Religious denomination Inter-denominational
Members of IAPS
Age range 4 – 13
No of pupils (day) 435
Fees per term (day) £1,290 – £1,640

A happy, caring, disciplined environment is the school's first priority. Pupils follow an extensive curriculum which includes information and design technology, drama, music and art. Older pupils are prepared for entrance/scholarship to all independent senior schools.

Teaching in the pre-prep (four to seven years) and lower school (seven to nine years) is form based, whilst pupils in the middle and upper schools are taught by subject specialists. French is taught from the age of six and pupils begin Latin at the age of nine.

Pupils are supported in their daily routine through a tutor scheme. Four houses encourage competition in work and games. The house system also provides an impetus for charity fund-raising.

Nationally and locally, St Faith's has an excellent reputation for its music, sport and academic achievements. It boasts an impressive list of awards to independent senior schools.

Pupils are able to take advantage of a wide range of extra-curricular activities and an early start and late stay programme complements the school day.

St Faith's is part of a registered charity for educating children.

The following independent colleges also offer GCSEs. Please refer to the Independent Sixth-Form Colleges section for details:

Cambridge Arts & Sciences

Cambridge Centre for Sixth Form Studies

The Grange School

Bradburns Lane, Hartford, Northwich, Cheshire CW8 1LU
Tel: 01606 74007 Fax: 01606 784581

Head Mr E S Marshall MA, LGSM
Founded 1933
Type Co-educational
Religious denomination Non-denominational
Members of HMC
Age range 4 – 18
No of pupils (day) 1,087
Girls 528; *Boys* 559
Junior 508; *Senior* 452; *Sixth form* 131
Fees per term (day) £875 – £1,225
Fees per annum (day) £2,625 – £3,675

Acknowledged as one of the top co-educational schools in Britain, the Grange is situated in the delightful village of Hartford, close to Chester, Warrington, Crewe and Knutsford.

Noted for its outstanding academic standards, the Grange has a highly qualified, experienced staff. The school offers pupils a balanced education preparing for GCSE, A level, university and Oxbridge entry. More than 23 A level subjects are available for study; pass rates consistently exceed 95 per cent.

Entry is by assessment at kindergarten, testing at junior level, by entrance exam at 11+, and by interview and GCSE results at 16+.

Facilities include an impressive design and information technology centre, science block of six laboratories, 20 acres of sports fields, tennis courts, rowing and a multi-purpose sports hall. Drama and music are taught to the highest level with five full-time teachers and peripatetic staff. Numerous clubs and societies flourish including the Duke of Edinburgh Award Scheme, badminton, photography, and pottery. Building work will be completed during 1996 to provide a modern languages block and purpose-built junior school.

St Joseph's School

St Stephens Hill, Launceston, Cornwall PL15 8HN
Tel: 01566 772988

Head P S Larkman LVO, MA
Founded 1915
Type Co-educational junior, girls' senior
Religious denomination Roman Catholic. All denominations welcome
Members of ISAI, BSA
Age range 3 – 16 *Boarders from* 7
No of pupils (day) 181; *(boarding)* 24
Girls 161; *Boys* 39
Junior 92; *Senior* 113
Fees per term (day) £835 – £1,195; *(boarding)* £1,920 – £2,590
Fees per annum (day) £2,208 – £3,129; *(boarding)* £5,124 – £6,840

St Joseph's School, Launceston, is an independent boarding and day school.

There is a self-contained junior school with a kindergarten, sharing many of the senior school's facilities.

The senior school, with its comprehensive intake, has earned a national academic reputation over the years. The secret of this success is small teaching groups and a well-qualified teaching staff.

Traditional Christian values are the cornerstone of St Joseph's School. A caring and well-ordered society allows children of all ages to develop to their full potential, in all aspects of the curriculum.

At St Joseph's we try to educate the whole person. If you would like to know more, please contact the headmaster's secretary on 01566 772988.

Austin Friars School

Etterby Scaur, Carlisle, Cumbria CA3 9PB
Tel: 01228 28042 Fax: 01228 810327

Head Mr M G Taylor MA (Hons)
Founded 1951
Type Independent
Religious denomination Roman Catholic
Members of SHMIS, ISIS, GBA
Age range 11 – 18 *Boarders from* 11 – 18
No of pupils (day) 120 girls; 151 boys; *(boarding)* 30 boys
Senior 216; *Sixth form* 85
Fees per term (day) £1,446; *(boarding)* £2,526
Fees per annum (day) £4,338; *(boarding)* £7,578

Austin Friars School is an independent Augustinian Catholic School founded in 1951. The school is situated in grounds overlooking the historic city of Carlisle and there are opportunities to take advantage of the cultural heritage of the area and for outdoor activities in the Lake District, Northumberland and Scotland.

Austin Friars aims to foster the personal development of its pupils spiritually, academically, socially and physically to enable them to take their place creatively in society.

The school has high expectations of its pupils and encourages them to develop their potential in a disciplined yet happy, positive and productive atmosphere and this is reflected in GCSE and A level examination results which are amongst the best in the North of England.

The school offers scholarships, bursaries and Assisted Places. Admission to the school for children of all denominations is from age 11 through to sixth form.

Motto: In Omnibus Caritas.

Casterton School

Casterton, Kirkby Lonsdale, Cumbria LA6 2SG
Tel: 015242 71202 Fax: 015242 71146

Head Mr A F Thomas MA (Cantab)
Founded 1823
Type Girls' independent school
Religious denomination Church of England
Members of GSA, GBGSA
Age range 8 – 18
Junior 42; *Senior* 225; *Sixth form* 85
Fees per annum (day) £4,920 – £5,664;
(boarding) £7,230 – £9,030

Set in the heart of the beautiful Lune Valley, Casterton is one of the oldest boarding schools for girls, having been founded in 1823. It has first-class facilities and an outstanding academic record (A level 99.2 per cent, GCSE 97.8 per cent, grades A – C). A traditional academic curriculum is offered which includes three modern languages, and separate sciences.

In 1993 Casterton had the highest GCSE pass rate in the country and was second in the *Financial Times* 'Value for Money' table.

Entry requirements and procedures: entry, which is possible at all ages from 8 to 16, is via an entrance examination. Academic and music scholarships are available and the school is a member of the Government Assisted Places Scheme. A limited number of day girls places is available. A separate pre-preparatory department caters for boys and girls aged four to seven on a daily basis.

The extra-curricular programme, which makes full use of the school's unique environment, includes riding, sailing and outdoor pursuits, as well as individual and team sports such as hockey, netball, lacrosse, tennis, rounders, athletics and swimming. Facilities include a heated indoor swimming pool and fully equipped riding centre.

Art, music and drama are particularly strong and a new creative arts centre is the latest project in a range of developments aimed at fostering a girl's individual talents. The school's ambitious building programme continues with a science and mathematics block which opened in 1995.

Casterton is a happy, friendly school where high standards of self-discipline are expected. Senior girls have a considerable degree of independence and are encouraged to take responsibility within the school.

Casterton School is a charitable trust, which exists for the education of girls.

St Anne's School Senior

Browhead, Windermere, Cumbria LA23 1NW
Tel: 01539 446164 Fax: 01539 488414

Head Mr C M G R Jenkins MA (Oxon)
Founded 1863
Type Independent day and boarding (girls)
Religious denomination Non-denominational
Members of GSA, GBGSA, Round Square
International Schools
Age range 11 – 18
No of pupils (day) 246
Senior 246 *Sixth form* 75
Fees per term (day) £400 – £2,017; *(boarding)*
£2,140 – £3,042
Fees per annum (day) £1,200 – £6,051;
(boarding) £6,420 – £9,126

Member of the world-wide Round Square
network of Kurt Hahn Schools.

Situated in the Lake District National Park,
with grounds of over 90 acres, St Anne's is a
recognised RYA Centre. The ethos of St Anne's
is based on the development of the individual
within a broad and challenging curriculum and
with over 60 extra-curricular activities, for
example major sports, swimming, fencing,
dance, voluntary service.

Curriculum: 11 – 13, including music and dance.
Many options for GCSE and A level: Oxbridge
entrance. Examinations possible in music,
dance, speech and drama, IT, typewriting and
word processing. Careers advice, work
experience and placement overseas.

Scholarships and awards available: academic,
music, dance, drama, art, travel and sport.

Academic and leisure facilities: purpose-built
science laboratories, new central library,
computer centre, the Jenkins Centre for the
Performing Arts – dance studio, music and so
on. The Crampton Theatre for drama,
art/pottery studios. All-weather astro-turf
pitch, 19 tennis courts, sports hall.

Entry requirements: entry is possible at all ages
from 11 – 16 via own entrance examinations.
Prospective pupils encouraged to spend a
day/night in school as a 'taster'.

St Anne's Elleray School

Windermere, Cumbria LA23 1AP
Tel: 01539 443308 Fax: 01539 488414

Head Mrs S Burkett Cooper BEd
Founded 1863
Type Independent boarding school for girls and
day school for boys and girls
Religious denomination Non-denominational
Members of GSA, GBGSA
Age range 3 – 11
Girls 105 *Boys* 35
Fees per annum (day) £1,200 *(boarding)* £7,350

Curriculum: form teachers for mathematics,
English, geography, drama and religious
education in classes with a ratio of 10:1.
Specialist subject teachers for art, science,
biology, singing, music, French, Latin, history,
dance, physical education, team and individual
games, swimming, design and information
technology, nutrition and health, sailing.

Entry requirements: evidence of intelligent
interest, curiosity, enthusiasm and friendliness
during a day spent at Elleray School, plus good
basic literacy and numeracy in older children.

Examinations offered, including Boards:
Common Entrance examinations; The Royal
Academy of Dancing examinations; The
Associated Board of the Royal School of Music
examinations.

Academic and leisure facilities: swimming pool,
lake frontage with boat houses and pavilion,
sailing and rowing boats, fell walking,
camping, orchestra, cookery, choir, dance,
computers, chess, calligraphy, theatre,
adventure playground, log cabins, craft, French
clubs, drama, gym club, athletics, tennis,
rounders, tree house, extensive grounds for
creative play. St Anne's Elleray School also
offers a first class nursery school and day
nursery for children from two to five years.

St Anne's School Educational Trust Ltd is a
registered charity, established to provide
education of the highest standards.

St Bees School

St Bees, Cumbria CA27 0DS
Tel: 01946 822263 Fax: 01946 823657

Head P A Chamberlain BSc
Founded 1583
Type Independent
Religious denomination Church of England
Members of HMC, GBA, BSA
Age range 11 – 18 *Boarders from* 11 – 18
No of pupils (day) 178; *(boarding)* 110
Girls 143; *Boys* 145
Junior 80; *Senior* 127; *Sixth form* 81
Fees per term (day) junior £1,951; senior £2,406
Fees per term (boarding weekly) junior £2,356; senior £3,331
Fees per term (boarding full) junior £2,558; senior £3,497

Curriculum: very broad during the first three years; drama, music, information technology, outdoor pursuits and all the usual academic subjects. Sixteen GCSE and 17 A level courses; over 95 per cent of leavers to degree courses.
Entrance: own examinations; Common Entrance; sixth form entrance requires minimum of five GCSEs.

Scholarships: academic and music at 11+. Art, music and sports into sixth form. Assisted places.
Sport and extra-curricular: outstanding sporting record and facilities. Lake District nearby for outdoor pursuits. Art, drama, music and numerous clubs and societies.
Boarding: much of the accommodation completely refurbished in 1993-4. Virtually all have single or shared study bedrooms.

Barlborough Hall School

Barlborough, Chesterfield, Derbyshire S43 4TJ
Tel: 01246 810511 Fax: 01246 570605

Head Mr Adrian J Taylor
Founded 1939
Type Co-educational boarding & day preparatory school
Religious denomination Roman Catholic but others welcome
Accredited by HMI
Age range 3 – 13 *Boarders from* 7
No of pupils (day) 134; *(boarding)* 26
Girls 72; *Boys* 88
Fees per term (day) Preparatory £1,606; pre-preparatory £884; *(boarding)* £2,257
Fees per annum (day) Preparatory £4,818; pre-preparatory £2,651; *(boarding)* £6,771

Barlborough Hall School is an independent Catholic co-educational day and boarding preparatory school situated in extensive grounds close to junction 30 of the M1.

The school offers a stimulating education of high quality for children in the 3–13 age range with an emphasis on academic, cultural and social development.

Telephone enquiries to arrange a personal visit to the school are always welcome.

- Academic excellence.
- Attractive environment and excellent sporting facilities, increasingly popular with day pupils.
- Strong traditions of music and drama.
- A Christian community with happy, confident children aware of the needs of others.

Mount St Mary's College

Spinkhill, Derbyshire S31 9YL
Tel: 01246 433388 Fax: 01246 435511

Head Mr B Fisher MA (Oxon)
Founded 1842
Type Co-educational boarding and day
Religious denomination Catholic/Jesuit
Members of HMC
Age range 13 – 18 *Boarders from* 13 (7+ at Barlborough Hall)
No of pupils (day) 96; *(boarding)* 194
Girls 97; *Boys* 198
Senior 206; *Sixth form* 110
Fees per term (day) £2,021; *(boarding)* £2,990
Fees per annum (day) £6,063; *(boarding)* £8,970

Mount St Mary's was founded in 1842 to provide an education for children.

Religious denomination: Roman Catholic but accepting other denominations.

Curriculum: academic studies more than cover the National Curriculum and the Education Reform Act 1988. The core curriculum consists of mathematics, physics, chemistry, biology and English. The other foundation subjects are history, geography, technology (CDT or computer studies), music, art, physical education with a minimum of one modern foreign language – French, Spanish and German. Also available are Latin, Greek, economics and politics.

Entry requirements: from the independent sector by Common Entrance at 13+ otherwise by report and interviews. Assisted places and scholarships are available at 13+ and 16+.

Examinations offered: a full range of GCSE and A level courses in the subjects previously noted.

Academic and sports facilities: the school has a wide range of excellent modern facilities including a fully equipped computer suite and a new library. A new science block opened in September 1994, also a refurbished languages suite, CDT area, theatre and assembly hall.

A wide range of activities is available including astronomy, photography and satellite radio communications. There is a strong tradition of music and drama at the college.

The college has an excellent sporting reputation with outstanding rugby success. The 1st XV have been finalists twice in the *Daily Mail* cup and there is a strong 'sevens' tradition. In recent years many players have represented their county and several have represented their country. The girls compete at top levels in hockey, netball and athletics. Swimming and tennis are also available.

Pupils also participate in the Duke of Edinburgh Award Scheme and in the Combined Cadet Force.

Boarding facilities: the boarders are housed in dormitories and in their own individual rooms at sixth form level. They are cared for by resident teachers and their families and there is a high standard of pastoral care. The school also allows weekly boarding. Many day pupils are keen to become boarders during their time at the college.

A daily coach service to the west side of Sheffield is provided.

Scholarships, exhibitions and bursaries: the policy of the governors is to provide one scholarship of £500 a year and two of £100 per annum. However, any student awarded a scholarship would, if necessary, be provided with an additional bursary to take up a scholarship place without hardship to the family. Scholarships are awarded by examination at 13+ for entry into Form 3. Sixth form scholarships are awarded to internal and external candidates on the results of GCSE examinations. Music scholarships, instrumental and organ, are offered at 13+ and sixth form.

Blundell's School

Tiverton, Devon EX16 4DN
Tel: 01884 252543 Fax: 01884 243232

Head Mr Jonathan Leigh MA
Founded 1604
Type Co-educational
Religious denomination Church of England
Members of HMC
Age range 11 – 18 *Boarders from* 11
No of pupils (day) 152 *(boarding)* 217
Girls 83; *Boys* 286
Senior 185; *Sixth form* 184
Fees per term (day) from £1,812 *(boarding)* £3,715
Fees per annum (day) £5,436; *(boarding)* £11,145

Blundell's, a very West Country co-educational school, combines balance, excellence, space and tradition to provide a unique package for 11 – 18-year-old day and boarding pupils.

The 100-acre campus, sited outside the market town of Tiverton, provides a glorious rural setting with the space and facilities to allow every pupil the maximum opportunity for individual development. Blundell's offers all traditional subjects at A level plus theatre studies, music, art, history of art, photography, and sports science. The main curriculum is underpinned by a full programme of supplementary courses and lectures at all levels. Blundell's impressive sporting reputation is widely known and its superb facilities are complemented by an unusually wide range of sporting and extra-mural activities to suit the interests of every pupil.

Life at Blundell's is supported by a very strong house structure where pupils live in a family environment, guided by their houseparents and tutors.

Edgehill College

Northdown Road, Bideford, Devon EX39 3LY
Tel: 01237 471701 Fax: 01237 425981

Head Mrs E M Burton BSc, AKC
Founded 1884
Type Co-educational independent
Religious denomination Methodist Foundation – all denominations welcome
Members of GSA
Age range 3 – 18 *Boarders from* 4+ – 18
No of pupils (day) 359; *(boarding)* 98
Girls 344; *Boys* 113
Junior 113; *Senior* 344; *Sixth form* 84
Fees per term (day) £845 – £1,755; *(boarding)* £2,290 – £3,190
Fees per annum (day) £2,535 – £5,265; *(boarding)* £6,870 – £9,570

Edgehill College overlooks the historic town of Bideford in beautiful north Devon. The main buildings, five residential houses, tennis courts, playing fields, gymnasium, sports hall, swimming pool, all-weather pitch and recreational gardens are situated in grounds extending over 50 acres. Home economics, textiles, design and technology and art have their own centres. The excellent teaching facilities include science laboratories, four computer rooms, language laboratory, drama/dance studio, lecture theatre, an extensive library, music room and a sixth form centre. Edgehill College prides itself on tradition, firm but friendly discipline and a keen sense of moral values.

Kelly College

Tavistock, Devon PL19 0HZ
Tel: 01822 613005 Fax: 01822 616628

Head M Turner MA
Founded 1877
Type Independent co-educational
Religious denomination Church of England
Members of HMC, GBA, BSA, ISIS
Age range 4 – 18 *Boarders from* 11
No of pupils (day) 250 *(boarding)* 140
Girls 170; *Boys* 220
Senior 290; *Sixth form* 100
Senior fees per term (day) from £1,695;
(boarding) from £3,635
Senior fees per annum (day) from £5,085;
(boarding) from £10,905

Curriculum: the lower school curriculum incorporates breadth and balance, introducing pupils to subjects offered later. GCSE courses commence in the fourth form with pupils taking seven to ten subjects. In the sixth form, most pupils take three subjects and general studies at A level. The majority leave to go on to degree courses.

Entry requirements: entry is by examination and/or interview at 11+ and 13+ and at sixth-form level.

Examinations offered: GCSE and A level courses (MEG and O&C Board as well as other boards).

Academic and leisure facilities: there are over 20 clubs and societies catering for an extensive range of academic and leisure interests.

Scholarships: awards are available for boys and girls applying for entry at 11 and 13 years and at sixth-form level for academic potential, music, art, science, sport, swimming and equestrian skills, and for all-round ability.

Boarding facilities: there are two boarding houses for boys and two for girls.

Junior school: Kelly has its own day junior school for 4 to 11 year olds situated half a mile from the main site.

Allhallows College

Rousdon, Lyme Regis, Dorset DT7 3RA
Tel: 01297 626100 Fax: 01297 626114

Principal K R Moore MA, FGS, CGeol
Founded 15th Century
Type Independent
Religious denomination Church of England
Age range 11 – 18
No of pupils (day) 50 *(boarding)* 120
Girls 50 *Boys* 120
Sixth form 40
Fees per term (day) Age 11 – 13 £1,300; age 13+
£1,600 *(boarding)* £3,200
Fees per annum (day) Age 11 – 13 £3,900; age
13+ £4,800 *(boarding)* £9,600

Entry: at 11+, 13+ and 16+ via Common
Entrance, or own tests. Scholarships and
bursaries are available at all levels.

Curriculum: lower school is based generally on
the requirements of National Curriculum KS3
and KS4. Most students sit nine GCSE subjects
at the end of Year 11 (fifth form).

A wide range of A level subjects is available,
including art, theatre studies, business studies
and geology. Most students go on to university
after A levels.

Extra-curricular activities: a wide range of
sports is coached making full use of the superb
new sports hall, extensive playing fields and the
nearby sea. As well as the Combined Cadet Force
and community service Allhallows has its own
fire service and coastguard service. Many other
activities are available, some making use of the
Undercliffs National Nature Reserve which
forms part of the college campus.

Croft House School

Shillingstone, Blandford Forum, Dorset DT11 0QS
Tel: 01258 860295 Fax: 01258 860552

Head Mr M P Hawkins BA, DEA
Founded 1941
Type Girls' independent
Religious denomination Church of England
Members of GSA, GBGSA
Age range 11 – 18
Fees per term (day) £2,225; *(boarding)* £3,250

Croft House is a small school set in the midst of
the Dorset countryside. Being a small school
means that every girl may be treated as an
individual. Croft House prides itself on the girls
it turns out – the aim of the school is to produce
happy, confident and articulate young ladies
able to take their place in the world equipped to
meet every challenge.

Facilities include a large, modern gymnasium,
a theatre and a new science block. There is also
a heated swimming pool. Riding has been long
established at Croft House and is one of the
main activities with many girls going on to gain
their BHSAI certificate.

As well as the normal curriculum leading to
GCSE and A level additional subjects include
word processing, textiles, child care and
development, and theatre studies. Girls
welcome at any age from 11 to 18. Sixth form
girls have study bedrooms.

The school is just two hours from Heathrow
and Gatwick and there is an escort service to
and from these London airports.

St Mary's School

Shaftesbury, Dorset SP7 9LP
Tel: 01747 852416 Fax: 01747 851557

Head Sister M Campion Livesey IBVM
Founded 1945
Type Girls' independent Roman Catholic
Religious denomination Roman Catholic
Members of GBGSA, GSA, BSA, ISIS
Age range 9 – 18 Boarders from 9
No of pupils (day) 100 *(boarding)* 200
Girls 300
Junior 31 *Senior* 269 *Sixth form* 67
Fees per term (day) £1,950 – £2,050; *(boarding)* £3,050 – £3,200
Fees per annum (day) £5,850 – £6,150; *(boarding)* £9,150 – £9,600

Curriculum: the school offers a broad and balanced curriculum with all girls learning Latin, science, technology and information technology from the age of 11. The average number of GCSEs is nine with all girls studying RE, English language and literature, French, mathematics and balanced science plus three options.

Entry requirements: own entrance exam and testimonial at 9+, 10+, 11+ and 14+. Common Entrance and testimonial at 12+ and 13+. Five grade C GCSEs and testimonial at 16+. Two sixth-form scholarships, music scholarships from 11+, and art scholarships from 13+.

Subject specialities: very good science facilities and very strong art and music department. Pass rate at GCSE is 97 per cent and A level 93 per cent. All pupils proceed to higher education with 90 per cent to university.

Facilities: from the age of nine in four senior boarding houses and one junior house, all with common rooms, quiet rooms and kitchens. Purpose-built sixth-form house. Music school, IT room, sports hall, drama facilities, swimming pool, 55 acres. County champions in netball and athletics.

Sherborne Preparatory School

Acreman Street, Sherborne, Dorset DT9 3NY
Tel: 01935 812097 Fax: 01935 813948

Head R T M Lindsay Esq
Founded 1885
Type Independent
Religious denomination Church of England, other faiths and denominations welcome
Members of IAPS
Age range 3 – 13+ Boarders from 7
Girls 54 *Boys* 130
Fees per term (day) Half-day nursery £405; Pre-preparatory £945; Preparatory £1,662 *(boarding)* £2,493

Sherborne Preparatory School is a completely independent establishment near the centre of Sherborne. There is a common boundary with Sherborne School for Girls and much of Sherborne School is close by. Many children go on to these two schools, as well as a wide variety of other senior independent schools.

A very high standard is achieved in many aspects of school life, in work, music, sport and drama. Twelve awards were gained in 1994. Children regularly gain places in the IAPS National Symphony Orchestra. Sporting successes include winning the Rosslyn Park Preparatory Schools Seven-a-side Rugby Tournament in 1992.

The aim of the school is to enable all children to discover and develop their talents.

The school has been coeducational since 1976. There is a separate girls' house, but classes are mixed. A pre-preparatory department was opened in 1993 and is in a splendid specially-designed building, dedicated in March 1995 by Archbishop Lord Runcie.

There are 15 acres of playing fields, tennis/netball courts and gardens. The Sherborne School swimming pool is used almost every day. Many of the staff live on or very near the campus.

Sherborne School for Girls

Bradford Road, Sherborne, Dorset DT9 3QN
Tel: 01935 812245 Fax: 01935 814973

Head Miss J M Taylor
Founded 1899
Type Independent
Religious denomination Church of England
Members of GSA, BSA, SHA
Age range 11 – 18; *Boarders from* 11
No of pupils (day) 18; *(boarding)* 418
Senior 258; *Sixth form* 160
Fees per term (day) £2,650; *(boarding)* £3,850
Fees per annum (day) £7,950; *(boarding)* £11,550 (Fees for 1995/6)

Average size of class: 21
Teacher/pupil ratio: 1:7.2
Curriculum: all the usual subjects up to GCSE or A level; 24 subjects offered at A level including the following, which are not offered at GCSE: economics, history of art, Italian, Russian and social biology.
Entry requirements and procedures: girls must pass 11+, 12+ or 13+ Common Entrance. Entrance into sixth form is competitive.

The school stands in its own grounds of 40 acres. Train service between Sherborne and Waterloo via Salisbury, Basingstoke, Woking (airport coach connection with Heathrow).
Scholarships, exhibitions and bursaries: six academic scholarships and two exhibitions are offered annually as a result of examination and interview; in addition there are two scholarships offered for outstanding promise in music. Sixth-form scholarship held in November. Closing date for 11+, 12+, 13+ and music scholarships is 1 December for examinations and auditions in late January or February. Winners of academic or music awards are offered emoluments related to the current fees. Details from the secretary.

Sherborne School for Girls is a charitable trust for the purpose of educating girls in a boarding environment.

Sherborne School International Study Centre

Newell Grange, Sherborne, Dorset DT9 4EZ
Tel: 01935 814743 Fax: 01935 816863

Head R W Mowat
Founded 1977
Type Boys' secondary independent
Religious denomination Non-denominational
Age range 10 – 16 *Boarders from* 10
No of pupils (boarding) 75
Boys 75
Junior 25; *Senior* 50
Fees per term (boarding) £5,100
Fees per annum (boarding) £15,300

The International Study Centre is a specialist section of Sherborne School and exists to prepare boys from other countries for admission to good English independent boarding schools.

Curriculum: pupils follow courses leading to the Common Entrance Examination (at 13 years) or GCSE (at 16 years). Most boys stay for only one or two years and by then have acquired a good foundation for high levels of success in the future.

Classes are small, with an average of six pupils. Intensive tuition in English (spoken and written) is an integral part of every course. Boys also study mathematics, physics, chemistry, biology and can choose additional subjects such as history, geography, design, art or French.

Facilities: the centre has excellent classrooms, laboratory and library facilities and is situated on a most attractive site in the heart of the historical town of Sherborne in the southwest of England. Access to London and to the London airports is easy by train or by road and takes about two hours. A full programme of sporting activities is organised for team and individual sports. Facilities for sport are first class, with pitches for football, rugby, hockey and cricket. There are indoor and outdoor courts for basketball, and good facilities for tennis, squash and badminton. Sherborne School also has a 25-metre indoor heated swimming pool. Frequent excursions are arranged at weekends.

Boarding facilities: the boarding house (for 75 boys) was built in 1991 and provides first-class student accommodation. Most boys are in comfortable single or double study/bedrooms, each of which has its own washbasin. The youngest boys have two dormitories, each for six boys. There is good provision of showers and toilets throughout the house, and two separate recreation rooms with television and table-tennis.

Fourth term: in July and August, the centre offers an intensive programme of English studies (30 lessons per week) in classes of six pupils, with English through mathematics and science included. These courses can be for two, four, six or eight weeks.

Success: although the centre offers a very high standard of accommodation and learning facilities, its world-wide reputation as the best introduction for overseas students to the English school system has come from the high quality of the education provided, and the astonishing success of its pupils during both their study time in Sherborne and in their future education. Please contact the Principal for further information.

Talbot Heath

Rothesay Road, Bournemouth, Dorset BH4 9NJ
Tel: 01202 761881 Fax: 01202 768155

Head Mrs C Dipple MA, MèsL, FRSA
Founded 1886
Type Day and boarding
Religious denomination Church of England
Members of GSA
Age range Pre-preparatory: 3 – 7 (co-educational); Juniors 7 – 11; Seniors 11 – 18; *Boarders from* 9 – 18
No of pupils (day) 541; *(boarding)* 29
Junior 151 (including pre-preparatory); *Senior* 419; *Sixth form* 96
Fees per term (day) £550 – £1,750; *(boarding)* full £2,310 – £3,050; weekly £2,390 – £2,970
Fees per annum (day) £1,650 – £5,250

Situated on an extensive woodland campus with good access to Bournemouth's town centre, Talbot Heath has been established for over a century, serving both local pupils and others. The school follows Anglican traditions but welcomes pupils of all faiths.

Academic standards are among the finest in Dorset, but students are equally encouraged towards high achievement in sport, music, creative/performing arts and technology.

Links with industry and the wider world are fostered through such varied activities as 'Young Enterprise Companies', work experience, the Duke of Edinburgh Award Scheme and international student exchanges. The school has an impressive record of charitable fund raising. The excellent and spacious facilities including the music school (1991), sports hall (1986) and the swimming pool, are used by both junior (under 11) and senior pupils.

The school enjoys a happy and positive atmosphere, having an exceptionally caring and dedicated staff with a very high proportion of qualified subject specialists.

Durham School

Durham City, County Durham DH1 4SZ
Tel: 0191 384 7977 Fax: 0191 383 1025

Head Mr M A Lang MA, FRSA
Type Boys' independent boarding/day with girls in sixth form
Religious denomination Church of England
Member of HMC
Age range 11 – 18 *Boarders from* 11
Fees per term (day) (11 – 13) £2,044 (13 – 18) £2,403 *(boarding)* (11 – 13) £3,065 (13 – 18) £3,605
Fees per annum (day) (11 – 13) £6,132 (13 – 18) £7,209 *(boarding)* (11 – 13) £9,195 (13 – 18) £10,815

Entry requirements and procedures: at 11 by examination, at 13 by Common Entrance, and at 16, both boys and girls, by GCSE results and interview.
Curriculum: all boys cover a wide range of subjects to GCSE with English, mathematics, French, physics, chemistry and biology being part of the core curriculum. All the normal A level subjects are offered in the sixth form plus AS levels, while pupils are also prepared for the Oxford and Cambridge entrance examinations.
Examinations offered: pupils normally take GCSE and A level on the MEG (Oxford and Cambridge) Board, but when suitable, other boards are often used.
Academic and leisure facilities: facilities for both work and play are excellent and up to date. In the last 15 years a physics block, a sports centre, a theatre, a classroom block, a new girls' house and a CDT centre have been built, while the facilities for the playing of games are first class.
Scholarships: see separate entry.
Boarding: there are five boarding houses, four senior, three for boys and one for sixth-form girls, and one for our junior boys.

Alleyn Court and Eton House School

Wakering Road, Great Wakering, Southend-on-sea, Essex SS3 0PW
Tel: 01702 582553 Fax: 01702 584574

Head Mr S Bishop and Mr P Green
Founded 1904
Type Independent day
Religious denomination Anglican
Members of IAPS, ISAI
Age range 2½ – 16
Girls 49; *Boys* 301
Fees per term (day) £589 – £1,520

The school offers an all-round education which combines the best of both the traditional and the modern. Courses are geared to Common Entrance and scholarship examinations at 13+ and then to GCSE. They can be tailored to the needs of each pupil. Pupils with specific learning difficulties are catered for. Normal entry is at three years to the pre-prep, and at 6, 11 or 13, but entry at other points is also possible. There are no formal examinations for entry. At GCSE all pupils study English language, English literature, mathematics, French, science (dual award), and computing plus three subjects chosen from art, design technology, history, geography, business studies, physical education, Latin, Spanish, drama and music. There is a new junior classroom block, modern science and technology building and a new sports hall anticipated in the near future. A large range of clubs and extra-curricular activities is provided. Scholarships may be awarded for outstanding academic, sporting or musical ability.

Bancroft's School

Woodford Green, Essex IG8 0RF
Tel: 0181 505 4821 Fax: 0181 559 0032

Head Dr P C D Southern MA
Founded 1737
Type Independent, co-educational day
Religious denomination Church of England
Members of HMC, SHA, IAPS
Age range 7 – 18
No of pupils (day) 937
Girls 486; *Boys* 451
Junior 196; *Senior* 523; *Sixth form* 218
Fees per term (day) £1,436 – £1,898
Fees per annum (day) £4,308 – £5,694

Bancroft's is a fully co-educational day school taking pupils from seven through to A level and university entrance. Its academic standards are high with generous provision of scholarships and other awards. About 90 per cent of pupils proceed to degree courses and most others enter employment in the City or other professional openings. The fields of music and drama are a great strength and at all levels the programme of extra-curricular activities is exceptional.

In September 1990 the preparatory department opened for boys and girls between the ages of 7 and 11. It occupies a completely new building on a secluded part of the main school site and enjoys many of the facilities as well as the atmosphere and sense of purpose of Bancroft's. Pupils from the preparatory department at the age of 11 will in the normal course of events transfer automatically, without examination, to the secondary part of the school.

Brentwood School

Ingrave Road, Brentwood, Essex CM15 8AS
Tel: 01277 212271 Fax: 01277 260218

Head John A B Kelsall
Founded 1557
Type Co-educational and boarding
Religious denomination Church of England
Members of HMC, GBA, IAPS
Age range 5 – 18 *Boarders from* 11
No of pupils (day) 968; *(boarding)* 55
Girls 301; *Boys* 722
Junior 306; *Senior* 461; *Sixth form* 256
Fees per annum (day) £5,787; *(boarding)* £10,110

Brentwood School offers its pupils the best of both worlds. Girls and boys are taught separately from 11 to 16 but combine for all other school activities and mix freely on the campus in a natural environment. The sixth form is fully co-educational. This is an almost unique system practised by a very small number of schools but which we regard as quite the best arrangement possible.

Academic standards are high with almost all sixth formers gaining places at university, 10 – 15 at Oxford or Cambridge.

The school is a caring, busy community. A broad education is offered with music, drama, sport, Combined Cadet Force and community service along with many other activities complementing academic work.

Future developments include an all-weather pitch, extended library, and indoor heated pool. Scholarships and bursaries are available. Prospective parents are most welcome to visit; the headmaster will be delighted to show you round.

Coopersale Hall School

Flux's Lane, off Steward's Green Road, Epping, Essex CM16 7PE
Tel: 01992 577133

Head Mr Nicholas Hagger MA (Oxon) and Mrs Frances Best BSc
Founded 1989
Type Private co-educational preparatory day school
Religious denomination Church of England
Age range 3 – 11
Girls 115; *Boys* 117
Fees per annum (day) £1,987.50 – £3,585

Curriculum: the children in the main school are taught English, reading/writing skills, mathematics, science, history, geography, scripture, art/craft, design/technology, music, dancing, drama, physical education and French (from 7). Children are prepared for the public school's and state examinations at 11.
Entry requirements: at 3, early registration. Entrance tests at 6.

Cranbrook College

Mansfield Road, Ilford, Essex IG1 3BD
Tel: 0181 554 1757 Fax: 0181 518 0317

Head Mr G T Reading MA, CertEd (Oxon), FRSA
Founded 1896
Type Boys' independent day, primary and secondary
Religious denomination Non-denominational
Members of ISAI, ISIS
Age range 4 – 16+
No of pupils (day) 205
Boys 205
Junior 86; *Senior* 119
Fees per term (day) £950 – £1,220
Fees per annum (day) £2,850 – £3,660

Curriculum: in the lower school, boys follow a general primary school course, and in the upper school they prepare for GCSEs.

Entry: the main entry is at age four, but older boys are admitted when vacancies exist. Entry below eight is subject to an informal test. At eight and over there is an entrance examination.
Examinations: GCSE (MEG and ULEAC).
Academic and leisure facilities: the school aims to provide a happy, ordered and secure environment in which, through academic work and a variety of sports and other activities, boys can reach the highest standards within their capability.
Governing body: Cranbrook College Educational Trust Limited, a registered charity set up to provide 'general instruction of the highest class' for pupils from Ilford and the surrounding area.

Dame Johane Bradbury's School

Ashdon Road, Saffron Walden, Essex CB10 2AL
Tel: 01799 522348

Head Mrs R M Rainey
Founded 1525
Type Independent preparatory
Religious denomination Non-denominational
Age range 4 – 11
No of pupils (day) 274
Girls 160; *Boys* 114
Junior 152
Fees per term (day) £785 – £1,040*
Fees per annum (day) £2,355 – £3,120*
(* as of September 1995)

The school was founded in 1525 and aims to provide a broad general education of a high standard. A high teacher/pupil ratio is maintained and the fully qualified staff, augmented by specialists, and in the younger forms by ancillary help, work as a team to provide a stimulating educational environment. French is introduced at the age of six and the school has a choir, orchestra and other instrumental groups. Creative potential is encouraged. Physical education includes gymnastics, tennis, netball, football, cricket, rugby, rounders, athletics and swimming.

There are extensive grounds and playing fields and a hard tennis/netball court. The spacious building provides large classrooms, a gym, dining room, science laboratory, design and technology area, music room, art centre, library, computer room and learning support room. There is a wide range of extra-curricular activities including chess, pottery, photography, ballet, jazz dance and judo. The school is a registered charity number 310872.

Ilford Ursuline High School

Morland Road, Ilford, Essex IG1 4QS
Tel: 0181 554 1995 Fax: 0181 554 9537

Head Miss J Reddington
Founded 1903
Type Secondary Independent Girls
Religious denomination Catholic
Members of GSA, GBGSA, SHA, ISBA
Age range 11 – 18
No of pupils (day) 360
Girls 360
Senior 310 *Sixth form* 50
Fees per term (day) £1,443
Fees per annum (day) £4,329

Curriculum: for the first three years a broad and balanced curriculum including the National Curriculum is followed leading to a full range of academic courses at GCSE and Advanced level. The Ilford Ursuline has a record for excellent examination results. Music and sport flourish together with drama and many school societies.

Entry requirements: entrance to the school is by examination, interview and a report received from the headteacher of the girls' previous school. The school participates in the Government Assisted Places Scheme.

The Ilford Ursuline High School belongs to the Roman Union of the Order of St Ursula, a charitable trust which provides a high standard of education for local girls of mainly Catholic denomination, although other faiths are welcomed.

New Hall School

Chelmsford, Essex CM3 3HT
Tel: 01245 467588 Fax: 01245 464348

Head Sister Margaret Mary CRSS
Founded 1642
Type Girls' Catholic day and boarding 11 – 18 plus preparatory (mixed) 4 – 11
Religious denomination Roman Catholic (other denominations welcome)
Members of GSA
Age range 4 – 18; *boarders from* 9 (girls only)
No of pupils: Preparatory 134; Senior 302; Sixth form 100
Senior (day) 217; *Boarding* 171
Fees per term (day) £1,020 – £2,201; *(full boarding)* £2,388 – £3,438; *(weekly boarding)* £2,388 – £3,370

Founded in 1642, New Hall School is a well-established Catholic independent boarding and day school for girls, which has recently launched its mixed preparatory school. The school embraces girls of varied religious beliefs and also welcomes a wide variety of academic abilities, believing that all will achieve their best and will put to good use their different talents.

The curriculum is broadly based in Years 7, 8 and 9. At GCSE level, the girls are asked to make a choice from 20 subjects including separate sciences, IT and drama. At sixth form level, 20 A level subjects plus non-A level sixth form courses are offered. Entry is by head's report, interview, current school work and current school's own examinations.

Above all, New Hall is a caring community where spiritual values underpin all that is offered. Strong pastoral care, high academic standards and superb facilities combine to ensure the provision of a broad-based and Christian education for life.

Oaklands School

8 Albion Hill, Loughton, Essex IG10 4RA
Tel: 0181 508 3517

Principal Mr Nicholas Hagger MA (Oxon) and
Head Mrs Ann Hagger
Founded 1937
Type Kindergarten and preparatory school
Religious denomination Anglican
Members of ISIS
Age range 3 – 11
Girls 167; *Boys* 70
Fees per annum (day) £2,100 – £3,240

A long-established school beside Epping Forest. Pre-reading, writing and number activities (kindergarten) lead to reading, writing skills and number/mathematics concepts. History, nature study, art/CDT, music, dancing, drama and physical education. Boys are prepared for entrance examinations at seven, girls for the public schools' or state examinations at 11, and for a broader curriculum in French, history/geography, science and computer science.

Entry requirements: at three, early registration. Entrance tests at six.

St Mary's School

91 Lexden Road, Colchester, Essex CO3 3RB
Tel: 01206 572544 Fax: 01206 576437

Head Mrs G M G Mouser MPhil
Founded 1908
Type Girls' day school
Religious denomination Inter-denominational
Members of GSA, GBGSA, ISIS
Age range 4 – 16
Fees per term (day) £880 – £1,230
Fees per annum (day) £2,640 – £3,690

Opportunity is provided throughout the school for each girl to develop her personality and academic potential to the full, advised as necessary by the school counsellor. The senior school offers a range of 22 GCSE subjects, including four modern languages. Participation in an extensive range of cultural and physical activities is encouraged.

Senior school specialist rooms include four laboratories, a networked computer room, and textiles, art and home economics facilities. The gymnasium, tennis and netball courts, and heated open-air swimming pool are supplemented by local sports facilities.

The nearby lower school has its own tennis and netball courts, sports field, adventure playground and nature trail.

Entry is by examination and interview. One full-fees scholarship to the senior school, tenable for five years, is awarded annually to a girl who will make a major contribution to school life.

Beaudesert Park School

Minchinhampton, Gloucestershire GL6 9AF
Tel: 01453 832072 Fax: 01453 836040

Head Mr J R W Beasley
Founded 1908
Type Independent preparatory
Religious denomination Church of England
Members of IAPS
Age range 4 – 13 *Boarders from* 8
No of pupils preparatory school 155; *(day)* 95;
(boarding) 60; pre-preparatory 124
Girls (preparatory) 62; *Boys* (preparatory) 93;
(pre-preparatory) 61
Fees per term (day) £1,050 – £2,100; *(boarding)*
£2,853 (from September 1995)

Curriculum: all normal subjects necessary for
Common Entrance and scholarship plus music,
drama, art, craft, design technology and wide
range of sport and activities for boys and girls.
Entry requirements and procedures: by interview
and short test.

Beaudesert Park is a co-educational
preparatory school in the Cotswolds, within
easy reach of Bristol, Gloucester, Cheltenham
and Cirencester, and near the M4 and M5. The
children thrive in a happy atmosphere amid
beautiful surroundings and the emphasis is on
the all-round development of each individual
child. Good scholarship record with small
classes. Excellent facilities include indoor
swimming pool, sports hall and design
technology department.

Bredon School

Pull Court, Bushley, Near Tewkesbury, Gloucestershire GL20 6AH
Tel: 01684 293156 Fax: 01684 258008

Head Mr Colin E Wheeler
Type Independent
Religious denomination Church of England
Age range 3 – 19 *Boarders from* 7
No of pupils (day) 121; *(boarding)* 179
Girls 63; *Boys* 237
Junior 55; *Senior* 181; *Sixth form* 65
Fees per term (day) £800 – £2,320; *(boarding)* £2,710 – £4,050
Fees per annum (day) £2,450 – £6,960; *(boarding)* £8,130 – £12,150

Curriculum: Bredon is a co-educational independent boarding and day school for 300 pupils. Bredon follows the National Curriculum and students sit the National Assessment Tests at the appropriate stages. Some pupils are able to benefit from the expertise of the Learning Support Centre staff, and the School is CReSTeD registered.

Entry requirements: there is no entrance examination, but prospective students are required to attend the school for interview with the headmaster. Acceptance is subject to the result of the interview and to a satisfactory report from the pupil's headmaster. Pupils are accepted from the age of five; direct entry into all other year courses is acceptable by arrangement with the headmaster.

Examinations offered: pupils are prepared for GCSE, A and A/S level in a wide variety of subjects depending on individual ability. The school also offers a broad range of the new General National Vocational Qualifications at Foundation, Intermediate and Advanced levels (the vocational A levels), in business, leisure, design, health and social care, manufacturing (engineering), NVQ (NAB) agriculture and horticulture.

Academic and leisure facilities: Bredon aims to provide a sound general education and has set out to educate the whole person rather than merely the academic pupil. Pupils are helped to achieve the academic standard of which they are capable by well-qualified staff operating in small classes. Bredon has class sizes of 6 – 15 pupils and the teacher/pupil ratio is 1:7. Pupils' character and interests are developed through extra-curricular and pastoral activities.

Excellent facilities exist in craft, design and technology, and computer studies. A farm unit provides the basis for agricultural studies. The school has recently opened a new sports hall, laboratories and classroom complex. The main school games are rugby football, cricket, cross-country and athletics. On one afternoon a week a wider choice is available, including hockey, weight-training, canoeing, fencing, soccer, squash, swimming and a number of other minor sports. There is a flourishing outdoor pursuits department, which operates throughout the year, culminating in major expeditions. The school is an independent centre for the Duke of Edinburgh's Award Scheme, and numerous holiday activities are organised.

Cheltenham Ladies' College

Cheltenham, Gloucestershire GL50 3EP
Tel: 01242 520691 Fax: 01242 227882

Head Miss Enid Castle BA
Founded 1853
Type Girls' boarding and day
Religious denomination Christian
Members of BSA, GSA, ISIS
Age range 11 – 18 *Boarders from* 11
No of pupils (day) 202; *(boarding)* 641
Senior 843; *Sixth form* 273
Fees per term (day) £2,600; *(boarding)* £4,095

Founded in 1853, the college flourished for most of its first 50 years under the guidance of Miss Dorothea Beale, its most famous principal, who believed that the education of girls was as important as that of boys. It was during these years that it acquired its beautiful buildings in the centre of Cheltenham, a pleasant spa town in the Cotswolds. Its early and sustained success drew girls from all over the country and boarding houses were established to house them. The college has continued to develop buildings and facilities of high quality, and ensured that the curriculum has kept pace with the best of modern educational thinking. Today the college provides an environment well-equipped to prepare girls for higher education and the working world of the twenty-first century.

The boarders are housed in comfortable boarding houses in the care of resident housemistresses and house staff. There are four boarding houses for sixth formers where house mistresses have a small teaching commitment. The housemistresses of the seven junior houses do not teach as they are fully committed to the welfare of the girls in their charge. There are also three day-girl houses.

There are nearly 100 full-time and 55 part-time teaching staff who head a very broad curriculum, including 24 subjects offered up to A level.

The music department is very strong offering tuition in many instruments and the opportunity to make music in orchestras, choirs and instrumental groups. A new sports hall and swimming pool have added to the wide range of sporting activities available while art and drama are popular and successful. A new, fully equipped editing suite opens in the autumn term 1995, and a new art and technology block is planned for 1997.

The college is fully networked and computers are used in every subject. Many other extra-curricular activities are on offer.

Girls normally enter the college between the ages of 11 and 13+ although older girls are accepted into the sixth form for Advanced level studies. Younger girls enter via Common Entrance examination or the scholarship examination. Sixth-form candidates work towards an entrance examination in the subjects they wish to study for Advanced level.

A number of scholarships, including sixth form, art and music scholarships, are awarded each year. Full details can be obtained from the Registrar.

Dean Close Junior School

Lansdown Road, Cheltenham, Gloucestershire GL51 6QS
Tel: 01242 512217 Fax: 01242 221195

Head Mr Ian F M Ferguson MA
Founded 1886
Type Co-educational preparatory
Religious denomination A Christian school with Evangelical Anglican foundation
Members of IAPS, ISIS
Age range 3+ – 13+ *Boarders from* 7
No of pupils (day) 144; *(boarding)* 82
Girls 97; *Boys* 129
Fees per term (day) £2,025 *(boarding)* £2,960

Dean Close Junior School is a Christian family school with outstanding facilities and caring staff committed to the development of the individual child in all aspects of education.

The school follows the Common Entrance base but firmly embraces the National Curriculum. An entry test in English and mathematics appropriate for the age is set but most children come and spend a day in the school.

Academic and music scholarships and exhibitions are offered at 11+.

There are four boarding houses run by house parents and two day houses all offering pastoral care of the highest order. The classrooms are modern and purpose-built and include two science laboratories, a computer centre and an art and technology department. The school hall, dining hall and playing fields all enable the children to enjoy first-class facilities, together with the swimming pool, gymnasium, artificial pitches and theatre in the senior school.

The vast majority of boys and girls move on to Dean Close School at 13+, so ensuring continuity and stability.

Dean Close School

Cheltenham, Gloucestershire GL51 6HE
Tel: 01242 522640 Fax: 01242 244758

Head C J Bacon
Founded 1886
Type Independent
Religious denomination Church of England
Members of HMC
Age range 12½ – 18 *Boarders from* 12½
No of pupils (day) 174; *(boarding)* 274
Girls 194; *Boys* 254
Sixth form 171
Fees per term (day) £2,845; *(boarding)* £4,075
Fees per annum (day) £8,535; *(boarding)* £12,225

Strong emphasis is placed on personal faith, mutual respect, service, integrity, friendship and the need to discover and develop individual talents. We endeavour to find and enhance these talents, whether they are creative, intellectual or athletic, employing the skills of a versatile and professional staff and our extensive facilities. We expect to see self-discipline, leadership and the use of personal initiative in every scholar. A co-educational system throughout the school provides a realistic and stable environment in which to mature.

Everyone – day and boarding – has a workroom or study, and the boarders are placed in small-sized houses with substantial study bedroom accommodation for the seniors. Impressive facilities include a superb indoor swimming pool, sports hall, two artificial grass pitches, a fine theatre/concert hall and a new art and design building. A new music school is currently being built. A wide range of A levels is available. Ninety-seven per cent of scholars go on to higher education with the best of these achieving Oxbridge places. Generous scholarships and bursaries are available.

Hatherop Castle Preparatory School

Hatherop, Near Cirencester, Gloucestershire GL7 3NB
Tel: 01285 750206 Fax: 01285 750430

Head Mr Paul Easterbrook BEd
Founded 1947
Type Preparatory school (with own nursery)
Religious denomination Church of England, others welcome
Members of ISAI, ISJC
Age range 2½ – 13 *Boarders from* 8
No of pupils (day) 267
Girls 159; *Boys* 108
Preparatory 119; *Pre-preparatory* 90; *Nursery* 57
Fees per term (day) £1,000 – £1,600; *(boarding)* £2,500

Curriculum: the curriculum is broad and offers the whole range of subjects. French is taught from age six and German from age 11. We aim for high standards and every child is encouraged to achieve their own potential. Every child is helped to become a considerate and intelligent young person.

Entry requirements: examination at 8+ and interview. Scholarships for day and boarding places available at eight. Otherwise by interview.

Examinations offered: Common Entrance and PSS levels at 11+, 12+ and 13+. Associated Music Board exams, LAMDA and English Speaking Board.

Academic and sports facilities: situated in the heart of the Cotswolds, Hatherop has beautiful grounds and plenty of space. Soccer, rugby, hockey, netball and tennis are played as well as athletics and swimming in own heated outdoor pool. Music and drama are given a high profile with regular concerts and productions.

The school has its own nursery which takes pupils from two and a half and gets them ready for main-stream schooling. Transition into the preparatory school is automatic.

Boarders live in well-furnished dorms and are an extension of the head and his wife's own family. The head's wife runs the boarding house and takes a special interest in all the pastoral welfare of the children.

The King's School

Pitt Street, Gloucester, Gloucestershire GL1 2BG
Tel: 01452 521251 Fax: 01452 385275

Head Peter R Lacey
Founded 1541
Type Co-educational boarding and day
Religious denomination Church of England
Members of HMC, SHMIS, SHA, GBA
Age range 4 – 19 *Boarders from* 11
No of pupils (day) 458; *(boarding)* 56
Girls 191; *Boys* 403
Junior 115; *Senior* 287; *Sixth form* 112
Fees per term (day) £680 – £1,890; *(boarding)* £1,950 – £3,030
Fees per annum (day) £1,494 – £5,241; *(boarding)* £7,059 – £8,853

The King's School occupies buildings in the shadow of Gloucester Cathedral. As well as providing the choristers for the cathedral's daily services, life at the school is centred around this ancient building, with music as a particular strength.

Junior, middle and senior departments cater for pupils aged from 3 to 18. There is a flourishing and expanding sixth form and about 12 per cent of the students have gained Oxbridge places in recent years. GNVQs were introduced in September 1994. GCSE results have been exemplary.

Boarders ensure a lively, cosmopolitan atmosphere and wide-ranging sports and activities keep the pupils enthusiastically occupied for seven days a week.

Rendcomb College

Rendcomb, Cirencester, Gloucestershire GL7 7HA
Tel: 01285 831213 Fax: 01285 831331

Head Mr John N Tolputt
Founded 1920
Type Co-educational independent boarding, weekly boarding and day
Religious denomination Church of England
Members of HMC, SHA, SHMIS
Age range 11 – 18 *Boarders from* 11 – 18
No of pupils (day) 59; *(boarding)* 187
Girls 79; *Boys* 167
Junior 47; *Senior* 130; *Sixth form* 68
Fees per term (day) £2,144 – £2,814; *(boarding)* £2,769 – £3,558

In its beautiful Cotswold setting, Rendcomb College combines the friendliness of a small school with excellent academic standards. Nearly all sixth-form pupils go on to universities and colleges and find that the many extra-curricular activities available at Rendcomb, which include drama and theatre studies, choral and instrumental music, the Duke of Edinburgh Award Scheme and cooking, help them to make the most of their time there.

Boarding accommodation is superb; every pupil from the fifth form upwards has a single, spacious study-bedroom and the recreational facilities are outstanding, enabling pupils to enjoy a wide range of sports, from the traditional team sports such as rugby, hockey and cricket, through to the more unusual sports of archery, fly-fishing, golf and clay pigeon shooting.

Pupils gifted academically, in sport and in the creative arts are especially welcome and details of scholarships, bursaries and assisted places are available on request.

Westonbirt School

Tetbury, Gloucestershire GL8 8QG
Tel: 01666 880333 Fax: 01666 880364

Head Mrs Gillian Hylson-Smith BA Hons, DipCEG
Founded 1928
Type Girls' independent boarding and day
Religious denomination Church of England
Members of GSA, BSA, Allied Schools, ISIS
Age range 11 – 18; *Boarders from* 11 – 18
No of pupils (day) 40; *(boarding)* 180
Girls 220
Sixth form 60
Fees per term (day) £2,312 *(boarding)* £3,595
Fees per annum (day) £6,936 *(boarding)* £10,785

Curriculum: the school offers a full range of subjects to provide a balanced education for all. Girls work in sets according to their ability. For GCSE all girls take nine to ten subjects (including English Language, English Literature, maths, two sciences and a modern language). There is a wide choice of A levels in the sixth form.

Entry requirements: Common Entrance or Westonbirt papers if entering higher up the school. Scholarships available on merit and bursaries awarded to clergy, diplomatic and services personnel.

Facilities: set in beautiful grounds in the heart of the Cotswolds, Westonbirt School is situated just off the M4 motorway, about an hour from Heathrow Airport.

The school buildings include a recently completed art, technology and science block, a comprehensive information technology centre, a music school, extensive games facilities and an indoor swimming pool.

Westonbirt cares about the all-round development of its girls and we place emphasis on pastoral care and building the confidence of our pupils as well as academic achievement.

Wycliffe College

Stonehouse, Gloucestershire GL10 2JQ
Tel: 01453 822432 Fax: 01453 827634

Head D C M Prichard MA
Founded 1882
Type Co-educational independent
Religious denomination Inter-denominational
Members of HMC
Age range 13 – 18 *Boarders from* 13
No of pupils (day) 135; *(boarding)* 210
Girls 109; *Boys* 236
Senior 175; *Sixth form* 172
Fees per term (day) £2,730; *(boarding)* £3,880 – £3,995
Fees per annum (day) £8,190; *(boarding)* £11,610 – £11,985

Wycliffe is currently spending £2.5 million on developments with a new £1m dining hall and sixth form hall of residence, comprising study bedrooms with en suite bathroom and fax facilities, now completed. Recently modernised accommodation offers a jacuzzi and sauna, and four more halls of residence are planned.

This pre-university college of the Cotswolds offers 90 activities and traditionally 90 per cent proceed to Higher Education. The careers department is a centre of excellence. GCSE is normally taken in ten subjects and a unique one-year Development Sixth Course is offered as well as the two year A level course.

Numerous awards given for talent in music, art, drama, design & technology, squash, rowing as well as academic subjects.

A full-time qualified teacher of English as a Foreign Language and a language development centre cater for foreign students and others in need.

With its junior school Wycliffe educates over 630 boarding/day pupils aged 3 – 18 in 60 acres of grounds.

Bedales School

Petersfield, Hampshire GU32 2HW
Tel: 01730 263286 Fax: 01730 267411

Head Alison Willcocks MA, BMus
Founded 1893
Type Co-educational boarding
Religious denomination Non-denominational
Members of HMC, SHMIS, GBA, IAPS
Age range 3 – 18 *Boarders from* 8
No of pupils (day) 75; *(boarding)* 327
Girls 207; *Boys* 190
Junior 169; *Senior* 397; *Sixth form* 132
Fees per term (day) £2,843; *(boarding)* £3,967
Fees per annum (day) £9,567; *(boarding)* £12,996

Bedales School was founded as a 'pioneer school' in 1893 by Mr J H Badley, and became co-educational shortly afterwards. It stands in an estate of 120 acres outside Petersfield, Hampshire, overlooking the South Downs.
Curriculum: senior school (13–18). Eighty in each year. In the first year, all follow a broad-based curriculum. There follows a two-year course leading to GCSE. All pupils study art, design and music in the first and second years and are required to take at least one of these subjects to GCSE. The usual range of subjects is offered. At A level, German, Latin, Spanish and theatre arts are offered in addition to usual subjects. In the sixth form a broad and interesting extended curriculum includes a compulsory modern language element for all.

Entry requirements and procedures: entry to the school at 3+, 4+, 8, 9, 10, 11, 13 and 16. Once accepted, pupils proceed to the next stage if they so wish, provided they perform satisfactorily. Entrance tests for newcomers at 10, 11 and 13 take the form of residential tests in January preceding the September entry. Entry at 8, 9 and 16 is by a series of one-day interviews.
Examinations offered including Boards: in addition to the usual range of GCSE and A levels, pupils can do the Association Board exams in speech, drama and music. Virtually all go on to further education, most to university, some to drama, art and music colleges, with 15 per cent per year at Oxbridge.
Academic and leisure facilities: 17 acres of playing fields offering cricket, football, hockey and netball. Six grass courts and three hard courts for tennis, squash court, heated and covered swimming pool, gym, and astro-turf pitch. The large sports hall accommodates all the indoor games. Outdoor work department is run by pupils and, in addition to growing trees, has over the years moved and restored two 18th-century barns which now form the base of the department and a centre for rural crafts and a bakery.
Scholarships and bursaries: music scholarships available from 11 and academic awards from 13. A number of awards available at sixth form level, and bursaries from 11 based on a means test. Scholarships are available at 13 and 16.

Ditcham Park School

Ditcham Park, Petersfield, Hampshire GU31 5RN
Tel: 01730 825659 Fax: 01730 825070

Head Mrs P M Holmes
Founded 1976
Type Co-educational day school
Religious denomination Christian (non-de-nominational)
Age range 4 – 16
No of pupils (day) 300
Girls 137; *Boys* 163
Junior 110; *Senior* 190
Fees per term (day) £1,020 – £1,710
Fees per annum (day) £3,060 – £5,130

Curriculum: National Curriculum plus French at nine, Latin at 12 and three separate sciences at 13. Varied and lively teaching, most pupils taking nine GCSE subjects out of a possible 16, obtaining in 1995 an average of 8 passes at grades A – C.

Entry requirements: headteacher's report plus our own test. Special examination for scholarship candidates (8+ and 11+).

Examinations offered: GCSE (Southern and Midland Examining Groups); Royal Schools of Music; Guildhall School of Speech and Drama.

Academic and leisure facilities: all teaching rooms, including a small theatre, are very well equipped. Full range of non-academic activities. In addition, outings to theatres and concerts and regular trips to the continent.

Dunhurst (Bedales Junior School)

Alton Road, Steep, Petersfield, Hampshire GU32 2DP
Tel: 01730 262984 Fax: 01730 267411

Joint Heads Mr and Mrs Michael Heslop
Founded 1902
Type Independent co-educational day and boarding
Religious denomination Non-denominational
Age range 8 – 13 *Boarders from* 8 – 13
No of pupils (day) 102; *(boarding)* 68 (boys and girls)
Girls 86; *Boys* 84
Junior 170
Fees per term (day) £1,981 – £2,132; *(boarding)* £2,937 – £3,123

Dunhurst, the junior school of Bedales, was founded in 1902 and occupies a part of the Bedales 150-acre estate in a rural setting just to the north of Petersfield. It follows the same general ethos as Bedales and is properly co-educational and non-denominational. The atmosphere is relaxed, friendly and purposeful with a great amount of tolerance, trust and genuine rapport between teachers and pupils. Visitors are struck by the fact that Dunhurst is an unusual school and has something unique to offer.

Dunhurst aims to achieve high academic standards and follows a broad educational programme built around the 'core' subjects of English, mathematics and science, but giving equal importance to physical education, art, pottery, textiles, workshop, computing, comparative religion, current affairs, geography, history, dance, drama and music. In addition to class music for all, pupils' practice time for individual instruments is fitted into their daily timetable. The aim is for pupils to achieve breadth of experience as well as excellence in many different areas.

Matches against other schools take place regularly in athletics, cricket, football, hockey, netball, rounders and occasionally swimming and tennis. A wide range of other sports and outdoor activities is offered as well.

Dunhurst makes full use of the first-rate facilities at Bedales which include a sports hall, an all-weather pitch and a covered swimming pool. This makes for an easy transition for pupils moving from Dunhurst to the senior school at the age of 13.

Applicants for both boarder and day places sit entrance tests for admission at the ages of 8+, 9+, 10+ or 11+.

Embley Park

Romsey, Hampshire SO51 6ZE
Tel: 01794 512206 Fax: 01794 518737 Junior School 01794 515737

Head David Chapman BA (Dunelm)
Founded 1947
Type Independent 3 – 18 co-educational
Religious denomination Church of England, all denominations welcome
Members of GBA, SHMIS, SHA, BSA
Age range 3 – 18 *Boarders from* 11
No of pupils (day) 260; *(boarding)* 100
Girls 110; *Boys* 250
Senior 230; *Sixth form* 50
Fees per term (day) £455 (nursery); £875 (junior); £1,845 (senior); *(boarding)* £3,090
Fees per annum (day) £5,535; *(boarding)* £9,270

Embley is a broad-ability school with an IQ threshold of 100, but still achieves, by small classes and setting in key subjects, approximately 75 per cent entry to higher education. The school sets its own entry test, but Common Entrance is used at 13+. At GCSE, a core curriculum is offered but separate subject sciences and two languages can still be attempted. Business studies and PE are alternative humanity options. At A level 17 subjects are offered with 25 per cent of the senior school aged 16+. More than £1 million has been spent on facilities since 1989, and these include purpose-built science laboratories and a 7000 square-foot sports hall. Forty per cent of the senior school boards. Scholarships available (HM Forces, clergy, teachers, single parents).

Commencing 1st September 1995, Embley has a Junior & Nursery School situated in Romsey on the old site of La Sagesse Convent.

Embley Park will therefore offer co-education from 3 – 18 years, day and boarding.

Farleigh School

Red Rice, Andover, Hampshire SP11 7PW
Tel: 01264 710766 Fax: 01264 710070

Head Mr J E Murphy BSc, PGCE
Founded 1953
Type Preparatory
Religious denomination Roman Catholic
Members of IAPS
Age range 3 – 13 *Boarders from* 8
No of pupils (day) 242; *(boarding)* 87
Girls 89; *Boys* 240
Fees per term (day) (main school: age 8 – 13) £1,980; *(boarding)* £2,789; (pre-preparatory) £1,020; (kindergarten) £452
Fees per annum (day) (main school: age 8 – 13) £5,940 *(boarding)* £8,367; (pre-preparatory) £3,060; (kindergarten) £1,356

Farleigh School is set in a rural estate close to the A303(M3) and within one and a half hours' driving time of London. Founded in 1953 as a boarding school for Catholic boys, Farleigh has gradually extended its scope to include day boys and girls and now welcomes girls as boarders in a newly refurbished wing. Most boarders are Roman Catholic but the school welcomes children of other Christian denominations.

The curriculum leads to the Common Entrance and scholarship examinations for senior schools and takes cognisance of the developing National Curriculum. Several scholarships are gained annually by pupils moving on to various leading independent schools. Facilities include three science laboratories, a large purpose-built sports hall, a computer room equipped with Archimedes 3020 computers and a newly equipped music suite with electronic keyboards linked to computer.

A wide range of activities is arranged after school hours and at weekends, giving boarders and day children alike a full and varied life. Many staff are residential and the pastoral team, headed by two house mothers, includes a qualified head matron and assistants.

Farnborough Hill

Farnborough Road, Farnborough, Hampshire GU14 8AT
Tel: 01252 545197

Head Sister Elizabeth McCormack RCE, BEd,
CertEd, DipPsych
Founded 1889
Type Day
Religious denomination Roman Catholic
Members of GSA
Age range 11 – 18
No of pupils (day) 520
Girls 520
Sixth form 110
Fees per term (day) £1,476
Fees per annum (day) £4,428

Farnborough Hill is housed in the historic home of the Empress Eugenie. Facilities include a chapel, gymnasium, indoor swimming pool, laboratories, technology workshops, and extensive playing fields. The school is committed to the education of the whole person in a caring, Christian environment. Academic standards are high; in 1995 the A level pass rate was 97 per cent and at GCSE 98 per cent of results were at grades A* – C. Among the many extra-curricular activities there is particular emphasis on sport and the creative arts. Entry is by examination taken in January for the following September. The school participates in the Government Assisted Places Scheme.

Forres Sandle Manor

Fordingbridge, Hampshire SP6 1NS
Tel: 01425 653181 Fax: 01425 655676

Head R P J Moore BA, PGCE
Type Independent co-educational preparatory
Religious denomination Church of England
Members of IAPS
Age range 3 – 13 *Boarders from* 7
No of pupils (day) 165; *(boarding)* 90
Girls 105; *Boys* 150
Fees per term (day) £596 – £1,995; *(boarding)*
£2,795
Fees per annum (day) £1,788 – £5,985;
(boarding) £8,385

Beautiful grounds, fine facilities, and dynamic, talented staff make Forres Sandle Manor hugely popular with both boarder and day children. Determined always to achieve the highest standards, we believe in the paramount importance of each child's happiness. We help individuals to fulfil their potential across a broad, modern curriculum and to maintain an excellent academic record.

Visitors are always impressed by outstanding music, the range and excellence of sports and activities and the modern facilities for teaching, learning and living. Above all they remember our happy, courteous and purposeful children. Send for our prospectus and come and meet us.

Forres Sandle Manor is a registered Charitable Trust for the education of children.

Lord Wandsworth College

Long Sutton, Near Odiham, Hook, Hampshire RG29 1TB
Tel: 01256 862482 Fax: 01256 862563

Head G de W Waller MA, MSc
Founded 1920
Type Independent
Religious denomination Non-denominational
Members of HMC, SHMIS, GBA
Age range 11 – 18 Boarders from 11
No of pupils (day) 134; *(boarding)* 341
Girls 43; *Boys* 432
Junior 79; *Senior* 396; *Sixth form* 150
Fees per term (day) £2,364 – £2,460; *(boarding)* £3,027 – £3,164
Fees per annum (day) £7,082 – £7,380; *(boarding)* £9,084 – £9,492

Curriculum: National Curriculum to GCSE with additional options such as classics. A levels and some AS levels.

Entry requirements: own exam at 11, Common Entrance at 13, interview and test at 16. Contact the headmaster's secretary for details.
Academic and leisure: set in 1200 acres of north Hampshire countryside. The college has modern facilities and a continuing building programme.
Scholarships: available for academic or musical excellence. Foundation support for children who have lost the support of one or both parents. Assisted places.
Boarding: four senior boys' houses, one girls' house, junior house.

Academic standards are high but the performing arts and sport are an important part of life at the school.

The Pilgrims' School

3 The Close, Winchester, Hampshire SO23 9LT
Tel: 01962 854189 Fax: 01962 843610

Head M E K Kefford MA, DipEd
Founded 1931
Type Boys' preparatory
Religious denomination Church of England
Members of IAPS, CSA
Age range 8 – 13
No of pupils (day) 100; *(boarding/weekly boarding)* 80
Boys 180
Fees per term (day) £1,975; *(boarding)* £2,705
Fees per annum (day) £5,925 *(boarding)* £8,115

Boys' preparatory school (IAPS) for boarders and day boys, incorporating the Choristers of Winchester Cathedral and the Quiristers of Winchester College who attend the school with choral scholarships to the value of half the boarding fee. There are exceptional facilities for music, sport and academic study, with excellent staff/pupil ratio and pastoral structure. The school is situated in beautiful buildings in the Cathedral Close with adjacent playing fields, and benefits additionally from the sporting and recreational facilities of Winchester College. For further information, please apply to the headmaster.

Rookesbury Park School

Wickham, Hampshire PO17 6HT
Tel: 01329 833108 Fax: 01329 835090

Head Miss L A Appleyard MA (Ed), CertEd
Founded 1929
Type Girls' preparatory
Religious denomination Church of England
Age range 3 – 13 *Boarders from* 7
No of pupils (day) 105; *(boarding)* 45
Fees per term (day) £515 – £1,790; *(boarding)* £2,215 – £2,605
Fees per annum (day) £1,565 – £5,370; *(boarding)* £6,645 – £7,815

Rookesbury Park School occupies the former manor house in the village of Wickham, set in an unrivalled setting of 14 acres overlooking farmland. The school was founded in 1929 and in 1961 it became an educational trust administered by a board of governors.

It is a friendly and flourishing school with a thriving nursery department offering small classes and a balanced curriculum. Well-equipped with science laboratory, computer and technology rooms, swimming pool, tennis courts and athletics field.

There are approximately 150 girls in the school which includes both day, weekly and full boarding. The girls are prepared for the Common Entrance examination to major independent schools and for independent senior schools scholarships. There is a large, well-qualified staff and the average class size is 18 pupils. Games played include netball, lacrosse, tennis, rounders, athletics and swimming.

The school has a very busy and stimulating extra-curricular programme in which all girls are encouraged to participate. There is a small school chapel and boarders attend the local parish church of St Nicholas.

Rookwood School

Weyhill Road, Andover, Hampshire SP10 3AL
Tel: 01264 352855

Head Mrs S Hindle BA Hons, FCollP
Founded 1934
Type Independent
Religious denomination Non-denominational
Members of ISAI
Age range 3 – 16 *Boarders from* 7 – 16 (girls only)
No of pupils (day) 250; *(boarding)* 25
Girls 182; *Boys* 93
Junior 210; *Senior* 65
Fees per term (day) £865 – £1,512; *(boarding)* £2,200 – £2,877
Fees per annum (day) £2,595 – £4,536; *(boarding)* £6,600 – £8,631

Rookwood School stands in eight acres of beautiful grounds within walking distance of Andover town centre and the station.

There is purpose-built accommodation for the three- to seven-year-olds with light, airy classrooms and an excellent pupil : teacher ratio.

In the main school, where boys can stay to 11 years and girls to 16, classes are small enough for plenty of individual attention. The computer room reflects the importance of information technology. There are two laboratories, a home economics and craft area, a hall/gymnasium, music room and art studio. The atmosphere everywhere including the boarding house is disciplined, busy and happy.

The school grounds provide the venue for a variety of sporting activities with netball/tennis courts, an outdoor heated swimming pool and facilities for hockey, football, cricket, rounders and athletics.

Stage productions involving all the pupils are a regular occurrence.

The school is a registered charity (number 307322A31-A) which exists for the education of children.

Stanbridge Earls

Romsey, Hampshire SO51 0ZS
Tel: 01794 516777 Fax: 01794 511201

Head Mr H Moxon MA, DipEd
Founded 1952
Type Co-educational boarding school
Religious denomination Inter-denominational
Members of GBA, SHMIS, BSA, corporate member British Dyslexia Association, CReSTeD
Age range 11 – 18 *Boarders from* 11
No of pupils (day) 17 *(boarding)* 175
Girls 41; *Boys* 142
Junior 46; *Senior* 137; *Sixth form* 33
Fees per term (day) £2,665 (junior); £2,915 (senior); *(boarding)* £3,550 (junior); £3,885 (senior)

Stanbridge Earls is on the edge of the New Forest. It has 48 acres of beautiful wooded grounds which contain a chain of small lakes. *Curriculum*: all the traditional subjects are offered up to GCSE level but there is a great variety of alternatives designed to develop the strengths and interest of every pupil. Thirteen subjects are available at A level. Many pupils are dyslexic but everyone takes GCSE and are expected to gain at least five C grades. A number of leavers go on to university and other centres of higher education.

Entry requirements: by interview, school report and where appropriate educational psychologists' report.

Examinations offered including boards: GCSE: SEG, MEG and NEA; A level: London and AEB.

Academic and leisure facilities available: the school has excellent facilities for all academic subjects. Accelerated learning centre for those with specific word learning difficulties, 12 experienced specialist teachers. Skilled remediation in maths is also available. There is a wide choice of games and the school has a large sports hall, indoor swimming pool, squash courts, floodlit tennis courts, vehicle engineering workshops and playing fields. Sailing is done from Lymington.

Stanbridge Earls is an educational charitable trust providing an education for boys and girls.

Wykeham House School

17 East Street, Fareham, Hampshire PO16 0BW
Tel: 01329 280178 Fax: 01329 823964

Head Mrs R M Kamaryc
Founded 1913
Type Independent day
Religious denomination Anglican – all welcome
Members of GSA, GBGSA
Age range 4 – 16
No of pupils (day) 300 girls
Fees per term (day) £963 – £1,290
Fees per annum (day) £2,889 – £3,870

The school occupies a prominent position in the centre of Fareham within easy access of the M27. Over 300 pupils are drawn from a wide catchment area, including Portsmouth, Southampton, Emsworth, Bishops Waltham and the Meon Valley. The school seeks to encourage a high academic achievement for each individual giving the pupils a strong sense of purpose and an appreciation of the value of sound, thorough work. An emphasis is placed on courtesy and concern for others. There is a strong sense of community with close contact between parents and school being actively encouraged. The teacher:pupil ratio is generous to allow every pupil individual attention. The curriculum aims to maintain standards and yet recognises the need to keep apace of educational developments and modern teaching techniques. Specialist rooms and three well-equipped laboratories are available. Two computer rooms and four networks provide excellent information technology opportunities for the entire school.

Bromsgrove School

Worcester Road, Bromsgrove, Hereford & Worcester B61 7DU
Tel: 01527 579679 Fax: 01527 576177

Head T M Taylor MA, DipEd
Founded 1553
Type Co-educational
Religious denomination Church of England
Members of HMC, IAPS
Age range 7 – 18 Boarders from 7
No of pupils (day) 742 *(boarding)* 354
Girls 441; *Boys* 658
Junior 424; *Senior* 672; *Sixth form* 257
Fees per term (day) £1,430 – £2,050; *(boarding)* £2,615 – £3,375
Fees per annum (day) £4,290 – £6,150; *(boarding)* £7,545 – £9,825

Curriculum: the school is at the forefront of curriculum development, whilst maintaining traditional teaching values. It prides itself on achieving high standards from pupils of a wide range of ability. It offers an impressive range of subjects, including design and technology, Spanish, business studies and the performing arts. With close monitoring of the academic progress of each pupils, the school obtains high academic success, with a pass rate of 92.5 per cent at A level, an average of 8.2 GCSE passes at A–C grade per student and important success at Oxbridge. Ninety-five per cent of pupils continue on to university.

Entry requirements: entry between ages seven to eleven is based upon assessment tests and at thirteen by interview and tests, or Common Entrance. Pupils entry into the sixth form is determined by their GCSE results.

Examinations offered: the school seeks to offer the most appropriate examination for each subject. A, AS and GCSE subjects are offered through the various examination boards. We have introduced a number of modular courses where appropriate and offer a GNVQ in business.

Careers: there is an excellent careers department. The school enjoys close links with industry and pupils undertake work experience placements. Pupils undertake self-appraisal and mock interview practice.

Academic and leisure facilities: the school is situated in a leafy, hundred acre, self-contained campus, near the town of Bromsgrove; it is easily accessible, being convenient for the motorway network (via M6/M5 or M40/M42) and Birmingham International Airport. There are excellent facilities for study and recreation. Academic facilities include a design centre, modern laboratories, music school and drama studio. In May 1994, the school opened a £2.5 million library and resources centre including 'state of the art' library, lecture theatre, careers room and information technology facilities.

The school is opportunity-orientated and provides a very wide range of extra-curricular and sporting activities.

Facilities include a heated indoor swimming pool, sports hall, floodlit 'all-weather' pitch and climbing wall, as well as extensive grass pitches within the campus. Sport, music and drama thrive as extra-curricular activities.

Boarding: while the school offers boarding and day education, the ethos is that of a vibrant boarding community. Every pupil has their own desk in their house, be it modern purpose-built accommodation or an older building which has been carefully modernised. A full programme of activities, cultural trips and expeditions is offered.

Hereford Cathedral School

Old Deanery, Cathedral Close, Hereford HR1 2NG
Tel: 01432 363522 Fax: 01432 363525

Head Dr H C Tomlinson BA, FRHistS, FRSA
Re-founded 1384
Type Co-educational day and boarding
Religious denomination Church of England
Age range 11 – 18 *Boarders from* 11 (8 in junior school)
No of pupils (day) 590; *(boarding)* 40
Girls 305; *Boys* 325
Junior 255; *Senior* 195; *Sixth form* 180
Fees per term (day) £1,510; *(boarding)* £2,660
Fees per annum (day) £4,530; *(boarding)* £7,980

History: Hereford Cathedral School, as other secular foundations, developed from the Song School and Library associated with the original Cathedral Church of the eighth century. The earliest extant record, however – the appointment of the first lay headmaster – is 1384. Cathedral and school remain in close harmony; morning assembly is held in the Cathedral, as are all major services and gatherings, and the choristers – who attend the junior school – are part of the Choral Foundation that maintains the reputation for musical excellence at Hereford.

Composition/numbers/boarding facilities: HCS is a Christian foundation in the Anglican tradition; each boy and girl is encouraged to explore Christian beliefs, although children of other faiths and different denominations are welcome. Six hundred pupils attend the school (160 in the sixth form), with a further 250 (aged 3 to 11) in the junior school, pre-preparatory and nursery class. Most are day pupils, but there is boarding provision for boys and girls, and a separate house for choristers.

Entry requirements and scholarships: admission is normally by entrance examination at 11+ or 13+, although tests can be arranged for transfer from other schools at 12+ and 14+. Students may be admitted to the sixth form to take Advanced level courses provided they have appropriate GCSE qualifications. A substantial number of scholarships (including art and music) and fee-assisted places are awarded each year.

Pastoral care: each pupil is assigned to a personal tutor in one of the day or boarding houses. The housemaster/mistress, assisted by tutors, ensures continuity of advice and care throughout the pupil's career.

Curriculum: the school provides a broad academic base. In the first two years all pupils take English, religious studies, mathematics, Latin, French, geography, history, information technology, chemistry, physics, biology, technology, music, drama, art, physical education and games. By delaying choices for as long as possible, the aim is to enable pupils to experience subjects in depth before making their course commitments.

Sixth-form students usually take three A levels, most also sitting a general studies paper. All undertake a non-specialist programme; with options including geology, Russian, information technology, current affairs, political theory, contemporary issues in science, German for business, magazine production, current affairs, linguistics, ecology, ethics, and public speaking. A strong careers team of senior staff includes a professional careers officer. Their advice is available throughout the school.

Music and drama: by participation in festivals and local orchestras, and the development of the music school as focus of music-making in the community, HCS enhances the strong musical tradition of the city. Dramatic performances play an important part in school life, pupils of all ages participating in many and varied productions, including large-scale musicals.

Sport: extensive playing fields, by the River Wye, accommodate cricket, rugby and hockey pitches. The school has tennis, squash and netball courts, and a gymnasium, and the use of the city's leisure centre, all-weather athletics track and hockey pitches, swimming baths and rowing club.

Outdoor pursuits: the school has its own Scout and Venture Scout Groups, Combined Cadet Force (all three services), and is an operating authority for Duke of Edinburgh Award Scheme.

Malvern Girls' College

Avenue Road, Great Malvern, Hereford & Worcester WR14 3BA
Tel: 01684 892288 Fax: 01684 566204

Head Dr Anne Lee
Founded 1893
Type Girls' boarding and day
Religious denomination Church of England
Members of GSA, BSA
Age range 11 – 18 *Boarders from* 11
No of pupils (day) 60; *(boarding)* 400
Girls 487
Sixth form 179
Fees per term (day) £2,600; *(boarding)* £3,900
Fees per annum (day) £7,800; *(boarding)* £11,700

Broad and varied curriculum. Entry is by school's own examinations or by Common Entrance. Overseas pupils may take examinations in their own schools or exam centres. Applications should be made to the registrar. Twenty subjects offered at A level, 16 at AS level and 25 at GCSE. Excellent facilities – one computer to seven pupils, indoor heated swimming pool, astro-turf games pitch, innovative sports dome, squash courts, athletics track.

Entry scholarships offered in academic subjects, music and art. Eight boarding houses have all been extensively refurbished in recent years. Separate houses for sixth form and a house for 11 and 12 year olds. School sanatorium has resident nursing staff.

St James's and The Abbey

West Malvern, Hereford & Worcester WR14 4DF
Tel: 01684 560851 Fax: 01684 569252

Head Miss E M Mullenger
Founded 1896
Type Girls senior independent day and boarding
Religious denomination Church of England
Members of GSA
Age range 11 – 18 *Boarders from* 11
No of pupils (day) 32; *(boarding)* 148
Sixth form 53
Fees per term (day) £2,436; *(boarding)* £3,654
Fees per annum (day) £7,308; *(boarding)* £10,962

St James's and The Abbey is a girls' school of approximately 200 in a beautiful setting on the western slopes of the Malvern Hills. Full, weekly or day boarding are all available and there is direct entry into the sixth form. The facilities for science, information technology, modern languages and creative arts are up-to-date and stimulating. The fifth and sixth form houses provide comfortable study bedrooms. The school has its own well-equipped theatre and offers theatre studies at GCSE and Advanced level.

Entry is by interview and Common Entrance or own entrance examination. Scholarships and bursaries are awarded.

A wide range of options within a broad curriculum, small classes and a lively and varied programme of weekend activities (including Duke of Edinburgh's Award) together with individual attention and encouragement, all contribute towards developing the girls both personally and academically. Pupils normally progress to higher education and much emphasis is laid on careers advice.

St Richard's

Bredenbury Court, Bredenbury, Nr Bromyard, Hereford & Worcester HR7 4TD
Tel: 01885 482491 Fax: 01885 488982

Head Mr R E H Coghlan
Founded 1921
Type Co-educational preparatory
Religious denomination Roman Catholic
Members of IAPS
Age range 4 – 13 *Boarders from* 7 – 13
No of pupils (day) 54; *(boarding)* 67
Girls 52; *Boys* 69
Fees per term (day) £274 – £1,614; *(boarding)*
£2,225 – £2,380
Fees per annum (day) £822 – £4,842; *(boarding)*
£6,675 – £7,140

Founded in 1921, St Richard's is a Catholic preparatory school of about 100 boys and girls situated in 35 acres of beautiful Herefordshire countryside. The school is of a size that combines a comfortable, busy and homely atmosphere with academic and spiritual excellence. A traditional character is based on the concept of an extended family.

Children are prepared for Common Entrance and scholarships to Catholic and other independent senior schools. Entry is between seven and ten. The average number in a class is 13.

St Richard's is experienced in looking after the needs of those from abroad. Children are escorted to/from London and arrangements are made for their escort on to Heathrow and other destinations.

Abbot's Hill School

Bunkers Lane, Hemel Hempstead, Hertfordshire HP3 8RP
Tel: 01442 240333 Fax: 01442 69981

Head Mrs J S Kingsley MA (Cantab), Barrister at Law, FRSA
Founded 1912
Type Girls' independent boarding, weekly boarding and day
Religious denomination Church of England
Members of GSA, GBGSA, BSA, AHIS
Age range 11 – 16 *Boarders from* 10 – 16
No of pupils (day) 80; *(boarding)* 70
Girls 150
Senior 150
Fees per term (day) £2,020; *(boarding)* £3,400 (weekly); £3,425 (full)
Fees per annum (day) £6,060; *(boarding)* £10,200 (weekly); £10,275 (full)

Abbot's Hill is set in 70 acres of parkland, 25 minutes from Euston and near junction 20 of the M25 and junction 5 of the M1. There are full and weekly boarders.
Curriculum: we follow the National Curriculum to Key Stage 3 and GCSE.

Entry requirements: examination and interview at 11, 12, 13.
Examinations offered: girls study for nine GCSE subjects: six core subjects and three from a choice of nine other subjects.
Academic and leisure facilities: a science, technology and humanities building was opened in 1991. There is a gymnasium/theatre, a concert hall, nine outdoor tennis courts, two indoor courts and an art/design building.
Scholarships: major and minor academic scholarships are offered, and minor scholarships in art, music and sport.
Boarding: Year 11 are in purpose-built study bedrooms, other years in attractive dormitories. There is a wide number of extra-curricular activities so weekly boarders develop interests and full boarders are ensured of an energetic and enjoyable weekend.

The staff/pupil ratio is 1:8.

Abbot's Hill charitable trust exists to provide high quality education for girls and junior boys.

Aldenham School

Elstree, Hertfordshire WD6 3AJ
Tel: 01923 858122 Fax: 01923 854410

Head Mr S Borthwick BSc, CPhys
Founded 1597
Type Independent
Religious denomination Church of England
(other denominations welcome)
Age range 11 – 18 *Boarders from* 13
No of pupils (day) 267; *(boarding)* 100
Girls 15; *Boys* 352
Junior 60; *Senior* 357; *Sixth form* 100
Fees per term (day) £1,665 (11+); £2,620 –
£3,110 (13+); *(boarding)* £3,820

Situated in its own beautiful 135-acre site in the Hertfordshire green belt, with excellent access to London, the M1 and the M25, Aldenham's particular reputation as a close-knit, small and supportive community with a strong boarding ethos makes it the very best environment for a high-quality all-round education encouraging children to enterprise.

The achievement of every child's academic potential remains central but the building of confidence comes too from the sport, music and drama, and by living and working together within the disciplined and vigorous community that is Aldenham today.

Aldenham has developed an extremely flexible array of day and boarding options.

The vast majority of pupils take nine GCSEs and three A levels with over 20 subjects offered in the sixth form.

The Arts Educational School

Tring Park, Tring, Hertfordshire HP23 5LX
Tel: 01442 824255 Fax: 01442 891069

Head Mrs J D Billing GGSM, CertEd, FRSA
Founded 1919
Type Boarding and day school
Religious denomination Inter-denominational
Members of SHA, BSA, ISAI
Age range 8 – 18 *Boarders from* 8
No of pupils (day) 60; *(boarding)* 160
Girls 210; *Boys* 10
Junior 100; *Senior* 70; *Sixth form* 50
Fees per term (day) £1,590 – £2,226; *(boarding)*
£2,756 – £3,604
Fees per annum (day) £4,770 – £6,678;
(boarding) £8,268 – £10,812

The Arts Educational School is one of the major performing arts schools in the United Kingdom and is housed in a magnificent Rothschild mansion set in 17 acres of beautiful parkland.

It is an independent school for boys and girls between the ages of 8 and 18 and entry is by audition and academic examination where the principal criterion is artistic talent. A few part scholarships are available for which every applicant is assessed at audition.

Its specialist subjects of dance, drama and music are complemented by a fine academic education thereby preparing pupils for a wide choice of routes into further education.

A preparatory department was opened in September 1993 and there has been an extensive development of sixth form courses during the past two years. The artistic curriculum in the lower school has been refined during the past year to introduce the Theatre Arts Course alongside the Dance Course making the school very much at the forefront of artistic education.

Students in the fourth and sixth forms study one of the following two-year vocational courses while taking their examinations in dance, drama and music.

The **Dance Course** is for those who wish to specialise in dance as performers, teachers or in other related areas.

The **Drama Course** is designed for pupils who are interested in theatre in a variety of ways: as potential actors, actresses or singers or from a more technical or academic point of view.

The **Musical Theatre Course** is for all rounders and places an equal emphasis on dance, drama and music.

There is a strong pastoral system in the school and as we are small in comparison to many schools, there is a family atmosphere.

Whatever the career or course chosen, the fusion of natural talent, creativity and personality with sound teaching and direction produces young communicators, well-equipped to grasp the many opportunities that lie ahead.

Bishop's Stortford College

10 Maze Green Road, Bishop's Stortford, Hertfordshire CM23 2QZ
Tel: 01279 758575 Fax: 01279 755865

Head S G G Benson MA
Founded 1868
Type Independent, fully co-educational from September 1995
Religious denomination Non-denominational
Members of HMC
Age range 13 – 18 *Boarders from* 13+
No of pupils (day) 200; *(boarding)* 130
Girls 45; *Boys* 285
Sixth form 141
Fees per term (day) £2,480 (max); *(boarding)* £3,440 (max)
Fees per annum (day) £7,440; *(boarding)* £10,320

Curriculum: the structure and discipline of a challenging academic curriculum demands much from all pupils. With a range of 14 subjects, everyone takes at least ten GCSEs, including common core subjects and three separate sciences. At A level, choices are made from 15 subjects in very flexible groups; extensive non-specialist options ensure breadth and balance in the sixth form.

Scholarships/assisted places/bursaries are awarded at 13+ and sixth form.

The 'small school' environment greatly strengthens pastoral care and emphasises individual encouragement. The extra-curricular facilities are extensive, with sport, music, art and drama all played and performed to the highest standards.

Though in a rural location, there is easy and quick access to Stansted, the M11 and M25.

Haberdashers' Aske's School for Girls

Aldenham Road, Elstree, Hertfordshire WD6 3BT
Tel: 0181 953 4261

Head Mrs P A Penney BA, FRSA, FIMgt, MInstD
Type Day school for girls
Religious denomination Church of England foundation
Member of GSA
Age range 4 – 18
Junior 300; *Senior* 600; *Sixth form* 240
Fees per term (day) junior £1,155; senior £1,380
Fees per annum (day) junior £3,465; senior £4,140

The senior school curriculum includes all academic subjects, with French and Latin compulsory from Year 7; German or Spanish from Year 8; music, art, technology and drama. Separate sciences are taught throughout the school. All girls take sport up to lower sixth.

Twenty-one advanced level subjects are offered with equally strong support for mathematics, sciences and arts. Extensive extra-curricular activities. Entry at 4+ and 5+ is by playgroup activity and interview: at 11+ and 16+ by examination and interview.

The school is purpose-built, with a new technology building, two language and twelve science laboratories, computer rooms (one with 38-station network) and large library with CD-ROMs. A splendidly equipped art and music building opened in 1995. There is a sports hall, indoor heated swimming pool, tennis courts and extensive playing fields. Junior girls have specialist teaching and facilities for science, music and physical education. Academic and music scholarships are available.

Haileybury

Hertford, Hertfordshire SG13 7NU
Tel: 01992 463353 Fax: 01992 467603

Head D J Jewell MA, MSc, FRSA
Founded 1862
Type Independent
Religious denomination Church of England
Members of HMC
Age range 11 – 18 *Boarders from* 13
No of pupils (day) 180; *(boarding)* 420
Girls 80; *Boys* 520
Junior 30; *Senior* 270; *Sixth form* 300
Fees per term (day) £2,045 – £3,075; *(boarding)* £4,240
Fees per annum (day) £6,135 – £9,225; *(boarding)* £12,720

Day boys admitted at 11, 13 and 16. Boarding boys admitted at 13 and 16. Girls admitted into sixth form.
Magnificent classical buildings set in a beautiful 500-acre campus of playing fields, woods and

farmland. Yet only 20 miles north of central London and one hour by road from Heathrow. Combines high academic standards with wide range of activities: especially art, music, drama and sport. Please contact the registrar for a prospectus.

Heath Mount School

Woodhall Park, Watton-at-Stone, Hertford, Hertfordshire SG14 3NG
Tel: 01920 830230 Fax: 01920 830357

Head Rev H J Matthews BSc, MA, PGCE
Founded 1817
Type Co-educational boarding and day
Religious denomination Church of England
Members of IAPS
Age range 3 – 13 *Boarders from* 7 – 13
No of pupils (day) 284; *(boarding)* 50
Girls 120; *Boys* 219
Fees per term (day) £1,240 – £1,936; *(boarding)* £2,268 – £2,429
Fees per annum (day) £3,720 – £5,808; *(boarding)* £6,804 – £7,287

Heath Mount School, established over 175 years ago, is located at Woodhall Park, a beautiful Georgian mansion in 40 acres of private parkland. The mansion's vast cellar areas have been imaginatively converted to house up-to-date technology, art and science laboratories and a flourishing sixth-form centre where pupils run their own business and coffee bar. The school also has its own purpose-built pre-prep and sports hall. Weekly and half-weekly boarding places are available as well as day places. Girls board at River House which is also on the estate. Leavers go to all the major public schools.

Lochinver House School

Heath Road, Potters Bar, Hertfordshire EN6 1LW
Tel: 01707 653064 Fax: 01707 653064

Head Patrick Atkinson
Founded 1947
Type Boys' day preparatory
Religious denomination Inter-denominational
Age range 4 – 13
No of pupils (day) 325
Boys 325

Lochinver House School was founded in 1947 and since that time its facilities have developed to provide a high-quality all-round education leading to Common Entrance and scholarship level.

Lochinver has playing fields on site, and a very successful music department. Boys are able to join choirs, instrumental groups, wind band and school orchestra.

During his school career, a boy will spend a certain amount of time in France. The cost of this and other curriculum-related trips such as outdoor pursuits is covered by the fees.

Lochinver has a fully integrated pastoral care system and offers a wide range of activities and a late-stay group for younger boys.

The Princess Helena College

Preston, Hitchin, Hertfordshire SG4 7RT
Tel: 01462 432100 Fax: 01462 432100

Head Mr John Jarvis OBE
Founded 1820
Type Secondary independent
Religious denomination Church of England
Age range 11 – 18 *Boarders from* 11
No of pupils (day) 45; *(boarding)* 105
Girls 150
Senior 110; *Sixth form* 40
Fees per term (day) £2,320; *(boarding)* £3,330
Fees per annum (day) £6,960; *(boarding)* £9,990

Curriculum: all subjects of the National Curriculum.
Languages: French, German, Spanish, Italian, Latin.

At GCSE all girls take English, English literature, mathematics, French and at least one science. GCSE options include geography, history, design technology, music, art, German, Spanish, Italian, Latin and drama. All the main academic subjects are also offered at A level.

Entry requirements and procedures: Common Entrance or own entrance examinations and interview. Five passes at C or above at GCSE for sixth-form entry.
Examinations offered: GCSEs and A levels; Cambridge First Certificate.
Academic and leisure facilities: design technology centre opened 1992. Magnificent sports hall with four badminton courts, plus heated swimming pool and extensive playing fields.
Scholarships: 11+, 12+, 13+ and sixth form. Minor awards available for music and art.
Boarding facilities: newly refurbished junior accommodation in small dormitories in the main Lutyens building. Single study bedrooms in the GCSE year. The separate sixth form house is an extremely attractive building which was opened in 1992 by our President, Her Royal Highness Princess Alice, Duchess of Gloucester.

Queenswood

Shepherds Way, Brookmans Park, Hatfield, Hertfordshire AL9 6NS
Tel: 01707 652262 Fax: 01707 649267

Head Mrs A M B Butler
Founded 1894
Type Girls' boarding and day
Religious denomination Inter denominational
Members of GSA, GBGSA, BSA
Age range 11 – 18 *Boarders from* 11
No of pupils (day) 60; *(boarding)* 335
Girls 395
Fees per term (day) £2,256; *(boarding)* sixth form £3,814; *others* £3,658

Queenswood School's convenient location near London in beautiful surroundings and with up-to-date facilities provides many opportunities. The school is a caring Christian community well known for its commitment to pastoral care. Our educational emphasis is increasingly on European connections, language confidence and information technology competence across the curriculum. Science, sport and music, Young Engineers and Young Enterprise are part of a forward-looking school which combines the stability and traditional values of a boarding school with an innovative approach to education inside and outside the classroom.

Queenswood offers day places to girls wishing to share in a vibrant boarding school environment.

Rickmansworth Masonic School

Rickmansworth Park, Rickmansworth, Hertfordshire WD3 4HF
Tel: 01923 773168 Fax: 01923 896729

Head Mrs I M Andrews MA
Founded 1788
Type Independent
Religious denomination Church of England
Members of GSA, GBGSA
Age range 4½+ – 18 *Boarders from* 7
No of pupils (day) 392; *(boarding)* 298
Girls 690
Junior 130; *Senior* 400; *Sixth form* 125; *Infant* 45
Fees per term (day) £920 – £1,787; *(boarding)*
£1,743 – £2,937

The school has exceptional facilities for academic work, including good laboratories, an unusually attractive circular library and separate areas for music, drama, craft and art and design. A two-year business studies course leads to GNVQ level 3. There is a fine chapel and sporting facilities include a heated indoor swimming pool, 18 tennis courts and superb playing fields within an estate of 315 acres.

There are 130 sixth form pupils and a wide-ranging curriculum is supported by a fully qualified staff. A favourable staff/pupil ratio of 1:12 ensures that pupils get much individual attention.

Rickmansworth is close to the M25 and has a London Transport/British Rail station. It is close to London (Heathrow) airport. The school's buildings are magnificent and purpose-built. The whole site is set among the beautiful backslope of the Chiltern hills. It is easily accessible and yet rural in outlook.

Boarding pupils are cared for in well-appointed and spacious houses. Dormitories and study bedrooms are carpetted and comfortably furnished. In each house there is a balanced number of boarders and day pupils.

The sixth-form house is a most agreeable residential and social centre. Fifth-form girls generally stay on and some new girls enter at sixth-form level. All sixth form pupils have single or shared study bedroom accommodation. Each year most sixth formers go on to do university degree courses and other programmes of higher education; others find careers in professional and commercial fields.

The school caters for girls who are above average in ability, but it is not narrowly academic. Extra-curricular activities include music, drama, public speaking and debating. Duke of Edinburgh Award activities, Guides, Brownies, dancing, sailing, games and other sporting activities all flourish, as well as a very large number of clubs and societies.

Admission is by the school's own entrance examination and interview. There are a number of general scholarships available for academic excellence and special talents in music and art. There are six foundation scholarships available each year at 11+ for daughters of freemasons.

The Rickmansworth Masonic School Charitable Trust exists for the advancement of education and the relief of need.

St Albans High School for Girls

Townsend Avenue, St Albans, Hertfordshire AL1 3SJ
Tel: 01727 853800

Head Mrs C Y Daly
Founded 1889
Type Independent
Religious denomination Church of England
Members of GSA, GBGSA, ISIS
Age range 7 – 18
No of pupils (day) 720
Girls 720
Junior 184; *Senior* 401; *Sixth form* 135
Fees per term (day) £1,300 – £1,570
Fees per annum (day) £3,900 – £4,710

Founded in 1889, the school is situated on a pleasant urban site. It is Christian by tradition and ethos, closely connected with St Albans Abbey. A broad academic education is provided, including all the subjects in the National Curriculum, in both junior and senior schools. Teaching methods are modern and extensive use is made of aids such as computers and audio-video equipment. Public examination results at GCSE and Advanced level reach high standards. Girls go on to a wide variety of careers, most via degree courses. Extra-curricular activities are plentiful: music and drama feature strongly. Facilities for physical education include playing fields and a new sports hall.

Entry requirements: examinations are set annually at ages 7, 11, and 16; intermediate ages sit appropriate examinations if and when places are available. Three academic scholarships and one music scholarship are available on entry at 11; a further three academic scholarships are available on entry to the sixth form.

St Albans High School for Girls is a registered charity.

St Christopher School

Barrington Road, Letchworth, Hertfordshire SG6 3JZ
Tel: 01462 679301 Fax: 01462 481578

Head Colin Reid MA (since 1981)
Founded 1915
Type Co-educational
Religious denomination Non-denominational
Members of GBA and SHMIS
Age range 2½ – 18 *Boarders from* 8 – 18
No of pupils (day) 302; *(boarding)* 167
Girls 180; *Boys* 289
Junior 95; *Senior* 342; *Sixth form* 90
Fees per term (day) £703 – £2,062; *(boarding)* £2,914 – £3,640
Fees per annum (day) £2,109 – £6,186; *(boarding)* £8,742 – £10,920

St Christopher School is situated in Letchworth, 35 miles north of London on the A1(M) with easy access to the M25 and all major airports. The fast trains from Kings Cross take 30 minutes. There is a domestic village atmosphere with most of the buildings in the 'Garden City' idiom and surrounded by attractive grounds.

The school provides a complete education from infancy to adulthood. Children of one family, whatever their ages, can attend the same school. With over 50 per cent of senior boys and girls boarding, the school provides day as well as boarding pupils with a wide range of opportunity throughout every day of the week.

Boarders live in family-style houses having breakfast, evening meal and supper with their houseparents. The diet is vegetarian. There is a strong community feel and many staff live in or adjacent to the school with their own children attending.

The school has long been noted for the value it places on the individual and for the encouragement of self-confidence. It attracts children (and parents) with strong independent attitudes and many children who need to be valued for themselves flourish at St Christopher. There is no school uniform worn apart from in games and all are referred to by first names.

The teaching is of a high standard and academic results are creditable. Most sixth formers proceed to a degree course and the school gives careful advice on future plans. St Christopher does not believe in artificial competition in academic work; thus there are no subject or form orders and no prizes.

The school is strong in the creative and performing arts as well as the core academic subjects such as science. There are excellent, purpose-built music facilities and a superb theatre which is run by pupils and used for drama teaching and performances by all ages.

There is a very wide range of sports, games and extra-curricular courses with a special emphasis on outdoor pursuits such as climbing, walking, camping and orienteering. There are major expeditions for all in each year group and regular opportunities to become involved in weekend trips.

The school has strong local support and pupils are involved in a range of ventures among the local community. There are strong international links and regular exchanges with schools in France, Germany and Austria and visits by sixth formers to development projects in Rajasthan, India.

St Edmund's College

Old Hall Green, Ware, Hertfordshire 5G11 1DS
Tel: 01920 821504 Fax: 01920 823011

Head D J J McEwen
Founded 1568
Type Independent
Religious denomination Roman Catholic
Members of HMC, GBA
Age range 3 – 18 *Boarders from* 7 – 18
No of pupils (day) 326; *(boarding)* 157
Girls 176; *Boys* 307
Junior 64; *Senior* 302; *Sixth form* 117
Fees per term (day) £1,695 – £2,040; *(boarding)*
£2,575 – £3,185;
Fees per annum (day) £5,085 – £6,120 *(boarding)*
£7,725 – £9,555

Curriculum: National Curriculum plus, including Latin.
Entry: entrance exam; Common Entrance; interview; contact the admissions secretary.
Exams: GCSE, A level, GNVQ, Oxbridge.
Facilities: IT centre and multimedia, nine laboratories, art and CDT, sports hall, music school and music laboratory, sixth-form centre, swimming pool. Two hundred acres of games fields.
Scholarships: awarded on basis of entrance exam. Assisted places.
Boarding: 7-13 in St Hugh's; 13-18 in Challoner and Poynter Houses in small rooms – singles in sixth form.

St Francis' College

The Broadway, Letchworth, Hertfordshire SG6 3PJ
Tel: 01402 070011 Fax: 01402 082301

Head Miss M Hegarty BA, HDipEd, DMS
Founded 1933
Type Girls' independent day and boarding
Religious denomination Christian (Roman Catholic foundation)
Members of GSA, GBGSA, ISIS
Age range 3 – 18 *Boarders from* 7+
No of pupils (day) 271; *(boarding)* 45
Junior 124; *Senior* 192; *Sixth form* 54
Fees per term (day) £1,040 – £1,675; *(boarding)*
£2,845 – £3,270

St Francis' College is situated in a very pleasant residential area of Letchworth Garden City within easy reach of London and Cambridge.
Curriculum: a broad academic education is offered in both the junior and senior schools. The college is well equipped with a fine theatre, information technology centre, art and drama studios. The majority of girls take ten subjects at GCSE and continue to A level and university. There is a wide range of sports, public speaking, music and drama on offer and pupils are encouraged to participate in The Duke of Edinburgh Award scheme, St John Ambulance and the Young Enterprise scheme.
Entry requirements: entry to the preparatory department by interview and assessment. Entrance to the senior school is by entrance examination at 11+ and 13+ and 16+. Intermediate ages sit an appropriate examination if and when places are available. A number of major and minor scholarships are awarded each year for entry 11+ and 13+. There is one music scholarship available each year. Awards are available for entry at 16+.
St Francis' College Trust is a registered charity which exists to provide education for girls.

St Martha's Senior School

Camlet Way, Hadley, Barnet, Hertfordshire EN5 5PX
Tel: 0181 449 6889 Fax: 0181 441 5632

Head Sister M Cecile Archer BA (Hons), PGCE
Founded 1947
Type Independent, girls'
Religious denomination Roman Catholic
Age range 11 – 18
No of pupils (day) 305
Girls 305
Senior 305; *Sixth form* 41
Fees per term (day) £1,050
Fees per annum (day) £3,150

St Martha's Senior School is a Catholic foundation under the direction of the Sisters of St Martha, which exists in order to promote the spiritual, aesthetic, intellectual and physical well-being of every girl put into its care, in the spirit of the Gospel. Girls are selected through an entrance examination and are placed in one of two parallel forms in which they will remain for the first five years. At the end of Year 7 (first year) girls are placed in different groups, based on ability, for French, mathematics and science. During the first three years pupils follow a common academic and creative course which includes all the requirements of the National Curriculum, with additions. At the end of the fifth year (Year 11) GCSE is taken, normally in eight subjects. Girls who wish to stay on then enter the sixth form, and can follow a wide variety of courses leading to A levels.

Sherrardswood School

Lockleys, Welwyn, Hertfordshire AL6 0BJ
Tel: 01438 714282

Head M C Lloyd MA
Founded 1928
Type Co-educational day and boarding
Religious denomination Church of England
Members of ISAI, ISIS
Age range 3 – 18 *Boarders from* 8
No of pupils (day) 286; *(boarding)* 32
Girls 147; *Boys* 172
Junior 198; *Senior* 121; *Sixth form* 20
Fees per term (day) £902 – £1,479; *(boarding)* £2,268 – £2,795
Fees per annum (day) £2,706 – £4,437; *(boarding)* £6,804 – £8,385

The school is situated in 25 acres of splendid parkland adjoining the A1(M). The junior and boarding departments are situated in a fine eighteenth-century listed building whilst the senior department has recently moved into new purpose-built accommodation on the same site. The school's games fields and swimming pool are shared between the two departments. Entry to the senior department is by examination, interview and report from previous school. A wide range of GCSE, A level and 16+ vocational courses is offered. Specialist facilities in purpose-built accommodation exists for sciences, technology, music, art, computers, food technology and art and design. A large number of clubs and extra-curricular activities run at lunchtime and after school. The boarding house is for approximately 40 boarders aged 8 – 18 and makes use of all the leisure and sports facilities on site. Two scholarships of up to half the fees are available dependent upon results in the entrance exam.

Stanborough School

Stanborough Park, Garston, Watford, Hertfordshire WD2 6JT
Tel: 01923 673268 Fax: 01923 893212

Head Dr A Luxton
Founded 1941
Type Independent
Religious denomination Seventh Day Adventist
Age range 3½ – 18 *Boarders from* 10
No of pupils (day) 173; *(boarding)* 42
Girls 102; *Boys* 113
Junior 97; *Senior* 98; *Sixth form* 20
Fees per term (day) £610 – £920; *(boarding)* £1,990 – £2,335
Fees per annum (day) £1,830 – £2,910; *(boarding)* £5,970 – £7,005

Stanborough School is a Christian co-educational school, committed to developing individual potential within a caring and well-disciplined environment. Entry is by interview, reports and examination and pupils are aged between 3½ and 18. Children of all religious backgrounds and cultures are welcomed.

In its programme and ethos the school nurtures community spirit and encourages responsibility and initiative. Exams offered include LAMDA, RSA, GCSE and A level. The boarding facilities offer ensuite facilities in twin rooms, while the extensive parkland and school gymnasium provide ample opportunity for varied leisure activities. Local facilities also allow for swimming and ice-skating, while close proximately to London, Heathrow and the M1, M25 and M40 make transportation easy.

The main school building includes excellent new facilities: a language laboratory, three science laboratories, an art room, including a pottery kiln, technology laboratory and a music room. There is a students' association and various clubs to encourage student leadership throughout.

Hull Grammar School

Cottingham Road, Hull, Humberside HU5 2DL
Tel: 01482 440144 Fax: 01482 441312

Head R Haworth MA (Cantab)
Founded c 1320
Type Co-educational day school
Religious denomination Church of England
Members of ISAI, ISIS
Age range 2½ – 18
No of pupils (day) 370
Girls 155; *Boys* 215
Junior 102; *Senior* 215; *Sixth form* 53
Fees per term (day) £750 – £1,275
Fees per annum (day) £2,250 – £3,825

The school became independent in 1988. It is the aim of the school to provide a stable, caring and disciplined environment in which excellence will be nurtured. One of the principal strengths of the school is the quality of the teachers, who aim to bring out the best in individual pupils according to their needs and abilities. While the principal target is academic achievement, this is set in the context of an all-round education. Academic scholarships are available at 11+ and 16+.

The school stands in its own grounds close to both Hull and Humberside Universities. Pupils travel from all parts of the Humberside region. The main building houses a fine assembly hall, classrooms, a spacious library, five fully equipped science laboratories, a large gymnasium and a computer centre. There are specialist facilities for music, craft, design and technology and home economics. A sixth form centre provides a common room and study room, and there is a specialist careers room.

St James' School

22 Bargate, Grimsby, South Humberside DN34 4SY
Tel: 01472 362093 Fax: 01472 351437

Head Mr D J Berisford
Founded 1880
Type Independent
Religious denomination Church of England
Age range 4 – 19 Boarders from 7
No of pupils (day) 186; *(boarding)* 64
Girls 95; *Boys* 155
Junior 93; *Senior* 122; *Sixth form* 35
Fees per annum (day) £2,235 – £5,710;
(boarding) full £6,168 – £7,983; weekly £5,772 – £7,584

Founded as the Choir School for St James Parish Church in 1880, St James' is a co-educational day and boarding school for 270 pupils from the age of four to 18. Small class sizes, a broad curriculum, specialist help for EFL and Learning Support together with a caring, homely atmosphere have all contribution towards a high academic standard for all ages. A wide range of subjects is offered at GCSE and A level, the results being well above the national average. Bursaries are awarded for outstanding academic and musical potential.

There is a strong, musical tradition: orchestras, choirs, choristers and numerous ensembles. Emphasis is also placed on a wide variety of sporting activities, drama, clubs, trips within Britain and abroad, the Duke of Edinburgh Award Scheme, which all help to develop the child into a happy, well-rounded individual.

Bembridge School

Hillway, Bembridge, Isle of Wight PO35 5PH
Tel: 01983 872101 Fax: 01983 872576

Head J High MA (Oxon)
Founded 1919
Type Co-educational
Religious denomination Non-denominational
Members of SHMIS
Age range 11 – 16
No of pupils (day) 118; *(boarding)* 125
Girls 73; *Boys* 170
Fees per term (day) £1,490 – £1,540; *(boarding)* £2,560 – £3,090
Fees per annum (day) £4,470 – £4,620; *(boarding)* £7,680 – £9,270

Curriculum: throughout the school this is based on the National Curriculum. All pupils take seven to ten GCSE courses which may include options such as German, business studies, CDT or drama, as well as the usual core subjects. After fifth form Bembridge pupils join the sixth form at neighbouring Ryde School where a very wide range of A level courses is available to them. Foreign pupils are prepared for EFL examinations. There is a well-established CReSTeD-recognised dyslexia centre, with specialist staff. Bembridge is a corporate member of the British Dyslexia Association. Study skills are taught at all levels in the school.
Entry requirements: entry by Common Entrance or Bembridge tests, supported by reports from the current school.
Academic and leisure facilities: excellent laboratory, classroom, library, art and CDT facilities. New computer centre in the junior department. IT facilities used extensively in the senior departments. Sports hall, squash courts, golf course. Fine playing fields in 100 acres of coastal grounds. A very wide range of activities includes choir, orchestra, drama club, archery, field sports club, canoeing, sailing and many other outdoor pursuits. The school is licensed as a centre for the Duke of Edinburgh Award Scheme.
Scholarships: a number of scholarships are awarded each year and at least one is reserved for music and one for art. Special allowances for members of Her Majesty's Armed Forces.
Boarding facilities: the junior boarders are accommodated in small, homely dormitories and there are games rooms and other areas for relaxation. The pupils are closely supervised by the matron and other resident staff. There are three boarding houses in the senior part of the school and the dormitories are divided into two- or three-bed units, while sixth formers have single study bedrooms. An SRN supervises the school sanatorium.

Almost all leavers go on to further studies.

Bembridge is a small school with a high staff to pupil ratio which allows individual attention and a flexible approach. The beautiful environment is ideal for those interested in the creative arts, outdoor pursuits or field studies.

Registered charity which exists to provide education for boys and girls.

Ashford School

East Hill, Ashford, Kent TN24 8PB
Tel: 01233 625171 Fax: 01233 647185

Head Mrs Patricia Metham BA (Bristol), JP
Founded 1898
Type Girls' independent boarding and day
Religious denomination Inter-denominational
Members of GSA, GBGSA, IAPS
Age range 2½ – 18 *Boarders from* 8
No of pupils (day) 438; *(boarding)* 80
Girls 518
Junior 181; *Senior* 377; *Sixth form* 115
Fees per term (day) £318 – £1,950; *(boarding)*
£3,007 – £3,493
Fees per annum (day) £954 – £5,850; *(boarding)*
£9,021 – £10,479

Curriculum: the school encourages girls to maintain breadth of interest and skills. Girls choose between eight and ten subjects, including separate or combined sciences, technology and a range of languages. Economics, business studies, human biology and theatre studies are among the 23 two-year courses available in the sixth form; 96 per cent go on to higher education. Girls develop 'real world' skills through work experience and active involvement in the immediate community and Europe. There are three artists in residence.

Entry requirements: school report and interview for the sixth form, supporting six or more A–C grades at GCSE. Written tests at 11 and 13. Test and interview for junior school at seven, informal interview at three and five. Academic and musical scholarships and assisted places.

Examinations offered: ULEAC, SEG and MEG Boards for GCSE. London, AEB and Cambridge Boards for Advanced and Advanced Supplementary levels. Girls are prepared for Oxbridge entry.

Academic and sports facilities: there are computer centres and IT networks in both senior and junior schools. A new language laboratory combines audio-visual and IT facilities, including e-mail. There are nine laboratories, two computer rooms, and a well-equipped, computer-aided design and technology centre.

There are 11 netball/tennis courts, playing fields, heated indoor pool, gym and sports hall. Music and drama work in a large performance hall and two smaller octagons. The 23-acre site in Ashford provides good recreation space and a nature study centre, with easy access from London, the continent and beyond.

Boarding: three boarding houses offer a friendly and supportive environment. Clubs and activities include a magic circle, jazz, video-making, art, cookery, drama, riding and a range of sports.

Ashford School Charitable Trust exists to provide high-quality education for girls.

Babington House School

Grange Drive, Chislehurst, Kent BR7 5ES
Tel: 0181 467 5537

Head Mrs E V Walter
Founded 1887
Type Co-educational day school to 7+. Girls to 16+
Religious denomination Non-denominational
Age range 3 – 16+
No of pupils (day) 206
Girls 150; *Boys* 56
Junior 150; *Senior* 70
Fees per term (day) £1,135 – £1,450
Fees per annum (day) £3,405 – £4,350

The school is deliberately small – class sizes average 16. With the exception of the laboratory, nursery and gymnasium, the school is contained within a large Victorian house. The curriculum reflects the National Curriculum but is not bound to it. Expectations are high. Most pupils take eight or nine GCSEs and individual tuition and examinations are taken in instrumental music, singing, elocution and dance. Sport covers tennis, netball, gymnastics, volleyball, badminton, trampolining, swimming, squash and skiing. All pupils proceed to higher education; mixed sixth forms, with neighbouring major boys' schools favoured (those receiving our 7+ transfers).

Informal interview and testing for entry at seven and under; from 7+, a half to full day's assessment. Scholarships and bursaries at 11+.

Pupils from abroad are largely the children of embassy staff and bankers. Entry may be agreed on full report from current school, where relevant. An interview with either or both parents is a prerequisite.

Beechwood School, Sacred Heart

Pembury Road, Tunbridge Wells, Kent TN2 3QD
Tel: 01892 529193 Fax: 01892 536164

Head Mr Trevor Hodkinson
Founded 1915
Type Boarding and day
Religious denomination Catholic
Members of GSA, GBGSA, SHA
Age range 3 – 18 girls, 3 – 7 boys *Boarders from* 9
No of pupils (day) 136; *(boarding)* 83
Girls 212; *Boys* 7
Junior 72; *Senior* 93; *Sixth form* 54
Fees per term (day) £850 – £2,110; *(boarding)* £2,720 – £3,535
Fees per annum (day) £2,550 – £6,330; *(boarding)* £8,160 – £10,605

Curriculum: broad-based curriculum up to National Curriculum Key Stage 3, including technology, drama, PSE, plus all subjects required by National Curriculum. Wide choice of subjects for GCSE and A level, including integrated business studies course for A level (business studies, computing, accounting and law). Careers advice throughout school and coaching in examinations skills and university entrance for all sixth formers.
Entry: by written application with school reports at any stage. An entrance examination at 11+ only.
Examinations: all main boards and subjects for GCSE and A level. EFL examinations for overseas students, including Cambridge first certificate proficiency and JNB. RSA examinations for sixth form.
Facilities: modern art and science block and computer wing, heated swimming pool, sports hall, two large auditoria. High proportion of single rooms for boarders, no dormitory accommodation. Sitting rooms for each age-group. Beautiful grounds including six tennis courts, games fields and gardens. Full programme of lunch-time and after-school activities. Special activity programme for boarders every weekend – sports trips, shopping, cinema.
Scholarships: academic, sports and arts scholarships available at 11+, 13+ and 16+. Details from head's secretary.
General: Beechwood School is one of the international network of Sacred Heart Schools. It is Catholic in its traditions, but welcomes girls of all religions. Academic results are excellent. All age-groups are taught in small sets and the pupil:teacher ratio is 8:1. There is a high level of pastoral care, every girl is assigned to a tutor for general supervision and a large residential staff cares for the boarders 24 hours a day. The majority of girls are English but the school welcomes applications from overseas students, believing that an international education and learning to live as world citizens is an essential part of preparing for adult life.

Bickley Park School

2 Southborough Road, Bickley, Bromley, Kent BR1 2DY
Tel: 0181 467 2195 Fax: 0181 467 2195

Head D J A Cassell
Founded 1918
Type Independent preparatory school for boys
Religious denomination Non-denominational
Members of IAPS, NAHT
Age range 3 – 14
No of pupils (day) 359
Girls 10 *Boys* 349
Fees per term (day) £530 – £1,830
Fees per annum (day) £1,590 – £5,490

The school, situated between Bromley and Chislehurst, was founded in 1918 and since 1962 it has been a charitable trust administered by a board of governors. The buildings are surrounded by pleasant grounds; close by is a large and excellent sports field.

There are three departments to the school: nursery (boys and girls 3 – 5 years), Parva (boys aged 5 – 8 years) and Park (boys aged 8 – 14 years). The aim is to develop each child through a broad, balanced and well-defined curriculum, enabling them to move forward with confidence and self-discipline to the next phase of education.

Initially there is no entry test, but if boys are over the age of five years, they are tested to ensure they are capable of benefiting from the education provided.

As well as preparing each boy ultimately for the Common Entrance examination, or a scholarship attempt, there are ample opportunities for extra-curricular activities.

Breaside Preparatory School

41– 43 Orchard Road, Bromley, Kent BR1 2PR
Tel: 0181 460 0916 Fax: 0181 466 5664

Head N G Murray
Founded 1950
Type Independent Preparatory
Religious denomination Inter-denominational
Age range 3 – 11
No of pupils (day) 215
Girls 53; *Boys* 162
Fees per term (day) £600 – £1,120
Fees per annum (day) £1,800 – £3,360

Breaside is a co-educational school with a well-established reputation for friendliness and a growing reputation for high achievement. On the Chislehurst side of Bromley it is easily reached from many parts of south-east London.

Curriculum: a strong emphasis is placed on individual attention in small classes. Children are prepared for all senior schools and those with additional promise sit scholarships. The broadly based curriculum aims to help children fulfil their potential. French is taught from reception and pupils are able to participate in the many games, clubs and activities. The school is well resourced and enjoys the support of belonging to Asquith Court Schools Ltd.

Entry requirements: interview and test after 5 years of age. The school is well worth a visit to experience the busy, caring environment which its dedicated staff create.

Cobham Hall

Cobham, Gravesend, Kent DA12 3BL
Tel: 01474 823371/824319 Fax: 01474 822995

Head Mrs Rosalind McCarthy
Founded 1962
Type Girls' independent senior
Religious denomination Inter-denominational
Members of GSA, GBGSA, Round Square
Age range 11 – 18 *Boarders from* 11 – 18
No of pupils (day) 20 *(boarding)* 180
Girls All
Sixth form 60
Fees per term (day) £2,200 (11 – 13), £2,750 (14+); *(boarding)* £4,285 (11 – 18)
Fees per annum (day) £6,600 (11 – 13), £8,250 (14+); *(boarding)* £12,855 (11 – 18)

Cobham Hall is a beautiful and historic building and is set in 150 acres of landscaped grounds. The school is conveniently situated close to the M25 within easy reach of Heathrow and Gatwick.

There is an unusually wide curriculum catering for the whole ability range. One hundred per cent of leavers go on to higher education.

The school offers junior (11+, 12+, 13+) and sixth form scholarships including four full scholarships for day girls. Enquiries to registrar for further details.

Combe Bank School

Sundridge, Sevenoaks, Kent TN14 6AE
Tel: 01959 563720 Fax: 01959 561997

Head Miss Nina Spurr (senior); Mrs E Marsden (preparatory)
Founded 1972
Type Girls' independent day school
Religious denomination Roman Catholic and Anglican
Members of GSA, GBGSA, ISIS
Age range 3 – 18
No of pupils (day) 404
Junior 191 *Senior* 213 *Sixth form* 43
Fees per annum (day) Nursery £1,785; Junior £4,188; Senior £5,460

Girls at Combe Bank work in exceptionally happy and beautiful surroundings, and it is a school where everyone has a chance of real achievement. We believe that each of our pupils, from the really academic to the girl whose gifts are more practical or social, needs to find an outlet for her talents and recognition of her efforts.

Small classes allow us to match teaching to intellect in all subjects, with excellent results. Pupils enjoy a sound and interesting programme of study, a full and active range of after-school activities, and a thorough and stimulating preparation for life in the Europe of the 21st century.

Dover College

Dover, Kent CT17 9RH
Tel: 01304 205969 Fax: 01304 242208

Head M P G Wright Esq BA
Founded 1871
Type Co-educational day and boarding
Religious denomination Church of England
Members of HMC, ISIS
Age range 11 – 18 *Boarders from* 13
No of pupils (day) 98; *(boarding)* 152
Girls 87; *Boys* 163
Junior (11 – 12) 25; *Senior (13 – 16)* 133; *Sixth form* 92
Fees per term (day) £1,235 – £2,050; *(boarding)* £3,840 (weekly £2,235 – £3,625)
Fees per annum (day) £3,705 – £6,150; *(boarding)* £11,520 (weekly £7,200 – £10,875)

Dover College was founded in 1871 and occupies the grounds of the ancient Priory of St Martin. The College Close with its medieval and modern buildings creates an attractive enclosed haven of tranquillity and learning. Pupils still use the original 12th century refectory and chapel. There has been a centre of learning on this site for 800 years. The college was granted a Royal Charter by His Majesty King George Vth in 1923 and the patron of the college is the Lord Warden of the Cinque Ports, currently Her Majesty Queen Elizabeth the Queen Mother.

The closest school to continental Europe, which can be reached in 40 minutes, there are four European capitals within three hours' drive by car, as well as excellent road and rail links to London and beyond.

Fully co-educational since 1975, Dover College caters for both local children and those from overseas, including a large component from continental Europe. The distinct atmosphere of the school is one of a small, caring environment with a European outlook. Pupils have many opportunities to travel, arranged through the European Studies department.

The main aims of the school are to encourage to the fullest possible extent the talents of each individual boy or girl and to prepare him or her for adult life. Special emphasis is placed upon the acquisition of the habits of industry, honesty, loyalty and decent behaviour.

The school is very positive academically and prides itself on value-added success. Individual guidance and supervision at all levels. The teacher/pupil ratio is low at 1:10 and classes are small. There is a special needs department for children with dyslexia or learning difficulties, as well as a qualified EFL teacher.

The college fields strong teams in the usual independent school games, and pupils have also competed at national level in athletics, fencing, judo and sailing. In addition, a wide range of clubs and societies take place in afternoons and evenings.

Entry requirements: Common Entrance, interview or reports. Scholarships and bursaries available for children with high academic, music, art or sporting ability. Assisted places and service discounts.

The Duke of York's Royal Military School

Dover, Kent CT15 5EQ
Tel: 01304 245024 Fax: 01304 245019

Head G H Wilson BA, MEd, FRSA
Founded 1803
Type Independent co-educational boarding school
Religious denomination Church of England
Members of GBA, BSA, SHMIS, ISIS
Age range 11 – 18 *Boarders from* 11
No of pupils (boarding) 490
Girls 102; *Boys* 388
Junior 138; *Senior* 242; *Sixth form* 110
Fees per term (boarding) £250
Fees per annum (boarding) £750

Curriculum: National Curriculum to GCSE. A level courses and BTEC National Diploma and Advanced GNVQ courses in engineering and business in sixth form.
Entry registration: one parent must have four years' service in the Armed Forces. Own entrance tests plus report from present school.
Range of fees: as at 1 September 95: boarding £250 per term. Independent co-educational boarding. Convenient for travel to Forces locations. Strong academic emphasis with two-year courses in sixth form.
Academic, leisure and boarding facilities: the Duke of York's is a magnificently resourced boarding school standing in 150 acres of attractive parkland two kilometres north of Dover. Accommodation and facilities are first class.

Leisure facilities include 13 tennis courts (all-weather and grass), excellent sports pitches, all weather hockey pitch, golf course, rifle ranges, cricket pavillion, badminton court, indoor pool and gymnasium, indoor cricket school and athletics track.

Dulwich Preparatory School, Cranbrook

Coursehorn, Cranbrook, Kent TN17 3NP
Tel: 01580 712179 Fax: 01580 715322

Head M C Wagstaffe BA (Hons), PGCE
Founded 1939
Type Independent preparatory school
Religious denomination Church of England
Members of IAPS
Age range 3 – 13 *Boarders from* 8
No of pupils (day) 463; *(boarding)* 74
Girls 259; *Boys* 274
Fees per term (day) £645 – £1,865; *(boarding)* £2,785 – £2,865

The school is under the same governing body as Dulwich College Preparatory School, London. The school is fully co-educational, taking pupils on a first come, first served basis. There is a strong academic tradition enabling children to achieve scholarships to top senior schools, with special needs help offered to those with learning difficulties. There is an emphasis on up-to-date teaching and the school has achieved notable successes in music and art.

Entry: at 3+ and 4; by testing from 7+ onwards.
Curriculum: National Curriculum followed. Usual subjects taught, plus French, art, CDT, drama, IT, music and physical education.
Examinations offered: pupils prepare for 11+, Common Entrance and scholarships.
Academic and leisure facilities: music school, art block and CDT centre. All-weather pitches, athletics track, playing fields, tennis courts, sports hall complex, two swimming pools.
Boarding facilities: from age eight, in three houses. Six to ten pupils in each dormitory. Travel to/from airports arranged, plus train travel to/from London escorted by staff.
Special needs: gifted children catered for. Remedial and dyslexia help given. Several staff specially trained.

Farringtons and Stratford House School

Perry Street, Chislehurst, Kent BR7 6LR
Tel: 0181 467 0256/5586 Fax: 0181 295 1575

Head Mrs B J Stock BA Hons
Founded 1911 (merged 1994)
Type Girls' kindergarten, junior and senior
Religious denomination Methodist
Members of GSA, GBGSA
Age range 3 – 18 *Boarders from* 7
No of pupils (day) 450 *(boarding)* 150
Girls 600 *Boys* 5 (in kindergarten only)
Kindergarten 45; *Junior* 210; *Senior* 255; *Sixth form* 87
Fees per term (day) £1,159 – £1,654; *(boarding)* £2,765 – £3,187
Fees per annum (day) £3,447 – £4,962; *(boarding)* £8,295 – £9,561

Farringtons and Stratford House welcomes girls of all abilities and helps them to achieve their full potential in academic study, examination performance, sport, music and drama. The school offers a wide curriculum at GCSE (91 per cent A–C grade in 1995), Advanced level (86 per cent pass rate in 1995) and in vocational courses. There is a strong sixth form, 90 per cent of whom took up degree courses after leaving us in 1995, and a happy, bustling junior school where girls grow in confidence as they acquire the first, basic skills. Our excellent facilities include a new technology block, purpose-built computer suites, newly-equipped science block, a satellite TV system for use in modern language learning, well-stocked libraries and careers room, heated swimming pool and a large, new sports hall adjacent to extensive playing fields. Extra-curricular activities abound for both boarders and day girls.

Friars School

Great Chart, Ashford, Kent TN23 3DJ
Tel: 01233 620493 Fax: 01233 620493

Head Mr P M Ashley BA, CertEd
Founded 1949
Type Co-educational day and boys' boarding
Religious denomination Non-denominational
Members of IAPS, ISIS
Age range 2½ – 13 *Boarders from* 7 – 13
No of pupils (day) 110; *(boarding)* 10
Girls 25; *Boys* 95
Fees per term (day) £400 – £1,775; *(boarding)* £2,475

Friars is a co-educational school catering for children from 2½ to 13 years of age. We aim to give all the children in our care a happy start to their school careers by developing in them the skills and personal qualities essential for a satisfying life. The very generous pupil:staff ratio ensures that each child is seen as an individual, with his or her own special talents, thus enabling them to achieve greater academic, sporting, musical or artistic success.

The school is set in 11 acres of very attractive grounds which include excellent facilities. There are new classroom blocks, all weather surfaces, an outdoor heated swimming pool, an excellent gymnasium and ample playing fields.

The boarding facilities are housed in a delightful Georgian house which has spacious dormitories, a quiet room and a games/television room. The school caters for both weekly and part boarders.

Greenhayes School for Boys

Corkscrew Hill, West Wickham, Kent BR4 9BA
Tel: 0181 777 2093 Fax: 0181 777 2093

Head D J Cozens BA
Founded 1931
Type Independent
Religious denomination Non-denominational
Age range 4½ – 11
No of pupils (day) 104
Junior 59
Fees per term (day) £825
Fees per annum (day) £2,475

Greenhayes is a traditional type of school which combines the aims of good discipline, care for the individual and sound teaching in the basics. *Curriculum*: a firm grounding in reading, language and maths is provided, together with coverage of all other core subjects, including French, music and games. Computers are in use in every class. Music includes singing and recorder tuition, while sports include gymnastics, swimming, football, cricket, and cross-country running. After-school activities include chess and table tennis. Boys are prepared for entrance examinations at 11 years to all the major local independent schools, especially Whitgift, Trinity, Dulwich College and St Dunstan's College, usually with a 100 per cent success rate. There is also a pre-school for boys and girls three to five years.
Entry requirements: for Form 1 – parental interview only. All other ages by interview/test.

Holmewood House

Langton Green, Tunbridge Wells, Kent TN3 0EB
Tel: 01892 862088 Fax: 01892 863970

Head D G Ives MA (Oxon)
Founded 1945
Type Co-educational day and boarding preparatory
Religious denomination Inter-denominational
Members of IAPS
Age range 3 – 13 *Boarders from* 7
Girls 155; *Boys* 293
Fees per term (day) £635 – £2,340; *(boarding)* £3,485

Entry requirements: entry to the school is by interview and test. Academic, music, art and sporting scholarships are offered annually to pupils currently attending state primary schools.

Curriculum: the school follows a broad-based curriculum designed to allow each pupil to fulfil his or her individual potential, while at the same time covering all aspects of the National Curriculum and the Common Entrance and scholarship examinations to independent schools by the age of 13. Full details of the curriculum are supplied with the school prospectus.

The school has regularly enjoyed outstanding academic, art and music successes with the quality and quantity of scholarships won to top independent schools, and through the Common Entrance examination.

Boarding: we operate a flexible boarding system, with both weekly and full boarding.

The housemistress and housemaster, with their respective families, live in flats adjacent to the girls' and boys' dormitories.

Pastoral care: the school is divided into six houses. Day pupils and boarders are mixed in the houses, so that day pupils are fully integrated into the life of the school. A tutor system ensures that each child is cared for and guided during his or her time at the school.

Sports and activities: expert coaching is given in a wide variety of sports including rugby, soccer, hockey, netball, cricket, tennis, shooting, athletics, gymnastics, orienteering, cross-country, golf, archery, fencing, judo, squash and swimming. Facilities include a heated swimming pool, three squash courts, an indoor .22 range, a full-size all-weather pitch and running track, and a magnificent new sports hall.

A new music school and theatre will be built in the near future.

Religious activities: the main aims of the school are to teach children the virtue of hard work and self-discipline in a Christian community and to encourage in them a healthy, independent spirit by allowing plenty of scope for self-expression in creative activities. The school is inter-denominational, but a sound Christian emphasis is put on the essentials for a happy, purposeful community of high personal standards and an understanding for the needs and feelings of others.

Kent College

Canterbury, Kent CT2 9DT
Tel: 01227 763231 Fax: 01227 764777

Head Mr E B Halse BSc (Econ)
Founded 1885
Type Independent
Religious denomination Methodist foundation, inter-denominational
Members of HMC
Age range 4 – 18 *Boarders from* 7
No of pupils (day) 304; *(boarding)* 200
Girls 211; *Boys* 293
Junior 115 (infant 63); *Senior* 523; *Sixth form* 152
Fees per term (day) £1,888; *(boarding)* £3,366
Fees per annum (day) £5,664; *(boarding)* £10,098

When Kent College was founded in 1885, just eight boys were enrolled on the first day. Now the school is fully co-educational with some 530 senior pupils, of whom 230 are boarders. Another 170 pupils attend the infant and junior school. Kent College is one of 14 Methodist secondary schools and this grouping gives much support and strength.

Kent College offers strong academic teaching within the context of a supportive Christian environment. The reputation for sport is outstanding for both boys and girls. Many pupils delight in the varied opportunities in music and drama. We offer a range of activities and are developing links in Eastern Europe. Both schools have dyslexia units which accept small numbers of intelligent dyslexic children each year. There is also the farm, enjoyed by all, in the most agreeable setting of the Moat Park Estate and Blean Woods.

Northbourne Park School

Betteshanger, Deal, Kent CT14 0NW
Tel: 01304 611215 Fax: 01304 619020

Head Mr F W Roche BEd (Hons), MA
Founded 1936
Type Preparatory
Religious denomination Church of England
Members of IAPS
No of pupils (day) 167; *(boarding)* 45
Girls 88; *Boys* 124
Fees per term (day) £1,070 – £1,915; *(boarding)* £2,680
Fees per annum (day) £3,210 – £5,745; *(boarding)* £8,040

Set in beautiful parklands in the Kentish countryside, there is easy access to Dover and the continent, and Gatwick and London are within an 80-minute drive.

Average size of class: 12

Teacher/pupil ratio: 1:10

Curriculum: we prepare children for Common Entrance and individual scholarship examinations. Geography is taught through the French language (French is taught from age 3).

A unique Anglo-French programme is producing bilingual pupils. Academic, choral, music, art and sports scholarships awarded.

Entry requirements and procedures: interview.

Rose Hill School

Culverden Down, Tunbridge Wells, Kent TN4 9SY
Tel: 01892 525591 Fax: 0892 533312

Head J G L Parker Esq BA, JP
Founded 1832
Type Preparatory
Religious denomination Inter-denominational
Members of IAPS, ISIS
Age range 3 – 13+
No of pupils (day) 202
Girls 66 *Boys* 136
Fees per term (day) Pre-prep £560 *Prep* £1,155
Main £1,810
Fees per annum (day) £5,235

Preparation for Common Entrance and scholarships to independent schools and for entry at 11+ and 13+ to excellent local grammar schools.

Magnificent situation on the fringe of the town. Purpose-built facilities and buildings throughout. Fully co-educational, the school aims to help each child fulfil his or her full potential according to the level of ability. Our primary concern is the individual whose well-being is ensured through strong pastoral care within a Christian atmosphere. Highly qualified and experienced staff cover computers, science, design technology, French, Latin, German, Greek, English, history, geography, RE, arts and crafts. Choirs and orchestra are strong. All the major girls' and boys' team games are played, together with tennis, squash, athletics, badminton, orienteering, basketball, gymnastics. The swimming pool and golf course are both popular.

A superb new building houses the pre-preparatory department.

A number of bursaries are available under the Grange Scholarship Foundation.

Entry requirements: tests and/or interviews according to age.

St Edmund's School, Canterbury

St Thomas's Hill, Canterbury, Kent CT2 8HU
Tel: 01227 454575 Fax: 01227 471083

Head A N Ridley Esq MA (Oxon)
Founded 1749
Type Co-educational 3 – 18 day/boarding
Religious denomination Church of England
Members of HMC, IAPS, CSA
Age range 3 – 18 *Boarders from* 7 (boys) 10 (girls)
No of pupils (day) 326; *(boarding)* 170
Girls 155; *Boys* 341
Junior 217; *Senior* 279; *Sixth form* 100
Fees per term (day) from £1,030; *(boarding)* from £2,770
Fees per annum (day) from £3,090; *(boarding)* £8,310

Curriculum: the junior school prepares pupils for the Common Entrance examination taken at the age of 13, and the most able do more advanced work with the opportunity for public school scholarships. Pupils joining the senior school in the lower fifth year (Year nine) follow a broad curriculum of 18 subjects. Normally, up to nine GCSE subjects are taken; thereafter St Edmund's offers a choice of 18 subjects at A level, from which students usually take three.
Entry: normally parents make an appointment with the junior school secretary or in the case of the senior school, the headmaster's secretary. A registration form is completed indicating the intended month (usually September) and year of entry. In the case of the junior school (three to 12/13 years of age) there are some tests and an interview at the school. Successful candidates will be formally offered a place. In the senior school, candidates will offer their Common Entrance examination results or GCSE grades (or predicted grades); alternatively, a report from their previous schools. A completed entrance form and deposit are then required. Detailed joining instructions are subsequently issued by the school.
Facilities: the junior and senior schools are located on the same magnificent 60 acre site – adjoining the University of Kent at Canterbury – which dominates the high ground just outside the city of Canterbury. Both schools are surrounded by an array of sports fields and are served by a newly built sports hall, tennis course and golf course. The schools boast fine, modern, purpose-built teaching facilities.
Scholarships: the junior school educates the choristers of Canterbury cathedral, who are full members of the school. Details of voice trials (held in the autumn) may be obtained from the cathedral organist, David Flood, on 01227 765219. Details of the generous academic, music, sports and art awards, together with bursaries, may be obtained from the school registrar.
Boarding: facilities at St Edmund's are located in houses close by – some with en suite facilities – for the girls, and accommodation for the boys is in the imposing main school building. A full complement of qualified and trained staff is on hand 24 hours a day.

St Lawrence College Junior School

Ramsgate, Kent CT11 7AF
Tel: 01843 591788 Fax: 01843 853271

Head Revd D D R Blackwell BSc
Founded 1884
Type Independent preparatory
Religious denomination Church of England
Members of IAPS
Age range 4 – 13 *Boarders from* 5
No of pupils (day) 107; *(boarding)* 39
Girls 55; *Boys* 91
Fees per term (day) £800 – £1,830; *(boarding)* £2,790
Fees per annum (day) £2,400 – £5,490; *(boarding)* £8,370

Curriculum: lower school teaching aims to lay solid foundations in basic numeracy and literacy, and spoken French is introduced at age seven. From age nine, the range of subjects studied widens, to include science, history, geography, scripture, music and art. Pupils are prepared for Common Entrance and public schools' scholarship examinations, within the context of the central criteria of the National Curriculum. Effort and achievement in each subject is assessed every three weeks. The academic and social life of the school is supported by a strong pastoral system.

Entry requirements and procedures: entry is by interview, supplemented by a test in mathematics and English. Scholarships are available for children at the age of 8+. Special bursaries are available for children of clergy and HM Forces.

Great emphasis is laid on encouragement, the development of enthusiasm and a happy family atmosphere. We aim to make learning fun and give each young person the opportunity to develop mind, body and spirit to the full.

Sevenoaks

Sevenoaks, Kent TN13 1HU
Tel: 01732 455133 Fax: 01732 456143

Head R P Barker MA
Founded 1432
Type Independent co-educational day and boarding
Religious denomination Inter-denominational
Members of HMC
Age range 11 – 18 *Boarders from* 11
No of pupils (day) 620; *(boarding)* 316
Girls 426; *Boys* 510
Junior 128; *Senior* (13 – 16) 410; *Sixth form* 398
Fees per term (day) £2,358; *(boarding)* £3,873
Fees per annum (day) £7,074; *(boarding)* £11,619

Sevenoaks is a co-educational, independent, day and boarding school, situated next to the 1,000 acres of Knole Park, 30 minutes from central London and Gatwick Airport, and an hour from Heathrow. Approximately one-third of the 940 students are boarders. Pupils worldwide enter at 11, 13 or 16, taking GCSEs, A levels and the International Baccalaureate. Sevenoaks aspires to high academic standards – most pupils go on to university – while providing excellent facilities for sport and extra-curricular activities. More than 50 scholarships are awarded annually for academic excellence, art, music, sport and all-round ability. Prospectus and further details from the registrar.

Sibton Park

Lyminge, Folkestone, Kent CT18 8HB
Tel: 01303 862284 Fax: 01303 863429

Head Mr C Blackwell BA, and Mrs Blackwell MA
Founded 1948
Type Preparatory
Religious denomination Inter-denominational
Members of IAPS, ISIS
Age range 1½ – 13 *Boarders from* 7 – 13
No of pupils (day) 60; *(boarding)* 45
Girls 85; *Boys* 20
Fees per term (day) £645 – £1,957; *(boarding)* £2,288 – £2,995

Curriculum: all National Curriculum subjects, plus Latin; extra-curricular include speech and drama, instrumental music, riding, ballet.
Entry requirements and procedures: interview and test.
Scholarships: King Hussein of Jordan scholarship; bursaries: forces, clergy.
Examinations offered: Common Entrance, scholarships, Kent Test, Cambridge English.
Academic and leisure facilities: 16th-century house forms nucleus of well-equipped school: hall, laboratory, computer room, music block, design technology and art studios, three tennis/netball courts, heated swimming pool. Unspoilt countryside surrounds extensive grounds: large lawns, spinney, assault course, children's gardens, pet area, stables, manege, cross country course.
Boarding facilities: girls live as extended family with the principals in main house with cheerful, homely, bedrooms and common-rooms. All travel arrangements made.

Sutton Valence School

Sutton Valence, Maidstone, Kent ME17 3HL
Tel: 01622 842281 Fax: 01622 844093
e-mail: sutton vs @ rmple.co.uk
http://www.rmple.co.uk/ednwch/sites/sutton vs

Head Mr N A Sampson
Founded 1576
Type Co-educational boarding and day school
Members of HMC
Religious denomination Church of England
Age range 11 – 18
No of pupils 400
Girls 140; *Boys* 260
Fees per annum (day) £7,095; *(boarding)* £11,085

Curriculum: all subjects to GCSE and A level. Ninety per cent stay on to A level. Ninety per cent of sixth-form leavers proceed to university.

Entry requirements and procedures: own junior entrance examination at 11+, Common Entrance examination or own examination at 13+, five good GCSE passes for sixth form. Ten assisted places at 11+ to 13+ each year: five at 16+ into the sixth form.

Sutton Valence School is set in a beautiful, safe, country village environment. It has extensive playing fields, a recent music school, a new astro-turf pitch, library and science block (including computer and electronics rooms). Boarding accommodation has recently been refurbished and a multimedia suite has opened to promote interactive learning.

Ursuline College

225 Canterbury Road, Westgate-on-Sea, Kent CT8 8LX
Tel: 01843 834431 Fax: 01843 835365

Head Sr Alice Montgomery DSU, MEd
Founded 1904
Type Independent co-educational
Religious denomination Roman Catholic
Members of ISIS, GSA, GBGSA, SHA, BSA
Accredited by ISJC
Age range 10 – 18 *Boarders from* 10 – 18
No of pupils (day) 165; *(boarding)* 185
Girls 200; *Boys* 150
Junior 90; *Senior* 158; *Sixth form* 102
Fees per term (day) £1,785; *(boarding)* £3,060 –
£3,521
Fees per annum (day) £5,355; *(boarding)* £9,180
– £10,563

The Ursuline College is a co-educational school for boarders and day pupils numbering some 400 pupils. This exciting new co-educational venture has come about as a result of the closure of St Augustine's College and The Abbey School in 1995 and the decision of the vast majority of the boys' parents to send their sons to the Ursuline Convent School which has been renamed **The Ursuline College**. There will be almost a 50 per cent division between boys and girls.

The new school has a combined history of over 200 years and offers parents the very best preparation for their children for the 21st century. There will be a co-educational junior department to the age of 11 as well as a fully integrated sixth form. A distinctive feature of the new school will be parallel single-sex lessons in the 11–16 age range, thus enabling parents to send their sons and daughters to the same school yet at the same time guaranteeing single-sex education during these important years.

Pupils are prepared for GCSE and A level public examinations. A wide variety of options is available, including foreign language exchange programmes. Examination pass rates are high and over 90 per cent of A level pupils proceed to university, including Oxford and Cambridge. The school has an excellent careers department which offers invaluable advice on university entrance and career prospects. Work experience is a feature of the Year 11 curriculum. Music, art and drama play an important part in the life of the school. There is a wide programme of activities, including well-organised weekends.

Government Assisted Places are available at 11+. In addition there is a ten per cent reduction for members of HM Forces as well as introductory service bursaries. Two scholarships and four bursaries are available each year to Catholic pupils entering year 7 (age 11). These are awarded on the results of the entrance examination which takes place towards the end of January.

The school stands in 16 acres of grounds and has been on the present site since 1904. There has been a continued programme of building to meet the challenge of education for a technological and scientific age. A new eight classroom block will be in position for the 1995-1996 academic year. Extensive accommodation for boy boarders has been purchased close to the school. The school has its own gym and sports facilities, but use is also made of the local excellent sports centre as well as local pitches for the major sports.

Registered charity number L1/245661A/1.

Bridgewater School

Drywood Hall, Worsley Road, Worsley, Manchester, Lancashire M28 2WQ
Tel: 0161 794 1463 Fax: 0161 794 3519

Head Dr B J Blundell
Founded 1950
Type Co-educational grammar
Religious denomination Non-denominational
Members of ISAI
Age range 3 – 18
No of pupils (day) 435
Girls 192; *Boys* 243
Junior 242; *Senior* 172; *Sixth form* 21
Fees per annum (day) £2,535 – £3,995

The school is a co-educational grammar school which follows the National Curriculum *plus*.

Entrance at age 11 to the senior school is by examination. Scholarship places are available. Entry into the sixth form depends upon five GCSE passes at grades A – C. Again scholarship places are available.

Full range of GCSE and A level subjects. High academic standard. Regular tests lead to first-class results. In 1992 through to 1995 Bridgewater School was the top co-educational grammar school in the government area league tables. Small classes and a happy atmosphere.

Beautiful location on green belt site. Excellent facilities for sports. £1.5 million development programme now complete, and new £1 million development currently in operation.

Leicester Grammar School

8 Peacock Lane, Leicester, Leicestershire LE1 5PX
Tel: 0116 291 0500 Fax: 0116 291 0505

Head J B Sugden MA (Cantab), MPhil
Founded 1981
Type Co-educational day grammar
Religious denomination Church of England
Members of HMC, GBA, SHA, ISIS, ISCO
Age range 10 – 18
No of pupils (day) 600
Girls 296; *Boys* 304
Junior 202; *Senior* 383; *Sixth form* 129
Fees per term (day) £1,360[*]
Fees per annum (day) £4,080[*]
([*] as of September 1995)

Curriculum: a broad core curriculum leads to ten GCSE subjects, options including three separate sciences, classics, second modern language, three humanities, art, music, drama, design and technology and physical education. Twenty A level subjects are offered in addition to a wide-ranging general studies course. Academic standards are high (95 per cent pass rate at GCSE and A level); 95 per cent of students enter higher education.

Entry: entry is at 10+, 11+, 13+, 14+ by IQ, English and mathematics tests; sixth-form entry is by interview and conditional offer.

Scholarships: academic and music scholarships, governors' and government-assisted places (up to 100 per cent) and sixth-form scholarships are offered.

Academic, leisure and religious activities: the Christian religion lies at the heart of the school's ethos (assemblies are held in Leicester Cathedral) but the school attracts students of all faiths. All students are encouraged to develop their individual talents; a strong tradition has been built up in music (60 per cent have instrumental lessons, various orchestras, bands, choirs), sport, drama, art and design and technology.

Ratcliffe College

Fosse Way, Ratcliffe-on-the-Wreake, Leicester, Leicestershire LE7 4SG
Tel: 01509 817000 Fax: 01509 817004

Head Father Keith Tomlinson STL, FRSA
Founded 1847
Type HMC independent co-educational
Religious denomination Roman Catholic
Members of HMC
Age range 10 – 18 *Boarders from* 11
No of pupils (day) 320; *(boarding)* 155
Girls 154; *Boys* 317
Junior 85; *Senior* 268; *Sixth form* 122
Fees per term (day) £1,608 (junior) – £2,022;
(boarding) £2,411 – £3,032
Fees per annum (day) £4,824 – £6,066;
(boarding) £7,233 – 9,096

Entry is by examination and interview. Academic standards are high and over 95 per cent of A level leavers go on to higher education. The school avoids specialisation as long as possible, but the boys and girls are divided into three or four units to enable the brighter pupils to be stimulated and the less academic child to be in a group where the work is not too demanding for him or her. Parents receive frequent reports. Scholarships for art, music and sport are offered, together with some bursaries and assisted places. There are reductions for siblings and discounts for members of the Armed Forces.

'The Newman', our purpose built junior department, was designed to ease the transition from primary to secondary school and will take 10+ pupils from September 1995.

Ratcliffe College is set in over 100 acres of rural Leicestershire. Without destroying the beauty of the original buildings, designed by Pugin and dating from the 19th century, the school has been considerably modernised and extended. This year there are 475 pupils, about one-third of whom are girls; just under half are boarders. An extensive range of games take place, including rugby, hockey, cricket, netball, rounders, tennis and athletics. Over half of our pupils learn to play a musical instrument and there are opportunities for them to join brass, dance and jazz bands. Leisure activities for all pupils include aerobics, badminton, cycling, Combined Cadet Force, the Duke of Edinburgh Award Scheme, fencing, squash, swimming, tennis and weight training; there are various clubs and societies. Pupils are encouraged to be caring and have consideration for others and there is a flourishing voluntary service unit.

The moral welfare and integrity of our pupils is paramount and the friendly spirit of Ratcliffe College aims to provide the best possible atmosphere in which young people can develop their talents, and keep up with the latest and best developments in the world of education, without ever losing sight of the ultimate objective, which is to produce young men and women whose Christian ideals fit them to take an active and constructive place in society.

Uppingham School

Uppingham, Leicestershire LE15 9QD
Tel: 01572 822216 Fax: 01572 822332

Head Dr Stephen Winkley
Founded 1584
Type Independent boarding
Religious denomination Church of England
Members of HMC
Age range 11 – 18 *Boarders from* 13 – 18
No of pupils (day) 30 *(boarding)* 585
Girls 140; *Boys* 475
Senior 270; *Sixth form* 330
Fees per annum (day) £7,650 *(boarding)* £12,750

Uppingham lies in a beautiful market town 50 minutes by rail from London. Boys admitted at 13+; boys and girls into sixth form. School numbers 615 with 330 in the sixth form.
Entry requirements: 30 scholarships offered at sixth form and 13+. These are academic, music, technology, art, and all-rounder. Also by Common Entrance or interview.
Curriculum: GCSE (98 per cent success in 1994). Then 25 subjects offered at A level (96 per cent success). Ninety per cent proceed to degree courses. Uppingham is renowned for the magnificence of its facilities for sport, music, drama and information technology.
Pastoral: Uppingham is 95 per cent boarding and is thus fully active at weekends with all facilities operational. Thirteen boarding houses: each number fewer than 50 and are run by houseparents and a tutor team. This ensures close monitoring of all pupils' academic and social development.

For prospectus and video ring 01572 822216 or fax 01572 822332, or write to the headmaster or registrar.

The following independent college also offers GCSEs. Please refer to the Independent Sixth-Form Colleges section for details:

Irwin College, Leicester

Falkner House

19 Brechin Place, London SW7 4QB
Tel: 0171 373 4501

Head Mrs Jacina Bird
Founded 1954
Type Preparatory
Religious denomination Christian
Members of IAPS, ISIS, NAHT
Age range 4 – 11
No of pupils (day) 140
Girls 140
Fees per term (day) £1,750
Fees per annum (day) £5,250

Curriculum: English, mathematics, science, computers, Bible studies, history, geography, French, German, Latin and classical studies, fine art, famous people, art and craft, music, singing, dance, drama, ballet, physical education (netball, tennis, rounders, swimming, judo, athletics, gymnastics).
Entry: interview and assessment.

The aims and objectives of the school are to provide a sound education for girls where academic standards are high; good manners are viewed as important; first-class tuition is given; the children are happy and enjoy school life. Kindness and consideration for others are regarded as essential. Great importance is attached to the maintenance of close co-operation between home and school in order to foster self-confidence in a happy atmosphere.

Garden House

53 Sloane Gardens, London SW1W 8ED
Tel: 0171 730 1652 Fax: 0171 730 0470

Joint Heads Mrs Rosemary Whaley and Mrs Wendy Challen
Founded 1954
Type Preparatory
Religious denomination Church of England
Age range 3 – 11
No of pupils (day) 310
Girls 250; *Boys* 60
Junior 310
Fees per term (day) £900 – £2,050
Fees per annum (day) £2,700 – £6,150

Curriculum: English, mathematics, reading, science, handwriting, poetry, history, geography, scripture, French, computing, current events, art, CDT, drama, singing and music, dancing, fencing and physical education (netball, tennis, rounders, gym and swimming).

The aim of the school is to provide a sound education in a happy, caring environment for girls from 3 to 11 and boys from 3. A high academic standard ensures a healthy number of scholarships (academic and musical among others). Visits to museums and galleries form an essential part of the school curriculum as do field studies and outward bound for the older girls and boys. Girls are prepared for entrance examinations for London day schools at 11+. Boys are prepared for entry to preparatory schools at 8+.

Glendower Preparatory School

87 Queen's Gate, London SW7 5JX
Tel: 0171 370 1927 Fax: 0171 244 8308

Head Mrs Barbara Humber
Founded 1895
Type Preparatory
Religious denomination Non-denominational
Members of IAPS
Age range 4 – 12
No of pupils (day) 178
Girls 178
Junior 90 *Senior* 88
Fees per term (day) £1,600
Fees per annum (day) £4,800

Glendower Preparatory School was established in 1895. It is a non-denominational day school for girls aged between four and 12 years. In 1969 Glendower became an educational trust administered by a board of governors.

Glendower is a small, family-orientated school with an atmosphere of enthusiasm and liveliness. It aims to maintain a high academic standard and, above all, to encourage every girl to approach all things with a determination to do her best. We try to instil a sense of courtesy and thoughtfulness for others, to encourage self-discipline and common sense, rather than to impose dogmatic rules. Girls are prepared for the entrance examinations for the London independent day schools at 11+, and for the various boarding schools at 12+. Discussions with the headmistress as to the choice of appropriate schools begin at the age of nine years.

The school has a science laboratory, art/CDT rooms, music room and library. There is a strong sporting tradition in the school and music and drama are flourishing departments. Entry – by interview at four; test and interview at eight years, or as vacancies occur.

Hill House International Junior School

Hans Place, London, SW1X 0EP
Tel: 0171 584 1331

Head Colonel Stuart Townend OBE, MA (Oxon)
Founded 1951
Type Co-educational day school
No of pupils (day) 1,050
Girls 43% *Boys* 57%
Fees per term (day) £3,800 – £4,900

Hill House was founded in 1951 and is fully co-educational, taking boys and girls from 3 to 14. It is an international school not only because it operates in two countries, England and Switzerland, but because half the places in the school are given to English boys and girls and half to non-English boys and girls.

The four principles

The school works on four principles. In order of priority they are:

1 Safety of the boy or girl.
2 Happiness at work and games.
3 Good manners and discipline.
4 Preparation for the next school.

Curriculum

The curriculum is English, boys and girls being prepared not only for entry into English public schools but also schools overseas. The main subjects in which a boy and girl should have at least one lesson each day are: English, maths, science, French. The supporting subjects requiring fewer lessons are: geography, history, biology, Latin, divinity, music, art, carpentry, computer programming and, for girls, ballet.

At a normal English preparatory school the boys play soccer, rugger and cricket with some athletics and swimming. Hill House has boys and girls from many countries and the policy is not to specialise but to teach all the boys and girls the basic principles of all games.

Swiss annex

Hill House has always had a permanent annex in Switzerland.

The house in Glion was purpose-built. The dormitory with french oak on the walls, its ceiling of polished Finnish pine and its view looking out, from a height of 2,500 ft, over the largest lake in Europe to the snow-capped mountains of Grammont and the 11,000 ft Dents du Midi, is unique.

The courses in Switzerland are optional and parents pay no extra fees. The school pays the air fares, all expenses at Glion, including laundry, excursions, ski-lifts and provides skis, ski-books, climbing-boots anoraks etc.

Queen's Gate School

133 Queen's Gate, London SW7 5LE
Tel: 0171 589 3587 Fax: 0171 584 7691

Head Mrs A M Holyoak CertEd
Founded 1891
Type Girls' independent day
Religious denomination Non-denominational
Members of GSA, SHA
Age range 4 – 18
No of pupils (day) 366
Junior 142 *Senior* 190 *Sixth form* 34
Fees per term (day) £1,160 – £1,712
£1,800 sixth form (Autumn 1995)

Curriculum and academic life: the curriculum is rich, varied, well balanced and as wide as possible during the years leading to the GCSE examinations, and is frequently reviewed to take into account new approaches to teaching and scientific and technological change.

All girls sit GCSE examinations in English language, English literature, mathematics, a modern language, and a science, and have the option of taking courses in additional science subjects, the humanities, a range of modern languages, classics, business studies, computer studies, art and design, graphic design, music and drama. Decisions on options are made after full consultation with parents.

Small classes ensure maximum guidance with course work and much individual attention. Each girl's work is frequently assessed and progress and achievement are carefully monitored. Detailed reports are written for parents.

Entry requirements and procedures: for junior school: girls enter the preliminary form aged four without formal testing, but visit the school for a morning of assessment in the spring term prior to the September entry. Girls wishing to enter after this take tests in maths and English. Girls in form 3 are required to pass the London Day Schools 11+ entrance examination before moving up into the senior school.

Senior school: girls sit the London Day School Examination at 11+ and the school's own entrance examinations at 12+, 13+ and 16+. Before acceptance all girls are interviewed.

Sixth form: girls entering the sixth form are required to have at least five GCSE passes, grades A–C.

Examinations offered: **GCSE**: MEG, SEG, ULEAC, NEAB. **A level**: Oxford, Cambridge, London.

Academic and leisure facilities: the school has well-equipped science and computer laboratories and is conveniently placed to take full advantage of the resources offered by central London education. It is within easy walking distance of the Science Museum, Geological and Natural History Museums and the Victoria and Albert Museum, Hyde Park and Kensington Gardens.

The girls play netball, hockey, lacrosse and tennis and, as well as having their own gymnasium, enjoy the facilities of local sports hall, athletics grounds and swimming pools.

Scholarships: one 8+ scholarship (external and internal), two internal sixth-form bursaries.

Queen's Gate School Trust is a registered charity which exists to provide high quality education for girls in central London.

Queen's College

43 – 49 Harley Street, London W1N 2BT

Head The Hon Lady Goodhart MA (Oxon)
Founded 1848
Type Independent girls' school
Religious denomination Church of England, others welcome
Members of GSA, GBGSA
Age range 11 – 18
No of pupils (day) 370
Fees per term (day) £1,940

Queen's College, founded in 1848 by Professor F D Maurice, was the first-ever academic institution to receive a charter for the education of women. Former students include Dorothea Beale, Sophie Jex-Blake, Gertrude Bell and Katherine Mansfield. Housed in beautiful 18th-century buildings in the very heart of London, the college is equipped with bright modern laboratories and facilities for the teaching of science, information technology and modern languages. We pay close attention to academic standards, with almost all girls going on to university, but we also encourage individuality, self-motivation and independence of mind, welcoming different talents, abilities and interests. We offer a very wide range and combination of subjects and opportunities to enjoy almost everything from art and music to information technology and visits abroad. Our location is one of our greatest assets, and all students benefit from London's galleries, museums, theatres, exhibitions and concerts. Admission is by examination and interview.

St James Independent Schools for Boys and for Girls

Registered Office: 91 Queens Gate, London SW7 5AB Tel: 0171 373 5688 Fax: 0171 835 0771
Other sites at 61 Eccleston Square SW1 Tel: 0171 976 6012 Fax: 0171 834 0471 and
19 Pembridge Villas W11 Tel: 0171 229 2253 Fax: 0171 792 1002

Founded 1975
Type Independent day schools for girls and for boys
Religious denomination All denominations welcome
Members of ISAI (Accredited ISJC)
Age range 4½ – 18
Girls 260; *Boys* 323
Boys (J) 127; *(S)* 196; *(6th)* 37
Girls (J) 122; *(S)* 138; *(6th)* 30
Fees per term (day) £1,100 – £1,585
Fees per annum (day) £3,300 – £4,755

Curriculum: the schools strive to put into practice what is universally considered sound educational principle; establishing firm foundations, nourishing the growth and encouraging the development of the whole person.

We start in the junior schools where, in addition to the best features of a traditional English education, pupils are taught Sanskrit (from the age of five), Ancient Greek (from eight) and philosophy. These subjects amplify and strengthen reading and the study of literature (which includes Shakespeare and the scriptures). Writing is based on fine calligraphy and mathematics begins with the learning of tables at the age of five. Art, singing, speech, drama and physical exercise are timetabled for all ages.

In the senior schools pupils take between eight and ten GCSEs, being introduced to the principles of their subjects as well as continuing their activities of singing, drama, speech and physical activity. The sixth forms offer a wide choice of A levels to which are added non-examination subjects such as philosophy, economics, modern history and law.

Music plays an important part in the life of the schools and there are regular dramatic productions and concerts. There are also regular school holidays for climbing, sailing and open-air projects as well as cultural visits abroad.

Each term a prominent member from public or business life is invited to deliver the senior school lecture.

Entry requirements: interview and test.
Examinations offered: GCSE (Midland Board); A levels (Oxford and Cambridge Board)
Academic and sports facilities: the schools are well equipped with libraries; laboratories and gymnasium. Being situated in central London students have easy access to museums and galleries. There is daily physical exercise, physical education for girls includes gymnastics, Aikido, athletics, lacrosse, netball and tennis. For the boys there are gymnastics, athletics, rugby, cricket and tennis. Team games are played at a fully-equipped sports field at Chiswick. Boys have an ACF unit, sailing and climbing clubs.
Religious activity: the schools are open to all religious denominations. They teach philosophy rather than religion, holding that the essential spiritual truths can be discovered in all religions. Children are introduced to the great scriptures of the world.

The schools are owned by the Independent Educational Association Limited, a charitable trust which aims to make the education of St James available to as many children as possible.

St Paul's Cathedral Choir School

2 New Change, London EC4M 9AD
Tel: 0171 248 5156 Fax: 0171 329 6568

Head Mr S A Sides BEd (Oxon)
Type of school Preparatory boys school
Religious denomination Church of England (admits day boys of all faiths)
Age range 7+ – 13
No of pupils (day) 60; *(boarding choristers)* 40
Fees per term (day) £1,640; *(boarding choristers)* £990
Fees per annum (day) £4,920; *(boarding choristers)* £2,970

There have been choristers at St Paul's for over nine centuries. The present school is a Church of England Foundation dating back over 100 years and is governed by the Dean and Chapter of St Paul's Cathedral. It caters for boys aged 7 – 13. The choir school expanded to include day boys in 1989 and the school accepts boys of all faiths. It offers a broad curriculum leading to scholarship and Common Entrance examinations. In the first three years the work is tailored to individual needs bearing in mind the wide variety of educational backgrounds from which boys come. The school has an excellent record in placing boys in the senior schools of their choice, many with music scholarships. Every opportunity is taken to make use of the school's proximity to museums, libraries, galleries, theatres and the numerous attractions which London has to offer.

The 40 chorister boarders are housed on the cathedral site and are fully integrated with the day boys for all their academic studies and games. The choristers' cathedral choral training offers them a unique opportunity to participate in the rich musical life of St Paul's and the City.

The school was rehoused in the 60s in purpose-built premises on the eastern end of the cathedral site. The facilities include a science laboratory, computers, an art room, music room and practice rooms, hall/gymnasium, common room and a TV/video room. All boys are encouraged to play a musical instrument (most boys play two) and there are musical appreciation and theory lessons and a school orchestra.

A wide variety of games is offered including field sports at local playing fields and weekly swimming lessons. The boys have their own playground and the use of the hall for indoor games and gymnastics.

Admissions procedure: prospective day boys of 7+ years in September are interviewed by the headmaster and given a short test, usually in February of the previous academic year. Voice trials and tests for chorister places are held in February, May and October for boys of nearly 7 years and upwards.

St Philip's School

6 Wetherby Place, London SW7 4NE
Tel: 0171 373 3944

Head H Biggs-Davison MA (Cantab)
Religious denomination Roman Catholic
Age range 7 – 13
No of pupils (day) 100
Fees per term (day) £1,445

Conveniently situated in South Kensington, St Philip's is the Catholic day preparatory school which, since 1934, has served central London. In a family atmosphere of small classes, boys between the ages of seven and thirteen are prepared for Common Entrance and scholarship exams for all public schools.

Visits to theatres, museums and art galleries take place regularly and competitive sport has always been a strong feature of life at St Philip's. Two afternoons per week, all boys play football, rugby, cricket, cross-country and athletics in due season, while swimming takes place once per week. After-school activities include judo and fencing.

St Philip's is accredited by the Mensa Foundation for Gifted Children.

Entry is by examination and interview. Please apply to the bursar for full details and a prospectus.

St Philip's School Trust Ltd exists to provide high quality education for boys.

Southbank International School

36–38 Kensington Park Road, London W11 3BU
Tel: 0171 229 8230 Fax: 0171 229 3784

Head Milton E Toubkin
Founded 1979
Type Independent co-educational
Members of ISJC, ECIS
Age range 4 – 18
No of pupils (day) 240
Girls 110; *Boys* 130
Junior 50; *Senior* 95; *Sixth form* 95
Fees per term (day) £1,200 – £3,160
Fees per annum (day) £3,600 – £9,480

Southbank International School offers an individualised academic programme to pupils aged 4 – 18. The school is located in Kensington, and has now established a reputation for its small classes, friendly atmosphere, and excellent academic results. Southbank is one of the few schools in London that offer students the opportunity to do the International Baccalaureate Diploma. The IB is growing in popularity as sixth formers seek a challenging, more broadly based curriculum as an alternative to traditional A levels. It enables students to study a wide range of academic subjects, including the creative arts, while specialising in three at a higher level. The IB is accepted by universities worldwide. The top British universities are now actively recruiting IB diploma holders. Southbank International School has 89 per cent pass rate for the IB, compared to a worldwide average of 70–75 per cent.

In September 1995 Southbank opened a new campus in Hampstead for pupils aged 3 – 12.

Admission is based on previous academic records, teacher references, a pupil profile and a parent statement. Interviews are recommended but not required.

The following independent colleges also offer GCSEs. Please refer to the Independent Sixth-Form Colleges section for details:

Ashbourne Independent Sixth Form College, W8

David Game Tutorial College, SW7

Davies, Laing and Dick, W2

Davies's College, WC1

Mander Portman Woodward, SW7

Abercorn Place School

28 Abercorn Place, London NW8 9XP
Tel: 0171 286 4785

Head Mrs A Greystoke BA (Hons)
Founded 1987
Type Nursery and preparatory school
Religious denomination Non-denominational
Members of NAHT
Age range 2½ – 13+
No of pupils (day) 200
Girls 90; *Boys* 110
Fees per term (day) £1,035 – £1,895
Fees per annum (day) £3,105 – £5,685

Abercorn Place School

The school is situated in leafy St John's Wood. Facilities include a new purpose-built science laboratory, computing room and art and CDT centre. Abercorn has the enviable reputation for developing young children into individuals with the confidence, self-discipline and talents to achieve across the curriculum. Whilst emphasis is placed upon basic skills in literacy and numeracy, the children are also taught and encouraged to participate in music, sport, computing, art and design technology. Academic skills are valued, and children are taught by a combination of traditional and modern methods.

Enthusiastic, qualified staff produce excellent academic results in a happy atmosphere.

Communication between the school and parents is encouraged in all aspects of school life.

The American School in London

2–8 Loudon Road, London NW8 0NP
Tel: 0171 722 0101 ext 222 Fax: 0171 586 6885

Head Dr Judith R Glickman
Founded 1951
Type Independent co-educational day
Age range 4 – 18
No of pupils (day) 1,244
Girls 591; *Boys* 653
Fees per annum (day) £8,275 – £9,750

The American School in London is a co-educational, non-profit institution which offers an outstanding American education. The curriculum leads to an American high school diploma, and the strong Advanced Placement program enables students to enter the top universities in the US, the UK and other countries.

The core curriculum of English, maths, science, and social studies is enriched with courses in modern languages, computer, fine arts, and physical education. Small classes allow teachers to focus on individuals; students are encouraged to take an active role in learning to develop the skills necessary for independent critical thinking and expression. Many extra-curricular activities including sports, music, drama, and community service are available for students of all ages.

The American School in London welcomes students of all nationalities, including non-English speakers below the age of 12, who meet the scholastic standards. Entry is at any time throughout the year.

The Cavendish School

179 Arlington Road, London NW1 7EY
Tel: 0171 485 1958 Fax: 0171 267 0098

Head Mrs L J Harris BA
Founded 1875
Type Girls' Catholic day preparatory, boys' pre-preparatory
Religious denomination Catholic
Members of IAPS
Age range 3 – 11
Girls 170; *Boys* 10
Fees per term (day) £1,225 – £1,384

Parents seeking a happy academic girls' preparatory school should consider The Cavendish School – an IAPS Catholic preparatory school housed in spacious Victorian school buildings and a modern block with three secluded playgrounds. Founded in 1875, The Cavendish School specialises in providing a well-balanced curriculum in a caring, family atmosphere. A broad range of subjects and extra-curricular activities (including French and Spanish, advanced French for bilingual pupils, ballet, jazz dancing, BAYS, science, gymnastics, short tennis and games) is taught by highly qualified, experienced staff. A pre- and after- school care facility is provided.

The school aims to stimulate the children's attainment of sound academic standards whilst also encouraging the development of their creative skills, confidence and happiness.

Devonshire House Preparatory School

2 Arkwright Road, Hampstead, London NW3 6AD
Tel: 0171 435 1916

Head Mrs S P T Donovan BEd (Hons)
Founded 1989
Type Preparatory and pre-preparatory day school
Religious denomination Non-denominational
Members of ISIS
Age range 2½ – 13
No of pupils (day) 300
Fees per term (day) £1,255 – £1,660

Curriculum: early literacy and numeracy are very important and the traditional academic subjects form the core curriculum. Specialist teaching and the combined sciences form an increasingly important part of the timetable as the children grow older. Expression in all forms of communication is encouraged with classes having lessons in art, music, drama, French, and information and design technology. Much encouragement is given to pupils to help to widen their horizons and broaden their interests. The school fosters a sense of responsibility amongst the pupils.

Entry requirements: the offer of places is subject to availability and to an interview. Children wishing to enter the school over the age of six will normally be required to take a formal written test.

Academic and leisure facilities: the school is situated in fine premises in the heart of Hampstead with their own walled grounds. The aim is to achieve high academic standards whilst developing enthusiasm and initiative throughout a wide range of interests. It is considered essential to encourage pupils to develop their own individual personalities and a good sense of personal responsibility.

Scholarships: the school offers academic and music scholarships.

Hampstead Hill School

St Stephen's Hall, Pond Street, London NW3 2PP and 53 Courthope Road, London NW3 2LE
Tel: 0171 435 6262

Head Mrs Andrea Taylor
Founded 1949
Type Pre-preparatory and nursery school
Age range 2 – 9
No of pupils (day) c 220
Girls c 80 *Boys* c 140
Fees per term (day) £1,500 (5 – 9 year olds)
Fees per annum (day) max £5,000 for under 5s for full 52 weeks a year, 9½ hours a day. Part-time available.

Hampstead Hill Pre-Preparatory School offers a wide curriculum and sound education, in very small classes, to prepare children for entrance examinations to junior public and preparatory schools at the ages of 7+ or 8+. Extended hours service available.

Hampstead Hill Nursery School offers part or full-day (nine and a half hours) care, fun and education for children aged two plus to five plus years.

There is a full creative, music and academic syllabus. Nursery School open 52 weeks a year, and holiday scheme available for all pupils over five years.

Fees at both schools payable weekly or monthly.

Heathside Preparatory School

16 New End, Hampstead, London NW3 1JA
Tel: 0171 794 5857

Head Ms M Remus and Mrs J White
Founded 1988
Type Independent preparatory school
Age range 2 – 13+
No of pupils (day) 86
Girls 36; *Boys* 50
Junior 31; *Senior* 55
Fees per term (day) £1,320
Fees per annum (day) £3,960

Curriculum: Heathside Preparatory School offers a full curriculum which concentrates on developing strong literacy, numeracy and social skills as well as preparing students for entry to secondary schools. In addition to core subjects the following courses are taught: French, computer studies, music, instrumental lessons, pottery, photography, drama and swimming.
Entry: admission is by interview with the headmistresses. Your child will also be invited to spend a day in the school.
Academic and leisure facilities: the school sets high academic standards whilst enabling children to express their creativity and talents. Extra-curricular activities include choir, chess club, debating society, photography/film club, computer club, pottery group, football team and a drama group.

Heathside has a record of remarkable exam results. Exam class teachers give extra tuition to candidates throughout the autumn and winter terms. The school also has a first-class record at taking latecomers and getting them up to the standard of London independent secondary schools.

Our special needs department provides support for pupils with dyslexia and other learning difficulties.

Housed in two historic buildings in the heart of Hampstead Village, we are only a few minutes walk from the Heath. Facilities include a hall with stage, a large art room, a computer laboratory, a photography dark room, a pottery kiln and several small rooms used for small group or individual tuition. The school has a well-stocked library.

Professor Higgins and Eliza Doolittle in Heathside's production of *My Fair Lady*

The King Alfred School

Manor Wood, North End Road, London NW11 7HY
Tel: 0181 457 5200 Fax: 0181 457 5249

Head Francis Moran MA (Cantab), PGCE
Founded 1897
Type Co-educational day school
Religious denomination Secular
Members of GBA
Age range 4 – 18
Girls 224; *Boys* 232
Junior 227; *Senior* 229; *Sixth form* 40
Fees per term (day) £1,260 – £2,150
Fees per annum (day) £3,780 – £6,450

The King Alfred School was founded in 1897 by a group of local parents as a 'rational school'. Their ideals (continuity, co-education, active rather than passive learning, no religious affiliation, partnership, true respect for children's needs) are valued and incorporated in today's practice. There is no uniform and children and staff are on first name terms. The school keeps artificial barriers and regulations to a minimum. It has opposed from the start the constraints of government-imposed curricula, trusting the insight and creativity of its own teachers to produce an environment where children of widely different abilities and character can all gain from their learning. GCSE results bear out this strategy – few fifth formers do not qualify for sixth forms. Because of its size, KAS can only offer Advanced levels, though it includes several less usual subjects. Most of the sixth form (in some years all) enter higher education.

Mill Hill and Belmont

The Ridgeway, Mill Hill, London NW7 1QS
Tel: 0181 959 1176 Fax: 0181 906 2614

Head Mr W R Winfield
Founded 1807
Type Independent boys boarding and day with co-educational sixth form
Religious denomination Non-denominational
Members of HMC, SHA, IAPS
Age range 7 – 18 *Boarders from* 13
No of pupils (day) 340; *(boarding)* 180
Girls 35; *Boys* 485
Junior 312; *Senior* 320; *Sixth form* 200
Fees per term (day) £2,510; *(boarding)* £3,880
Fees per annum (day) £7,530; *(boarding)* £11,640

Curriculum: pupils enter the senior school at 13 and take GCSEs three years later. The core subjects are separately streamed; the pace and level of teaching are therefore suited to individuals' abilities. Half the boys go on exchange to France, Germany and/or Spain, the remainder follow an integrated programme including fieldwork for one week at the school's field study centre in Dentdale.

Sixth form pupils take three or four A levels. Suitable candidates are prepared for entry to Oxford and Cambridge. Over 95 per cent go on to higher education thanks to an A level pass rate of over 96 per cent.

Entry requirements: 13+ entry is by entrance scholarship, Common Entrance or our own assessments; entry to the sixth form is dependent on GCSE results, interviews and the previous school's testimonial. Government Assisted Places are available. The school offers up to 12 academic and music scholarships annually. Further information on entrance procedures can be obtained from the registrar.

Academic facilities: teachers have their own specialist classrooms. The teacher/pupil ratio of 1:10 means that sets average eighteen and sixth form sets average ten. The school has a large number of Apple Macintosh computers situated in four suites and is linked to Internet. Music and drama are high profile activities with programmes throughout the year. Extra-curricular activities and societies include community service, Duke of Edinburgh Award Scheme, Combined Cadet Force, public speaking, philosophy and cookery.

Sports, games and leisure facilities: the school is situated in 120 acres of parkland on the edge of London. The generous playing fields are matched by a sports hall, two swimming pools, squash courts, fives courts, an all weather pitch and indoor range. Competitive excellence is highly valued and coaching skills are exceptional.

Pastoral care: pupils are allocated to one of nine houses, four of which are boarding. A house master is the first link between parents and the school. Each pupil also has a tutor and close links with parents are maintained through regular meetings and reports.

For further information please contract: Mr R Laxworthy, the registrar.

The Mount School

Milespit Hill, Mill Hill, London NW7 2RX
Tel: 0181 959 3403 Fax: 0181 959 1503

Head Mrs Margaret Pond
Founded 1926
Type Girls
Members of ISIS, ISJC, GBGSA
Age range 5 – 18
No of pupils (day) 400
Girls 400
Junior 50; *Senior* 290; *Sixth form* 60
Fees per term (day) Junior £1,060; Senior £1,185
Fees per annum (day) Junior £3,180; Senior £3,555

The school is set in five acres of grounds in a designated green belt area near Mill Hill East station and the 240 and 221 buses. A new purpose-built laboratory block was completed in January 1994 together with the installation of a suite for 'PC' computers with CD-ROM facilities. Good use is made of exhibitions and theatres in London.

The school follows the National Curriculum and each pupil is encouraged to strive for her personal best. A wide range of GCSE and A level subjects is offered. The EFL department helps overseas students with their English and other academic studies if necessary.

North Bridge House School

Preparatory and Senior Schools (*10 – 16 years*), 1 Gloucester Avenue, London NW1 7AB (further sites at Netherhall Gardens and Fitzjohns Avenue, NW3)
Tel: 0171 267 6266

Principal W H Wilcox
Founded 1939
Type Co-educational
Religious denomination non-denominational
Age range 2½ – 16
Girls 419 *Boys* 490
Fees per annum (day) £5,250

The school comprises four buildings, two of them large Victorian houses close to Swiss Cottage, Hampstead, and two others, including a large late Victorian building with a separate modern addition in the ground, prominently fronting the approach to Regents Park at Parkway.

North Bridge House provides a complete education from nursery at two and a half years to 16+. It continues to be a large and successful preparatory school with an outstanding record in the public school entrance and scholarship examinations. This year 37 boys went to St Paul's Boys School, Westminster, UCS, Highgate, City of London or St Alban's. 27 of the girls went on to South Hampstead, City of London, Francis Holland, Queen's College, St Paul's and Channing.

In the senior department those who prefer to stay on or who join at 11+ are prepared for the GCSE examinations and entry into the sixth forms of the London public day schools. Boys and girls have been offered sixth-form places in many of these schools including Westminster, the City of London Schools for Boys and Girls, South Hampstead, Francis Holland, Channing, Highgate and Mill Hill.

The Royal School, Hampstead

65 Rosslyn Hill, London NW3 5UD
Tel: 0171 794 7707 Fax: 0171 431 6741

Principal Mrs C A Sibson BA (Oxon)
Founded 1855
Type Girls' independent boarding and day
Religious denomination All faiths welcome
Age range 4 – 18 *Boarders from* 7
Girls 188
Junior 70; *Senior* 118
Fees per term (day) £1,050 – £1,230; *(boarding)* £2,034 – £2,890 (weekly boarding £1,762 – £2,290)

The school was founded on its present site in 1855. The patron is HRH Princess Alexandra, the Hon Lady Ogilvy, GCVO. The school is a small independent boarding and day school for girls. The school's curriculum includes the core subjects leading to GCSE and A level examinations and is compatible with the National School Curriculum. It also includes two foreign languages and three science subjects. There is a well-qualified and largely resident staff which gives an overall pupil to teacher ratio of 10:1. The maximum size for all classes is 22 girls.

Entry requirements: entry to both the senior and junior department is by interview, previous school reports and an entrance test when applicable. Scholarships are available at 11 years and for sixth form entry.

Examinations offered: GCSE, AS, A levels, Pitmans and RSA.

We provide a caring, happy and secure environment with pleasant and spacious surroundings. The school has comfortable modern boarding accommodation and a large garden. There are excellent sports facilities and London's nearby educational, cultural and recreational centres are visited regularly. An assembly is held each morning and all faiths are welcome.

The Royal School, Hampstead, exists to provide a sound and broad-based education which prepares girls both to meet and cope with the challenges of the 1990s.

St Margaret's

18 Kidderpore Gardens, Hampstead, London, NW3 7SR
Tel: 0171 435 2439

Head Mrs S Meaden
Founded 1884
Type Day girls
Religious denomination Church of England
Members of ISAI
Age range 5 – 16
No of pupils (day) 135
Girls 135
Junior 50; *Senior* 85
Fees per term (day) £1,170 – £1,385
Fees per annum (day) £3,510 – £4,155

St Margaret's offers a high standard of teaching in small classes. Pupils follow the national curriculum. French begins in the infant class, and in the senior school Spanish, Russian and classical civilisation are offered. All girls go on to full time sixth-form education, recent leavers are now studying at St Paul's Girls School, South Hampstead High School, Fine Arts College and Camden School for Girls. The girls frequently visit London theatres, art galleries, and concert halls. Extra-curricular activities include gym and drama clubs, self defence, first aid, batik classes and horse riding. Girls may have individual instrumental and speech and drama lessons.

Entrance is by interview at ages five and six and by interview and written test from the age of seven. A prospectus is available from the school and Suzanne Meaden is happy to see prospective parents at any time.

Christ's College Blackheath

4 St Germans Place, Blackheath, London SE3 0NJ
Tel: 0181 858 0692 Fax: 0181 858 7778

Head R Bellerby
Founded 1823
Type Independent
Religious denomination Non-denominational
Age range 3 – 18 *Boarders from* 8
No of pupils (day) 120; *(boarding)* 60
Girls 90; *Boys* 90
Junior 60; *Senior* 80; *Sixth form* 40

Christ's College has a reputation for firm but fair discipline and is well known for the politeness and courtesy of its pupils. Blackheath is a well-preserved village on the edge of hundreds of acres of open parkland, adjoining Greenwich Park, the site of the original Royal Greenwich Observatory.

The school observes the best of the National Curriculum, but does so selectively and pupils have additional options – for example those wishing to study the three sciences separately to GCSE may do so while others opt for a single or double integrated science. There is a full range of subjects available at GCSE and A level, and a limited range at AS level.

Thirty scholarships are awarded each year, usually to form 1 (Year 7), form 5 (Year 1) or form 6 (Year 12). Admittance is by reference, interview and examination.

The headmaster was appointed in 1994, but has been a head of other schools since 1975. He and his wife, who looks after student welfare, have a wealth of experience. They live in the school grounds and are available to students and parents seven days a week.

Dulwich College

London SE21 7LD
Tel: 0181 693 3601 Fax: 0181 693 6319

Head Mr A C F Verity
Founded 1619
Type Independent
Religious denomination Church of England
Members of HMC, GBA, BSA, ISIS
Age range 7 – 18 *Boarders from* 10
No of pupils (day) 1,390; *(boarding)* 90
Junior 155; *Senior* 865; *Sixth form* 370
Fees per annum (day) £5,811 – £6,135; *(boarding)* £12,270 (weekly £11,775)

Broad academic curriculum to GCSE and A level. The great majority of pupils proceed to university. Admission at 7+ on aptitude test, interview and school report, and at 10+, 11+ and 13+ on written examination, interview and school report; at 16+ on interview, school report and six or more passes at GCSE with grade A or B in English language and the three subjects to be studied at A level.

Annual vacancies: 7+ 40, 10+ 20, 11+ 90, 13+ 60, 16+ 25.

Situated in leafy suburbs close to good rail links. Well-equipped library, science, language and computing laboratories, workshops, music and art schools, sports hall, swimming pool, squash courts, theatre and extensive playing fields. Art, music and drama flourish. A number of one-half and one-third of tuition fees scholarships for academic ability, music and art. Three well-equipped boarding houses; one or two one-half of boarding fees scholarships available. Broad social and ethnic mix.

Ibstock Place, The Froebel School

Clarence Lane, Roehampton, London SW15 5PY
Tel: 0181 876 9991 Fax: 0181 878 4897

Head Mrs Franciska Bayliss, Froebel CertEd,
FRSA
Founded 1894
Type Co-educational day
Religious denomination Non-denominational
Members of ISAI
Age range 3 – 16
No of pupils (day) 448
Girls 256; *Boys* 192
Junior 256; *Senior* 192
Fees per term (day) £550 (nursery) – £1,750
(senior)
Fees per annum (day) £1,650 (nursery) – £5,250
(senior)

Ibstock Place, The Froebel School, will celebrate
50 years at Roehampton in 1996. In the last ten
years the school has grown considerably as
demand for educational continuity has
increased and the reputation of the school has
widened. Academic standards are high, with a
wide choice of GCSE subjects, and results are
consistently good. The great majority of pupils
leave with excellent qualifications to continue
their education at tertiary colleges or in sixth
forms at independent day and boarding schools.
Sport, music, art and drama flourish
throughout the school.

Newton Prep

149 Battersea Park Road, London SW8 4BH
Tel: 0171 720 4091 Fax: 0171 498 9052

Head Mr R G Dell MA (Oxon)
Founded 1991
Type Co-educational preparatory
Religious denomination Non-denominational
Age range 3 – 13
No of pupils (day) 250
Girls 100; *Boys* 150
Junior 250
Fees per term (day) £905 – £1,805
Fees per annum (day) £2,715 – £5,415

Newton Prep, a co-educational day preparatory
school, is especially geared to the needs of bright
and gifted children in the age range of 3 – 13.

With entry based upon cognitive ability, and
special programmes to meet the individual
needs of bright children, it is possible to
accelerate the learning process in its broadest
sense without children feeling pressured.

The Newton Prep curriculum fosters the
physical, mental and spiritual lives of its pupils,
and provides an education that is excellent,
exciting and ethical. We aim to nurture souls
and especially those souls who display talents
beyond the ordinary.

Redcliffe School

47 Redcliffe Gardens, London SW10 9JH
Tel: 0171 352 9247 Fax: 0171 352 6936

Head Miss Rosalind Cunnah MA
Founded 1948
Type Pre-preparatory and preparatory
Religious denomination Inter-denominational
Members of IAPS; accredited by ISJC
Age range Boys 4 – 8; girls 4 – 11
No of pupils (day) 97
Girls 60 *Boys* 37
Fees per term (day) £1,540
Fees per annum (day) £4,200

Small, friendly school catering for a range of abilities, with a playground. Basic skills accentuated plus many creative and practical activities. Music, French, science and art specialist teachers. Outings to museums and theatres.

Entry requirements: children are assessed at three years of age for entry at four. Entry for subsequent years is by test. Scholarships are available for girls entering at seven plus.

Rosemead Preparatory School

70 Thurlow Park Road, West Dulwich, London SE21 8HZ
Tel: 0181 670 5865 Fax: 0181 761 9159

Head Mrs R L Lait BA, CertEd
Founded 1942
Type Day
Religious denomination Non-denominational
Age range 3 – 11
No of pupils (day) 260
Girls 131; *Boys* 129
Junior 260
Fees per term (day) £1,000 – £1,190
Fees per annum (day) £3,000 – £3,570

Rosemead is a well-established preparatory school with a fine record of academic achievement. Children are prepared for entrance to independent London day schools at age 11 years, many gaining awards and scholarships. The school has a happy, family atmosphere with boys and girls enjoying a varied, balanced curriculum which includes maths, English, science, French, information technology, arts and humanities. Music and drama are strong subjects with tuition available in most orchestral instruments and various music groups meeting frequently. A full programme of physical education includes gymnastics, most major games, dance and (from six years) swimming. Classes make regular visits to places of interest. A residential field studies course is arranged for the junior pupils along with various school holidays. Main entry to the school is at ages three and four years following informal assessment. The school is administered by a board of governors elected annually by the parents.

St Dunstan's College

Stanstead Road, Catford, London SE6 4TY
Tel: 0181 690 1274 Fax: 0181 314 0242

Head Mr J D Moore
Founded 1888
Type Independent co-educational day school
Religious denomination Church of England
Members of HMC
Age range 4 – 18
No of pupils (day) 800
Fees per term (day) £1,155 – £1,790
Fees per annum (day) from £3,465

Curriculum: a full academic curriculum is offered with over 20 subjects offered at both A level and GCSE. A level subjects include politics, business studies, economics, theatre studies and physical education in addition to the usual academic subjects.

Entry requirements and procedures: the principal points of entry are at 4, 7, 11 and 16 for both boys and girls. Entry at the ages of 9 to 13 is on the basis of a competitive exam held in the spring of each year with a termly examination at 8+; individual assessments apply at other ages.

Examinations offered: GCSE, A level, S level and Oxbridge entry.

Academic and leisure facilities: a sixth-form suite is available for older pupils. Teaching is in well-appointed and comfortable classrooms, laboratories and information technology rooms.

Scholarships: we have several scholarships and bursaries, and 25 government-assisted places to award at 11+. There are an additional five Assisted Places to award to sixth-form candidates.

The Arts Educational London Schools

Cone Ripman House, 14 Bath Road, Chiswick, London W4 1LY
Tel: 0181 994 9366 Fax: 0181 994 9274

Principal Mr Peter Fowler MA
Founded 1919
Type Independent day school
Religious denomination Non-denominational
Members of ISAI
Age range 8 – 18
Fees per annum (day) £5,562 (includes lunch);
(preparatory) £3,750

The Arts Educational London School is one of the UK's leading centres of education and training for the performing arts of the theatre.

At the co-educational day school which is part of this superbly equipped complex, talented boys and girls follow a balanced curriculum that combines a sound academic education, IT computer studies and excellent vocational training.

Curriculum: the courses closely follow the National Curriculum covering normal academic studies, plus vocational subjects, which are taught to GCSE level – 75 per cent of entrants attaining A–C grades last year.

Additional studies: specialist vocational tuition covers information technology, art, music, choir, dance and drama, leading to examinations set by recognised boards and associations. Appropriate religious studies are also covered.

In a caring, friendly environment, the school offers excellent preparation for either higher academic studies or further professional training.

Entry requirements: entry is by audition and personal interview.

Ashbourne Middle School

17 Old Court Place, London W8 9PL
Tel: 0171 376 0360

Head M J Hatchard-Kirby MSc BApSc
Founded 1981
Age range 10 – 16
No of pupils (day) 40
Fees per annum (day) £7,875

Established in 1981 and co-educational, Ashbourne works in very small groups whose size never exceeds ten. The commitment to small groups offers real opportunities for individual attention to those students who have previously lacked motivation and need a closely supervised, structured approach to work.

Wonderfully situated near Kensington Gardens and Hyde Park, which provide facilities for games, the school is a few minutes away from the excellent museums of Natural History and Science and Geology, and the Victoria and Albert Museum.

The curriculum is wide-ranging and includes information technology, art, outings, trips

abroad, and thinking skills. Students are prepared for Common Entrance and then GCSE examination. The school aims to unlock potential and in 1993 achieved the best GCSE results in the borough. Ashbourne offers the opportunity for change; many an academic career has been revitalised because of the individual attention offered by small groups, the insistence on aiming high and working hard.

Avenue House

70 The Avenue, Ealing, London, W13 8LS
Tel: 0181 998 9981 Fax: 0181 991 1533

Head Carolyn Barber
Type Co-educational pre-preparatory and preparatory school
Religious denomination Non-denominational
Fees per term (day) Half day £600; Full day £1,200
Fees per annum (day) Half day £1,800; Full day £3,600

Avenue House is a happy, caring, academic school situated in a quiet leafy area of Ealing.

Founded in January 1995, the aim of this co-educational pre-preparatory and preparatory school is to provide an environment where each child can realise his or her educational potential to the full. Pupils are encouraged to develop their own individual talents and personalities, enabling them to become self-confident, enthusiastic and caring children who learn to value the importance of diligent work from an eary age.

Pupils are taught in small classes where they can achieve their full potential in academic subjects, music, drama, sport and public examinations. All pupils are monitored individually and frequent meetings with parents and the school are actively encouraged. We believe a positive approach to learning leads to excellence.

Children in the nursery are taught in a stimulating environment. Apart from being introduced to their numbers and a variety of initial reading schemes, French, computers, cooking, drama, PE, art, craft, music and movement form a vital part of the nursery sessions. Weekly swimming lessons are given at the Gurnell Swimming Pool by specialist instructors.

The preparatory school curriculum, whilst adhering closely to the National Curriculum, is based on the need to prepare pupils for the relevant public examination of the parents' choice. In conjunction with the traditional academic subjects computers, music, art, craft, drama, swimming, gymnastics and games are taught. Although the emphasis is still on developing all the children's talents, we also believe in the traditional values of courtesy, kindness and consideration for others.

In addition to its own library and purpose-built gymnasium the school has the use of a purpose-built science laboratory. The school also offers a pre- and after-school care service for parental convenience.

Educational visits play an important rôle in helping children relate their class work to the real world. For this reason the pupils are taken on outings where they can benefit from having first-hand knowledge of London and its surrounding area.

At Avenue House we believe a happy child is most likely to succeed.

Beacon House School

15 Gunnersbury Avenue, Ealing, London W5 3XD
Tel: 0181 992 5189

Head Mrs Mary Milner BA (Hons)
Founded 1946
Type Mixed independent day school
Age range 3 – 11
No of pupils (day) 150
Girls 120; *Boys* 30
Junior Kindergarten and transition 50; senior 100
Fees per term (day) £454 – £1,010
Fees per annum (day) £1,362 – £3,030

Curriculum: children in the upper school are prepared for entrance into other schools, special attention being paid to a sound grounding in English, mathematics and junior science. The National Curriculum is also covered. The syllabus includes art design and technology, history, geography, religious education, French and music.

Computers are among the resources available. Physical education takes place twice weekly and children in Forms 5 and 4 are taken swimming weekly. Every morning and lunchtime there is a 20 minute garden break.

Entry requirements: entry is non-competitive, in order of registration.

Extra-curricular activities include recorder, choir, chess and elocution classes. All forms in the senior school have an outing each term to a theatre or place of interest chosen to complement their studies, and entertain their parents annually.

Liaison between home and school is supplemented by twice-yearly parents' form meetings. A very personal, friendly atmosphere prevails.

Broomwood Hall

74 Nightingale Lane, London SW12 8NR
Tel: 0181 673 1616 Fax: 0181 675 7805

Head Mrs K A H Colquhoun BEd, DipT
Founded 1984
Type Co-educational pre-preparatory, girls preparatory
Religious denomination Church of England
Members of IAPS
Age range 4 – 8 boys; 4 – 12 girls
No of pupils (day) 282
Girls 172; *Boys* 110
Fees per term (day) £1,500 – £1,760

We are a co-educational pre-preparatory and preparatory school for children from the age of four until eight (boys) and 11+ or 12+ (girls).

Located midway between Clapham and Wandsworth Commons, the school was established in 1984 to prepare children for entry to the well known boys' preparatory and girls' public schools. We continue to do this, although an increasing number of children now go on to London day schools.

The curriculum is a structured, traditional one leading up to Common Entrance and scholarship examinations at 11+ and 12+. It is designed to cater for children of all abilities, setting a high academic standard for able children but encouraging the less able without applying undue pressure.

We offer one scholarship each year for a girl (aged eight) from the state system, to study for Common Entrance.

Clifton Lodge Preparatory School

8 Mattock Lane, Ealing, London W5 5BG
Tel: 0181 579 3662

Head D A P Blumlein
Founded 1979
Type Boys' preparatory
Religious denomination Christian
Age range 4 – 13
No of pupils (day) 160
Junior 40 *Senior* 120
Fees per term (day) £1,400 – £1,496
Fees per annum (day) £4,200 – £4,450

Clifton Lodge is a school that stands for standards: standards of proper behaviour, and standards of personal achievement.

We believe that boys want to be a success in life and this they can only obtain by hard work, confidence in their own ability and a properly disciplined approach, whatever the activity. Clifton Lodge seeks at all times to impart these values.

The school is geared to give much individual attention, with boys being able to work at their own level, enabling them to realise their own potential.

The curriculum is based on the need to prepare boys for entry to public school at 13+ through the Common Entrance examination, public school scholarships or other equivalent examinations, and Clifton Lodge is justifiably proud of its excellent record of success in these. Whereas this provides the core of the academic programme, nevertheless we consider it essential to educate all pupils as broadly as possible and much time is also given to music (regular choral and instrumental recitals are given), sport (football, rugby, cricket, tennis athletics, etc) and drama, these avenues providing boys with valuable opportunities to develop further talents and to guild up their self-confidence.

The school is of Christian denomination and the daily assembly, attended by the whole community, is based around these ideas.

Choral scholarships: the school has an established choral tradition and choristerships to the value of one third of the basic fees are available to boys who become full choristers.

International School of London

139 Gunnersbury Avenue, London W3 8LG
Tel: 0181 992 5823 Fax: 0181 993 7012

Head Richard Hermon MA
Founded 1972
Type Co-educational day school
Age range 4 – 19
No of pupils (day) 200
Girls 90; *Boys* 110
Junior 80; *Senior* 95; *Sixth form* 25
Fees per term (day) £1,730 – £2,780
Fees per annum (day) £5,190 – £8,340

Curriculum: the programme from nursery to GCSE follows English lines, but special consideration is given to native languages other than English. English as a second language is taught where necessary. In the primary school, mother tongue language programmes are available in Arabic, Danish, French and Italian; at the secondary level, Arabic, French, Danish, Italian, Japanese, Portuguese, Spanish and other languages are offered as needed.

Entry requirements: ISL accepts students at all ages and at any time during the academic year. Admission is based on previous school records and a personal interview, if possible.

Examinations: GCSE and the International Baccalaureate

Academic and leisure facilities: the school has a spacious playground and a separate nursery playground. The school uses the sports fields of the adjacent Gunnersbury Park and the swimming and sports facilities of nearby Brentford Leisure Centre. Many extra-curricular activities and sports options are available.

Scholarships: bursaries are available.

Transportation: door-to-door bus service is available.

Kensington Park School

10 Pembridge Square, London W2 4ED
Tel: 0171 221 5748

Head Richard Walker
Founded 1988
Type Independent
Age range 11 – 18
No of pupils (day) 90
Girls 40; *Boys* 50
Junior 60; *Senior* 30
Fees per term (day) £1,830
Fees per annum (day) £5,490

Curriculum: the first three years follow a curriculum of English, mathematics, science, French, history, geography, computing, art, design and technology and sport. In the fourth form students take a core of English, mathematics, physics, chemistry, biology and a language (French or Spanish) together with options from a choice of seven subjects. There is a maximum class size of 12.

Entry requirements: entrance is through a one-day extended interview during which written work in mathematics and English is completed.

Examinations offered: the school is a centre for ULEAC (London), MEG and SEG, and offers GCSE examinations in all the normal subjects.

Facilities: situated in magnificent period buildings in Notting Hill Gate, the school is equipped with an art studio, science laboratories, dark room and a computer centre.

Scholarships: a limited number of bursaries are available for parents who require financial support.

Latymer Upper School

King Street, Hammersmith, London W6 9LR
Tel: 0181 741 1851 Fax: 0181 748 5212

Head Mr C Diggory BSc, CMath, FIMA, FRSA
Type Independent boys, Co-educational Sixth Form school
Religious denomination Christian non-denominational
Members of HMC
Age range 7 – 18
No of pupils (day) 1071
Boys 1071
Preparatory 130; *Senior* 686; *Sixth form* 255
Fees per term (day) £1,934
Fees per annum (day) £5,802

Entry requirements: boys must be registered by early December. Competitive examinations and interviews are held for entry at 7, 8, 11 and 13, and at 16 for the sixth form for boys and, from 1996, for girls. Academic and music scholarships are offered every year. The school participates in the assisted place scheme. The syllabus and past papers in mathematics and English are available from the registrar, along with further details.

Curriculum: a full range of academic subjects is offered to GCSE and A level. Languages include Latin, Greek, French, German and Spanish (European work experience and exchanges are run every year). Science is taught as separate subjects by subject specialists. Results are strong, and all boys go to university. A school-wide computer network is used to assist the boys in many subjects. Form sizes of 22 boys and teaching group sizes often smaller than that ensure the personal attention of staff. The Latymer Preparatory School has just been developed from the preparatory department and has its own extensive facilities and riverside site for the 7 – 11 age range.

Pastoral care: the school has a strong tradition of excellent pastoral care. The school has three divisions (lower school, middle school, sixth form) led by a head of division who is responsible for those in the division. Teams of form tutors deliver a coherent programme promoting involvement in the community, charity work, and the personal, social and academic development of their form.

Music and drama: these activities play a large part in the life of the school. There are several orchestras and choirs and two concerts each term.

There are five major drama productions each year, and opportunities for all to perform in **Gild** events. Some orchestras and drama productions are run jointly with The Godolphin and Latymer School.

Sport: there are fine facilities for sport. The school has a boat house on site with a direct river access, a large sports hall, a squash court and an indoor swimming pool on site. The playing fields are two miles away at Wood Lane. Emphasis is on involvement, participation and choice.

The school does well in the major sports of rugby, soccer, rowing, cricket and athletics and runs more than one team per year group. We also offer other sports such as fencing, swimming and golf to cater for individual interests. The school maintains excellent fixture lists in all major sports.

Outdoor pursuits: every pupil has the opportunity to have a residential experience and do outdoor pursuits as part of the annual school activities week or with schools' Scouts. A very active Parents Gild ensures that no one is excluded from an activity for financial reasons.

The Duke of Edinburgh Award Scheme flourishes in the school with several achieving the Gold Award each year.

Amberleigh Preparatory School

398 Wilbraham Road, Chorlton-cum-Hardy, Manchester, Greater Manchester M21 0UH
Tel: 0161 881 1593

Head Mr P F Hayden CertEd
Founded 1925
Type Preparatory
Religious denomination Non-denominational
Members of ISAI
Age range 4 – 11
No of pupils (day) 115
Girls 40; *Boys* 76

Amberleigh is proud of its reputation for being a friendly, happy school which thrives upon firm discipline and a keen desire to see that our children make the most of their talents. Each child progresses at his or her own pace through a reading and number scheme based on individual books and mathematical cards. No child is ever held back; all are encouraged to work to the limit of their capacities. The junior classes work at a keen pace and prepare thoroughly for the entrance examinations of independent secondary schools and local education authority selection procedures. A teacher is also allocated three afternoons each week to give help in reading and mathematics to children who need extra support in these subjects mainly because of joining the school at age seven or eight. There is also a house point credit and rewards system in the junior school which awards points for satisfactory work and sporting prowess. There are seven classes of average size 20 pupils. Preparation for independent and local authority selection procedures form an integral part of the curriculum. Over the past three years 90 per cent of our 11-year-old pupils have gained places at independent or maintained grammar schools. Pupils participate in normal games, athletics and swimming. Elocution and dancing are taught and LAMDA and RADA examinations may be taken. Our aim is to inculcate joy in hard work and a proper respect for the happiness of fellow pupils. After-school care is available from the end of school until 5.30pm each day.

The following independent college also offers GCSEs. Please refer to the Independent Sixth-Form College section for details:

Abbey Tutorial College, Manchester

Streatham House School

2 Victoria Road West, Blundellsands, Liverpool, Merseyside L23 8UQ
Tel: 0151 924 1514

Head Mrs C Baxter
Founded 1925
Type Independent
Religious denomination Non-denominational
Age range 2½ – 16
No of pupils (day) 212
Girls 179; *Boys* 33
Junior 48; *Senior* 61
Fees per term (day) £420 – £995
Fees per annum (day) £1,260 – £2,985

Streatham House School is a small school with a friendly atmosphere. There is a high teacher-pupil ratio and individual attention is given to each child. Traditional values of discipline, good manners and concern for other people are encouraged.

The school has a flourishing kindergarten department where strong emphasis is placed on music and art, as well as preparing for the introduction of more formal learning through imaginative structured play.

The infant/junior school gives a firm grounding in the basic subjects and develops in children a keen interest in science. Much of the teaching is cross-curricular and classroom displays are particularly lively.

The senior school offers a wide range of subjects to GCSE level, producing excellent examination results. Learning is taken out of the classroom through field-work, theatre or museum visits and educational trips abroad.

We are able to accept pupils with moderate physical handicaps as far as our buildings permit.

American Community Schools, England

Hillingdon Court, 108 Vine Lane, Hillingdon, Uxbridge, Middlesex UB10 0BE
Tel: 01895 259771 Fax: 01895 810634

Head Mr B Duncan
Founded 1967
Type Co-educational
Religious denomination Non-sectarian
Members of New England Association of Schools
and Colleges, ISJC, ECIS, NE/SA, IB
Age range 4 – 18
No of pupils (day) 570
Girls 271; *Boys* 299
Junior 370; *Senior* 200
Fees per semester (day) £2,375 – £4,370
Fees per annum (day) £4,750 – £8,740

The three American Community Schools, founded in 1967, are non-sectarian co-educational schools for students between the ages of four and eighteen. The Middlesex campus is located in Hillingdon 15 miles from London and is accessible by London Underground. A door-to-door bus service is provided by the school.

Student body/faculty

Approximately 46 per cent of the 570 students are American, 10 per cent are Canadian and the remaining 44 per cent represent 32 other nationalities. There are 78 full-time teachers on the faculty, all holding a university degree. The student faculty ratio is 8:1.

Admissions

New students are accepted subject to space being available in all grades throughout the year on the basis of a completed application form and previous school records (with a provision for testing prior to grade placement when necessary).

Academic program

The traditional American curriculum, offering a wide range of subjects is designed to lead to an American High School Diploma. Experienced university counselling is provided by the Academic Dean and all examinations required for admission to American universities are administered by the school.

In addition the school provides courses leading to the International Baccalaureate Diploma, a recognised qualification for entry to universities throughout the world including Britain. It also offers advanced standing in American universities. The high-level courses are equivalent to A level standards.

English as a second language:

The school offers a program for those students in the secondary school whose native language is not English.

The Campus

The school is situated in an 11-acre campus which provides the students with a first class gymnasium, playing fields and tennis courts. The historic main house is situated in landscaped gardens. 'Pavilions', a welcome addition to the campus, was constructed in spring and summer of 1993, and contains twelve classrooms, and the usual support units.

Student activities

A full range of sports are offered including basketball, tennis, track and field, soccer, rugby, swimming and volleyball. Other activities available are Student Council Yearbook, music, computers, drama, video, scouting etc.

Accreditation

The school is accredited by the New England Association of Schools and Colleges, ISJC, and holds membership in the International Baccalaureate Organisation.

St Helen's School

Eastbury Road, Northwood, Middlesex HA6 3AS
Tel: 01923 828511 Fax: 01923 835824

Head Mrs D M Jenkins MA (Cantab), CPhys
Founded 1899
Type Girls' Independent day and boarding
Religious denomination Christian based, all faiths welcome
Members of GSA, GBGSA
Age range 4+ – 18 *Boarders from* 8+ – 18
No of pupils (day) 906; *(boarding)* 60
Girls 966
Junior 353; *Senior* 613; *Sixth form* 171
Fees per term (day) £1,012 – £1,591; *(boarding)* full £2,643 – £2,998; weekly £2,536 – £2,891
Fees per annum (day) £3,036 – £4,773; *(boarding)* full £7,929 – £8,994; weekly £7,608 – £8,673

Founded in 1899 St Helen's is a flourishing school with 966 girls. The school has three departments – preparatory, junior and senior – with excellent boarding facilities for 62 pupils. Pleasantly located in a 22-acre green site, we offer a wide range of sporting facilities, including a heated swimming pool.

The ethos of St Helen's is to foster excellence within a friendly and supportive community. All girls are encouraged to succeed and there is a wide range of extra-curricular activities to complement the academic curriculum which is broad and balanced. Girls acquire skills in both information and design technology and there is a particularly strong emphasis on languages, science and mathematics. Music, drama and art play a significant role in school life.

We have an excellent record of academic success and almost all our sixth formers enter higher education, many gaining Oxbridge places. At Advanced level, our girls achieved a pass rate of 99 per cent, 71 per cent achieving A or B grades, and our GCSE pass rate was also 99 per cent, with 62 per cent gaining A & A* grades.

St Helen's offers weekly as well as full boarding facilities. Weekend activities for the boarders include riding, tennis, swimming and windsurfing. There is a senior boarding house with study bedrooms and one further boarding house. Each house has its own housemistress and assistant housemistress.

The close links between St Helen's and our brother school Merchant Taylors, mean that our pupils receive all the benefits of single-sex education with the advantage of contact with a highly successful boys' school.

Opportunities for European work experience and substantial links with industry mean that our pupils are well prepared to embark on life in the 21st century.

Entry to St Helen's is competitive by examination and interview. Scholarships and Assisted Places are available. We are a Christian foundation but we are a cosmopolitan community and we welcome girls of all faiths.

Northwood is 30 minutes from central London on the Metropolitan Line. It is easily accessible from the M1, M4 and M25, is only 30 minutes drive from Heathrow Airport, and is approximately an hour from Gatwick and Luton Airports. Coach services are available from Ealing, Beaconsfield/Gerrards Cross, Harrow, Mill Hill and Radlett/Elstree areas.

St Martin's School

40 Moor Park Road, Northwood, Middlesex HA6 2DJ
Tel: 01923 825740 Fax: 01923 835452

Head Mr M J Hodgson MA, CertEd
Founded 1922
Type Boys' preparatory day school
Religious denomination Church of England
Members of IAPS, ISIS
Age range 3 – 13
Junior 125; *Senior* 245
Fees per annum (day) £1,425 – £4,770

Curriculum: boys entering the pre-preparatory at four and the main school at seven are taught by class teachers. Subject specialists take over at nine. We have the benefit of science laboratories, art and design rooms and excellent computer facilities.

Entry requirements: all candidates take an assessment test.

Examinations offered: children are prepared successfully for Common Entrance or scholarship entrance to senior schools.

Academic and sports facilities: St Martin's offers an all-round education. We enjoy an enviable reputation in games and competitive sports. Our choirs, orchestra and stage productions are deservedly renowned, and our activities programme caters for a wide range of hobbies.

Our pastoral system encourages children to learn self-reliance and a sense of responsibility in a happy family atmosphere.

Langley Preparatory School and Nursery

Beech Hill, 11 Yarmouth Road, Thorpe St Andrew, Norwich, Norfolk NR7 0EA
Tel: 01603 433861 Fax: 01603 702639

Head Mr P J Weeks BEd(Hons), CertEd, M(Coll)P
Founded 1910
Type Co-educational day school
Religious denomination Non-denominational
Members of IAPS, ISIS
Age range 2 – 12
No of pupils (day) 125
Girls 35; *Boys* 90
Fees per term (day) £670 – £1,315

The school is situated in five acres of attractive grounds. Its proximity to the centre of Norwich makes it ideal for parents working in or near the city.

Our aim is to allow each child to reach his or her full potential.

A broad curriculum is followed and classes rarely exceed 16. All National Curriculum subjects are taught.

There are purpose-built rooms for art, science and information technology. A design technology studio is the most recent development. There is also a swimming pool. As well as the traditional team games orienteering is offered as an extra-curricular activity. The school has been Norfolk's Schools' League Champions for the past six years.

Music, speech and drama are also strong elements on the curriculum. The school has an annual concert, Christmas production and regularly takes part in local speech and drama competitions.

A range of after school clubs are also available.

Langley School

Langley Park, Norwich, Norfolk NR14 6BJ
Tel: 01508 520210 Fax: 01508 528058

Head S J W McArthur BSc, MA, CertEd, FCollP
Founded 1910
Type Independent
Religious denomination Inter-denominational
Members of SHMIS, BSA, GBA, ISIS
Age range 10 – 18 *Boarders from* 10 – 18
No of pupils (day) 183 *(boarding)* 64
Girls 53 *Boys* 213
Senior 206 *Sixth form* 60
Fees per term (day) £1,485 – £1,820; *(boarding)* £2,885 – £3,500; *(weekly boarding)* £2,470 – £2,840
Fees per annum (day) £4,455 – £5,460; *(boarding)* £8,655 – £10,500; *(weekly boarding)* £7,410 – £8,520

Entry requirements: interview, report from previous school and entrance tests at 10, 11, 12 and 13. Also Common Entrance. At 16 candidates must have completed satisfactory a GCSE course. A range of academic, music, art, technology and sports scholarships are also awarded annually.

Situated in superb grounds of 50 acres near Norwich, Langley is approximately 100 miles north east of London and close to Norwich Airport for international connections via Amsterdam. The school provides transport for an extensive local area for day pupils.

Langley offers a traditionally English independent school education taught by experienced graduate staff with emphasis on good manners, high standards of academic work and encouraging pupils to partake in as wide a range of experiences as possible.

Classes are small with an average staff to pupil ratio of 1:9. Currently 21 subjects are available at GCSE, including all the sciences, information systems, Spanish, and Latin. The sixth form prepares pupils for A levels leading to university entry and careers in the professions or in industry. A three-tier curriculum which now includes GNVQ advanced business enables pupils to select from a wide range of options.

The impressive facilities, which include craft, design and technology centre, lecture theatre, assembly hall, large sports hall and well equipped purpose-built classrooms, have recently been supplemented by the opening of a new science centre equipped with the latest technology and containing eight laboratories and a computing suite.

There are extensive playing fields, 12 tennis courts and a nine-hole golf course. The main games are rugby, hockey, athletics, cricket, tennis, netball and rounders. Langley has a good record of pupils achieving representative honours at local, regional and national levels.

An Arts Umbrella programme offers pupils the opportunity to experience theatrical and musical productions in London and other centres, supplementing the school's internal provisions.

The aim of the school is to provide a full education, academically, socially and culturally, to encourage pupils to develop their talents and own personality, to use time wisely, to achieve a high standard of self-discipline; and to draw out and train the qualities of leadership. There is an active Combined Cadet Force, Parents' Association and Past Pupils' Society.

Northamptonshire Grammar School

Pitsford Hall, Pitsford, Northamptonshire NN6 9AX
Tel: 01604 880306 Fax: 01604 882212

Head Dan Hanson
Founded 1989
Type Independent boys' day grammar school
Religious denomination Non-denominational
Age range 7 – 18
No of pupils (day) 200
Junior 40; *Senior* 120; *Sixth form* 40
Fees per annum (day) £4,830

Northamptonshire Grammar School, set in 26 acres of park land, is the only independent selective day school for boys aged 7 – 18 in the county. Boys are fully extended and motivated by highly qualified and enthusiastic staff in classes small enough to allow individual attention. The emphasis on high academic standards ensures that boys leave fully prepared for higher education.

The school day is from 8.40am to 5.20pm. There are daily school bus services from Northampton and Daventry. Entry to the school is by examination in February. Scholarships are awarded at 11+, 13+ and 16+. A limited number of bursaries is available.

Up to the age of 11, all boys are taught by a class teacher in a separate junior department which has its own head. The junior department acts as a bridge for boys entering the senior school, with which it shares some facilities and teaching staff. Specialist teaching in the junior department is presently available in games, drama, gymnastics, French, music, art and IT. The sports include rugby, hockey, cricket, cross-country running, athletics and rounders. All boys are taught the recorder and many learn to play other instruments. Extra speech lessons are also available. Between 3.30pm and 5.20pm optional extra-curricular activities, supervised prep and tea are available.

In the senior school there are three sections – lower, middle and sixth form – each with its own leader. All boys are allocated to a tutor who monitors his work regularly. Form tutors stay with their forms until the end of each section. From the age of 11 a strong emphasis is placed upon the development of skills and understanding that will be needed for smooth progress up to GCSE and A level.

The senior school has an extensive sporting programme including abseiling, badminton, cross-country running, fishing, five-a-side soccer, golf, martial arts, sailing, squash, swimming, tennis, wall-climbing and weight training. The school has been county rugby champion at two age levels for the last three years.

Service to the community is an integral part of the school's philosophy. During each academic year money is raised for a variety of charities. In the last 12 months money has been raised for BBC Children in Need, Northampton Shelter, Sir Malcolm Sargent Cancer Fund for Children and Unicef.

The extra-curricular activities programme gives boys the opportunity to broaden their horizons and includes chess, choir, computing, conversational Russian and Spanish, debating and public speaking, drama and music, ecology, expeditions, first aid, magazine, radio astronomy, radio-controlled cars, the sixth-form discussion group, the yearbook and wargaming. At present over 60 boys are involved in the Duke of Edinburgh's Award Scheme and last year four boys received their Gold Award.

Throughout the school, classroom teaching is punctuated with visits to places of local and national interest. In the junior school, all boys go to frontier camp. In the senior school, all boys in the first year visit Hadrian's Wall for a week. In the second year, they spend a week in Normandy, and third- and fourth-years have the opportunity to travel to Germany. Overseas skiing and walking expeditions have been arranged and last summer the 1st XV toured South Africa.

Northamptonshire Grammar School, which is a registered charity, exists to provide high quality education to boys in the county.

Wellingborough School

Northamptonshire NN8 2BX
Tel: 01933 222427 Fax: 01933 271986

Head F R Ullmann
Founded 1595
Type Independent
Religious denomination Church of England
Members of HMC, IAPS, GBA, BSA
Age range 3 – 18 *Boarders from* 13
No of pupils (day) 710; *(boarding)* 50
Girls 280; *Boys* 480
Pre-prep 120; *Junior* 240; *Senior* 390; *Sixth form* 140
Fees per term (day) £830 – £1,725; *(boarding)* £2,790 – £3,100
Fees per annum (day) £2,480 – £5,175; *(boarding)* £8,370 – £12,600

Average size of class: 16:20
Teacher/pupil ratio: 1:10
Curriculum:

3 – 7: sound foundation across National Curriculum.

8 – 18: English, French, German, (senior school), Latin, classical studies (senior school), history, geography, mathematics, physics, chemistry, biology, information technology, art, design technology, drama, music, RE and physical education leading to GCSE (eight to nine subjects) and A levels. All sixth-form pupils are prepared for university entrance.

Entry requirements and procedures: entry for junior and senior schools by examination and interview. Scholarships and DFE assisted places at 11, 13 and 16. Bursaries for special talents (eg music, art and sport).

Facilities: include comfortable boarding accommodation for senior boys and girls, 40 acres of playing fields with a modern sports hall, squash and tennis courts and swimming pool. Outdoor activities include Combined Cadet Force and Duke of Edinburgh Award. School week: five day teaching, games coaching and Combined Cadet Force timetable. Comprehensive weekday and independent weekend activities programme. All pupils involved from age eight.

Situated close to M1 and A1-M1 link with easy access to all parts of UK and main airports. Wellingborough School Foundation, which is a charity, exists to provide and conduct in or near Wellingborough in the County of Northamptonshire a day and boarding school for boys and girls.

Winchester House Preparatory School

High Street, Brackley, Northamptonshire NN13 7AZ
Tel: 01280 702483 Fax: 01280 706400

Head Mr D R Speight MA (Oxon)
Founded 1875
Type Boarding and day co-educational preparatory school
Members of IAPS
Age range 3 – 14
No of pupils (day) 170; *(boarding)* 90 (8–14)
Fees per term (pre-preparatory) £1,200; *(day)* £2,200; *(boarding)* £2,910

Curriculum: subjects required for scholarships, Common Entrance and the National Curriculum are taught, including IT, art, music, pottery, craft, design technology and Latin. Greek is also taught to the scholars during their last two years. Each year group in the main school is divided into sets for each subject to ensure that every child works at the right level and faces suitable challenges leading to success at their entrance exams.

An impressive number of scholarships to the leading independent schools are won each year. *Entry requirements:* entry to the school is by interview. Children entering the main school at eight should be able to read and write, and have a basic knowledge of arithmetic. Scholarships are offered to academic, artistic and musical pupils.

Academic and leisure facilities: the academic facilities are excellent; a new library, IT and English department; a modern music school; well-equipped art, pottery and CDT workshops; a much used theatre; designated laboratories and subject classrooms.

There are extensive games pitches, hard playing surfaces, four tennis courts, two squash courts, a heated swimming pool, a small bore rifle range, a school hall and a six hole golf course. Cricket, rounders, rugby, netball and hockey are the major games. We also offer athletics, badminton, basketball, canoeing, clay pigeon shooting, dance, go- karting, ice-skating, riding, sailing and 'scouting'. Other leisure activities include modelling, photography and philately. There are three annual camps, a canal trip, a ski trip and various expeditions.

A new purpose-built boarding house for girls has been extended to provide further accommodation. The boys have three boarding 'houses' with comfortable well furnished dormitories.

There is also a nationally recognised pre-preparatory department of 90 children aged three to eight.

The following independent college also offers GCSEs. Please refer to the Independent Sixth-Form Colleges section for details:

Bosworth Tutorial College, Northampton

Abingdon School

Abingdon, Oxfordshire OX14 1DE
Tel: 01235 531755 Fax: 01235 536449

Head M StJohn Parker
Founded 1256
Type Boys' independent day and boarding
Religious denomination Church of England
Others welcome
Members of HMC
Age range 11 – 18; *Boarders from* 11 – 18
No of pupils (day) 620; *(boarding)* 140
Boys 760
Junior 125 (11 – 13); *Senior* 635; *Sixth form* 250
Fees per term (day) £1,754; *(boarding)* £3,283
Fees per annum (day) £5,262; *(boarding)* £9,849

Curriculum: broad studies to 16, average ten GCSE passes, over 20 A level choices plus AS and stimulating general studies. Sixth form of 250, 97 per cent university entry, Oxford and Cambridge 20–25 per cent.
Entry requirements and procedures: school's examination at 11, Common Entrance at 13,

GCSE results for sixth form. Academic, music, art, sixth-form scholarships, assisted places and bursaries are available.

The school is situated in spacious grounds in the centre of the small town of Abingdon, near Oxford, with fast motorway communications, and bus runs from Abingdon to Heathrow. Weekly boarding is increasingly popular and the day boy area is served by an extensive network of buses.

A £2.5 million teaching and sixth-form building opened in 1994, the climax of a 17-year development programme to include an assembly hall and theatre, sports hall, laboratories, technology centre and the renovation of the boarding houses and study bedrooms.

The school is noted for academic, musical and artistic excellence, wide sporting and leisure opportunities, and a friendly atmosphere.

Bloxham School

Bloxham, Banbury, Oxfordshire OX15 4PE
Tel: 01295 720206 Fax: 01295 721897

Head Mr David K Exham MA
Founded 1860
Type Boarding and day (co-educational sixth form)
Religious denomination Church of England
Members of HMC, ISIS, BSA
Age range 11 – 18 *Boarders from* 13
No of pupils (day) 88; *(boarding)* 255
Lower school 24; *Sixth form* 150
Fees per term (day) £3,085; *(boarding)* £3,950; *(Lower school)* £2,095

Bloxham School is one of Britain's best independent smaller boarding and day schools with a co-educational sixth form.

The school is in North Oxfordshire, only three miles from the M40 motorway, close to London and Birmingham Airports and 25 miles from Oxford. Forty-five per cent board and 25 per cent are day pupils.

Bloxham School expects pupils to do well. GCSEs achieved in fifth form – average 8.0; A levels achieved in sixth form – average 3.5; pass rates for 1994 95.2 per cent at A level; 85.1 per cent at GCSE (A–C).

Ninety per cent of Bloxhamists go on to university. Each year five or six apply to Oxford or Cambridge and a good proportion is accepted (four in 1995).

There are fine facilities for academic work, sport, recreation and living. Recent developments include the music school, new information technology suite, new dining room and kitchens, an extended art school, the new indoor swimming pool, all weather hockey pitch and tennis courts. A fine new technology centre will be completed in 1996. With a well-qualified teaching staff, the school offers a supportive and friendly environment with individual tutors for each pupil. Every boy and girl is encouraged to fulfil their potential inside the classroom and through the wide range of other activities which are available.

Scholarships: we offer five Government Assisted Places at 13+, and at 11+, 13+ and 16+ academic, art, music and design technology scholarships which may be supplemented by a bursary according to the financial needs of parents.

Cokethorpe

Witney, Oxfordshire OX8 7PU
Tel: 01993 703921 Fax: 01993 773499

Head P J S Cantwell
Founded 1957
Type Independent
Religious denomination Inter-denominational
Members of SHMIS
Age range 9 – 18 *Boarders from* 11 – 18 (boys only)
No of pupils (day) 156; *(boarding)* 55
Girls 40; *Boys* 171
Junior 55; *Senior* 125; *Sixth form* 31
Fees per term (day) £1,350 – £2,620; *(boarding)* £3,165 – £3,980

A broad academic and vocational curriculum is followed to GCSE. Traditional A levels and GNVQ Level 3 are available to the sixth form. Small classes provide everyone with the opportunity of fulfilling their potential. Extra help is available in the learning support department. Entry requirements are interview and headteacher's report at the age of nine, interview and assessment at 11 and 13 years with Common Entrance for preparatory school candidates.

Examinations: GCSE, A level, GNVQ level 3. The design technology building contains the library, art, ceramics, information technology and design technology facilities. There are also modern laboratories, a new music school, and sixth form facilities. The new sports hall provides first rate facilities for a wide range of indoor sports, including cricket, hockey and tennis. There is a wide range of extra-curricular activities within 40 acres of grounds. Scholarships are awarded on entrance assessment. Bursaries are available on application for details. Two boarding houses with resident housemasters and house tutors provide a high degree of personal attention and pastoral care.

d'Overbroeck's

Beechlawn House, Park Town, Oxford, Oxfordshire OX2 6SN
Tel: 01856 310000 Fax: 01856 52296

Joint Heads J D G Noel BA, CertEd
R M Knowles MA, DPhil
Founded 1947
Type Co-educational sixth form
Religious denomination Non-denominational
Age range 16 – 19
No of pupils (day) 120; *(boarding)* 100
Girls 105; *Boys* 115
Fees per term (day) £3,055; *(boarding)* £4,255

d'Overbroeck's has a distinctive character which sets it apart from many schools and makes it attractive to those seeking an education that is more personalised inside the classroom and less structured outside it than that offered by many institutions. The staff-student ratio is 1:4. Supervision is close and personal.

The academic programme is highly flexible and ensures that the college is particularly suitable for both the academically weak and the very gifted. Almost all GCSE and A level subjects may be studied in any combination. Teaching takes place either in small groups or an individual basis.

Considerable guidance from experienced staff is given to those making an application to higher education and the numbers gaining entry to university are very high.

The college has a range of excellent facilities including science and computer laboratories. Students enjoy a varied sporting programme and the cultural and social benefits of being in the centre of Oxford.

Headington School

Oxford, Oxfordshire OX3 7TD
Tel: 01865 741968 Fax: 01865 60268

Head Miss E M Tucker MA (Cantab)
Founded 1915
Type Girls' day and boarding
Religious denomination Church of England
Members of GSA
Age range 4 – 18 *Boarders from* 9+
No of pupils (day) 550; *(boarding)* 200
Junior 220; *Senior* 550; *Sixth form* 160
Fees per term (day) £1,508; *(boarding)* £3,010
Fees per annum (day) £4,524; *(boarding)* £9,030

Curriculum: National Curriculum GCSE; plus classics and German or Spanish. Economics, history of art, politics, theatre studies, environmental science, GNVQ business studies added at A level, as well as GCSE Italian.
Entry requirements: Common Entrance 11+, 12+, 13+. School examination 14+, 16+.
Academic and leisure facilities: new library, science laboratories, information technology rooms, art/design and music blocks. Strong music, sport, drama, Duke of Edinburgh Award Scheme, boat club, covered swimming pool, sports hall.
Scholarships: 11+, 12/13+, 16+ half fee entry scholarships. Music scholarship: tuition on two instruments.
Boarding facilities: two hundred boarders: four houses, one for upper sixth, three for mixed ages including lower sixth; all houses have homely atmosphere.

Kingham Hill School

Kingham, Chipping Norton, Oxfordshire OX7 6TH
Tel: 01608 658999 Fax: 01608 658658

Head Mr M H Payne BSc, PGCE
Founded 1886
Type Co-educational boarding and day
Religious denomination Church of England
Members of SHMIS, GBA, ISJC
Age range 11 – 18 *Boarders from* 11
No of pupils (day) 15; *(boarding)* 186
Girls 46; *Boys* 160
Junior 35; *Senior* 127; *Sixth form* 41
Fees per term (day) £1,840 – £1,895; *(boarding)* £3,068 – £3,159
Fees per annum (day) £5,520 – £5,685; *(boarding)* £9,204 – £9,477

Curriculum: a broad spectrum of subjects at junior level leading to a wide choice of GCSE subjects. In the vocationally oriented sixth form a selection of A levels and GNVQs is offered.
Academic and leisure facilities: these are excellent, providing the staff with all the equipment they need to make learning interesting. Computer department, purpose-built technology centre, music school. Very successful SpLD department. Main games (rugby, soccer, cricket, hockey) plus netball, rounders, tennis, covered heated swimming pool, gymnasium, shooting range, assault course. Scouts, Combined Cadet Force, and Duke of Edinburgh Award Scheme.
Scholarships: art and music. Bursaries for those with a boarding need.
Boarding facilities: seven separate boarding houses. Numbers restricted to 35 in each house.

Millbrook House

Milton, Abingdon, Oxfordshire OX14 4EL
Tel: 01235 831237 Fax: 01235 821556

Head S R M Glazebrook
Founded 1955
Type Preparatory
Religious denomination Church of England
Members of CReSTeD
Age range 7 – 14 *Boarders from* 7
No of pupils (day) 6 *(boarding)* 50
Girls 5 *Boys* 50
Fees per term (day) £2,200 *(boarding)* £3,200

Specialised tuition for children who receive help for dyslexia and other learning problems or for those who need that little extra help. There is a high pupil/teacher ratio 8:1. Emphasis on personal attention and confidence building.

All major sports are offered including cricket, soccer, rugby, tennis and swimming.

Continuous success to all principal Public Schools and more importantly, finding the right school for the individual. Holiday courses also available.

Rye St Antony

Pullen's Lane, Headington Hill, Oxford, Oxfordshire OX3 0BY
Tel: 01865 62802 Fax: 01865 63611

Head Miss A M Jones
Founded 1930
Type Independent girls' boarding and day school
Religious denomination Roman Catholic
Members of GSA
Age range 3 – 18 *Boarders from* 8
No of pupils (day) 250; *(boarding)* 130
Girls 380
Junior & Nursery 80; *Senior* 225; *Sixth form* 75
Fees per term (day) £750 – £1,750; *(boarding)* £2,450 – £2,850
Fees per annum (day) £2,250 – £5,250; *(boarding)* £7,350 – £8,550

Rye St Antony is situated a mile out of Oxford in 12 acres of fine grounds on Headington Hill overlooking the city. The school was founded as a lay Catholic school and is run as an educational charitable trust.

The nursery and junior school are an integral part of the main school, and pupils are steadily introduced to the specialist teaching and facilities of the senior school.

A range of 20+ GCSE subjects is offered from which each girl chooses nine to ten subjects. Teaching in additional subjects is arranged as required.

20+ subjects are available at A level, and AS subjects are offered according to demand. Most girls stay on to take three A level subjects, subsequently going on to higher education.

Throughout the school girls are encouraged to develop their talents in music, art, drama and sport. Many girls also participate in the Duke of Edinburgh's Award Scheme, 20 students achieved the Gold Award this year.

Entry requirements and procedures:

Nursery and junior school: interview and school's own assessment.

Senior school: interview and Common Entrance examination at 11+; school's own entrance examination at other ages.

Sixth form: interview, report and GCSE results.

St Mary's, Wantage

Wantage, Oxfordshire OX12 8BZ
Tel: 01235 763571 Fax: 01235 760467

Head Mrs S Bodinham BSc, AKC
Founded 1873
Type Girls' independent boarding
Religious denomination Church of England
Member of GSA
Age range 11 – 18 *Boarders from* 11 – 18
No of pupils (boarding) 230
Girls 230
Senior 185 *Sixth form* 75
Fees per term (day) £2,400; *(boarding)* £3,620
Fees per annum (day) £7,200; *(boarding)* £10,860

Curriculum: **GCSE**: all girls take English, French, mathematics, combined science and religious studies, plus two optional subjects. **A level**: art history, theatre studies, economics, business studies and politics, in addition to GCSE subjects. All girls do IT. Office technology and administrative studies offered in sixth form when all girls follow course leading to Diploma of Achievement.

Entry requirements: Common Entrance at 11+, 12+, 13+, plus interview. Five GCSE passes for sixth-form entry. Prospectus from admissions secretary (ext 207).
Examinations offered: excellent academic record. A level pass rate in 1995: 87 per cent; 71 per cent grades A – C; GCSE pass rate: 82 per cent; 70 per cent grade A*, A, B, 33 per cent grades A, A*.
Academic and leisure facilities: five science laboratories, language laboratory, art and craft rooms, music wing; wide range of clubs and other recreational activities. Strong art, drama, music and sports departments. Instruction on all musical instruments and in speech and drama.
Scholarships: one sixth form and three scholarships at 13+: one academic + two for music/art/sports awarded annually.
Boarding facilities: full boarding. Eleven-year olds in own area, and sixth form in separate buildings (with study bedrooms).

Wychwood School

74 Banbury Road, Oxford, Oxfordshire OX2 6JR
Tel: 01865 57976 Fax: 01865 56806

Head Mrs M L Duffill
Founded 1897
Type Independent
Religious denomination Non-denominational
Age range 11 – 18 *Boarders from* 11 – 18
No of pupils (day) 80; *(boarding)* 80
Girls 160
Senior 160; *Sixth form* 40
Fees per term (day) £1,450; *(boarding)* £2,295

Wychwood was established in Oxford in 1897. Girls can make use of the cultural advantages of a university city. Wychwood is a charitable trust set up for educational purposes and offers a wide range of education in a very understanding and, for senior members, mature atmosphere. The girls take an active part in the school council where they may put forward ideas of their own, and state their opinions on matters raised. There is a natural form of discipline which, balanced between freedom and trust, is appreciated and not resented. The small size of Wychwood allows every girl to be treated as an individual, and we wish to apply to every girl the method best suited to her mental capacity and temperament and to judge her by her own possible standard of attainment. We wish our teachers to lead each girl to think and work independently, instead of being a passive recipient of instruction, to fix their eyes upon her future good rather than upon her success as a pupil, and to be ready to sacrifice the credit she might bring to the school if, by so doing, they can further her welfare in later life. An easy and natural relationship with adults and a happy atmosphere are considered to be of vital importance, so that each girl retains her individuality. There is in our system as little a break as possible in the continuity of the girl's life, as life at home and school training should be of the same quality and directed to the same end.

The following independent colleges also offer GCSEs and equivalent. Please refer to the Independent Sixth-Form Colleges section for details:

Abacus College, Oxford

Cherwell Tutors, Oxford

St Clare's, Oxford

Bedstone College

Bucknell, Shropshire SY7 0BG
Tel: 01547 530303 Fax: 01547 530740

Head Michael S Symonds BSc, CPhys, MInstP,
FRSA, PGCE
Founded 1948
Type Co-educational boarding and day
Religious denomination Church of England
Members of SHMIS, ISAI, GBA, BSA
Age range 3½ – 18 *Boarders from* 7
No of pupils (day) 23; *(boarding)* 174
Girls 80 *Boys* 117
Junior 30 *Senior* 167; *Sixth form* 36
Fees per term (day) £1,445 – £2,002; *(boarding)*
£2,173 – £3,213
Fees per annum (day) £4,131 – £5,721;
(boarding) £6,210 – £9,180

For half a century, Bedstone College has prepared young people to enter the outside world with the best academic qualifications within their scope, well-developed personal skills and self- confidence. The college was amongst the first independent schools to become fully co-educational and the warm family atmosphere that successful co-education produces is immediately obvious to any visitor. That family atmosphere is further enhanced with more than 80 per cent of scholars being boarders, and the day scholars being fully integrated within their respective boarding houses.

Today, the college caters for young people between the ages of 3 and 18 in the pre-preparatory, preparatory and senior schools.

Set in the heart of Britain on the common borders of Shropshire, Herefordshire, and Powys, the college is a haven of peace far from the distracting influences of urban life and yet easily accessible from all parts of the country.

Academic work is at the heart of every school and Bedstone has developed a broad-based and challenging curriculum designed to meet the needs of its scholars, preparing them to live and work in a rapidly changing world.

In the preparatory department (for 7–11-year-olds) the emphasis is very much on learning the basic skills of literacy and numeracy. The majority of lessons will be taken by the class teacher but in the sciences, modern languages, technology, music and sport, the scholars will be taught by specialist teachers who also teach in the senior college.

Once scholars join the main body of the college they are offered a broad pattern of academic work which goes beyond the requirements of the National Curriculum. The selection of subjects to be pursued at GCSE is made at the end of the third year (National Curriculum Year 9). The more able scholars are expected to follow a course leading to examination in ten GCSE subjects, whilst those who are less able will follow a course leading to examinations in six, seven, or eight GCSE subjects. Progress is closely monitored.

Class sizes up to GCSE are between 15 and 18. The staff : scholar ratio is a very generous 1:9.

The college is very aware of the difficulties that dyslexia can cause and takes a whole-school approach to the problem. Central to such help is the highly regarded learning support unit. The unit also caters for the small number of scholars from abroad who receive intensive tuition in English as a Second Language (ESL).

In the sixth form there are almost twenty-five A and AS level courses to choose from. The majority of scholars will choose three subjects plus general studies. Many of the A levels are now modular and allow for greater flexibility in course design and provide the benefit of an early indication of final grades which is of great value when applying to university.

In addition to the full range of sporting and musical activities, the college also offers over twenty-four leisure activities including horse-riding, clay-pigeon shooting, hover-craft building and golf.

Concord College

Acton Burnell Hall, Shrewsbury, Shropshire SY5 7PF
Tel: 01694 731631 Fax: 01694 731389

Head Anthony L Morris
Founded 1949
Age range 12+ *Boarders from* 12
No of pupils (day) 10; *(boarding)* 240
Girls 120; *Boys* 140
Senior 260; *Sixth form* 200
Fees per term (day) £1,410; *(boarding)* £3,950

Courses offered: GCSE and A levels in mathematics, further mathematics, economics, physics, chemistry, biology, history, political studies, art, English, French, German, law, accounting.
Nature of tuition: lectures; small groups; tutorials. Average size of group: 10. Student/teacher ratio: 10:1.

Concord College has a reputation for excellent examination results. Now managed by an educational trust, Concord has an impressive campus with attractive buildings, playing fields and gardens. It has modern and well-equipped laboratories, a computer room, library and an engineering workshop.

Its graduate teachers work hard with the students and provide a sympathetic but disciplined environment. In addition to lessons, students attend supervised private study for three hours each day. Students are carefully prepared for their examinations and are advised and assisted in gaining university places. The college has been particularly successful in preparing students for university entrance in engineering, accountancy, law and the medical sciences.

One and two year GCSE and A level courses are offered. Co-educational sports are voluntary with good facilities for badminton, basketball, rugby, riding, swimming, soccer, tennis and weight training. Other popular leisure pursuits are ballroom dancing, aerobics, chess, drama and music.

A truly international college, there were students from 50 countries attending the college in 1994–95. Most are privately financed but some are sponsored by governments and other official agencies. The students are ambitious and conscientious and this creates an environment in which our British students greatly benefit from the energetic and purposeful competition.

The college remains open during Christmas, Easter and half term holidays. There is no additional charge for students who wish to stay.

The Bell-Concord educational charitable trust exists to provide high quality co-educational boarding education.

Moreton Hall

Weston Rhyn, Oswestry, Shropshire SY11 3EW
Tel: 01691 773671 Fax: 01691 778552

Head Jonathan Forster
Founded 1912
Type Independent girls' boarding and day
Religious denomination Church of England
Members of SHA, GSA, GBGSA, ISCO, ISIS
Age range 10 – 18 *Boarders from* 10
No of pupils (day) 20; *(boarding)* 260
Girls 280
Sixth form 100
Fees per annum (day) £7,590; *(boarding)*
£10,950

Curriculum: going well beyond the National Curriculum, some 20 subjects are available at GCSE, varying from traditional academic subjects such as Latin and the sciences, to practical subjects such as drama, dance and physical education. Modern languages available include French, German, Italian, Spanish and Russian. A levels in history of art, social biology, politics, business studies and theatre studies extend the range of the curriculum. GNVQ level 3 leisure and tourism (equivalent to two A levels) is available based at Moreton Hall Travel and can be taken with a conventional A level course. Information technology is integrated into teaching at all levels.

Entry requirements: girls are admitted to the school, normally in September, at the age of 11, either by Common Entrance or by the school's entrance examination, which is held at the end of January each year. This examination requires no knowledge of foreign languages and is designed to test potential ability rather than factual recall. Sixth form entrance is by examination and interview and numbers are limited. All applications should be addressed to the Principal.

Examination offered: GCSE (MEG, SEG, NEAB, London), A level (Oxford, JMB, London). RSA (computer literacy), ABRSM, LAMDA. Over three quarters of second year sixth form students go on to university.

Academic and leisure facilities: Moreton Hall has recently completed an ambitious building programme and has facilities of the highest quality designed to provide the right environment for the education of girls in the 1990s.

The new laboratories and art and design centre are housed within a short distance of the central classroom, careers and library complex. A new networked IT department has opened up this year.

In 1989, an exceptionally well-equipped sports centre was completed comprising a sports hall and floodlit tennis courts. These new facilities, along with heated swimming pool, tennis courts, nine-hole golf course and playing fields are set in 100 acres of beautiful parkland at the foot of the Berwyn hills. The school offers a wide range of sporting options, including lacrosse, netball, hockey, cricket, tennis and athletics. Sailing and riding are also popular.

Moreton Enterprises and Moreton Hall Travel both offer girls real business experience. Moreton Enterprises, supervised by professional advisers, runs the tuck shop, pay phones, minibuses, Midland Bank branch office and school farm. Moreton Hall Travel has a full British Rail ticket agency and organises all school travel. Both businesses form training centres for GNVQ examinations.

Scholarships: a number of scholarships worth between 5 per and 50 per cent will be made to pupils at 11+, 12+ and 13+. Sixth form scholarships and bursaries, given in memory of Miss Bronwen Lloyd-Williams, are awarded to girls entering lower sixth or to assist a pupil in the school to complete her education. Awards for music, drama, art and for outstanding sporting talent are made at 11+, 12+, 13+ and 16+.

Boarding facilities: younger girls are housed in the Norton-Roberts building under the supervision of a resident housemistress, two assistant housemistresses and a matron. As pupils progress up the school, the dormitories are gradually replaced by double and finally single study bedrooms, as girls move from middle school houses to the second year sixth house, Lloyd-Williams. Boarding houses at Moreton Hall are all linked informally with houses at Shrewsbury School, pupils meeting regularly for social and cultural occasions.

Packwood Haugh

Ruyton-XI-Towns, Shrewsbury, Shropshire SY4 1HX
Tel: 01939 260217 Fax: 01939 260051

Head P J F Jordan MA St John's College Cambridge, CertEd
Founded 1892
Type Preparatory and pre-preparatory
Religious denomination Church of England
Members of IAPS
Age range 4 – 13 *Boarders from* 7
No of pupils (day) 90; *(boarding)* 130
Girls 90; *Boys* 130
Fees per term (day) £908 (pre-preparatory) – £2,090; *(boarding)* £2,688
Fees per annum (day) £2,724 (pre-preparatory) – £6,270; *(boarding)* £8,064

Curriculum preparation for Common Entrance and scholarship examinations to senior schools. (On average 14 scholarships per annum won.)

There is an entry assessment test and scholarships are available by examination.

The aim of the school, by offering a wide range of activities in all aspects of school life, is to bring out the best in every child.

There are 65 acres of grounds with extensive playing fields, floodlit astro-turf, swimming-pool, nine-hole golf course, tennis, squash court, gymnasium, shooting, a purpose-built music school, CDT and a new computer centre with multimedia facilities.

The boys are housed in the main building, the girls have a new boarding house. It is a full week boarding school with busy and well-organised week-ends, and regular exeats. There is a strong emphasis on pastoral care, good behaviour and good manners.

All Hallows School

Cranmore Hall, Shepton Mallet, Somerset BA4 4SF
Tel: 01749 880227 Fax: 01749 880709

Head Mr C J Bird
Founded 1938
Type Independent co-educational (boarding and day)
Religious denomination Roman Catholic
Members of IAPS, NAHT
Age range 3 – 14
No of pupils (day) 138; *(boarding)* 76
Girls 89; *Boys* 125
Fees per term (day) Pre-preparatory £900; Full day £1,800 *(boarding)* £2,760

Set in rural surroundings in beautiful Somerset countryside, yet close to the major cities of Bath and Bristol, All Hallows pioneered Catholic boarding co-education for preparatory school age children.

Christian principles are integrated into daily life so that all Christian denominations are welcomed into the ecumenical life of this Roman Catholic foundation.

Professionally-qualified, family-orientated staff, many of whom reside in the school, provide for the academic and pastoral welfare of the children.

Distinctive opportunities, at no extra cost, exist for the academically gifted and those with learning difficulties through the Learning Support Unit and/or specialist tutors. The school has a happy and deliberate mix of boarders and day pupils. Attractive flexibility exists between boarding and day arrangements. There is a purposeful and busy extra-curricular programme which is organised by all staff and runs each evening after school and at weekends.

The school enjoys regional and national sporting success in gymnastics, hockey and athletics, as well as competitive fixtures against local opposition in all the usual team sports. Excellent facilities allow the children and staff to discover talent and develop potential, including a recently built sports hall, chapel, art studio, classroom block and information technology centre.

All Hallows' fully independent status from any one particular senior school, plus adherence to the Common Entrance and prep schools' scholarship syllabus, enables parents and the Headmaster to select the most appropriate senior school to suit a particular child's needs. In the last few years we have sent pupils to over 40 different schools.

All Hallows is a charitable trust (registered charity no 310281).

Bruton School for Girls

Sunny Hill, Bruton, Somerset BA10 0NT
Tel: 01749 812277 Fax: 01749 812537

Head Mrs J M Wade
Founded 1900
Type Independent day and boarding
Religious denomination Non-denominational
Members of GSA, GBGSA, BSA, ISIS
Age range 8 – 18 *Boarders from* 8 – 18
No of pupils (day) 320; *(boarding)* 220
Girls 540
Junior 55; *Senior* 400; *Sixth form* 85
Fees per term (day) Junior £1,050; senior £1,262; *(boarding)* Junior £2,118; senior £2,330
Fees per annum (day) Junior £3,150; senior £3,786; *(boarding)* Junior £6,354; senior £6,990

The school stands in a beautiful 40-acre site on the outskirts of Bruton and all curriculum subject areas are housed in specialist accommodation.

We provide an excellent academic education and a wide variety of extra-curricular activities in a friendly atmosphere, enabling each girl to achieve her potential. Our careers advice is extensive and our pupils proceed to a wide variety of higher education courses.

The girls in our sixth form are offered a choice of over 20 A level subjects, complemented by a varied general studies course, with excellent study and leisure facilities for both boarders and day girls.

We have five boarding houses, each with a happy, family atmosphere, and excellent facilities, supervised by well qualified and trained staff. Boarding arrangements are flexible to meet the needs of families.

Our junior department has small classes in newly refurbished accommodation, and shares the specialist facilities of the senior school, to which girls transfer at 11+.

Millfield Junior School (Edgarley Hall)

Glastonbury, Somerset BA6 8LD
Tel: 01458 832446 Fax: 01458 833679

Head Mr Richard Smyth
Founded 1946
Type Co-educational preparatory
Religious denomination Inter-denominational
Members of IAPS
Age range 8 – 13 *Boarders from* 8
No of pupils (day) 200; *(boarding)* 240
Girls 170; *Boys* 270
Fees per annum (day) £6,330; *(boarding)* £9,735

Average size of class: 13
Teacher/pupil ratio: 1:8
Curriculum: small teaching groups augment a broad curriculum. Beyond the Common Entrance syllabus, art, technology, music, computing, drama, chess and personal and social education are timetabled. The foreign language department offers a language

awareness course for younger pupils, and a choice of French, German, Latin and Spanish from the age of ten.

Entry requirements and procedures: entry by interview with Headmaster and a report from present school or by examination set in January each year for bursary places.

Subject specialities and academic track record: excellent scholarship and Common Entrance results are gained to Millfield and other well-known senior schools.

Specialist help is provided by the language development centre for pupils with specific learning difficulties.

Academic and leisure facilities offered: Edgarley provides staff and pupils with excellent modern facilities and equipment for academic work, music, drama, sport and over 90 activities.

Perrott Hill School Trust Ltd

North Perrott, Crewkerne, Somerset TA18 7SL
Tel: 01460 72051 Fax: 01460 78246

Head Mr J E A Barnes
Founded 1946
Type Preparatory
Religious denomination Church of England
Members of IAPS
Age range 3 – 13 *Boarders from* 7+
No of pupils (day) 109; *(boarding)* 37
Girls 37; *Boys* 109
Fees per term (day) £540 – £1,808; *(boarding)* £2,513
Fees per annum (day) £1,620 – £5,424; *(boarding)* £7,539

Perrott Hill is a co-educational, day and boarding school set in the heart of the Somerset countryside and is serviced by excellent road and rail networks.

Small classes and excellent academic facilities are reflected by an outstanding scholarship record, and a 100 per cent placement of pupils in their first choice public schools for the past six years.

Experienced and highly qualified staff form the backbone of Perrott Hill.

The children are able to use the extensive facilities which include a new CDT/art block and computer centre with expert help to hand. Other facilities include a recently established pre-preparatory department, music centre, recreation rooms, rifle shooting range, pet house and attractive grounds which include woods. Scholarships for academic, musical and all-round ability are offered annually.

Games and extra-curricular activities utilise the school's 25 acres of space to ensure a positive framework for a happy and successful educational environment for every child.

Abbots Bromley School of S Mary and S Anne

Abbots Bromley, Near Lichfield, Staffordshire WS15 3BW
Tel: 01283 840232 Fax: 01283 840988

Head Alan J Grigg BA, MPhil
Founded 1874
Type Independent girls
Religious denomination Church of England
Members of GSA, GBGSA
Age range 5 – 18 *Boarders from* 7
No of pupils (day) 120; *(boarding)* 170
Girls 290
Junior 50; *Senior* 240; *Sixth form* 65
Fees per term (day) £840 – £2,370; *(boarding)*
£3,005 – £3,555
Fees per annum (day) £2,520 – £7,110;
(boarding) £9,015 – £10,665

Curriculum: broad curriculum, 20 subjects at
GCSE and 18 at A level including business
studies, sociology, economics. Virtually all
sixth formers go on to degree courses. Small
classes, low pupil:teacher ratio.
Entry requirements and procedures: head's
report, English and mathematics tests for entry
into senior school.
Examinations offered: GCSE, A/S, A level, some
BTEC and RSA.
Scholarships: academic, music, ballet, sport,
riding.
Academic and leisure facilities:
• high academic standard and achievement;
• new computerised library facilities;
• sports facilities: sports hall, indoor pool, all-
  weather courts, tennis and netball courts;
• equestrian centre + BHS training facilities to
  AI standard;
• music – three orchestras, three choirs and
  links with CBSO;
• ballet and modern dance – 110 taught up to
  instructor level – own ballet studio;
• speech and drama – 35 LAMDA gold medals
  in the last six years;
• drama in school theatre and concert hall;
• Duke of Edinburgh air cadets, canoeing,
  water polo.
Boarding facilities:
• sixth form study bedrooms;
• five senior boarding houses;
• one junior boarding house.

Denstone College Preparatory School

Smallwood Manor, Uttoxeter, Staffordshire ST14 8NS
Tel: 01889 562083 Fax: 01889 568682

Head Mr A C Ninham
Type Co-educational, independent
Religious denomination Church of England
Members of Woodard Corporation, IAPS
Age range 3 – 13 *Boarders from* 8
No of pupils (day) 144; *(boarding)* 44
Girls 68; *Boys* 120
Junior 116; *Senior* 72
Fees per term (day) £806 – £1,771; *(boarding)* £2,221 – £2,373
Fees per annum (day) £2,418 – £5,313; *(boarding)* £6,663 – £7,119

The school is situated ten miles from Denstone College at Smallwood Manor in wooded grounds of 60 acres. There are eight computers, art and handicraft rooms, two science laboratories, an indoor .22 range and games room. Facilities include a fine gymnasium and assembly hall, a new classroom block, together with a new music room and eight practice rooms. The chapel was dedicated in 1979. Sports facilities are excellent and include a new covered heated pool and two new hard tennis courts. Rugby, hockey and netball are the main games and cricket, athletics and rounders are the main summer games. There are active Cub and Brownie packs, as well as facilities for computing, chess, athletics, basket-ball, drama, mechanics, riding and badminton. The pupils are encouraged to use their leisure time constructively. There is also a tutor system in the school, whereby each member of staff maintains a close interest in about a dozen pupils during their time at the school.

There is also a pre-preparatory for boys and girls aged between three and seven. The pre-preparatory is for day pupils only, and they work from 8.30am until 3.30pm for Monday to Friday.

Denstone College Preparatory School is part of the Woodard Schools Midlands Division Ltd Charitable Trust which exists to provide a Christian education for people who might not otherwise be able to afford it.

St Bede's School

Bishton Hall, Wolseley Bridge, Near Stafford, Staffordshire ST17 0XN
Tel: 01889 881277 Fax: 01889 882749

Head Mr H C B C Stafford Northcote
Founded 1936
Type Independent preparatory
Religious denomination Roman Catholic
Age range 2½ – 13½
Fees per term (day) £800 – £1,500; *(boarding)* £1,980
Fees per annum (day) £2,400 – £4,500; *(boarding)* £5,940

St Bede's is a co-educational preparatory school offering a thorough and balanced education in a happy, family environment. All pupils are encouraged to develop their character and abilities fully, with particular attention being given to the individual requirements of each child. The school has an excellent academic record and many pupils achieve scholarships to top schools when their years here come to fruition. The classes at St Bede's are small, allowing close personal contact between staff and pupils, and ensuring a high degree of individual attention. The National Curriculum is closely followed from the nursery school upwards. St Bede's pupils live as members of a family and are taught courtesy and consideration for others. Academic and sports scholarships are available.

The Yarlet Schools

Yarlet, Near Stafford, Staffordshire ST18 9SU
Tel: 01889 508240

Head Mr R S Plant
Founded 1873
Type Boys and girls preparatory and pre-preparatory school
Religious denomination Church of England
Members of IAPS
Age range 3 – 13 *Boarders from* 7
No of pupils (day) 65; *(boarding)* 40
Girls 15; *Boys* 90
Fees per term (day) £1,295 – £1,950; *(Pre-preparatory* £905); *(boarding)* £2,390
Fees per annum (day) £3,885 – £5,850 *(Pre-preparatory* £2,715); *(boarding)* £7,170

Entry requirements: ability to read and write and do elementary sums.

The school stands 400 feet up in open countryside on the A34 midway between Stafford and Stone.

The main subjects taught are English, history, geography, scripture, mathematics, science, French, Latin, music, art and CDT.

Alexanders International School

Bawdsey College, Bawdsey, Near Woodbridge, Suffolk IP12 3AZ
Tel: 01394 411633 Fax: 01394 411357

Director Niels Toettcher
Founded 1975
Type Co-educational boarding
Religious denomination International
Accredited by British Council, DFE registered
Members of ARELS
Age range 10 – 18 *Boarders from* 10
No of pupils (boarding) 100
Girls 40 *Boys* 60
Fees per annum (boarding) £9,000

Range of GCSE/IGCSE subjects with fully integrated English language support at all levels to make it easier for overseas pupils to join us without losing any valuable study time. A levels in maths, science, IT, business studies, art and geography.

Beginners in English accepted in lower school. Entry by interview and assessment. Full range of internationally recognised English language exams available.

Situated on coast of Suffolk, with 160 acres of grounds and a private beach, between the River Deben and the sea.

Over 35 nationalities represented each year at Alexanders.

Framlingham College

Framlingham, Nr Woodbridge, Suffolk IP13 9EY
Tel: 01728 723789 Fax: 01728 724546

Head Mrs G M Randall BA
Founded 1864
Type Independent
Religious denomination Church of England but other denominations welcome
Members of HMC, GBA, IAPS(JNR)
Age range 4 – 18 *Boarders from* 8
No of pupils (day) 140 (senior); *(boarding)* 300
Girls 160; *Boys* 280
Junior 301 (pre-preparatory) *Senior* 440 *Sixth form* 150
Fees per term (day) £900 – £2,072; *(boarding)* £2,546 – £3,229
Fees per annum (day) £2,700 – £6,216; *(boarding)* £7,638 – £9,687

The curriculum at Framlingham (and its junior school, Brandeston Hall) is inter-related to give a broadly-based, well-rounded, continuous education from 4 to 18 years of age. It is designed to prepare pupils for GCSE, A level, Oxbridge and other examinations. The school believes in high expectations, maintaining the school as a community and the fulfilment of individual potential. Overseas pupils (currently 25 in total) are carefully integrated into the life of the school. They receive a traditional British education, but their different cultures also give a much appreciated breadth and experience to home-based students.

Entry to the junior school is by test and interview and transfer to the college is at 13+. Common Entrance, scholarship examination and/or interview form the normal means of entry to the college at 13+, GCSE results and interview at 16+. Overseas students apply initially on the basis of a current principal's report. Enquiries regarding scholarships are invited. Government Assisted Places are available at 13+ and 16+.

St Felix

Southwold, Suffolk IP18 6SD
Tel: 01502 722175 Fax: 01502 722641

Head Susan Campion
Founded 1897
Type Independent girls
Religious denomination Non-denominational
Members of GSA
Age range 11 – 18 *Boarders from* 9
No of pupils (day) 84; *(boarding)* 145
Fees per term (day) £2,235; *(boarding)* £3,435

We believe in the value of single sex education for girls; our results reflect the advantage of single sex schools. We have a 92 per cent pass rate at Advanced level in 1994. Equally importantly, our girls are given every encouragement and opportunity to develop confidence, independence and a sense of adventure.

Entry is at 11+, 12+ and 13+, through the Common Entrance examination. Older girls are admitted on the basis of school reports. Entry into the sixth form is through GCSE results and interview.

The extensive curriculum is traditional in bias and includes the three separate sciences, classics (Latin and Greek), four modern languages (French, Spanish, German and Russian), supported by a strong programme of two and three dimensional art, design technology, information technology and music. There is a wide range of weekend and evening activities, societies and clubs – among them riding, karate, drama, modern dance, flower arranging, golf, survival course.

The school offers organ, general music and academic scholarships and exhibitions worth 33 per cent and 20 per cent. Services discount may be available.

Woodbridge School

Woodbridge, Suffolk IP12 4JH
Tel: 01394 385547 Fax: 01394 380944

Head Mr S H Cole MA CPhys, MInstP
Founded 1662
Type Independent
Religious denomination Church of England
Members of HMC, SHMIS, IAPS
Age range 4 – 18 *Boarders from* 13
No of pupils (day) 708; *(boarding)* 36
Girls 380; *Boys* 364
Junior 245; *Senior* 499; *Sixth form* 162
Fees per term (day) £1,784; *(boarding)* £2,932
Fees per annum (day) £5,352; *(boarding)* £8,746

Woodbridge School in Suffolk has facilities unrivalled by any other school in the region. A new building opened in 1994 housing the library, IT centre, English and mathematics departments, and the modern language department which incorporates two language laboratories. This year a floodlit all-weather hockey pitch and tennis courts will be completed. In recent years the junior school, The Abbey, for pupils aged 4 to 11, has also benefited from extensive new buildings.

Woodbridge is very proud of its co-educational identity, and has recently celebrated the twentieth anniversary of the entry of girls into the school. High standards are expected from all pupils, and most leave at the age of 18 to follow degree courses at universities. In addition to academic work great emphasis is placed on extra-curricular activities. There are full fixture lists for boys and girls. The creative arts are important to the life of the school. All pupils have the chance to play a musical instrument, and there are innumerable choirs, orchestras, bands and smaller ensembles. Art and drama are important, as is the Seckford scheme where pupils engage in a wide range of activities designed to encourage self-reliance, team-work and leadership.

American Community Schools, England

Heywood, Portsmouth Road, Cobham, Surrey KT11 1BL
Tel: 01932 867251 Fax: 01932 869789

Head Mr T Lehman
Founded 1967
Type Co-educational
Religious denomination Non-sectarian
Members of New Eng Ass of Sch & Coll, ISJC, ECIS, NE/SA, IB
Age range 3 – 18 *Boarders from* 12 – 18
No of pupils (day) 1,091; *(boarding)* 95
Girls 556; *Boys* 630
Junior /middle 779; *Senior* 407
Fees per semester (day) £1,625 – £4,370; *(boarding)* £6,375 – £7,155
Fees per annum (day) £3,500 – £8,740; *(boarding)* £12,750 – £14,310

The three American Community Schools, founded in 1967, are non-sectarian co-educational schools for students between the ages of three and eighteen. The Surrey school is located in Cobham, 25 miles from London and is accessible by British Rail. Door-to-door busing is available.

Student body/faculty: approximately 60 per cent of the 1,186 students are American, 6 per cent Canadian and the remaining 34 per cent represent 42 other nationalities. There are 116 full-time teachers on the faculty, all holding a university degree. The student faculty ratio is 10:1.

Admissions: new students accepted in all grades throughout the year on the basis of a completed application form and previous school records (with a provision prior to grade placement when necessary).

Academic program: the traditional American curriculum, offering a wide range of subjects is designed to lead to an American High School Diploma. Experienced university counselling is provided by the academic dean and all examinations required for admission to American universities are administered by the school.

The school provides courses leading to the International Baccalaureate Diploma, a recognised qualification for entry to universities in Britain, Europe and for advanced standing in American universities. Students may also pursue college-level studies through the American-based Advanced Placement (AP) program.

An English as a Second Language Program is available for non-English speaking applicants between the ages of six and fifteen.

The Campus: the 128-acre campus occupies a former country estate. A dining hall/auditorium, a new middle school (1990), a new high school (1992) and the new lower school completed for occupation in the Fall of 1995, complement the main house (1804). Sports facilities include a gymnasium, tennis courts, a golf course, adventure playground and picnic/barbecue areas.

Student activities: as well as the full range of sports offered, other activities include Student Council, Yearbook, music, computers, drama, video, cheerleading and scouting.

Accreditation: the school is accredited by the New England Association of Schools and Colleges, ISJC, and holds membership in the International Baccalaureate Organisation.

Boarding: both five and seven day boarding at the Surrey campus for 120 students in two separate wings. The well-appointed bedrooms are equipped with wall-to-wall carpeting, private bathrooms, built-in cupboards, desks, lamps, bookcases, bedside units and dressing tables. Amenities such as communal lounges and kitchenettes together with 24-hour health care readily available, as are live-in house parents who are able to give advice and act as a link between students and parents helping to make life for boarders as comfortable as possible.

American Community Schools, England

Woodlee, London Road (A30), Egham, Surrey TW20 0HS
Tel: 01784 430611 Fax: 01784 430626

Head Mrs K Alderdice
Founded New school – opened August 1995
Type Co-educational
Religious denomination Non-sectarian
Age range 3 – 14
No of pupils (range) 112
Girls 53; *Boys* 59;
Fees per semester (day) £1,625 – £4,370; *(boarding)* £6,375 – £7,155
Fees per annum (day) £3,500 – £8,740; *(boarding)* £12,750 – £14,310

The American Community Schools, founded in 1967, are non-sectarian co-educational schools for students between the ages of 3 and 18. The Woodlee campus is located in Egham, Surrey, is 18 miles from London and is accessible by British Rail. The school is conveniently placed in relation to Heathrow Airport and the M25 motorway. A door-to-door bus service is provided by the school.

Approximately 60 per cent of the 112 students are American, the remaining 40 per cent representing 16 other nationalities. There are 15 full-time teachers on the faculty, all holding a university degree. The student-faculty ratio is 6:1.

New students are accepted subject to space being available in all grades throughout the year, and on the basis of a completed application form and previous school records (with a provision for testing prior to grade placement when necessary).

Academic program:

The traditional American curriculum offering a wide range of subjects is available. Learning support and programs for gifted students are also provided, with specialists included on the staff. Class sizes are small with individual support and guidance being provided. Modern language instruction is offered beginning in grade 1. Computers are used throughout the school as a learning tool.

The school is situated on a 21-acre campus which provides the students with a purpose-built environment, including gymnasium, all-weather, floodlit tennis courts, dining hall, laboratory and playing fields. The library is fully computerised with CD-ROM materials available.

A full range of sports are offered, including basketball, tennis, track and field, soccer, softball and volleyball. Other activities available are student council, yearbook, music, computers, Scouting and intra-mural sports.

Boarding:

There is provision for boarding on the campus. Modern purpose-built facilities are available with single room accommodation for students being offered.

Amesbury

Hazel Grove, Hindhead, Surrey GU26 6BL
Tel: 01428 604322 Fax: 01428 717184

Head Nigel Taylor BSc, MA
Founded 1870
Type Co-educational day
Religious denomination Church of England
Members of IAPS
Age range 3 – 13 *Boarders from* 10
No of pupils (day) 150; *(boarding)* 20
Girls 50; *Boys* 120
Junior 170
Fees per term (day) pre-prep £1,245; *preparatory* £1,245 – £2,025; *nursery* £85 per session; *(boarding)* £495 supplement

Amesbury is a co-educational preparatory school for day pupils and weekly boarders aged 3–13. The catchment area covers Hindhead/Haslemere, Petersfield, Liphook, Farnham and Guildford.

Academic standards are high, although music, art, drama and sport all feature prominently. The Keffold Centre (places strictly limited), offering specialist support for dyslexic pupils, has a national reputation.

Set in 25 acres, the main building was designed by Sir Edward Lutyens (1917). Since then development of the excellent facilities has included the addition of two purpose-built classroom blocks, science laboratories and specialist teaching rooms (opened 1980, 1986 and 1992). The pre-preparatory school, opened in 1988, was extended in 1990. A floodlit all-weather surface was added in 1990 and phase one of the current building programme, a new sports hall, is currently underway.

Belmont School

Feldemore, Holmbury St Mary, Dorking, Surrey RH5 6LQ
Tel: 01306 730852 Fax: 01306 731220

Head David Gainer BEd Hons (London)
Founded 1870
Type Independent
Religious denomination Church of England
Members of IAPS
Age range 4 – 13 *Boarders from* 7
No of pupils (day) 217; *(boarding)* 43
Girls 63; *Boys* 197
Fees per term (day) £890 – £1,725; *(boarding)* +
£790

A very happy co-educational IAPS school for children aged four to thirteen and a half, with good weekly boarding facilities from seven upwards. No Saturday school leads to full family weekend.

Excellent academic and sporting traditions in a caring, friendly environment. Beautiful grounds in rural Surrey within easy reach of central London. A magnificent 'home from home'.

A purpose-built Dyslexia Unit (Moon Hall) with highly trained specialist staff. Sixty-acre estate with playing fields, all-weather hockey pitch, sports hall and open air swimming pool.

Completely refurbished main house, with extensive modern facilities. Fully-equipped computer room and new art and CDT area. New dining room building recently completed.

Emphasis on broad curriculum and exposure to very wide range of extra-curricular activities. Very good interaction between day and boarding pupils.

Further information and prospectus from the headmaster's secretary.

Box Hill School

Mickleham, Dorking, Surrey RH5 6EA
Tel: 01372 373382 Fax: 01372 363942

Head Dr R A S Atwood BA, PhD
Founded 1959
Type Independent
Religious denomination Non-denominational
Members of SHMIS, ISCO, Round Square
Age range 11 – 18 *Boarders from* 11 – 18
No of pupils (day) 106; *(boarding)* 163
Girls 93; *Boys* 176
Senior 184; *Sixth form* 70
Fees per term (day) £2,050; *(weekly boarding)* £3,280; *(boarding)* £3,400
Fees per annum (day) £6,150; *(weekly boarding)* £9,840; *(boarding)* £10,200

Average size of class: 15
Teacher/pupil ratio: 1:8.5
Entry requirements and procedures: interview; written tests in maths and English; confidential report from previous school; Common Entrance where appropriate.
Educational extras: most extras are genuinely personal (*ie* transport, toiletries, clothes). Some A level texts must be purchased and all sixth form parents are asked to provide £40 to £50 for cultural outings and theatre trips.
Curriculum: wide range of subjects in Years 7 to 9 including art, music, computing, design, expeditions to Hadrian's Wall, Pilgrim's Way, the Lakes combine academic work with outdoor pursuits. Years 10 and 11: choice of 17 subjects at GCSE. Form 6: choice of 17 subjects at A level.
Subject specialities and academic track record: Strong in traditional subjects as well as art, drama, computing, design/technology, outdoor pursuits; two full-time dyslexia specialists. English courses run for overseas students, plus a one-year pre-A level course.
Examinations offered including Boards: wide choice at both GCSE and A level. No attempt to force pupils into a mould; curriculum adapted to individuals. Small tutor groups.
Destination and career prospects of leavers: about three-quarters of A level leavers go on to degree courses. Others to a wide range of professions, art courses and other colleges.
Academic and leisure facilities include: a new science block, design/technology block; computing and electronics rooms, drama studio, multi-purpose hall/gymnasium, 35 acres of playing fields with outdoor heated swimming pool, plus usual classrooms and laboratories.

Termly exchanges and visits with sister schools in Germany, Australia, Switzerland, USA and Canada offer unique opportunities, particularly for languages. Project work undertaken in India.

The school is situated in an attractive country village, within easy distance of Gatwick and Heathrow airports and the M25, and 45 minutes from central London by train.

The school is a registered charity providing a broad education for children both boarding and day.

Scholarships, exhibitions and bursaries: ten scholarships are awarded each year for sixth form entry. Awards may be made in Years 7–11 in recognition of academic, musical, artistic or sporting potential. In cases of exceptional financial need, bursaries are available for all year groups.

Canbury School

Kingston Hill, Kingston upon Thames, Surrey KT2 7LN
Tel: 0181 549 8622 Fax: 0181 974 6018

Head Mr J G Wyatt
Founded 1982
Type Secondary co-educational day
Religious denomination Non-denominational
Members of ISAI
Age range 10 – 16
No of pupils (day) 50
Girls 13; *Boys* 37
Senior 50
Fees per term (day) £1,575

Curriculum: we cover a full range of GCSE subjects, most pupils taking a total of eight or nine.
Entry requirements: there are tests in English, maths and verbal reasoning. The headmaster interviews each candidate. A trial day or two at the school can be arranged.

Subjects offered: English, maths, French, science, technology, geography are the main National Curriculum subjects. Business studies, history and religious education are studied. German and Russian are possible additional languages. Drama, art and music are studied seriously. A classroom assistant helps EFL pupils.
Facilities: modern technology, computer and art facilities are available. The school minibus transports pupils to a wide range of sports facilities within the borough.

Canbury School is different in placing emphasis on smallness of size. No class has more than 12 pupils. Full concentration is placed on bringing out the special talents of each pupil. Pupils participate in the school council which makes decisions in some areas of school life.

Caterham School

Harestone Valley Road, Caterham, Surrey CR3 6YA
Tel: 01883 343028 Fax: 01883 347795

Head R A E Davey MA
Founded 1811
Religious denomination United Reformed Church (open to all)
Members of HMC, IAPS, Assisted Places Scheme
Age range 3 – 18
No of pupils (day) 700
Fees per term (day) £1,295 – £1,932; *(boarding)* £3,532 – £3,732

Caterham School has enjoyed a long and distinguished history. The school's high placing in the academic league table demonstrates its awareness of the importance of examination results – as does the remarkably high percentage of sixth formers going on to university – but it also recognises that examinations are not all that matters. The substantial boarding element of the school means that the advantages of boarding education are available to all its pupils. The school's achievements in sport, music and drama testify to its concern with an all-round education. Whether as boarders or day pupils, boys and girls from three to 18 will find at Caterham a friendly and stimulating environment designed to educate for life as well as for academic success.

Claremont Fan Court School

Claremont Drive, Esher, Surrey KT10 9LY
Tel: 01372 467841 Fax: 01372 471109

Principal Patricia B Farrar
Founded 1979
Type Co-educational
Religious denomination Christian Science
foundation, day pupils from all religions
Age range 3 – 18 *Boarders from* 11
No of pupils (day) 623; *(boarding)* 19
Girls 332; *Boys* 310
Junior (first and middle) 272; *Senior* 370
including sixth form; *Sixth form* 61
Fees per term (day) £555 – £1,895; *(boarding)*
£2,880 – £2,995
Fees per annum (day) £1,485 – £5,400;
(boarding) £8,640 – £8,985

Claremont Fan Court is a co-educational day and boarding school for pupils from three to 18. While all boarders (from the age of 11) come from a Christian Science background, day pupils come from many religions. The school is owned and run by an educational foundation with charitable status. It was formed by Christian Scientists but has no formal connection with the Christian Science Church and Christian Science is not taught.

The foundation of the school rests upon a love for children and a deep appreciation of their God-given potential. The school maintains a high standard of academic expectation and achievements at all levels, but it also places importance on a friendly atmosphere in which the pupils' own confidence and individuality can develop. Pupils are helped to overcome, as far as possible, attitudes of self-limitation and negative opinions as to their capabilities. The school does not permit the use of alcohol, tobacco or drugs in any of its activities. It maintains a firm policy on Christian moral values and encourages children to express them in daily life. Parents are expected to endorse the standards required of pupils.

Claremont Fan Court is situated in 90 acres of the famous Claremont estate. The First School

has its own purpose-built building in its own section of the estate. The Middle School is based mainly in its own building in The Close but shares some facilities with the Senior School which is based in Claremont mansion.

The curriculum is broadly-based and the National Curriculum is generally followed throughout the school. A strong emphasis is put on mathematics and language in the early years and academic expectations are high. There is a tutorial system throughout the Senior School which closely monitors the pastoral and academic welfare of each student. Music, drama and sport play an integral part in the child's whole education. Pupils are prepared for all stages of Associated Board Music and Poetry Society Speech and Drama examinations.

Activities include outings to art galleries, concerts, films and theatres. Students go skiing, off-shore sailing and attend personal development courses participating too in the Duke of Edinburgh Award Scheme. The sixth form centre provides relaxation, recreation and study facilities in the historic surroundings of White Cottage.

Entrance is by examination and interview with the principal. Academic scholarships are available at year 7, year 9 and sixth form level and other financial assistance is sometimes available at other levels.

Cranleigh Preparatory

Horseshoe Lane, Cranleigh, Surrey GU6 8QH
Tel: 01483 273666 Fax: 01483 277136

Head Malcolm Keppie MA
Founded 1881
Religious denomination Church of England
Age range 7 – 13 *Boarders from* 7
No of pupils (day) 103; *(boarding)* 77
Boys 180
Fees per term (day) £2,090; *(boarding)* £2,770
Fees per annum (day) £6,270; *(boarding)* £8,310

The school stands in its own beautiful 30 acres of grounds. Mr and Mrs Keppie live in the main building with the boarding masters and matron. The school is a boarding school, the benefits of which are available to the day boys. Across the road is Cranleigh School to which two-thirds of the boys proceed.

Boys enter aged seven or eight after an entry test, and are prepared for Common Entrance or scholarships. A broad, balanced but academic curriculum includes computing, art and design, pottery, woodwork, metalwork and music, and many timetabled activities. The science labs, music school and sports hall are recently built.

Sport is strong and varied. Rugby, soccer, hockey, cricket, tennis, swimming and athletics are the main sports, among many others. Musical life includes three choirs and an orchestra.

Boarding life is busy and fun, with committed staff, full weekends, and regular exeats.

New classrooms, changing rooms and computer room in 1996.

Cranleigh School

Cranleigh, Surrey GU6 8QQ
Tel: 01483 273997 Fax: 01483 267398

Head Mr T A A Hart MA
Founded 1865
Type Independent
Religious denomination Church of England
Members of HMC, SHA, GBA, ISBA
Age range boys 13 – 18; girls 16 – 18 *Boarders from* 13
No of pupils (day) 83; *(boarding)* 430
Girls 73; *Boys* 440
Sixth form 265
Fees per term (day) £3,110; *(boarding)* £4,140
Fees per annum (day) £9,330; *(boarding)* £12,420

Cranleigh is an energetic school, reputed for its warm, caring community atmosphere. There is a strong focus on personal development, and pupils are encouraged to make the most of their varied potential, to relish challenge, to feel they are known as individuals and to become talented and wise adults in a fast- changing world.

A great strength is drawn from the fact that Cranleigh operates as a strong boarding community, where day pupils are fully integrated and open boarding is a policy.

Attractively located, less than an hour from Gatwick, Heathrow, London and the south coast, Cranleigh's exceptional facilities including three theatres, a golf course and horse-riding, are set within 250 acres of rolling Surrey countryside.

Croham Hurst School

79 Croham Road, South Croydon, Surrey CR2 7YN
Tel: 0181 686 7347 Fax: 0181 688 0841

Head Miss S C Budgen
Founded 1899
Type Independent girls' school, selective
Members of GSA, ISIS
Age range 4 – 18
Girls 500
Junior 180; *Senior* 320
Fees per term (day) £740 – £1,530
Fees per annum (day) £2,220 – £4,590

Croham Hurst occupies an attractive open site and is easily accessible by public transport.

The school maintains a reputation for high academic achievement and is committed to developing the individual potential of each girl. We have a proven record of excellent results at GCSE and A level and an established tradition of university entrance, including Oxbridge.

Many girls begin their education in the lively, stimulating environment of the on-site junior school. This is sustained in the senior school by the broad curriculum in the first three years, where National Curriculum subjects are supplemented by classical studies, Latin, German, Spanish and textiles. We offer an extensive range of option courses, providing a choice from 24 subjects at GCSE and 20 at A level. Girls are encouraged to achieve high standards and their learning is supported by small teaching groups and the flexibility to provide 'tailor-made' timetables in order to accommodate the needs of the individual. Pupils' personal talents and interests can be extended through an exciting programme of extra-curricular activities.

Entrance is by interview and test relevant to age. Government Assisted Places and scholarships, including sixth-form scholarships, are available.

Duke of Kent School

Ewhurst, Cranleigh, Surrey GU6 7NS
Tel: 01483 277313 Fax: 01483 273862

Head R K Wilson MA
Founded 1976
Type Co-educational preparatory
Religious denomination Inter denominational
Members of IAPS
Age range 4 – 13 *Boarders from* 7 – 13+
No of pupils (day) 55; *(boarding)* 100
Girls 55; *Boys* 100
Fees per annum (day) £2,250 – £5,760, Pre-preparatory £3,015; *(boarding)* £7,365 – £8,235

Curriculum: in addition to the main subjects required for Common Entrance, the curriculum includes art, music, drama, CDT, computer studies, study skills, hobbies, and a structured games programme for all pupils.
Entry requirements: non-competitive placement tests and interviews at the school. Bursaries and scholarships available.

Please contact the school for further details.

The school is owned by the RAF Benevolent Fund, and is sited in a beautiful setting in the Surrey hills, with easy access to Heathrow, Gatwick and the south coast. It has outstanding facilities including science and computer laboratories, modern classroom block, music school, workshops, heated indoor swimming pool, sports hall, spacious playing fields and grounds.

Dunottar Day School for Girls

High Trees Road, Reigate, Surrey RH2 7EL
Tel: 01737 761945 Fax: 01737 779450

Head Miss Jane Burnell BSc, CBiol, MIBiol, PGCE, FRSA
Founded 1926
Type Independent girls
Religious denomination Non-denominational, Christian
Members of GSA, ISIS
Age range 4 – 18
No of pupils (day) 435
Girls 435
Junior 127; *Senior* 308; *Sixth form* 48
Fees per term (day) £920 – £1,510
Fees per annum (day) £2,760 – £4,530

Dunottar is situated in 15 acres of beautiful grounds on the outskirts of Reigate. It is convenient for mainline stations and bus routes.

Seventeen GCSE subjects, including three separate sciences, and 22 A level subjects including theatre studies and sociology are included in the broad curriculum. The school has very strong sporting and music traditions. Teaching is given in a wide range of musical instruments and girls are encouraged to join the school orchestras and choirs. Extra tuition is available in drama and dance. There are excellent on-site games facilities including a large indoor heated swimming pool and playing fields.

Entrance examinations are held in January and February for entry the following September. Girls are accepted directly into the sixth form. Academic scholarships are available at 11+ and musical scholarships at 11+ and 14+ for seven and four years' duration respectively. A number of sixth form awards are available each year. Dunottar was the top Surrey school throughout East and Mid-Surrey for GCSE in 1994.

Edgeborough

Frensham, Near Farnham, Surrey GU10 3AH
Tel: 01252 792495 Fax: 01252 795156

Head Mr R A Jackson MA, PGCE (Cantab)
Founded 1906
Type Co-educational preparatory day and boarding
Religious denomination Church of England
Members of IAPS
Age range 3 – 13 *Boarders from* 7 – 13
No of pupils (day) 190; *(boarding)* 50
Girls 70; *Boys* 170
Ages 3 – 7 85; *Ages* 8 – 13 155
Fees per term (day) £1,100 – £2,285; *(boarding)* £2,705 – £2,990

Edgeborough is a lively and welcoming school set in beautiful grounds. It offers a continuous education for boys and girls from 3 to 13.

The school comprises four main departments: nursery, pre-preparatory (now sited in an attractive new purpose-built lodge); junior and senior. All pupils follows a co-ordinated academic programme culminating in Common Entrance or public school scholarship at 13.

Awards are won every year to major Public Schools.

There is every opportunity for children to excel in all areas helped by an enthusiastic and dedicated staff. There are excellent facilities including swimming pool, golf course and an open-air theatre.

The boarding community is well-established and enjoys modern, well-appointed accommodation.

Entry is by parental interview at the nursery and pre-preparatory stages and by an assessment morning at seven or eight.

Ewell Castle School

Church Street, Ewell, Surrey KT17 2AW
Tel: 0181 393 1413 Fax: 0181 786 8218

Head Mr R A Fewtrell MA, JP, FRSA
Founded 1926
Type Independent day school
Religious denomination Church of England
Members of SHMIS, IAPS, GBA
Age range 3 – 18
No of pupils (day) 450
Girls 30; *Boys* 420
Junior 140; *Senior* 250; *Sixth form* 60
Fees per term (day) £392 – £1,475
Fees per annum (day) £1,176 – £4,425

Curriculum: Years 7 – 9 (age 11 – 13): a broad curriculum incorporating National Curriculum requirements.
Years 10 – 11 (age 14 – 16): core curriculum: mathematics, English, foreign Language and a science plus a wide ranging option scheme.

Sixth form: co-educational. Twenty A level and AS level courses. High level of entry to degree courses.

Small class sizes. Setting by ability in major subjects from age 11 – 16.
Entry requirements: interview and tests at junior school. Interview, report from present school, written tests in mathematics and English for entry to senior school at 11+ and 13+. Common Entrance where appropriate.
Scholarships: scholarships and other awards are available at all levels including the sixth form.
Examinations offered: GCSE (Midland, Southern and LEAG). AS, A level (London and AEB).
Academic and leisure facilities: extension of science and design and technology facilities. Sports centre. Apple Macintosh computer networks used. Comprehensive range of extra curricular and sporting activities. Drama and music productions annually. Foreign exchanges, field trips and sports tours abroad.

Frensham Heights School

Rowledge, Farnham, Surrey GU10 4EA
Tel: 01252 792134 Fax: 01252 794335

Head Mr Peter M de Voil
Founded 1925
Type Co-educational
Religious denomination Non-denominational
Members of HMC, BSA
Age range 3 – 18 *Boarders from* 11
No of pupils (day) 166; *(boarding)* 133
Girls 172; *Boys* 169
Junior (4 – 11) 61; *Senior* 169; *Sixth form* 87
Fees per term (day) £2,490; *(boarding)* £3,890
Fees per annum (day) £7,470; *(boarding)* £11,670

Frensham Heights is a fully co-educational HMC boarding (full or weekly) and day school 360 pupils aged 4 – 18. The school's philosophy endorses liberal values and promotes strong personal relationships and respect for the individual. It achieves distinguished results in the performing and creative arts. Classes are small and academic results excellent. The school is situated in beautiful grounds near Farnham, Surrey, 50 minutes from London by train and 40 miles from Heathrow and Gatwick airports.

Greenacre School for Girls

Sutton Lane, Banstead, Surrey SM7 3RA
Tel: 01737 352114 Fax: 01737 352114

Head Mrs P M Wood
Founded 1933
Type Girls' independent day
Religious denomination Non-denominational
Members of GSA, GBGSA, ISIS, ISBA
Age range 3 – 18
No of pupils (day) 393
Girls 393
Junior 179; *Senior* 167; *Sixth form* 47
Fees per term (day) £420 – £1,660
Fees per annum (day) £1,260 – £4,980

Greenacre was founded in 1933 and provides a full education based on traditional methods, while preparing girls for the ever-changing world in which they live. The staff are caring and dedicated. They believe that the individual matters and that each girl has her own talents. High academic achievements are expected, as are good manners and discipline.

A wide range of subjects is available at both GCSE and A level, and while the majority of girls go on to higher education, full careers advice is available. There are excellent facilities for a variety of sports. After-school activities include computer, debating, drama and music clubs, as well as the Duke of Edinburgh Award scheme.

Entry at 11+ by formal test and interview; at 16 by GCSE and interview. Scholarships are offered at 11+ and sixth-form entry. Bursaries are awarded at the discretion of the governors. Discounts for siblings.

Hoe Bridge School

Hoe Bridge and The Trees Ltd, Hoe Place, Old Woking Road, Woking, Surrey GU22 8JE
Tel: 01483 760018 Fax: 01483 757560

Head R W K Barr
Type Preparatory
Religious denomination Church of England
Members of IAPS
Age range 7 – 13 *Boarders from* 7
No of pupils (day) 196; *(boarding)* 10
Girls 15; *Boys* 181
Fees per term (day) £1,700 – £1,955; *(boarding)*
£2,550 – £2,805
Fees per annum (day) £5,100 – £5,865;
(boarding) £7,650 – £8,415

Hoe Bridge School preserves the best of traditional values, whilst taking advantage of twentieth century progress. The curriculum ranges from Latin to computing and design and technology, covering the requirements for Common Entrance and incorporating the demands of the National Curriculum.

The school is fortunate in having an experienced, well-qualified and committed staff who can offer a broad curriculum and stimulating environment. This provides opportunities for those who are academically able and also for those whose abilities are of a creative, practical or sporting nature.

Entry is by assessment and interview. Children are prepared for Common Entrance and for scholarship examinations to senior independent schools.

The extensive grounds of the school provide enviable facilities for games and outdoor pursuits, including rugby, association football, hockey, netball, cricket, athletics, tennis, swimming, archery, shooting, dance and movement, Scouts, putting and croquet.

A large multi-purpose, two-storey sports hall accommodates gymnastics, plays, concerts, judo, badminton and table tennis. Within this building there are also classrooms and laboratories. Other classrooms are housed within the mansion. All classrooms are spacious and well-designed. No class has more than 18 pupils. The majority of subjects have well-equipped, specialist classrooms.

Weekly boarding is available in a purpose-built boarding wing.

Parents are kept informed of their child's progress through termly reports and termly parents' evenings. There is a thriving social committee run by the parents. The school aims to develop the potential of the children in whatever activity they undertake and encourages personal responsibility for others. Hoe Bridge has its own pre-preparatory school 'the Trees' situated in the grounds which caters for children between the ages of three and eight.

King Edward's School

Witley, Wormley, Godalming, Surrey GU8 5SG
Tel: 01428 682572

Head Rodney J Fox
Founded 1553
Type Co-educational independent boarding
Religious denomination Church of England
Members of HMC
Age range 11 – 18 *Boarders from* 11
Junior 56 boys; 46 girls; *Senior* 145 boys; 132 girls; *Sixth form* 59 boys; 70 girls
Fees per term (day) £2,080; *(boarding)* £2,990

Average size of class: 20 maximum
Teacher/pupil ratio: 1:8
Curriculum: English literature, English language, biology, chemistry, physics, French, German, Latin, geography, history, economics, maths, religious studies, information technology, art, music, CDT-1, CDT-2, home economics, drama, physical education and electronics.

Entry requirements and procedures: either Common Entrance at 13 or our own entry examination in English, maths, and verbal reasoning; at age 11 and also sixth form entry.

Founded in 1553 by King Edward VI in rural countryside on the borders of Surrey, Sussex and Hampshire. Children who have a need for boarding education may be eligible for bursaries.

King Edward's School charitable trust provides a structured approach to education and offers substantial bursaries to children whose home circumstances make boarding a real need.

Kingston Grammar School

70 London Road, Kingston upon Thames, Surrey KT2 6PY
Tel: 0181 546 5875 Fax: 0181 547 1499

Head Mr C D Baxter MA
Founded 1561
Type Independent co-educational
Religious denomination Church of England but all faiths welcomed
Members of HMC
Age range 10 – 18
No of pupils (day) 604
Girls 208; *Boys* 396
Junior 25; *Senior* 441; *Sixth form* 138
Fees per term (day) £1,710 – £1,795
Fees per annum (day) £5,130 – £5,385

Curriculum: in years 1 and 2 pupils follow a wide course choosing from 12 subjects including Latin, French, German and technology. In the third year an option scheme introduces Spanish. Further options are undertaken in the fourth year where the pupils select nine subjects for GCSE. A number take mathematics in the fourth year. In the sixth a comprehensive range of A levels and some A/S levels are available. At all levels pupils receive careers advice and have a timetable constructed based on their options.

Entry requirements: entry at 10+ and 11+ is by examination in January, at 13+ by Common Entrance or our own examination. At 16+ entrance is by interview and GCSE results. Assisted Places and academic, art, music and sports awards are available.

Kingston Grammar School Foundation, a registered charity, exists to provide high quality education for girls and boys.

Marymount International School

George Road, Kingston upon Thames, Surrey KT2 7PE
Tel: 0181 949 0571 Fax: 0181 336 2485

Head Sister Rosaleen Sheridan RSHM
Founded 1955
Type Girls' independent day and boarding school
Religious denomination Roman Catholic multi faith
Members of Sisters of the Sacred Heart of Mary
Age range 11 – 18 *Boarders from* 11 – 18
No of pupils (day) 95; *(boarding)* 105
Girls 200
Middle School 40; *High School* 160
Fees per term (day) £2,300 – £2,500; *(boarding)* £4,116 – £4,450

Established in 1955 by the Sisters of the Sacred Heart of Mary, Marymount International School in Kingston, Surrey is an independent day and boarding school for 200 girls, aged 11 – 18 (grades 6 – 12), representing forty different nationalities.

Small classes and individual attention enable students to attain their full personal and academic potential.

Courses are based on the American college preparatory curriculum, offered in conjunction with the International Baccalaureate Middle Years' Programme (grades 6 – 10). Students in grades 11 – 12 may elect to follow the IB diploma syllabus, leading to UK university admission and US college credit. Ninety-eight per cent of our graduates go on to third-level education in the UK and abroad.

Oakfield School

Coldharbour Road, Pyrford, Woking, Surrey GU22 8SJ
Tel: 01932 342465 Fax: 01932 342465

Head Mrs Rosaline Brothers
Founded 1910
Type Independent day
Age range 2½ – 16
No of pupils (day) 180
Girls 145; *Boys* 35
Junior 90; *Senior* 90
Fees per term (day) £640 – £1,147
Fees per annum (day) £1,920 – £5,241

Oakfield is a caring community within which each child is valued. The school has an average class size of 14 allowing us to promote the individual development of our pupils.

The school is set in attractive, rural surroundings yet is easily accessible by road and rail.

Excellent examination results in GCSE, RSA, RADA and Common Entrance. Broad curriculum including science, information technology and French from the age of three. Regular open evenings and written reports.

There is a nursery department which provides a secure, structured environment from which to make the transition to infant school. After school clubs make life easier for working mothers.

All staff hold first aid certificates. We enjoy the tremendous support provided by our parents' association.

Parsons Mead School

Ottways Lane, Ashtead, Surrey KT21 2PE
Tel: 01372 276401 Fax: 01372 278796

Head Miss E B Plant
Founded 1897
Type Independent
Religious denomination Church of England
Members of GSA, BSA, AHIS
Age range 3 – 18 *Weekly boarders from* 8+
No of pupils (day) 360; *(boarding)* 10
Girls 370
Junior 110; *Senior* 220; *Sixth form* 40
Fees per term (day) £1,675; *(weekly boarding)* £2,943
Fees per annum (day) £5,025; *(weekly boarding)* £8,829

Parsons Mead has excellent facilities including a new science block, new technology suite, drama studio, sports hall and outdoor pool. Girls gain excellent GCSEs and A levels and go on to degree courses. Theatre studies, classical civilisation, Latin, business studies, economics and psychology are also offered. There are specialist rooms for all subjects. As well as the sports hall and swimming pool there are five netball/tennis courts, two hockey pitches and an athletics track. Girls regularly represent their county in athletics, swimming, tennis, hockey and netball. Music and drama flourish. There are two major productions each year. There are many clubs and societies: Young Enterprise, Young Engineers, table tennis, computing, mathematics, art, technology. Older pupils join in the Duke of Edinburgh Award scheme and Combined Cadet Force. There are regular visits at home and abroad including an annual ski trip.

Entry is by assessment and interview according to age. There is a formal entrance examination at 11+.

Prior's Field

Godalming, Surrey GU7 2RH
Tel: 01483 810551 Fax: 01483 810180

Head Mrs J M McCallum BA (Hons)
Founded 1902
Religious denomination Inter-denominational
Members of GSA
Age range 11 – 18 *Boarders from* 11 – 18
No of pupils (day) 215; *(boarding)* 115
Girls 215
Senior 175; *Sixth form* 40
Fees per term (day) £2,185; *(boarding)* £3,270
Fees per annum (day) £6,555; *(boarding)* £9,810

Located close to Charterhouse, within 20 miles of Heathrow and Gatwick, Prior's Field offers an academic curriculum at GCSE. Photography, media, business and theatre studies, textiles and art history are offered at A level, plus science and arts subjects. Most leavers proceed to university.

Reduced fee places for service daughters and scholarships are offered annually. Young Enterprise, Duke of Edinburgh Schemes and educational visits encourage self reliance.

Sports include lacrosse, hockey, netball and regional standard tennis. There are frequent dramatic and musical performances, a jazz group and public speaking teams.

Individual study bedrooms for senior girls. Entry at 11, 13 and 16.

Priory School

Bolters Lane, Banstead, Surrey SM7 2AJ
Tel: 01737 354479 Fax: 01737 370537

Head Ian R Chapman
Founded 1921
Type Boys' preparatory
Members of IAPS
Age range 3 – 13
No of pupils (day) 183
Boys 188
Fees per term (day) nursery (morning only) £540; Pre-preparatory £970; main school £1,430

Boys are prepared for any of the senior independent schools. The aim is to provide a sound, well-balanced course of education to prepare boys for a smooth transfer to their next school at age 13+. The curriculum reflects this aim and in so doing includes all school games and physical activities as a normal and necessary part of every boy's life. A multi-purpose sports hall enhances the facilities, as does a specialist science block. In 1995 a new nursery block was opened to provide education for boys aged 3+. Transfer to the pre-preparatory department is at 5+. In addition, a new science block has also been completed and this will open in September 1996. There is a strong emphasis on music and at least one drama production is held each term. Although most boys are prepared for a sound Common Entrance performance, a large number of scholarships have been won. The essential groundwork of a good education lies in the experienced pre-preparatory department which the school possesses. Traditional values and standards run parallel with modern teaching methods and an extensive range of educational visits is arranged throughout the year.

Reed's School

Sandy Lane, Cobham, Surrey KT11 2ES
Tel: 01932 863076 Fax: 01932 866289

Head D E Prince MA (Cantab)
Founded 1813
Type Boys' boarding and day and sixth form girls
Religious denomination Church of England
Members of HMC, SHMIS
Age range 11 – 18
No of pupils (day) 200 *(boarding)* 150
Girls 20; *Boys* 330
Junior 60; *Senior* 220; *Sixth form* 70
Fees per term (day) £2,162 – £2,580; *(boarding)* £2,883 – £3,413
Fees per annum (day) £6,486 – £7,740; *(boarding)* £8,649 – £10,239

Reed's School is a boarding and day school for boys aged 11 – 18 with a limited sixth-form day girl entry. The school also includes 30 Dutch day pupils aged 11 – 15, the children of parents working in England.

The school is situated just off the A3(M) in 55 acres of Surrey heath and woodland within easy reach of Heathrow and Gatwick airports. Although the ethos of the school is directed towards academic achievement, it offers a wide range of recreational games and activities. Pupils also participate in the Duke of Edinburgh Award Scheme and there is a Combined Cadet Force contingent.

Curriculum: There is a permanent full-time teaching staff of 33 including a school chaplain and pupils are prepared for GCSE and A level examinations. The school has the latest facilities for design and technology, computing, printing and electronics and enjoys a strong musical tradition. Religious instruction is in accordance with the principles of the Church of England.

Entry requirements and procedure: pupils may be registered at any time and entry is at ages 11+, 12+, 13+ and sixth-form. Entry at 11+ and 12+ is by the school's own tests, whilst that at 13+ is normally by Common Entrance. Sixth form entry is determined by GCSE results, school report and interview.

Examinations offered: GCSE, A level, AS level, MEG, SEG, NEA, Cambridge.

Scholarships: academic, music, art and technology scholarships up to half fees are offered in January and May each year for pupils entering at 11+ and 13+ respectively. Sixth-form scholarships of similar value are offered in February each year.

Bursaries: foundation bursaries are available to boys who are in need of a boarding education who have lost the support of one or both parents.

Academic and leisure facilities: seven science laboratories, specialist classrooms for languages, CDT, art, music, geography and printing. Full facilities for rugby, hockey, cricket, tennis, squash, swimming, including sports hall, swimming pool, artificial hockey pitch and nine tennis courts, sixth-form centre, theatre.

There are eight Department for Education and Science Assisted Places a year.

Applications should be made to the headmaster.

Ripley Court School

Rose Lane, Ripley, Surrey GU23 6NE
Tel: 01483 225217

Head Mr J W N Dudgeon
Founded 1893
Type Co-educational boarding and day preparatory school
Religious denomination Non-denominational
Members of IAPS, NAHT
Age range 4 – 14 *Boarders from* 8
No of pupils (day) 245, *(boarding)* 18
Girls 15, *Boys* 248
Fees per term (day) £896 – £1,441, *(boarding)* £2,213
Fees per annum (day) £2,559 – £3,693, *(boarding)* £6,324

Ripley Court School was founded in 1893 and became an educational trust in 1969. The centenary is being celebrated during the course of the 1993/1994 academic year.

Ripley Court is a Queen Anne house, bounded on four sides by 20 acres of attractive grounds. It lies 25 minutes from London on the old Portsmouth Road and is 25 minutes' drive from both Heathrow and Gatwick.

Children go on to a wide range of senior schools and, while children of high ability are encouraged to work towards scholarships, equal care and attention is given to all.

A pre-preparatory section caters for children between the ages of four and seven years, and the main school continues their education through to 14 years. Boys and girls may be day children and boys may be weekly or full boarders.

For further information please contact the school secretary.

The Royal School

Hindhead, Surrey GU26 6BW
Tel: 01428 605407 Fax: 01428 607977

Head Mr Colin Brooks
Founded September 1995, (formerly The Grove and Royal Naval Schools, founded in the late 1800s)
Type Independent boarding & day school for girls
Religious denomination Church of England
Members of GSA, GBGSA
Age range 5 – 18 *Boarders from* 7
No of pupils (day) 264 *(boarding)* 156
Girls 420
Junior 102 *Senior* 273 *Sixth form* 45
Fees per term (day) £1,155 – £2,019; *(boarding)* add £1,150 per term

The Royal School, Hindhead, (formerly The Grove School and The Royal Naval School) combines over 300 years of tradition for excellence. Set in 50 acres of beautiful parkland, 12 miles south of Guildford, the school is within easy reach of two international airports and sited adjacent to the main A3 trunk road, midway between London and Portsmouth. We offer an exceptional standard of education for girls, with many opportunities for them to develop their talents. We aim to prepare young women for the 21st century by developing the skills, self-awareness and confidence they will require throughout their adult lives.

Our preparatory school, known as 'The Grove', is a lively, flourishing establishment for 4 to 11-year-olds, with a strong emphasis on traditional teaching and sensitive pastoral care.

We prepare girls to Common Entrance at 10+, for entry to The Royal School or other major public schools. Over the last few years, many new facilities have been built and we are pleased to announce a further development to provide a new general purpose hall and improved facilities for science, art and computer studies.

The Royal School offers an exceptionally wide range of GCSE and GCE A level options, and has consistently achieved exceptional success in public examinations. This year we are once again in the top 200 schools in the United Kingdom.

Ever mindful of the needs of parents, The Royal School offers a range of after-school care and boarding facilities. Our day girls come from an ever-wider area, using our fleet of modern minibuses, which travel to Farnham and Haslemere stations, as well as the outlying, more rural, areas.

Classes are small, averaging less than 15 girls. Facilities for computer studies, modern languages, performing arts, science and sport are excellent and many after-school activities are offered, including opportunities for young engineers, the Duke of Edinburgh Award Scheme, computer studies, astronomy, art, music, drama and competitive sports.

To visit the school is to be assured of a warm welcome. We are informal and always keen to support parents in what we know is a difficult decision for them to make. For further information please telephone: 01428 605407.

St Andrew's School Woking

Church Hill House, Horsell, Woking, Surrey GU21 4QW
Tel: 01483 760943 Fax: 01483 740314

Head Mr A N Brownridge BA, PGCE
Founded 1937
Type Independent preparatory
Religious denomination Church of England
Accredited by ISJC
Age range 3 – 13
No of pupils (day) 160
Girls 12 *Boys* 148
Fees per term (day) £1,995
Fees per annum (day) £5,985

Broad curriculum including IT, Latin and music. The school accepts boys and girls at three years and there is scholarship entry at seven years. Children are prepared for independent senior schools entrance and scholarship exams (St Andrew's has an outstanding record over recent years in gaining top awards at Winchester, Eton, Sherborne, Bradford, Wellington). Main school games are soccer, hockey, cricket but there is a wide variety of other activities. Teaching is in a modern purpose-built block. There is a heated swimming pool and ample playing fields on site (11 acres). This day school operates a very long working day, five days a week.

St Catherine's School

Bramley, Guildford, Surrey GU5 0DF
Tel: 01483 893363 Fax: 01483 893003

Head Mrs C M Oulton MA Oxon
Founded 1885
Type Girls' independent
Religious denomination Church of England
Members of GSA, IAPS
Age range 4 – 18 *Boarders from* 9
No of pupils 630
Fees per annum (boarding) £9,255

St Catherine's School has an excellent record at both A level and GCSE. Most of the 630 girls go on to university and there is a regular Oxbridge entry. High standards of behaviour and good manners are fostered, and a network of house mistresses and tutors provides extensive pastoral support. Girls are encouraged and expected to work hard to achieve their full potential.

Teaching facilities are excellent, and include well-equipped laboratories for science, languages, and computer studies. The school has an unrivalled reputation for sport, music and art. Games facilities include floodlit hard courts, indoor heated pool, multi-gym and gymnasium. A new art centre is under construction.

Access to the A3 and Guildford station is good, and day girls attend from a wide catchment area. School coaches run to and from Woking and Farnham daily. Heathrow and Gatwick are within easy reach, and transport is arranged for girls travelling abroad.

St Edmund's School

Portsmouth Road, Hindhead, Surrey GU26 6BH
Tel: 01428 604808 Fax: 01428 607898

Head Mr A Fowler-Watt MA
Founded 1874
Type Boys' preparatory – boarding and day
Religious denomination Church of England
Members of IAPS
Age range 5 – 13 *Boarders from* 7
No of pupils (day) 60 (Pre-preparatory 55); *(boarding)* 35
Fees per term (day) from £1,200; *(boarding)* from £2,750
Fees per annum (day) from £3,600; *(boarding)* from £7,050

Boys are prepared for Common Entrance and scholarships to all major public schools. All major sports are played plus golf, sailing, sculling, riding, squash and swimming.

Extensive range of cultural activities with special emphasis on music, drama and public speaking. Wide range of hobbies and leisure pursuits. Set in gracious woodlands, the school has excellent facilities including golf course, tennis courts, indoor heated pool and its own chapel. Boarders enjoy a caring family atmosphere and overseas pupils and sons of service personnel are particularly welcome.

Little St Edmund's caters for boys and girls from the ages of 2 to rising 5. They enjoy all the facilities that St Edmund's has to offer but remain safe and secure in their own special accommodation set in the beautiful grounds. We offer flexible hours to suit busy working parents and remain open during the holidays for holiday care.

St John's

Epsom Road, Leatherhead, Surrey KT22 8SP
Tel: 01372 372021 Fax: 01372 386606

Head Mr C H Tongue
Founded 1851
Type Independent
Religious denomination Church of England
Members of HMC
Age range 13 – 18 *Boarders from* 13
No of pupils (day) 270; *(boarding)* 130
Girls 50; *Boys* 350
Senior 215; *Sixth form* 185
Fees per term (day) £2,400; *(boarding)* £3,500
Fees per annum (day) £7,200; *(boarding)* £10,500

Since its foundation in 1851, St John's has grown from a small boarding school for the sons of clergy to a thriving boarding and day school with a special tradition and atmosphere.

Today the school has 400 pupils aged 13 – 18, including 50 sixth-form girls.

Academic achievement is paramount. However, St John's is a small, friendly community whose aim is to develop all pupils' talents and active participation in the many cultural, creative and sporting activities is strongly encouraged. The school's musical tradition – three choirs, two bands, a string quartet and an orchestra – is complemented by the theatre which fosters acting potential in house and school plays. Rugby, cricket and football are the major boys' games but a great many other sports flourish. In total there are more than 50 sports and activities on offer.

Christian values are at the heart of school life and the chapel supports a strong pastoral system based on houses and small tutor groups.

St Teresa's School

Effingham Hill, Dorking, Surrey RH5 6ST
Tel: 01372 452037/454896 Fax: 01372 450311

Head Mr L Allan BA, MEd, PGCE, FRSA
Founded 1928
Type Independent day and boarding
Religious denomination Roman Catholic
Members of GSA, IAPS, SHA, GBGSA, BSA
Age range (preparatory school) 2 – 11; *(senior school)* 11 – 18
No of pupils (day) 392; *(boarding)* 140
Fees per term (day) £1,690; *(boarding)* £3,595
Fees in prep school on sliding scale

St Teresa's is situated in beautiful rural surroundings within easy reach of London and with good access to the A3, M25 and major airports. From preparatory to sixth form, pupils are given broad and balanced foundations which prepare them for life. Girls of all denominations are welcome.

Twenty GCSE and A level subjects are on offer with 60+ extra curricular activities. The school is strongly academic with outstanding examination results. Success in music, art, sport and public speaking is unrivalled.

Scholarships are available in the preparatory department and at 11+, 12+, 13+ and for sixth-form entry. Boarders in each year group have their own common rooms with television and video and sixth formers live and work in a separate modern purpose-built centre. Our aim is that each girl should find enjoyment in learning and develop as an individual, well prepared to face the future with confidence.

Surbiton High School

Surbiton Crescent, Kingston upon Thames, Surrey KT1 2JT
Tel: 0181 546 5245 Fax: 0181 547 0026

Head Miss M G Perry
Founded 1884
Type Girls' day school
Religious denomination Church of England
Members of GSA
Age range 4 – 18
No of pupils (day) 912
Girls 804; *Boys* 108
Junior 354; *Senior* 11 – 18 558; 11 – 16 450;
Sixth form 108
Fees per term (day) £967 – £1,613
Fees per annum (day) £2,901 – £4,839

Founded in 1884 and owned by the Church Schools Company, Surbiton High School stands in a quiet area of Surbiton in pleasant landscaped rounds. The school is known for being a good academic school achieving very creditable results each year. The 1995 A level pass rate was 100 per cent, GCSE 97.2 per cent (A–C). We offer a friendly, caring environment where individuals are valued and encouraged to develop their talents to the full.

Entry procedure and scholarships: parents of prospective pupils should contact the admissions secretary. Open days are held during the autumn term. Entry to the school is by examination and interview. At 11+ academic, music and sports scholarships are offered. At 16+ academic scholarships are offered.

Curriculum: Surbiton uses a range of teaching techniques, with an emphasis on individual study to encourage all girls to achieve high standards and develop an enthusiastic, problem-solving approach to their work. A broad curriculum is followed with a high profile given to information technology, modern languages and science. Girls take subjects over and above the National Curriculum with Latin, Greek, drama and Spanish being offered. In the sixth form our challenging general studies programme includes Japanese, psychology, community awareness and many sports.

Extra-curricular activities: Surbiton has a sports hall and extensive playing fields. There are established teams in netball, hockey and tennis plus rowing, judo, squash, badminton and skiing.

The school offers many extra-curricular activities with strong performance traditions in music and drama. Peripatetic tuition is offered in all instruments, voice and speech and drama. Other clubs include debating, technology, ceramics, photography, classics, stamp, and young enterprise.

The sixth form is based in a newly opened self-contained centre with a computerised library and study facilities. Sixth formers play an active role in the running of the school. Specialist careers and university guidance is given throughout. Most pupils take up degree courses.

Surbiton High School has both a junior girls' and junior boys' school situated in close proximity to the senior school. A new junior girls' school opened in January 1994 with many specialist facilities for art, science, music and technology.

TASIS England American School

Coldharbour Lane, Thorpe, Surrey TW20
Tel: 01932 565252 Fax: 01932 564644

Head Mr Lyle Rigg
Founded 1976
Type College preparatory day and boarding
Religious denomination Non-denominational
Boarders from 12
No of pupils (day) 515 *(boarding)* 155
Girls 330 *Boys* 340
Junior 390 *Senior* 280
Fees per annum (day) £7,000 – £8,185;
(boarding) £13,500

Located on a beautiful 35-acre campus 18 miles south of London, TASIS England offers an American College preparatory curriculum to day and boarding students from grades Pre-K to 12, and has built exceptional facilities for art, drama, music, computers, and sports. Small classes and a dedicated faculty provide students with individual attention and help. The curriculum includes English as a Second Language courses and advanced placement courses for students seeking college credit. The school's extensive travel program offers opportunities for students to experience first hand the culture riches of Europe.

Woldingham School

Marden Park, Woldingham, Surrey CR3 7YA
Tel: 01883 349431 Fax: 01883 348653

Head Dr P Dineen
Founded 1842
Type Independent
Religious denomination Roman Catholic (all denominations welcome)
Members of GSA, BSA
Age range 11 – 18 *Boarders from* 11
No of pupils (day) 101; *(boarding)* 428
Girls 529
Senior 282; *Sixth form* 132
Fees per term (day) £2,309; *(boarding)* £3,802
Fees per annum (day) £6,927; *(boarding)* £11,436

Curriculum: most girls take nine to ten GCSEs. All acquire at least a 'working knowledge' of two European languages and take science to 16+ either on an integrated or separate subject basis. The aim is to provide 'breadth and balance' so that alternative academic pathways are available at 16+. Sixth formers study three to four A level subjects as well as general courses. AS options are also available.
Entry requirements and procedures: as a Roman Catholic school in the ecumenical tradition, Woldingham welcomes members of other traditions in sympathy with its educational philosophy. Girls normally enter at 11+ having taken the Common Entrance Examination. This age group also attend at school for a one-day informal assessment during the previous autumn. A few vacancies may be available in other years (the Registrar will provide details). Sixth form entrants should be capable of taking at least three A levels (or an equivalent blend of A and AS subjects).
Examinations and Boards offered: at GCSE, A level, Oxbridge and US College Entrance. All students take degree or equivalent courses.
Boarding facilities: girls are organised on a year group basis, pastoral supervision and support being provided by senior teachers (heads of years) and assistants. At Marden House 110 boarders, aged 11 – 13, share small dormitories. Senior house accommodates girls aged 13 – 17, about half of them in single study-bedrooms. Opened in 1992 Berwick House provides outstanding facilities for upper sixth girls. A new sports centre opened in 1995

Yateley Manor

51 Reading Road, Yateley, Camberley, Surrey GU17 7UQ
Tel: 01252 873298 Fax: 01252 860029

Head Francis Howard MA (Cantab), DipEd (Oxon)
Founded 1947
Type Preparatory
Religious denomination Church of England
Members of IAPS
Age range 3 – 13
No of pupils (day) 490
Girls 171; *Boys* 319
Fees per term (day) £469 – £1,569
Fees per annum (day) £1,407 – £4,707

Curriculum: Yateley Manor is an academic co-educational day preparatory school offering the full range of subjects, arts and sport, necessary for senior school Common Entrance and scholarship examinations. Pupils come from a wide local catchment area, served by school buses, and proceed mainly to academic senior schools via normal entry or scholarships. With an enormous range of extra-curricular activities, the school offers a wide, stimulating environment in which children can grow to become happy, confident and fulfilled people.

Entry requirements: children enter the junior school at three or four, via an informal assessment. There is another entry to the main school at seven, through interview and written assessment, as a result of which academic and music scholarships are awarded. Entry is possible at any age subject to vacancies.

Academic and leisure facilities: the school is extremely well-equipped generally, with outstanding libraries, science and computer facilities, excellent music, art and drama rooms, and superb sports buildings.

The following independent college also offers GCSEs. Please refer to the Independent Sixth-Form Colleges section for details:

Cambridge Tutors College, Croydon

Ardingly College

Haywards Heath, West Sussex RH17 6SQ
Tel: 01444 892577 Fax: 01444 892266

Head James Flecker; *Master of Junior School*
Peter Thwaites
Founded 1858
Type Co-educational
Religious denomination Church of England
Members of IAPS, HMC, ISIS, Woodard Schools
Age range 2½ – 18 *Boarders from* 7+
No of pupils (day) 269; *(boarding)* 330
Girls 247; *Boys* 352
Junior 149; *Senior* 450; *Sixth form* 171
Fees per term (day) Pre-preparatory £400 –
£1,000; Junior £1,750 – £1,875; Senior
£3,065; *(boarding)* Junior £2,750; Senior
£3,880

One College

Ardingly College is one of Britain's leading independent co-educational boarding and day schools. There is a single campus which is shared by the junior school of about 100 boys and 70 girls from 2½ – 13, and the senior school of about 260 boys and 200 girls from 13 – 18.
Location

The school is set in lovely English countryside, only 35 miles from central London, 18 miles north of Brighton and just nine miles from Gatwick Airport, which makes it particularly attractive to those who live overseas.

Ardingly is an academic school. As a general pattern, pupils will be expected to take nine GCSEs in the fifth form and three A levels in the sixth form. Class sizes throughout the school are small – fewer than 20 pupils for GCSE and about 12 per set for A levels.

Eighty per cent of all Ardinians go on to further education. Ten or so candidates apply for Oxford or Cambridge and a good proportion is accepted each year. This sets a high standards of expectation throughout the school. Ardinians are taught very much as individuals. There is splendid pastoral care with individual tutors for each pupil and a well-organised house system.

Most subjects studied here are the traditional ones common to many schools, but there are some, particularly in the sixth form, which are fairly unusual (English Language, theatre studies, fine art, craft art, archaeology, statistics and physical education).

Ardingly has an enviable reputation for excellence in sport, music and the creative arts. Outside the classroom there is a tremendous range of activity and pupils are encouraged to sample as much of it as they possibly can.
Scholarships: we offer five government assisted places at 11+, as well as academic, all-round, art, craft, design and technology, drama, language, music science and sports scholarships, which may be supplemented by a discretionary bursary.

Battle Abbey School

Battle, East Sussex TN33 0AD
Tel: 01424 772385 Fax: 01424 773573

Head D J A Teall BSc (Newcastle)
Founded 1912
Religious denomination Christian
Age range 2½ – 18 *Boarders from* 8
No of pupils (day) 150 *(boarding)* 50
Girls 100; *Boys* 100
Junior 80; *Senior* 120; *Sixth form* 20
Fees per term (day) £1,030 – £1,875; *(boarding)* £2,430 – £3,030
Fees per annum (day) £3,090 – £5,625; *(boarding)* £7,290 – £9,090

The school is big enough to encourage healthy competition and to develop the social skills and awareness of others learnt by being part of a lively community. It is on the other hand small enough to have many of the attributes of a large family. Teaching classes are small throughout the school, allowing individual attention and the opportunity for all pupils to achieve their maximum potential.

The school is privileged to occupy one of the most famous historical sites in the world, that of the 1066 Battle of Hastings. The main school building is the 15th century Abbot's house belonging to the Abbey of St Martin founded by the Conqueror himself. It has been beautifully modernised, and is typical of the school's happy blend of traditional values with up-to-date facilities.

Grouped around this building are well equipped specialist rooms including science laboratories, technology areas and a computer room equipped with state of the art, industry-standard hardware and software. The dormitories are bright and cheerful, many having magnificent views over the surrounding countryside. The sixth form pupils have study-bedrooms and their own common room and are treated very much as the young adults that they are.

The school has an indoor heated swimming pool, extensive sports fields and a large, artificial grass, all-weather playing area. Music and drama also have an important place in the curriculum; there is at least one major dramatic production every year. There are ample opportunities for developing skills and hobbies; private coaching is available in many subjects including riding, sailing, and instrumental music. Activity groups, which are a regular feature of weekends, include a wide variety of pursuits and there is the opportunity to follow the Duke of Edinburgh Award Scheme. There are frequent visits to theatres, art galleries and other places of interest.

Battle is only 57 miles from London on the main railway line to Hastings. Gatwick, Heathrow, and the Channel ports are within easy reach. There is accompanied travel to and from London at the beginning and end of each term and half-term.

All-rounder scholarships of up to 50 per cent are available and there is an automatic 12 per cent bursary for serving members of Her Majesty's Forces.

Brighton College and Brighton College Junior School

Eastern Road, Brighton, East Sussex BN2 2AL
Tel: 01273 697131

Heads Mr J D Leach MA, Mr G Brown DipMus, CertEd, LTCL
Founded 1845
Type Co-educational boarding and day
Members of HMC, SHA
Age range 3 – 18 *Boarders from* 13
Junior 343; *Senior* 474; *Sixth form* 170
Fees per annum (day) £2,460 – £7,854; *(boarding)* £7,230 – £11,940

Curriculum: Junior School: the usual CE curriculum including computing, CDT, art, home economics, music and Latin. Dovetailing with National Curriculum as appropriate.

Senior School: in Year 1, a broad curriculum including the above subjects plus German and electronics. In Year 2 pupils choose ten or eleven subjects to study for GCSE from a range of options. For A level the choice widens to include economics, business studies, classical civilization, history of art, geology, Spanish and Greek with some AS subjects and general studies course. Physical education and RS are taught throughout and are also GCSE options.

Entry requirements: entry tests at 8+ and 11+ (including assisted places) for junior school. Common Entrance/scholarships exam or special test at 13+ for senior school. Interview and report, minimum five GCSE C grades for sixth form entry. Four scholarships and five assisted places also offered.

Examinations offered: GCSE: MEG, LEAG, SEG. AS and A level: O&C, AEB, London.

Academic and leisure facilities: sports: rugby, hockey, cricket, netball, rounders, tennis, swimming, water polo (own indoor heated pool), football, cross-country, athletics, fencing, judo, sailing, golf, shooting, riding, squash, basketball, badminton (sports hall).

Music and drama: orchestra, bands, choirs and ensembles. Regular internal and external concerts. Termly dramatic productions including musicals.

Activities and societies: include chess, bridge, public speaking, debating, travel, law, archaeology, ecology, canoeing, life saving, rugby league (JS), art, pottery, dry skiing, needlework, JS newspaper, College Times, photography, snooker, calligraphy, gardening, puppeteering.

Brighton College is a registered charity and exists to provide a high quality education for boys and girls.

Burgess Hill School

Keymer Road, Burgess Hill, West Sussex RH15 0EG
Tel: 01444 241050 Fax: 01444 870314

Head Mrs Rosemary Lewis BSc
Founded 1906
Type Independent girls' school
Religious denomination Inter-denominational
Age range 3 – 18 *Boarders from* 13+ (year nine)
No of pupils (day) 510; *(boarding)* 50
Girls 560
Junior 200; *Senior* 290; *Sixth form* 70
Fees per term (day) £855 – £1,840; *(boarding)* £2,775 – £3,095
Fees per annum (day) £2,565 – £5,520; *(boarding)* £9,285

Burgess Hill School stands in 12 acres of beautiful grounds close to the centre of the town and is a 30-minute drive from Gatwick.

The excellent facilities include a new purpose built 17-classroom and new science and technology block, music centre and art and design centre. The sixth form have their own centre with individual study areas, common rooms and an HE centre holding extensive careers advice.

The main aim of the school is to challenge our students to achieve goals well beyond their own expectations in all the activities they pursue. We educate for life and develop consideration for others, a love of learning, self-esteem and self-discipline. The curriculum is broad and challenging and relevant to the needs of young people. There is a wide choice of subjects both at GCSE and A level.

There are three beautiful boarding houses adjoining the school grounds. The rooms and common rooms are spacious, light and pleasantly furnished and the atmosphere is informal and friendly.

The school also runs a daily bus service to and from a number of outlying districts including Turners Hill, Henfield, Cowfold, Lewes, Uckfield and Newick.

For further details please contact the Registrar.

Christ's Hospital

Horsham, West Sussex RH13 7YP
Tel: 01403 211293 Fax: 01403 211580

Head Mr R C Poulton
Founded 1552
Type Co-educational
Religious denomination Church of England
Members of HMC
Age range 11 – 18
No of pupils (boarding) 819
Girls 328; *Boys* 481
Junior 346; *Senior* 463; *Sixth form* 220
Fees per term (boarding) Nil – £3,563
Fees per annum (boarding) Nil – £10,688

Christ's Hospital is an extraordinary school offering a full boarding education in an ethos of care.

Entry is at age 11+. All children must qualify in an entrance examination. A few places are available for sixth-form entry. A wide range of subjects are offered around a compulsory core. Out- of-school activities are boundless in grounds of 120 acres and the superb new sports centre. Parents pay a contribution according to family income. Many pay nothing at all (if income is below £10,650). Others pay on a sliding scale. 1995 results: A level 93 per cent pass, GCSE 79 per cent ABC grades.

Cottesmore School

Buchan Hill, Pease Pottage, West Sussex RH11 9AU
Tel: 01293 520648 Fax: 01293 614784

Head M A Rogerson MA (Cantab)
Founded 1894
Type Preparatory
Religious denomination Church of England
Age range 7 – 13 *Boarders from* 7 – 13
No of pupils (boarding) 140
Girls 47; *Boys* 93
Fees per term (boarding) £2,910
Fees per annum (boarding) £8,730

Cottesmore is an all boarding school, situated a mile from exit 11 of the M23, ten minutes from Gatwick Airport and one hour from central London and Heathrow Airport.

Curriculum: boys and girls are taught together in classes averaging 14 in number. The teacher/pupil ratio is 1:9. Children are fully prepared for Common Entrance and scholarship examinations.

Music: the musical tradition is strong – more than 80 children learn a variety of instruments; there is a chapel choir, a school orchestra, and there are several musical ensembles.

Drama: several plays are produced every year, with major productions open to parents.

Sport: the major games are association and rugby football, cricket, hockey, netball and rounders. Numerous other sports are taught and encouraged. They include tennis, squash, golf, riding, athletics, cross country running, swimming, windsurfing, fishing, boating, gymnastics, shooting, judo, archery and trampolining. The school competes at national level in several of these sports.

Recent development: there is a 20 metre indoor heated swimming pool, a computer room containing twelve BBC Master Econet-linked computers, an art studio and a new building containing six classrooms including a science laboratory and a specially equipped language room.

Hobbies and activities: these include pottery, photography, stamp collecting, chess, bridge, model-making, model railway, tenpin bowling, gardening, ballet, modern dancing, drama, craft, carpentry, printing, cooking and debating.

The boys and girls lead a full and varied life and are encouraged to take part in as wide a variety of activities as possible. With a third of the children having parents living and working abroad, weekends are a vital part of school life and are made busy and fun for all.

Entry requirements: entry is by headmaster's interview and a report from the previous school. For a prospectus and more information, please write or telephone the headmaster's secretary, Mrs Karen Stafford.

Dorset House School

The Manor, Church Lane, Bury, Pulborough, West Sussex RH20 1PB
Tel: 01798 831456 Fax: 01798 831141

Head A L James BA (Oxon)
Founded 1781
Type Boys' boarding and day preparatory school
Religious denomination Church of England
Members of IAPS
Age range 4 – 13 *Boarders from* 8+
No of pupils (day) 79; *(boarding)* 40
Boys 119
Junior 119
Fees per term (day) £1,110 – £2,235; *(boarding)* £2,680
Fees per annum (day) £3,330 – £6,705; *(boarding)* £8,040

Curriculum: boys are prepared for Common Entrance and public school scholarships. The demands of the National Curriculum and GCSE are always kept in mind and we aim to keep abreast of new developments.

Entry: entry is by interview and subject only to places being available.

Based in Bury Manor, a beautiful 16th century building on the banks of the River Arun, the school has excellent facilities for academic studies, music, art and sport. A strong traditional emphasis in teaching is maintained. In addition to the core subjects, music, art, technology and computing all find a place in the timetable. Cricket, rugby and soccer are the main school games but hockey, athletics and swimming also play a large part. Professional coaching is available in tennis and judo. The family atmosphere at this small school gives children a sense of friendship, security and enthusiasm, while preparing them for entry into the best public schools in England.

Farlington School

Strood Park, Horsham, West Sussex RH12 3PN
Tel: 01403 254967 Fax: 01403 272258

Head Mrs P M Mawer BA
Founded 1896
Type Independent girls
Religious denomination Church of England (but open to all denominations)
Members of GSA, GBGSA
Age range 4 – 18 *Boarders from* 8
No of pupils (day) 310 *(boarding)* 35
Girls 345
Junior 100 *Senior* 197 *Sixth form* 48
Fees per term (day) £840 – £1,570 (preparatory school); £1,930 (senior school); *(boarding)* £3,080
Fees per annum (day) £5,790; *(boarding)* £9,240

Curriculum: broadly-based academic curriculum. Wide range of subjects offered at GCSE; 18 subjects at A level, including sociology and theatre studies. General studies AS studied by all sixth formers. 80+ per cent go on to high degree course.
Entry requirements and procedures: our own exam + interview.

Examinations offered: GCSE, A level, AS level, RSA French. In 1995 A level pass rate was 92.4 per cent; GCSE pass rate was 94.5 per cent.
Academic and leisure facilities: new science building with five purpose-built laboratories, fully-equipped for KS3 and KS4. All-weather pitch, outdoor heated swimming pool, student-run farm.
Scholarships: music, academic, sixth form.
Boarding facilities: weekly or full in small, friendly boarding house.
Special features: current National Schools' Riding Association champions; county and national sports success, particularly volleyball. Young Enterprise Company 1995 North Sussex regional winner. Strong drama tradition with annual production at Horsham Arts Theatre.

Lavant House-Rosemead

Chichester, West Sussex PO18 9AB
Tel: 01243 527211 Fax: 01243 530490

Head Mrs M Scott
Founded 1952
Type Independent
Religious denomination Christian
Age range 3 – 18 (Boys 3 – 8) *Boarders from* 8
(girls only)
No of pupils (day) 146; *(boarding)* 52
Fees per term (day) £450 – £1,850
(boarding) £2,625 – £3,290

Lavant House-Rosemead is an independent school for up to 200 pupils, of whom approximately a quarter are boarders. Lavant House was founded in 1952 with the aims of combining a high level of academic education with a wide range of general activities in an open, friendly, caring, almost family environment, based on Christian values. Rosemead joined after closing in Littlehampton in July 1995. The school is divided into two: the junior school, Stanier House, for boys 3 – 8 and girls 3 – 11, and the senior school, Lavant House-Rosemead, which takes girls as boarders from 8 – 18 and as day pupils from 11 – 18.

The school stands in its own grounds of 53 acres at the foot of the Sussex Downs, three and a half miles from the cathedral city of Chichester with which the school has many links. The main school is housed in an 18th century building, which accommodates the administration, the library, the dormitories and the dining room. There are modern classrooms and science blocks and an assembly hall/gymnasium, with an adjoining squash court. A recent extension houses the computer, language and home economics rooms.

Pupils in the junior school are prepared for Common Entrance. For part of the day they work and play in French under the guidance of a native French speaker. Entry to the senior school is usually by the 11+ Common Entrance, or by interview and the appropriate examination. The headmistress interviews all prospective pupils for both the junior and senior school. In the senior school there is a wide common curriculum leading to a variety of GCSE and A level courses. Information and business studies courses are available in the sixth form. In a flourishing art department, painting, drawing, batik, lino-printing and pottery are taught. The long tradition of success at drama, both in individual and group performances, has led to the opening of a drama studio to support preparation for GCSE and A level drama.

The school aims to help each and every pupil reach his (junior school) or her full potential and provide an all-round education, and for this purpose everyone is expected to take part in a wide range of extra-curricular activities.

Mayfield College

Mayfield, East Sussex TN20 6PL
Tel: 01435 872041 Fax: 01435 873544

Head Mr C P Vroege FRCO, GBSM, ARCM, PGCE
Founded 1868
Type Secondary boarding and day
Religious denomination Roman Catholic
Members of ISAI, BSA
Age range 11 – 18
No of pupils (day) 40; *(boarders)* 80
Sixth form 40
Fees per term (day) £1,000 – £2,140; *(boarding)*
£2,025 – £3,950

Situated on a beautiful 100 acre site in the Sussex Weald, the college offers good facilities, attention to individual needs and a strong sense of community with traditional values.
Average size of classes: 10
Teacher/pupil ratio: 1:5
Curriculum: a broad curriculum is followed in the first three years, followed by the normal degree of specialisation for GCSE and A level. The school also offers agricultural studies (there is a small farm) and specialist help is available for pupils with specific learning difficulties. The International Study Centre caters for those students who need to improve their English before entering the main school. Co- educational sixth form.
Entry requirements co-educational sixth form: entry at any age is by interview (when possible), school reference and either Common Entrance or Mayfield Tests with good GCSE grades for sixth form. EFL is available if required at all levels of the college.

Michael Hall School

Kidbrooke Park, Forest Row, East Sussex RH18 5JB
Tel: 01342 822275 Fax: 01342 826004

Head Chairman of College of Teachers (rotating position)
Founded 1925
Type Steiner
Religious denomination Non-denominational (Christian)
Members of Steiner Schools Fellowship
Age range 3 – 18 *Boarders from* 8
No of pupils (day) 446; *(boarding)* 56
Girls 240; *Boys* 262
Junior (4 – 6) 88, (6 – 14) 306; *Senior* (14 – 18) 88 *Sixth form* 27 + 20 EFL
Fees per term (day) £525 – £1,225; *(boarding)* £2,300 – £2,675
Fees per annum (day) £1,575 – £3,675; *(boarding)* £6,900 – £8,025 (inclusive of tuition)

One of over 600 Steiner or Waldorf schools worldwide, Michael Hall aims to be as truly comprehensive as is possible within national parameters. We are open to girls and boys 3 – 18, providing a broad education and a healthy balance of artistic, academic and practical activities. The unique and well-established curriculum responds to each developmental phase of childhood, stimulating a joy in learning and making competitive testing unnecessary. Specialists ensure excellence in the upper school. We offer GCSE, GNVQ, A level and EFL courses. Entry is by interview with reference to previous school reports.

Micklefield Wadhurst

With the Legat School of Classical Ballet, Mayfield Lane, Wadhurst, East Sussex TN5 6JA
Tel: 01892 783193 Fax: 01892 783638

Heads Mr Eric Reynolds BA (Hons), PGCE
Founded Micklefield 1910, Wadhurst 1930
Type Senior girls' boarding and day
Religious denomination Christian foundation
Members of GSA, BSA
Age range 10 – 18 *Boarders from* 11
No of pupils (day) 60; *(boarding)* 120
Girls 180; *Boys* Legat only
Senior 180; *Sixth form* 49
Fees per term (day) £2,070 – £2,140; *(boarding)* £3,340 – £3,370
Fees per annum (day) £6,210 – £6,420; *(boarding)* £10,020 – £10,110

Traditional GCSE and A level curriculum with broad range of subjects, vocational courses in childcare and catering. Legat offers professional dance training. Specialist help for dyslexic pupils. Common Entrance examination or own entrance tests. Audition for entry into Legat. Purpose-built science block, information technology laboratory, home economics building for food technology and textiles, spacious art/CDT department. Sports hall, heated indoor swimming pool, two games fields, six tennis courts, dance studios, ten music practice rooms. School chapel, scholarships for academic ability, music, drama, art, sport. Bursaries for clergy, missionaries, armed forces. Shared dormitories for younger pupils, study bedrooms in sixth form centre.

Moira House Junior School

Upper Carlisle Road, Eastbourne, East Sussex BN20 7TE
Tel: 01323 644144 Fax: 01323 649720

Head Mrs Ann Harris
Founded 1875
Type Independent day and boarding
Religious denomination Inter-denominational
Members of GSA, BSA, GBGSA
Age range 2 – 11 *Boarders from* 8
No of pupils (day) 85 *(boarding)* 5
Girls 90
Junior 90
Fees per term (day) £1,070 – £1,790; *(boarding)* £3,420
Fees per annum (day) £3,210 – £5,370; *(boarding)* £10,260
Kindergarten fees: £7 per session

The junior school is very much part of Moira House, but retains its individual identity. Whilst sharing the swimming pool, games fields, Swann Hall and dining room it has its own library, activities centre, gardens and pets. Entry may be at any age, from Kindergarten. Tests in mathematics and English are given to girls over seven, preferably during a day visit to school. Curriculum includes French, swimming, performing arts, in addition to sound foundations in English, mathematics and science. From nine, girls receive specialist teaching in preparation for 11+, Common Entrance before moving to the senior school. Scholarships are offered from eight. A wide-ranging activity programme complements the curriculum. The growth of self-confidence and self-reliance is encouraged within a happy, friendly atmosphere. Day girl participation is welcomed in the junior boarding house.

Moira House

Upper Carlisle Road, Eastbourne, East Sussex BN20 7TE
Tel: 01323 644144 Fax: 01323 649720

Head Adrian Underwood BA (Hons), MA, FRSA
Founded 1875
Type Independent girls' boarding and day
Religious denomination Inter-denominational
Members of GBGSA, GSA, BSA
Age range 3 – 18 *Boarders from* 8
No of pupils (day) 250; *(boarding)* 130
Girls 380
Junior 100; *Senior* 190; *Sixth form* 90
Fees per term (day) £1,070 – £2,300; *(boarding)*
£3,420 – £3,570
Fees per annum (day) £3,210 – £6,900;
(boarding) £10,260 – £10,710

Foundation: Moira House was founded in 1875 by Mr and Mrs Charles Ingham, regarded in their time as gifted pioneers in the field of female education.

Situation: we are situated on high ground in Eastbourne, near Beachy Head, with views over the sea. Our grounds open directly on to the Sussex Downs.

Facilities: each subject has its own resource at base and there has been an extensive building programme over the last 15 years. All our sports facilities are on site, including a 25-metre indoor heated pool. We are members of the local David Lloyd Club for racket sports.

Faith: the school is inter-denominational and the majority of the school attends Family Service at the parish church, whose vicar is our chaplain and prepares girls for Confirmation.

Boarding: we have three boarding houses including a separate sixth form house and a separate junior house.

Curriculum: in the junior school we offer a wide curriculum, whilst preparing for the 11+ Common Entrance examination for transfer to the senior school. In the senior school, we follow formal academic courses in the normal curriculum in arts and sciences. There are 20 GCSE examination subjects, 18 A level examination subjects, including business studies, law and politics.

Careers counselling: the strong programme of careers counselling has been developed by our senior master, Howard Barlow, well known as author of *How To Pass A Levels*.

Drama, music and sport: these have always been strengths of our school. Plays and concerts are regularly performed, both in school and in the community of Eastbourne. We have a strong programme of inter-school sport, including a biennial hockey tours to the USA and the West Indies.

Activity: over 30 activities are offered each term in a strong programme which include the Duke of Edinburgh Award, the Young Enterprise Scheme, Shakespeare on the Platform, Youth Parliament and community service.

International links: there are usually three exchanges each year plus skiing and outdoor pursuits in Europe.

Entry: entry is by examination and interview at any age to the junior school and the senior school at 11+, 13+ and 16+. Scholarships and bursaries are available. Please refer to the scholarships section.

Charitable status: Moira House School is a registered charity (no 307072). It exists to provide excellent education for young women.

Newlands Manor School

Sutton Place, Seaford, East Sussex BN25 3PL
Tel: 01323 890309 Fax: 01323 490100

Head Mr Brian F Underwood MA, DipEd (Oxon)
Founded 1978
Type Co-educational boarding and day
Religious denomination Non-denominational
Age range 13 – 18
No of pupils (day) 95
Girls 80; *Boys* 170
Sixth form 62
Fees per term (day) £1,890; *(boarding)* £2,985 – £3,395
Curriculum: there are more than 20 subjects on the curriculum which is in accordance with nationally recognised guidelines. A balanced curriculum is encouraged whilst at A level the sciences and mathematics (pure and applied) are particularly strong. Classes are small and our aim is to enable each individual boy and girl to achieve maximum potential. Specialist help is available for dyslexic or EFL pupils. All pass rates are well above national averages. Science is studied as three separate subjects. Entry is by Common Entrance at 13 or by interview and report from previous school. Entry is possible at any stage.

There are a number of scholarships and bursaries for academic, artistic, musical and sporting excellence. The school has a particularly strong record in art, music and computing. Current members of the school include a member of the England Girls' Cricket Squad and an international sailing champion. There are opportunities for many other sports including basketball, soccer, hockey, netball, volleyball, rugby football, athletics, golf, squash, badminton, horse riding, tennis and cross-country running.

There is a strong choral tradition.

Examinations offered: GCSE (MEG, LEAG, SEG, AEB), A and AS levels (Cambridge, AEB, SEG, LEAG, Oxford).

The majority of leavers progress to higher education at leading universities and colleges in the United Kingdom and abroad. A small proportion directly enter the services or the professions each year.

The school is a friendly, happy and well-equipped community fostering the essential qualities of industry, tolerance, independence and self-discipline. Emphasis is placed on individual encouragement within a 'small school'.

Newlands Manor is situated in pleasant grounds and enjoys a semi- rural location on the edge of a coastal town with very easy access to Gatwick and Heathrow airports. London is 1 hour 25 minutes by rail.

The school is fully co-ordinated with Newlands Preparatory School on the same campus, thus enabling regular contact between brothers and sisters of different ages.

The Newlands Schools exist to provide education for boys and girls.

Registered Charity No 297606.

Roedean School

Brighton, East Sussex BN2 5RQ
Tel: 01273 603181 Fax: 01273 676722

Head Mrs Ann Longley MA
Founded 1885
Type Girls' independent boarding school
Religious denomination Church of England (all faiths welcome)
Members of GSA, GBGSA, BSA, SHA
No of pupils 430
Sixth form 160
Fees per term (day) £2,455 *(boarding)* £4,325

Average size of class: 18
Teacher/pupil ratio: 1:8
Curriculum: a full spectrum of subjects is offered with minimal setting against one another, enabling real choice, balance and flexibility for GCSE, A and AS level. Much emphasis is placed on providing girls with individual programmes of academic and extra-curricular activities.
Entry requirements and procedures: entry at 11+, 12+, 13+ is by Common Entrance; at 14+ by Roedean examinations; and sixth form entry is by interview. A limited number of day places available throughout the school.
Subject specialities and academic track record: 99per cent pass rate at A level; 99 per cent pass rate at GCSE (grades A*–C). Strength across the curriculum.
Examinations and boards offered are: A level – Cambridge and London Boards. GCSE – Midland, London and Southern Groups. Leavers go on to universities, colleges of higher education, art schools, etc.
Academic and leisure facilities: new theatre and performing arts complex for music, drama and dance. Careers room, library/resource centres, design/DT centre, computer/IT laboratory, nine specialist science laboratories, new humanities centre, modern languages mini-laboratories, art studio, sports hall, indoor heated swimming pool, squash courts, extensive playing fields.

Roedean is set on Downs overlooking the sea between Brighton and Rottingdean. Good road and rail links with London and its airports.

St Andrew's Preparatory School

Meads, Eastbourne, East Sussex BN20 7RP
Tel: 01323 733203

Head Mr H Davies Jones MA (Oxon)
Founded 1877
Type Preparatory and pre-preparatory
Religious denomination Church of England
Members of IAPS
Age range 3 – 13 *Boarders from* 7
No of pupils (day) 401
Girls 147; *Boys* 254
Fees per term (day) £500 – £1,780; *(boarding)* £2,575

Average size of class: 15
Teacher/pupil ratio: 1:10
Curriculum: a broad curriculum is followed.
Entry requirements and procedures: early registration is necessary to secure a pre-preparatory place. All entrants to the preparatory school will sit an informal test for placing purposes.

The fee includes all compulsory extras.

Subject specialities and academic track record: the Common Entrance and scholarship record is good.

Limited numbers of academic scholarships are available for eight and nine year olds. A competitive examination is held at the beginning of March.

Academic/sports/leisure facilities available: the school has theatre/gymnasium complex which also includes a 20m indoor heated swimming pool. Other sports facilities include tennis courts, a climbing wall and ample grass space for games. Instruction is offered in riding, sailing, golf and squash. A creative arts centre was opened in 1986 with workshops for CDT, an art room and a photographic dark room. There is a computer centre, an extensive library, and a music school with an auditorium and many practice rooms. A shooting range/pavilion and Scout headquarters was opened in 1993.

The school has its own chapel.

The school aims to help each child fulfil his or her potential in the classroom and outside it.

St Bede's at The Dicker

Near Hailsham, East Sussex BN27 3QH
Tel: 01323 843252 Fax: 01323 442628

Head R A Perrin
Founded 1978
Type Co-educational
Religious denomination Inter-denominational
Members of SHMIS, GBA
Age range 12½ – 19 *Boarders from* 12½ – 19
No of pupils (day) 160; *(boarding)* 290
Girls 40 per cent; *Boys* 60 per cent
Senior 160; *Sixth form* 180
Fees per term (day) £2,250 *(boarding)* £3,800

St Bede's is set in the village of Upper Dicker in the countryside. The buildings and playing fields occupy four sites around this small village and in all spread over some 75 acres.

It enjoys a staff:pupil ratio of 1:8. The academic standards are high and most sixth formers go on to degree courses.

Entry is at 12½ – 14 by Common Entrance or interview and school's own entrance test. Direct entry is encouraged into the sixth forms and entry at any level can be arranged.

Curriculum: St Bede's provides an extremely wide-ranging programme, both in its academic and in its extra-curricular activities. It is thus possible for programmes to be tailored to the individual's needs to an unusually high degree.

There is a total of 30 GCSE (Key Stage 4) subjects available and as well as the usual subjects Latin, Spanish, Italian, oriental languages, art, business studies, CDT, drama, home economics, integrated humanities, IT, music, physical education, photography and rural sciences are offered.

85 per cent stay on to the sixth form. Most GCSE subjects are offered at A level plus economics, history of art, horticultural science, pure and applied maths, media studies and theatre studies. Computer studies, geology, psychology, RE, sociology and statistics are available at AS level and the school also offers a few carefully selected BTEC, GNVQs level 3 (vocational courses) recognised as A level equivalents.

All sixth-form leavers go on to university and other institutions of higher education including universities in continental Europe and the USA.

The arts: in music, drama and art, St Bede's achieves an exceptionally high standard both in performances and public examinations.

The club activities programme: an extensive club activities programme includes many sporting and games playing opportunities and these are open to all students. For those who enjoy sport there are extensive fixture lists against other schools and clubs organised each term. The school has particularly strong teams in football, netball, tennis, squash and swimming. A 25 metre competition pool has recently been built and the school has its own practice golf course and riding stables. However, games are not compulsory and in all there are currently over 85 club activities organised and professionally staffed ranging from the Army Cadet Force, Duke of Edinburgh Award Scheme, numerous outdoor pursuits and activities within the fields of art, drama, music, journalism, science, agriculture, technology, engineering and social services.

Boarding facilities: there are five boarding houses and within these, the student's welfare is closely looked after by housemasters and housemistresses in conjunction with resident house tutors and matrons. Students are in small dormitories for the first and second year and the fifth form (Year 11) upwards have study bedrooms. All boarding houses have a recreational common room and student kitchen.

The boarders' house is more than a place to live in; its staff are responsible for all the day to day arrangements of a student's life at school and provide tutors to keep a personal eye on the student's progress at weekly confidential meetings. Each student's fortnightly record diary and half-termly internal progress reports provide background material for these meetings.

Scholarships and bursaries: A generous number of academic and arts scholarships are available and certain scholarships may be awarded to those entering the sixth form.

St Leonards–Mayfield School

The Old Palace, Mayfield, East Sussex TN20 6PH
Tel: 01435 873652 Fax: 01435 872627

Head Sister Jean Sinclair
Founded 1850/1872
Type Independent
Religious denomination Roman Catholic
Age range 11 – 18 *Boarders from* 11
No of pupils (day) 210; *(boarding)* 315
Girls 525
Senior 365; *Sixth form* 160
Fees per term (day) £2,300; *(boarding)* £3,450

Curriculum: broadly based to GCSE with a strong core. At A level there is free choice from 25 subjects, two classical, five modern languages are offered with extra-curricular Japanese. Strong mathematics and science, excellent art, ceramics.
Entry: Common Entrance, 11+, 12+, 13+ with report.
Facilities: library with 18,000 volumes, indoor heated pool, all-weather pitch, new music school, riding facilities, comfortable boarding houses, first class food, dedicated, experienced staff.
Scholarships: means tested at 11+, 13+.
Boarding: mainly full boarders but we are happy to meet increased parental demand for weekly boarding. Boarders are normally Roman Catholic; visiting priests celebrate masses each weekend. Strong supportive community encourages development of the individual.

St Mary's Hall

Eastern Road, Brighton, East Sussex BN2 5JF
Tel: 01273 606061 Fax: 01273 620782

Head Mrs P J James BA
Founded 1836
Type Independent day and boarding school
Religious denomination Church of England
Members of GSA, GBGSA, ISIS
Age range 3 – 18 *Boarders from* 8
No of pupils (day) 323; *(boarding)* 78
Girls 389; *Boys* 12
Junior 140; *Senior* 263; *Sixth form* 54
Fees per term (day) £390 – £1,980; *(boarding)*
£2,325 – £2,985
Fees per annum (day) £1,170 – £5,940;
(boarding) £6,975 – £8,955

St Mary's Hall was founded in 1836 for the daughters of the Church of England clergy. The school is proud of its traditions of care and respect for the individual and also of its capacity to incorporate the best of modern education. There is a well-appointed CDT room and a computer room equipped with a Nimbus network system. Excellent art and craft facilities include a pottery kiln and a dark room, while for drama productions there is a computerised stage lighting system. All playing fields are on the site and there is a 25 metre indoor heated swimming-pool.

Sixteen subjects are offered at GCSE; pupils normally take between eight and ten. A wide variety of subjects is offered at A level including theatre studies, history of art, law, economics and business studies. A large number of girls go on to take degree courses in mathematics and science. Boarding accommodation ranges from the Regency splendour of Sussex Square to a modern purpose-built house in the grounds, which also provides a day-centre for the sixth form.

St Mary's Hall has the fine chapel of St Mark's and each day begins with an act of Christian worship, though all faiths are treated with respect. All dietary needs are catered for. With about 400 pupils, it is possible to know each girl as an individual although the school is large enough to maintain good facilities, to stimulate a lively pursuit of music, drama and the visual arts and to have graduate specialists teaching in the senior school.

St Mary's Hall is a charity established to promote the education of children of any age. Entrance is by examination. Academic and music scholarships, clergy and forces bursaries, and government assisted places are available. Prospective pupils are welcome to spend a day at the school, or 24 hours if boarding is being considered.

Seaford College, Petworth

Petworth, West Sussex GU28 0NB
Tel: 01798 867392 Fax: 01798 867606

Head R C Hannaford BSc, MIBiol
Founded 1884
Type Boys boarding and day; day girls in sixth
Religious denomination Church of England
Members of SHMIS, GBA
Age range 11 – 18 *Boarders from* 11 – 18
No of pupils (day) 75; *(boarding)* 224
Girls 4 day in sixth form
Sixth form 100
Fees per term (day) Junior £1,755; Senior £1,975; *(boarding)* Junior £2,750; Senior £3,210

Curriculum: pupils are prepared for the full range of GCSE and A level subjects. We also offer the BTEC Diploma (GNVQ) in Business and Finance and A level technology. Students attend a week's work experience in a company of their choice. Frequent visits to France and Germany are organised throughout the college. There is a new purpose-built centre supporting the fine tradition of art and technology at the college. A new computer centre opens in September 1995. Qualified dyslexia support is available.

Entry requirements and procedures: Common Entrance, interview and scholarships.
General: the college is situated in its own 320 acre park which dates back to Elizabeth I and a twelfth century church is now the college chapel. This outstanding site is at the foot of the South Downs between Petworth and Chichester. For those living abroad, Heathrow and Gatwick Airports and the Portsmouth ferry terminal are all within an hour's drive.

Seaford is based on the traditional House system. Each housemaster supported by his assistants and academic tutors oversees a pupil's progress in all aspects of life in the community. A boy can expect to have a single or double study bedroom from the age of 14.

The college has an outstanding sporting record with boys representing not only their county, but also attaining divisional and national level. We also offer A level sports studies.

Significant attainments have been made by the Chapel Choir with frequent international tours which have always featured receptions at the invitation of the British Ambassador, including Washington, Moscow and Paris, and Brussels.

A programme of activities is offered at weekends. The large Combined Cadet Force maintains an exciting training programme and the college uses a base on the edge of Exmoor for adventure and academic studies.

Entrance scholarships are held in February each year and special bursaries are available for members of HM Forces. Open days are held each term.

For further information apply to the Registrar.

Slindon College

Slindon House, Slindon, Arundel, West Sussex BN18 0RH
Tel: 01243 814320 Fax: 01243 814647

Head Mr Peter D Morris BEd, MA (Oxon)
Founded 1972
Type Boarding and day
Religious denomination Non-denominational
Members of ISAI
Age range 11 – 18 *Boarders from* 11
No of pupils (day) 20; *(boarding)* 80
Boys 100
Junior 40; *Senior* 45; *Sixth form* 15
Fees per term (day) £1,995; *(boarding)* £3,050
Fees per annum (day) £5,985; *(boarding)* £9,150

Curriculum: a broad-based, balanced curriculum is offered with English, mathematics, science, information technology and games being compulsory in Years 7 – 11.

In Years 7, 8 and 9, in addition, all boys study art, design technology, drama, geography, history, music and personal and social education (including religious studies). Many also take French.

GCSE options are: art and design, rural science, design, drama, French, geography, history, home economics, motor vehicle studies and music.

A good selection of subjects is offered at Advanced level. The one year sixth form course includes four complementary elements: core curriculum, vocational courses, work experience and community service.

Each boy has to select at least two afternoon activities per week from a wide range including squash, cycling, drama, basketball, football, golf, windsurfing, canoeing and the Duke of Edinburgh Award Scheme.

Entry requirements: Boys may enter Slindon College at any age from eleven. There is no entrance examination, the headmaster preferring to judge a boy's ability at interview and through the inspection of recent school reports and exercise books.

For A level studies, predicted GCSE grades are requested.

Tuition for a limited number of boys with special educational needs including dyslexia and ADD/ADHD.

Examinations offered: examinations at GCSE, AS and A level are offered through the established examination boards. Additionally, AEB Basic, RSA CLAIT and Cambridge EFL examinations are offered.

Academic and leisure facilities: facilities include an information technology room, three science laboratories, three rooms for design work, two art rooms and a pottery room, music and music practice rooms, a library, two special needs rooms, an observatory and classrooms for all subject areas. Motor vehicle maintenance, poultry breeding and rearing, and a tropical butterfly house all feature in the school's extra-curricular programme.

There are football and rugby pitches, a junior hockey area, a floodlit hardplay area, an outdoor heated swimming pool, two squash courts an 14 acres of land.

Scholarships: children of service personnel receive a fee reduction of 10 per cent as do second and third sons. A number of scholarships and bursaries available subject to conditions.

Boarding facilities: there are two boarding houses, each with its own common room and games room. The juniors live in comfortable dormitories and the seniors mostly in double study bedrooms. The house staff know each boy very well and emphasis is placed on creating a caring, secure, family atmosphere.

Sompting Abbotts School

Church Lane, Sompting, Lancing, West Sussex BN15 0AZ
Tel: 01903 235960

Principal Mrs P M Sinclair
Head Mr R M Johnson
Founded 1921
Type Preparatory
Age range 3 – 13 *Boarders from* 7 – 13
No of pupils (day) 160; *(boarding) (weekly)* 15
Boys 15
Fees per term (day) £675 – £1,295; *(boarding)* £1,895
Fees per annum (day) £2,025 – £3,885; *(boarding)* £5,685

The school is set in 30 acres and is situated on the south slope of the South Downs just north of Worthing.

Fifteen fully-equipped staff take care of the boys.

The pre-preparatory department and nursery class cater for boys between the ages of three and eight, and is located in its own self-contained building, which has large attractive classrooms.

Boys in the preparatory department are prepared for Common Entrance to all independent schools. The main sports played are cricket, association and rugby football. Facilities include gymnasium, tennis courts, swimming pool and a shooting range. School transport is available.

Temple Grove

Heron's Ghyll, Uckfield, East Sussex TN22 4DA
Tel: 01825 712112 Fax: 01825 713432

Heads Mr M G N Lee MA (Cantab), DipEd and Mrs J E Lee BA, CertEd
Founded 1810
Type Co-educational preparatory school and pre-preparatory department
Religious denomination Church of England
Age range 3 – 13 *Boarders from* 8
No of pupils (day) 145; *(boarding)* 25
Girls 80; *Boys* 90
Junior 143; *Senior* 27
Fees per term (day) £1,265 – £2,230; *(boarding)* £2,295 – £2,730
Fees per annum (day) £3,795 – £6,690; *(boarding)* £6,885 – £8,190

Temple Grove is a fully co-educational preparatory school with a well-balanced and extensive curriculum taking children from 3 – 13.

There is a well-established boarding tradition alongside a thriving intake of day pupils.

The school day is designed to enable pupils to partake in a vast array of extra mural activities in the evenings and Saturday mornings on an optional basis.

The 40 acres of grounds includes lakes and woodlands, first class playing fields, swimming pool, tennis courts, a floodlit all-weather surface and gardens. There is a chapel, spacious gymnasium and newly completed theatre, CDT centre and music school.

Soccer and rugby football, netball, rounders, cricket, tennis, athletics and swimming are the main games. Other activities include judo, fencing, dancing, golf, computing, electronics, drama, art and craft, shooting, photography and instrumental music.

A prospectus will be sent on request and parents are warmly invited to view the school.

Windlesham House

Washington, Pulborough, West Sussex RH20 4AY
Tel: 01903 873207 Fax: 01903 873017

Acting Heads Julie and Stephen Goodhart
Founded 1837
Type Full boarding co-educational preparatory school
Religious denomination Church of England
Age range 7 – 13 *Boarders from* 7 – 13
No of pupils (boarding) 295
Girls 123; *Boys* 178

Curriculum: very broad curriculum offered to enable all children to discover and develop their individual strengths and talents.
Entrance requirements: no entrance examination. Parents seeking a place for their child at Windlesham should contact the registrar.
Academic/leisure facilities: at least 60 activities to choose from during the year. We have a theatre, indoor swimming pool, chapel, tennis and squash courts, extensive playing fields and grounds.
Boarding: this is very much a family school where all the children board. Everything is done to encourage the children's individuality and promote a warm and friendly atmosphere. Relationships between staff and children are excellent and our aim is to give every child a happy and fulfilled time at Windlesham.

The following independent college also offers GCSEs. Please refer to the Independent Sixth-Form Colleges section for details:

Bellerby's College, Hove

Craigievar High School

37 Roker Park Road, Sunderland, Tyne & Wear SR6 9PL
Tel: 0191 548 5468

Head Mrs M Chadwick
Founded 1974
Type Private independent
Religious denomination Inter-denominational
(Islam and Christian taught)
Age range Girls 2½ – 18 Boys 4 – 7
No of pupils (day) 50
Girls 40; *Boys* 10
Junior 36; *Senior* 14
Fees per term (day) £400 – £800
Fees per annum (day) £1,200 – £2,400

Craigievar High School has been open for 21 years and is a small school for girls aged 4 to 18 years. Boys are accepted 4 - 7 years. The nursery department accepts both boys and girls. We follow the national curriculum and offer in addition classics, dance, drama and music involving strings, woodwind and piano.

Small classes give children individual attention. The aim of the school is to give every students a broad academic education and to help each person to fulfil their talents. Our philosophy is to produce a happy and stimulating environment.

Eastcliffe Grammar School

The Grove, Gosforth, Newcastle upon Tyne, Tyne & Wear NE3 1NE
Tel: 0191 285 4873

Head G D Pearson BA (Hons), DipEd, FRSA
Founded 1946
Type Independent co-educational day
Religious denomination Christian non-denominational
Age range 3 – 18
No of pupils (day) 230
Girls 60; *Boys* 170
Junior 55; *Senior* 151; *Sixth form* 24
Fees per term (day) £800 – £1,360
Fees per annum (day) £2,400 – £4,080

Eastcliffe admits boys and girls from the age of three and offers a wide range of educational opportunities within a positive family atmosphere. Entry to the junior school is by assessment and interview. Candidates for the senior school are admitted by entrance examination and interview. All candidates are encouraged to spend a day with an appropriate class. Founded in 1946, the school is situated in a pleasant, residential suburb and is easily reached by car and public transport. Classes are small and particular emphasis is placed upon developing the abilities and aptitudes of individual children. There is a strong academic tradition and good facilities for the sciences, humanities, creative and performing arts, design technology and sports.

Many children join the school in the junior department and proceed by assessment rather than a formal entrance examination to the senior school. Fourteen subjects are offered at GCSE level. In the sixth form courses are offered to A, and AS level with some lower sixth classes for new or resit GCSEs. Applications for the sixth form are welcomed from home and overseas students and special help is available with English as a foreign language. There is a wide programme of extra-curricular activities.

Bilton Grange

Dunchurch, Rugby, Warwickshire CV22 6QU
Tel: 01788 810217 Fax: 01788 810122

Head Quentin G Edwards
Founded 1873
Type Co-educational boarding day preparatory and pre-preparatory
Religious denomination Church of England
Members of IAPS
Age range 4 – 13 Boarders from 8 – 13
No of pupils (day) 200; *(boarding)* 92
Girls 116; *Boys* 176
Junior 98; *Senior* 174; *Sixth form* 45
Fees per term (day) £789 – £2,292; *(boarding)* £2,865
Fees per annum (day) £2,361 – £6,876; *(boarding)* £8,595

Set in 156 acres of parkland and offering some of the best facilities in the country, Bilton Grange has a proud tradition of academic, sporting and artistic achievement. The entry is non-selective but about 25 per cent of the boys and girls move on to their senior schools with awards. The curriculum is broad and innovative and we lead the field in design and information technology. Our design and technology facility is a regional centre for the Nuffield Foundation. The pre-preparatory is housed in a separate building with excellent specialist facilities. Boarding is available from eight in very attractive modernised rooms and washing facilities, with resident adult support care and a full weekend programme.

The Kingsley School

Beauchamp Avenue, Leamington Spa, Warwickshire CV32 5RD
Tel: 01926 425127 Fax: 01926 831691

Head Mrs M A Webster BA, MEd, FRSA
Founded 1884
Type Independent girls' day school, with boys 2½ – 7
Religious denomination Church of England (all faiths welcome)
Members of GSA, GBGSA, ISIS
Age range 2½ – 18
No of pupils (day) 585
Girls 579; *Boys* 6
Junior 131; *Senior* 370; *Sixth form* 84
Fees per term (day) Senior £1,415
Fees per annum (day) £4,245

Kingsley provides girls from 2½ to 18 with a high quality well-balanced education in a friendly, disciplined environment. Boys from 2½ prepared for entry to local schools at seven. Teacher:pupil ratio of 1:10 allows personal attention from specialist staff and impressive academic results.

Curriculum: Twenty-two GCSE options include: separate sciences, Latin and Greek, IT, business studies, physical education and drama. Twenty-two A levels include: economics, business studies, computing, psychology, theatre studies and textiles.
Entry requirements: school examination and interview at 11+.
Examinations offered: GCSE, A level, A/S level, RSA-CLAIT.
Academic and leisure facilities: computer rooms, multimedia work stations, CD Roms with Ecctis 2000, Internet. New sixth-form science laboratory and common room. Flourishing performing arts with drama and dance studios. Wide range of sports (12 County representatives). Duke of Edinburgh Award Scheme (more than 80 Gold Awards). 1995 Gawcott cross-country and Junior ISIS Riding Competition winners. Expeditions, field courses and foreign exchanges.
Scholarships: scholarships, art and music exhibitions and government assisted places.

Pattison College

90 Binley Road, Coventry, West Midlands CV3 1FQ
Tel: 01203 455031

Principal Miss B Pattison
Founded 1949
Type Theatre Arts
Age range 3 – 16+ *Boarders from* 10
Fees per term (day) £550 – £995; *(boarding)* £1,600 – £1,830
Fees per annum (day) £1,650 – £2,785; *(boarding)* £4,800 – £5,490

Pattison College accepts pupils from three years to 16 years for general education which may be combined with optional theatre arts tuition leading to GCSE examinations in nine subjects.

From 16+ we offer a three year professional student course in dance, drama and singing which may be combined with A level studies. On completion of this course students may choose to work in the world of cabaret and musical theatre or teach.

Boarders are accepted from the age of ten and live in a spacious house in a residential area, close to the school.

Entry is by interview and assessment.

The Blue Coat School

Somerset Road, Edgbaston, Birmingham, West Midlands B17 0HR
Tel: 0121 454 1425 Fax: 0121 454 7757

Head Brian P Bissell
Founded 1722
Type Co-educational preparatory
Religious denomination Church of England
Members of IAPS, ECIS, BSA, ISJC accredited
Age range 3 – 13 *Boarders from* 7 – 13
No of pupils (day) 326 *(boarding)* 74
Girls 174; *Boys* 226
Pre-prep 160; *Junior* 240 (to 13+)
Fees per term (day) £960 – £1,460; *(boarding)* £2,230
Fees per annum (day) £2,880 – £4,380; *(boarding)* £6,690

An exceptionally well-equipped Midlands preparatory school, which has four purpose-built boarding houses (two for girls and two for boys) set in attractive grounds of 15 acres, with sports fields, hard courts and a heated indoor swimming pool.

Through the specialist-based teaching programme, which incorporates the National Curriculum, children are prepared for entrance examinations and scholarships, and the school awards its own academic and music scholarships at eleven years of age.

Children can enjoy a wide range of extra-curricular pursuits. Throughout, there is sensible discipline and a happy, purposeful atmosphere. Fast road and rail routes and the proximity of Birmingham International Airport ensure easy access for UK and overseas parents.

Royal Wolverhampton School

Penn Road, Wolverhampton, West Midlands WV3 0EG
Tel: 01902 341230 Fax: 01902 344496

Head Mrs B A Evans
Founded 1850
Type Independent
Religious denomination Church of England
Members of SHMIS, SHA, GBA
Age range 2½ – 18 *Boarders from* 7
No of pupils (day) 157 (junior 223); *(boarding)* 140 (junior 12)
Girls 125 (junior 88); *Boys* 172 (junior 147)
Junior 235; *Senior* 217; *Sixth form* 80
Fees per term (day) £830 – £1,725*; *(boarding)* £2,370 – £3,015*
Fees per annum (day) £2,490 – £5,175*; *(boarding)* £7,110 – £9,045* (*Fees quoted from September 1995)

The Royal School is an independent co-educational school located on the outskirts of Wolverhampton. Recent developments include new junior and senior boarding houses, a new dining hall and kitchen, a new technology centre and three computer networks.

The school follows the National Curriculum at all stages. Eighteen A level subjects are available in the sixth form. There is a strong Combined Cadet Force with Army and RAF sections.

Scholarships are available at age 11, 13 and 16 for academic merit, sport and music. Entry to junior school and pre-preparatory is by entry test; to senior school by our own entrance examination. Foundation scholarships are available to children who have lost one or both parents.

The Royal School is a registered charity.

Tettenhall College

Wood Road, Tettenhall, Wolverhampton, West Midlands WV6 8QX
Tel: 01902 751119 Fax: 01902 741940

Head Dr P C Bodkin
Founded 1863
Type Independent
Religious denomination Inter-denominational
Members of HMC, SHMIS
Age range 7½ – 18 *Boarders from* 8 – 18
No of pupils (day) 261; *(boarding)* 73
Girls 118; *Boys* 216
Junior 134; *Senior* 245; *Sixth form* 66
Fees per term (day) £1,504 – £1,880; *(boarding)*
£2,503 – £3,049
Fees per annum (day) £4,517 – £5,640;
(boarding) £7,509 – £9,147

The curriculum is effectively the National Curriculum with minor amendments. Entry is by assessment or Common Entrance. A full range of GCSE and A/AS levels subjects is offered. There are two main libraries, an IT room and a sixth form study area. Music school, art studio, theatre, sports hall, squash courts, indoor swimming pools, extensive playing fields. Academic, music and art scholarships and concessionary fees for the children of the clergy and service personnel. There are two girls' and two boys' boarding houses. Pastoral care is of a high quality and there are extensive recreational facilities and weekend activities.

Dauntsey's School

High Street, West Lavington, Devizes, Wiltshire SN10 4HE
Tel: 01380 818441 Fax: 01380 813620

Head Mr C R Evans MA
Founded 1542
Type Independent
Religious denomination Inter-denominational
Members of HMC
Age range 11 – 18 *Boarders from* 11 – 18
No of pupils (day) 339 *(boarding)* 284
Girls 276; *Boys* 347
Junior 218 (11 – 14); *Senior* 405 (14 – 18) *Sixth form* 186
Fees per term (day) £2,164; *(boarding)* £3,514
Fees per annum (day) £6,492; *(boarding)* £10,542

Dauntsey's is a very happy and successful co-educational independent school. Excellent facilities are available for academic work, music, drama, art and sport. There are several new buildings: sports hall, swimming pool, CDT and maths centres, science laboratories, humanities area, art studios and an all-weather hockey and tennis surface. There have recently been major extensions to the boarding houses, music school and dining hall. Outward-bound activities flourish including a very active sailing club which sails the famous *Jolie Brise*.

There is an emphasis on pastoral care and Christian values although worship is not narrowly denominational. There is a flexible system on exeats for boarders.

Careers advice is thorough and there is a programme of work experience. Most pupils go on to university and each year about ten go to Oxbridge.

Visitors are always welcome. Please contact the academic registrar for a prospectus and details of the entry procedure.

The Godolphin School

Milford Hill, Salisbury, Wiltshire SP1 2RA
Tel: 01722 333059 Fax: 01722 411700

Head Mrs Hilary Fender
Founded 1726
Type Girls independent
Religious denomination Church of England
Members of GSA
Age range 7 – 18 *Boarders from* 11
No of pupils (day) 240; *(boarding)* 209
Girls 449
Junior 47; *Senior* 402; *Sixth form* 102
Fees per term (day) £1,733 – £2,152; *(boarding)* £3,593
Fees per annum (day) £5,199 – £6,456; *(boarding)* £10,779

Godolphin occupies 16 acres of playing fields and gardens only a ten minute walk from the centre of Salisbury. Its buildings range from fine Victorian to state of the art technology blocks, purpose-built boarding houses, a new preparatory school, a huge four studio art block and a thriving music department.

The school has an academic tradition and most girls continue to further education (including Oxbridge). Life, however, is not dictated solely by examination results; consequently, there are 22 sports (some played to a national competitive standard), over 75 per cent play an instrument, the art department is open to all and there are activities from astronomy or conservation to cookery and jewellery design.

Our ultimate aim is to produce happy, capable, intelligent people and so self-worth, thoughtfulness, responsibility, humour and a sense of purpose are highly prized attributes actively fostered through excellent staff, well-established pastoral care and plenty of one to one attention.

The International School of Choueifat

Ashwicke Hall, Marshfield, Near Chippenham, Wiltshire SN14 8AG
Tel: 01225 891841 Fax: 01225 891011

Director Mr Salah Ayche
Founded 1886
Type Independent boarding
Religious denomination Non-denominational
Age range 9 – 18+ *Boarders from* 9 – 18+
No of pupils (boarding) 98
Girls 12; *Boys* 86
Fees per annum (boarding) £8,700 – £9,500
(September 1995)

The International School of Choueifat is situated in superb grounds of 150 acres in the heart of Wiltshire within easy reach of London. It offers courses leading to GCSE and A levels. It also prepares for SAT, Achievement and Advanced Placement Test.

The school stresses mathematics, sciences and bilingualism. Its primary objective is to prepare students for university, and it has placed students in some of the most prestigious universities of the western world.

Intensive courses are offered to new students who may have problems in some subjects before they join a regular class. Besides academic work, students enjoy a wide variety of extra-curricular activities.

The sports complex includes a heated swimming pool. The extra-curricular activities include a cultural enrichment programme.

Kingsbury Hill House

34 Kingsbury Street, Marlborough, Wiltshire SN8 1JA
Tel: 01672 512680

Head Mr M Innes-Williams
Founded 1946
Type Day co-educational preparatory and pre-preparatory
Age range 3 – 13
No of pupils (day) 120
Girls 60; *Boys* 60
Junior 120
Fees per term (day) £540 – £1,545
Fees per annum (day) £2,525 – £4,540

Kingsbury Hill House School occupies a fine double fronted Georgian house situated close to the eastern end of Marlborough's historic High Street. Further classrooms, a large gymnasium, science room and art school are located around the enclosed formal gardens, which include a large playground and tennis/netball court. Sporting facilities are located on site and in the outstanding settings of Marlborough Common and Savernake Forest nearby.

The school has nursery, pre-preparatory and preparatory departments and prepares children for CEE and scholarship at 11+, 12+ and 13+. The school maintains a fine academic tradition, but also believes that loyalty, a sense of fair play, and good manners are as important for the development of the child. The school provides a happy and stimulating start to education so that children may develop within a firm, yet friendly environment and achieve excellence in academic sporting and creative pursuits thus developing a spirit of independence.

Leaden Hall School

70 The Close, Salisbury, Wiltshire SP1 2EP
Tel: 01722 334700 Fax: 01722 410575

Head Mrs Diana Watkins MA
Founded 1937
Type Preparatory
Religious denomination Christian
Members of IAPS
Age range 3 – 12 *Boarders from* 7
No of pupils (day) 172; *(boarding)* 30
Girls 202
Fees per term (day) £965 – £1,160; *(boarding)* £2,080
Fees per annum (day) £2,895 – £3,480; *(boarding)* £6,240

Set in the cathedral close, Leaden Hall provides a single sex education for girls. We believe that we are educating the successful women of the 21st century and are therefore determined to ensure that the girls are adaptable and open to change. High standards are encouraged in all areas of a broad curriculum designed to prepare children for the Common Entrance examinations, scholarships, and county 11+ and 12+ selections. Our day girls are able to participate in all the boarders' activities and this can include the fun of staying at school overnight. Our family atmosphere generates a warm and friendly environment where self-confidence can flourish.

Norman Court

(formerly named Northaw School)
Norman Court, West Tytherley, Near Salisbury SP5 1NH
Tel: 01980 862345 Fax: 01980 862082

Head K N Foyle BA *Deputy Head* R H Williams BEd
Type Co-educational boarding and day
No of pupils: (Main school) 140; *(day)* 60; *(boarding – full and weekly)* 80; *(pre-preparatory)* 50
Fees per term (day) £1,940; *(boarding)* £2,610; *(pre-preparatory)* £920

We are a well-established co-educational boarding and day school located in idyllic surroundings near to Andover, Salisbury and Winchester. With excellent facilities and small classes, children are encouraged to have a strong work ethos.

Children are prepared for scholarships or 11+, 13+ Common Entrance and LEA schools. We have 100 per cent Common Entrance results to a variety of leading senior independent schools.

Norman Court has an extensive building programme to add to and improve many of its facilities in all areas of the school, which include the academic, pastoral, music and sports facilities.

A visit is essential to savour the happy family atmosphere of work and play in a disciplined framework.

Norman Court School is a registered charity no 307426 for the education of children.

Pinewood School

Bourton, Swindon, Wiltshire SN6 8HZ
Tel: 01793 782205 Fax: 01793 783476

Head Mr H G C Boddington
Founded 1875
Type Preparatory
Religious denomination Church of England
Members of IAPS, ISIS
Age range 4 – 13 *Boarders from* 8
No of pupils (day) 162 *(boarding)* 34
Girls 72; *Boys* 124
Fees per term (day) from £950; *(boarding)* £2,650
Fees per annum (day) from £2,850; *(boarding)* £7,950

Pinewood offers the advantages of a small school (average class size is 14) with outstanding facilities, set in splendid rural surroundings. The school is divided between day children and boarders; both boys and girls flourish in the happy, caring atmosphere. A major building programme has recently produced a new music school, art room and workshop, as well as classrooms, kitchens and changing rooms. Academic results are impressive, with scholarships gained to senior schools and individual attention offered to the weaker pupil. A wide range of games and activities mean that every child is able to find an area of enjoyment and, hopefully, of excellence. A new and successful development has been a pre-preparatory department started in September 1993.
Entry requirements: assessment at 7+. Interview with headmaster.

Stonar School

Cottles Park, Atworth, Near Melksham, Wiltshire SN12 8NT
Tel: 01225 702309 Fax: 01225 790830

Head Mrs S Hopkinson BA (Oxon)
Founded 1895
Type Girls' independent
Religious denomination Church of England
Age range 4 – 18 *Boarders from* 8
No of pupils (day) 225; *(boarding)* 255
Girls 480
Junior 79; *Senior* 307; *Sixth form* 104
Fees per term (day) £780 – £1,763; *(boarding)* £2,914 – £3,182
Fees per annum (day) £2,340 – £5,289; *(boarding)* £8,742 – £9,546

Profile: Stonar is a user-friendly school preparing today's girls for life in the 21st century. The school combines traditional values and emphasises sound learning in a structured and purposeful community with access to up-to-the-minute IT, industrial know-how, sensitive and well-informed careers advice and a rich provision of extra-curricular opportunities in drama, music and sport. As the venue of the annual British ISODE competition Stonar enjoys national renown for its equestrianism.
Entry: at four to ten by informal interview, at 11 – 13 by entry exam in Common Entrance; at 14 – 18 by interview and school reference.
Curriculum: based on National Curriculum plus early emphasis on basic literacy and numeracy. French taught from the age of six and Latin from nine. Computer network. Senior girls take eight to ten GCSE subject. A levels offered in most GCSE subjects plus business studies, politics and social biology. Eighty five per cent of leavers go on to higher education.
Scholarships available. Specialised help for small number of dyslexic pupils.

Ackworth School

Ackworth, Pontefract, West Yorkshire WF7 7LT
Tel: 01977 611401 Fax: 01977 616225

Head Martin J Dickinson MA (Cantab)
Founded 1779
Type Boarding and day
Religious denomination Society of Friends (Quakers)
Members of HMC, SHMIS, BSA, ISIS
Age range junior 7 – 11; senior 11 – 18 *Boarders from* 11
No of pupils (day) 265; *(boarding)* 140
Girls 253 *Boys* 179
Fees per term (day) junior school £951; senior school £1,772; *(boarding)* £3,111

The original 18th century buildings provide a spacious and striking focal point for an up-to-date and forward-looking school which is extremely well-resourced. A staffing ratio of 1:10 brings an emphasis on individual development which underpins the school's academic success (90 per cent pass rate at A level in 1995). The school offers a wide range of extra-curricular activities with outstanding sporting and musical activities. Ackworth is a well-ordered and happy school.

Entry is by academic test. Scholarships (academic, music, art) or assisted places available.

Ampleforth College Junior School

The Castle, Gilling East, York, Yorkshire YO6 4HP
Tel: 01439 788238 Fax: 01439 788538

Head Rev J A Sierla OSB
Founded 1914
Type Independent preparatory
Religious denomination Roman Catholic
Members of IAPS
Age range 8 – 13
No of pupils (day) 13; *(boarding)* 107
Boys 120
Fees per term (day) £1,725 – £2,180; *(boarding)* £2,805
Fees per annum (day) £5,175 – £6,540; *(boarding)* £8,415

Curriculum: full range of subjects aimed towards GCSE, including sciences, languages, mathematics, classics, art, design, IT and music (choral and instrumental).
Entry requirements: interview and academic assessment.
Examinations offered: Ampleforth Entrance Examination and scholarships.

Academic and leisure facilities: a 14th-century castle converted to a fine country house with spacious grounds facing Ampleforth College across the valley, with its own playing fields, sports hall, golf course, and indoor heated pool. Sports include rugby, cricket, swimming, golf, riding and archery. Musically strong with two choirs, an orchestra, and chamber group.
The Ampleforth Abbey Trust is a registered religious and educational charity.

Ashville College

Harrogate, North Yorkshire HG2 9JP
Tel: 01423 566358 Fax: 01423 505142

Head M H Crosby
Founded 1877
Type Independent co-educational day and boarding
Religious denomination Methodist
Members of HMC
Age range 4 – 18 *Boarders from* 7
No of pupils (day) 550; *(boarding)* 150
Girls 290; *Boys* 410
Junior 165 *Senior* 415 *Sixth form* 120
Fees per term (day) Pre-prep £800; Junior £1,050 – £1,300; Senior £1,560; *(boarding)* Junior £2,658; Senior £2,918
Fees per annum (day) Pre-prep £2,400; Junior £3,150 – £3,900; Senior £4,680; *(boarding)* Junior £7,974; Senior £8,754

Ashville College is a co-educational day and boarding school on the edge of Harrogate: pupils age range is 4 – 18. It is a Methodist School and retains close links with the Methodist Church.

Its grounds are extensive and attractive with fine views into south Yorkshire. Facilities are excellent: boarding houses are modern, well-equipped and up-to-date. There is a fine sports hall and swimming pool, purpose-built music and drama centre. The latest addition is a sixth form centre with study and recreational provision for A level and BTEC students.

Class sizes average about 22, though that decreases the higher up the school the pupil goes.

The atmosphere of the school is purposeful, students are encouraged to develop their talents and fulfil their potential.

Aysgarth School

Bedale, North Yorkshire DL8 1TF
Tel: 01677 450240 Fax: 01677 450736

Head Mr J C Hodgkinson MA
Founded 1877
Type Preparatory
Religious denomination Church of England
Member of IAPS
Age range 4 – 13 *Boarders from* 8
No of pupils (day) 5 *(main school)*; 23 *(pre-preparatory)*; *(boarding)* 90 *(main school)*
Girls (pre-prep) 7; *Boys* 111
Fees per term (pre-preparatory) £800; *(main school, day)* £1,920; *(boarding)* £2,742
Fees per annum (pre-preparatory) £2,400; *(main school, day)* £5,760; *(boarding)* £8,226

Aysgarth School is a boarding school for boys aged from 8 – 13. The school stands in 50 acres of lovely grounds in the foothills of the Yorkshire Dales. There is a good train service north and south and boys are escorted to Edinburgh, London and stations in between at the beginning and end of terms and exeats. A minibus runs to Dumfriesshire. Boys are prepared in small classes for all the major public schools. The buildings are purpose-built and fully-equipped. There is a fine chapel, a modern sports hall and a thriving music department. About three quarters of the boys learn a musical instrument. The facilities include extensive playing fields, rifle range, heated indoor swimming pool, squash court, fives courts and tennis courts. The main games are cricket, soccer and rugby football. A pre-preparatory department opened in September 1993 for boys and girls up to the age of eight.

Ayton School

High Green, Great Ayton, North Yorkshire TS9 6BN
Tel: 01642 722141 Fax: 01642 724044

Head Alice Meager BA (Hons), MA
Founded 1841
Type Co-educational
Religious denomination Quaker
Members of GBA, SHA
Age range 4 – 18 *Boarders from 9*
Girls 106; *Boys* 143
Junior 84; *Senior* 140
Fees per term (day) £815 – £1,475 *(boarding)*
£2,785 (weekly); £3,165 (full)

This small school is situated on the northern edge of the North Yorkshire Moors National Park, yet close to major road, bus, rail and air terminals. Ayton offers good facilities from the early years through to GCSE. A broad general curriculum avoiding narrow specialisation is provided and GCSE science is delivered as three separate sciences. The school is well known for its achievements in drama and music. Most pupils are day scholars from the area south of Cleveland, but the boarding house caters for weekly and full boarders from nine years of age. At every level we consider individual attention and a personal caring attitude to be all important. The school uses its own qualifying examinations in English and mathematics and a confidential reference from the child's present school when considering entries. Some bursary scholarship help may be available.

Brantwood Independent School for Girls

1 Kenwood Bank, Sheffield, Yorkshire S7 1NU
Tel: 0114 258 1747 Fax: 0114 258 1847

Head Mrs E M Swynnerton BA (Hons), DipEd
Founded 1910
Type Independent
Members of ISAI
Age range 4 – 16
No of pupils (day) 190
Girls 190
Junior 90; *Senior* 100
Fees per term (day) £910 – £1,125
Fees per annum (day) £2,730 – £3,375

Brantwood School offers its pupils small class sizes and individual attention.
Senior school curriculum: English language, English literature, history, geography, French, German, mathematics, IT, technology, physics, chemistry, biology, RE, art, music, drama, physical education, games.
Junior school curriculum: English, mathematics, science, technology, IT, history, geography, RE, art, speech training, drama, ballet, music, physical education, games, French.
Examination Boards: NEAB, ULEAC, MEG, IDTA, LAMDA. Awards: BAGA. St John's, swimming awards.
Senior school entry: entrance test. *Junior entry*: individual interview.
The school believes in a system which values each child, building on their strengths and supporting weaknesses. We encourage individual development and aim to maximise success in public examinations.

Giggleswick School

Settle, North Yorkshire BD24 0DE
Tel: 01729 823545 Fax: 01729 824187

Head Anthony Millard
Founded 1512
Type Boarding and day
Religious denomination Church of England
Members of HMC
Age range 3 – 18 *Boarders from* 8
No of pupils (day) 74 *(boarding)* 363
Girls 158 *Boys* 279
Junior 132 *Senior* 187 *Sixth form* 118

Giggleswick School, set in the heart of magnificent Dales scenery, has a new day pre-preparatory department, Mill House (3 – 7), a preparatory school, Catteral Hall, (8 – 13) and the senior school, (13 – 18). We offer high academic standards and a great deal more. The school believes wholeheartedly in boarding and offers a full programme of activities in the evenings and at weekends. Day pupils can take advantage of all the benefits of boarding.

Curriculum, examinations, entry, scholarships: National Curriculum. Usual A levels plus theatre studies, sports studies, design and economics and politics. New alternative post 16, 1 year course, 'The Development Sixth'. Entry by interview and tests. Scholarships and assisted places.

Academic, leisure and boarding facilities: well-resourced departments. Indoor swimming pool, sports halls, squash and five courts, fitness room and climbing wall. Extensive playing fields and facilities for outdoor pursuits. Strong art, music, drama and design.

Superb refurbishment programme has set excellent standards of personal accommodation and communal facilities.

Harrogate Ladies' College

Clarence Drive, Harrogate, North Yorkshire HG1 2QG
Tel: 01423 504543 Fax: 01423 568893

Acting Head Mr Geoffrey Hazell MA (Cantab)
Founded 1893
Type Senior boarding and day
Religious denomination Church of England
Members of GSA, GBGSA, BSA, ISIS
Age range 10 – 18 *Boarders from* 10 – 18
No of pupils (day) 150; *(boarding)* 200
Girls 350
Senior 255 *Sixth form* 95

Situated close to the town centre, the college enjoys a secure residential location with beautiful countryside nearby.

It has a reputation for excellent all–round education and offers over 20 GCSE and A level subjects. Academic results are impressive and outstanding academic and sporting facilities include a design and technology centre, art room, music block, swimming pool, sports hall, multi-gym and a sixth form centre. Emphasis given to pastoral care and the breadth of extra-curricular activities ensures a busy and fulfilling lifestyle.

Entry is by entrance test and school report. Scholarships, bursaries and assisted places are available.

The Mount School

Dalton Terrace, York, North Yorkshire YO2 4DD
Tel: 01904 622275 Fax: 01904 627518

Head Barbara J Windle MA (Cantab)
Founded 1831
Type Independent girls
Religious denomination Society of Friends (Quaker)
Age range 3 – 18 *Boarders from* 11
No of pupils (day) Senior 115; Junior 76; *(boarding)* 120
Girls 235
Senior 171; *Sixth form* 64
Fees per term (day) Senior £1,985; Junior £790 – £1,225; *(boarding)* Senior only £3,230
Fees per annum (day) Senior £5,955; Junior £2,370 – £3,675; *(boarding)* Senior only £9,690

Main fee is fully inclusive of all standard requirements. Broad-based curriculum leading to GCSE core of English, maths, science and a modern language with wide choice of additional subjects. Choice of 20 A levels with combination of A level and A/S level possible (all follow a full general studies course). Strong academic, music and drama tradition leads 99 per cent of sixth form leavers to degree courses, including Oxbridge.

Facilities: excellent facilities for music, science, and maths, arts and technology. Specialist classrooms for all; sixth form studies. Beautiful grounds, sports facilities, 25 metre indoor pool. IBM compatible computers available throughout the school (one computer for five girls). Boarding, weekly and day school, separate sixth form house with its own study area. Direct train link with Manchester airport and easy access to Leeds/Bradford. London an hour and forty minutes by train.

Close to York's historic centre, The Mount makes good use of the city's cultural activities and offers an ethos of high standards, hard work, friendliness and all the benefits of a small, caring Quaker school.

Pocklington School

West Green, Pocklington, York, North Yorkshire YO4 2NJ
Tel: 01759 303125 Fax: 01759 306366

Head Mr J N D Gray
Founded 1514
Type Co-educational independent
Religious denomination Church of England
Members of HMC
Age range 7 – 18 *Boarders from* 10
No of pupils (day) 610; *(boarding)* 143
Girls 285; *Boys* 468
Junior 125; *Senior* 628; *Sixth form* 201
Fees per term (day) £1,340 – £1,614; *(boarding)*
£2,399 – £2,896

Curriculum: a full range of academic subjects is studied up to GCSE.

Entry requirements and procedures: by school entrance tests, by examinations by Common Entrance at 13+ or by interview and school report. Entry to A level courses is by acquisition of five GCSEs at grade C or above and by interview.

Examinations offered: GCSE, A level, AS levels in some subjects.

Academic and leisure facilities: full academic facilities, indoor heated swimming pool, 70 acre grounds, sports hall, squash courts, lawn tennis courts, CDT centre incorporating art, theatre, library, sixth form centre, boarders social area.

Scholarships: at junior school, 11, 13 and 16 for academic. At 11, 13 and 16 for art, music and design.

Boarding facilities: all boarding houses are spacious and comfortable and have been recently refurbished. Boarders' social centre (five roomed cottage).

Queen Ethelburga's College

Thorpe Underwood Hall, Ouseburn, York, Yorkshire YO5 9SZ
Tel: 01423 331480 Fax: 01423 331007

Head Mrs G L Richardson
Founded 1912
Type Girls' boarding and day school
Religious denomination Church of England
Age range 2½ – 18 *Boarders from* 6 – 18
No of pupils (day) 140 *(boarding)* 160
Girls 276; *Boys* 24
Junior 100; *Senior* 155; *Sixth form* 45
Fees per term (day) £499 – £2,259; *(boarding)*
£2,359 – £3,499
Fees per annum (day) £1,497 – £6,777;
(boarding) £7,077 – £10,497

Broad-range curriculum following National Curriculum's key subjects. Entry to preparatory school by assessment and interview. Entry to senior school by Common Entrance and interview. Prepares pupils in preparatory school for Common Entrance and girls in senior school for GCSE and A level exams. BHASI stages 1, 2 and 3 in own equestrian centre.

Purpose-built technical block housing science laboratories, home economics, art and design technology areas, lecture theatre. Leisure facilities include indoor heated pool, fitness area, own riding stables and sports pitches. Participation in Duke of Edinburgh Award Scheme and other outdoor pursuits.

Scholarships for academic excellence at 11, 12, 13, 16. Separate computer and business centres. Riding scholarship available from 8 – 16. New boarding area, experienced house staff. Own medical centre.

Queen Margaret's School

Escrick Park, York, Yorkshire YO4 6EU
Tel: 01904 728261 Fax: 01904 728150

Head Dr G A H Chapman
Founded 1901
Type Girls' independent boarding
Religious denomination Church of England
Members of GSA, BSA
Age range 11 – 18 *Boarders from* 11 – 18
No of pupils (day) 25; *(boarding)* 325
Girls All
Sixth form 100
Fees per term (day) £2,158; *(boarding)* £3,406
Fees per annum (day) £6,474; *(boarding)* £10,218

Queen Margaret's encourages excellence. Over 90 per cent of the girls are full boarders and enjoy a superb range of extra-curricular activities, particularly at weekends. A commitment to Christian and academic values earns it a first-class reputation and a high academic rating. Most girls enter the sixth form and proceed to higher education. Well-qualified staff help provide the friendly atmosphere which develops breadth as well as depth of education. The school has excellent facilities for creative and performing arts plus seven newly refurbished science laboratories. Physical education is an integral part of the curriculum and teams excel at lacrosse, hockey and tennis. There are all-weather tennis courts, two squash courts, indoor and outdoor swimming pools, a sports hall, riding school and a nine-hole golf course.

Queen Mary's School

Baldersby Park, Topcliffe, Thirsk, North Yorkshire YO7 3BZ
Tel: 01845 577425 Fax: 01854 577368

Heads Mr and Mrs P Belward
Founded 1925
Type Independent
Religious denomination Church of England
Members of IAPS, ISIS
Age range 3 – 16 *Boarders from* 7
No of pupils (day) 120; *(boarding)* 130
Girls 250
Junior 150; *Senior* 100
Fees per term (day) £645; *(boarding)* £2,510
Fees per annum (day) £1,935; *(boarding)* £7,530

Preparatory and senior boarding, weekly and day school for girls, with a lively nursery and pre-preparatory department, situated at Baldersby Park, a beautiful mansion in 40 acres of glorious Hambleton countryside of north Yorkshire.

At all ages girls have the benefit of being taught by highly qualified, dedicated staff. Teaching is to small groups in well-equipped rooms and every girl receives the individual attention to develop her mind and character to her full potential. Groups are arranged to cater for the full compass of ability and high standards are consistently achieved. Modern educational thinking is balanced with the best traditional practice. The four cornerstones of the school's founder of hard work, public spirit, trustworthiness, and good manners, strongly colour the character of everyday school life.

Academic and music scholarships are available at 11+, 12+ and 13+ to the value of one third fees per year.

For further information and prospectus please contact the school secretary.

Read School

Drax, Near Selby, North Yorkshire YO8 8NL
Tel: 01757 618248 Fax: 01757 617432

Head Mr A J Saddler MA
Type Independent co-educational boarding and day
Members of ISAI, ISIS, BSA
Age range 5 – 18 *Boarders from* 8
Junior 40; *Senior* 175; *Sixth form* 30
Fees per term (day) Pre-preparatory £865, Junior £1,100, Senior £1,205; *(boarding)* Junior £2,260, Senior £2,485

Curriculum: years 1–9: full, traditional curriculum incorporating best of National Curriculum. Years 10–11: GCSE; generous options scheme available. Sixth form: all traditional A level subjects available.

Entry requirements: places offered on basis of scholarship examinations, interview and school report.
Examinations offered: GCSE, A/S, A via NEAB, AEB.
Academic and sports facilities: the mostly Edwardian buildings have been modernised in recent years. Since 1980, a major additional building programme has been undertaken providing Moloney Hall, Norfolk House (residential) and refurbished laboratories and computer laboratory. A new teaching block for arts subjects was opened in 1993; new tennis courts built in 1993. New indoor sports area opened 1995.

Ripon Cathedral Choir School

Whitcliffe Lane, Ripon, North Yorkshire HG4 2LA
Tel: 01765 602134 Fax: 01765 608760

Head Mr R H Moore
Founded 1960
Type Independent
Religious denomination Church of England
Members of ISIS, IAPS, CSA
Age range 4½ – 13 *Boarders from* 8
No of pupils (day) 101; *(boarding)* 20
Girls 46; *Boys* 55
Fees per term (day) £1,110 – £1,615; *(boarding)* £2,045 – £2,205
Fees per annum (day) £3,330 – £4,845; *(boarding)* £6,135 – £6,615

Children aged 4½ – 7: are taught by formal and informal methods with a wide range of activities.

Children aged 8 – 13½: study all Common Entrance and scholarship subjects and also art and design, computing, music, physical education, games and swimming.
Entry requirements: interview.
Examinations offered: entry and Common Entrance (academic, music and art scholarships) to senior independent schools.
Academic and sports facilities: spacious playing fields, tennis court and large sports hall. Activities include drama, Cubs, Scouts, Brownies and Guides, chess, computing, bicycling and sport. Music is taught to a high level with a wide range of instruments and ensembles.

Rishworth School

Rishworth, West Yorkshire HX6 4QA
Tel: 01422 822217 Fax: 01422 823231

Head M J Elford BSc
Founded 1724
Type Co-educational day and boarding
Religious denomination Church of England
Members of SHMIS, GBA
Age range 4 – 18 *Boarders from* 11
No of pupils (boarding) 134
Girls 274; *Boys* 363
Fees per term (day) £798 – £1,600; *(boarding)*
£2,660 – £ 3,096

Average size of class: 15
Teacher/pupil ratio: 1:12

Curriculum: full range of subjects leading to preparation for GCSE at all levels, A level, university entrance, and vocational courses.
Entry requirements and procedures: entry at 11 by entrance exam. Entry at other times subject to interview and satisfactory reports from previous school, some scholarships and bursaries available.

Rishworth School stands in 130 acres of a beautiful Pennine valley, six miles south-west of Halifax and close to the M62.

Rishworth School is a registered charity existing to provide high quality education.

St Hilda's School

Sneaton Castle, Whitby, North Yorkshire YO21 3QN
Tel: 01947 600051 Fax: 01947 603490

Head Mrs M Blain BEd, MA
Founded 1914
Type Independent co-educational
Religious denomination Church of England
Members of ISAI, SHA
Age range 2½ – 18 *Boarders from* 7
No of pupils (day) 145; *(boarding)* 96
Girls 148; *Boys* 93
Junior 113; *Senior* 128; *Sixth form* 34
Fees per term (day) £925 – £1,525; *(boarding)*
£2,360 – £2,825
Fees per annum (day) £2,670 – £4,350;
(boarding) £6,600 – £8,070

Average size of class: 13. Teacher/pupil ratio:
1:8.
Curriculum: broad range of subjects at GCSE and A level to include music, theatre studies, IT.
Entry requirements and procedures: by interview if under 11 years, by school examination 11 – 13 years. Older pupils to sixth form on GCSE results and references.
Academic, art, music and drama scholarships available at 11, 13 and 16 years.

Scarborough College

Filey Road, Scarborough, North Yorkshire YO11 3BA
Tel: 01723 360620 Fax: 01723 377265

Head T Kirkup
Founded 1898
Type Co-educational day and boarding
Religious denomination Christian non-denominational
Members of SHMIS, IAPS, GBA, BSA
Age range 4 – 18 *Boarders from* 6
No of pupils (day) 485 *(boarding)* 94
Girls 259 *Boys* 320
Junior 166 *Senior* 413 *Sixth form* 85
Fees per term (day) £784 – £1,637 *(boarding)* £2,179 – £3,019
Fees per annum (day) £2,352 – £4,911 *(boarding)* £6,537 – £9,057

The curriculum takes due account of the National Curriculum but is more rounded. Entry to Lisvane is by interview and aptitude test and to college by competitive examination at 11+ and 13+ or by reference, interview and aptitude at other stages. For public examinations, 19 subjects are offered for GCSE and 17 at A level.

Facilities at both schools are excellent for teaching, sport and extra-curricular activities. Newly added buildings include a music, science and technology block at Lisvane and a multi-purpose hall at the college. These are part of an on-going, ten-year strategic plan.

The teaching complement is 50 allowing each pupil to achieve a great deal of individual attention. The framework of rules is simple and straightforward. It is in this disciplined but friendly environment that the individual can prosper best.

Rathdown School

Glenageary, County Dublin, Ireland
Tel: 00 353 1 2853133

Head Miss Stella G Mew MA, HDipEd (Hons)
Founded 1973
Type Independent school
Religious denomination Protestant (all faiths accepted)
Members of Irish Schoolmasters Association, European Secondary Heads' Association
Age range 3½ – 18
No of pupils (day) 320; *(boarding)* 90
Fees per term (day) junior school IR£285 – IR£520; senior school IR£550; *(boarding)* IR£1,650

Rathdown School offers superb value for UK or overseas pupils as it is grant-aided, so fees remain low while standards are high. Senior pupils gain direct entry to UK universities (including Oxbridge) with Leaving Certificate qualifications. Results are excellent, and there is a wide range of subject choice.

Sports and music are well catered for, and boarding and school facilities extremely good.

The school prospectus details all courses and options.

St Leonards and St Katharines Schools

St Andrews, Fife KY16 9QU
Tel: 01334 472126 Fax: 01334 476152

Head Mrs Mary James
Type Boarding
Religious denomination Non-denominational
Members of GSA, GBGSA, SHA, ISBA, HAS
Age range 7 – 18; *Boarders from* 7
No of pupils (day) 67; *(boarding)* 265
Girls 332
Senior 233; *Sixth form* 100
Fees per term (day) St Katharines – from £1,100;
St Leonards – 2,075; *(boarding)* St Katharines –
£2,974; St Leonards – £3,925
Fees per annum (day) St Katharines – from
£3,300; St Leonards – £6,225; *(boarding)* St
Katharines £8,922; St Leonards – £11,775

A broad range of subjects is offered including English, mathematics, the three sciences, design and technology, IT, art and design, three mainstream languages, classics, history, geography, economics and politics, physical education and religious studies. The academic curriculum produces outstanding results. The majority of girls stay on into the sixth form and thereafter 95 per cent or more proceed to university. This curriculum, together with the personal and social education programme run by an outstanding careers department, is thereafter buttressed by a series of activities. A specially-built music school enables orchestra, choirs and other musical groups to run on a formal and informal basis. There are regular visits abroad by choirs and orchestras. The standard of drama in the school is also extremely strong and in 1995 a drama group from St Leonards won a major award at the Edinburgh Festival Fringe. There are three squash courts, an indoor swimming pool, recently refurbished, and extensive playing fields as well as a gymnasium. The standard of games is high and girls are selected each year to represent Scotland in lacrosse, fencing or athletics. The ski team participates annually in the British Schools' Invitation Ski Race in France. There is a sailing club and the school has its own golf club, as also it is heavily engaged in the Duke of Edinburgh Award Scheme. The enthusiastic involvement of pupils in these activities builds the confidence which is the hallmark of a St Leonards' girl. Pupils reside in boarding houses and the level of pastoral care is excellent.

St Katharines, the junior school of St Leonards, shares its ethos and facilities. Entrance is at 7+ for both boarding and day pupils. St Leonards and St Katharines are linked for fee purposes with Merchiston Castle School and the schools collaborate both socially and academically. Entry into St Leonards is at any age by means of Common Entrance or the school's own examination. Entry into the sixth form is by means of six GCSEs at grade C or above. Both schools follow an English curriculum. Several scholarships and bursaries are available and St Leonards and St Katharines participate in the Assisted Places Scheme. The schools are a registered charity and exist to provide an excellent education for girls.

Albyn School for Girls

17–23 Queens Road, Aberdeen, Grampian AB9 2PA
Tel: 01224 322408 Fax: 01224 209173

Head Miss Norma H Smith
Founded 1867
Type Girls' day school
Religious denomination Non-denominational
Members of GBGSA, HAS, SHA
Age range 2½ – 18
No of pupils (day) 425
Girls 415; *Boys* 10
Junior 185; *Senior* 240; *Sixth form* 70 (V and VI) (included in 240)
Fees per term (day) £770 – £1,308
Fees per annum (day) £2,310 – £3,925
After-school club facilities and all-year-round nursery.

Curriculum: lower school: follows the Scottish 5 – 14 programme. Specialist teaching in music, art, physical education, home economics and French.

Upper school: general course in UI and II leading to Scottish examinations (standard grade, higher grade, CSYS and SCOTVEC modules).

Entry: school examination, interview and/or school reports.
Academic and leisure facilities: set in attractive Victorian buildings housing classrooms, spacious library and art studios with purpose-built infant/nursery department, hall with music/drama facilities. Gymnasium, music room, home economics block, new laboratories (completed August 1992) and computing laboratory opened August 1994. Spacious playground, tennis/netball courts on site with playing fields.

Extra-curricular activities are many and varied and include debating, choir, orchestra, art club, drama, chess, scripture union, mathematics and classics clubs, the Duke of Edinburgh Award Scheme, young enterprise and many sporting activities.
Scholarships: scholarships for entry to UI awarded for outstanding talent (eg art, music, academic).

Albyn participates in the assisted places scheme.

Gordonstoun School & Aberlour House

Gordonstoun School, Elgin, Grampian IV30 2RF
Tel: 01343 830445 Fax: 01343 830241

Head Mr M C S-R Pyper BA
Founded 1934
Type Co-educational boarding and day
Religious denomination Inter-denominational
Members of HMC, GBA, BSA
Age range 8 – 18 Boarders from 8
No of pupils (day) 40; *(boarding)* 520
Girls 260; *Boys* 300
Junior 120; *Senior* 440; *Sixth form* 180
Fees per term (day) £1,880 – £2,603; *(boarding)* £2,745 – £4,035
Fees per annum (day) £5,640 – £7,809; *(boarding)* £8,235 – £12,105

Both schools, founded by Kurt Hahn in the 1930s, aim to prepare young people for life in a changing world. Thus an education to ensure the best academic qualifications sees equal emphasis placed on the development of personal qualities through the encouragement of the cultural, physical, social and spiritual faculties of every boy and girl.

The school estates set in Morayshire and Strathspey provide environments of unparalleled opportunity with an expectation to participate in and contribute to an all-embracing curriculum. Our motto is 'Plus est en vous' and we aim to prove the truth of this to all who come here. There are also international summer school courses offering EFL, adventure, sports, computers.

St Margaret's School for Girls

17 Albyn Place, Aberdeen, Grampian AB9 1RH
Tel: 01224 584466 Fax: 01224 585600

Head Miss L M Ogilvie
Founded 1846
Type Independent girls' day
Religious denomination Inter-denominational
Members of GSA, GBGSA, HAS, SHA, ISBA
Age range 3 – 18
No of pupils (day) 421
Girls 416; *Boys* 5
Junior 187; *Senior* 234; *Sixth form* 109 (V and VI)
Fees per term (day) £232 – £1,234
Fees per annum (day) £696 – £3,702

The curriculum is broad and leads to the Scottish Examination Board Standard Grade, Higher and CSYS examinations, with equal opportunities in sciences, and arts.

Entry is by test and interview. One scholarship is available in VI Senior.

St Margaret's has excellent facilities including well-equipped specialist accommodation. Extensive playing fields at Summerhill are currently being upgraded with the addition of a new pavilion and a new classroom extension is underway at Albyn Place.

Extra-curricular opportunities include Young Investigators, Young Engineers, drama, debating, orchestras, choirs and Duke of Edinburgh Award Scheme. The school is small enough to care about the individual, and develop her potential, yet large enough to provide a varied curriculum. Girls are taught to respect others, to be adaptable to change, aim for the highest standards, and have a sense of fun.

Fettes College

Carrington Road, Edinburgh, Midlothian EH4 1QX
Tel: 0131 332 2281 Fax: 0131 332 3081

Head Mr M T Thyne MA, FRSE
Founded 1870
Type Independent co-educational boarding and day school
Religious denomination Inter-denominational
Members of GBA, HMC, BSA, ISBA
Age range 10 – 18 *Boarders from* 10
No of pupils (day) 109; *(boarding)* 378
Girls 211; *Boys* 264
Junior 101; *Senior* 384; *Sixth form* 164
Fees per term (day) £1,745 – £2,745; *(boarding)* £2,785 – £4,085
Fees per annum (day) £5,235 – £8,235; *(boarding)* £8,355 – £12,255

Curriculum: GCSE – (Midland Examining Group and NEA). Core subjects: English, mathematics, French, religious studies. Optional subjects: physics, chemistry, biology, history, geography, Latin, French, German, Greek, Spanish, drama, art, technology, music, PE, design and technology.

A level (Oxford and Cambridge Board and London) and Scottish Higher. A full range of subjects at each. Pass rate for 1995 in A level 99 per cent, Higher 82 per cent, GCSE 21 per cent A* and 52 per cent A* and A grades. Ten per cent of upper sixth leavers go to Oxford or Cambridge and 95 per cent of all leavers go on to higher education.

The college provides excellent facilities for games, art, technology, music and drama. Principal ages of entry are 10 – 13 and 16 through scholarship, Common Entrance, or own entrance examinations.

Fettes is situated on an 85-acre campus, with extensive playing fields, and is near the centre of Edinburgh – one of the most culturally active cities in the world. There is excellent access by road, rail and air.

Loretto

Musselburgh, Midlothian EH21 7RE
Tel: 0131 665 2567 Fax: 0131 653 2773

Head Keith J Budge
Founded 1827
Type Independent
Religious denomination Non-denominational
Age range co-educational 8 – 18 *Boarders from* 8
No of pupils (day) 10; *(boarding)* 310
Girls 65; *Boys* 255
Junior 80; *Senior* 320; *Sixth form* 155
Fees per term (day) £2,580 (£1,946*); *(boarding)* £3,870 (£2,900*)
Fees per annum (day) £7,740 (£5,838*); *(boarding)* £11,610 (£8,700*)
* Junior school fees

Loretto School lies in the outskirts of the small town of Musselburgh, on the Firth of Forth. Musselburgh is the birthplace of the game of golf and there are 40 golf courses within a radius of 15 miles.

Here Lorettonian boys and girls aged from 8 to 18 have the freedom of 80 acres of lawns, trees and playing fields whilst also being close to the main A1 south, only six miles from Edinburgh, and less than half an hour's drive from Edinburgh Airport.

Loretto remains a deliberately small school with 320 boys and girls aged 13 to 18 – the Upper School – and 80 boys and girls aged 8 to 13 – the Nippers. We firmly believe that full co-education will prepare Lorettonians for the adult world of their generation. A school of this small size allows each pupil to be both known by everyone and feel part of a community, whilst at the same time being large enough to be able to offer the widest possible range of academic, cultural and athletic opportunities. Within the community, much emphasis is placed on the maintenance of Christian values and standards.

The school has developed steadily over the years to meet the changing requirements of contemporary education. Specially designed boarding houses, a modern theatre, a study library as well as a fiction library, a sports hall, squash courts and new classroom have all been built.

An impression of the buildings and grounds may be had from the prospectus. However, a visit to the school for a discussion with the headmaster followed by a tour of the facilities with present pupils is needed to gain an insight into the special and happy atmosphere of Loretto.

Merchiston Castle School

Colinton, Edinburgh, Midlothian EH13 0PU
Tel: 0131 441 1567 Fax: 0131 441 6060

Head D M Spawforth MA (Oxon)
Founded 1833
Type Boys' boarding and day
Religious denomination Inter-denominational
Members of HMC
Age range 10 – 18 *Boarders from* 10
No of pupils (day) 122; *(boarding)* 284
Boys 406
Junior 68; *Senior* 338; *Sixth form* 141
Fees per term (day) £1,770 – £2,480; *(boarding)*
£2,770 – £3,835
Fees per annum (day) £5,310 – £7,440;
(boarding) £8,310 – £11,505

Balanced curriculum leading to GCSE, A levels or Highers. Very wide range of subjects offered. Subject specialities and academic track record: English, history, languages, maths, science, technology, music, art and design, drama – strongly featured. Also careers guidance. A level pass rate – 100 per cent. Examinations offered including boards are: GCSE (MEG), A level (Oxford and Cambridge), Higher (SEB). Destinations and career prospects of leavers: 87 per cent go on to degree courses including Oxford and Cambridge.

Academic and leisure facilities include a chapel with full-time chaplain, libraries, computing and electronics departments, music school, art and design centre, theatre, careers centre, science block, large sports hall, large indoor swimming pool, squash courts, fives courts, tennis courts, extensive playing fields – rugby, cricket, athletics, Combined Cadet Force, Duke of Edinburgh Award Scheme, work experience and leadership courses.

One of Scotland's leading independent schools, situated in Colinton, four miles from the centre of Edinburgh. Set in 100 acres of exceptionally beautiful grounds close to the Pentland Hills.

St Denis and Cranley School

Ettrick Road, Edinburgh, Lothian EH10 5BJ
Tel: 0131 229 1500 Fax: 0131 229 5753

Head Mrs Jennifer M Munro MA, DipRE
Founded 1858
Type Independent girls' boarding and day
Religious denomination Inter-denominational
Members of GSA, SHA, HAS, ISBA
Age range 5 – 18 *Boarders from* 8
No of pupils (day) 110; *(boarding)* 50
Girls 180; *Boys* Nursery only
Junior 50; *Senior* 110; *Sixth form* 35 – 40
Fees per term (day) £725 – £1,495; *(boarding)*
£2,380 – £3,050
Fees per annum (day) £2,175 – £4,485;
(boarding) £7,140 – £9,150

St Denis and Cranley School, set in lovely grounds in the heart of Edinburgh, has a strong tradition of high achievement in all areas of school life. Small classes throughout the school, and a vital and friendly atmosphere where the individual is valued, help each girl to fulfil her potential whatever her ability and to grow in self-confidence and personal integrity.

Entry requirements: interview for lower juniors, test papers for girls 8 – 12. Report for girls over 12. Interview where possible. Separate papers for scholarship entry – general, art, music at age 12 or 16.
Examinations offered: SCE: standard, higher, sixth year studies; GCSE: A levels; RSA; LAMDA and AB.
Academic and leisure facilities: all facilities are on one site including boarding houses, academic buildings, new science and technology block, sports hall and assembly hall/theatre.

Hockey, tennis, badminton, squash, basketball, athletics and swimming are offered. A wide range of extra-curricular activities are available, including choir, orchestra and instrumental groups, drama, skiing, riding and the Duke of Edinburgh Award Scheme. This session Teviot Playcare has been opened: an all-day childcare facility for children of 3 months upwards for 50 weeks of the year.

The following independent college also offers GCSEs. Please refer to the Independent Sixth-Form Colleges section for details:

Basil Paterson College, Edinburgh

Glenalmond College

Perth, Tayside PH1 3RY
Tel: 01738 880442 Fax: 01738 880410

Head Mr I G Templeton
Founded 1841
Type Independent day and boarding
Religious denomination Episcopelian/non-denominational
Members of HMC
Age range 12 – 18 *Boarders from* 12
No of pupils (day) 34, *(boarding)* 255
Girls 53; *Boys* 236
Junior 18; *Senior* 153; *Sixth form* 118
Fees per term (day) £1,995 – £2,600; *(boarding)* £2,995 – £3,990
Fees per annum (day) £5,895 – £7,980; *(boarding)* £8,985 – £11,970

Full range of subjects to GCSE, choice of A level or Scottish Highers in sixth form.

Common Entrance, junior and sixth form entrance exams.

Very strong music, art, theatre.

Splendid facilities for technology and there are excellent computing opportunities.

Golf course, salmon river, artificial ski-slope, indoor and outdoor shooting, skiing, water sports enhance a wide range of sports facilities. Glenalmond is also strong on public speaking. There are good European links.

Easy access to Glasgow and Edinburgh and to airports.

Art, music and academic scholarships and bursaries are available for service children and clergy children.

The college is a registered charity providing quality education for boys and girls.

Lathallan School

Botherton Castle, Johnsaven, By Montrose, Tayside DD10 0HN
Tel: 01561 362220 Fax: 01561 361695

Head Mr Philip Fawkes
Founded 1928
Type Preparatory
Religious denomination Inter-denominational
Members of IAPS
Age range 5 – 13 *Boarders from* 7
No of pupils (day) 80; *(boarding)* 60; *total* 140
Girls 55; *Boys* 85
Fees per term (day) £1,239 – £1,778; *(boarding)* £2,749 – £2,812

Lathallan Preparatory School is superbly situated in a baronial castle on the north east Scottish coast. Standing in 60 acres of playing fields, woodland and private beach, the school is within easy access of Dyce Airport and Montrose station.

Lathallan has an excellent academic reputation and has taken an initiative in the teaching of modern languages.

The standard of accommodation is high, the children enjoy good health and a full and rewarding day, and the school has all the benefits of a rural location.

There are many supervised evening and weekend activities, among them skiing, ornithology, needlework, fishing, archery, badminton, carpentry and leatherwork. Ballet, horse-riding, Scottish country dancing, creative arts, piping, drumming and judo are taught by qualified instructors, and two thirds of the children learn at least one musical instrument.

Parents are encouraged to feel that they share in the education of their children and boarding school becomes an extension of home, enriching family relationships. Lathallan has charitable status and exists to provide the highest quality of education; it has all the hallmarks of a well-established and successful preparatory school.

Morrison's Academy

Ferntower Road, Crieff, Tayside PH7 3AN
Tel: 01764 653885 Fax: 01764 655411

Head Mr H A Ashmall MA, MLitt, FIMgt, MMIM
Founded 1860
Type Co-educational day and boarding
Religious denomination Inter-denominational
Members of HMC, GBA, HAS, ISBA
Age range 5 – 18 *Boarders from* 8
No of pupils (day) 426; *(boarding)* 79
Girls 219; *Boys* 286
Junior 134; *Senior* 303; *Sixth form* 68
Fees per term (day) £750 – £1,215; *(boarding)* £3,173 – £3,530
Fees per annum (day) £2,250 – £3,645; *(boarding)* £9,519 – £10,590

Location: Morrison's Academy, within easy reach of Edinburgh and Glasgow airports is situated in a small town in central Scotland, whose inhabitants take a pride in the school's achievements, as well as an interest in the students from other countries who have added so much to the community that is Morrison's and Crieff.

Profile: Morrison's Academy was established in 1860 to provide education opportunities for day and boarding pupils. Five other teaching blocks covering both primary and secondary syllabuses now complement the original old school building, on a ten acre site.

Facilities: eleven modern science laboratories and five computer laboratories give students a strong introduction to these subjects while a music centre was opened in 1990. An on-site games complex includes an indoor swimming pool, a gymnasium and a games hall and there are seven superb all-weather tennis courts. A few minutes from the teaching campus the school has 30 acres of playing fields and two modern pavilions.

Accommodation: boarding is available from eight years to 19 years. The separate houses for girls and boys are supervised by housemistresses and housemasters directly responsible to the principal. Accommodation is excellent with facilities both for study and relaxation. With the help of the boarders' social club, young people from many nations have the opportunity to live and work together in a learning atmosphere.

Courses: the school has an excellent record of academic success and prepares students for the Scottish Examination Board's examinations as well as London A levels.

Former students have gone on to universities throughout the United Kingdom and professional appointments throughout the world.

We are proud to report our students have a distinguished record of success. This success has come from shared hard work by them and their teachers, the excellent learning facilities provided, the secure environment in which they live and their allocation to a senior counsellor who monitors progress and gives assistance with university applications.

Please contact the Principal for further information.

The school is a recognised charity providing education.

Rannoch School

Rannoch, By Pitlochry, Tayside PH17 2QQ
Tel: 01882 632332 Fax: 01882 632443

Head Michael Barratt MA
Founded 1959
Type Independent co-educational secondary
Religious denomination Inter-denominational
Members of SHMIS, Round Square
Age range 10 – 18 *Boarders from* 10 – 18
No of pupils (day) 10 *(boarding)* 250
Girls 65; *Boys* 195
Junior 45; *Senior* 215; *Sixth form* 80
Fees per term (day) £1,830; *(boarding)* £2,900 –
£3,450
Fees per annum (day) £5,490; *(boarding)* £8,700
– £10,350

Rannoch School, in its magnificent highland setting, encourages every boy and girl to develop their own talents and fosters in all a sense of adventure, self-reliance and responsibility to the community.

Rannoch pupils have now gained 500 Duke of Edinburgh's gold awards.

Above all, however, Rannoch is a school which helps young people of whatever academic ability from a strong university candidate – places have been gained at Oxford and Cambridge over the last two sessions – to those for whom success at Standard Grade and GCSE would be a real achievement. Specialist support tuition is always available in English and mathematics.

Rydal Penrhos School

Colwyn Bay, Clwyd LL29 7BT (Co-ed Division); LL28 4DA (Girls' Division); LL8 7BP (Prep)
Tel: 01492 530155 (Co-ed); 530333 (Girls); 530381 (Prep)
Fax: 01492 531872 (Co-ed and Prep); 533198 (Girls)

Head (Co-educational division) Mr N W Thorne BEd (Oxon), MSc (London); (Girls' Division) Mr C J Allen, MA, MSc (Oxon)
Founded 1880
Type Day & boarding, preparatory & senior
Religious denomination Methodist
Members of HMC, GSA, IAPS
Age range 2½ – 18 (co-educational); 11 – 18 (girls only) *Boarders from* 7
No of pupils (day) 472; *(boarding)* 357
Girls 441; *Boys* 388
Junior 250; *Senior* 579; *Sixth form* 175
Fees per term (day) £588 – £2,408; *(boarding)* £1,438 – £3,328
Fees per annum (day) £1,764 – £7,224; *(boarding)* £4,314 – £9,984

In 1995, Rydal School and Penrhos College joined together under the name of Rydal Penrhos. The school accepts boys and girls between the ages of 2½ and 18, both as boarders and day pupils. At the transfer to the senior school at the age of 11, girls have the unique option of continuing in a co- educational setting or proceeding to our girls-only division. Families who have children with a wide spread of school ages and who may need different styles of education may therefore look to Rydal Penrhos for all their requirements.

The school is blessed with a safe environment of the most outstanding natural beauty. With the sea on the doorstep and with a backcloth of grandeurs which form the Snowdonia National Park, pupils and parents could not wish for a more inspiring setting for both study and recreation.

This setting enables us to provide a most impressive programme of activities outside classroom hours. None the less, it is academic study which is the educational mainspring of the school. Most sixth formers proceed to degree courses, including Oxbridge, and the school is proud of the distinguished achievements of former pupils and the examination successes achieved year on year by current pupils. The Senior School's girls division, for example, topped the 1994 GCSE league tables for North and Mid-Wales.

Scholarships are awarded to pupils aged 11, 12, and 13; and at age 16 for entry to the sixth form. Awards are made for general academic ability as well as for more specialist abilities in music, art and design, science and French. The school participates in the Government's Assisted Places Scheme.

As you would expect, teaching facilities are of the highest order with excellent additional provision for musicians, artists and those interested in drama. Sporting honours are won regularly by Rydal Penrhos pupils at both county and national level. With two 25m indoor heated swimming pools, a full range of courts and gymnasia, fleets of sailing craft and some of the most impressive pitches in the region, the school is able to cultivate a foundation of fitness in each pupil which will continue into adult life.

Entry to the preparatory school is by interview (and school report where appropriate). Entry to the senior school is by written test, interview with the Headmaster and school report.

The school has many years' experience of welcoming pupils from other countries and publishes a separate brochure (available in seven languages) which gives detailed information of interest to parents and pupils who live overseas.

Llandovery College

Llandovery, Dyfed SA20 0EE
Tel: 01550 720315 Fax: 01550 720168

Head Dr C E Evans
Founded 1848
Type Independent
Religious denomination Church in Wales
Age range 11 – 18 *Boarders from* 11
No of pupils (day) 73; *(boarding)* 168
Girls 73; *Boys* 168
Junior 57; *Senior* 103; *Sixth form* 81
Fees per term (day) £1,840 – £2,068; *(boarding)* £2,686 – £3,170
Fees per annum (day) £5,520 – £6,204; *(boarding)* £8,058 – £9,510

Founded and endowed by Dr Thomas Phillips in 1848 to provide a classical, liberal and scientific education, the college is beautifully sited amidst magnificent countryside. Academically, Llandovery is one of the most distinguished schools in Wales – standards are high and examination results consistently good. The staff:pupil ratio is about 1:8. Approximately 80 per cent of pupils leaving proceed to higher education. A special unit for able, dyslexic children was opened in 1992. Daily worship and a weekly Eucharist Service are held in the college chapel.

A recent development programme has provided a new sports hall, computer networks, a library and a design technology centre. Work on a new performing arts theatre is currently in progress. The college boasts outstanding records in sport and in outdoor pursuits with a high success rate in the Duke of Edinburgh's Award Scheme.

Government Assisted Places and scholarships are available for academically able pupils.

Howell's School Llandaff

Cardiff Road, Llandaff, Cardiff, South Glamorgan CF5 2YD
Tel: 01222 562019 Fax: 01222 578879

Head Mrs C J Fitz BSc
Founded 1860
Type Girls' independent
Religious denomination Non-denominational
Members of GSA, GPDST
Age range 4 – 18
No of pupils (day) 698
Girls 689
Junior 127; *Senior* 562; *Sixth form* 139
Fees per term (day) £976 (junior); £1,328 (senior)

Established in 1860, Howell's School occupies a commanding site in the cathedral village of Llandaff, a suburb of Cardiff, the capital city of Wales. The splendid mid-Victorian Gothic building has been enlarged and adapted. In 1991 a new technology centre was added; also a music department with a magnificent concert hall and a practice wing (20 practice rooms) and electronic recording studies. The boarding houses have now become an exclusive sixth form centre with ample facilities for study, leisure and teaching. A sound education in the grammar school tradition is provided. Academic standards are high and results good. Over ninety per cent of girls go on to degree courses, including Oxbridge. All girls in Year 12 take the Diploma of Achievement. French, German, Welsh and Latin are offered throughout the school and many girls take GCSE in more than one language. There are regular exchanges with France and Germany. Italian, Spanish, Russian and Japanese are also taught in the sixth form. Very strong in music and drama. High standards are achieved in netball, hockey, lacrosse, tennis, swimming, athletics and cross country. Some involvement in local community schemes. Work experience and work shadowing are available in Years 9, 11 and 12 including an opportunity to take part in European work experience in Year 12.

Haberdashers' Monmouth School for Girls

Hereford Road, Monmouth, Gwent NP5 3XT
Tel: 01600 714214

Head Dorothy L Newman BA
Founded 1892 as a sister school to Monmouth School
Type Independent girls' boarding and day
Religious denomination Anglican, Church of Wales
Members of GSA
Age range 7 – 18 *Boarders from* 11, 13 or sixth form
No of pupils (day) 518; *(boarding)* 132
Girls 557 in main school, 93 in preparatory dept
Senior 557 *Sixth form* 168
Fees per term (day) £1,167 – £1,525[*]; *(boarding)* £2,424 – £2,782[*]
Fees per annum (day) £3,501 – £4,575[*] *(boarding)* £7,272 – £8,346[*]
[*] higher figures denote sixth-form fees

Curriculum: as for Monmouth School with the increased number of A levels, AS levels as above. Shared teaching with Monmouth School.

Entry requirements and procedures: age 7 and 11+, own exam; 13+ scholarship or own exam; sixth-form entry by scholarship or via GCSE and interview.
Examinations offered: as Monmouth School.
Academic and leisure facilities: recent building include science block (1994), indoor swimming pool (1992), preparatory department (1990) and indoor sports hall (1989). Classrooms and laboratories are extensive, with special sixth-form provision. Specialist workshops are provided for CDT and drama.
Scholarships: academic and music scholarships and bursaries at all normal entry levels.
Boarding facilities: recently upgraded accommodation on the school site includes a junior house and modern senior study bedrooms.
Location: as Monmouth School.

Monmouth School

Monmouth, Gwent NP5 3XP
Tel: 01600 713143 Fax: 01600 772701

Head Tim H P Haynes
Founded 1614
Type Independent boys' boarding and day
Religious denomination Anglican, Church in Wales
Members of HMC
Age range 11 – 18 *Boarders from* 11 or 13
No of pupils (day) 387; *(boarding)* 183
Boys 570
Senior 570; *Sixth form* 170
Fees per term (day) £1,636[*] *(boarding)* £2,725[*]
Fees per annum (day) £4,908[*] *(boarding)* £8,175[*]
[*] as of 1 September 1995

Curriculum: broadly-based curriculum. Classics from 11+. Pupils take at least nine GCSEs. Modern languages include French, German, Spanish and Russian. Information technology taught to all juniors. Twenty-eight subjects available at A level, 18 at AS level, plus full general studies programme. Combined sixth form timetable allows shared teaching pro-gramme with Haberdashers' Monmouth School for Girls.
Entry requirements and procedures: 11+, own exam; 13+, CEE, scholarship or own exam; sixth form entry by scholarship or via GCSE and interview.
Examinations offered: GCSE (MEG, WJEC, NEAB); A and AS level (O&C, OUDLE, ULEAC, UCLES, NEAB); Oxford entrance and Cambridge STEP examinations.
Academic and leisure facilities: recent buildings include science block (1983), library (1987), music school (1989), technology centre (1991), maths centre (1994), IT centre (1995). Well-equipped sports hall, 23–acre sports ground.
Scholarships: academic and music scholarships and bursaries at all normal entry levels, senior sports scholarships.
Boarding facilities: all boarding and day houses have been recently upgraded.
Located in the Wye Valley border town of Monmouth. Easy motorway access to the Midlands, Avon and south Wales.

St David's College

Llandudno, North Wales LL30 1RD
Tel: 01492 875974 Fax: 01492 870383

Head William Seymour MA
Founded 1965
Type Boys' secondary
Religious denomination Inter-denominational
Members of SHMIS, GBA
Accredited by ISJC
Age range 11 – 18 *Boarders from* 11 – 18
No of pupils (day) 60; *(boarding)* 160
Boys 220
Junior 30; *Senior* 140; *Sixth form* 50
Fees per term (day) £2,163; *(boarding)* £3,326
Fees per annum (day) £6,489; *(boarding)* £9,978

Spectacularly situated on the edge of Snowdonia, St David's provides a broad education with an emphasis on developing confidence and self-esteem. In addition to a wide curriculum we offer an outstanding Outdoor Pursuits programme including training for instructor certificates. We are an RYA centre. Our Cadogan Centre has thirty years' experience and expertise supporting dyslexic pupils and our 'whole school' approach to dyslexia achieves commendable results. Information technology is strongly developed and a full range of City & Guilds computer-aided design courses available.
St David's College exists for secondary education with a Christian framework.

Christ College Brecon

Brecon, Powys LD3 8AG
Tel: 01874 623359 Fax: 01874 611478/623913

Head Mr S W Hockey MA (Cantab), FIOD
Founded 1541 by Henry VIII
Type Independent co-educational full & weekly boarding & day
Religious denomination Anglican
Members of HMC, GBA, ISIS, BSA
Age range 11 – 18 *Boarders from* 11
No of pupils (day) 80; *(boarding)* 265
Girls 55; *Boys* 290
Junior (11 – 13) 65; *Senior (13 – 18)* 280; *Sixth form* 130
Fees per term (day) £2,430; *(boarding)* £3,135
Fees per annum (day) £7,290; *(boarding)* £9,405

Curriculum: GCSE: choice from 20 subjects. A level: 24 subjects available, including archaeology, business economics, PE, technology and art with wide subject choice including: photography, graphic design and printmaking.
Entry: 11-14 and 16+ test in English, maths, reasoning and reading. 13+: scholarship or Common Entrance. 16+: Heads report and at least five GCSE grade A – C passes.
Facilities: classrooms are mostly new or refurbished. Excellent modern concert hall/theatre. Very wide range of games (20). High grade rugby. County maintained cricket facilities. Choice of 40 extra-curricular activities. Sailing and water-skiing on Llangorse Lake. Golf at Cradoc. Mountain activities in surrounding National Park (Brecon Beacons). Superb sports hall. Tartan athletics track. Hockey all-weather pitch.
Scholarships: academic and music awards at 11+, 13+ and 16+. All-rounder award at 13+. Sports awards at 16+ (all sports eligible).
Bursaries: armed forces and clergy.
Government Assisted Places: available annually.
Summary: Small, happy family school with excellent academic record (1994 A level 97 per cent pass rate). Teacher/pupil ratio 1:9. Safe, beautiful, accessible location.

British School of Brussels

Leuvensesteenweg 19, 3080 Tervuren, Belgium
Tel: 00 32 2 767 4700 Fax: 00 32 2 767 8070

Head Jennifer M Bray MA
Founded 1969
Type British International School
Religious denomination Non-denominational
Members of HMC, IAPS, ECIS, COBISEC
Age range 3 – 18
No of pupils (day) 980
Girls 457; *Boys* 523
Junior 464; *Senior* 376; *Sixth form* 140
Fees per term (day) BF 48,000 – 241,000[*]
Fees per annum (day) BF 120,000 – 603,000[*]
([*]payable in Belgian francs)

The school provides a British-style education within a European context, catering for students between the ages of three and 18; approximately 70 per cent are British but over 60 nationalities are represented. Entrance is non-selective. The purpose-built early years unit offers the security of a small school within a larger school community. The curriculum leads to the GCSE and A level examinations as well as to GNVQs and almost all students proceed to universities or colleges of higher education world-wide. Well-resourced careers and learning support departments, computing facilities and libraries, support the curriculum. Instrumental music lessons are available. There are extensive indoor and outdoor sports facilities and an arts centre theatre that seats 240. BSB is a community school and offers adult education classes and holiday courses for children. There is a school bus service and a host family scheme operates for those who live too far for daily travel.

British School of Paris

Senior School, 38 Quai de l'Ecluse, 78290 Croissy Sur Seine, Paris, France
Tel: 00 33 1 34 80 45 90 Fax: 00 33 1 39 76 12 69
Junior School, 78380 Bougival, France
Tel: 00 33 1 39 69 78 21 Fax: 00 33 1 30 82 47 49

Head Mr Martin Honour
Founded 1954
Type Independent
Religious denomination Anglican
Members of HMC, IAPS, EClS
Age range 4 – 18 *Boarders from* 11
No of pupils (day) 600; *(boarding)* 25
Girls 305; *Boys* 320
Junior 315; *Senior* 310; *Sixth form* 70
Fees per annum (day) 58 – 77,000 FF; *(boarding)* + 10,000 FF

The British School of Paris caters for English-speaking children of over 30 nationalities (about 70 per cent of them British) from ages 4 – 18. It is a non-profit association in France and is managed by a board of governors under the patronage of His Excellency the British Ambassador.

The school is on two different sites in the western suburbs of Paris. The junior school occupies a beautiful wooded site overlooking the Seine valley and boasts many modern facilities including new indoor swimming pool and a play area with synthetic turf. Studies are based on the British National Curriculum with emphasis on English, maths and science, and of course, the French language. Various sports, music and drama and many extra curricular activities are also provided.

At the senior school the first part of a three phase development programme comprising four spacious modern laboratories and associated practical area opened in January 1989. This development continued with the construction of a new teaching block, a refectory and a sports hall. Students enter at the age of 11 and for the first three years, a broad general education is maintained in line with the National Curriculum. Pupils are prepared for the GCSE and A level examinations in a comprehensive range of subjects. A level courses are supplemented by a general studies programme.

Music and drama are encouraged; the new music centre has teaching and practice facilities and a well-equipped electronic studio. Specialist teachers visit the school to provide individual lessons in a wide range of instruments. Highly professional drama productions, ranging from Shakespeare to musicals such as 'My Fair Lady' take place in a local theatre. The school's membership of the International Schools Theatre Association enables pupils to take part in drama workshops in a variety of countries.

The school has had considerable sporting success in recent years, winning the International Schools' Sports Tournament competition in girls' field hockey in 1988, 1989 and 1990 and boys' rugby in 1989. Our international fixture lists provide an incentive to gain a place in school teams. As well as local matches our teams travel regularly to Belgium, Holland, Germany, Britain and Austria and, on occasions, have been as far afield as the Czech Republic and Canada.

The British School is co-educational throughout with almost equal numbers of boys and girls. Each section has about 300 pupils, with a two form entry into the senior school. Most are day pupils, although a growing number of senior school pupils live, under school supervision, with carefully chosen French and occasionally English, 'host families'. This is of particular interest to pupils who come to Paris to do their A levels and especially if they are studying French.

Small overall numbers, modest class sizes and a supportive pastoral system, mean that new pupils integrate quickly and find themselves well motivated in their work. Academic standards have improved steadily in recent years and compare favourably with good academic schools in Britain. Ninety per cent of sixth formers go on to higher education in Britain and elsewhere, with a regular intake to Oxford and Cambridge.

The British School in the Netherlands

Jan v Hooflaan 3, (2252 BG) Voorschoten, Netherlands 2252 BG
Tel: 00 31 71 5616958 Fax: 00 31 71 5617144

Head Michael J Cooper BA, MIBiol, FRSA
Founded 1935
Type International co-educational day school
Members of COBISEC, HMC, ECIS
Age range 3 – 18
No of pupils (day) 1,200
Junior 3 – 11 710; *Senior* 380; *Sixth form* 110
Fees per term (day) Hfl1,955 – 6,510 (£752 – £2,411)*
Fees per annum (day) Hfl5,865 – 19,530 (£2,172 – £7,233)*
*calculated at Hfl2.7 to the pound.

The British School, located in The Hague and Voorschoten, is an international, co-educational day school following a British curriculum with extensive facilities for children aged 3 – 18 years. It offers GCSE, A and AS level examinations in a wide range of subjects.

Pupils learn Dutch at five years, French at ten years plus German and Spanish at eleven years. They travel widely on cultural and field trips and participate in international sports fixtures, debating competitions and a host of extra-curricular activities.

Admission is granted throughout the year following an interview.

Kings College

Paseo de los Andes, 28761 Madrid, Spain
Tel: 00 91 803 4800 Fax: 00 91 803 6557

Head Dr G R Percy
Founded 1969
Type Co-educational day and boarding
Religious denomination Non-denominational
Members of HMC
Age range 2 – 18
No of pupils (day) 1,200; *(boarding)* 36
Fees per term (day) Ptas151,000 – 325,000

British co-educational day and boarding school, with optional Spanish validation. Preparation for IGCSE and GCE A level, also BUP and COU. Eighty-three teachers plus over one thousand two hundred pupils of many nationalities, from two to 18 years (36 boarders). Modern purpose-built school surrounded by countryside but well connected to Madrid. Five science laboratories, computer centre, libraries, music rooms, sport facilities, two gymnasia, riding school, heated indoor swimming pool and stables. Two boarding houses with full-time resident staff. Full range of extra-curricular activities including ballet, craft, drama, guitar, judo, piano, riding, swimming and tennis. School bus service and meals.

King's College Infant School: Prieto Ureña, 22. 28016 Madrid. Telephone 91-3592758. Headmaster: Dr G R Percy.

A second infant department of the above King's College for two to six-year-olds.

Aiglon College

1885 Chesières-Villars, Switzerland
Tel: 00 41 25 35 27 21 Fax: 00 41 25 35 28 11

Head Mr Richard McDonald MA (Oxon)
Founded 1949
Type Co-educational boarding
Religious denomination Christian allegiance
Members of HMC, Round Square, ECIS, COBISEC
Age range 11 – 18 *Boarders from* 11
No of pupils (day) 12; *(boarding)* 273
Girls 125; *Boys* 160
Junior 40; *Senior* 159; *Sixth form* 86
Fees per term (day) Sfr9,115 – 12,325; *(boarding)*
Sfr14,754.40 – 17,618.40
Fees per annum (day) Sfr30,045 – 36,975;
(boarding) Sfr44,263.50 – 52,365.70

The British International School in Switzerland, is situated in the French-Swiss Alps and has 285 boarders, (150 boys and 130 girls) age 11 to 18. The headmaster is an overseas member of The Headmaster's Conference and the school is registered as a non-profit making trust in Switzerland, the UK, USA and Canada.

Founded in 1949, Aiglon's aim is to show our boys and girls the integrity needed to know how to cope with adversity and to also show them how to be aware of their responsibilities to the community. The academic programme is rigorous and prepares students for British GCSE and A level examinations as well as the American College Board. Aiglon students are currently enrolled in leading universities on both sides of the Atlantic. Academic study is complemented by a high degree of pastoral care and a challenging programme of sports and outdoor activities including skiing and mountain expeditions. The school has six senior boarding houses with a separate junior school for 50 boys and girls, aged 11 – 13, all situated on a south facing slope at 4,000 ft. Facilities include a large theatre and gym, four laboratories for science and languages, three libraries, tennis courts and two playing fields. The school also has access to swimming pools, a skating rink, a sports centre with indoor tennis and squash courts, and extensive ski slopes.

Admission is through the school's entrance tests or the Common Entrance Examinations and a small number of places is also available in the lower sixth for candidates with good GCSE qualifications.

Language summer schools in English and French combined with outdoor activities are offered in July and August.

Further information may be obtained from the head of admissions.

Brillantmont International College

Avenue Secrétan 16, 1005 Lausanne, Switzerland
Tel: 00 41 21 312 4741 Fax: 00 41 21 320 8417

Head Françoise Frei-Huguenin
Founded 1882
Type International
Members of ECIS, FSEP, AVDEP
Age range 14 – 19 *Boarders from* 14 – 19
No of pupils (day) 50 *(boarding)* 90
Girls 100 *Boys* 40
Senior 50 *Sixth form* 20
Fees per term (day) Sfr5,000 *(boarding)* Sfr13,300
Fees per annum (day) Sfr15,000 *(boarding)* Sfr40,000

Brillantmont prepares students to GCE; IGCSE and A levels (Cambridge Board) in English, French, German, Italian, Spanish, maths, biology, chemistry, physics, computer studies, history, economics, art.

Located in the centre of Lausanne, the French speaking area of Switzerland, Brillantmont has a reputation for teaching languages and offers a wide variety of cultural and sporting events.

Our strengths are: – to offer an excellent preparation for university; – to have an international students' body from 35 nations; – to offer tuition in small classes; – to have a boarding school where the development of the student's personality and talents is a major concern.

Students are accepted on school reports.

Franklin College, Switzerland

Via Ponte Tresa 29, Sorengo (Lugano), Switzerland 6924
Tel: 00 41 91 993 0101 Fax: 00 41 91 994 4117

Head Dean Timothy Keating
Founded 1968
Type University program
Members of Middle States Association of Schools and Colleges, ECIS
Age range 18 – 28
No of pupils (day) 25 *(boarding)* 200
Girls 125 *Boys* 100
Fees per term (day) Sfr13,950 *(boarding)* Sfr17,450
Fees per annum (day) Sfr27,900 *(boarding)* Sfr34,900

Curriculum: Franklin College Switzerland is an accredited, four-year US university program which offers the US Bachelor of Arts degree in a variety of majors including international management, international economics, international relations, visual and communication arts, foreign languages. A special feature of the academic program is individualized majors combining any two of nine subject areas. Also offered is an accelerated MBA degree in cooperation with Long Island University in New York.

Facilities: the Franklin campus features a private villa located in a park overlooking Lake Lugano. Campus facilities include an auditorium, library, computer and science laboratories, art studios, student centre/cafeteria and student resident apartments.

Boarding facilities: the college has a variety of furnished student apartments which range from individual studios to shared apartments for two to five students. All students are guaranteed housing.

Entry requirements: admission is in August or January. Applicants must have a secondary school diploma or equivalent examinations, with a background in college preparatory courses.

Scholarships: Franklin has need and merit-based financial aid available to academically qualified students.

Institut Château Mont-Choisi

Bd de la Forêt, Ch des Ramiers 16, 1009 Pully-Lausanne, Switzerland
Tel: 00 41 21 728 8777 Fax: 00 41 21 728 8864

Heads Jenö Pusztaszerri, Dr B Hourcade
Founded 1885
Type Co-educational day, girls' boarding
Members of Swiss Federation of Private Schools, accredited by ECIS, NEASC
Age range 12 – 20 *Boarders from* 12
Fees per annum (day) SFr17,000; *(boarding)* SFr42,500

Curriculum: complete American High School Program, grades 9–12. University counselling and placement. CEEB examinations: PSAT, SAT, ACH and AP. Post High School graduation year (13th year), European studies (language and culture).

Intensive French program (certificates and diplomas of the Alliance Française), Intensive English-ESL-program (Cambridge First Certificate and Proficiency) and TOEFL.

Business studies (Diplomas and Certificates of the London Pitman Institute); entry preparation for Hotel and Tourism schools. Elective courses in modern languages (Spanish, German and Italian) in computer studies and in art.

Wide range of activities include jazz, music, cookery, tennis, group sports, cultural tours, field-trips and seasonal sporting activities (skiing, etc).

Summer course includes the study of French and English, computer studies, cookery and a full program of non-academic activities and sports. The teacher/student ratio is 1:9.

Entry requirements and procedures: for admittance to the school, each student must submit an enrolment form, the most recent school reports, a recommendation from the former school's principal, along with a letter certifying the applicant's good standing and character, and the enrolment fee. Château Mont-Choisi welcomes a personal interview and visit to the school when possible.

Academic and leisure facilities: the facilities of Château Mont-Choisi comprise six buildings with 14 classrooms (six of which are video equipped), language, science, computer and photo laboratories, a 5,000 volume library, a studio art room, a music room, and a standard chef's kitchen. The château, the main building, contains large lounges, study and music rooms, and a gymnasium equipped for fitness and general entertainment. A modern dining room and cafeteria are located in the Rosemont. The newest annexe, the Wellingtonia, offers rooms which are particularly well-designed, including a living room and the library. The facilities include a tennis court and heated swimming pool.

John F Kennedy International School – Switzerland

CH-3792 Saanen-Gstaad, Switzerland
Tel: 00 41 30 4 13 72 Fax: 00 41 30 4 89 82

Head Mr William Lovell
Founded 1949
Type International preparatory school
Religious denomination Non-denominational
Age range 5 – 14 *Boarders from* 6 – 14
No of pupils (day) 30 *(boarding)* 26
Girls 28 *Boys* 28
Junior 56
Fees per term (day) Sfr9,150 *(boarding)* Sfr16,500
Fees per annum (day) Sfr18,300 *(boarding)* Sfr33,000

Founded in 1949 in the beautiful alpine village of Saanen, three kilometers from the world famous resort of Gstaad, this is an English language boarding and day school for 50–60 students between the ages of five and 14.

It features a 1:3 staff-to-student ratio and enjoys a family-like atmosphere in an international environment.

The school strives to provide its students with a firm foundation of academic skills, work habits and the attitudes necessary for success in university-preparatory secondary schools. In addition, a conscious effort is made to foster a 'global viewpoint' and to take the learning process beyond the classroom through field trips, cultural activities and sports, including daily skiing in winter.

A summer camp, held in July and August is aimed at children 7 – 12 years and combines language instruction in English and French with a variety of sports, outdoor activities and camping.

The John F Kennedy School is accredited by the Department of Education of the Canton of Bern.

Keswick School

School House, Keswick, Cumbria CA12 5NF
Tel: 01768 772173 Fax: 01768 774813

Head H W Allen MA (Cantab)
Founded Earliest record c 1400
Type Voluntary aided co-educational comprehensive
Religious denomination Non-denominational
Members of BSA, STABIS
Age range 11 – 18 *Boarders from* 14 – 18
Girls 459; *Boys* 503
Sixth form 97; boys, 106; girls, 73
Fees per term (boarding) £1,250 – £1,300 (tuition fees paid by DFEE/LEA)

Curriculum: the National Curriculum is followed, leading to GCSE. A, AS levels, GNVQs, BTEC courses and a programme of general studies are available in the sixth form.

Entry requirements and procedures: by interview and school report.

Situated in the Lake District, the school has an excellent record of academic success, unsurpassed opportunities for outdoor education, and caring support for all students. The Keswick School Charitable Trust exists to provide high-quality education for local boys and girls.

Colchester Royal Grammar School

6 Lexden Road, Colchester, Essex CO3 3ND
Tel: 01206 577971/2/3 Fax: 01206 549928

Head Mr S A C Francis MA
Founded 1539, by Royal Charter
Type Boys' grant-maintained selective
Religious denomination Non-denominational
Age range 11 – 18 *Boarders from* 11
No of pupils (day) 667; *(boarding)* 18
Boys 667
Sixth form 183
Weekly boarding £950 a term
Full boarding £1,470 a term

Site, atmosphere and aims: delightful setting in mature gardens in pleasant residential area. Substantial playing fields. School recently received first-class Ofsted inspection report. Orderly, caring, friendly atmosphere.

Curriculum: record of outstanding academic success. In 1995 the school came first in the Daily Express National A Level League for State Schools and ninth in that of the Sunday Times; 19 Oxbridge places. Broad curriculum, wide range of GCSE subjects and 19 A levels. Sixth form minority studies, with local Girls' High.

Entry requirements and procedures: 11+ entry by test. Occasional vacancies for ages 12 – 14. Sixth form entry by conditional offers from GCSEs.

Academic and leisure facilities: school redecorated, refurbished extensively. Good facilities. Strong games, music, drama.

Boarding facilities: family atmosphere boarding in pleasant, comfortable house. Good study facilities. Ideal opportunities for sixth formers.

Links: good liaison with parents, old boys, industry, universities.

Access: easy access to M25, London, Stansted, Gatwick, Heathrow, Harwich, Dover. Regular train service to London Liverpool Street: 50 minutes.

Cranbrook

Cranbrook, Kent IN17 3JD
Tel: 01580 712163 Fax: 01580 715365

Head Mr P A Close MA, FRSA
Founded 1518
Type Grant-maintained mixed day/boarding grammar
Religious denomination Non-denominational
Members of STABIS, BSA
Age range 13 – 18 *Boarders from* 13
No of pupils (day) 459; *(boarding)* 275;
Girls 329; *Boys* 405
Sixth form 280
Fees per term (boarding) £1,620
Fees per annum (boarding) £4,860

High academic standard: 94 per cent of GCSE results A–C grades; 93 per cent pass rate at A level; 80 per cent of students proceed to university/polytechnic. Music, art and drama thrive, whilst boys' and girls' teams compete at the highest levels in all major sports. Musical activities include an orchestra, big band, choral society and chamber group, whilst for drama we have a 400 seat newly-renovated theatre. For the creative arts there are fine facilities including a new design and technology centre. Arrangements for sports are excellent with plentiful playing fields, heated swimming pool, squash and tennis courts, astro- turf pitch and a sports hall with dance studio, multi-gym and climbing wall. Many outdoor pursuits, including Combined Cadet Force.

Entry at 13+ by selection test/Common Entrance and interview. Day pupils must be resident in Scheme of Education Area.

Further details may be obtained from the registrar.

Cranbrook School (GM) existing to promote education in Cranbrook.

Sir Roger Manwood's

Manwood Road, Sandwich, Kent CT13 9JX
Tel: 01304 613286 Fax: 01304 615336

Head Mr I Mellor MA
Founded 1563
Type Grant-maintained grammar
Members of BSA, STABIS
Age range 11 – 18 *Boarders from* 11
No of pupils (day) 600; *(boarding)* 70
Girls 345; *Boys* 325
Sixth form 160
Fees per term (day) No tuition fees *(boarding)* £1,532
Fees per annum (day) No tuition fees *(boarding)* £4,596

Sir Roger Manwood's School, in the ancient Cinque Port of Sandwich, is a rare combination of mixed grammar school and boarding school. Entrance is by testing in English and mathematics. The school has an excellent academic track record; A level and GCSE pass rates were 94 per cent in 1995. There are numerous sports, clubs and societies, catering for a wide range of enthusiasms, and the school has good and spacious facilities, including a swimming pool. It is situated within easy reach of the channel ports and London.

The King's School

Brook Street, Grantham, Lincolnshire NG31 6RP
Tel: 01476 63180 Fax: 01476 590953

Head Mr S Howarth
Founded 1528
Type Boys' grant-maintained grammar
Religious denomination Multi-denominational
Members of BSA, STABIS
Age range 11 – 18 *Boarders from* 11+
No of pupils (day) 850; *(boarding)* 70
Sixth form 200

'A good school by any standards' – OFSTED report 1993. King's is a grant-maintained grammar school with no fees for tuition. It has a strong tradition of academic, cultural and sporting achievement including a Combined Cadet Force and Duke of Edinburgh Award Scheme. Eighty per cent of pupils go on to degree courses. The school offers excellent career counselling and has recently become affiliated to the London Livery Company of Information Technologists. The boarding house for 70 is an attractive, fully-modernised detached house set in its own grounds. It provides an ideal environment for personal, social and academic development at minimum cost.

The King's School charity exists to provide high-quality education for boys.

The Minster School

Nottingham Road, Southwell, Nottinghamshire NG25 0HG
Tel: 01636 814000 Fax: 01636 814788

Head Mr P J Blinston MEd
Founded 956
Type Voluntary aided comprehensive school with boarding
Religious denomination Church of England
Age range 11 – 18 *Boarders from* 8
Girls 645; *Boys* 730
Junior 22; *Senior* 1132; *Sixth form* 221
Fees per term (boarding) £1,350

Entry requirements and procedures: as the only maintained, all-ability school in the county with boarding accommodation, the school does not hold formal selection tests for boarders for the main school and initial application for admission is by letter to the headmaster.
Curriculum: the curriculum is broad and caters for the needs of all abilities. The junior department follows a full primary school curriculum with emphasis on music. There is full provision for the National Curriculum in the main school and a full range of GCSE and A level subjects is offered. A high number of sixth formers go on to higher education. Earlier this year the school featured on local and national news following its impressive performance in the 1993 external examinations. This thriving historic school maintains strong academic, musical and sporting traditions.

Sports centre attached to main part of school. Over 200 pupils engaged in Duke of Edinburgh Award Scheme in last year. 11 Gold, 23 Silver, 61 Bronze awards. French exchange with twin town of Sees. German study work abroad as part of GCSE.

A school which has had strong connections with Southwell Minster for over 1,000 years. 70+ boarders in two houses, within walking distance of both sites of the school. New suite for girls' boarding opened in September 1990.

Sexey's School

Bruton, Somerset BA10 0DF
Tel: 01749 813393 Fax: 01749 812870

Head Mr S Burgoyne MA
Founded 1891
Type Grant-maintained co-educational boarding and day
Religious denomination Church of England
Members of BSA, STABIS
Age range 11 – 18
No of pupils (day) 420
Girls 195; *Boys* 225
Fees per term (boarding) £1,330

Average size of class: 19 (sixth form: 11)
Teacher/pupil ratio: 1:11
Curriculum: GCSE core (English, mathematics and science). Foundation (art, music, physical education, French, technology, geography, history, Latin, drama and German also offered). A level: 16 major subjects.

Entry requirements and procedures: at age 11 and 13 interview with headmaster, with reports and samples of work from previous school. Sixth form admission is on the basis of five C grades at GCSE.

Readily accessible by train and road from London and the west country, on edge of pleasant small town. Extensive sports facilities and extra-curricular activities.

A statutory charity under grant maintained legislation which exists to provide boarding education for boys and girls aged 11 – 18.

Gordon's School

West End, Woking, Surrey GU24 9PT
Tel: 01276 858084

Head Mr D P Mulkerrin MA
Type Grant maintained
Religious denomination All
Age range 11 – 18
No of pupils (day) 300; *(boarding)* 150
Fees per term (day boarding) £998; *(full boarding)* £1,816; *(weekly boarding)* £1,635

Gordon's School was founded in 1885 at the express wish of Queen Victoria, as the National Memorial to General Gordon. Since its foundation the school has been privileged to have the reigning monarch as its patron.

Originally a boys' boarding school, today Gordon's is a grant maintained, co-educational school catering for some 300 boarders and day pupils. Our average class size of 16 means that every boy and girl is truly known and treated as an individual, and their particular talents recognised and nurtured.

At Gordon's, great importance is placed on the quality of teaching in the classroom because we strongly believe that schools are first and foremost centres for learning. Academic standards are good with a high value added factor in exam results. In terms of ethos, we are known as a school where traditional values still matter – we insist on high standards, self-discipline, courtesy and good manners

from our pupils. The key to our success is very high expectations.

With its unique historical traditions and superb boarding facilities situated in 50 acres of Surrey parkland, Gordon's offers pupils a very full life. There is the intellectual challenge in the classroom, competition on the sports field, and creative fulfilment in music, art, dance and drama. Individual enthusiasms are readily met in over thirty clubs and societies which range from swimming to chess, and from horse riding to ballet, to our highly successful Combined Cadet Force. Throughout, the Gordon's emphasis is on hard work, high expectations – and a great deal of enjoyment! As a school, we are known for a particular strength in developing personality, character and confidence in youngsters to enable them to cope fully with the modern world.

Because Gordon's is a boarding school with grant maintained status, parents pay for the accommodation element only; they do not pay tuition fees. As such the school is seen by many parents as an attractive alternative to independent boarding schools. It offers high quality boarding education at an affordable price while at the same time having the traditional values and excellence of many of the prestigious independent schools.

Royal Alexandra and Albert School

Gatton Park, Reigate, Surrey RH2 0TW
Tel: 01737 642576 Fax: 01737 642294

Head Mr R Bushin MA (Cantab), MA (Educ)
Founded 1758
Type Voluntary aided co-educational
Religious denomination Protestant
Age range 7 – 18 *Boarders from* 7
No of pupils (day) 31; *(boarding)* 369
Girls 167; *Boys* 233
Junior 85; *Senior* 282; *Sixth form* 33

Curriculum: excellent facilities for all National Curriculum subjects. There is a wide choice of options for GCSE including core National Curriculum subjects. IT is taught throughout the school and pupils' skills are of an exceptionally high standard, with one PC to every seven pupils.
Entry requirements and procedures: by interview, entry test and school report.
Sixth form: sixth formers attend Reigate or East Surrey Colleges to pursue A level, GNVQ or other vocational courses.

Sports/games/leisure facilities: the school's 250 acre parkland setting offers outstanding facilities for rugby, soccer, hockey, athletics, tennis and netball plus indoor, heated 25m × 4 lane swimming pool, sports hall and gymnasium. The school's competitive sporting record is excellent. In addition there is an activities centre for ACF, Sea Cadets, Scouts, Guides, St Johns, Crusaders. Angling, sailing and canoeing on lakes. Excellent orchestra. BHS approved riding school.

The school is jointly maintained by Surrey LEA and Royal Alexandra and Albert Foundation. Set in 250 acre estate at Gatton Park, Reigate.

Places available for full boarders, weekly boarders, day boarders (with all meals and supervised prep) and day pupils.

Cambridge Arts & Sciences (CATS)

Round Church Street, Cambridge, Cambridgeshire CB5 8AD
Tel: 01223 314431 Fax: 01223 467773

Head Miss Elizabeth Armstrong BA (Hons)
Founded 1985
Type Independent sixth-form and tutorial college
Religious denomination Non-denominational
Accredited by BAC
Age range 15 – 19 *Boarders from* 16
No of pupils (day) 50; *(boarding)* 115
Girls 88; *Boys* 77
Senior 12; *Sixth form* 153
Fees per term (day) £2,500 – £3,000; *(boarding)* £3,600 – £4,100
Fees per annum (day) £7,500 – £9,000; *(boarding)* £10,800 – £12,300

The college is set in a central campus which surrounds the Cambridge Union. Facilities include six art studios, three science laboratories, a photographic studio, dark room, video editing suite and computer laboratory. There are two libraries and a careers room. All students are members of the Cambridge Union – the forum for undergraduate debates – and they attend its lectures and debating workshops. The curriculum covers all subjects and there are no restrictions on the combinations which are studied; the college is a centre for most examining boards. Class sizes are limited to seven and the staff/student ratio is 1:3. A premium is placed on individual attention and students have a personal tutor who monitors well-being and progress. Residential and day students are admitted; entry is by interview and school reference. CATS is a thriving community with a dynamic, family atmosphere. In the last two years all applicants have secured places in higher education.

Cambridge Centre for Sixth Form Studies

1 Salisbury Villas, Station Road, Cambridge, Cambridgeshire CB1 2JF
Tel: 01223 316890 Fax: 01223 358441

Head Co-principals Dr Dawson and Mr Redhead
Founded 1981
Type Independent sixth form
Members of CIFE
Accredited by BAC
Age range 14 – 19 *Boarders from* 14
No of pupils (day) 65; *(boarding)* 130
Girls 90; *Boys* 105
Senior (GCSE year) 20; *Sixth form* 175
Fees per annum (day) £8,295 – £8,670[*] *(boarding)* £11,355 – £12,915[**] *Fees based on 3 A levels (without bursary)

A sixth-form college in the fullest sense, students come to CCSS both for two-year A level and GCSE courses, and for intensive one-year and short-term retake programmes. An extensive range of subjects is offered and subject choice is unrestricted. The key to the college's academic strength is the teaching structure: students are taught in small classes (maximum seven), and have, in addition, weekly individual tutorials with their subject teachers which prove invaluable in developing skills and confidence and in ironing out difficulties. All students, whatever the length of their stay, benefit from the college's strong tradition of pastoral care, and are also able to participate in a comprehensive range of sporting and extra-curricular activities. An unusual facility is a beautifully located field-centre in the Hebrides. Approximately one-third of students are local and the college provides fully supervised accommodation in its own houses for the 130 students needing to board.

Irwin College

164 London Road, Leicester, Leicestershire LE2 1ND
Tel: 0116 255 2648 Fax: 0116 285 4935

Head Mr A J Elliott BA (Oxon), MPhil (Cantab)
Founded 1975
Type Independent tutorial college
Religious denomination Non-denominational
Accredited by BACIFHE
Age range 13 – 24 *Boarders from* 14 – 24
No of pupils (day) 30 *(boarding)* 20
Girls 17 *Boys* 33
Junior 7 *Senior* 12 *Sixth form* 31
Fees per annum (day) £5,040 *(boarding)* £8,910

Irwin College is located in elegant Victorian buildings opposite a large park near the centre of Leicester, with three comfortable residences five minutes away. We hold A level and GCSE courses for UK and overseas students. We provide close academic and pastoral supervision, requiring committed and conscientious study in a warm, friendly and supportive environment. Students are treated as young adults and given every encouragement to excel in extra-curricular pursuits (sports, debates, music etc) as well as academically. Every student has an individual tutor available for consultation over university entrance, future careers and personal matters. Staff are qualified, experienced professionals sensitive to young people's needs.

Classes are small with four students being the average size, thus ensuring a large measure of individual attention for each member. Examinations are held every Saturday morning and lessons are structured closely around syllabuses. Our approach seeks to enhance our students' knowledge, social skills, maturity and general happiness.

Ashbourne Independent Sixth Form College

17 Old Court Place, London, W8 4PL
Tel: 0171 376 0360 Fax: 0171 937 2207

Head M J Hatchard-Kirby MSc, BApSc
Founded 1981
Age range 16 – 19
No of pupils (day) 150
Fees per term (day) £2,675 – £3,250

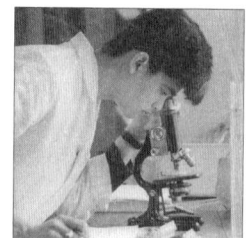

Ashbourne Sixth Form College was founded in 1981 and is now one of London's leading sixth-form colleges with about 150 students each year engaged in one-year, two-year or 'short retake' courses at GCSE and A level.

The college was originally renowned for its grade-improvement record at O and A level and its specialisation in mathematics and the sciences. The emphasis now is still firmly on results (the college expects to achieve 40 per cent A/B grades in examinations) and offering expert exam-based coaching in all major subjects.

David Game Tutorial College

69 Notting Hill Gate, London W11 3JS
Tel: 0171 584 7580/9097 Fax: 0171 584 2637

Head David Game MA (Oxon), MPhil (London)
Founded 1974
Type Independent sixth-form college, accredited by BACIFHE
Age range 14 – 25 *Boarders from* 16

Curriculum and examinations: the college specialises in preparation for entry to British universities.

All major GCE A level and GCSE subjects are offered: mathematics, sciences and business-related subjects are particular strengths.

The majority of students take one-year courses in GCSE or A levels. However, one and a half and two-year programmes are available.

Intensive retake and Easter revision courses are also offered.

An alternative to A levels is the one-year university foundation programme. This is of modular structure and continuously assessed. September and January starts give university entrance in October following.

Academic and leisure facilities: small classes, performance-related teaching, individual student attention and personal counselling are distinctive features. The Director of Studies gives assistance and support with UCAS entries.

Teaching facilities: the college is housed in purpose-designed premises immediately adjacent to Notting Hill Gate underground station. It has excellent library, laboratory and computing facilities.

Boarding facilities: the college has a range of student residences conveniently located in West London. Selected family accommodation is also available.

Davies, Laing & Dick Independent Sixth Form College (DLD)

10 Pembridge Square, London W2 4ED
Tel: 0171 727 2797 Fax: 0171 792 0730

Co-Principals Peter W Boorman MA (Cantab);
Elizabeth Rickards MA (St Andrews)
Founded 1931
Type Independent
Members of CIFE
Accredited by BAC
Age range 16 – 20
No of pupils (day) 250
Girls 130; *Boys* 120
Senior 250; *Sixth form* 250
Fees per term (day) from £550 (one course) to
£2,600 (3 A levels)
Fees per annum (day) from £1,539 (one course)
to £7,800 (3 A levels)

Davies, Laing and Dick is a leading tutorial college housed in a large Victorian building in Pembridge Square, some five minutes' walk from Kensington Gardens. The student roll is currently 250 students: approximately half of these students are sixth formers spending two years preparing for A levels; the other half are A level retake students re-sitting to secure university places on over-subscribed degree courses such as medicine, law or English at premier league universities. There is also a GCSE department specialising in one year GCSE courses. Those wishing to do GCSEs over a two year period can be accommodated in the junior school, Kensington Park School.

Apart from the traditional school subjects, a wide range of unusual subjects is offered at A level including photography, psychology, film and media studies, Russian, and theatre studies. There is a portfolio art course for students wishing to go on to a Foundation course at Art School. Students are expected to be strongly committed to their studies. They are supported in this by excellent study facilities: three laboratories, a light and spacious art studio, a fully staffed library, an additional study area/exams room and a computer room; support is also extended through a vigilant personal tutor system. Fortnightly reports in all subjects, daily class attendance monitoring, and where necessary, timetabled supervised study ensure that students are able to achieve their potential. Each student attends a course in study skills whilst they are at DLD. Teachers are highly qualified and carefully chosen for their ability to communicate and encourage; they have the highest professional standards. The average set size is 5:1.

There is a sports and social programme; lectures and extra mural visits are frequently organised. An accommodation officer is able to arrange accommodation with host families, or in student residences and flats.

High standards of teaching are the norm at DLD; in turn we expect high standards from our students in terms of commitment to study, behaviour and courtesy. Appointments to visit the college can be made both during the academic year as well as in the Easter and Summer holidays.

Davies's College

25 Old Gloucester Street, Queen Square, London WC1N 3AF
Tel: 0171 430 1622 Fax: 0171 430 9212

Head Mr Andrew T Williams
Founded 1927
Type Independent
Age range 15+
No of pupils (day) 130
Girls 60 *Boys* 70
Senior 130
Fees per term (day) See text
Fees per annum (day) See text

Davies's College is an independent day school, located in a quiet garden square in central London, conveniently close to both Holborn and Russell Square underground stations.

Established in 1927, the college offers the following courses:

A level and GCSE retake courses: there are three different types of retake course depending on the subjects and examination boards involved: a) a course offered over one year; b) a course from September to November/January; c) a course from January to June.

Examination techniques and timed essays form an essential part of these courses.

Fees are based on length of programme and number of subjects studied.

One-year A level and GCSE courses: students may study up to six GCSEs or three A levels over one year from a wide range of subjects.

A level fees range from £3,289 for one subject to £9,103 for three. GCSE fees for up to six subjects are £6,490.

Two-year GCSE programme: students on the two-year GCSE programme study up to eight subjects. English and mathematics are compulsory, but the remaining GCSEs may be chosen from a wide variety of subjects. All students also attend arts and crafts and physical education classes as part of the curriculum. £4,950 for up to eight subjects, £1,760 for each additional GCSE.

Two-year A level programme: students study for three A levels. In addition, all students may choose either general studies A/S level or information technology skills courses in their first year. Up to three subjects, £5,670; £3,289 for each additional A level.

Student facilities: the college has two study rooms, one of which is supervised, for private study, library and photocopying facilities, an information technology centre and separate laboratories for biology, chemistry and physics.

Careers advice: careers seminars are held regularly and representatives from business and industry visit frequently to discuss career prospects. Visits are also made by admissions tutors from a number of medical schools and universities to give information on admissions policies, minimum grade requirements and subject choices.

Admissions policy: entry to the college is based on examination results (where appropriate) in addition to interview and a reference from the student's previous school.

Ealing Tutorial College

28A New Broadway, Ealing, London W5 2AX
Tel: 0181 579 6668 Fax: 0181 567 8688

Head Mr Neil Cownden BSc
Founded 1992
Type Sixth-form college
Age range 16+
No of pupils (day) 64
Girls 34; *Boys* 30
Sixth form 64
Fees for 1 term per A level retake £1,801 inc VAT;
fees for 3 term per A level retake £2,224 inc VAT
Fees for one year course £2,929 inc VAT

At Ealing Tutorial College students are prepared for A level examinations in mathematics and the sciences. The majority of our students apply to read medicine, dentistry, pharmacy, physiotherapy and opthalmic optics although a significant proportion do apply for other degree level subjects. Specialist help from the principal, teaching staff and guest lecturers is given to students applying for medicine and dentistry, especially when the student is resitting one or more A levels.

The college's academic record shows a pass rate of over 95 per cent, 44 per cent with A grade, with over 73 per cent of all grades achieved at A or B (and 92 per cent at A to C grade).

Most students at the college come from the London area but a small number of students seeking specialist help with their medical school applications come from further afield. Mature students are welcome and the college has a very good record of placing such students on medical courses.

Mander Portman Woodward

24 Elvaston Place, London SW7 5NL
Tel: 0171 584 8555 Fax: 0171 225 2953

Principals Dr Nigel Stout MA, DPhil and Miss Fiona Dowding MA
Founded 1973
Type Independent fifth and sixth-form college
Religious denomination Non-denominational
Members of CIFE
Accredited by BAC
No of pupils (day) 400
Girls 200; *Boys* 200
Sixth form 330
Fees per term (day) 7 GCSEs: £3,241; 3 A levels: £3,057

A co-educational college in Kensington (nearest tube Gloucester Road) with approximately 400 students. One- and two-year courses as well as short retake courses are offered in a wide range of arts and science GCSE and A level subjects. Preparation is given for fourth and seventh term Oxford and Cambridge entrance. Facilities include four science laboratories, computer room, art and pottery studios, music room, stage, library and reading rooms, two canteens and a sports hall. Teaching in small classes of seven or fewer. Individual tuition is also available by arrangement. Each student has a director of studies to monitor progress and give advice on further education and employment opportunities. Help given in finding accommodation. Our buildings provide a particularly comfortable environment and do not have an institutional atmosphere.

Westminster Tutors

82 Old Brompton Road, South Kensington, London SW7 3LQ
Tel: 0171 584 1288 Fax: 0171 584 2637

Co-Principals Peter Brooke BA, MLitt and Jane Darwin MA, BLitt
Founded 1934
Type Tutorial College
Age range 16 – 19
No of pupils (day) 60
Girls 30; *Boys* 30
Sixth form 60
Fees per term (day) from £1025 per subject
Fees per annum (day) from £2,880 per subject

Westminster Tutors is well known and widely respected as a small co-educational tutorial college with excellent examination results and a tradition of close personal attention to the individual needs of students. We have always concentrated on the arts and social science subjects and mathematics, aiming for high academic achievement in a friendly informal atmosphere. We specialise in A level subjects taken as both full courses and intensive re-take courses. We also offer Christmas and Easter revision courses. The college is situated in attractive premises in the lively Old Brompton Road, three minutes' walk from South Kensington underground station and Hyde Park. College facilities include a library, a common room and a kitchen where tea and coffee are available. The library is being extended, concentrating on books that are directly relevant to the courses taught, and students are encouraged to suggest additional titles they think may be helpful.

Abbey Tutorial College, Manchester

Main Building: 20 Kennedy Street, Manchester, Greater Manchester M2 4BY
Tel: 0161 236 6386 Fax: 0161 236 1086
Science Building: 6 – 12 Fountain Street, Manchester, Greater Manchester M2 2AA
Tel: 0161 839 7332 Fax: 0161 839 7334

Head Dominic Jordan BA (Cantab)
Founded 1990
Type Independent
Age range 14 – 19+
No of pupils (day) 120
Girls 60 *Boys* 60
Fees per term (day) £1,750 – £2,800
Fees per annum (day) £5,250 – £8,400

Curriculum: all mathematics and science subjects, many social science and arts subjects at Advanced level and GCSE. Laboratory classes are included where appropriate.

Abbey Tutorial College opened in Manchester in 1990 and rapidly established itself as the North West's leading centre for mathematics and the sciences, with an impressive reputation for university entrance and exceptional results. With more space available, it has been possible to increase the number of courses offered by the college, to include many arts, humanities and social science subjects, as well as GCSEs.

Many of the students enrolled at Abbey are retaking A levels to raise their grades to those required for medicine, dentistry, law and other highly competitive university courses. Retake courses last four or nine months and the results have been exceptional: 95 per cent of intensive resit examinations taken in 1995 resulted in A – C grades.

Abbey also offers a comprehensive range of two-year A level courses at the college for students who wish to prepare for these examinations over the customary two-year study period. These places are aimed at motivated, ambitious students who require A or B grades for entrance to university. Due to the high standard of applicants for these places, entrance is by interview only. There are generous bursaries and scholarships available.

At Easter we provide a series of courses covering both A levels and GCSEs to external students who need extra help prior to their summer exams. Some may have gaps in their knowledge which may need to be filled; however, the majority lack confidence in applying their knowledge to examination questions.

It is our aim to motivate these students with an intensive and demanding series of tutorials, workshops and examination practice sessions. Previous years' successes have demonstrated that revision in a highly structured group environment is far more effective than working alone without support.

Furthermore, Abbey have organised a series of medical seminars for January 1996, at which doctors, consultants and admissions tutors will give expert advice and help to all would-be medics.

Now based at our magnificent new premises in the heart of Manchester's thriving commercial centre, Abbey is well placed to meet the educational challenges of the twenty-first century.

Tuition takes place in small groups (maximum eight students per group) in an informal yet disciplined atmosphere. Students on all courses follow a tailor-made programme which is centred exclusively on the examination. Abbey monitors each student carefully throughout the course as well as comprehensively guiding them through the complete UCAS procedure.

Bosworth Tutorial College

9–12 St Georges Avenue, Northampton, Northamptonshire NN2 6JA
Tel: 01604 719988 Fax: 01604 791418

Joint heads Mark A V Broadway BSc, PGCE; Sheilagh McIntosh CertEd, Dip Maths Assn
Founded 1977
Type Tutorial and sixth-form college
Age range 14+ *Boarders from* 14+

Bosworth is a fully residential and day college, overlooking parkland in the centre of Northampton. The emphasis is very much on hard work in a relaxed, mature and caring environment. Teaching is in small groups of typically five or six in number with regular testing.

A wide range of A levels and GCSE subjects is offered with great flexibility in subject combinations. Courses are usually over one year, two years or 18 months, but we are often able to cater for mid-term entries. The college is an examination centre for most of the examining boards and careful assistance is given to university applications.

The intensive, academic activity is counter-balanced by a comprehensive programme of optional sporting and social events.

Residential students live in the college fully supervised by a warden, or if they prefer, with one of our carefully selected families, who all live nearby. We also offer small, independent houses to our mature students, sharing with three or four others. Whichever accommodation students choose, all meals are taken within the college.

Our individual approach enables us to cater for students of all abilities – those struggling to make the grade as well as Oxford and Cambridge candidates.

Abacus College

Threeways House, George Street, Oxford, Oxfordshire OX1 2BJ
Tel: 01865 240111 Fax: 01865 247259

Head Laraine Brown
Founded 1968
Type Independent secondary
Religious denomination Non-denominational
Members of BACIFHE
Age range 13 – 18 *Boarders from* 16+
No of pupils (day) 30; *(boarding)* 90
Girls 45; *Boys* 75
Senior 20; *Sixth form* 100
Fees per term (day) £610 – £3,050; *(boarding)* £1,545 – £3,862
Fees per annum (day) £1,830 – £9,150; *(boarding)* £4,635 – £12,625

Curriculum and examinations: Abacus College has been preparing students for GCE A level and GCSE examinations for 25 years and is recognised as efficient by the British Accreditation Council for Independent Further and Higher Education (BACIFHE). A broad range of subjects is offered and tuition is in small groups or on a one-to-one basis. The principal, deputy principal and all key tutors are experienced graduates with a minimum of five years with the college. *Entry requirements*: students should contact the college with their qualifications and attend an interview where possible.
Academic and leisure facilities: the college's purpose-built facilities include excellent classrooms, laboratory, library and computer room, plus a comfortable students' common room.
Scholarships: the Roland Hazell Scholarship – details of the scholarship may be obtained from the Principal.
Boarding: accommodation is available in hostels or with families and is full board or self-catering.

Cherwell Tutors

Greyfriars, Paradise Street, Oxford, Oxfordshire OX1 1LD
Tel: 01865 242670 Fax: 01865 791761

Head Paul J Gordon
Founded 1973
Type Tutorial college
Religious denomination All
Age range 16+ *Boarders from* 16+
No of pupils (day) 20; *(boarding)* 140
Girls 75; *Boys* 85
Senior 20; *Sixth form* 140
Fees per term (day) c £2,750; *(boarding)* c £3,750
Fees per annum (day) £8,250; *(boarding)* £11,250

Cherwell Tutors, founded in 1973, is a small semi-residential tutorial establishment situated in the heart of Oxford, specialising in preparing boys and girls under close personal supervision for entrance into higher education.

Usually, 150 pupils join Cherwell each academic year to be prepared for the GCSE, A level and Oxbridge entrance examinations.

Cherwell Tutors' distinction is that of tuition geared to the needs of the individual, where tutorials for each pupil are supported by seminars and trials held weekly; revision classes and practicals for those studying natural science and art.

Accommodation arrangements are made. Pupils may stay in one of Cherwell's four hall of residence or with a family.

Provision is made for all sport at Cherwell.

St Clare's, Oxford

139 Banbury Road, Oxford, Oxfordshire OX2 7AL
Tel: 01865 52031 Fax: 01865 513359

Head Mrs Margaret Skarland BA, PGCE
Founded 1953
Type International college
Members of ECIS; Accredited by BAC
Age range 16+ *Boarders from* 16
No of pupils (day) 15; *(boarding)* 267
Girls 172 *Boys* 110
Sixth form 168, and 114 above
Fees per annum Charged in two instalments per year *(day)* £8,020; *(boarding)* £12,820 – £13,040

St Clare's is an international, co-educational, residential college in Oxford. Founded in 1953, it has grown out of a scheme to establish links between British and European students after the war. The college is a registered charity which aims to promote international understanding and high academic standards in its students. Around 300 students from around 40 countries study during the academic year, the largest national group being British. The minimum age is 16, and the atmosphere is informal and friendly, encouraging personal responsibility. The college is located in a pleasant residential area about one mile from Oxford city centre, and occupies 18 Victorian houses to which purpose- built facilities have been added. These include an outstanding academic resources centre (30,000 volumes, audio-visual centre, computers), opened in May 1995, and four science laboratories, art studio, hall and student club. Students live in college houses under the care of a resident warden.

Courses are offered at pre-university and university levels, and in English language. The two year pre-university (sixth form) course leads to the International Baccalaureate diploma, designed to educate the whole person and to qualify for entrance to the world's most demanding universities. Students choose six subjects, providing a programme balanced in depth and breadth. They also complete a research project, follow a course in critical thinking and engage in extra-curricular activities.

A one-year university foundation course is also offered for students with appropriate academic qualifications.

Teaching staff are selected for their strong academic background and teaching skills. Many are involved in IB curriculum development and examining and the college (which has offered the IB since 1977), regularly assists schools introducing the programme. The staff student ratio is around 1:7.

There is an extensive programme of social, cultural, service and sporting activities, and students are encouraged to avail themselves fully of all the opportunities which Oxford provides.

Entry is on the basis of academic results, interview and confidential school record. Scholarships and bursaries are awarded by examinations, held in January.

Almost all IB diploma students proceed to higher education in Britain or elsewhere assisted by two higher education advisers.

Cambridge Tutors College

Water Tower Hill, Croydon, Surrey CR0 5SX
Tel: 0181 688 5284/7363 Fax: 0181 686 9220

Principal D N Wilson BA, MLitt (Oxon), MIL, FCollP
Founded 1958
Type Sixth form/tutorial
Religious denomination Non-denominational
Age range 16+
No of pupils (day) 240
Girls 125; *Boys* 115
Senior (GCSE) 20; *Sixth form* 220
Fees per term (day) £2,483
Fees per annum (day) £7,450

The college was founded by graduates of Cambridge University and is widely recognised as one of the country's foremost tutorial establishments. It has built up a solid reputation for the excellence of its A level results in the sciences and mathematics and in business-related subjects such as accounts, economics and law. The college has been particularly successful in gaining a high number of places for its students at British medical schools. In 1993 the college was chosen by King's College London to run its prestigious international science foundation year course.

Cambridge Tutors bases its teaching on the tutorial system, where students work in very small groups of average six (maximum eight). This enables them to receive greater individual attention from the tutor and makes it easier for them to participate in class discussion. The academic discipline is tough, but students are prepared to accept this in return for the more relaxed and informal social environment of the tutorial college.

Students take weekly tests in all of their subjects under strict exam conditions. This ensures that they have regular practice in producing quality answers under pressure of time and also allows subject tutors to monitor whether what is taught is being adequately digested and understood. A comprehensive programme of study skills is designed to teach students how to study effectively, by analysing the processes and techniques of learning (eg improving memory, reading (scanning) skills, note-taking, organising work schedules, revision and exam techniques).

The 34 specialist tutors have a combined service of over 400 years, and the college prides itself on a dedicated, stable and consistent teaching staff. Of the 145 degree-course applicants in 1994, 52 per cent gained places at the top 10 universities and 73 per cent gained places at the top 25 universities. The overall percentage gaining places at old and new universities was 94 per cent.

The college is situated in an attractive parkside location near the centre of Croydon and is only five minutes' walk from East Croydon Mainline Station and within easy reach of central London, Gatwick and Heathrow airports.

Hurtwood House

Holmbury St Mary, Dorking, Surrey RH5 6NU
Tel: 01483 277416 Fax: 01483 267586

Head K R B Jackson
Founded 1969
Type Independent VI form college
Religious denomination Multi-denominational
Members of ARELS
Age range 15 – 18 *Boarders from* 15 – 18
No of pupils (boarding) 250
Girls 125 *Boys* 125
Sixth form 250
Fees per term (boarding) £4,500 – £5,500
Fees per annum (boarding) £13,500 – £16,500

Hurtwood House combines the best of public school with the best of sixth form college. It is the only public school which specialises in the sixth form and provides a mature boarding community and a stepping-stone between school and university for 16 – 18 year old boys and girls.

Curriculum: two-year A level courses are available in mathematics, further mathematics, physics, chemistry, biology, English, French, German, history, politics, law, economics, accounting, history of art, business studies, sociology, Spanish, media studies, theatre studies, art and music technology.

University entrance: Hurtwood House has an outstanding record for the successful placement of students in universities throughout the country. More than 95 per cent of applicants go on to higher education each year.

Academic and leisure facilities: teaching is in small classes. The student/teacher ratio is 6:1 and the average class size is ten. The maximum amount of attention is focused on the needs of the individual. Emphasis is placed on teaching students how to study effectively. Great attention is paid to detail and students have their work assessed and graded in every subject every week. They received regular counselling from house staff and progress is monitored at weekly staff meetings. Reports are sent to parents twice a term. Examination results are exceptionally good at all levels. Excellent facilities include an extensive reference library and resource centre, modern science laboratories and classrooms which are equipped to the highest standards. The school also has its own purpose-built theatre and TV/film studio.

There is a full programme of cultural, social and leisure activities. A wide range of sports includes football, cricket, tennis, rugby, netball, volleyball, basketball, hockey, riding, swimming and squash. The college has its own playing fields, theatre, common rooms, TV rooms etc.

The house itself is a fine Edwardian building with a magnificent estate of more than 50 acres of playing field, private woodlands and gardens. It is close to Guildford and is only one hour from London by rail or road and close to Heathrow and Gatwick airports.

Boarding facilities: Hurtwood House is fully residential and provides a secure and caring environment for its students, all of whom live and sleep at the college in one of the five school houses, each set in its own beautiful grounds about five minutes away from the central building. The study bedrooms are all comfortably equipped and furnished. Supervision and welfare in each house is in the hands of the housemaster and their assistants who also live on the school premises and are responsible day and night for the health, welfare and happiness of the students.

Overseas students: there are 250 boys and girls in the college. Two-thirds of these come from England and the remainder from 30 or 40 different countries.

Bellerbys College

44 Cromwell Road, Hove, East Sussex BN3 3ER
Tel: 01273 723911 Fax: 01273 328445

Head Mr L Denholm MA, MEd, DipRSA
Founded 1959
Type Sixth form college
Age range 15+ *Boarders from* 15+
Fees per term (boarding) £3,375 – £3,950
Fees per annum (boarding) £11,500 – £11,850

Bellerbys College offers an alternative to the conventional school sixth form.

Our guiding principle is to help students achieve the highest grades of which they are capable in a friendly, informal atmosphere. The development of individual abilities, skills and knowledge through personal tuition in small classes (average eight) enables students to fulfil their potential in public examinations. A high proportion of students go on to university.

Bellerbys College is situated in a residential area close to Hove town centre and welcomes students from many countries as well as the UK.

A level programmes commence in September, January and April. The largest intake is September and many students complete three A levels in one year.

GCSE courses and one term or one year resit courses commence in September.

The college has boarding accommodation supervised by residential staff. An optional sporting and social programme is offered.

Bellerbys College is accredited by the BAC and is a member of CIFE.

Basil Paterson College

Dugdale-McAdam House, 22–23 Abercromby Place, Edinburgh, Lothian EH3 6QE
Tel: 0131 556 7695 Fax: 0131 557 8503

Head Mr Robin R Mackenzie MA
Founded 1929
Type Independent tutorial college
Accredited by BAC
Age range 16+
No of pupils (day) 37
Girls 15; *Boys* 22
Fees per term (day) A levels from £920; SCE Highers from £707 per term; GCSEs from £565 per term

Basil Paterson College occupies a spacious 19th century building in Edinburgh's famous Georgian new town, five minutes from the city centre. Its three schools (School of Academic Studies, School of Secretarial and Business Studies and Edinburgh Language Foundation) combine to offer a unique range of courses for British and overseas students.

The School of Academic Studies offers a wide range of courses in preparation for SCE, GCE and GCSE examinations. The permanent staff consists of mature, qualified and experienced teachers, all of whom are specialists in their fields. Each conduct small classes, thus allowing students individual attention. Student advisers are present to monitor progress, offer advice and assist with academic and personal matters.

The school is accredited by the British Accreditation Council. A full social programme is on offer to students from all three schools. Students have free access to a golf and country club which has extensive leisure facilities.

The Old Vicarage

Marden, Tonbridge, Kent TN12 9AG
Tel: 01622 832200 Fax: 01622 832200

Head Mrs P G Stevens LRAM (S&D)
Founded 1986
Type Girls' boarding and day
Boarders from 16+, no upper limit
No of pupils (day) variable *(boarding)* maximum 12
Girls All
Fees per term (boarding) General course £2,300 + VAT (day students negotiable)
Short courses £250 – £350 per week
VAT does not apply to English as a Foreign Language but is applicable at the standard rate on all other fees

A small friendly school for girls 16+. Country area. Just under an hour from London. Choice of courses and subjects available throughout the year.

General course: in two or three terms. Academic and practical subjects including English language and literature, secretarial skills, speech and drama, art and crafts, fashion and dressmaking, cookery, sugarcraft. Additional subjects as required. Examinations available.

Short course: on weekly basis including intensive English and choice of subjects from general course. All suitable for foreign and British girls. Full board and free time to travel if desired while accommodation retained.

Inchbald School of Design

7 Eaton Gate, London SW1W 9BA
Tel: 0171 730 5508 Fax: 0171 730 4937

Head Mrs Jacqueline Duncan
Founded 1960
Type Design education
Accredited by British Accreditation Council
Age range 17 – 50+
No of pupils (day) 80 (plus those on short courses in holidays)
Girls Variable *Boys* Variable
Fees per term (day) Vary according to course

The school is the leading establishment of its kind, specialising in the education of interior and garden design, and the history of design. Courses, ranging in length from three day to three years, are career-oriented and suit all levels – elementary, through to advanced intermediate and professional. Qualifications range from ten-week certificate, one-year diploma, two-year high diploma, to three-year masters diploma. Applicants living in the UK are asked to attend interview with the course director. Those applicants living abroad at time of application complete a questionnaire.

Scholarships: for exceptional applicants in demonstrable financial difficulty, the principal may at her discretion waive a percentage of the course fees.

KLC School of Interior Design

KLC House, Springvale Terrace, London W14 0AE
Tel: 0171 602 8592 Fax: 0171 602 1964

Head Jenny Gibbs FRSA, MSCD, AIDDA
Founded 1980
Type Interior design education
Accredited by British Accreditation Council
No of pupils (day) Diploma course – 30; Certificate course – 20; Specialist day courses/workshops – 30
Fees Diploma course – 3 terms @ £2,175 ex VAT (Career Development Loans available)
Scholarship An annual scholarship place is available

Officially recognised by the British Accreditation Council and affiliated to the London campus of Huron University, KLC is a leading school of interior design and enjoys an international reputation. All tutors are practising professionals and each student's work is monitored by a personal tutor to ensure that he or she develops his or her potential to the full. Career guidance and counselling plus the benefit of an active Alumni Association enable students to maintain contact with KLC after they have graduated.

UK applicants are asked to attend an interview; overseas applicants are required to complete an application form and are then interviewed by telephone.

Normal entry standard is five subjects at GCSE/O level and two subjects at A level but mature students are encouraged.

The Princess Christian College

26 Wilbraham Road, Fallowfield, Manchester, Greater Manchester M14 6JX
Tel: 0161 224 4560 Fax: 0161 256 4142

Principal Mrs E Rigby
Founded 1901
Type Nursery training college
Members of ANTC
Age range 16+ *Boarders from* 16+
No of pupils (boarding) 50
Fees per annum (day) £5,400 (less tax relief);
(boarding) £6,750 (less tax relief)

This small, friendly college is well located in a pleasant residential area of south-west Manchester, close to Manchester University, with easy access to motorway networks, intercity rail and coach services and Manchester International Airport. The family atmosphere of the college owes much to the mature surroundings of the Victorian house which has been its home since 1919 and extended to meet increasing needs.

The college offers quality training on a residential or daily basis to students aged 16+ whose chosen profession is childcare. Flexible learning packages, with theoretical input and a wide variety of experience placements, meet every need. Available over one or two years, courses lead to a range of qualifications:

- The Certificate in Childcare and Education (CACHE)
- The NNEB Diploma in Nursery Nursing
- NVQ (Childcare) Level II or III
- The internationally renowned Princess Christian Certificate.

Entry requirements are as flexible as the courses and will be discussed at interview.

St Aldates College

Rose Place, Oxford, Oxfordshire OX1 1SB
Tel: 01865 240963 Fax: 01865 242783

Head Mrs Pauline Martin
Founded 1975
Type Business and Career skills
Members of IBTA
Age range 16 – 30
No of pupils (boarding) 200
Fees per term (day) From £1,335

Set in the heart of Oxford, St Aldates offers a comprehensive range of business courses designed to give students the practical skills necessary for rewarding careers. Courses offered include:

1) 9 month Business Studies diploma
2) 9 month Executive PA diploma
3) 9 month Media PA diploma
4) 9 month Media Management diploma
5) 3 month Intensive Career Skills courses (particularly suitable for those in their gap year).

Training keeps in close touch with new technology and the changing needs of business. Each course includes extensive computer skills training using the latest PC Windows-based software, as well as CD-ROM and the global Internet. Students on nine month courses also have the opportunity to practise their skills in a work experience placement arranged by the college as part of their course. In addition, all students receive careful careers counselling and instruction in interview technique from our in-house recruitment professionals.

As a result St Aldates graduates are highly regarded by employers and each year many receive excellent job offers even before they complete their course.

Boveridge House School

Cranborne, Wimborne, Dorset BH21 5RU
Tel: 01725 517218

Head Miss P Harper
Founded 1966
Type Private
Age range 8 – 19; *Boarders from* 8 – 19
No of pupils (day) 1; *(boarding)* 33
Girls 16; *Boys* 18
Junior 3 classes *Senior* 3 classes
Fees per term (day) £1,900 *(boarding)* £4,000
Fees per annum (day) £5,700 *(boarding)* £12,000

School for children with learning difficulties and related medical problems, following a modified GCSE school curriculum.

Older pupils follow life skills programme. Tuition given in music, riding and outdoor activities. Boveridge House School also offers riding holidays and remedial tuition in English language and mathematics during school holidays.

Boveridge House is an elegant Georgian mansion offering the highest standards of care and accommodation to students. There is an Arabic-speaking member of staff.

RNIB New College

Whittington Road, Worcester WR5 2JX
Tel: 01905 763933 Fax: 01905 763277

Principal Mrs Helen Williams
Founded 1867
Type Non-maintained special
Religious denomination Church of England
Age range 10 – 19 *Boarders from* 10
No of pupils (day) 3; *(boarding)* 118
Girls 60; *Boys* 60
Senior 90; *Sixth form* 38

We are a residential co-educational school for pupils with a visual impairment who are academically able. Pupils may have an additional disability.

Pupils follow the National Curriculum working towards GCSE and A levels. Entry is by assessment. Those hoping to join the school in September are usually assessed during the preceding spring term but individuals can always be assessed at the age and time correct for the pupils.

Pupils live in family units of 15/16 with a residential house parent and support staff. Living skills and leisure activities are considered to be important aspects of life here. Pupils in Years 12 and 13 live in a university-style hostel and are encouraged to lead an independent life.

Maple Hayes Hall Dyslexia School

Abnalls Lane, Lichfield, Staffordshire WS13 8BL
Tel: 01543 264387 Fax: 01543 262022

Head Dr E Neville Brown
Founded 1982
Type Independent DFE approved
Religious denomination Inter-denominational
Members of ISIS, ISAI, ISJC, ECIS
Age range 7 – 17
No of pupils (day) 30 girls and boys *(boarding)* 90 boys
Girls day only
Fees per term (day) £2,575; *(boarding)* £3,250 – £3,700
Fees per annum (day) £7,725 *(boarding)* £9,750 – £11,100

Maple Hayes Hall is one of the select few schools for dyslexics and underachievers which is inspected by OFSTED and approved by the Department for Education. The school is set in extensive grounds near Lichfield and caters for up to 120 children from 7 to 17 years. We have a worldwide reputation for our unique and effective teaching methods and for our examination results. After taking GCSE with us, most students go on to higher education at college or university.

We provide a good all-round education without the stigma of withdrawal to a special unit and our youngsters compete well in the Midland and National Independent School sports championships.

Children's learning is under the supervision of a chartered psychologist and an assessment service is available. Private and LEA placements are welcome. In addition to bursaries for private placements, there is a generous bursary scheme for children of very high intelligence. Admission is by interview and psychologist's report.

St Mary's

Wrestwood Road, Bexhill on Sea, East Sussex TN40 2LU
Tel: 01424 730740 Fax: 01424 733575

Principal David Cassar MA, MIMgt
Founded 1922
Type Independent DFE Approved special school
Religious denomination Christian foundation
Age range 7 – 16 *Boarders from* 7
No of pupils (day) 15; *(boarding)* 75
Girls Yes; *Boys* Yes
Junior 7; *Senior* 16
Fees per term (day) £5,754; *(boarding)* £8,632
Fees per annum (day) £17,262; *(boarding)* £25,896

St Mary's Wrestwood Educational Trust is a registered charity which exists to provide high quality education, therapy and care in a residential setting, for boys and girls with special educational needs which includes speech and language disorders and quite complex and unique conditions and syndromes.

We follow the National Curriculum differentiated where necessary, plus a comprehensive Life Skills programme. We have a team of speech and language therapists, an art therapist, a physiotherapist, an occupational therapist, specialist teachers for the hearing- impaired, and a high ratio of qualified and experienced care and nursing staff.

Referrals are normally made through local education departments. Private referrals are also accepted.

St Mary's is situated in a semi-rural location in Sussex near the sea. It is set in attractive buildings in woodland on the outskirts of Bexhill. Children are referred from all parts of the country.

The school is registered charity number 307021/A.

Bedford School

Burnaby Road, Bedford, Bedfordshire MK40 2TU
Tel: 01234 340444 Fax: 01234 340050

Head Dr I P Evans
Founded 1552
Type Independent
Religious denomination Church of England
Members of HMC
No of pupils (day) 853; *(boarding)* 247
Boys 1100
Junior 392; *Senior* 708; *Sixth form* 286
Fees per term (day) £2,335 *(boarding)* £3,715
Fees per annum (day) £7,005 *(boarding)* £11,145

Scholarships tenable at Bedford School
At 11+: two major scholarships of up to 50 per cent remission of fees; and two minor scholarships of up to 25 per cent remission. Also exhibitions of £500 per annum.
At 13+: up to nine major and minor scholarships ranging from 25 per cent to 50 per cent remission. Also a number of exhibitions available for all-round qualities.

Common Entrance Exhibitions of £600 per annum are available for candidates who perform particularly well in the Common Entrance Examination.

Music scholarships: a number of instrumental music scholarships of up to 50 per cent remission of fees plus free instrumental tuition. Music exhibitions of free instrumental tuition. One organ scholarship of up to 50 per cent remission of fees for a candidate for the lower sixth form.

Other awards: one minor scholarship of up to 30 per cent remission and two minor exhibitions of £500 per annum for boys showing outstanding ability in art, drama, design technology, or information technology.

One sixth-form scholarship offering remission of up to one third remission of fees.

The Grange School

Bradburns Lane, Hartford, Northwich, Cheshire CW8 1LU
Tel: 01606 74007 Fax: 01606 784581

Head Mr E S Marshall MA, LGSM
Founded 1933
Type Co-educational school
Age range 4 – 18
No of pupils (day) 1,087
Sixth form 131
Fees per annum (day) kindergarten (1) £2,625; prep school (2–6) £2,925; senior & sixth form £3,675

Scholarships and bursaries: attractive scholarships and bursaries are offered by the school. All pupils taking the senior school entrance examinations at 11+ years are eligible for scholarships awards. These are awarded for high academic merit at the headmaster's discretion. Bursaries are also awarded for academic merit and are means-related.

At Year 1 scholarship entry to the senior school is available in music, drama and sport.

Seven prestigious scholarships of up to 50 per cent fee remission are awarded by competitive examination, to prospective sixth form candidates.

The Grange School Hartford Ltd Charitable Trust exists to provide high quality education for local boys and girls.

St Anne's School Educational Trust Limited

Browhead, Windermere, Cumbria LA23 1NW
Tel: 015394 46164 Fax: 015394 88414

Head Mr C M G R Jenkins
Founded 1863
Type Independent day and boarding (girls)
Religious denomination Non-denominational
Members of GSA, GBGSA, Round Square International Schools
Age range 3 – 18 *Boarders from* 8
No of pupils (day) 140; *(boarding)* 210
Girls 330; *Boys* 20 (3 – 11 years)
Junior 100; *Senior* 250; *Sixth form* 75
Fees per term (day) £400 – £2,017; *(boarding)* £2,140 – £3,042
Fees per annum (day) £1,200 – £6,051; *(boarding)* £6,420 – £9,126

Scholarships, exhibitions and bursaries:
Sixth form: three academic scholarships 50 per cent, 35 per cent and 20 per cent (closed) of the full fees. Four minor awards: music, art, drama and sport.

13+: three academic scholarships up to 50 per cent of the full fees.

11+: three academic scholarships up to 50 per cent of the full fees.

11+/13+: music scholarships (up to 25 per cent of the full fees) and minor awards for music, drama and sport.

9+: academic scholarship at 10 per cent for two years. Music award of 5 per cent for two years.

Bursaries: 5 per cent service bursaries. There are a number of bursaries available for those with special needs.

St Anne's School Educational Trust, a registered charity, exists to provide education of the highest standards.

Durham School

Durham, County Durham DH1 4SZ
Tel: 0191 384 7977 Fax: 0191 383 1025

Head Mr M A Lang MA, FRSA
Founded 1414
Religious denomination Church of England
Member of HMC
Age range 11 – 18
No of pupils (day) 180; *(boarding)* 141
Girls 39; *Boys* 284
Junior 27; *Senior* 297; *Sixth form* 138
Fees per term (day) £1,695 – £2,473; *(boarding)*
£3,231 – £3,802
Fees per annum (day) £5,085 – £7,419;
(boarding) £9,693 – £11,406

A generous range of academic, music and art scholarships are available. Each year, five or six King's Scholarships are open to boys under 14 on 1st September. These are worth up to half fees for a boarder or a day boy and can be increased to full fees in case of need.

Further academic exhibitions, music and art scholarships and exhibitions are also awarded, both to those aged 13 and to those aged 11.

Burkitt Scholarships are awarded to entrants to the sixth form and can be won by both boys and girls.

The competitions for all the awards take place in late February or early March.

Clerical Bursaries may be awarded to the sons of Church of England clergy, and assisted places were awarded for the first time in 1989.

Winchester College

College Street, Winchester, Hampshire SO23 9NA
Tel: 01962 854328 Fax: 01962 842972

Head J P Sabben-Clare MA (Member of HMC, SHA)
Founded 1382
Type Boys boarding/day school
Religious denomination Church of England
Age range 13 – 18 *Boarders from* 13
Senior 681 (including sixth form); *Sixth form* 283
Fees per annum (day) £9,966; *(boarding)* £13,290

Scholarships, exhibitions and bursaries: the examination of candidates for scholarships, exhibitions and awards will begin at the college on Monday 13 May: about 15 scholarships and about six exhibitions will be offered. Scholarships have a basic value of half of the full fee. Exhibitions have a maximum value of one-third of the full fee. Candidates must be under 14 and at least 12 on 1 September 1996. Entry forms, which must be returned by 22 April, are obtainable from the Master In College, Winchester College, College Street, Winchester, Hampshire SO23 9NA.

Examinations for sixth form awards and places begin on Friday 2 February 1996. Entry forms, which must be returned by 20 November 1995, are obtainable from the headmaster (address as above).

Winchester College is a charitable trust which exists for the advancement of education and activities connected therewith.

St Albans School

Abbey Gateway, St Albans, Hertfordshire AL3 4HB
Tel: 01727 855521 Fax: 01727 843447

Head A R Grant MA (Cantab)
Founded 948
Type Independent senior boys' day school with co-educational sixth form
Religious denomination Non-denominational
Members of HMC, GBA, ISIS
Age range 11 – 18
No of pupils (day) 650
Girls 40; *Boys* 610
Senior 440; *Sixth form* 210

Twenty assisted places under the DFE scheme are awarded each year to entrants at 11+. Five are available for entrants to the sixth form. All assisted places are means-tested. A variable number of academic scholarships worth up to 50 per cent of the annual fees is awarded on academic merit at 11+, 13+ and 16+. Scholarships for music and art are offered at 13+. Bursaries towards music tuition are provided for pupils from each year in the school. Further details of all awards from the headmaster.

The school is a registered charity and aims to provide an excellent education enabling pupils to achieve the highest standard of academic success according to ability, and to develop their character and personality so as to become caring and self-disciplined adults.

The King's School

Canterbury, Kent CT1 2ES
Tel: 01227 595501 Fax: 01227 595595

Head The Revd Canon A C J Phillips
Founded 597
Type Co-educational
Religious denomination Church of England
Members of HMC
Age range 13 – 18 *Boarders from* 13 – 18
No of pupils (day) 129; *(boarding)* 605
Girls 290; *Boys* 444
Senior 439; *Sixth form* 295
Fees per term (day) £2,294; *(boarding)* £4,265
Fees per annum (day) £8,835; *(boarding)* £12,795

Scholarships, exhibitions and bursaries: up to 20 scholarships are awarded to 13+ entrants (boys and girls) of up to 50 per cent fees which may then be made up by a bursary for those in need, regular music scholarships and a number of discretionary awards are offered annually. Academic and music and art scholarships are also available for boy and girl pupils entering the sixth form. For particulars apply to the admissions secretary.

The King's School Charitable Trust exists to provide high quality education for boys and girls 13 – 18.

Millfield

Street, Somerset BA16 0YD
Tel: 01458 442291 Fax: 01458 447276

Head C S Martin
Founded 1935
Type Independent co-educational boarding and day
Religious denomination Multi-denominational
Members of HMC
Age range 13 – 19 *Boarders from* 13
No of pupils (day) 296; *(boarding)* 953
Girls 516; *Boys* 733
Senior 1,249; *Sixth form* 491
Fees per term (day) £2,770; *(boarding)* £4,440
Fees per annum (day) £8,310; *(boarding)* £13,320

Academic: approximately 20 awards are made at 13+ on the results of written examinations.

A further 20 may be awarded on the basis of GCSE results and Millfield examination.

Music: auditions are held in February for 15 scholarships and exhibitions, open to candidates for 13+ or 16+ entry.

Art: three scholarships, open to 13+ and 16+ candidates, are made annually on the assessment of portfolio collection.

Further awards are available to candidates showing good academic strength in music, art, games, drama or dance.

Awards are offered up to a maximum of 50 per cent fees; they may be supplemented further where need can be demonstrated.

Millfield School's preparatory school, Edgarley Hall, prepares boys and girls from the age of eight for entrance to Millfield; pupils are eligible for all Millfield 13+ awards.

Box Hill School

Mickleham, Dorking, Surrey RH5 6EA
Tel: 01372 373382 Fax: 01372 363942

Head Dr R A S Atwood BA, PhD
Founded 1959
Type Independent
Religious denomination Non-denominational
Members of SHMIS, ISCO, Round Square
Age range 11 – 18 *Boarders from* 11 – 18
No of pupils (day) 106 *(boarding)* 163
Girls 93 *Boys* 176
Senior 184 *Sixth form* 70
Fees per term (day) £2,050; *(weekly boarding)* £3,280; *(boarding)* £3,400
Fees per annum (day) £6,150; *(weekly boarding)* £9,840; *(boarding)* £10,200

Ten sixth-form scholarships, each the value of £500 per term, may be awarded annually by the Headmaster. Scholarships will be given to those who merit them on the basis of good character, all round contribution to the life of the School, and the ability to tackle three A levels successfully over a two year course. Good art or music would be strong recommendations, but ability and willingness to contribute to dramatic productions, expeditions, social services, sports, debating and similar activities would also be valued.

Parents should apply in writing to the Headmaster. For those already in the school, awards would be made on the basis of reports from teaching staff involved in academic work, activities and clubs, and in Houses. For pupils entering the sixth form from other schools, the awards would be made on the basis of an interview with the Headmaster and Head of Sixth Form, and on a full confidential report on character and academic work from the Head of their present school.

All offers of scholarships are dependent upon the successful candidate achieving at least five GCSE passes at Grade C or better.

Ardingly College

Haywards Heath, West Sussex RH17 6SQ
Tel: 01444 842577 Fax: 01444 892266

Head James Flecker
Founded 1858
Type Co-educational, boarding and day
Religious denomination Church of England
Members of ISIS, HMC
Age range 13 – 18 *Boarders from* 13
No of pupils (day) 150; *(boarding)* 310
Girls 195; *Boys* 265
Sixth form 189
Fees per term (day) £3,063; *(boarding)* £3,880
Fees per annum (day) £9,145; *(boarding)* £11,640

Ardingly College is a co-educational boarding and day school for boys and girls aged 2½–18, and is divided into pre-prep (2½–7), junior (7–13) and senior (13–18) schools which run independently but share a campus and have close links.

There is splendid pastoral care in all three schools, and individual tutors for each pupil and a well-organised House system in the junior and senior schools.

Ardingly is an academic school; as a general pattern, pupils will be expected to take nine GCSEs in the fifth form and three A levels in the sixth form. Class sizes throughout the school are small – fewer than 20 pupils for GCSE and about 12 per set for A levels.

We offer a wide range of scholarships at 13+ and 16+: academic art, CDT, drama, languages (16+ only), music, Oxbridge (16+ only), sciences (16+ only) and sport.

Ardingly College (Junior School)

Haywards Heath, West Sussex RH17 6SQ
Tel: 01444 842577 Fax: 01444 892200

Head Peter Thwaites
Founded 1858
Type Co-educational, boarding and day
Religious denomination Church of England
Members of IAPS, Woodard
Age range 7 – 13 *Boarders from* 7
No of pupils (day) 95; *(boarding)* 50
Girls 75; *Boys* 70
Junior 34; *Senior* 111
Fees per term (day) £1,750 – £1,875; *(boarding)* £2,750
Fees per annum (day) £5,750 – £5,625; *(boarding)* £8,250

Ardingly College Junior School is run as an independent preparatory school for boys and girls between the ages of 7 and 13 with nursery and pre-preparatory classes catered for in the 'Farmhouse' for 2½–7 year olds.

At Ardingly we provide an education which caters for a wide range of children; from the strongly academic, to those whose strengths are in the creative arts, to those who show their prowess in a more athletics way.

Pupils are prepared for Common Entrance and the destination for most of them is the senior school at Ardingly.

Many facilities are shared by both junior school and senior school, which gives access to a much greater range of activities inside and outside the classroom than is normally available to preparatory school.

The junior school awards academic, all-round, music and sports scholarships, and in addition to this, a number of Assisted Places at 11+.

Moira House School

Upper Carlisle Road, Eastbourne, East Sussex BN20 7TE
Tel: 01323 644144 Fax: 01323 649720

Head of Senior School: Adrian Underwood BA (Hons), MA, FRSA
Head of Junior School: Mrs A Harris BEd (Hons), ARCM

The Ingham Scholarships: the senior school

Three Sixth-Form Scholarships worth up to 75 per cent of the fees are available each year.

Four Ingham Academic Scholarships worth up to 50 per cent of the fees for either day girls or boarders are available each year.

Two Ingham scholarships worth up to 50 per cent of the fees for either day girls or boarders are available each year.

In addition, *Second Scholarships* are offered in all these categories.

The junior school

A number of *Ingham Academic and Music Scholarships* worth up to 50 per cent of the fees are available.

In addition *Second Scholarships* are offered in the Junior School.

Application

Full details for the Ingham Sixth-Form and Senior School Scholarships are available from the headmaster's secretary.

Full details for the Ingham Junior School Scholarships are available from the secretary of the headmistress of the Junior School.

Aiglon College

1885 Chesières-Villars, Switzerland
Tel: 00 41 25 35 27 21 Fax: 00 41 25 35 28 11

Head Mr Richard McDonald MA (Oxon)
Founded 1949
Type Co-educational boarding
Religious denomination Christian allegiance
Members of HMC, Round Square, ECIS, COBISEC
Age range 11 – 18 *Boarders from* 11
No of pupils (day) 9 *(boarding)* 279
Girls 120; *Boys* 159
Junior 35; *Senior* 154; *Sixth form* 99
Fees per term (day) Sfr9,115 – Sfr12,325;
(boarding) Sfr14,754.50 – Sfr17,618.90
Fees per annum (day) Sfr30,045 – Sfr36,975;
(boarding) Sfr44,263.50 – Sfr52,856.70

Scholarships and bursaries: a number of scholarships are offered annually, each amounting to approximately one half remission of fees. A number of bursaries is also available for deserving candidates who do not qualify for a scholarship. One scholarship may be awarded to a candidate who, as well as meeting the school's academic requirements, shows particular promise in skiing. Awards are made on the results of Common Entrance and/or Aiglon entrance exam, school recommendation and interview. Further information may be obtained from the head of admissions.

PART FOUR: REFERENCE SECTION

4.1
EXAMINATIONS AND TRAINING

Common Entrance

The Common Entrance examination forms the basis of entry to most independent senior schools, although some schools set their own entrance exams. Traditionally it is taken by boys at the age of 13 and by girls at the age of 11. However, with the growth of co-education at senior level the divisions have become less sharply defined and the examinations at 11+, 12+ and 13+ are open to both boys and girls.

The Common Entrance papers are set centrally by the Independent Schools' Examinations Board, which comprises members of the Headmasters' Conference (HMC), the Girls' Schools Association (GSA) and the Incorporated Association of Preparatory Schools (IAPS). The papers are marked, however, by the individual schools, which have their own marking schemes and set their own entry standards. Common Entrance is not an exam which candidates pass by reaching a national standard. Generally speaking, highly academic schools will normally look for a mark of 60+; those catering for children of more average ability will accept 50+.

With the introduction of GCSEs and the National Curriculum, the content of the Common Entrance papers has undergone regular review and the Independent Schools Examinations Board has adapted syllabuses to bring them into line with National Curriculum requirements.

Candidates are entered for Independent Schools Examinations by their junior or preparatory schools. Parents whose children attend state primary schools should apply to the Independent School Examinations Board direct, ideally four months before the scheduled examination date. Some pupils may need additional coaching for the exam if they are not attending an independent preparatory school. To be eligible, pupils must normally have been offered a place by a senior school subject to their performance in the exam. Pupils applying for scholarships may be required to pass Common Entrance before sitting the scholarship exam. Candidates normally take the exam in their own junior or preparatory schools.

At 11+ the Common Entrance exam consists of papers in English, mathematics and science, and is designed to be suitable for all pupils, whether they attend independent or state schools. At 12+ papers are set in English, mathematics, science and elementary French. Most pupils who take the exam at 13+ come from independent preparatory schools. Compulsory subjects are English, mathematics, science, French, history, geography and religious studies. Latin and Greek are optional subjects although some schools require Latin.

The examination for 13+ entry takes place in February, March, June and November. For entry at 11+ the exam is held in January. For further information on Common Entrance, or copies of past papers, contact: The Administrator, Independent Schools Examinations Board, Jordan House, Christchurch Road, New Milton, Hampshire BH25 6QJ *Tel*: 01425 621111, *Fax*: 01425 620044.

General Certificate of Secondary Education (GCSE)

The GCSE examination is open to anyone, but is normally taken by pupils at the age of 16. The structure of the examination has been adapted to comply with National Curriculum requirements. The GCSE forms the principal means of assessment of the two years preceding GCSE examinations (Key Stage 4) from 14–16. One of the chief features of GCSE is the focus on positive achievement. Pupils are assessed on the basis of what they can demonstrate of their knowledge and skills, rather than being penalised for inadequacies.

Coursework also forms a part of most GCSE syllabuses, enabling pupils to gain credit from work done during the year rather than exclusively on the basis of exam performance.

GCSE results are reported on a scale of grades from A* – G.

Increasing use is being made of 'differentiated' examination papers, ie a series of tiered papers targeted at different ranges of ability within the A* – G range of the grading scale.

Most pupils of average ability take eight or nine GCSE subjects, although some may take 10 or 11. Very able pupils may take some GCSE exams after one year. Pupils are asked to choose their subjects at 13. Schools can offer advice on those they think most suitable.

Further information and dates of examinations may be obtained from the six GCSE Examining Boards: **Northern Examinations and Assessment Board**, Devas Street, Manchester M15 6EX *Tel*: 0161 953 1180; **Midland Examining Group**, Syndicate Buildings, 1 Hills Road, Cambridge CB1 2EU *Tel*: 01223 553311; **University of London Examinations and Assessment Council**, Stewart House, 32 Russell Square, London WC1B 5DN *Tel*: 0171 331 4000; **Southern Examining Group**, Stag Hill House, Guildford, Surrey GU2 5XJ *Tel*: 01483 506506; **Welsh Joint Education Committee**, 245 Western Avenue, Cardiff CF5 2YX *Tel*: 01222 265000; **Northern Ireland Council for the Curriculum, Examinations and Assessment**, Beechill House, 42 Beechill Road, Belfast, Northern Ireland BT8 4RS *Tel*: 01232 704666.

GCE A levels

GCE A levels normally involve a further two years of study after GCSE and are taken at 18. In most cases pupils must have passed a GCSE exam in the subjects they wish to take, but some A levels, for example law, may not have been studied before students reach sixth-form level and can be started from scratch.

Most pupils take three subjects, some take two and a few very able ones four. A levels demand more individual, in-depth study than GCSEs and place greater emphasis on traditional study skills and presentation. Subject choices should be made with care and schools will be able to advise. Students should try to think ahead to possible routes or areas of study after A levels, since entry to specific higher education courses or areas of employment may demand certain subjects or a certain combination of subjects.

A levels are normally assessed by examination, for which grades are awarded A – E. Grade N denotes narrow failure. Grade U (Unclassified) is not certificated.

Some schools also now offer GNVQs (General National Vocational Qualifications), sometimes known as 'vocational A levels'. There are three levels – Foundation, Intermediate and Advanced. GNVQs are discussed in more detail below.

AS levels

AS levels are designed to be taken in conjunction with GCE A levels, as a means of broadening the curriculum for sixth-form students beyond the confines of a three-subject course. Students are encouraged to take AS levels in subjects which complement their A level studies and allow continued study of separate but relevant other subjects. A student studying A levels in modern languages might be encouraged to take one or two AS levels in mathematics or economics.

AS levels are studied in the same depth as A levels, but in terms of volume of material covered they only take up about half the time. Two AS levels are therefore taken as the equivalent of one A level. A frequent combination is two A levels and two AS levels, which allows some flexibility while also making up the required number of points needed for university applications. AS levels are well-recognised and accepted by universities, but for some courses admissions tutors may specify A levels rather than AS levels in given subjects. Students keen to apply for specific courses should check the entry requirements before confirming their A and AS level choices.

Further information on GCE A and AS levels, together with dates for the forthcoming examination sessions, may be obtained from the following Examining Boards: **The Associated Examining Board**, Stag Hill House, Guildford, Surrey GU2

5XJ *Tel*: 01483 506506; **Northern Examinations and Assessment Board**, Devas Street, Manchester M15 6EX *Tel*: 0161 953 1180; **Oxford and Cambridge School Examination Board**, Purbeck House, Purbeck Road, Cambridge CB2 2PU *Tel*: 01223 411211; **University of Oxford Delegacy of Local Examinations**, Ewert House, Summertown, Oxford OX2 7BZ *Tel*: 01865 54291; **University of Cambridge Local Examinations Syndicate**, Syndicate Buildings, 1 Hills Road, Cambridge CB1 2EU *Tel*: 01223 553311; **University of London Examinations and Assessment Council**, Stewart House, 32 Russell Square, London WC1B 5DN *Tel*: 0171 331 4000; **Welsh Joint Education Committee**, 245 Western Avenue, Cardiff CF5 2YX *Tel*: 01222 265000; **Northern Ireland Council for the Curriculum, Examinations and Assessment**, Beechill House, 42 Beechill Road, Belfast, Northern Ireland BT8 4RS *Tel*: 01232 704666.

Scottish Certificate of Education

In Scotland, most independent schools, particularly the city day schools, prepare students for the Standard Grade examinations taken at 16+. Higher Grade examinations taken at 17+ or 18+ represent one further year of study and form the basis for entry to Higher Education.

The Scottish curriculum at Higher Grade is generally broader in scope than the English GCE A level system. Pupils quite frequently take up to five or six Higher Grade subjects. Awards are indicated by one of four grades, A – D. The C/D boundary represents the pass/fail division. Scottish universities generally demand four or five Highers for entry to degree courses, which are also acceptable as the basis for applications to English universities.

In practice many students stay on after Highers to complete the Certificate of Sixth Year Studies at 18+. The CSYS is similar to GCE A level studies in that it encourages more individual study and greater specialisation in preparation for studies at Higher Education level. Most syllabuses require submission of a dissertation or project. Students normally take two or three CSYS subjects in which they must already hold a Higher Grade pass and may also take additional Highers at the same time. Results are expressed in terms of a five-point ranking A–E or are ungraded. Ungraded results are not certificated.

For further information about the Scottish Certificate of Education Standard or Higher Grades, or the CSYS, contact: **Scottish Examination Board**, Ironmills Road, Dalkeith, Midlothian EH22 1LE *Tel*: 0131 663 6601.

The International Baccalaureate

The IB is recognised and accepted by universities worldwide. It is offered by a small number of independent and state schools and colleges in the UK, a full list of which appears below. Worldwide there are some 600 state and independent schools offering the IB programme in 82 countries. The emphasis is on breadth, specialisation in specific areas, international understanding and critical thinking skills.

The IB can be an attractive alternative to A levels for academically able students. It is a two-year course, broader in scope and more demanding than a GCE A level syllabus and consists of six subject groups:

Group 1	Language A1 (first language) including the study of selections from world literature.
Group 2	Language A2, B or *ab initio* (second language) or a second language A1.
Group 3	Individuals and Societies – history, geography, economics, philosophy, psychology, social anthropology, business and organisation, information technology in a global society.
Group 4	Experimental Sciences – biology, chemistry (HL), general chemistry (SL), applied chemistry (SL), physics, environmental systems, design technology.
Group 5	Mathematics – mathematics (HL), mathematical studies (SL), mathematical methods (SL), advanced mathematics (SL).
Group 6	One of the following options – art/design, music, theatre arts, Latin, Classical Greek, computer science.

Candidates for the Diploma must offer one subject from each of the above groups and offer at least three and not more than four of the six subjects at Higher Level (HL) and the others at Subsidiary Level (SL).

Language A1 is designed for students for whom the language is normally their best one. Language A2 is for study by speakers with a high level of competence in the language. Language B is designed for study by students with some previous experience of learning the language. *Ab initio* is a foreign language learning programme for students with no previous experience of the language and who do not normally live in a country where the language is spoken.

Instead of Group 6 candidates may offer a third modern language, a second subject from Group 3, a second subject from Group 4 or advanced mathematics (SL).

Candidates must also submit an extended essay in one of the IB specified subjects, follow a course in the theory of knowledge and take part in activities representing creativity, action and service.

One pilot programme is currently underway – history and culture of the Islamic world.

In line with the IB's international emphasis, all subjects are offered in English, French and Spanish.

Each examined subject is graded on a scale of 1 (minimum) to 7. Award of the Diploma requires a minimum total of 24 points out of 45 and satisfactory completion of the theory of knowledge course, the extended essay and CAS.

For further information on the IB contact: **International Baccalaureate Office** Dr Ian Hill, Regional Director for Europe/Africa/Middle East, Route des Morillons 15, CH-1218 Grand-Saconnex, Geneva, Switzerland *Tel*: +41 22 791 0274 *Fax*: +41 22 791 0277.

The following schools and colleges are authorised to participate in the International Baccalaureate in the United Kingdom:

ENGLAND

Cambridgeshire

Impington Village College
New Road
Impington
Cambridge CB4 4LX
Tel: 01223 232835
Fax: 01223 235114
Warden: Mrs Sylvia West
IB Co-ordinator: Dr Kevin M Purday
IB No: 0579

Cheshire

Margaret Danyers College
North Downs Road
Cheadle Hulme
Cheadle
Cheshire SK8 5HA
Tel: 0161 485 4372
Fax: 0161 488 4354
Head: Harry Tomlinson
IB Co-ordinator: Mrs Helen B Hurst
IB No: 0545

Warrington Collegiate Institute
Crab Lane
Padgate
Warrington
Cheshire WA2 0DB
Tel: 01925 814343
Fax: 01925 816077
Principal: Dr Smith
IB Co-ordinator: David Cooper
IB No: 0735

Cumbria

Ullswater High School
Wetheriggs Lane
Penrith
Cumbria CA11 8NG
Tel: 01768 64377
Fax: 01768 890037
Head: David A Robinson
IB Co-ordinator: Mrs Hilary M Lanham
IB No: 0687

Devon

Exeter College
Hele Road
Exeter
Devon EX4 4JS
Tel: 01392 384087
Fax: 01392 210282
Principal: Dr J G Capey
IB Co-ordinator: Susan E A Temple
IB No: 0695

Essex

Anglo-European School
Willow Green
Ingatestone
Essex CM4 0DJ
Tel: 01277 354018
Fax: 01277 355623
Head: R Reed
IB Co-ordinator: Ms D A Inkersole
IB No: 0078

Hereford and Worcester

Malvern College
College Road
Malvern
Worcestershire WR14 3DF
Tel: 01684 892333
Fax: 01684 572398
Head: Roy de C Chapman
IB Co-ordinator: Dr René P Filho
IB No: 0641

Hertfordshire

Hockerill Anglo-European School
Dunmow Road
Bishops Stortford
Hertfordshire CM23 5HX
Tel: 01279 658451
Fax: 01279 755918
Head: Paul Andrews
IB Co-ordinator: Frank Ruggiero
IB No: 0815

Oaklands College, School of Arts and Sciences
St Peters Road
St Albans
Hertfordshire AL1 3RX
Tel: 01727 847070
Fax: 01727 847071
Head: Dr Rod F Cooper
IB Co-ordinator: Mrs F Julie Tidey
IB No: 0593

Kent

Sevenoaks School
Sevenoaks
Kent TN13 1HU
Tel: 01732 455133
Fax: 01732 456143
Head: R P Barker
IB Co-ordinator: Janet Thomas
IB No: 0102

London

Hammersmith and West London College
Gliddon Road
Baron's Court
London W14 9BL
Tel: 0181 741 1688
Fax: 0181 741 2491
Head: Mrs Illis
IB Co-ordinator: Gillian Mayo
IB No: 0021

International School of London
139 Gunnersbury Avenue
London W3 8LG
Tel: 0181 992 5823
Fax: 0181 993 7012
Head: Dr R Ghusyani
IB Co-ordinator: Huw Davies
IB No: 0057

La Retraite Roman Catholic Girls' School
Atkins Road
Clapham Park
London SW12 0AB
Tel: 0181 673 5644
Fax: 0181 675 8577
Head: Mrs M Howie
IB Co-ordinator: Ms A Reeves
IB No: 0833

Southbank International School
36-40 Kensington Park Road
London W11 3BU
Tel: 0171 229 8230
Fax: 0171 229 3784
Head: Milton E Toubkin
IB Co-ordinator: Mrs Hanne Simon
IB No: 0309

Merseyside

Broadgreen Community Comprehensive School
Queen's Drive
Liverpool
Merseyside L13 5UQ
Tel: 0151 228 6800
Fax: 0151 220 9256
Head: Ian P Andain
IB Co-ordinator: Dai W Thomas
IB No: 0639

Middlesex

The American Community School
108 Vine Lane
Uxbridge
Middlesex UB10 0BE
Tel: 01895 259771
Fax: 01895 256974
Head: Brian Duncan
IB Co-ordinator: Mrs Renata E Delshadian
IB No: 0152

St Dominic's Sixth Form College
Mount Park Avenue
Harrow-on-the-Hill
Middlesex HA1 3HX
Tel: 0181 422 8084
Fax. 0181 422 3759
Principal: John L Lipscomb
IB Co-ordinator: Mrs J Lynch
IB No: 0141

Oxfordshire

The Henley College
Deanfield Avenue
Henley-on-Thames
Oxfordshire RG9 1UH
Tel: 01491 579988
Fax: 01491 410099
Principal: Graham O J Phillips
IB Co-ordinator: Robin Milne
IB No: 0557

St Clare's
139 Banbury Road
Oxford OX2 7AL
Tel: 01865 52031
Fax: 01865 310002
Principal: Mrs Margaret Skarland
IB Co-ordinator: Nick Lee
IB No: 0041

Surrey

The American Community School
'Heywood'
Portsmouth Road
Cobham
Surrey KT11 1BL
Tel: 01932 867251
Fax: 01932 869791
Head: T Lehman
IB Co-ordinator: Craig Worthington
IB No: 0431

Marymount International School
George Road
Kingston upon Thames
Surrey KT2 7PE
Tel: 0181 949 0571
Fax: 0181 336 2485
Principal: Sr Rosaleen Sheridan

IB Co-ordinator: Dr Brian Johnson
IB No: 0128

West Midlands

The City Technology College
P O Box 1017
Cooks Lane
Kingshurst
Birmingham B37 6NZ
Tel: 0121 770 8923
Fax: 0121 770 0879
Principal: Mrs Valerie P Bragg
IB Co-ordinator: Arnet Edwards
IB No: 0568

Stourbridge College
Hagley Road
Old Swinford
Stourbridge
West Midlands DY8 1QU
Tel: 01384 378531
Fax: 01384 397319
Principal: David Toeman
IB Co-ordinator: Sally Firman
IB No: 0683

North Yorkshire

Yorkshire Coast College
Lady Edith's Drive
Scarborough
North Yorkshire YO12 5RN
Tel: 01723 372105
Fax: 01723 500923
Principal: Stan Dey
IB Co-ordinator: Mrs Kim Jutsum
IB No: 0739

Northern Ireland

Lagan College
44 Manse Road
Castlereagh
Belfast
Northern Ireland BT8 4SA
Tel: 01232 401810
Fax: 01232 703269
Principal: Dr B K Lambkin
IB Co-ordinator: Miss Anne Rowe
IB No: 0549

SCOTLAND

Dumfries & Galloway

Lockerbie Academy
Lockerbie
Dumfriesshire DG11 2AL
Tel: 01576 202626
Fax: 01576 203032
Rector: Andrew M Blake
IB Co-ordinator: Graham J Herbert
IB No: 0753

WALES

Clwyd

Llandrillo College
Llandudno Road
Colwyn Bay
Clwyd LL28 4HZ
Tel: 01492 546666
Fax: 01492 543052
Principal: Huw Evans
IB Co-ordinator: Carolyn Williams
IB No: 0640

South Glamorgan

United World College of the Atlantic
St Donat's Castle
Llantwit Major
South Glamorgan CF6 9WF
Tel: 01446 792345
Fax: 01446 794163
Principal: Colin D O Jenkins
IB Co-ordinator: J Roger Fletcher
IB No: 0017

West Glamorgan

Swansea College
Ty Coch Road
Sketty
Swansea
West Glamorgan SA2 9EB
Tel: 01792 206871
Fax: 01792 208137
Principal: Cyril M Lewis
IB Co-ordinator: D Hibbs
IB No: 0614

General National Vocational Qualifications (GNVQs) and National Vocational Qualifications (NVQs)

The GNVQ and NVQ framework has been introduced to try to standardise the wide range of vocational and training qualifications offered by a variety of awarding bodies. The awards offered by bodies such as the Business and Technology Education Council (BTEC), City and Guilds, and Royal Society of Arts (RSA) are gradually being replaced by new-style NVQ and GNVQ qualifications.

GNVQs are awarded at three levels: Foundation, Intermediate and Advanced, and are designed to develop knowledge and skills in broad vocational areas rather than in specialist activities. They are useful for young people seeking additional training who have not yet decided on a specific career. GNVQs are awarded by three bodies – BTEC, City and Guilds and RSA – and are generally available at Intermediate and Advanced level in ten occupational areas: leisure and tourism, manufacturing, health and social care, business, art and design, the built environment, science, hospitality and catering, engineering and information technology.

NVQs are concerned more directly with skills required in the workplace and are based on standards set through broad consultation among employers. They are awarded by about 130 different bodies, including those mentioned above. NVQs focus on being able to meet standards and can be taken in a range of contexts, for example, at work, during spare time or at college. Many young people do NVQs as part of youth training and some schools are also beginning to offer NVQs or NVQ units. There are some 750 now available in a wide range of occupations. NVQs are awarded at five levels. Level 1 is the simplest, representing basic knowledge and skills. Achievement of an NVQ Level 5 demands competence at senior management level.

GNVQs and NVQs are assessment-based qualifications based on a modular approach, which allows students to complete specific units gradually and build up their qualifications in the way which best meets their needs.

For further information, students may contact the awarding body of the qualification in which they are interested, careers advisers, schools and colleges offering courses which lead to that qualification or industry training organisations. The National Council for Vocational Qualifications can also offer help and is based at 222 Euston Road, London NW1 2BZ Tel: 0171 728 1914.

In Scotland there is a similar system of Scottish Vocational Qualifications (SVQs) and General SVQs. Information about these may be obtained from the Scottish Vocational Education Council (SCOTVEC), Hanover House, 24 Douglas Street, Glasgow G2 7NQ Tel: 0141 248 7900.

BTEC Qualifications

The Business and Technology Education Council (BTEC) approves programmes in a wide range of employment-related study areas. The main ones include agriculture, beauty therapy, business and finance, caring services, computing and information systems, construction, design, distribution, engineering, home economics, horticulture, hotel and catering, housing, information technology, leisure services, management, media, performing arts, science and travel and tourism.

Programmes leading to BTEC qualifications are run in schools, colleges and universities all over England, Wales and Northern Ireland, although a separate, similar system operates in Scotland. The Scottish Vocational Education Council (see above) can offer further information.

Qualifications are awarded at different levels. First Certificates and Diplomas offer basic skills to students aged 16+. National Certificates and Diplomas form the next level. In most cases students must already hold a First Certificate or Diploma or four GCSEs at grade C or above. Higher National Certificates and Diplomas form the highest level and are generally taken by students aged 18+ who will be expected to hold appropriate qualifications or demonstrate relevant experience before they are accepted on to the course. Study programmes are available on a full-time, part-time or sandwich basis.

BTEC GNVQs are currently available at Foundation, Intermediate and Advanced levels in art & design, business, construction and the built environment, health and social care, leisure and tourism, manufacturing, hospitality and catering and science. There is also a limited introduction of five further subjects. As appropriate GNVQ and NVQs are introduced into the BTEC framework, the certificates and diplomas outlined above will be gradually phased out.

Further information is available from BTEC Customer Enquiry Unit, Central House, Upper Woburn Place, London WC1H 0HH *Tel*: 0171 413 8400.

City & Guilds

City & Guilds is a long-established vocational assessment and awarding body, offering qualifications in over 500 subjects, at all levels from basic skills to the highest standards. In all cases these emphasise the practical application of skills and knowledge. Some have been designed specifically for young people aged 14 – 18. They can be taken at school, college or at a local training centre.

City & Guilds offer a variety of GCSEs in technology, design and technology, and information systems.

General National Vocational Qualifications (see above) are offered in art and design, business, health and social care, leisure and tourism, manufacturing, construction and the built environment, hospitality and catering, science, distribution, engineering, information technology, media: communication and production, and management studies. GNVQs in land-based industries/environment and performing arts are under development and should be available from 1996.

In addition, traditional City & Guilds qualifications are available in a range of subjects, including communication skills, computing, engineering, graphic design, languages, media and science.

City & Guilds also offers certification through Pitman Qualifications in areas which include accounting, business studies, shorthand, typing and word processing.

All City & Guilds qualifications for pupils under 16 have been approved by the Secretary of State for Education and the content approved by the Schools Curriculum and Assessment Authority.

For further information contact the Customer Services Enquiry Unit, City & Guilds, 1 Giltspur Street, London EC1A 9DD *Tel*: 0171 294 2468.

RSA Examinations Board

RSA offers a range of qualifications, courses for which are widely available in schools and colleges. The main areas covered include accounting, administration, book-keeping, business, customer service, information technology, languages (particularly for business purposes), marketing, retailing, secretarial, finance and wholesaling and warehousing. Some awards are made on the basis of examination performance, often for students following courses on a full-time basis at schools and colleges; others are based on coursework or assessments. NVQs (see above) are also an important part of the RSA awards framework. Further details are available from RSA's Customer Information Bureau, RSA Examinations Board, Westwood Way, Coventry CV4 8HS *Tel*: 01203 470033.

4.2
SCHOLARSHIPS

The following information is based on information provided by schools. Further details of scholarships available at individual schools may be found in Part Three: Scholarships. The abbreviations used are as follows:

A	Art	I	Instrumental music
AA	Academic ability	O	All round ability
D	Drama	S	Science
G	Games	6	VIth Form entry

ENGLAND

Avon

Badminton School	6 A AA D G I O S
Bath High School GPDST	6 AA
Bristol Cathedral School	6 AA I
Bristol Grammar School	6 AA I
Clifton College	6 A AA I O
Clifton College Preparatory School	AA G I O
Clifton High School	6 AA I S
Colston's Collegiate School	6 I O
Colston's Girls' School	6 AA I O
Downside School	6 A AA I O
The Hall School Sidcot	AA
King Edward's School, Bath	6 AA
Kingswood Day Preparatory School	AA I
Kingswood School	6 A AA G I
Monkton Combe Junior School	AA O
Monkton Combe School	6 A AA I O
Paragon School	O
The Park School	AA
Prior Park College	6 A AA I
Queen Elizabeth's Hospital	6 AA I
The Red Maids' School	6 AA I
Redland High School	6 A AA G I O S
The Royal School	6 A AA D G I O S
St Ursula's High School	AA
Sidcot School	6 AA I O
Westwing School	O

Bedfordshire

Bedford High School	6
Bedford Modern School	AA I
Bedford School	6 A AA D I O
Bedford Preparatory School	AA
Dame Alice Harpur School	G I S
Moorlands School	A AA I

Berkshire

The Abbey School, Reading	6 AA
Bearwood College	6 A AA D G I O
Bradfield College	6 A AA I O
Brockhurst School	AA
Cheam Hawtreys	AA
Claires Court School	A AA I O

Dolphin School	A AA D I
Douai School	6 A AA I S
Downe House School	6 AA I
Eton College	6 AA I
Heathfield School	6 A AA I O S
Hemdean House School	AA I O
Herries School	AA
Highfield School	AA
Holme Grange School	AA O
Hurst Lodge	6 A AA D I O
Langley Manor School	G I O
Lambrook	A AA G I O
Leighton Park School	6 A AA I
Licensed Victuallers' School	6 AA O S
Long Close School	AA O
Luckley-Oakfield School	6 AA I
Maidenhead College Claires Court Girls	6 A AA I O
Marist Convent Senior School	6
The Oratory Preparatory School	AA G I
The Oratory School	A AA I
Padworth College	6 AA
Pangbourne College	6 A AA D G I O
Papplewick	AA I
Priors Court Preparatory School	AA
Queen Anne's School	6 A AA I O
Reading Blue Coat School	6 AA I
St Andrew's School, Reading	I
St Gabriel's School	I O
St George's, Ascot	AA I
St George's School, Windsor	I
St Joseph's Convent School	6 AA
St Mary's School, Ascot	6 I S
St Piran's Preparatory School	AA
Stubbington House	AA G O
Thorngrove School	AA I O
Wellington College	6 A AA I S

Buckinghamshire

Ashfold School	A AA G I
Bury Lawn School	I
Gateway School	O
Godstowe Preparatory School	AA
Hampden Manor School	AA O
High March School	AA
Holy Cross Convent	6 O

Buckinghamshire (continued)

Ladymede	AA G I
Maltmans Green School	AA
Milton Keynes Preparatory School	AA
Pipers Corner School	6 I
St Mary's School, Gerrards Cross	AA G
Stowe School	6 A AA I O S
Swanbourne House School	A AA G I O
Thornton Gollege Convent of Jesus and Mary	AA
Wycombe Abbey School	6 AA I

Cambridgeshire

Dean Grange Preparatory School	AA O
Kimbolton School	6 A AA G I O
King's College School	I
The King's School, Ely	6 A AA I O
Kirkstone House School	A AA I O
Laxton School	AA I
The Leys School	A AA I O
Oundle School	6 A AA I O
The Perse School	AA
The Perse School for Girls	6
Peterborough High School	6 AA
St Faiths School	O
St John's College School	I
St Mary's School, Wantage	6 A AA I O
Wisbech Grammar School	I

Channel Islands

Elizabeth College, Guernsey	I O
St Michael's Preparatory School	AA
Victoria College, Jersey	AA

Cheshire

Abbey Gate College	6 AA D G I O
Cheadle Hulme School	A D I
Culcheth Hall	AA
The Grange School	6 AA D G I
Hammond School	AA I
The King's School, Canterbury	6 A AA I
The King's School, Macclesfield	6 AA I S
Mostyn House School	6 AA O
Mount Carmel School	6 A I
North Cestrian Grammar School	AA
The Ryleys	AA O
St Ambrose College	6 I O
Terra Nova School	AA

Cleveland

Red House School	AA
Teesside High School	6
Yarm School	6 AA I

Cornwall

The Duchy Grammar School	6 AA O
Polwhele House School	AA I
Roselyon School	AA
St Joseph's School, Launceston	AA
St Petroc's School	A AA G I O
Treliske School	AA G I O
Tremough Convent School	6 AA I O
Truro High School	6 AA O
Truro School	6 A AA I

Cumbria

Austin Friars School	A AA
Harecroft Hall School	AA
Hunter Hall School	AA O
Lime House School	6 G O
St Anne's	6 A AA D G I
St Bees School	6 A AA G I
Sedbergh School	6 A AA I

Derbyshire

Derby High School	6 AA I O
Normanton School	6 AA G I O
Ockbrook School	6
Repton Preparatory School	I
Repton School	6 A AA I
St Anselm's	AA I
St Elphin's School	6 AA I

Devon

The Abbey School, Torquay	AA O
Blundell's School	6 A AA D I O
Bramdean Grammar School	6 I
Bramdean Preparatory & Grammar School	AA G I O
The Dolphin School	O
Edgehill College	6 A AA I
Exeter Cathedral School	I
Exeter School	6 AA I
Gramercy Hall School	A AA G I S
Grenville College	6 A AA G I O S
Kelly College	6 A AA G I O
Lanherne School	O
The Maynard School	I
Mount House School	AA O
Plymouth College	6 A AA G I
St Aubyns School	AA O
St Bernard's Preparatory School	G O
St John's School, Sidmouth	AA
St Margaret's Exeter	AA I
St Michael's, Barnstaple	A AA G
Shebbear College	6 A AA G O
Stoodley Knowle Convent School	6 AA
Stover School	6 AA I O
Tower House School	A AA D G I O
Trinity School	A AA D G I O
West Buckland Preparatory School	AA G I
West Buckland School	6 A AA G I O
Wolborough Hill School	G I

Dorset

Allhallows College	6 A AA I O
Bryanston School	6 A AA I
Canford School	6 A AA I O
Castle Court Preparatory School	AA I
Claycsmore Preparatory School	A AA I
Claycsmore School	6 A AA I O
Croft House School	6 A AA D I
Dumpton School	A AA G I O
Homefield School	AA I
Homefield School (Preparatory)	AA I
Milton Abbey School	6 A AA I O
Newell House School	AA
The Old Malthouse	AA
The Park School	AA I O
Port Regis	A AA G I O
St Antony's-Leweston School	6 A AA D I
St Dunstan's Abbey School	A AA D I
St Martin's School, Bournemouth	AA
St Mary's School, Shaftesbury	6 A I
St Monica's School	AA I O
St Peter's School, Exmouth	AA
Sherborne Preparatory School	AA
Sherborne School	6 A AA I O S
Sherborne School for Girls	6 AA I
Talbot Heath	6 AA I
Thornlow Senior School	A AA
Wentworth Milton Mount	6 AA

County Durham

Barnard Castle School	6 A AA I O
Bow School	AA G I O
The Chorister School	I
Durham High School	6 AA
Durham School	6 A AA G I O
Hurworth House School	AA O
Polam Hall	6 AA I

Essex

Alleyn Court and Eton House School	A AA G I
Bancrofts School	6 AA I
Bell House School	AA
Brentwood School	6 A AA I
Chigwell School	6 A AA I
Colchester Boys High School	A AA G I O
Felsted Preparatory School	AA
Felsted School	6 A AA I
Friends' School	6 O
Holmwood House	A AA D G I O
Ilford Ursuline High School	AA I O
New Hall School	6 A AA D I O S
Park School for Girls	AA
St Cedd's School, Chelmsford	I
St John's School	AA
St Margaret's School, Halstead	AA O
St Mary's School, Colchester	O
St Nicholas School, Harlow	AA

Gloucestershire

The Abbey School, Tewkesbury	I
Berkhamstead School	AA
Bredon School	6 AA G O
Cheltenham College	6 A AA G I O S
Cheltenham College Junior School	A AA D G I O
The Cheltenham Ladies' College	6 A AA I
Dean Close Junior School	AA I
Dean Close School	6 A AA G I S
The Dormer House PNEU School	O
Hatherop Castle Preparatory School	AA G I O
The King's School	6 A AA G I
Rendcomb College	6 A AA D G I
The Richard Pate School	O
Rose Hill School	I
St Edward's School, Cheltenham	6 A AA D G I O S
Selwyn School	6 AA D G I
Westonbirt School	6 AA I O
Wycliffe College	6 A AA D G I O
Wycliffe College Junior School	A AA D G I

Hampshire

The Atherley School for Girls	6 AA
Ballard College	6 AA I
Ballard Lake Preparatory School	A AA G I O
Bedales School	I S
Boundary Oak School	AA I
Churchers College	6 AA I
Convent of Our Lady of Providence	6
Daneshill House	AA I
Ditcham Park School	AA
Dunhurst (Bedales Junior School)	I
Durlston Court	A AA G I
Embley Park School	6 A AA G I O
Farleigh School	AA
Farnborough Hill	6 AA
Forres Sandle Manor	AA I O
The Gregg School	AA I
Hordle House	AA I
King Edward VI School	AA I
La Sagesse Convent	O
Littlefield School	AA G O
Lord Wandsworth College	6 A AA I O
Mayfield Preparatory School	AA O
Mayville High School	AA
Meoncross School	O
Moyles Court School	AA O
North Foreland Lodge	S
The Pilgrims School	I
The Portsmouth Grammar School	A AA I
Portsmouth High School GPDST	6 AA
Prince's Mead School	I O
Rookesbury Park School	AA I
Rookwood School	AA
St Mary's College, Southampton	AA
St Nicholas School, Fleet	6 AA I
St Swithun's School	6 AA I
Stanbridge Earls School	A AA
Stockton House School	O
The Stroud School	A AA G I O
Winchester College	6 AA I
Wykeham House School	AA

Hertfordshire

Abbot's Hill	A AA G I O
Aldenham School	6 A AA G I O
Aldwickbury School	AA
The Arts Educational School, Tring	D I
Beechwood Park	AA I
Berkhamsted Junior School	AA
Berkhamsted School	6 A AA I
Berkhamsted School for Girls	AA I
Bishop's Stortford College	6 A AA I O
Egerton-Rothesay School	A AA G I
Haberdashers' Aske's School	AA I
Haberdashers' Aske's School for Girls	AA I
Haileybury College	6 A AA I O
Haresfoot Preparatory School	A AA D O
Haresfoot Senior School	AA O
Heath Mount School	AA I O
The Junior School, Bishop's Stortford College	A AA I O
Kingshott	AA
Lockers Park	A AA G I O
Northfield School	6
The Princess Helena College	6 A AA I
Queenswood	6 AA G I
The Rickmansworth Masonic School	6 A AA I
St Albans High School	6 I O
St Albans School	6 A AA I
St Andrew's Montessori School	AA O
St Columba's College	6 AA
St Edmund's College	6 I
St Francis' College	6 AA I
St Margaret's School	6 A AA I O S
St Nicholas House	O
Sherrardswood School	6 AA
Stanborough School	6
Stormont	AA
Westbrook Hay	A AA G I O
York House School	AA

Hereford & Worcester

Abberley Hall	A AA G I
The Alice Ottley School	6 AA I
Bromsgrove Lower School	AA I O
Bromsgrove School	6 A AA G I O
Dodderhill School	AA I
The Downs School	AA I O
The Elms	AA G O
Green Hill School	O
Hawford Lodge School	AA
Heathfield School	AA
The Hereford Cathedral Junior School	AA I
The Hereford Cathedral School	6 A AA I
Hillside School	AA
Hillstone School (Malvern College Junior School)	A AA I
Holy Trinity School	6 AA
The King's School, Worcester	6 AA I
The Knoll School	AA
Lea House School	AA
Malvern College	6 A AA G I O
Malvern Girls' College	6 A AA I
Moffats School	AA I O
Royal Grammar School Worcester	6 AA I O
St James's & The Abbey	6 A AA D I O
St Mary's Convent School, Worcester	6 AA I O
St Richard's	AA
Whitford Hall School	O

North Humberside

Hull Grammar School	6 AA O
Hull High School	AA O

South Humberside

St James' School	6 AA G I O

Isle of Man

The Buchan School	AA I O
King William's College	6 AA I O

Isle of Wight

Bembridge School	A AA I
Ryde School with Upper Chine	6 AA O

Kent

Ashford School	6 AA I
Babington House School	AA O
Baston School	I O
Benenden School	6 A AA I
Bedgebury School	6 A AA G I
Beechwood School Sacred Heart	6 AA G I O
Bethany School	6 A AA G I
Bishop Challoner School	6 AA
Breaside Preparatory School	AA
Bromley High School GPDST	6 AA I
Cobham Hall School	6 AA O
Combe Bank School	6 O
Croft Hall (Hill School Junior Department)	G O
Derwent Lodge School for Girls	AA
Dover College	6 A AA G I O
Farringtons & Stratford House	6 AA I
Friars School	AA G I
Gad's Hill School	AA
Hilden Grange School	A AA G I
Holmewood House	A AA G I O
Holy Trinity College	6 AA I
The Junior School, St Lawrence College	AA
Kent College	6 AA I O
Kent College	6 AA D I O
King's Preparatory School, Rochester	AA I
King's School	A AA I
Marlborough House School	A AA G I O
Merton Court Preparatory School	AA D G I
Northbourne Park School	A AA G I O
Rose Hill School	A AA G I O
Sackville School	A AA D G I O S
St Christopher's School, Canterbury	O
St Edmund's Junior School	A AA G I O
St Edmund's School, Canterbury	A AA G I O
St Lawrence College in Thanet	6 AA I
St Mary's College, Folkestone	I
St Michael's School	A AA G I
Sevenoaks School	6 A AA G I O S
Sibton Park	AA I O
Sutton Valence Junior School	AA
Sutton Valence School	6 A AA G I
Tonbridge School	A AA I
Walthamstow Hall	6 AA I
Wellesley House School	AA G I
Westbrook House School	AA G I
West Heath School	6 A AA G
Yardley Court	AA I

Lancashire

Arnold School	6 AA I
Bentham School	6 A AA G I O S
Bolton School (Boys' Division)	6 I
Bolton School (Girls' Division)	6 I O
Bury Grammar School	6 AA
Bury Grammar School (Girls')	6 AA
Casterton School	6 AA I O
Elmslie Girls' School	6 AA I
The Hulme Grammar School	6 AA
King Edward VII School, Lytham St Annes	6 AA I
Kirkham Grammar School	6 AA I
Moorland School	O
Oakhill College	AA
Queen Elizabeth's Grammar School	6
Queen Mary School	AA I
Rossall Preparatory School	A AA I O
Rossall School	6 A AA I O S
St Anne's College Grammar School	AA
St Joseph's Convent School	AA D G I
Scarisbrick Hall School	6 AA
Stonyhurst College	6 A AA I
Westholme School	6 AA

Leicestershire

Grace Dieu Manor School	AA
Leicester Grammar School	6 AA I
Leicester High School For Girls	6 AA I

Loughborough Grammar School	AA I
Loughborough High School	AA I
Nevill Holt School	A AA I
Oakham School	6 A AA D I
Ratcliffe College	6 A AA G I
Stoneygate School	AA
Uppingham School	6 A AA I O

Lincolnshire

The Cathedral School	I
The Fen Preparatory School	AA
Maypole House	AA G O
St Hugh's School	A AA G I O
St Joseph's School, Lincoln	I
Stamford High School	6 A AA D G I
Stamford School	6 A AA I O
Stonefield House	AA O
White House School	O
Witham Hall	AA I O

London

Abercorn Place	O
Alleyn's School	6 A AA I
The Arts Educational Schools	D
Ashbourne Middle School	AA
Belmont (Mill Hill Junior School)	I
Blackheath High School GPDST	6 A AA I S
Channing School	6 AA
Christs College	6 AA O
City of London School	6 AA I
City of London School for Girls	6 AA I
Clifton Lodge	I
Colfe's School	6 A AA I
Collingham	6
Devonshire House Preparatory School	AA I
Dulwich College	6 A AA I
Durston House	AA O
Ealing College Upper School	AA
Eaton Square School	O
Eltham College	6 AA I
Emanuel School	6 AA I
Falkner House	I
Forest Girls' School	6 AA I
Forest Junior School	AA I
Forest School	6 AA I
Francis Holland School, SW1	6 AA
Francis Holland School, NW1	6 I
Friern Barnet Grammar School	AA
Garden House School	AA I O
The Godolphin and Latymer School	I
The Hampshire School (Kensington Gardens)	AA I O
The Hampshire School (Knightsbridge Under School)	AA O
The Hampshire School (Knightsbridge Upper School)	AA I O
Harvington School	D I
Hazelhurst School for Girls	AA
Heathside Preparatory School	AA
Hellenic College of London	6
Highgate School	6 AA I
Ibstock Place, The Froebel School	I
International Community School	6 AA
International School of London	6 O
Italia Conti Academy of Theatre Arts	D
James Allen's Girls' School	6 A AA I O
Keble Preparatory School	AA O
Kensington Park School	AA
The King Alfred School	O
King's College Junior School	AA I
King's College School	6 AA I
Latymer Upper School	6 AA I
Lycee Francais Charles de Gaulle	6
Mill Hill School	AA I O
More House	AA I
The Mount School	6 AA O
Newton Preparatory School	AA S
Normanhurst School	AA O
Northcote Lodge	AA
North Bridge House Upper School	AA
Notting Hill and Ealing High School GPDST	6 AA I O
Palmers Green High School	AA I
Putney High School	6 AA I
Putney Park School	A AA I
Queen's College	6 A AA I

London (continued)

Queen's Gate School	6 O
Redcliffe School	O
Riverston School	AA G I O
The Roche School	AA
Rosemead Preparatory School	AA
Royal School, Hampstead	AA
St Augustine's Priory	6
St Dunstan's College	6 AA I O
St Paul's Cathedral Choir School	I
St Paul's Girls' School	A AA I
St Paul's Preparatory School	I
St Paul's School	6 AA I
St Philip's School	O
Sinclair House School	O
South Hampstead High School	6 AA
Southbank International School	O
Streatham Hill and Clapham High School	6 AA I S
Sydenham High School	6 AA I
Sylvia Young Theatre School	D I
Thomas's Preparatory School Clapham	A AA D G I
Trevor Roberts'	I
University College School	AA I
The Village School	AA
Westminster Abbey Choir School	I
Westminster Cathedral Choir School	I
Westminster School	6 AA I
Westminster Under School	AA I
Wimbledon High School	6 AA
Woodside Park School	AA G I O

Greater Manchester

Ash Lea Grammar School	AA
Branwood Preparatory School	O
Bridgewater School	6 O
Chetham's School of Music	I
Manchester High School for Girls	AA
Manchester Jewish Grammar School	AA
Norman House School	AA
Rosecroft School Didsbury	O
St Bede's College	6 AA I
William Hulme's Grammar School	6 AA I

Merseyside

Avalon Preparatory School	AA
The Belvedere School GPDST	6 AA
Birkenhead High School GPDST	6 AA
Birkenhead School	6 AA I
Kingsmead School	AA I
Liverpool College	6 AA I O
Merchant Taylors' School	6 AA O
Merchant Taylors' School for Girls	6 O
St Edward's College, Liverpool	6 AA I O
St Mary's College, Liverpool	6
Streatham House School	AA
Tower College	AA
Tower Dene Preparatory School	AA D I O

Middlesex

Alpha Preparatory School	
The American Community Schools	
Buckingham College Senior School	6 AA
Halliford School	AA
Hampton School	A AA I
Harrow School	A AA I
Heathfield School	6 AA I
The John Lyon School	AA G I
The Lady Eleanor Holles School	6 AA I O
Merchant Taylors' School	6 AA I
Newland House School	AA I O
North London Collegiate School	AA I
Northwood College	6 AA
The Purcell School	I
St David's School, Ashford	6 A AA G I
St Helen's School for Girls	6 A AA I

Norfolk

Eccles Hall School	I
Glebe House School	A AA G I O

Gresham's Preparatory School	AA
Gresham's School	6 A AA D G I S
Hethersett Old Hall School	I O
Langley Preparatory School & Nursery	AA I
Langley School	6 A AA G I
The Norwich High School for Girls GPDST	6 AA I
Norwich School	6 AA I
Riddlesworth Hall	A AA I
Taverham Hall	AA I
Thetford Grammar School	AA
Wood Dene School	AA

Northamptonshire

Great Houghton Preparatory School	AA
Maidwell Hall	A AA G I O
Northampton High School	6 AA
Northamptonshire Grammar School	6 AA I
Quinton House	6 AA O
St Peter's School	AA
Wellingborough School	6 A AA G I
Winchester House School	A AA I

Northumberland

Longridge Towers School	6 AA I

Nottinghamshire

Coteswood House School	A AA D G I O
Dagfa House School	O
Lorne House	O
Nottingham High School	AA
Nottingham High School for Girls	6 AA
Orchard School	AA
Ranby House	AA
Trent College	6 A AA D G I O
Wellow House School	A AA G I O
Worksop College	6 A AA G I O

Oxfordshire

Abacus College	AA
Abingdon School	A AA I
Bloxham School	6 A AA I O S
Bruern Abbey School	AA
Carmel College	6 A AA I
Christ Church Cathedral School	I
Cokethorpe School	6 AA I O
Cranford House School	AA I O
Ferndale School	AA
Headington School	6 AA I
Josca's Preparatory School	AA
Kingham Hill School	A I
Magdalen College School	AA I
New College School	I
Our Lady's Convent Senior School	A AA I
Oxford High School GPDST	6 AA I
Radley College	A AA I
Rye St Antony School	O
St Clare's, Oxford	6 AA O
St Edward's School, Oxford	6 A AA I O
St Mary's School, Wantage	6 A AA I O
School of S Helen & S Katharine	6 AA I
Shiplake College	A
Sibford School	6 I
Summer Fields	O
Tudor Hall School	6 AA I
Wychwood School	A AA I

Shropshire

Adcote School	6
Bedstone College	6 AA I
Bellan House Preparatory School	AA I O
Ellesmere College	A AA I O S
Moor Park School	AA
Moreton Hall	6 A AA D G I O
The Old Hall School	AA
Oswestry Junior School	AA I O
Oswestry School	6 AA G
Packwood Haugh	AA
Prestfelde Preparatory School	AA I
Shrewsbury High School	6
Shrewsbury School	6 A AA I
Wrekin College	6 A AA D G I O

Somerset

Brunton School for Girls	6 AA I O
Buckland School	I
Chard Independent School	AA
Chilton Cantelo School	O
Edgarley Hall	AA I O
King's Bruton Pre-Preparatory & Junior School	O
King's College, Taunton	6 A AA I O S
King's Hall School	AA G I
King's School, Bruton	6 A AA I O
Millfield School	6 A AA I O S
The Park School	A AA D I
Perrott Hill School	AA I O
Queen's College	6 AA I O
Queen's College Junior School	AA I O
Rossholme School	AA D G I O
St Christopher's, Burnham-on-Sea	I O
St Martin's Independent School	AA
Taunton Preparatory School	A AA I O
Taunton School	6 A AA I
Wellington School	AA I
Wells Cathedral Junior School	I
Wells Cathedral School	6 AA I

Staffordshire

Abbotsholme School	6 A AA G I O
Brooklands School	AA
Denstone College	6 A AA I O
Denstone College Preparatory School	A AA I
Howitt House School	AA
Lichfield Cathedral School (St Chad's)	AA I
Newcastle-under-Lyme School	6 AA
St Dominic's Independent Junior School	AA
St Dominic's Priory School	6 O
St Dominic's School	6 AA
St Joseph's College, Stoke-on-Trent	6 AA
School of S Mary and S Anne	6 A AA G I O

Suffolk

The Abbey School, Woodbridge	A AA I
Amberfield School	A AA I
Cherry Trees School	AA D I
Culford School	6 AA I
Eversley School	AA
Fairstead House School	O
Finborough School	6
Framlingham College	6 A AA D I O S
Framlingham College Junior School	AA I
Hillcroft Preparatory School	AA I
Ipswich High School GPDST	6 AA
Ipswich School	A AA I
Moreton Hall	AA I
Old Buckenham Hall School	A AA I
Orwell Park	A AA D G I S
Royal Hospital School	6 A AA I
St Felix School	6 AA I
St George's School	AA I
St Joseph's College, Ipswich	AA I O
School of Jesus and Mary	AA I
South Lee Preparatory School	AA
Stoke College	I
Woodbridge School	6 A AA I

Surrey

Aberdour School	AA
Amesbury School	AA G I
Barfield School	O
Barrow Hills School	AA O
Belmont School	AA
Box Hill School	6 A AA G I O
Burys Court School	I
Canbury School	AA O
Caterham School	6 AA I
Caterham School Preparatory	AA I O
Charterhouse	6 A AA I O
City of London Freemen's School	AA I
Claremont Fan Court School	6 AA G I O
Commonweal Lodge School	6 AA I O
Cranleigh Preparatory School	AA
Cranleigh School	6 A AA I
Croham Hurst School	6 AA
Croydon High School GPDST	6 AA

Cumnor House School	AA G I
Duke of Kent School	O
Dunottar School	6 AA I
Eagle House	AA I
Edgeborough	O
Epsom College	6 A AA I O
Essendene Lodge School	O
Ewell Castle School	6 AA G O
Feltonfleet School	A AA I O
Frensham Heights School	6 A AA D I O S
Greenacre School for Girls	6 AA
Guildford High School (Church Schools Co Ltd)	6 AA I
Hawley Place School	A AA D G I O S
Homefield Preparatory School	AA
King Edward's School Witley	6 A AA I
Kingston Grammar School	6 A AA G I
Kingswood House School	AA
Lanesborough	I
Lyndhurst School	AA
Manor House School	AA G O
Marymount International School	AA
Milbourne Lodge School	AA I
Notre Dame School	6 AA O
Notre Dame Senior School	6 AA O
Oakfield	A AA O
Old Palace School of John Whitgift	6 AA I
Parkside School	AA
Parsons Mead	6 AA
Prior's Field School	6 A AA D I
Reed's School	6 A AA I O
Reigate Grammar School	AA I
Reigate St Mary's Preparatory and Choir School	I
Rokeby School	A AA G I
Royal Grammar School	6 AA I
Royal Russell School	6 AA
The Royal School	6 I O
St Andrew's School, Woking	AA G I
St Catherine's School, Camberley	AA
St Catherine's School, Guildford	6 AA G I
St Edmund's School, Hindhead	AA
St George's College, Weybridge	6 AA I O
St Hilary's School, Godalming	AA I
St John's School	6 A AA I
St Maur's Convent School	6 AA I O
St Michael's School	AA
St Teresa's Preparatory School	AA
St Teresa's School	6 A AA G I O
Shaftesbury Independent School	6 AA
Sir William Perkins's School	6 AA I
Surbiton High School	6 AA G I
Sutton High School (GPDST)	6 AA O
Tormead School	6 AA
Trinity School	6 A AA I
Whitgift School	6 AA I
Wispers School	AA D G I
Yateley Manor Preparatory School	AA I
Yehudi Menuhin School	I

East Sussex

Battle Abbey School	AA O
Bodiam Manor School	AA G I
Brighton and Hove High School GPDST	6 AA
Brighton College	6 A AA G I O
Buckswood Grange	AA I O
Claremont School	A AA D G I O
Eastbourne College	6 A AA I
The Fold School	AA O
Greenfields School	A AA D G I O
Mayfield College	6 AA G I O
Micklefield Wadhurst incorporating the Legat School of Classical Ballet	6 A AA D G I O S
Moira House Junior School	O
Moira House Senior School	AA I
Newlands Manor School	6 A AA G I O S
Newlands Preparatory School	A AA D G I O S
The Old Grammar School	6
Roedean School	6 A AA I
St Andrew's School, Eastbourne	AA G O
St Aubyn's	AA G
St Bede's, Eastbourne	A AA D G I O
St Bede's School	6 A AA D G I O
St Leonards-Mayfield School	A AA I
St Mary's Hall	6 AA I
Skippers Hill Manor Preparatory School	AA O
Temple Grove with St Nicholas School	A AA G I O

511

East Sussex (continued)

Vinehall School	AA I O
Westerleigh	AA I O

West Sussex

Ardingly College	6 A AA D G I O S
Ardingly College Junior School	AA G I
Arundale Preparatory School	I
Burgess Hill School	6 AA I
Copthorne School	AA G I
Dorset House School	I
Farlington School	6 AA I
Great Ballard School	A AA D G I O
Great Walstead	AA G I
Handcross Park School	AA G I
Hurstpierpoint College	6 A AA G I O
Lancing College	6 A AA I O
Lavant House Rosemead	6 A AA
Oakwood School	AA D G I
Our Lady of Sion School	6 A AA D G I O S
Pennthorpe School	AA
The Prebendal School	I
Seaford College	6 A AA G I O
Shoreham College	AA G I O
Slindon College	6 AA O
Stoke Brunswick	AA I O
The Towers Convent School	AA
Westbourne House School	I
Windlesham House	AA G I
Worth School	6 AA I O S

Tyne and Wear

Argyle House School	
Ascham House School	AA
Central Newcastle High School GPDST	6 AA
Dame Allan's Boys School	AA
Dame Allan's Girls School	AA
Eastcliffe Grammar School	6 A AA I O
Grainger Grammar School	AA
The King's School	6 A AA I
La Sagesse Convent High School	6 AA G O
Newcastle Preparatory School	O
Newcastle Upon Tyne Church High School	AA I
Royal Grammar School	I
Sunderland High School	6 AA I
Westfield School	6 A AA D G I
Wolstanton Preparatory School	AA

Warwickshire

Abbotsford School	AA
Arnold Lodge School	A I O
Bilton Grange	AA G I O
Emscote Lawn School	A AA I O
The King's High School for Girls	AA I
The Kingsley School	6 A AA I O
New College	O
Princethorpe College	6 A AA I
Rugby School	6 A AA I O
Warwick School	6 A AA I
Wroxall Abbey School	6 A AA G I O

West Midlands

Ardenhurst School	AA I
Bablake School	6
Birchfield School	AA
The Blue Coat School	AA I
Edgbaston Church of England College	6 AA I O S
Edgbaston College, Birmingham	AA I
Edgbaston High School for Girls	6 AA I
Eversfield Preparatory School	AA
Hallfield School	AA I
Highclare School	O
Holy Child School	AA
Hydesville Tower School	AA I O
King Edward VI High School for Girls	6 AA
King Edward's School, Birmingham	6 A AA I O
King Henry VIII School, Coventry	6 AA I
Norfolk House School	AA

The Royal Wolverhampton Junior School	AA I
The Royal Wolverhampton School	6 AA G I
St Martin's School, Solihull	6 AA I
Solihull School	6 A AA I O S
Tettenhall College	6 A AA D G I O S
Wolverhampton Grammar School	AA I

Wiltshire

Dauntsey's School	6 A AA I O
The Godolphin School	6 A AA I O
Grittleton House School	AA
The International School of Choueifat	AA
Kingsbury Hill House	AA O
La Retraite Leehurst School	6 O
Leaden Hall	A AA I
Marlborough College	6 A AA I O
Salisbury Cathedral School	AA I
St Mary's School	A AA I
Sandroyd	G I O
Stonar School	6 A AA D G I O S
Warminster School	6 AA O

North Yorkshire

Ampleforth College	6 AA I
Ampleforth College Junior School	AA I O
Ashville College	6 AA I O
Aysgarth Preparatory School	I
Ayton School	6 AA I O
Bootham School	6 A AA I O S
Catteral Hall	AA I
Cundall Manor School	AA G I
Fyling Hall School	6 O
Giggleswick School	6 A AA D G I O
Harrogate Ladies' College	6 A AA I O
Howsham Hall	AA G O
The Minster School	I
The Mount School	6 AA I
Pocklington School	6 A AA I
Queen Ethelburga's College	6 A AA D G I
Queen Margaret's School	6 AA I
Queen Mary's School	AA I
Read School	6 AA
Red House School	AA
Ripon Cathedral Choir School	AA I O
St Hilda's School	6 A AA D I
St Martin's School	AA
St Olave's School (Junior of St Peter's)	AA
St Peter's School	6 AA I
Scarborough College	6 A AA I O
Terrington Hall	A AA G I O
Woodleigh School	A AA D G I
York College for Girls	6 AA I O

South Yorkshire

Birkdale School	6 AA I
Mount St Mary's College	6 AA I O
Sheffield High School GPDST	6 AA

West Yorkshire

Ackworth School	6 A AA I
Batley Grammar School	AA
Bradford Girls' Grammar School	AA I
Bronte House School	A AA I
Clevedon House	AA I
Fulneck School	6 AA O
Gateways School	6 AA O
Hipperholme Grammar School	6 AA
Kayes' College	AA
Leeds Girls' High School	AA I
Leeds Grammar School	6 AA I
Moorlands School	A AA G I
North Leeds & St Edmund's Hall Preparatory School	AA
Queen Elizabeth Grammar School	6 AA I
Rishworth School	6 AA
St David's School	A AA D G I O S
Shaw House School	O
Silcoates School	6 AA I
Wakefield Girls' High School	6
Westville House Preparatory School	O
Woodhouse Grove School	6 A AA G I

NORTHERN IRELAND

County Antrim

Campbell College	A AA I
Hunterhouse College	AA
Methodist College	6 I

County Down

Rockport Preparatory School	AA

County Tyrone

Royal School Dungannon	6 AA O

SCOTLAND

Borders

Beaconhurst Grange	O
St Mary's Preparatory School	O

Central

Dollar Academy	O

Fife

New Park School	AA
St Katherines Girls Preparatory School	AA O
St Leonards School	6 A AA G I

Grampian

Aberlour House	AA
Albyn School for Girls	A AA G I O
Gordonstoun School	6 AA I O
Robert Gordons College	6 AA
St Margaret's School for Girls	AA

Lothian

Cargilfield	AA O
Clifton Hall	AA O
The Edinburgh Academy	6 A AA I
Edinburgh Academy Preparatory School	AA
Fettes College	AA I
George Heriot's School	AA
George Watson's College	AA I

Loretto Junior School	O
Loretto School	6 A AA I O
The Mary Erskine School	AA I
Merchiston Castle School	6 A AA I O S
St Denis and Cranley School	6 AA
St George's School for Girls	6
St Margaret's, Edinburgh	6 AA I
St Mary's Music School, Edinburgh	I
Stewart's Melville College	AA I

Strathclyde

Drumley House School	AA
Glasgow Academy	6 AA O
The High School of Glasgow	AA
Hutchesons' Grammar School	6 AA
Keil School	A AA I
The Kelvinside Academy	6 AA
Lomond School	6 AA I
Park Lodge School	AA
St Oswald's School	A AA D G I O S
Wellington School	AA

Tayside

Ardvreck School	AA
Butterstone School	O
Craigclowan Preparatory School	AA O
Croftinloan School	AA I O
Glenalmond College	6 A AA I O
Kilgraston School	6 A AA I
Lathallan School	A AA D G I O
Morrison's Academy	6 AA
Rannoch School	6 AA G I O
Strathallan School	A AA I O

WALES

Clwyd

Howell's School, Denbigh	6 AA D G I
Ruthin School	6 A AA D G I O S
Rydal Penrhos Preparatory School	AA
Rydal Penrhos Senior School	6 A AA I
Rydal Penrhos Senior School Girls' Division	6 AA I S

Dyfed

Llandovery College	6 AA G I
Netherwood School	AA I
St Michael's School	AA G I O

Mid Glamorgan

St Clare's Convent, Porthcawl	AA
St John's School	AA O

South Glamorgan

The Cathedral School	I
Howell's School, Cardiff	6 AA I
Kings Monkton School (Primary)	AA
Kings Monkton School and College	AA O
New College and School	A AA G I
Our Lady's Convent School	O
St John's College	I
Westbourne Schools	AA I O S

West Glamorgan

Ffynone House School	6 A AA D G I O S

Gwynedd

St David's College	A AA G I

Gwent

Haberdashers' Monmouth School for Girls	6 AA I
Monmouth School	6 AA G I O
Rougemont School	6 AA O
St John's-on-the-Hill	A AA D G I O

Powys

Christ College	6 AA I O
St David's School, Brecon	AA I O

FURTHER EDUCATION

London

KLC School of Interior Design	A

OVERSEAS

Switzerland

Aiglon College	AA G
Franklin College	AA

4.3
BURSARIES AND RESERVED ENTRANCE AWARDS

The following is compiled from information provided by schools. Further information about awards made by individual schools may be found in Part Three: Scholarships. The abbreviations used are as follows:

C	Choral		FO	Foreign Office
E	Christian Missionary or		H	Financial or domestic hardship
	full-time worker		M	Medical profession
F	Her Majesty's Forces*		T	Teaching profession
			+	The Clergy

*F1 – The Royal Navy F2 – The Royal Marines F3 – The Army F4 – The Royal Air Force

ENGLAND

Avon

Badminton School	H T
Bristol Cathedral School	H
Clifton College	+ F H T
Clifton College Preparatory School	+ F T
Clifton High School	H
Colston's Girls' School	H
The Downs School	+ F
Downside School	H
Fairfield PNEU School	H
King Edward's School, Bath	H
Kingswood School	+ F H
Mander Portman Woodward	H
Monkton Combe Junior School	+ E H
Monkton Combe School	+ E H T
Overndale School	H
Paragon School	H
Prior Park College	H
Queen Elizabeth's Hospital	H
Redland High School	H
The Royal School	F
Tockington Manor	F T
Westwing School	F H

Bedfordshire

Bedford High School	H
Bedford Modern School	H
Bedford School	+ H T
Bedford Preparatory School	H
Dame Alice Harpur School	H
Moorlands School	H T

Berkshire

The Abbey School	H

Bearwood College	F H
The Brigidine School	H
Brockhurst School	F
Dolphin School	H
Douai School	H
Downe House School	H
Elstree School	+ T
Eton College	H
Heathfield School	H
Hemdean House School	H
Highfield School	H
Horris Hill	H
Hurst Lodge	F FO
Lambrook	+ F H T
Leighton Park School	+ H
Licensed Victuallers' School	H
Long Close School	H
The Oratory Preparatory School	H
Pangbourne College	H
Presentation College	H
Priors Court Preparatory School	+ E F H
Queen Anne's School	+ T
Reading Blue Coat School	H
St Andrew's School, Reading	+
St Joseph's Convent School, Reading	H
St Mary's School, Ascot	H
St Piran's Preparatory School	E H
Stubbington House	H
Upton House School	H
Wellington College	H

Buckinghamshire

Ashfold School	F
Bury Lawn School	H
Caldicott	H T
Gayhurst School	+ E H T
Hampden Manor School	T

Buckinghamshire (continued)

Heatherton House School	H T
Ladymede	+ F H
Milton Keynes Preparatory School	H
Pipers Corner School	F
St Mary's School, Gerrards Cross	+
Stowe School	H
Swanbourne House School	+ F

Cambridgeshire

Dean Grange Preparatory School	+ F FO T
Kimbolton School	+ H
The King's School, Ely	+ H
Laxton School	H
The Leys School	F H
Oundle School	H
The Perse School for Girls	H
Peterborough High School	F
St John's College School	H

Channel Islands

St George's Preparatory School	H
St Michael's Preparatory School	+ H

Cheshire

Abbey Gate College	H
Beech Hall School	+ E H
Culcheth Hall	H
The Grange School	H
Hillcrest Grammar School	H
Hulme Hall Schools	H T
The King's School, Chester	H
The King's School, Macclesfield	H
Loreto Convent Grammar School	H
Mount Carmel School	H
Oriel Bank High School	H
Pownall Hall School	+ T
The Queen's School	H
Ramillies Hall School	F
St Hilary's School, Alderley Edge	H
Terra Nova School	+ F
Yorston Lodge School	+

Cleveland

Yarm School	H

Cornwall

Roselyon School	H
St Petroc's School	+ F T
Treliske School	H
Tremore Christian School	+ E H
Tremough Convent School	+
Truro High School	+
Truro School	F H

Cumbria

Austin Friars School	F H
Harecroft Hall School	+ F H
Hunter Hall School	H
Lime House School	+ E F H
St Anne's, Windermere	F H
St Bees School	+ F H
Sedbergh School	H

Derbyshire

Derby High School	+ E H
Normanton School	F H T
Repton School	H
St Anselm's	+ F
St Elphin's School	+ F
Stancliffe Hall	+ E F T

Devon

Blundell's School	F H
Bramdean Grammar School	+ H
Bramdean Preparatory & Grammar School	+ H
The Dolphin School	+ E H
Edgehill College	+ E F H
Exeter Cathedral School	+ H
Exeter School	H
Gramercy Hall School	M
Grenville College	+ F H
Kelly College	+ F H T
The Maynard School	H
Mount House School	H
Mount St Mary's Convent School	H
Plymouth College	H
St Aubyns School	+ E F
St John's School	F
St Margaret's Exeter	+ H
St Michael's, Barnstaple	+ H
St Wilfrid's School, Exeter	H
Sands School	H
Shebbear College	+ E F H T
Stoodley Knowle Convent School	H
Stover School	F H
Tower House School	H
Trinity School	+ E F H
West Buckland Preparatory School	+ F
West Buckland School	+ F H

Dorset

Allhallows College	+ F H T
Bryanston School	H
Canford School	+ F1 H
Castle Court Preparatory School	+ E
Claysmore Preparatory School	+ E F H
Claysmore School	+ E F H T
Croft House School	+ F T
Dumpton School	+ H
Homefield School	F H
Homefield School (Preparatory)	F H
Knighton House	+ E T
Newell House School	+ H T
The Park School	H
St Antony's-Leweston School	H
St Mary's School, Shaftesbury	H
St Monica's School, Poole	+ F H T
Sherborne Preparatory School	F H
Sherborne School	F
Sherborne School for Girls	H
Talbot Heath	H
Thornlow Junior School	F
Thornlow Senior School	F
Wentworth Milton Mount	+ E H

County Durham

Barnard Castle School	F H
The Chorister School	+ H
Durham High School	+ H
Durham School	+
Hurworth House School	H
Polam Hall	H

Essex

Alleyn Court and Eton House School	+ H T
Bancrofts School	H
Brentwood School	H
Colchester Boys High School	H T
Cranbrook College	T
Dame Johane Bradbury's School	H
Felsted Preparatory School	F
Holmwood House	H
Ilford Ursuline High School	H
New Hall School	F FO H
Raphael Independent School	H
St John's School, Billericay	H
St Margaret's School, Halstead	H
St Michael's School, Leigh on Sea	+
St Nicholas School, Harlow	H T

Gloucestershire

Beaudesert Park	F
Cheltenham College	H T
Cheltenham College Junior School	H
The Cheltenham Ladies' College	H
Dean Close Junior School	+ E F H T
Dean Close School	+ E F T
Hatherop Castle Preparatory School	F H
The King's School, Gloucester	+ F H
Rendcomb College	F H
The Richard Pate School	T
Rose Hill School	+ F H
St Clotilde's School	H
St Edward's School, Cheltenham	H
Selwyn School	+
Westonbirt School	+ E F FO
Wycliffe College	F1 F3 F4 FO H T
Wycliffe College Junior School	F H

Hampshire

Ballard Lake Preparatory School	H
Bedales School	H
Churchers College	H
Daneshill House	H T
Ditcham Park School	T
Dunhurst (Bedales Junior School)	H
Durlston Court	F H
Embley Park School	+ F F2 H T
Farnborough Hill	H
Forres Sandle Manor	F
The Gregg School	H
Highfield School	+ E
Hordle House	H
King Edward VI School, Southampton	H
La Sagesse Convent	H
Littlefield School	H
Lord Wandsworth College	H
Mayfield Preparatory School	F3 F4 H T
The Pilgrims School	+
The Portsmouth Grammar School	H
Rookesbury Park School	H
St Benedict's Convent School	H
St Nicholas School, Fleet	+
St Swithun's School, Winchester	H
Salesian College	H
Stanbridge Earls School	H
The Stroud School	+
Walhampton School	+ E H
West Hill Park Preparatory School	H

Hertfordshire

Abbot's Hill	+ F H T
Aldenham School	H
Beechwood Park	+ F H
Berkhamsted Junior School	H
Berkhamsted School	F3 H M T
Berkhamsted School for Girls	H
Bishop's Stortford College	F H T
Edge Grove School	+ E F FO H M T
Egerton-Rothesay School	H
Haberdashers' Aske's School	H
Haberdashers' Aske's School for Girls	+ H
Haileybury College	+ F3 H T
Heath Mount School	F T
The Junior School, Bishop's Stortford College	+ E F H M T
The Little Folks Lab	H
Lockers Park	F
The Princess Helena College	+ F H
St Albans High School	+ H
St Columba's College, St Albans	H
St Edmund's College, Ware	F
St Francis' College, Letchworth	H
St Margaret's School, Watford	+ F H
Sherrardswood School	F
Westbrook Hay	F
York House School	H T

Hereford & Worcester

Abberley Hall	+ H T
The Alice Ottley School	+
Aymestrey School	+ T
Bromsgrove Lower School	F H
Bromsgrove School	F H M T

Croftdown	+ F T
The Downs School	+ F
The Elms	+ F H T
Green Hill School	+ H
Hawford Lodge School	+
The Hereford Cathedral Junior School	+
The Hereford Cathedral School	+ F H T
Hillside School	H
Hillstone School (Malvern College Junior School)	F
The King's School, Worcester	+ F H
Malvern College	F H T
Moffats School	+ F H T
Royal Grammar School Worcester	F H
St James's & The Abbey	F H
St Mary's Convent School, Worcester	H
St Richard's, Bromyard	F
Winterfold House	+ F H T

North Humberside

Hymers College	H

South Humberside

Brigg Preparatory School	+
St James' School, Grimsby	+ F T

Isle of Man

The Buchan School	F
King William's College	+ F H T

Isle of Wight

Bembridge School	F H
Ryde School with Upper Chine	H
Westmont School	+ H

Kent

Bedgebury School	+ F H
Beechwood School Sacred Heart	H
Bethany School	+ E F
Bromley High School GPDST	H
Cobham Hall School	H
Croft Hall (Hill School Junior Department)	+ F H T
Derwent Lodge School for Girls	+ H
Dover College	F H M T
Duke of York's Royal Military School	F
Farringtons & Stratford House	+ F H
Friars School	F FO
Hilden Grange School	H T
The Hill Preparatory School	F H T
Holmewood House	F
Holy Trinity College	H
Junior King's School	+
The Junior School, St Lawrence College	+ F
Kent College, Canterbury	+ F H
Kent College, Pembury	+ E F H
Vernon Holme (Kent College Infant & Junior School)	+ E F H
King's Preparatory School, Rochester	+ T
King's School, Rochester	+ T
Marlborough House School	+ F T
Merton Court Preparatory School	H T
Northbourne Park School	F H
Rose Hill School	H
Sackville School	H
St Edmund's Junior School, Canterbury	+ F FO
St Edmund's School, Canterbury	+ F FO
St Lawrence College in Thanet	+ E F
St Michael's School, Sevenoaks	T
Sevenoaks School	H
Sibton Park	+ F H T
Solefield School	T
Sutton Valence School	F H T
Tonbridge School	H
Ursuline College	F
Walthamstow Hall	+ E H
Wellesley House School	+ H T
West Heath School	H

Kent (continued)

Westbrook House School	+ F
Yardley Court	+ H

Lancashire

Arnold School	H
Beech House School	H
Bentham School	+ F H T
Bolton School (Boys' Division)	H
Bolton School (Girls' Division)	H
Bury Grammar School (Girls')	H
Casterton School	+ H
Elmslie Girls' School	H
Heathfield School	H
The Hulme Grammar School	H
The Hulme Grammar School for Girls	H
Kirkham Grammar School	F H
Moorland School	F H
Queen Elizabeth's Grammar School	+ H
Queen Mary School	+
Rossall Preparatory School	+ F H
Rossall School	+ E F H
St Mary's Hall, Stonyhurst	F H
Stonyhurst College	H
Westholme School	H T

Leicestershire

Grace Dieu Manor School	F
Leicester Grammar School	H
Leicester High School For Girls	H
Loughborough Grammar School	+ E F H
Loughborough High School	H
Manor House School	+ H
Nevill Holt School	+ F H T
Oakham School	H
PNEU School, Loughborough	+
Ratcliffe College	F H
Stoneygate School	+ E H
Uppingham School	+ H

Lincolnshire

Maypole House	F1 F2 F3
St Hugh's School, Woodhall Spa	+ F H T
Stamford High School	H
Stamford School	H T
Witham Hall	F H T

London

The American School in London	H T
Arnold House School	H
The Arts Educational Schools	H
Ashbourne Middle School	H
Belmont (Mill Hill Junior School)	H
Blackheath High School GPDST	H
The Cavendish School	H
Channing School	+ H
Christs College	E F H
City of London School	T
City of London School for Girls	H
Colfe's School	H
Collingham	H
Dallington School	H
Dulwich College Preparatory School	H
Durston House	H
Ealing College Upper School	H
Eaton House The Manor	H
Eltham College	E H
Emanuel School	H T
Finton House School	H
Forest Girls' School	+
Forest Junior School	+ F
Forest School	+ F
Francis Holland School, SW1	+ H
Francis Holland School, NW1	+
Garden House School	H
The Godolphin and Latymer School	H
The Hampshire School (Knightsbridge Under School)	+
Hampstead Hill Pre-Preparatory & Nursery School	H
Hellenic College of London	H

Hereward House School	+
Highgate Junior School	+ T
Highgate School	+ H T
International School of London	H
James Allen's Girls' School	H
King Fahad Academy	H
King's College School	H
Latymer Upper School	H
Lyndhurst House Preparatory School	H
Mander Portman Woodward	H T
Mill Hill School	+ F
More House	H
The Mount School	H
The Norwegian School	F FO
Notting Hill and Ealing High School GPDST	H
Palmers Green High School	H
The Pointer School	H
Putney High School	H
Putney Park School	H
Queen's College	H
Riverston School	+
The Roche School	H
Royal Ballet School	H
St Benedict's School	H
St Christina's RC Preparatory School	H
St James Independent School for Girls	H
St Paul's Girls' School	H
St Paul's Preparatory School	H
St Paul's School	H
St Philip's School	H
Sarum Hall	H
Sinclair House School	H
South Hampstead High School	H
Southbank International School	H
Streatham Hill and Clapham High School	H
Sydenham High School	H
Sylvia Young Theatre School	H
Trevor Roberts'	H
University College School	H
The Village School	+ H
Westminster Cathedral Choir School	H
Westminster School	H T
Willington School	H
Willoughby Hall School	H
Wimbledon High School	H
Woodside Park School	H

Greater Manchester

Ash Lea Grammar School	H
The Manchester Grammar School	H
Manchester High School for Girls	H
Manchester Jewish Grammar School	H
Rosecroft School Didsbury	H T
St Bede's College	H
William Hulme's Grammar School	H
Withington Girls' School	H

Merseyside

Avalon Preparatory School	H
The Belvedere School GPDST	H
Birkenhead School	+ H T
Highfield School	H
Kingsmead School	+ E F H T
Kingswood School	H
Liverpool College	+ E F H
Merchant Taylors' School	H
Merchant Taylors' School for Girls	H
St Mary's College, Liverpool	H
Streatham House School	H
Sunnymede School	H T
Tower Dene Preparatory School	H

Middlesex

Alpha Preparatory School	T
The American Community Schools	+ E H
Buckingham College Senior School	H
Hampton School	H
Harrow School	+ E H T
Heathfield School	H
The Lady Eleanor Holles School	H
The Mall School	+ H
Merchant Taylors' School	H
Newland House School	H

Middlesex (continued)

North London Collegiate School	H
Orley Farm School	+
The Purcell School	H
Quainton Hall School	+ H T
St Catherine's School, Twickenham	H
St David's School, Ashford	F M T

Norfolk

Cawston College	F
Convent of the Sacred Heart	+ H
Eccles Hall School	F H
Glebe House School	+ F4
Gresham's Preparatory School	H
Gresham's School	H T
Langley School	H
The Norwich High School for Girls GPDST	H
Norwich School	H
Taverham Hall	+ F
Thetford Grammar School	H
Wood Dene School	H

Northamptonshire

Beachborough School	H
Falcon Manor	F
Great Houghton Preparatory School	+ H T
Maidwell Hall	E H T
Northampton High School	+
Northamptonshire Grammar School	H
Quinton House	H
St Peter's School, Kettering	H
Wellingborough School	H
Winchester House School	T

Northumberland

Longridge Towers School	+ F FO
Mowden Hall School	H

Nottinghamshire

Bramcote School	+ F T
Grosvenor School	+ F
Lorne House	H T
Nottingham High School for Girls	H
Ranby House	F H
Trent College	+ F H
Wellow House School	H
West Bridgford High School	E H T
Worksop College	+ H

Oxfordshire

Abingdon School	H
Bloxham School	+ H T
Carmel College	H
The Carrdus School	H T
Cokethorpe School	H
Cranford House School	H
Headington School	+
Josca's Preparatory School	H
Kingham Hill School	+ E F
Magdalen College School	H T
Our Lady's Convent Senior School	H
Oxford High School GPDST	H
Rye St Antony School	H
St Clare's, Oxford	H
St Edward's School	+ F
School of S Helen & S Katharine	H
Shiplake College	F T
Sibford School	+ H

Shropshire

Adcote School	+ F H
Bedstone College	F H
Bellan House Preparatory School	+ F T
Ellesmere College	+ H T
Kingsland Grange	+ H T
Moor Park School	H T

Moreton Hall	+ E F FO H T
Oswestry Junior School	F T
Oswestry School	F T
Packwood Haugh	+ F H T
Prestfelde Preparatory School	+ F H T
Queen's Park School	H
Shrewsbury School	H
Wrekin College	F H T

Somerset

Buckland School	H
Chilton Cantelo School	F FO
Edgarley Hall	H
King's Bruton Pre-Preparatory & Junior School	+
King's College, Taunton	+ H
King's Hall School	+ F
King's School, Bruton	+ H T
Millfield School	H
The Park School	+ E F H
Perrott Hill School	H
Queen's College, Taunton	+ F H
Queen's College Junior School, Taunton	+ F H
Rossholme School	H
St Christopher's, Burnham-on-Sea	F H
St Martin's Independent School, Crewkerne	H
Taunton Preparatory School	+ F H T
Taunton School	+ E F H
Wells Cathedral Junior School	+
Wells Cathedral School	+ H

Staffordshire

Abbotsholme School	+ E F FO H T
Denstone College	+ F H T
Denstone College Preparatory School	F3 F4 H
Edenhurst School	+ T
Howitt House School	+ H T
Lichfield Cathedral School (St Chad's)	+
Maple Hayes Hall Dyslexia School	H
Newcastle-under-Lyme School	H
St Bede's School, Stafford	H
St Dominic's Priory School, Stafford	H
School of S Mary and S Anne	+ F H T
Stafford Grammar School	H
Yarlet Hall	+ F1 F3 F4 T

Suffolk

Barnardiston Hall Preparatory School	+ F T
Culford School	+ F H
Eversley School	+
Fairstead House School	H
Finborough School	F H
Framlingham College	H
Framlingham College Junior School	H
Hillcroft Preparatory School	H
Ipswich High School GPDST	H
Ipswich School	H
Moreton Hall	F FO
Old Buckenham Hall School	+ T
Royal Hospital School	F1 F2
St Felix, Southwold	F
St George's School, Southwold	+ F T
School of Jesus and Mary	H
South Lee Preparatory School	H

Surrey

Aberdour School	+ T
Aldro School	H
Box Hill School	H
Canbury School	H
Caterham School	+ E F FO H T
Caterham School Preparatory	+ E F FO H T
Charterhouse	H
Cheswycks School	+
Claremont Fan Court School	H
Clewborough House Preparatory School	F H
Commonweal Lodge School	H
Coworth Park School	+
Cranleigh School	F FO
Croydon High School GPDST	H

Surrey (continued)

Downside Preparatory School	+ T
Drayton House School	H
Duke of Kent School	F
Dunottar School	H
Elmhurst Ballet School	F1 F3 F4 H
Epsom College	H M
Essendene Lodge School	H
Ewell Castle School	H
Frensham Heights School	H
Glenesk School	H
Greenacre School for Girls	H
Guildford High School (Church Schools Co Ltd)	+ H
Halstead Preparatory School	H
Haslemere Preparatory School	T
The Hawthorns School	+
Holy Cross Preparatory School	H T
King Edward's School Witley	+ E H
Kingston Grammar School	H
Kingswood House School	+ H T
Longacre Preparatory School	H
Lyndhurst School	H
Marymount International School	H
Milbourne Lodge School	+
Notre Dame Senior School	H
Oakfield	H
Old Palace School of John Whitgift	+ H
Parkside School	F FO H T
Parsons Mead	+ F
Prior's Field School	F H
Priory School	H
Reed's School	H
Reigate St Mary's Preparatory and Choir School	H
Rokeby School	T
The Royal Alexandra and Albert School	+ F FO H T
Royal Grammar School, Guildford	H
The Royal School, Hindhead	H
St Andrew's School, Woking	H
St Catherine's School, Guildford	H
St John's School, Leatherhead	+
St Maur's Convent School, Weybridge	H
St Michael's School, Oxted	+ F
St Teresa's Preparatory School	H
St Teresa's School	F H T
Sanderstead Junior School	H
Scaitcliffe School	H
Shaftesbury Independent School	+ E H
Shrewsbury House School	T
Sir William Perkins's School	H
Stowford	H
Surbiton High School	+ H
Sutton High School (GPDST)	H
TASIS England American School	H
Tormead School	H
Trinity School	H
Whitgift School	+ H
Wispers School	F
Yehudi Menuhin School	H

East Sussex

Ashdown House School	+ T
Battle Abbey School	F
Bricklehurst Manor Preparatory	H
Brighton and Hove High School GPDST	H
Brighton College	+ F3 H T
Brighton College Junior School	+ F3
Buckswood Grange	F
Claremont School	H M
Eastbourne College	H
The Fold School	H
Mayfield College	F H
Micklefield Wadhurst incorporating the Legat School of Classical Ballet	+ E F H T
Moira House Junior School	+ F H T
Moira House Senior School	+ E F H T
Mowden School	+ H T
Newlands Manor School	F FO H T
Newlands Preparatory School	F H
Roedean School	H
St Andrew's School, Eastbourne	F
St Aubyn's, Brighton	+ T
St Bede's School, Hailsham	F H T
St Leonards-Mayfield School	H

St Mary's Hall	+ F H
Skippers Hill Manor Preparatory School	H
Temple Grove	H
Vinehall School	+ E F
Westerleigh	H T
Wilton House School	F FO

West Sussex

Ardingly College	+ F H T
Ardingly College Junior School	H T
Burgess Hill School	H
Christs Hospital	+ F1 F2 F4 H
Copthorne School	H
Cottesmore School	H
Dorset House School	F H T
Fonthill	H
Great Ballard School	F
Great Walstead	+ E F H T
Hurstpierpoint College	+ E F H T
Lancing College	+ F1 F2 H
Lavant House Rosemead	F H
Oakwood School	F1 F3 F4 H
Our Lady of Sion School	H
St Margaret's Senior School Convent of Mercy, Midhurst	+
St Peter's School, Burgess Hill	H
Seaford College	F H
Shoreham College	+ F
Slindon College	F H
Stoke Brunswick	F H
Tavistock & Summerhill School	H

Tyne and Wear

Argyle House School	+ H
Central Newcastle High School GPDST	H
Dame Allan's Boys School	H
Dame Allan's Girls School	H
Eastcliffe Grammar School	H
Fulwell Grange Christian School	+ E
The King's School	+ H
Newcastle Preparatory School	H
Newcastle Upon Tyne Church High School	+
Newlands School	H
Sunderland High School	+ H
Westfield School	H

Warwickshire

Arnold Lodge School	H T
Bilton Grange	+ F H T
Emscote Lawn School	+ H T
The King's High School for Girls	H
The Kingsley School	+ H
New College	E H
Rugby School	H
Warwick School	H
Wroxall Abbey School	H

West Midlands

Bablake School	H
The Blue Coat School	+ E F H T
Edgbaston Church of England College	+
Edgbaston High School for Girls	H
Eversfield Preparatory School	+
Hallfield School	+ T
Hydesville Tower School	F T
Newbridge Preparatory School	+
Pattison's College	F3 F4 H
The Royal Wolverhampton Junior School	F H
The Royal Wolverhampton School	F H
Solihull School	+
Tettenhall College	+ F H T
West House School	+ T
Wolverhampton Grammar School	H

Wiltshire

Dauntsey's School	H
The Godolphin School	H
Grittleton House School	H
La Retraite Leehurst School	H
Leaden Hall	+
Marlborough College	+ F H
Pinewood School	+ T
St Mary's School, Calne	+ H
Sandroyd	H T
Stonar School	T
Warminster School	+ F H

North Yorkshire

Ampleforth College	H
Ampleforth College Junior School	H
Ashville College	+ E F H T
Aysgarth Preparatory School	+ F H T
Ayton School	+ F H
Bootham School	H
Catteral Hall	F H
Cundall Manor School	F FO
Giggleswick School	F H T
Grosvenor House School	+ F T
Harrogate Ladies' College	H
Howsham Hall	+ H T
Malsis School	+ T
Pocklington School	F H T
Queen Ethelburga's College	+ F
Queen Margaret's School	+
Queen Mary's School	+ F H
Read School	H
Red House School, York	H
Ripon Cathedral Choir School	F

St Hilda's School, Whitby	+ E F H
St Martin's School, York	F
St Olave's School (Junior of St Peter's)	F H T
St Peter's School, York	+ F H
Scarborough College	F H
Terrington Hall	+ F H
Woodleigh School	F
York College for Girls	+ H

South Yorkshire

Birkdale School	H
Mount St Mary's College	H
Rudston Preparatory School	H
Sheffield High School GPDST	H
Westbourne Preparatory School	H

West Yorkshire

Ackworth School	H
Batley Grammar School	H
Bradford Girls' Grammar School	H
Bradford Grammar School	+ H
Bronte House School	+ F
Clevedon House	F H
Fulneck School	+ F H
Gateways School	H
Hipperholme Grammar School	H
Leeds Grammar School	H
Queen Elizabeth Grammar School	H
Rishworth School	+ F
St David's School, Huddersfield	H
Silcoates School	+ E
Wakefield Girls' High School	H
Woodhouse Grove School	+ F H

NORTHERN IRELAND

County Antrim

Cabin Hill School	+ E F H
Methodist College	+

County Armagh

The Royal School	+

County Down

The Holywood Rudolf Steiner School	H
Rockport Preparatory School	+ H

County Londonderry

Coleraine Academical Institution	+ E

County Tyrone

Royal School Dungannon	+ E F H

SCOTLAND

Borders

St Mary's Preparatory School	F H

Central

Queen Victoria School	F

Fife

St Leonards School	+ F H T

Grampian

Aberlour House	H
Gordonstoun School	F H
Robert Gordons College	H
St Margaret's School for Girls	H

Lothian

Cargilfield	F H
Clifton Hall	F H T
The Edinburgh Academy	H
Fettes College	H
George Heriot's School	H
George Watson's College	+

The High School of Glasgow	H

Lothian (continued)

Loretto Junior School	F
Loretto School	+ F1 F3 F4 FO H M T
The Mary Erskine School	H
Merchiston Castle School	+ F H T
The Rudolf Steiner School	H
St Denis and Cranley School	+ E F
St George's School for Girls	+
St Serf's School	H

Strathclyde

Craigholme School	+
Drumley House School	H
Glasgow Academy	+ H

Hutchesons' Grammar School	H
Keil School	+ F H
Laurel Bank School	H
Lomond School	F
The Park School	H
St Aloysius' College	H

Tayside

Ardvreck School	F H T
Craigclowan Preparatory School	H T
Croftinloan School	+ E F H T
Glenalmond College	+ F H T
The High School of Dundee	+ H
Kilgraston School	T
Lathallan School	F FO H T
Rannoch School	+ F H T
Strathallan School	F T

WALES

Clwyd

Howell's School, Denbigh	F H
Ruthin School	+ F H
Rydal Penrhos Preparatory School	+ E F H
Rydal Penrhos Senior School	+ E F H
Rydal Penrhos Senior School Girls' Division	+ F

Dyfed

Llandovery College	+ F
Netherwood School	H
St Michael's School	H

Mid Glamorgan

St John's School, Porthcawl	H

South Glamorgan

The Cathedral School, Cardiff	+ H
Elm Tree House School	H
Kings Monkton School (Primary)	H

St John's College, Cardiff	H

West Glamorgan

Emmanuel Grammar School	+ E
Ffynone House School	H

Gwent

Monmouth School	F H
Rougemont School	H
St John's-on-the-Hill	F

Gwynedd

St David's College, Llandudno	F H
St Gerard's School	H
Tower House	F3 F4

Powys

Christ College	+ F H

FURTHER EDUCATION

London

Inchbald School of Design	H

OVERSEAS

Switzerland

Aiglon College	H
Franklin College	H

522

4.4
THE ASSISTED PLACES SCHEME

List of Participating Schools

Details of the Assisted Places Scheme are given on page 35. The following list of participating schools is the most up-to-date available at the date of publication. Each school is defined as B (Boys'), G (Girls') or M (Mixed). In Scotland the letter P denotes a preparatory school. (M) denotes mixed entry at sixth-form level. The normal ages of entry are shown for each school. In a few cases entry at 11 may be to a junior department or an associated preparatory school with transfer to the main school at 13. Schools which offer boarding places to assisted pupils are indicated by the letter 'b'. All enquiries about assisted places should be directed to the Head of the individual schools concerned.

ENGLAND

Avon

Bath High School	G 11 & VI
Bristol Cathedral School	B(M) 11 & VI
Bristol Grammar School	M 11 & VI
Clifton College, Bristol	Mb 11
Clifton High School, Bristol	Gb 11
Colston's Collegiate School, Bristol	Mb 11
Colston's Girls' School, Bristol	G 11 & VI
King Edward's School, Bath	B(M) 11
Kingswood School, Bath	Mb 11
Monkton Combe School, Bath	Mb 11
Prior Park College, Bath	Mb 11
Queen Elizabeth's Hospital, Bristol	Bb 11 & VI
The Red Maids' School, Bristol	Gb 11 & VI
Redland High School, Bristol	G 11 & VI

Bedfordshire

Bedford High School, Gb 11	13 & VI
Bedford Modern School	Bb 11
Bedford School	Bb 11
The Dame Alice Harpur School, Bedford	G 11–18

Berkshire

The Abbey School, Reading	G 11 & VI
Bradfield College, Reading	B(M)b VI
Douai School, Reading	Mb 11
Downe House School, Newbury	Gb 11 & 12
Leighton Park School, Reading	Mb 11 & 13
Marist Convent Senior School, Ascot	G 11
Pangbourne College, Reading	Bb 11
St Joseph's Convent School, Reading	G 11 & VI
Wellington College, Crowthorne	B(M)b 11

Buckinghamshire

Stowe School, Buckingham	B(M)b VI

Cambridgeshire

Kimbolton School, Huntingdon	Mb 11
Laxton School, Peterborough	M 11
The Leys School, Cambridge	B(M)b 11
The Perse School for Boys, Cambridge	B(M) 11
The Perse School for Girls, Cambridge	G 11 & VI
St Marys School, Cambridge	Gb 11 & VI
Wisbech Grammar School	M 11

Cheshire

Cheadle Hulme School, Cheadle	M 11 & VI
The King's School, Macclesfield	M 11
The King's School, Chester	B 11 & VI
Loreto Convent Grammar School, Altrincham	G 11
Mount Carmel School, Cheshire	G 11
The Queen's School, Chester	G 11 & VI
Stockport Grammar School	M 11 & VI
St Ambrose College, Altrincham	B 11 & VI

Cleveland

Teesside High School, Stockton-on-Tees	G 11
Yarm School	B(M) 11

Cornwall

Truro High School	Gb 11 & VI
Truro School	Mb 11 & VI

Cumbria

Austin Friars, Carlisle	Mb 11
Casterton School, Carnforth	Gb 11
St Bees School	Mb 11
Sedbergh School	Bb 11 & VI

Derbyshire

Derby High School	G 11
Repton School	Mb 13 & VI

Devon

Edgehill College, Bideford	Mb 11 & VI
Exeter School	B(M)b 11
The Maynard School, Exeter	G 11
Plymouth College	B(M)b 11
St Margaret's Exeter	G 11
West Buckland, Barnstaple	B(M)b 11

Dorset

Canford School, Wimborne	B(M)b 13 & VI
Talbot Heath, Bournemouth	Gb 11

Durham

Barnard Castle School	Mb 11
Durham School	B(M)b 11 & 13
Polam Hall School, Darlington	Gb 11

Essex

Bancroft's School, Woodford Green	M 11 & VI
Brentwood School	Mb 11 & VI
Chigwell School	B(M)b 11
Felsted School, Dunmow	Mb 11
Friends' School, Saffron Walden	Mb 11
Ilford Ursuline High School, Ilford	G 11 & VI

Gloucestershire

The Cheltenham Ladies' College	Gb 11
Rendcomb College, Cirencester	Mb 11
Wycliffe College, Stonehouse	Mb 11

Hampshire

Bedales School, Petersfield	Mb VI
Churcher's College, Petersfield	M 11
Farnborough Hill, Farnborough	G 11
King Edward VI School, Southampton	M 11
Lord Wandsworth College, Basingstoke	B(M)b 11
The Portsmouth Grammar School	M 11 & VI
Portsmouth High School, Southsea	G 11 & VI
St Swithun's School, Winchester	Gb VI
St John's College, Southsea	B(M)b 11
Salesian College, Farnborough	B 11
Winchester College	Bb 13

Hereford and Worcester

The Alice Ottley School, Worcester	G 11 & VI
Bromsgrove School, Bromsgrove	Mb 11 & 13
The Hereford Cathedral School	Mb 11
The King's School, Worcester	Mb 11
Malvern College	Mb 11
Royal Grammar School Worcester	Bb 11

Hertfordshire

Aldenham School, Elstree	B(M)b 13 & VI
Berkhamsted School	Bb 11
Berkhamsted School for Girls	G 11 & VI
Bishop's Stortford College	B(M)b 11
Haberdashers' Aske's School for Girls, Elstree	G 11 & VI
Haberdasher's Aske's School, Elstree	B 11 & VI
Haileybury, Hertford	Bb(M) 11
St Albans School	B(M) 11 & VI
St Albans High School	G 11 & VI
St Edmund's College, Ware	Mb 11 & VI
St Margaret's School, Watford	Gb 11 & 13

North Humberside

Hymers College, Hull	M 11

Isle of Wight

Ryde School with Upper Chine	M 11

Kent

Ashford School	Gb 11 & VI
Bromley High School	G 11 & VI
Dover College	Mb 11
Kent College, Canterbury	Mb 11
King's School, Rochester	Mb 11
St Lawrence College in Thanet, Ramsgate	Mb 11
Sevenoaks School	Mb 11
Sutton Valence School, Maidstone	Mb 11
Tonbridge School	Bb VI
Ursuline College, Westgate-on-Sea	Gb 11
Walthamstow Hall, Sevenoaks	Gb 11 & VI

Lancashire

Arnold School, Blackpool	Mb 11 & VI
King Edward VII School, Lytham	B 11
Kirkham Grammar School, Preston	Mb 11 & VI
Queen Elizabeth's Grammar School, Blackburn	B(M) 11
Queen Mary School, Lytham	G 11
Rossall School, Fleetwood	Mb 11 & VI
Stonyhurst College	B(M)b 11
Westholme School, Blackburn	G 11

Leicestershire

Leicester Grammar School	M 11
Loughborough Grammar School	Bb 11
Loughborough High School	G 11
Oakham School	Mb 11 & 13
Ratcliffe College, Leicester	Mb 11

Lincolnshire

Stamford High School	Gb 11 & VI
Stamford School	Bb 11

London

Alleyn's School, SE22	M 11
Blackheath High School, SE3	G 11 & VI
City of London School, EC4	B 11 & VI
City of London School for Girls, EC2	G 11 & VI
Colfe's School, SE12	B(M) 11
Dulwich College, SE21	Bb 11
Eltham College, SE9	B(M)b 11
Emanuel School, SW11	B 11
Forest School, E17	Bb 11 & VI
Francis Holland School, NW1	G 11
The Godolphin and Latymer School, W6	G 11 & VI
Highgate School, N6	Bb 11 & VI
James Allen's Girls' School, SE22	G 11
King's College School, SE19	B 11
Latymer Upper School, W6	B 11 & VI

London (continued)

Mill Hill School, NW7	B(M)b 11
Notting Hill and Ealing High School, W13	G 11 & VI
Putney High School, SW15	G 11 & VI
Queen's College, W1	G 11 & VI
St Benedict's School, W5	B(M) 11 & VI
St Dunstan's College, SE6	B 11 & VI
St Paul's Girls' School, W6	G 11 & VI
St Paul's School, SE13	Bb 11
South Hampstead High School, NW3	G 11 & VI
Streatham Hill and Clapham High School, SW2	G 11 & VI
Sydenham High School, Westwood Hill, SE26	G 11 & VI
University College School, NW3	B 11 & VI
Westminster School, SW1	B(M)b 11
Wimbledon High School, SW19	G 11 & VI

Greater Manchester

Bolton School (Boys' Division)	B 11 & VI
Bolton School (Girls' Division)	G 11 & VI
Bury Grammar (Boys)	B 11 & VI
Bury Grammar (Girls)	G 11 & VI
The Hulme Grammar School (Boys'), Oldham	B 11 & VI
The Hulme Grammar School (Girls'), Oldham	G 11 & VI
The Manchester Grammar School	B 11 & VI
Manchester High School for Girls	G 11 & VI
St Bede's College, Manchester	M 11 & VI
William Hulmes' Grammar School, Manchester	M 11 & VI
Withington Girls' School, Manchester	G 11 & VI

Merseyside

The Belvedere School, Liverpool	G 11 & VI
Birkenhead High School	G 11 & VI
Birkenhead School	B 11
Liverpool College	M 11 & VI
Merchant Taylor's School, Liverpool	B 11
Merchant Taylor's Girls' School, Liverpool	G 11 & VI
St Edward's College, Liverpool	M 11 & VI
St Mary's College, Liverpool	M 11

Middlesex

Hampton School, Hampton	B 11
The Lady Eleanor Holles School, Hampton	G 11 & VI
Merchant Taylors' School, Northwood	Bb 11
North London Collegiate School, Edgware	G 11 & VI
St Helen's School for Girls, Northwood	Gb 11

Norfolk

Gresham's School, Holt	Mb VI
The Norwich High School for Girls,	G 11 & VI
Norwich School	B 11

Northamptonshire

Northampton High School	G 11
Wellingborough School	Mb 11

Nottinghamshire

Nottingham High School	B 11 & VI
Nottingham High School for Girls	G 11
Trent College, Nottingham	Mb 11
Worksop College	Mb 11 & 13

Oxfordshire

Abingdon School	Bb 11
Bloxham School, Banbury	B(M)b 13
Carmel College, Wallingford	Mb 11
Headington School, Oxford	Gb 11
Magdalen College School, Oxford	Bb 11
Oxford High School	G 11 & VI
School of S Helen and S Katharine, Abingdon	Gb 11 & VI

Shropshire

Ellesmere College	B(M)b 11
Shrewsbury High School	G 11 & VI
Wrekin College, Telford	Mb 13

Somerset

Bruton School for Girls	Gb 11 & VI
King's School, Bruton	B(M) 11 & 13
Queen's College, Taunton	Mb 11
Taunton School	Mb 11 & VI
Wellington School	Mb 11
Wells Cathedral School	Mb 11

Staffordshire

Denstone College, Uttoxeter	Mb 11
Newcastle under Lyme School	M 11
School of St Mary & St Anne, Rugeley	Gb 11
Stafford Grammar	M 11
St Joseph's College, Stoke on Trent	M 11

Suffolk

Culford School, Bury St Edmunds	Mb 11
Framlingham College	Mb 13
Ipswich School	B(M)b 11 & VI
Ipswich High School	G 11 & VI
St Felix School, Southwold	Gb 11 & 12
St Joseph's College, Ipswich	B(M)b 11 & VI
Woodbridge School	Mb 11 & VI

Surrey

Caterham School	Mb 11
Charterhouse, Godalming	B(M)b VI
City of London Freemen's School, Ashtead	Mb 13
Cranleigh School	B(M)b 11
Croham Hurst School, South Croydon	G 11
Croydon High School, South Croydon	G 11 & VI
Epsom College	B(M)b 11
Guildford High School for Girls	G 11
King Edward's School Witley, Godalming	Mb 11
Kingston Grammar School	M 11
Old Palace School of John Whitgift, Croydon	G 11 & VI
Reed's School, Cobham	B(M)b 11 & 13
Reigate Grammar School	B 11 & VI
Royal Grammar School, Guildford	B 11 & VI
St Catherine's School, Guildford	Gb 11
St John's School, Leatherhead	B(M)b 13 & VI
St Maur's Convent School, Weybridge	Gb 11
St George's College, Weybridge	B(M)b 11 & VI
Sir William Perkins' School, Chertsey	G 11 & VI
Surbiton High School	G 11
Sutton High School	G 11 & VI
Tormead School	G 11 & VI
Trinity School of John Whitgift, Croydon	B 11 & VI
Whitgift School, South Croydon	B 11 & VI

East Sussex

Brighton and Hove High School, Brighton	G 11
Brighton College	Mb 11 & VI
St Mary's Hall, Brighton	Gb 11

West Sussex

Ardingly College, Haywards Heath	Mb 11
Burgess Hill School for Girls	Gb 11
Christ's Hospital School, Horsham	Mb 11 & VI
Hurstpierpoint College, Hassocks	Mb 11 & 13

Tyne and Wear

Central Newcastle High School, Newcastle upon Tyne	G 11 & VI
Dame Allan's Boys' School, Newcastle upon Tyne	B(M) 11
Dame Allan's Girls' School, Newcastle upon Tyne	G(M) 11 & VI
The King's School, North Shields	M 11
La Sagesse Convent School, Newcastle upon Tyne	G 11
Newcastle upon Tyne Church High School	G 11
Royal Grammar School, Newcastle upon Tyne	B 11

Warwickshire

The King's High School for Girls, Warwick	G 11 & VI
Kingsley School, Leamington Spa	G 11
Warwick School	Bb 11

West Midlands

Bablake School, Coventry	M 11 & VI
Edgbaston Church of England College	G 11
Holy Child School, Birmingham	G 11
King Edward's School, Birmingham	B 11
King Edward VI High School for Girls, Birmingham	G 11 & VI
King Henry VIII, Coventry	M 11 & VI
Solihull School	B(M) 11 & G VI
Wolverhampton Grammar School	M 11

Wiltshire

Dauntsey's School, Devizes	Mb 11
The Godolphin School, Salisbury	G 11

North Yorkshire

Ashville College, Harrogate	Mb 11
Bootham School, York	Mb 11
Giggleswick School, Settle	Mb 11 & 13
Harrogate Ladies' College	Gb 11
The Mount School, York	Gb 11
Pocklington School, York	Mb 11
St Peter's School, York	Mb 11
Scarborough College	Mb 11

South Yorkshire

Mount St Mary's College, Sheffield	Mb 11
Sheffield High School GPDST	G 11 & VI

West Yorkshire

Ackworth School, Pontefract	Mb 11
Batley Grammar School	B(M) 11
Bradford Girls' Grammar School	G 11
Bradford Grammar School	B(M) 11 & 13
Hipperholme Grammar School, Halifax	M 11
Leeds Girls' High School	G 11 & VI
Leeds Grammar School	B 11
Queen Elizabeth Grammar School, Wakefield	Bb 11
Silcoates School, Wakefield	Mb 11
Wakefield Girls' High School	G 11
Woodhouse Grove School, Apperley Bridge	Mb 11

SCOTLAND

Borders

St Mary's School, Melrose	MP 5-14

Central

Beaconhurst Grange, Stirling	MP 3-14
Dollar Academy	M 5-18

Dumfries and Galloway

Kilquhanity House School, Castle Douglas	M 5-18

Fife

New Park School, St Andrews	MP 4-14
St Katharines Girls' Preparatory School, St Andrews	G 7-12
St Leonards School, St Andrews	G 12-18

Grampian

Aberlour House School, Aberlour	MP 8-13
Albyn School for Girls, Aberdeen	G 3-18
Gordonstoun School, Elgin	M 13-18
Lathallan School, Montrose	MP 5-13
Robert Gordon's College, Aberdeen	M 5-18
St Margaret's School for Girls, Aberdeen	G 3-18

Lothian

Belhaven Hill, Dunbar	BP 7-13
Cargilfield, Edinburgh	MP 3-13
Clifton Hall, Newbridge	MP 3-13
Stewart's Melville College, Edinburgh	B b 11-18
The Edinburgh Academy	B 3-18
Fettes College, Edinburgh	M 10-18
George Heriot's School, Edinburgh	M 4-18
George Watson's College, Edinburgh	M 3-18
Loretto School, Musselburgh	B(M) B 8-18
The Mary Erskine School, Edinburgh	G 3-18 M 3- 12
Merchiston Castle School, Edinburgh	B 11-18
The Rudolf Steiner School of Edinburgh	M 3-18
St Denis and Cranley School, Edinburgh	G 5-18
St George's School for Girls, Edinburgh	G 3-18
St Margaret's School, Edinburgh	G 3-18 B 3-8

Strathclyde

Belmont House, Glasgow	B 3-18
Craigholme School, Glasgow	G 3-18 B 3-8
Drumley House School, Ayr	MP 3-13
Fernhill School, Glasgow	G 4-18 B 4-11
Glasgow Academy	M 4-18

Strathclyde (continued)

Hamilton College	M 4–18
The High School of Glasgow	M 3–18
Hutchesons' Grammar School, Glasgow	M 5–18
Keil School, Dumbarton	M 10–18
The Kelvinside Academy, Glasgow	B 4–18
Laurel Bank School, Glasgow	G 3–18 B3–7
Lomond School, Helensburgh	M 3–19
Park Lodge School, Helensburgh	MP 2–12
The Park School, Glasgow	G 3–18
St Aloysius College, Glasgow	M 8–18
St Columba's School, Kilmacolm	M 3–18
Wellington School, Ayr	G 3–18

Tayside

Ardvreck School, Crieff	MP 4–14
Butterstone School, Blairgowrie	GP 2–13
Craigclowan Preparatory School, Perth	MP 4–13
Croftinloan Preparatory School, Pitlochry	MP 7–14
Glenalmond College, Perth	B 12–18 G 16–18
The High School of Dundee	M 5–18
Kilgraston School, Perth	G 5–18
Morrison's Academy, Crieff	M 6–18
Rannoch School, Pitlochry	M 10–18
Strathallan School, Perth	M 10–18

WALES

Clwyd

Howell's School, Denbigh	Gb 11 & VI
Rydal Penrhos, Colwyn Bay	Mb Gb 11

Dyfed

Llandovery College	Mb 11

Gwent

Haberdashers' Monmouth School for Girls, Monmouth	G 11 & VI
Monmouth School	Bb 11

Powys

Christ College, Brecon	B(M)b 11

South Glamorgan

Howell's School, Cardiff	G 11 & VI

4.5
SPECIALIST SCHOOLS

Schools in the directory which specialise in the theatre, dance or music are listed below. For full details about entrance requirements and the curriculum parents are advised to contact schools direct.

Arts schools

The Arts Educational Schools, London W4
The Arts Educational Schools, Tring
Barbara Speake Stage School, London W3
Italia Conti Academy of Theatre Arts, London EC1
McKee School of Education, Dance and Drama, Liverpool
Ravenscourt Theatre School, London W6
Sylvia Young Theatre School, London NW1
Woodlee Academy Theatre School, London N1

Dance schools

Elmhurst Ballet School, Camberley
Hammond School, Chester
Micklefield Wadhurst incorporating the Legat School of
   Classical Ballet, Wadhurst
The Royal Ballet School, London W14
The Urdang Academy of Ballet, London WC2
Stonelands School of Ballet, East Sussex

Music schools

Chethams' Schools of Music, Manchester
The Purcell School, Harrow
St Mary's Music School, Edinburgh
The Yehudi Menuhin School, Cobham

4.6
SINGLE-SEX SCHOOLS

BOYS' SCHOOLS

ENGLAND

Avon

Bristol Cathedral School, Bristol 10-18 (Co-ed VIth form)
Downside School, Bath 10-18
King Edward's Junior School, Bath 7-11
King Edward's School, Bath, Bath 7-18 (Co-ed VIth form)
The Park School, Bath 3-11 (Girls nursery only)
Queen Elizabeth's Hospital, Bristol 11-18

Bedfordshire

Bedford Modern School, Bedford 7-18
Bedford School, Bedford 13-18
Bedford Preparatory School, Bedford 7-12
Rushmoor School, Bedford 4-16

Berkshire

Bradfield College, Reading 13-18 (Co-ed VIth form)
Brockhurst School, Newbury 6-13
Cheam Hawtreys, Newbury 7-13
Claires Court School, Maidenhead 10-17
Crosfields School, Reading 4-13
Elstree School, Reading 3-13
Eton College, Windsor 13-18
Haileybury Junior School, Windsor 7-14
Horris Hill, Newbury 8-13
Lambrook, Bracknell 4-13
Ludgrove, Wokingham 8-13
The Oratory School, Reading 11-18

Papplewick, Ascot 7-13
Presentation College, Reading 5-18 (Co-ed VIth Form)
Reading Blue Coat School, Reading 11-18 (Co-ed VIth form)
Ridgeway School (Claires Court Junior), Maidenhead 4-11
St Edwards School, Reading 7-14
St George's School, Windsor 7-13
St John's Beaumont, Windsor 4-13
Sunningdale School, Sunningdale 8-13
Wellington College, Crowthorne 13-18 (Co-ed VIth form)

Buckinghamshire

The Beacon School, Amersham 3-13
Caldicott, Farnham Royal 7-13
Davenies School, Beaconsfield 5-13
Gayhurst School, Gerrards Cross 4-13
Hampden Manor School, Great Missenden 4-13 (Girls 4-7)
Kingscote School, Gerrards Cross 4-7
Stowe School, Buckingham 13-18 (Co-ed VIth form)
Thorpe House School, Gerrards Cross 4-13

Cambridgeshire

The Perse School, Cambridge 7-18 (Co-ed VIth form)

Channel Islands

De La Salle College, Jersey 4-18

Elizabeth College, Guernsey 7-18 (Girls 16-18)
Victoria College, Jersey 11-19 (VIth with Jersey Girls College)
Victoria College Preparatory School, Jersey 7-11

Cheshire

Altrincham Preparatory School, Altrincham 4-12
The King's School, Chester 7-18
North Cestrian Grammar School, Altrincham 11-18
Pownall Hall School, Wilmslow 3-13
The Ryleys, Alderley Edge 3-13 (Weekly boarding only)
St Ambrose College, Altrincham 11-18
St Ambrose Preparatory School, Altrincham 4-11
Sandbach School, Cheshire 11-18

Cleveland

Yarm School, Yarm 5-18 (Co-ed VIth form)

Cumbria

Sedbergh School, Sedbergh 11-18

Devon

Bramdean Grammar School, Exeter 11-17 (Co-ed VIth form)
Bramdean Preparatory & Grammar School, Exeter 7-11
Exeter Preparatory School, Exeter 7-11
Exeter School, Exeter 11-18 (Co-ed VIth form)
Mount House School, Tavistock 7-14

Dorset

Milton Abbey School, Blandford Forum 13-18
The Old Malthouse, Swanage 4-13 (Girls 4-7)
Sherborne School, Sherborne 13-18

County Durham

Bow School, Durham 4-13
The Chorister School, Durham 4-13 (Day girls)
Durham School, Durham 11-18 (Co-ed VIth form)
Hurworth House School, Darlington 4-16

Essex

Chigwell School, Chigwell 7-18 (Co-ed VIth form)
Colchester Boys High School, Colchester 3-16 (Girls 4-11)
Cranbrook College, Ilford 4-16
Daiglen School, Buckhurst Hill 4-11
Loyola Preparatory School, Buckhurst Hill 4-11 (Nursery 3-4)
St Aubyn's School, Woodford Green 4-13
Widford Lodge, Chelmsford 4-13 (Co-ed 2-4)

Gloucestershire

Cheltenham College, Cheltenham 13-18 (Co-ed VIth Form)
Cheltenham College Junior School, Cheltenham 3-13 (Girls 3-10)

Hampshire

Boundary Oak School, Fareham 3-13 (Girls 3-9)
Lord Wandsworth College, Basingstoke 11-18 (Co-ed VIth form)
The Pilgrims School, Winchester 8-13
St John's College, Southsea 4-18 (Co-ed VIth form)
St Mary's College, Southampton 3-18
St Neot's School, Basingstoke 3-13 (Day girls 3-13)
Salesian College, Farnborough 11-18
Winchester College, Winchester 13-18

Hereford & Worcester

Abberley Hall, Worcester 2-13 (Girls 2-7)
Aymestrey School, Worcester 7-13
Royal Grammar School Worcester, Worcester 7-18

Hertfordshire

Aldenham School, Elstree 11-18 (Co-ed VIth form)
Aldwickbury School, Harpenden 4-13 (Girls 4-7)
Beechwood Park, St Albans 4-13 (Girls 4-7)
Berkhamsted Junior School, Berkhamsted 7-13
Berkhamsted School, Berkhamsted 10-18 (Co-ed VIth form)
Edge Grove School, Aldenham 2-13 (Girls 2-7)
Haberdashers' Aske's School, Elstree 7-18
Haileybury College, Hertford 11-18 (Co-ed VIth form)
Lochinver House School, Potters Bar 4-13
Lockers Park, Hemel Hempstead 7-13
Northwood Preparatory School, Rickmansworth 4-13
St Albans School, St Albans 11-18 (Co-ed VIth form)
St Columba's College, St Albans 11-18
York House School, Rickmansworth 4-13

Kent

Bickley Park School, Bromley 8-13
Greenhayes School for Boys, West Wickham 4-11 (Girls 3-5)
Harenc School Trust, Sidcup 3-11
The New Beacon School, Sevenoaks 5-13
St Ronan's, Hawkhurst 3-13 (Girls 3-8)
Solefield School, Sevenoaks 4-13
Tonbridge School, Tonbridge 13-18
Yardley Court, Tonbridge 7-13

Lancashire

Bolton School (Boys' Division), Bolton 8-18
Bury Grammar School, Bury 7-18
The Hulme Grammar School, Oldham 7-18
King Edward VII School, Lytham St Annes 3-18
Queen Elizabeth's Grammar School, Blackburn 7-18 (Co-ed VIth form)
St Mary's Hall, Stonyhurst 7-13
Stonyhurst College, Clitheroe 13-18 (Girls 16-18)

Leicestershire

Loughborough Grammar School, Loughborough 10-18
Uppingham School, Oakham 13-18 (Co-ed VIth form)

Lincolnshire

Stamford School, Stamford 8-18 (Co-ed 4-8)

London

Arnold House School, NW8 5-13
Belmont (Mill Hill Junior School), NW7 7-13
City of London School, EC4 10-18
Clifton Lodge, W5 4-13
Colfe's School, SE12 7-18 (Co-ed 3-6 and 16-18)
Dulwich College, SE21 7-18
Dulwich College Preparatory School, SE21 3-13 (Girls 3-5)
Durston House, W5 4-13
Ealing College Upper School, W13 11-18 (Co-ed VIth form)
Eaton House School, SW1 4-9
Eaton House The Manor, SW4 2-13 (Girls 2-4)
Eltham College, SE9 7-18 (Co-ed VIth form)
Emanuel School, SW11 10-19 (Co-ed VIth form; girls aged 10+, 11+ accepted from September 1996)
The Falcons Pre-Preparatory School, W4 3-8
Forest Junior School, E17 7-13 (Day girls 7-11)
Forest School, E17 13-18
Friern Barnet Grammar School, N11 10-16
The Hall School, NW3 5-13
Hereward House School, NW3 4-13
Highgate Junior School, N6 7-13

Highgate School, N6 13-18
Islamic College London, E1 11-16
Keble Preparatory School, N21 4-13
King's College Junior School, SW19 7-13
King's College School, SW19 13-18
Latymer Upper School, W6 7-18
Lubavitch House Senior School for Boys, N16 11-18
Lyndhurst House Preparatory School, NW3 7-13
Mechinah Liyeshivah Zichron Moshe, N16 11-16
Menorah Grammar School, NW11 11-18
Mill Hill School, NW7 13-18 (Co-ed VIth form)
Northcote Lodge, SW11 7-13
Pardes Grammar Boys' School, N3 5-17
St Angelo Preparatory School, W5 4-13
St Anthony's Preparatory School, NW3 6-13
St Benedict's Junior School, W5 4-11
St Benedict's School, W5 11-18 (Co-ed VIth form)
St James Independent School for Boys, SW7 4-10
St James Independent School for Boys, SW1 10-19
St Paul's Cathedral Choir School, EC4 7-13
St Paul's Preparatory School, SW13 7-13
St Paul's School, SW13 13-18
St Philip's School, SW7 7-13
Streatham Modern School, SW16 3-12
Sussex House School, SW1 8-13
Talmud Torah Yetev Lev, N16
Talmud Torah Jewish School, N16 3-11
Tower House School, SW14 5-13
University College School, NW3 11-18
University College School, Junior Branch, NW3 7-12
Westminster Abbey Choir School, SW1 7-13
Westminster Cathedral Choir School, SW1 8-13
Westminster School, SW1 13-18 (Co-ed VIth form)
Westminster Under School, SW1 8-13
Wetherby School, W2 4-8
Willington School, SW19 4-13
Wimbledon College Prep School, SW19 7-13
Yetev Lev Day School for Boys, N16 3-13

Greater Manchester

The Manchester Grammar School, Manchester 11-18
Manchester Jewish Grammar School, Manchester 11-18
Tashbar School, Salford 5-11

Merseyside

Birkenhead School, Birkenhead 3-18
Merchant Taylors' School, Liverpool 7-18

Middlesex

Alpha Preparatory School, Harrow 4-13 (Girls 4-11)
Buckingham College Lower School, Kenton 4-11
Buckingham College Senior School, Harrow 11-18 (Co-ed VIth form)
Denmead School, Hampton 3-13
Halliford School, Shepperton 11-19 (VIth with local girls' school)
Hampton School, Hampton 11-18

Harrow School, Harrow on the Hill 13-18
Hounslow College, Feltham 10-19
The John Lyon School, Harrow 11-18
The Mall School, Twickenham 4-13
Merchant Taylors' School, Northwood 11-18
Orley Farm School, Harrow 4-13 (Girls 4-6)
Quainton Hall School, Harrow 4-13
St John's Northwood, Northwood 4-13
St Martin's School, Northwood 3-13

Norfolk

Norwich School, Norwich 8-18 (Co-ed VIth form)
Town Close House Preparatory School, Norwich 3-13
   (Girls 3-8)

Northamptonshire

Maidwell Hall, Northampton 3-13 (Girls 3-8)
Northamptonshire Grammar School, Pitsford 7-18

Nottinghamshire

Al Karam Secondary School, Retford 11-18
Nottingham High School Preparatory School, Nottingham
   7-11
Nottingham High School, Nottingham 11-18
West Bridgford High School, Nottingham 5-18 (Co-ed VIth
   form)

Oxfordshire

Abingdon School, Abingdon 11-18
Bloxham School, Banbury 13-18 (Day boys 11-13, co-ed
   VIth form)
Bruern Abbey School, Oxford 8-13
Christ Church Cathedral School, Oxford 4-13
Cothill House Preparatory School, Abingdon 8-13
Josca's Preparatory School, Abingdon 4-13 (Girls 4-7)
Magdalen College School, Oxford 9-18 (Boarding for
   Choristers only)
Moulsford Preparatory School, Wallingford 7-13
New College School, Oxford 7-13
Radley College, Abingdon 13-18
St Edward's School, Oxford 13-18 (Co-ed VIth form)
Shiplake College, Henley-on-Thames 13-18
Summer Fields, Oxford 8-13

Shropshire

Ellesmere College, Ellesmere 10-18 (Girls 10-13 and 16-18)
Kingsland Grange, Shrewsbury 4-13
Prestfelde Preparatory School, Shrewsbury 3-13
Shrewsbury School, Shrewsbury 13-18

Somerset

King's School, Bruton 13-18 (Co-ed VIth form)

Suffolk

Ipswich School, Ipswich 11-19 (VIth form day girls)
Old Buckenham Hall School, Ipswich 3-13
St Joseph's College, Ipswich 11-18 (Boarding from 13,
   co-ed VIth form)

Surrey

Aldro School, Godalming 7-13
Charterhouse, Godalming 13-18 (Co-ed VIth form)
Chinthurst School, Tadworth 3-13
Cranleigh Preparatory School, Cranleigh 7-13
Cranleigh School, Cranleigh 13-18 (Co-ed VIth form)
Cranmore School, Leatherhead 3-13
Cumnor House School, South Croydon 4-13
Downsend School, Leatherhead 7-13
Downside Preparatory School, Purley 3-14
Eagle House, Camberley 4-13 (Girls 4-7)
Elmhurst School, South Croydon 4-11
Ewell Castle School, Epsom 3-18 (Girls 3-11 and 16-18)
Hall Grove School, Bagshot 4-14
Haslemere Preparatory School, Haslemere 5-14
Homefield Preparatory School, Sutton 5-13
King's House School, Richmond 4-13
Kingswood House School, Epsom 3-13
Lanesborough, Guildford 4-13
Milbourne Lodge School, Esher 8-13
More House School, Farnham 10-16
Oakhyrst Grange School, Caterham 3-11
Parkside School, Cobham 4-14 (Co-ed 2-5)
Priory School, Banstead 3-13
Reed's School, Cobham 11-18 (Co-ed VIth form)
Reigate St Mary's Preparatory and Choir School, Reigate
   3-13
Rokeby School, Kingston-upon-Thames 4-13
Royal Grammar School, Guildford 11-18
St Andrew's School, Woking 3-13 (Girls 3-4)
St Edmund's School, Hindhead 7-13 (Co-ed day 2-6)
St George's College, Weybridge 11-18 (Co-ed VIth form)
St George's College Junior School, Weybridge 2-11 (Girls
   2-7)
St John's School, Leatherhead 13-18 (Co-ed VIth form)
Scaitcliffe School, Egham 3-13 (Day Girls 3-7)
Shrewsbury House School, Surbiton 7-13
Surbiton Preparatory School, Surbiton 5-11
Trinity School, Croydon 10-18
Whitgift School, South Croydon 10-18
Woodcote House School, Windlesham 7-14

East Sussex

Mayfield College, Mayfield 11-18 (Day girls)

Mowden School, Hove 7-13
St Aubyn's, Brighton 7-14
St Christopher's School, Hove 5-14

King Edward's School, Birmingham 11-18
Solihull School, Solihull 7-18 (Co-ed VIth form)
West House School, Birmingham 3-13

West Sussex

Brambletye School, East Grinstead 7-14
Dorset House School, Pulborough 4-13
Lancing College, Lancing 13-18 (Co-ed VIth form)
Seaford College, Petworth 11-18 (Day boys 11-13, co-ed VIth form)
Slindon College, Arundel 11-18
Sompting Abbotts, Lancing 3-13
Worth School, Crawley 9-18

Wiltshire

Sandroyd, Salisbury 8-13 (A few day places)
Swan School for Boys, Salisbury 3-11

North Yorkshire

Ampleforth College, York 13-18
Ampleforth College Junior School, York 8-13
Aysgarth Preparatory School, Bedale 8-13 (Coed Day 3-8)
Grosvenor House School, Harrogate 3-14 (Sisters by arrangement)
Howsham Hall, York 5-14
Malsis School, Skipton 7-14

Tyne and Wear

Argyle House School, Sunderland 3-16
Ascham House School, Newcastle upon Tyne 4-13
Dame Allan's Boys School, Newcastle upon Tyne 8-18 (Co-ed VIth form)
Newlands School, Newcastle upon Tyne 4-14
Royal Grammar School, Newcastle upon Tyne 8-18

South Yorkshire

Birkdale School, Sheffield 4-18 (Co-ed VIth form)
Westbourne Preparatory School, Sheffield 4-13

Warwickshire

Warwick School, Warwick 7-18

West Yorkshire

Batley Grammar School, Batley 11-18 (Co-ed VIth form)
Bradford Grammar School, Bradford 8-18 (Co-ed VIth form)
Ghyll Royd School, Ilkley 3-11
Leeds Grammar School, Leeds 7-18
Queen Elizabeth Grammar School, Wakefield 7-18

West Midlands

Birchfield School, Wolverhampton 4-13
Chetwynd House School, Sutton Coldfield 4-12
Eversfield Preparatory School, Solihull 3-13

NORTHERN IRELAND

County Antrim

Cabin Hill School, Belfast 4-13
Campbell College, Belfast 11-18
Royal Belfast Academical Institution, Belfast 11-18

County Down

Bangor Grammar School, Bangor 11-18

County Londonderry

Coleraine Academical Institution, Coleraine 11-19

SCOTLAND

Central

Queen Victoria School, Dunblane 10-18

Edinburgh Academy Preparatory School, Edinburgh 3-11
  (Girls 3-5)
Merchiston Castle School, Edinburgh 10-18
Stewart's Melville College, Edinburgh 11-18

Lothian

Belhaven Hill, Dunbar 7-13
The Edinburgh Academy, Edinburgh 11-18 (Co-ed VIth
  form)

Strathclyde

Belmont House, Glasgow 3-18
The Kelvinside Academy, Glasgow 4-18

WALES

Gwent

Monmouth School, Monmouth 11-18

Powys

Brookland Hall School & Golf Academy, Welshpool 11-16

Gwynedd

St David's College, Llandudno 11-18

GIRLS' SCHOOLS

ENGLAND

Avon

Badminton School, Bristol 5-18
Bath High School GPDST, Bath 4-18
Clifton High School, Bristol 3-18 (Boarders 16-18, day
  boys 3-11)

Colston's Girls' School, Bristol 10-18
The Red Maids' School, Bristol 11-18
Redland High School, Bristol 4-18
The Royal School, Bath 3-18 (Boys 3-7)
St Ursula's High School, Bristol 3-18 (Boys 3-11)
Westwing School, Bristol 4-18

Bedfordshire

Bedford High School, Bedford 7-18
Dame Alice Harpur School, Bedford 7-18
St Andrew's School, Bedford 5-16

Berkshire

The Abbey School, Reading 4-18 (Boys 4-7)
The Brigidine School, Windsor 3-18 (Boys 3-7)
Downe House School, Newbury 11-18
Eton End PNEU, Slough 3-12 (Boys 3-7)
Heathfield School, Ascot 11-18
Hurst Lodge, Sunningdale 3-18 (Boys 3-7)
Luckley-Oakfield School, Wokingham 11-18
Maidenhead College Claires Court Girls, Maidenhead 3-18
 (Boys 3-7)
Marist Convent Senior School, Ascot 11-18
Marlston House School, Newbury 6-13
Padworth College, Reading 14-20
Queen Anne's School, Reading 11-18
St Gabriel's School, Newbury 3-16 (Boys 3-8)
St George's School, Ascot 11-18
St Joseph's Convent School, Reading 11-18
St Joseph's Preparatory School, Reading 3-11 (Boys 3-7)
St Mary's School, Ascot 11-18
Upton House School, Windsor 3-11 (Boys 3-7)

Buckinghamshire

Godstowe Preparatory School, High Wycombe 4-13 (Boys
 4-8)
Heatherton House School, Amersham 3-13 (Boys 3-5)
High March School, Beaconsfield 3-13 (Boys 3-7)
Holy Cross Convent, Gerrards Cross 5-18
Maltmans Green School, Gerrards Cross 3-13
Pipers Corner School, High Wycombe 4-18
St Mary's School, Gerrards Cross 3-18
Thornton College Convent of Jesus and Mary, Milton
 Keynes 3-16 (Boys 3-7)
Wycombe Abbey School, High Wycombe 11-18

Cambridgeshire

The Perse School for Girls, Cambridge 7-18
Peterborough High School, Peterborough 4-18 (Boys 4-8)
St Mary's School, Cambridge 11-18

Channel Islands

Beaulieu Convent School, Jersey 4-18
Helvetia House School, Jersey 4-11
The Ladies' College, Guernsey 3-18 (Boys 3-7)

Cheshire

Bowdon Preparatory School For Girls, Altrincham 2-12
Cransley School, Northwich 3-16 (Boys 3-11)
Culcheth Hall, Altrincham 3-18
Hammond School, Chester 11-16
Loreto Convent Grammar School, Altrincham 11-18
Loreto Convent Preparatory School, Altrincham 4-11
 (Boys 4-7)
Mount Carmel School, Alderley Edge 4-18
Oriel Bank High School, Stockport 3-16
The Queen's School, Chester 5-18 (Boys 5-8)
St Hilary's School, Alderley Edge 3-18
Wilmslow Preparatory School, Wilmslow 3-11

Cleveland

Teesside High School, Stockton-on-Tees 3-18

Cornwall

St Joseph's School, Launceston 3-16 (Boys 3-11)
Tremough Convent School, Penryn 3-18 (Boys 3-11)
Truro High School, Truro 3-18 (Boys 3-5)

Cumbria

St Anne's, Windermere 3-18 (Boys 3-11)

Derbyshire

Derby High School, Derby 3-18 (Boys 3-11)
Ockbrook School, Derby 3-18 (Boys 3-11)
St Elphin's School, Matlock 3-18 (Co-ed junior school)

Devon

The Maynard School, Exeter 7-18
Mount St Mary's Convent School, Exeter 3-18 (Boys 3-7)
St Dunstan's Abbey School, Plymouth 4-18 (Boys 4-7)
St Margaret's Exeter, Exeter 5-18
Stoodley Knowle Convent School, Torquay 4-18
Stover School, Newton Abbot 10-18

Dorset

Croft House School, Blandford Forum 11-18
Hanford School, Blandford Forum 7-13
St Antony's-Leweston School, Sherborne 11-18
St Mary's School, Shaftesbury 9-18

Sherborne School for Girls, Sherborne 12-18
Talbot Heath, Bournemouth 3-18
Wentworth Milton Mount, Bournemouth 11-18

County Durham

Durham High School, Durham 4-18 (Boys 4-7)
Polam Hall, Darlington 4-18
St Anne's Convent High School, Bishop Auckland 3-16 (Boys 4-11)

Essex

Bell House School, Brentwood 3-16 (Boys 3-7)
Braeside School for Girls, Buckhurst Hill 4-16
Ilford Ursuline High School, Ilford 11-18
New Hall School, Chelmsford 4-18 (Boys day 4-11)
Park School for Girls, Ilford 7-18
St Hilda's School, Westcliff-on-Sea 3-16 (Boys 3-7)
St Mary's Hare Park School, Romford 3-11 (Boys 3-7)
St Mary's School, Colchester 4-16

Gloucestershire

The Cheltenham Ladies' College, Cheltenham 11-18
Gloucestershire Islamic School, Gloucester 5-16
Kitebrook House, Moreton-in-Marsh 4-13 (Boys 4-8)
St Clotilde's School, Lechlade 3-18 (Boarders from 11, day boys 3-9)
Selwyn School, Gloucester 3-18 (Boys 3-11)
Westonbirt School, Tetbury 11-18

Hampshire

The Atherley School for Girls, Southampton 3-18 (Boys 3-11)
Convent of Our Lady of Providence School, Alton 4-18 (Co-ed junior school)
Farnborough Hill, Farnborough 11-18
La Sagesse Convent, Romsey 3-16 (Boys 3-11)
Mayville High School, Southsea 2-16 (Boys 2-8)
North Foreland Lodge, Hook 11-18
Portsmouth High School GPDST, Southsea 4-18
Rookesbury Park School, Wickham 3-13
Rookwood School, Andover 3-16 (Day boys 3-11)
St Benedict's Convent School, Andover 3-16
St Nicholas School, Fleet 4-16 (Boys 4-7)
St Swithun's School, Winchester 11-18
Sherborne House School, Eastleigh 3-11 (Boys 3-8)
Wykeham House School, Fareham 4-16

Hereford & Worcester

The Alice Ottley School, Worcester 3-19
Croftdown, Malvern 3-12
Dodderhill School, Droitwich 9-16
Holy Trinity School, Kidderminster 3-18
Malvern Girls' College, Malvern 11-18
The Margaret Allen School, Hereford 3-11
St James's & The Abbey, Malvern 11-18
St Mary's Convent School, Worcester 3-18 (Boys 3-8)

Hertfordshire

Abbot's Hill, Hemel Hempstead 11-16
Berkhamsted School for Girls, Berkhamsted 3-18
Convent of St Francis de Sales, Tring 2-17 (Boys 2-12)
Haberdashers' Aske's School for Girls, Elstree 4-18
Northfield School, Watford 2-18 (Boys 2-7)
The Princess Helena College, Hitchin 11-18
Queenswood, Hatfield 11-18
The Rickmansworth Masonic School, Rickmansworth 4-18
Rickmansworth PNEU School, Rickmansworth 3-11 (Boys 3-7)
St Albans High School, St Albans 7-18
St Francis' College, Letchworth 3-19 (Boys 3-7)
St Hilda's School, Bushey 3-11
St Hilda's School, Harpenden 2-11
St Margaret's School, Watford 4-18
St Martha's Senior School, Barnet 11-18
St Nicholas House, Hemel Hempstead 3-11 (Boys 3-7)
Stormont, Potters Bar 4-11

North Humberside

Hull High School, Hull 3-18 (Boys 4-11)

Kent

Ashford School, Ashford 3-18
Babington House School, Chislehurst 3-16 (Boys 3-7)
Baston School, Bromley 3-18
Bedgebury School, Cranbrook 3-18 (Boys Day 3-7)
Beechwood School Sacred Heart, Tunbridge Wells 3-18 (Boys 3-7)
Benenden School, Cranbrook 11-18
Bromley High School GPDST, Bromley 4-18
Cobham Hall School, Gravesend 11-18
Combe Bank School, Sevenoaks 3-18
Derwent Lodge School for Girls, Tonbridge 7-11
Farringtons & Stratford House, Chislehurst 3-18
Gad's Hill School, Rochester 3-18 (Boys 3-11)
The Granville School, Sevenoaks 3-11
Holy Trinity College, Bromley 3-18 (Boys 3-5)
Kent College, Pembury 3-18
Shernold School, Maidstone 3-13
Sibton Park, Folkestone 2-13 (Boys 2-8)
Ursuline College, Westgate-on-Sea 11-18
Walthamstow Hall, Sevenoaks 3-18
West Heath School, Sevenoaks 11-18
West Lodge Preparatory School, Sidcup 3-11 (Boys 3-7)

Lancashire

Bolton School (Girls' Division), Bolton 4-18
Bury Grammar School (Girls'), Bury 4-18 (Boys 4-7)
Casterton School, Carnforth 4-18 (Boys 4-7)
Elmslie Girls' School, Blackpool 3-18
The Hulme Grammar School for Girls, Oldham 7-18
Queen Mary School, Lytham St Annes 7-18
Westholme School, Blackburn 4-18 (Boys 4-8)

Leicestershire

Leicester High School For Girls, Leicester 3-18
Loughborough High School, Loughborough 11-18
Our Lady's Convent School, Loughborough 3-18 (Boys 3-5)

Lincolnshire

St Joseph's School, Lincoln 4-18 (Boys 4-11)
Stamford High School, Stamford 4-18 (Boys 4-8)

London

Blackheath High School GPDST, SE3 4-18
Bute House Preparatory School for Girls, W6 4-11
Channing Junior School, N6 5-11
Channing School, N6 11-18
City of London School for Girls, EC2 7-18
Falkner House, SW7 4-11
Forest Girls' School, E17 11-18
Francis Holland School, SW1 4-18
Francis Holland School, NW1 11-18
Garden House School, SW1 3-11 (Boys 3-8)
Glendower Preparatory School, SW7 4-12
The Godolphin and Latymer School, W6 11-18
Grange Park Preparatory School, N21 3-11
Harvington School, W5 3-16
Hazelhurst School For Girls, SW20 4-16 (Co-ed 4-7)
James Allen's Girls' School, SE22 11-18
Kensington Prep School for Girls, W8 4-11
Lady Eden's School, W8 3-11
Madni Girls School, E1 12-18
More House, SW1 11-18
The Mount School, NW7 5-18
Notting Hill and Ealing High School GPDST, W13 5-18
Palmers Green High School, N21 3-16
Pembridge Hall, W2 4-11
Putney High School, SW15 4-18
Putney Park School, SW15 4-16 (Boys 4-8)
Queen's College, W1 11-18
Queen's Gate School, SW7 4-18
Royal School, Hampstead, NW3 4-18
St Augustine's Priory, W5 4-18
St Christina's RC Preparatory School, NW8 3-11 (Boys 3-7)
St Christopher's School, NW3 4-11
St James Independent School for Girls, SW7 4-10
St James Independent School for Girls, W11 10-18
St Joseph's Convent School, E11 4-11

St Margaret's School, NW3 5-16
St Mary's Hampstead, NW3 3-11 (Boys 3-7)
St Paul's Girls' School, W6 11-18
Sarum Hall, NW3 3-11 (Boys 3-5)
South Hampstead High School, NW3 4-18
Streatham Hill and Clapham High School, SW16 4-18
The Study Preparatory School, SW19 4-11
Sydenham High School, SE26 4-18
Ursuline Convent Preparatory School, SW20 4-13 (Boys 4-7)
The Village School, NW3 4-11
Virgo Fidelis Convent, SE19 3-18 (Boys 3-8, with option to stay until 11)
Wimbledon High School, SW19 5-18

Greater Manchester

Bolton Muslim Girls School, Bolton 0-0
Jewish High School for Girls, Salford 11-18
Manchester High School for Girls, Manchester 4-18
Rosecroft School Didsbury, Manchester 3-16 (Boys 3-7)
Withington Girls' School, Manchester 7-18

Merseyside

The Belvedere School GPDST, Liverpool 3-18
Birkenhead High School GPDST, Birkenhead 4-18
Marymount Convent School, Wallasey 3-11
Merchant Taylors' School for Girls, Liverpool 4-18
Streatham House School, Liverpool 2-16 (Boys 2-11)

Middlesex

Heathfield School, Pinner 3-18
Jack and Jill School, Hampton 3-7 (Boys 3-5)
The Lady Eleanor Holles School, Hampton 7-18
North London Collegiate School, Edgware 4-18
Northwood College, Northwood 4-18
Peterborough & St Margaret's High School, Stanmore 4-16
St Andrew's Senior Girls' School, Harrow 8-16 (Boys 8-10)
St Catherine's School, Twickenham 3-16
St David's School, Ashford 3-18
St Helen's School for Girls, Northwood 4-18

Norfolk

Hethersett Old Hall School, Norwich 7-18
The Norwich High School for Girls GPDST, Norwich 4-18
Notre Dame Preparatory School, Norwich 3-12 (Boys 3-8)
Riddlesworth Hall, Diss 2-13 (Boys 2-8)
Thorpe House School, Norwich 3-16
Wood Dene School, Norwich 2-16 (Boys 2-11)

Northamptonshire

Northampton High School, Northampton 3-18
St Peter's School, Kettering 3-16 (Co-ed 3-11)

Nottinghamshire

Hollygirt School, Nottingham 4-16
Nottingham High School for Girls, Nottingham 4-18

Oxfordshire

The Carrdus School, Banbury 3-11 (Boys 3-8)
Cranford House School, Wallingford 3-16 (Boys 3-7)
Headington School, Oxford 4-18 (Co-ed 4-7)
Our Lady's Convent Senior School, Abingdon 11-18
Oxford High School GPDST, Oxford 9-18
Rye St Antony School, Oxford 8-18
St Mary's School, Wantage 11-18
School of S Helen & S Katharine, Abingdon 9-18
Tudor Hall School, Banbury 11-18
Wychwood School, Oxford 11-18

Shropshire

Adcote School, Shrewsbury 5-18
Moreton Hall, Oswestry 11-18
Shrewsbury High School GPDST, Shrewsbury 4-18

Somerset

Bruton School for Girls, Bruton 8-18
Rossholme School, Highbridge 7-16 (Co-ed 3-7)
St Christopher's, Burnham-on-Sea 3-13 (Boys 3-11)

Staffordshire

St Dominic's Priory School, Stone 3-18 (Boys 3-8)
St Dominic's School, Stafford 2-18 (Co-ed 2-7)
School of S Mary and S Anne, Abbots Bromley 5-18

Suffolk

Amberfield School, Ipswich 3-16 (Boys 3-7)
Ipswich High School GPDST, Ipswich 4-18 (Boys 4-7)
St Felix School, Southwold 11-18
St George's School, Southwold 2-11 (Boys day only)
School of Jesus and Mary, Ipswich 3-16 (Boys 3-7)

Surrey

Bramley School, Tadworth 3-12
Commonweal Lodge School, Purley 4-18
Croham Hurst School, South Croydon 4-18
Croydon High School GPDST, South Croydon 4-18
Downsend Girls' Preparatory School, Leatherhead 7-11
Dunottar School, Reigate 4-18
Flexlands School, Woking 3-11 (Boys 3-4)
Greenacre School for Girls, Banstead 3-18
Guildford High School (Church Schools Co Ltd), Guildford 4-18
Halstead Preparatory School, Woking 3-11
Hawley Place School, Camberley 2-16 (Boys 2-11)
Laverock School, Oxted 3-11
Manor House School, Leatherhead 3-16 (Boys 3-8)
Marymount International School, Kingston-upon-Thames 11-18
Micklefield School, Reigate 2-12 (Boys 2-7)
Notre Dame Preparatory School, Cobham 2-11 (Boys 2-6)
Notre Dame School, Lingfield 2-18 (Boys 2-11 & 16-18)
Notre Dame Senior School, Cobham 11-18
Old Palace School of John Whitgift, Croydon 4-18
Old Vicarage School, Richmond 4-11
Parsons Mead, Ashtead 3-18
Prior's Field School, Godalming 11-18
Rowan Preparatory School, Esher 3-11
The Royal School, Hindhead 5-18
Ryde's Hill Preparatory School, Guildford 3-11 (Boys 3-7)
St Catherine's School, Camberley 3-12 (Boys 3-5)
St Catherine's School, Guildford 4-18
St Ives, Haslemere 3-11 (Boys 3-5)
St Maur's Convent School, Weybridge 2-18 (Boys 2-7)
St Michael's School, Oxted 3-18 (Boys 3-8)
St Teresa's Preparatory School, Effingham 2-11
St Teresa's School, Dorking 3-18 (Boys 3-5)
Seaton House, Sutton 3-11 (Boys 3-5)
Sir William Perkins's School, Chertsey 11-18
Stanway School, Dorking 3-13 (Boys 3-8)
Surbiton High School, Kingston-upon-Thames 4-18 (Boys 4-11)
Sutton High School (GPDST), Sutton 4-18
Tormead School, Guildford 4-18
Wispers School, Haslemere 11-18
Woldingham School, Caterham 11-18

East Sussex

Brighton and Hove High School GPDST, Brighton 4-18
Deepdene School, Hove 2-11 (Boys 2-7)
Micklefield Wadhurst incorporating the Legat School of Classical Ballet, Wadhurst 10-18 (Boys Ballet only)
Moira House Junior School, Eastbourne 2-11
Moira House Senior School, Eastbourne 11-18
Roedean School, Brighton 11-18
St Leonards-Mayfield School, Mayfield 11-18
St Mary's Hall, Brighton 3-18 (Boys 3-8)
Stonelands School of Ballet, Hove 3-16 (Boys 3-5, boarders from 7)

West Sussex

Burgess Hill School, Burgess Hill 3-18
Farlington School, Horsham 4-18
Lavant House-Rosemead, Chichester 3-18 (Boys 3-8)
St Margaret's Senior School Convent of Mercy, Midhurst 11-16
The Towers Convent School, Steyning 3-16

Tyne and Wear

Central Newcastle High School GPDST, Newcastle upon Tyne 4-18
Craigievar School, Sunderland 2-18 (Boys 4-7)
Dame Allan's Girls School, Newcastle upon Tyne 8-18 (Co-ed VIth form)
La Sagesse Convent High School, Newcastle upon Tyne 3-18
Newcastle Upon Tyne Church High School, Newcastle upon Tyne 3-18
Westfield School, Newcastle upon Tyne 3-18

Warwickshire

The King's High School for Girls, Warwick 10-18
The Kingsley School, Leamington Spa 2-18 (Boys 2-7)
St Joseph's School, Kenilworth 4-18 (Boys 4-11)
Wroxall Abbey School, Warwick 2-18 (Boys day 2-7)

West Midlands

Edgbaston Church of England College, Birmingham 3-18
Edgbaston High School for Girls, Birmingham 2-18
Highclare School, Birmingham 3-18 (Boys 3-7 and 16-18)
Holy Child School, Birmingham 3-18 (Boys 3-11)
King Edward VI High School for Girls, Birmingham 11-18

Newbridge Preparatory School, Wolverhampton 3-11 (Boys 3-4)
St Martin's School, Solihull 3-18

Wiltshire

The Godolphin School, Salisbury 7-18 (Boarding from 11)
La Retraite Leehurst School, Salisbury 2-18 (Boys 2-7)
Leaden Hall, Salisbury 3-12
St Mary's School, Calne 11-18
Stonar School, Melksham 4-18

North Yorkshire

Belmont-Birklands School, Harrogate 2-11 (Boys 2-4)
Harrogate Ladies' College, Harrogate 10-18
The Mount School, York 11-18 (Day boys)
Queen Ethelburga's College, York 2-18 (Day boys 2-11)
Queen Margaret's School, York 11-18
Queen Mary's School, Thirsk 3-16
York College for Girls, York 3-18 (Boys 3-8)

South Yorkshire

Ashdell Preparatory School, Sheffield 4-11
Brantwood Independent School for Girls, Sheffield 4-17
Sheffield High School GPDST, Sheffield 4-18

West Yorkshire

Bradford Girls' Grammar School, Bradford 3-18
Gateways School, Leeds 3-18
Leeds Girls' High School, Leeds 3-19 (Boys 3-8)
Moorfield School, Ilkley 2-11
Wakefield Girls' High School, Wakefield 4-18

NORTHERN IRELAND

County Antrim

Hunterhouse College, Belfast 5-19
Victoria College Belfast, Belfast 4-18

SCOTLAND

Fife

St Katharines Girls Preparatory School, St Andrews 7-12
St Leonards School, St Andrews 12-18

Grampian

Albyn School for Girls, Aberdeen 3-18 (Boys 3-5)
St Margaret's School for Girls, Aberdeen 3-18 (Boys 3-5)

Lothian

The Mary Erskine School, Edinburgh 11-18
St Denis and Cranley School, Edinburgh 5-18
St George's School for Girls, Edinburgh 3-18 (Boys 3-5)
St Margaret's, Edinburgh 3-18 (Boys day 3-8)

Strathclyde

Craigholme School, Glasgow 3-18 (Boys 3-8)
Fernhill School, Glasgow 4-18 (Junior boys only)
Laurel Bank School, Glasgow 3-18 (Boys 3-4)
The Park School, Glasgow 3-18

Tayside

Butterstone School, Blairgowrie 2-13
Kilgraston School, Perth 5-18

WALES

Clwyd

Howell's School, Denbigh 3-18
Rydal Penrhos Senior School Girls' Division, Colwyn Bay 11-18

South Glamorgan

Elm Tree House School, Cardiff 3-11 (Boys 3-7)
Howell's School, Cardiff 4-18
Our Lady's Convent School, Cardiff 3-16

Gwent

Haberdashers' Monmouth School For Girls, Monmouth 7-18

4.7
RELIGIOUS AFFILIATION

The following index lists all schools specifying a particular religious denomination. However, it should be noted that this is intended as a guide only and that many of the schools listed also welcome children of other faiths. Schools which claim to be non- or inter-denominational are not listed. Parents should check precise details with individual schools. A full list of each school's entries elsewhere in the book is given in the main index at the back.

Buddhist

Dharma School, Brighton
Shi-Tennoji School In UK, Bury St Edmunds

Christian

Alder Bridge School, Reading
All Saints School, Leicester
The Ark School, Reading
Barnsley Christian School, Barnsley
Benty Heath School and Kindergarten, South Wirral
Bushey Place School, Norwich
Cedar School, London
Chorcliffe Preparatory School, Chorley
Christian School (Takeley), Bishop's Stortford
Clifton Lodge, London
Edgbaston College, Birmingham
Emmanual Christian School, Oxford
Emmanuel School, Exeter
Emmanuel School, Derby
Eversfield Preparatory School, Solihull
Eversley School, Southwold
Falkner House, London
The Family School, Canterbury
Filgrave School, Newport Pagnell
Gateway Christian School, Ilkeston
Georgina Perkins, Bedford
Grange Park Preparatory School, London
Grangewood Independent School, London
Haslemere Preparatory School, Haslemere
Heswall Preparatory School, Wirral
King of Kings School, Manchester
King's School, Plymouth
The King's School, Nottingham
Kings Park Christian School, Leigh
Kings School, Harpenden

The King's School, Witney
Kingsfold Christian School, Preston
Kwabena Montessori School, Farnborough
Lea House School, Kidderminster
Leeds Christian School, Leeds
Lorenden Preparatory School, Faversham
Lucton Pierrepont School, Leominster
Marlin Montessori School, Berkhamsted
Michael Hall, Forest Row
Monton Preparatory School,
Mountjoy House School, Huddersfield
New Life Christian School, Croydon
New Life Christian School, East Grinstead
Notre Dame School, Lingfield
The Octagon School, London
Priory School, Sandown
Regency Preparatory School, Macclesfield
River School, Worcester
St Andrew's Montessori School, Bushey
St Catherine's Preparatory School, Stockport
St Christophers School, Totnes
St David's School, Brecon
St Hilda's School, Westcliff-on-Sea
St John's Senior School, Enfield
St Oswald's School, Alnwick
Shepherds Community School, London
Stonefield House, Lincoln
Stowford, Sutton
Sunflower Montessori School, Twickenham
Torwood House School, Bristol
Tremore Christian School, Bodmin
Trinity School, Stalybridge
Vine School, Southampton
Willington School, London

Christian Science

Claremont Fan Court School, Esher

Church in Wales

Llandovery College, Llandovery
Lyndon School, Colwyn Bay

Church of England

Abberley Hall, Worcester
Abbey Gate College, Chester
Abbey Gate School, Chester
The Abbey School, Tewkesbury
The Abbey School, Woodbridge
Abbot's Hill, Hemel Hempstead
Aberdour School, Tadworth
Abingdon School, Abingdon
Adcote School, Shrewsbury
Airthrie School, Cheltenham
Aldenham School, Elstree
Aldro School, Godalming
Aldwickbury School, Harpenden
The Alice Ottley School, Worcester
Alleyn Court and Eton House School, Southend-on-Sea
Alleyn's School, London
Allhallows College, Lyme Regis
Amberfield School, Ipswich
Ambleside PNEU School, Cheam
Amesbury School, Hindhead
Ardenhurst School, Solihull
Ardingly College, Haywards Heath
Ardingly College Junior School, Haywards Heath
Arnold House School, London
Ashbourne PNEU School, Ashbourne
The Atherley School for Girls, Southampton
Attenborough Preparatory School, Nottingham
Aymestrey School, Worcester
Aysgarth Preparatory School, Bedale
Ballard College, New Milton
Ballard Lake Preparatory School, New Milton
Bancrofts School, Woodford Green
Barnardiston Hall Preparatory School, Haverhill
Baston School, Bromley
Beachborough School, Brackley
The Beacon School, Amersham
Bearwood College, Wokingham
Beaudesert Park, Stroud
Bedford School, Bedford
Bedford Preparatory School, Bedford
Bedgebury School, Cranbrook
Beech Hall School, Macclesfield
Beechenhurst Preparatory School, Liverpool
Beechwood Park, St Albans
Beeston Hall School, Cromer
Bellan House Preparatory School, Oswestry
Belmont School, Dorking
Benenden School, Cranbrook
Berkhampstead School, Cheltenham
Berkhamsted Junior School, Berkhamsted
Berkhamsted School, Berkhamsted
Bethany School, Cranbrook
Bickies, Tonbridge
Bilton Grange, Rugby
Birchfield School, Wolverhampton
Bloxham School, Banbury

The Blue Coat School, Birmingham
Blundell's School, Tiverton
Bodiam Manor School, Robertsbridge
Bow School, Durham
Bradfield College, Reading
Bradford Grammar School, Bradford
Brambletye School, East Grinstead
Bramcote School, Scarborough
Bramcote School, Retford
Bramley School, Tadworth
Brentwood School, Brentwood
Brigg Preparatory School, Brigg
Brighton College, Brighton
Brighton College Junior School, Brighton
Brighton College Junior School (Pre-preparatory), Brighton
Bristol Cathedral School, Bristol
Broadwater Manor School, Worthing
Brockhurst & Marlston House Pre-Preparatory School, Newbury
Brockhurst School, Newbury
Bromsgrove Lower School, Bromsgrove
Bromsgrove Pre-preparatory School, Bromsgrove
Bromsgrove School, Bromsgrove
Bronte School, Gravesend
Brookland Hall School & Golf Academy, Welshpool
Broomfield House, Richmond
Broomham School, Hastings
Broomwood Hall School, London
Bruern Abbey School, Oxford
Burys Court School, Reigate
Caldicott, Farnham Royal
Cameron House, London
Canford School, Wimborne
Casterton School, Carnforth
The Cathedral School, Cardiff
The Cathedral School, Lincoln
Cawston College, Norwich
Chafyn Grove School, Salisbury
Chard Independent School, Chard
Charterhouse, Godalming
Cheam Hawtreys, Newbury
Cheltenham College, Cheltenham
Cheltenham College Junior School, Cheltenham
Cheswycks School, Camberley
Chigwell School, Chigwell
Chilton Cantelo School, Yeovil
The Chorister School, Durham
Christ Church Cathedral School, Oxford
Christ College, Brecon
Christs College, London
Christs Hospital, Horsham
Claremont School, St Leonards-on-Sea
Clayesmore Preparatory School, Blandford Forum
Clayesmore School, Blandford Forum
Clifton College, Bristol
Clifton College Preparatory School, Bristol
Colston's Collegiate School, Bristol
Coniston, Reigate
Conway Preparatory School, Boston
Coopersale Hall School, Epping
Copthorne School, Crawley
Cothill House Preparatory School, Abingdon
Cottesmore School, Pease Pottage
Coventry Preparatory School, Coventry
Cranford House School, Wallingford
Cranleigh Preparatory School, Cranleigh
Cranleigh School, Cranleigh
The Crescent School, Rugby
Croft House School, Blandford Forum

The Croft School, Stratford upon Avon
Croftdown, Malvern
Cumnor House School, South Croydon
Cumnor House School, Haywards Heath
Cundall Manor School, York
Dair House School Trust Ltd, Slough
Daneshill House, Basingstoke
Dean Close Junior School, Cheltenham
Dean Close School, Cheltenham
Deepdene School, Hove
Denstone College, Uttoxeter
Denstone College Preparatory School, Uttoxeter
Derby High School, Derby
Dodderhill School, Droitwich
The Dormer House PNEU School, Moreton-in-Marsh
Dorset House School, Pulborough
Dover College, Dover
Downe House School, Newbury
Downside Preparatory School, Purley
Dragon School, Oxford
Duke of York's Royal Military School, Dover
Dulwich College, London
Dulwich College Preparatory School, London
Dulwich College Preparatory School, Cranbrook
Dumpton School, Wimborne
Durham High School, Durham
Durham School, Durham
Durlston Court, New Milton
Eagle House, Camberley
Eastbourne College, Eastbourne
Edenhurst School, Newcastle-under-Lyme
Edgbaston Church of England College, Birmingham
Edge Grove School, Aldenham
Edgeborough, Farnham
Edgehill School, Newark
Elizabeth College, Guernsey
Elmhurst Ballet School, Camberley
The Elms, Malvern
Elmslie Girls' School, Blackpool
Elstree School, Reading
Emanuel School, London
Embley Park School, Romsey
Emscote Lawn School, Warwick
Epsom College, Epsom
Eton College, Windsor
Eton End PNEU, Slough
Ewell Castle School, Epsom
Exeter Cathedral School, Exeter
Exeter Preparatory School, Exeter
Exeter School, Exeter
Fairfield PNEU School, Bristol
Fairholme Preparatory School, St Asaph
Farlington School, Horsham
Felsted School, Dunmow
Feltonfleet School, Cobham
The Fen Preparatory School, Sleaford
Flexlands School, Woking
Fonthill, East Grinstead
Forest Girls' School, London
Forest Junior School, London
Forest School, London
Forres Sandle Manor, Fordingbridge
Foxley PNEU School, Reading
Framlingham College, Woodbridge
Framlingham College Junior School, Woodbridge
Francis Holland School, London
Francis Holland School, London
Friern Barnet Grammar School, London
Gatehouse School, London

Gayhurst School, Gerrards Cross
Giggleswick School, Settle
Glebe House School, Hunstanton
The Godolphin School, Salisbury
Godstowe Preparatory School, High Wycombe
Grainger Grammar School, Newcastle upon Tyne
Great Ballard School, Chichester
Grenville College, Bideford
Gresham's Preparatory School, Holt
Gresham's School, Holt
Grey House Preparatory School, Basingstoke
Guildford High School (Church Schools Co Ltd), Guildford
Haberdashers' Aske's School for Girls, Elstree
Haileybury College, Hertford
Haileybury Junior School, Windsor
The Hall School, London
Hallfield School, Birmingham
Halstead Preparatory School, Woking
Hammond School, Chester
Hampden Manor School, Great Missenden
Handcross Park School, Haywards Heath
Hanford School, Blandford Forum
Harrogate Ladies' College, Harrogate
Harrow School, Harrow on the Hill
Hatherop Castle Preparatory School, Cirencester
Hazelwood School, Oxted
Headington School, Oxford
Heathfield School, Ascot
Helvetia House School, Jersey
Hemdean House School, Reading
The Hereford Cathedral Junior School, Hereford
The Hereford Cathedral School, Hereford
Hethersett Old Hall School, Norwich
Highfield School, Liphook
Highgate Junior School, London
Highgate Pre-Preparatory School, London
Highgate School, London
Hilden Grange School, Tonbridge
Hilden Oaks School, Tonbridge
Hillstone School (Malvern College Junior School), Malvern
Hollington School, Ashford
Holme Grange School, Wokingham
Holme Park Preparatory School, Kendal
Hordle House, Lymington
Horris Hill, Newbury
Howell's School, Denbigh
Hull Grammar School, Kingston-Upon-Hull
Hurstpierpoint College, Hassocks
Innellan House, St Andrews School Group, Pinner
International Community School, London
Ipswich Preparatory School, Ipswich
Ipswich School, Ipswich
James Allen's Girls' School, London
James Allen's Preparatory School, London
Junior King's School, Canterbury
The Junior School, St Lawrence College, Ramsgate
Kelly College, Tavistock
Kelly College Junior School - St Michael's, Tavistock
King Edward's School, Birmingham
King Edward's School Witley, Godalming
King William's College, Castletown
King's Bruton Pre-Preparatory & Junior School, Yeovil
King's College, Taunton
King's College Junior School, London
King's College School, London
King's College School, Cambridge
King's Hall School, Taunton
King's Preparatory School, Rochester, Rochester
King's School, Bruton

King's School, Rochester
The King's School, Chester
The King's School, Macclesfield
The King's School, North Shields
The King's School, Gloucester
The King's School, Worcester
The King's School, Canterbury
The King's School, Ely
Kingham Hill School, Oxford
Kingscote School, Gerrards Cross
Kingshott, Hitchin
Kingsland Grange, Shrewsbury
The Kingsley School, Leamington Spa
Kirkstone House School, Peterborough
Knighton House, Blandford Forum
The Knoll School, Kidderminster
The Lady Eleanor Holles School, Hampton
Lambrook, Bracknell
Lancing College, Lancing
Landry School, Ingatestone
Lanesborough, Guildford
Lanherne School, Dawlish
Lavant House Rosemead, Chichester
Laxton Junior School, Peterborough
Leicester Grammar Junior School, Leicester
Leicester Grammar School, Leicester
Leicester High School For Girls, Leicester
Licensed Victuallers' School, Ascot
Lichfield Cathedral School (St Chad's), Lichfield
Littlemead Grammar School, Chichester
Liverpool College, Liverpool
Lockers Park, Hemel Hempstead
Long Close School, Slough
Lorne House, Retford
Luckley-Oakfield School, Wokingham
Ludgrove, Wokingham
Lustleigh School, Newton Abbot
Lyonsdown School Trust Ltd, Barnet
Magdalen College School, Oxford
Maidwell Hall, Northampton
The Mall School, Twickenham
Malsis School, Skipton
Malvern College, Malvern
Malvern Girls' College, Malvern
Manor House School, Honiton
Manor Preparatory School, Abingdon
Mansfield Lodge, Ilford
Margaret May Schools Ltd, Sevenoaks
Marlborough College, Marlborough
Marlborough House School, Hawkhurst
Merchant Taylors' School, Northwood
Merton House (Downswood), Chester
Micklefield Wadhurst incorporating the Legat School of
    Classical Ballet, Wadhurst
Millbrook House, Abingdon
Milton Abbey School, Blandford Forum
The Minster School, York
Monkton Combe Junior School, Bath
Monkton Combe School, Bath
Monmouth School, Monmouth
Moorland School, Clitheroe
Moreton Hall, Oswestry
Morley Hall Preparatory School, Derby
Moulsford Preparatory School, Wallingford
Mount House School, Tavistock
Mowden School, Hove
Moyles Court School, Ringwood
Nevill Holt School, Market Harborough
The New Beacon School, Sevenoaks

New College School, Oxford
New School, Exeter
Newcastle Upon Tyne Church High School, Newcastle
    upon Tyne
Newell House School, Sherborne
Norfolk House School, London
Norman Court, Salisbury
North Foreland Lodge, Hook
Northampton High School, Northampton
Northbourne Park School, Deal
Northcote Lodge, London
Northgate House School, Chichester
Northwood Preparatory School, Rickmansworth
Nower Lodge School, Dorking
Oakham School, Oakham
Oakland Nursery School, Banstead
Oaklands School, Loughton
Oakwood School, Chichester
Old Buckenham Hall School, Ipswich
The Old Hall School, Telford
The Old Malthouse, Swanage
Old Palace School of John Whitgift, Croydon
Old Vicarage School, Richmond
Oriel Bank High School, Stockport
Orley Farm School, Harrow
Oundle School, Peterborough
Packwood Haugh, Shrewsbury
Pangbourne College, Reading
Papplewick, Ascot
Park Hill School, Kingston-upon-Thames
Parsons Mead, Ashtead
Pennthorpe School, Horsham
Perrott Hill School, Crewkerne
The Perse School, Cambridge
Peterborough & St Margaret's High School, Stanmore
Peterborough High School, Peterborough
The Pilgrims School, Winchester
Pinewood School, Swindon
Pipers Corner School, High Wycombe
Plumtree School, Nottingham
Pocklington School, York
The Prebendal School, Chichester
Prestfelde Preparatory School, Shrewsbury
Prince's Mead School, Winchester
The Princess Helena College, Hitchin
Prospect House School, London
Putney Park School, London
Quainton Hall School, Harrow
Queen Anne's School, Reading
Queen Elizabeth's Grammar School, Blackburn
Queen Ethelburga's College, York
Queen Margaret's School, York
Queen's College, London
The Querns School, Cirencester
Radley College, Abingdon
Ranby House, Retford
Rathvilly School, Birmingham
Ravenscourt Theatre School, London
Read School, Selby
Reading Blue Coat School, Reading
Red House School, York
Reddiford, Pinner
Reed's School, Cobham
Reigate St Mary's Preparatory and Choir School, Reigate
Rendcomb College, Cirencester
Repton Preparatory School, Derby
Repton School, Repton
The Rickmansworth Masonic School, Rickmansworth
Riddlesworth Hall, Diss

Ripon Cathedral Choir School, Ripon
Rishworth School, Rishworth
Rodney School, Newark
Roedean School, Brighton
Rose Hill School, Wotton-under-Edge
Roselyon School, Par
Rossall Preparatory School, Fleetwood
Rossall School, Fleetwood
Rossholme School, Highbridge
Rosslyn School, Birmingham
Roxeth Mead School, Harrow
Royal Russell School, Croydon
The Royal School, Hindhead
The Royal School, Bath
Royal School, Hampstead, London
The Royal Wolverhampton Junior School, Wolverhampton
The Royal Wolverhampton School, Wolverhampton
Rugby School, Rugby
Rushmoor School, Bedford
Russell House School, Sevenoaks
Ruthin School, Ruthin
Ryde School with Upper Chine, Ryde
Sackville School, Tonbridge
Saddleworth Preparatory School, Oldham
St Agnes PNEU School, Leeds
St Albans High School, St Albans
St Andrew's School, Woking
St Andrew's School, Eastbourne
St Andrew's School, Reading
St Andrew's School, Rochester
St Andrew's Senior Girls' School, Harrow
St Anselm's, Bakewell
St Aubyns School, Tiverton
St Bede's, Eastbourne
St Bees School, Egremont
St Catherine's School, Guildford
St Christopher's, Burnham-on-Sea
St Christopher's School, Hove
St Christopher's School, Epsom
St Christopher's School, Wembley
St Colette's School, Cambridge
St David's School, Purley
St David's School, Ashford
St Dunstan's Abbey School, Plymouth
St Dunstan's College, London
St Edmund's Junior School, Canterbury
St Edmund's School, Hindhead
St Edmund's School, Canterbury
St Edward's School, Oxford
St Elphin's School, Matlock
St Francis School, Pewsey
St Gabriel's School, Newbury
St Helen's School for Girls, Northwood
St Hilary's School, Alderley Edge
St Hilda's School, Harpenden
St Hilda's School, Whitby
St Hilda's School, Wakefield
St Hugh's School, Woodhall Spa
St James' School, Grimsby
St James's & The Abbey, Malvern
St John's College School, Cambridge
St John's Northwood, Northwood
St John's School, Sidmouth
St John's School, Billericay
St John's Preparatory School, Lichfield
St Lawrence College in Thanet, Ramsgate
St Margaret's Exeter, Exeter
St Margaret's School, London
St Margaret's School, Watford

St Martin's School, Northwood
St Martin's School, Bournemouth
St Mary's Hall, Brighton
St Mary's Preparatory School, Tenbury Wells
St Mary's School, Gerrards Cross
St Mary's School, Wantage
St Mary's School, Calne
St Mary's School, Colchester
St Michael's, Barnstaple
St Michael's School, Sevenoaks
St Michael's School, Leigh-on-Sea
St Michael's School, Oxted
St Neot's School, Basingstoke
St Nicholas House, Hemel Hempstead
St Nicholas School, Fleet
St Olave's School (Junior of St Peter's), York
St Olaves Preparatory School, London
St Paul's Cathedral Choir School, London
St Paul's Girls' School, London
St Paul's Preparatory School, London
St Paul's School, London
St Peter's School, York
St Peter's School, Kettering
St Petroc's School, Bude
St Piran's Preparatory School, Maidenhead
St Ronan's, Hawkhurst
St Ronan's, Bridport
St Swithun's School, Winchester
St Wystan's School, Repton
Salisbury Cathedral School, Salisbury
Sancton Wood School, Cambridge
Sanderstead Junior School, South Croydon
Sandroyd, Salisbury
Sarum Hall, London
School of S Helen & S Katharine, Abingdon
School of S Mary and S Anne, Abbots Bromley
Seaford College, Petworth
Sedbergh School, Sedbergh
Selwyn School, Gloucester
Sexey's School
Sherborne Preparatory School, Sherborne
Sherborne School, Sherborne
Sherborne School for Girls, Sherborne
Sherrardswood School, Welwyn Garden City
Shiplake College, Henley-on-Thames
Shoreham College, Shoreham-by-Sea
Shrewsbury House School, Surbiton
Shrewsbury School, Shrewsbury
Sibton Park, Folkestone
Silchester House School, Maidenhead
Silverhill School, Bristol
Sir Anthony Brown's School, Brentwood
Slapton Pre-Preparatory School, Towcester
Snaresbrook College, London
Solefield School, Sevenoaks
Solihull School, Solihull
Sompting Abbotts, Lancing
Southdown Pre-Preparatory School and Nursery, Steyning
Southfield PNEU School & Starting Points, Halesworth
Spratton Hall, Northampton
Stamford School, Stamford
Stanway School, Dorking
Stoke Brunswick, East Grinstead
Stonar School, Melksham
Stonelands School of Ballet, Exeter
Stoneygate School, Leicester
Stourbridge House School, Warminster
Stover School, Newton Abbot
Stowe School, Buckingham

The Stroud School, Romsey
Stubbington House, Ascot
The Study School, New Malden
Summer Fields, Oxford
Sunderland High School, Sunderland
Sunningdale School, Sunningdale
Sunnyside School, Worcester
Surbiton High School, Kingston-upon-Thames
Surbiton Preparatory School, Surbiton
Sussex House School, London
Sutton Valence School, Maidstone
Swanbourne House School, Milton Keynes
Talbot Heath, Bournemouth
Taverham Hall, Norwich
Temple Grove, Uckfield
Thetford Grammar School, Thetford
Thomas's Kindergarten, London
Thomas's Kindergarten, Battersea, London
Thomas's Preparatory School, London
Thorpe Hall School, Southend-on-Sea
Thorpe House School, Gerrards Cross
Thorpe House School, Norwich
Tockington Manor, Bristol
Tonbridge School, Tonbridge
Town Close House Preparatory School, Norwich
Trent College, Nottingham
Trevor Roberts', London
Trinity School, Teignmouth
Truro High School, Truro
Tudor Hall School, Banbury
Twyford School, Winchester
Uppingham School, Oakham
Upton House School, Windsor
Victoria Park Preparatory School, Shipley
Walhampton School, Lymington
Walmsley House School, Bedford
Warminster School, Warminster
Warwick Preparatory School, Warwick
Warwick School, Warwick
Wellesley House School, Broadstairs
Wellingborough School, Wellingborough
Wellington College, Crowthorne
Wellington School, Wellington
Wells Cathedral Junior School, Wells
Wells Cathedral School, Wells
West Bridgford High School, Nottingham
West Buckland School, Barnstaple
West End School, Harrogate
Westbourne House School, Chichester
Westbrook Hay, Hemel Hempstead
Westbrook House School, Folkestone
Westminster Abbey Choir School, London
Westminster School, London
Westminster Under School, London
Weston Favell Preparatory School, Northampton
Westonbirt School, Tetbury
Widford Lodge, Chelmsford
The Willow School, London
Wilton House School, Battle
Winchester College, Winchester
Winchester House School, Brackley
Wisbech Grammar School, Wisbech
Witham Hall, Bourne
Wolborough Hill School, Newton Abbot
Woodbridge School, Woodbridge
Woodcote House School, Windlesham
Woodleigh School, Malton
Worksop College, Worksop
Wrekin College, Telford

Wroxall Abbey School, Warwick
Wycombe Abbey School, High Wycombe
Wykeham House School, Fareham
Yardley Court, Tonbridge
Yarlet Hall, Stafford
Yateley Manor Preparatory School, Camberley
York College for Girls, York
York House School, Rickmansworth
Yorston Lodge School, Knutsford

Church of Scotland

Glasgow Academy, Glasgow

Episcopelian

Glenalmond College, Perth

Greek Orthodox

Hellenic College of London, London

Jewish

Akiva School, London
Carmel College, Wallingford
Gateshead Jewish Primary School, Gateshead
CKHR Immanuel College, Bushey
Jewish High School for Girls, Salford
Jewish Preparatory School, London
Kerem House, London
The Kerem School, London
Lubavitch House Senior School for Boys, London
Manchester Jewish Grammar School, Manchester
Mathilda Marks-Kennedy School, London
Mechinah Liyeshivah Zichron Moshe, London
Menorah Grammar School, London
Pardes Grammar Boys' School, London
Talmud Torah Jewish School, London
Talmud Torah Yetev Lev, London
Tashbar School, Salford
Yesodey Hatorah Jewish School, London
Yetev Lev Day School for Boys, London

Methodist

Ashdown Lodge, Apperley Bridge
Ashville College, Harrogate

Bronte House School, Bradford
Culford School, Bury St Edmunds
Edgehill College, Bideford
Farringtons & Stratford House, Chislehurst
Kent College, Canterbury
Kent College, Pembury
Vernon Holme (Kent College Infant & Junior School),
    Canterbury
Kingswood Day Preparatory School, Bath
Kingswood School, Bath
The Leys School, Cambridge
Methodist College, Belfast
Priors Court Preparatory School, Newbury
Queen's College, Taunton
Queen's College Junior School, Taunton
Rydal Penrhos Preparatory School, Colwyn Bay
Rydal Penrhos Senior School, Colwyn Bay
Shebbear College, Beaworthy
Treliske School, Truro
Truro School, Truro
Woodhouse Grove School, Apperley Bridge

Moravian

Fulneck School, Pudsey

Muslim

Al Hijrah School, Birmingham
Al Karam Secondary School, Retford
Balham Preparatory School, London
Bolton Muslim Girls School, Bolton
Coventry Muslim School, Coventry
Darul Uloom Islamic High School & College, Birmingham
Gloucestershire Islamic School, Gloucester
Islamic College London, London
Jamahiriya School, London
Madni Girls School, London

Pentecostal

Emmanuel Christian School, Fleetwood

Quaker

Ackworth School, Pontefract
Ayton School, Great Ayton
Bootham School, York
Friends' School, Saffron Walden
Friends' School, Lisburn
Leighton Park School, Reading
The Mount School, York

The Mount School Junior Department, York
Sibford School, Banbury
Sidcot School, Winscombe

Roman Catholic

All Hallows, Shepton Mallet
Ampleforth College, York
Ampleforth College Junior School, York
Austin Friars School, Carlisle
Barlborough Hall School, Chesterfield
Barrow Hills School, Godalming
Beechwood School Sacred Heart, Tunbridge Wells
Bishop Challoner School, Bromley
The Brigidine School, Windsor
Bury Catholic Preparatory School, Bury
Carleton House Preparatory School, Liverpool
The Cavendish School, London
Claires Court School, Maidenhead
Combe Bank School, Sevenoaks
Convent of Our Lady of Providence School, Alton
Convent of St Francis de Sales, Tring
Convent of the Sacred Heart, Swaffham
Convent Primary School, Rochdale
Cranmore School, Leatherhead
De La Salle College, Jersey
Douai School, Reading
Downside School, Bath
Eccleston School, Birmingham
Farleigh School, Andover
Farnborough Hill, Farnborough
FCJ Primary School, Jersey
Fernhill School, Glasgow
Grace Dieu Manor School, Leicester
Holy Child School, Birmingham
Holy Cross Convent, Gerrards Cross
Holy Cross Preparatory School, Kingston-upon-Thames
Holy Trinity College, Bromley
Holy Trinity School, Kidderminster
Ilford Ursuline High School, Ilford
Kilgraston School, Perth
La Retraite Leehurst School, Salisbury
La Sagesse Convent, Romsey
La Sagesse Convent High School, Newcastle upon Tyne
Laleham Lea Preparatory School, South Croydon
Loreto Convent Grammar School, Altrincham
Loreto Convent Preparatory School, Altrincham
Loyola Preparatory School, Buckhurst Hill
Maidenhead College Claires Court Girls, Maidenhead
Marist Convent Senior School, Ascot
Marymount International School, Kingston-upon-Thames
Moor Park School, Ludlow
More House, London
More House School, Farnham
Moreton Hall, Bury St Edmunds
Mount Carmel School, Alderley Edge
Mount St Mary's College, Sheffield
Mount St Mary's Convent School, Exeter
Mylnhurst Convent School, Sheffield
New Hall School, Chelmsford
Notre Dame Preparatory School, Cobham
Notre Dame Preparatory School, Norwich
Notre Dame Senior School, Cobham
Oakhill College, Blackburn
The Oratory Preparatory School, Reading

The Oratory School, Reading
Our Lady of Sion School, Worthing
Our Lady's Convent Junior School, Abingdon
Our Lady's Convent Preparatory School, Kettering
Our Lady's Convent School, Cardiff
Our Lady's Convent School, Loughborough
Our Lady's Convent Senior School, Abingdon
Our Lady's Preparatory School, Crowthorne
Presentation College, Reading
Princethorpe College, Rugby
Prior Park College, Bath
Prior Park Preparatory School, Swindon
Ratcliffe College, Leicester
Rosecroft School Didsbury, Manchester
Ryde's Hill Preparatory School, Guildford
Rye St Antony School, Oxford
Sacred Heart Preparatory School, Bristol
Sacred Heart R.C. Primary School, Wadhurst
St Aloysius' College, Glasgow
St Ambrose College, Altrincham
St Ambrose Preparatory School, Altrincham
St Andrew's Preparatory School, Edenbridge
St Anne's Convent High School, Bishop Auckland
St Anthony's Montessori School, Sunderland
St Anthony's Preparatory School, London
St Anthonys School, Cinderford
St Antony's Leweston Preparatory School, Sherborne
St Antony's-Leweston School, Sherborne
St Audrey's Convent School, Wisbech
St Augustine's Priory, London
St Bede's College, Manchester
St Bede's School, Stafford
St Benedict's Convent School, Andover
St Benedict's Junior School, London
St Benedict's School, London
St Bernard's Preparatory School, Slough
St Catherine's Preparatory School, Stockport
St Catherine's School, Twickenham
St Christina's RC Preparatory School, London
St Clare's Convent, Porthcawl
St Clotilde's School, Lechlade
St Columba's College, St Albans
St Dominic's Independent Junior School, Stoke-on-Trent
St Dominic's Priory School, Stone
St Edmund's College, Ware
St Edward's College, Liverpool
St Edward's School, Cheltenham
St Francis' College, Letchworth
St George's College, Weybridge
St George's College Junior School, Weybridge
St Gerard's School, Bangor
St John's Beaumont, Windsor
St John's College, Cardiff
St John's College, Southsea
St John's Nursery School, Tadworth
St Joseph's College, Stoke-on-Trent
St Joseph's College, Ipswich
St Joseph's Convent, Chesterfield
St Joseph's Convent School, Broadstairs
St Joseph's Convent School, London
St Joseph's Convent School, Reading
St Joseph's Convent School, Burnley
St Joseph's Dominican Convent, Pulborough
St Joseph's Preparatory School, Ipswich
St Joseph's Preparatory School, Reading
St Joseph's Preparatory School, Nottingham
St Joseph's School, Launceston
St Joseph's School, Kenilworth
St Joseph's School, Hertford

St Leonards-Mayfield School, Mayfield
St Margaret's Junior School Convent of Mercy, Midhurst
St Margaret's Senior School Convent of Mercy, Midhurst
St Martha's Senior School, Barnet
St Martin's School, York
St Mary's College, Southampton
St Mary's College, Liverpool
St Mary's College, Folkestone
St Mary's Convent School, Worcester
St Mary's Hall, Stonyhurst
St Mary's Hampstead, London
St Mary's Hare Park School, Romford
St Mary's School, Ascot
St Mary's School, Shaftesbury
St Mary's School, Cambridge
St Maur's Convent School, Weybridge
St Monica's School, Carlisle
St Paul's Convent, Sutton Coldfield
St Philip's School, London
St Philomena's Preparatory School, Frinton-on-Sea
St Pius X Preparatory School, Preston
St Richard's, Bromyard
St Teresa's Preparatory School, Effingham
St Teresa's School, Dorking
St Teresa's School, Princes Risborough
St Thomas Garnet's School, Bournemouth
St Ursula's High School, Bristol
St Winefride's Convent School, Shrewsbury
Salesian College, Farnborough
Stella Maris Junior School, Stockport
Stonyhurst College, Clitheroe
Stoodley Knowle Convent School, Torquay
Thornton College Convent of Jesus and Mary, Milton Keynes
The Towers Convent School, Steyning
Tremough Convent School, Penryn
Trinity School, Teignmouth
Ursuline Convent Preparatory School, London
Ursuline College, Westgate-on-Sea
Vinehall School, Robertsbridge
Virgo Fidelis Convent, London
Vita Et Pax School, London
Westminster Cathedral Choir School, London
Wimbledon College Prep School, London
Winterfold House, Kidderminster
Woldingham School, Caterham
Worth School, Crawley

Seventh Day Adventist

Dudley House School, Grantham
Fletewood School, Plymouth
The John Loughborough School, London
Stanborough School, Watford

United Reformed Church

Caterham School, Caterham
Caterham School Preparatory, Caterham
Silcoates School, Wakefield

4.8
EDUCATIONAL ASSOCIATIONS AND USEFUL ADDRESSES

The Allied Schools
42 South Bar Street
Banbury
Oxon OX16 9XL
Tel 01295 256441
General Manager: David Harris

Provision of financial services and advice to member schools and of secretariat for the Governing Bodies of those schools. The Allied Schools include:

Stowe School
Wrekin College
Canford School

Harrogate Ladies' College
Westonbirt School
Riddlesworth Hall

Association of Heads of Independent Schools
Abbot's Hill School
Bunkers Lane
Hemel Hempstead
Herts HP3 8RP
Honorary Secretary: Mrs J Kingsley

Membership of AHIS is open to heads of girls' and co-educational junior independent schools which are accredited by the Independent Schools Joint Council (see below).

Association of Nursery Training Colleges
Norland College
Denford Park
Hungerford
Berks RG17 0PQ
Tel 01488 682252

Provides information on careers in child care, as nannies, as nursery workers and on National Vocational Qualifications (NVQs) in child care and education offered in the three independent nursery training colleges: Norland College, Hungerford, Chiltern Nursery Training College, Reading and Princess Christian College, Fallowfield.

Association of Tutors Incorporated
Sunnycroft
63 King Edward Road
Northampton NN1 5LY
Tel 01604 24171 Fax 01604 24718
Secretary: Dr D J Cornelius

The professional body for independent tutors. Members provide advice and individual tuition to students at all levels of education. The tutoring may be supplementary to full course provision or may be on a full course basis.

Boarding Schools Association (BSA)
Ysgol Nant
Valley Road
Llanfairfechan
Gwynedd LL33 0ES
Tel 01248 681403
General Secretary: Michael Kirk

The BSA is concerned that boarding education remains a healthy and relevant resource readily available to all who need it, within the range of educational provision in this country.

British Association for Early Childhood Education
BAECE Headquarters
111 City View House
463 Bethnal Green Road
London E2 9QY
Tel 0171 739 7594

A charitable association which advises on the care and education of young children from birth to nine years. The association also publishes booklets and organises conferences for those interested in early childhood education.

British Dyslexia Association
98 London Road
Reading
Berkshire RG1 5AU
Tel 01734 668271
(Helpline/Information Service 10am–5pm weekdays)

Choir Schools Association
The Minster School
Deangate
York YO1 2JA
Tel 01904 625217 Fax 01904 632418
Administrator: Caroline Legard

An association of schools educating cathedral and collegiate boy and girl choristers. Membership comprises the following schools:

The Abbey School, Tewkesbury
Bristol Cathedral School, Bristol
The Cathedral School, Cardiff
The Cathedral School, Lincoln
The Chorister School, Durham
Christ Church Cathedral School, Oxford
Exeter Cathedral School, Exeter
Hereford Cathedral Junior School, Hereford
The King's School, Gloucester
The King's School, Worcester
King's College School, Cambridge
The King's School, Ely
King's Preparatory School, Rochester
Lanesborough, Guildford
Lichfield Cathedral School, Lichfield
Magdalen College School, Oxford
The Minster School, York
New College School, Oxford
Norwich School, Norwich

The Pilgrim's School, Winchester
The Prebendal School, Chichester
Reigate St Mary's Preparatory and Choir School, Reigate
Ripon Cathedral Choir School, Ripon
St Edmund's Junior School, Canterbury
St George's School, Windsor
St James's School, Grimsby
St John's College School, Cambridge
St Mary's Music School, Edinburgh
St Paul's Cathedral Choir School, London, EC4
Salisbury Cathedral School, Salisbury
Wells Cathedral School, Wells
Wells Cathedral Junior School, Wells
Westminster Abbey Choir School, London, SW1
Westminster Cathedral Choir School, London, SW1

Associate Members

Chetham's School of Music, Manchester
King Edward VI School, Chelmsford
Warwick School, Warwick

Conference for Independent Further Education (CIFE)
Buckhall Farm
Bull Lane
Bethersden
Near Ashford
Kent TN26 3HB
Tel/Fax 01233 820797
Secretary: Myles Glover, MA

CIFE, founded in 1973, is a professional association for independent colleges of further education which specialise in preparing students (mainly over statutory school leaving age) for GCSEs, A and AS levels and university entrance. In addition, some colleges offer English language tuition for students from abroad and degree-level tuition. The aim of the association is to promote good practice and safeguard adherence to strict standards of professional conduct and ethical propriety. Full membership is open to colleges which have been accredited either by the British Accreditation Council for Independent Further and Higher Education (BAC) or by the Independent Schools Joint Council. Candidate membership is available to colleges seeking accreditation by either body within three years which otherwise satisfy

CIFE's own stringent criteria for membership. All CIFE colleges, of which there are currently 31 spread throughout England, with concentrations in London, Oxford, and Cambridge, have to abide by exacting codes of conduct and practice; and the character and presentation of their published exam results are subject to regulation, the accuracy of the information presented requiring in addition to be validated by BAC as academic auditor to CIFE. Colleges in full membership are subject to re-inspection from time to time by their accrediting bodies. Further information and a list of colleges are available from the secretary.

CReSTeD (Council for the Registration of Schools Teaching Dyslexic Pupils)
9 Elgy Road
Gosforth
Newcastle-upon-Tyne NE3 4UU
Chairman: M W Vallance

The CReSTeD Register is to help parents and those who advise them to choose schools for dyslexic children. Its main supporters are the British Dyslexia Association and the Dyslexia Institute who, with others, established CReSTeD to produce an authoritative list of schools, both maintained and independent, which have been through an established registration procedure, including a visit by the CReSTeD-selected consultant.

The Dyslexia Institute Ltd.
133 Gresham Road
Staines
Middlesex TW18 2AJ
Tel 01784 463851

A registered educational charity with teaching, assessment and teacher-training centres throughout England. The aim of the Institute is to help dyslexics of all ages overcome their difficulties in learning to read, write and spell and to achieve their potential. Information may be obtained by sending a stamped addressed envelope to the Information Officer at the address above.

The Governing Bodies Association and the Governing Bodies of Girls' Schools Association (GBA and GBGSA)
The Coach House
Pickforde Lane
Ticehurst
East Sussex TN5 7BJ
Tel/Fax 01580 200855
Secretary: D G Banwell

The aims of the association are to advance education in independent schools, to discuss matters concerning the policy and administration of independent schools and to encourage co-operation between their governing bodies. For details please contact the Secretary.

The Girls' Schools Association (GSA)

130 Regent Road
Leicester LE1 7PG
Tel 0116 254 1619 Fax 0116 255 3792
President: Miss Margaret Rudland
General Secretary: Ms Sheila Cooper

The GSA exists to represent the 245 schools whose Heads are in membership. Its direct aim is to promote excellence in the education of girls. This is achieved through a clear understanding of the individual potential of girls and young women. Over 110,000 pupils are educated in schools which cover day and boarding, large and small, city and country, academically elite and broad based education. Scholarships, bursaries and assisted places are available in most schools.

The Girls' Public Day School Trust (GPDST)

26 Queen Anne's Gate
London SW1H 9AN
Tel 0171 222 9595

The GPDST is a Registered Charity (No 1026057). It was founded in 1872 as a pioneer of girls' education. Today the Trust has over 18,000 pupils attending its 25 member schools:

Bath High School, Bath
Birkenhead High School, Birkenhead
Blackheath High School, London SE3
Brighton and Hove High School, Brighton
Bromley High School, Bromley
Croydon High School, Croydon
Heathfield School, Pinner
Howells School, Cardiff
Ipswich High School, Ipswich
Kensington Preparatory School for Girls, London W8
The Belvedere School, Liverpool
Central Newcastle High School, Newcastle–upon–Tyne
Norwich High School, Norwich
Nottingham High School for Girls, Nottingham
Notting Hill and Ealing High School, London W13
Oxford High School, Oxford
Portsmouth High School, Portsmouth
Putney High School, London SW15
Sheffield High School, Sheffield
Shrewsbury High School, Shrewsbury
South Hampstead High School, London NW3
Streatham Hill and Clapham High School, London SW16
Sutton High School, Sutton
Sydenham High School, Sydenham, London SE26
Wimbledon High School, London SW19

GPDST schools are non-denominational. Entry is by interview and test appropriate to the pupil's age. All schools have a junior department. Kensington is a preparatory school only. GPDST schools offer Assisted Places at 11+ and at sixth-form level. For further details contact schools direct or contact the GPDST office for a general prospectus.

The Headmaster's Conference (HMC)
1 Russell House
Bepton Road
Midhurst
West Sussex GU29 9NB
Membership Secretary: R N P Griffiths
Secretary: V S Anthony, 130 Regent Road, Leicester LE1 7PG

Membership of HMC consists of 239 heads of major boys' and co-educational independent schools. The objects of the annual meeting are to discuss matters of common interest to members.

The Incorporated Association of Preparatory Schools (IAPS)
11 Waterloo Place
Leamington Spa
Warwickshire CV32 5LA
Tel 01926 887833
General Secretary: John Morris

IAPS is the professional association of headmasters and headmistresses of preparatory schools in the UK and overseas. Membership is open to suitably qualified heads and deputy heads of schools accredited by the Independent Schools Joint Council.

Independent Business Training Organisation (IBTA)
c/o Mr S Edwards
15 King Edward Street
Oxford OX1 4HT

IBTA has been established as an association of the leading private business and secretarial colleges with the objective of promoting the highest possible standards of commercial training in the UK. The Association offers a free advisory service to prospective students to help them select a suitable course and college of study.

The Independent Schools Association Incorporated (ISAI)
Boys' British School
East Street
Saffron Walden
Essex CB10 1LS
Tel 01799 523619
Secretary: Timothy Ham

Membership of ISAI is limited to the heads of schools which are not under the direct control of the Department for Education. The Association aims to co-operate with other bodies which stand for professional freedom in education and to maintain for independent schools due recognition by government and the general public of their place in the educational life of the nation.

The Independent Schools Bursars' Association (ISBA)
Woodlands
Closewood Road
Denmead
Waterlooville
Hants PO7 6JD
Tel 01705 264506
Secretary: D J Bird

Membership of ISBA includes 600 independent secondary schools. Objectives include the promotion of administrative efficiency and exchange of information between schools.

The Independent Schools Careers Organisation (ISCO)
12A Princess Way
Camberley
Surrey GU15 3SP
Tel 01276 21188 Fax 01276 691833

ISCO aims to assist careers staff in schools, assist employers in making career opportunities and qualifications known, to advise students and their parents on careers, higher education and opportunities available and to arrange courses for staff and pupils. For further information please contact the Administrative Director at the address above.

Independent Schools Examinations Board
Jordan House
Christchurch Road
New Milton
Hants BH25 6QJ
Tel 01425 621111

Details of the Common Entrance examinations (see the section on "Examinations and Training") are available from the Administrator at the address above. For copies of past papers, contact CE Publications Ltd at the same address, or on 01425 610016.

The Independent Schools Information Service (ISIS)
56 Buckingham Gate
London SW1E 6AG
Tel 0171 630 8793
Director: D J Woodhead

Established by the associations of independent schools to provide information about schools to parents and the media.

Independent Schools Joint Council (ISJC)
Grosvenor Gardens House
35-37 Grosvenor Gardens
London SW1W 7BS
Tel 0171 630 0144 Fax 0171 931 0036
General Secretary: Dr Arthur Hearnden OBE

ISJC is a federation of the following associations:

Governing Bodies Association (GBA)
Governing Bodies of Girls' Schools
  Association (GBGSA)
Headmasters' Conference (HMC)
Girls' Schools Association (GSA)
Society of Headmasters and
  Headmistresses of Independent
  Schools (SHMIS)

Incorporated Association of Preparatory
  Schools (IAPS)
Independent Schools' Association
  Incorporated (ISAI)
Independent School Bursars' Association
  (ISBA)

The total membership of ISJC comprises about 1400 schools. ISJC considers matter of policy and administration common to its members and when required speaks collectively on their behalf. It represents its members in joint discussions with the Department for Education and with other organisations and endeavours to represent the collective view of members on independent education.

The Round Square Schools
Box Hill School
Dorking
Surrey RH5 6EA
Tel 01737 246108 Fax 01737 240416
Secretary: Kay Holland

An international group of schools which follow the principles of Kurt Hahn, founder of the Salem School in Germany and Gordonstoun in Scotland. There are now 23 member schools in nine countries: Australia, Canada, England, Germany, India, Kenya, Scotland, Switzerland and the United States. Member schools arrange regular exchange visits for pupils and undertake aid projects in India, Kenya, Venezuela and Eastern Europe. All member schools uphold the five principles of outdoor adventure, community service, education for democracy, international understanding and environmental conservation. UK member schools are as follows:

Cobham Hall, Gravesend (Girls')
St Annes, Windermere (Girls')
Westfield, Newcastle upon Tyne (Girls')
Abbotsholme, Uttoxeter (Co-ed)

Box Hill, Dorking (Co-ed)
Gordonstoun, Elgin (Co-ed)
Rannoch, Pitlochry (Co-ed)

The Secondary Heads Association (SHA)
130 Regent Road
Leicester LE1 7PG
Tel 0116 247 1797 Fax 0116 247 1152
General Secretary: J Sutton

SHA represents the majority of Heads and Deputy Heads in all types of secondary schools and colleges.

The Service Children's Education Authority (SCEA)
HQ DGAGC
Worthy Down
Winchester
Hants SO21 2RG
Tel 01962 887934

An education information service for parents serving in HM Forces.

The Society of Headmasters and Headmistresses of Independent Schools (SHMIS)
The Coach House
34A Heath Road
Upton-by-Chesher
Cheshire CH2 1HX
Tel/Fax 01244 379649
Secretary: I D Cleland

A society of 70 schools, most of which have a strong boarding element.

Steiner Schools Fellowship
Kidbrooke Park
Forest Row
East Sussex RH18 5JB
Tel 01342 822115 Fax 01342 826004
Chairman: Christopher Clouder (After hours 01342 822158)

The Steiner Schools Fellowship represents the 26 autonomous Steiner (or Waldorf) Schools for normal children in the UK and Eire. There are over 600 schools world-wide. Key characteristics of the education include: careful balance in the artistic, practical and intellectual content of the curriculum; examinations 'taken in stride'; co-educational from 4 to 18 years; shared Steiner curriculum for all pupils - minimal specialisation before A levels; teaching based on Steiner's anthroposophical approach to the nature of the human being; co-operative school management - usually a variable parent payment scheme. Steiner education is rapidly gaining in popularity and credence in many areas of the world.

The Woodard Schools
1 The Sanctuary
Westminster
London SW1P 3JT
Tel 0171 222 5381
Registrar: P F B Beesley

The Woodard Corporation has 36 schools throughout the country, including 11 Associated schools. All have an Anglican foundation and together they form the largest group of Church Schools in England and Wales.

Member Schools

Southern Division

Ardingly College, Haywards Heath
Ardingly College Junior School,
   Haywards Heath
Bloxham School, Banbury
Hurstpierpoint College, Hassocks
Lancing College, Lancing

Midland Division

Denstone College, Uttoxeter
Denstone College Preparatory School,
   Uttoxeter
Ellesmere College, Ellesmere
Prestefelde, Shrewsbury
Ranby House, Retford
St Hilary's, Alderley Edge

School of S Mary and S Anne, Rugeley
Worksop College, Worksop

Western Division

The Cathedral School, Cardiff
Grenville College, Bideford
King's College, Taunton
King's Hall School, Taunton
St Margaret's School, Exeter

Northern Division

The King's School, North Shields
Queen Mary's School, Thirsk

Eastern Division

Peterborough High School, Peterborough
St James's School, Grimsby

Associated Schools

Bow School, Durham
Durham School, Durham

Affiliated Schools

Archbishop Michael Ramsey School,
   London (Voluntary Aided)
Bishop of Hereford's Bluecoat School,
   Tupsley (Voluntary Aided)
Bishop Stortford School, Kettering
Cawston College, Norwich
Derby Boys High School, Derby

Derby Girls High School, Derby
Elmslie Boys School, Blackpool
Queen Ethelburga's School, Harrogate
Queen Margaret's School, York
St Elphin's School, Matlock
St Peter's Collegiate School,
   Wolverhampton (Voluntary Aided)

GLOSSARY OF ABBREVIATIONS
APPEARING IN SCHOOL PROFILES

AHIS	Association of Heads of Independent Schools
ANTC	Association of Nursery Training Colleges
ARELS	Association of Recognised English Language Services
AVDEP	Association Vaudoise des Ecoles Privees
BAC	British Accreditation Council for Independent Further and Higher Education
BSA	Boarding Schools Association
CIFE	Conference for Independent Further Education
COBISEC	Council of British International Schools in the European Community
CReSTeD	Council for the Registration of Schools Teaching Dyslexic Pupils
CSA	Choir Schools Association
ECIS	European Council of International Schools
FSEP	Federation Suisse des Ecoles Privees
GBA	Governing Bodies Association
GBGSA	Governing Bodies, of Girls' Schools Association
GPDST	Girls' Public Day School Trust
GSA	Girls' Schools Association
HAS	Head Teachers' Association of Scotland
HMC	Headmasters' Conference
IAPS	Incorporated Association of Preparatory Schools
IB	International Baccalaureate
IBTA	Independent Business Training Organisation
ISAI	Independent Schools Association Incorporated
ISBA	Independent Schools Bursars' Association
ISCO	Independent Schools Careers Organisation
ISIS	Independent Schools Information Service
ISJC	Independent Schools Joint Council
NAHT	National Association of Head Teachers
NE/SA	Near East/South Asia
NEASC	New England Association of Schools and Colleges
SHA	Secondary Heads Association
SHMIS	Society of Headmasters and Headmistresses of Independent Schools
STABIS	State Boarding Schools Information Service

MAIN INDEX

A

B

C

D

E

F

G

H

I

J

K

L

M

N

O

P

Q

R

S

T

U

V

W

Y

BUSINESS REPLY SERVICE
Licence No. WD 598

GABBITAS EDUCATIONAL CONSULTANTS Ltd.,
CARRINGTON HOUSE,
126-130 REGENT STREET,
LONDON
W1E 7EZ

BUSINESS REPLY SERVICE
Licence No. WD 598

GABBITAS EDUCATIONAL CONSULTANTS Ltd.,
CARRINGTON HOUSE,
126-130 REGENT STREET,
LONDON
W1E 7EZ

BUSINESS REPLY SERVICE
Licence No. WD 598

GABBITAS EDUCATIONAL CONSULTANTS Ltd.,
CARRINGTON HOUSE,
126-130 REGENT STREET,
LONDON
W1E 7EZ

READER ENQUIRY CARD

If you would like further information about our Advisory, Guardianship or other Services, please complete and return this card. No stamp is necessary if posted within the UK.

Name:

Address:

Tel:

Please indicate which area of our services might interest you:

Please tell us where you obtained a copy of this Guide:

Bookshop/Library (name and town):

School/advisory service etc. (please give details),

Borrowed from friend/relative:

READER ENQUIRY CARD

If you would like further information about our Advisory, Guardianship or other Services, please complete and return this card. No stamp is necessary if posted within the UK.

Name:

Address:

Tel:

Please indicate which area of our services might interest you:

Please tell us where you obtained a copy of this Guide:

Bookshop/Library (name and town):

School/advisory service etc. (please give details),

Borrowed from friend/relative:

READER ENQUIRY CARD

If you would like further information about our Advisory, Guardianship or other Services, please complete and return this card. No stamp is necessary if posted within the UK.

Name:

Address:

Tel:

Please indicate which area of our services might interest you:

Please tell us where you obtained a copy of this Guide:

Bookshop/Library (name and town):

School/advisory service etc. (please give details),

Borrowed from friend/relative:

READER ENQUIRY CARD

If you would like further information about our Advisory, Guardianship or other Services, please complete and return this card. No stamp is necessary if posted within the UK.

Name:

Address:

Tel:

Please indicate which area of our services might interest you:

Please tell us where you obtained a copy of this Guide:

Bookshop/Library (name and town):

School/advisory service etc. (please give details),

Borrowed from friend/relative: